A GIFT OF FIRE

SOCIAL, LEGAL, AND ETHICAL ISSUES IN COMPUTING

SARA BAASE
San Diego State University

An Alan R. Apt Book

Prentice Hall, Upper Saddle River, New Jersey 07458

Library of Congress Cataloging-in-Publication Data
Baase, Sara.
    A gift of fire : social, legal, and ethical issues in computing /
Sara Baase.
        p.   cm.
    "An Alan R. Apt book."
    Includes bibliographical references and index.
    ISBN 0-13-458779-0
    1. Computers—Social aspects. 2. Computers—Moral and ethical
aspects. I. Title.
QA76.9.C66B3   1997
303.48'34–dc21
                                                96-45254
                                                CIP

Publisher: Alan Apt
Production Editor: Mona Pompili
Editor-in-Chief: Marcia Horton
Assistant Vice President of Production
    and Manufacturing: David W. Riccardi
Managing Editor: Bayani Mendoza de Leon

Development Editor: Sondra Chavez
Manufacturing Buyer: Donna Sullivan
Creative Director: Paula Maylahn
Art Director: Heather Scott
Cover Designer: Daniel Will-Harris
Editorial Assistant: Toni Chavez

© 1997 by Prentice-Hall, Inc.
Simon & Schuster / A Viacom Company
Upper Saddle River, New Jersey 07458

The author and publisher of this book have used their best efforts in preparing this book. These efforts include the development, research, and testing of the theories and programs to determine their effectiveness. The author and publisher shall not be liable in any event for incidental or consequential damages in connection with, or arising out of, the furnishing, performance, or use of these programs.

Printed in the United States of America

10   9   8   7   6   5   4   3   2

ISBN 0-13-458779-0

PRENTICE-HALL INTERNATIONAL (UK) LIMITED, *London*
PRENTICE-HALL OF AUSTRALIA PTY. LIMITED, *Sydney*
PRENTICE-HALL CANADA, INC., *Toronto*
PRENTICE-HALL HISPANOAMERICANA, S.A., *Mexico*
PRENTICE-HALL OF INDIA PRIVATE LIMITED, *New Delhi*
PRENTICE-HALL OF JAPAN, INC., *Tokyo*
SIMON & SCHUSTER ASIA PTE. LTD., *Singapore*
EDITORA PRENTICE-HALL DO BRASIL, LTDA., *Rio de Janeiro*

To Keith

For more than I can say

PREFACE

This book is intended for two audiences: students preparing for careers in computer science and students in the humanities and social sciences who are interested in issues that arise from computer technology. It also has much to offer to computer professionals and the general public. The book has no technical prerequisites.

Courses on social and ethical issues

Many universities offer courses with titles such as "Ethical Issues in Computing" or "The Social Impact of Computers." These courses vary quite a bit in content and focus. Some focus primarily on ethical issues (issues the student may face directly as a computer professional), whereas others address the wider social, political, and legal issues related to computers. The bulky subtitle of this book gives a hint of my preference. I believe it is useful and important for students to learn about the social, legal, philosophical, political, constitutional, and economic issues (and the historical background of the issues) related to computers—issues they may face as members of a complex technological society, not just in their professional lives. The issues are relevant to being a responsible computer user (professional or personal) and member of the public who may serve on a jury, debate social and political issues with friends, or influence legislation. Thus, for example, I think it is important to cover the implications of censorship laws for the Internet, government policy about encryption, the problems of protecting intellectual property in cyberspace, the risks of new technologies, and so on.

The last chapter of this book covers ethical issues for computer professionals. The basic ethical principles in computing are not different from ethical principles in other professions or other aspects of life: honesty, responsibility, fairness. However, within any profession, there are special kinds of problems and issues that arise. Thus there is a need to develop and discuss "applied ethics" and guidelines for the profession. I believe students will find the discussion of ethical issues for computer professionals more interesting and useful if it has as background the discussions of the social and legal issues and controversies in the first nine chapters. Both the information students gain from the earlier chapters and the practice in analyzing the issues help prepare them to discuss ethical problems.

Controversies

This book presents controversies and alternative points of view: privacy vs. access to information, privacy vs. law enforcement, freedom of speech vs. control of content on the Net, market-based vs. regulatory solutions, and so on. I encourage my students to explore the arguments on all sides and to be able to explain why they reject the ones they reject before they take a position. I believe this approach prepares them to tackle new controversies; they can figure out the consequences of various proposals, generate arguments for each side, and evaluate them. I encourage students to think in principles, rather than case by case, or at least to see that the same principle appears in different cases even if they choose to take different positions on them. For example, one issue that comes up several times, in different contexts throughout the book, is whether or not a device, technique, or a whole technology should be banned or severely restricted because people can use it for illegal or harmful actions as well as benign ones.

I intentionally mention controversies about which I know people in a class will have strongly held positions on opposite sides. One point I try to make by doing so is that when designing a law or policy about control of content on the Net, or about privacy, for example, we must recognize the diversity of opinions and personal preferences. Whether we advocate restrictive or loose policies, we should remember that they will be applied to people whose activities and opinions we agree with, and to those we find objectionable.

Each of the chapters in this book could easily be expanded to a whole book. I have had to leave out many interesting topics and examples. In some cases, I mention an issue, example, or position with little or no discussion. I hope some of these will spark further reading and debate. Some reviewers of early drafts of the book recommended that I include (or expand the discussion of) a number of topics. Some examples are the fundamental justifications for and controversies about freedom of speech, mandatory AIDS testing (related to the issue of public safety vs. privacy), and the role of Christian organizations in efforts to censor the Internet. I omit them from this book (or mention them only briefly) because the essence of these controversies has little to do with computers. Often the discussion in the book necessarily includes political and philosophical issues, but I have tried (with some difficulty because of my enthusiasm for these issues) to focus specifically on the connections between the issues and computer technology.

My point of view

Any writer on subjects such as those in this book has some personal opinions, positions, or biases. I have a strong bias in favor of the Bill of Rights. I also have a generally positive view of technology, including computer technology. Don Norman, psychologist and Fellow at Apple Computer, has observed that most people who have written books about technology "are opposed to it and write about how horrible it is."[*] I am not one of those people. I think that technology, in general, has been a major factor in bringing physical well-being, liberty, and opportunity to hundreds of millions of people. Perhaps critics of technology miss some of the most impressive and fundamental benefits because they are so used to them that they take them for granted. Think about the products we use, the food we eat, and the people we talk to in a day—and consider how different a day would be without modern communication, transportation, refrigeration, and plumbing. That does not mean technology is without problems. Most of this book focuses on problems. We must recognize and study them so that we can reduce the negative effects of computer technology and increase the positive ones.

When this book was about 70% complete, I attended a National Science Foundation-sponsored workshop on Ethical and Professional Issues in Computing. Keith Miller, one of the speakers, gave the following outline for discussing ethical issues (which he credited to a nun who had been one of his teachers years ago): "What? So what? Now what?" It struck me that this is a good summary of how I had written most of the larger sections of this book. I often begin with a description of *what* is happening, sometimes including a little history. Next comes a discussion of why there are concerns and what the new problems are *(so what?)*. Finally I give some commentary or perspective and some current and potential solutions to the problems *(now what?)*.

An early reviewer of this book objected to one of the quotations I include at the beginning of a section because he thought it was untrue. So perhaps I should make it clear that I agree with many of the quotations I have placed at the beginnings of chapters and various sections of the book—but not with all of them. I chose some to be provocative and to remind students of the variety of opinions on some of the issues.

Class activities

I designed and teach a course in the Department of Mathematical and Computer Sciences at San Diego State University on the issues in this book. I require a book report, a term paper (that includes a site visit or interviews), weekly homework, and an oral presentation by each student. We do several mock trials in class, for example, for hackers who unintentionally cause serious damage, for sexual harassment on a university's computer bulletin board system, and so on. The students are very enthusiastic about these activities. (I have included a few in the Exercises sections, marked as Class Exercises.) Students can satisfy my course's oral presentation requirement by volunteering for roles in class activities or by presenting 15-minute talks in class about their term papers.

Some examples in this book are so current that details will change before or soon after publication. I don't consider this to be a serious problem. Specific events do not change most of the underlying issues and arguments. (A few of the exercises in the book ask the reader to research some of the legal cases mentioned to find out if they have been resolved.) I encourage my students to bring in newspaper clippings (or online news stories)

---

[*]Quoted in Jeannette DeWyze, "When You Don't Know How to Turn On Your Radio, Don Norman Is On Your Side," *The San Diego Reader*, December 1, 1994, p. 1.

about relevant issues to discuss in class. When the students begin to stay alert for relevant news, they seem impressed to find how many ties there are between the course and current events.

Additional sources and Web page for this textbook

A note on the notes and references: The endnotes at the ends of the chapters include sources for specific information in the text and, occasionally, additional information and comment. I usually put one endnote at the end of the paragraph with the sources for the whole paragraph. The lists of references at the ends of the chapters provide short samplings of the material available on the topics covered in this book. I have included some of the references that I used, some that I think are particularly useful or interesting for various reasons, and some that are not likely to be found elsewhere. I have made no attempt to be complete, but I include references to bibliographies complied by others. Although there is a huge amount of information online, I have cited, mostly, material published in hardcopy (i.e., books, journals, and newspapers). This is partly because these sources are stable, whereas online files and links may change. I mention several World Wide Web sites (such as the Electronic Frontier Foundation) that have extensive archives of relevant material.

I have set up a World Wide Web page for this book, www-rohan.sdsu.edu/ faculty/giftfire. It contains material for instructors using the book, including course materials (e.g., sample assignments), discussion topics, links to many documents and other sites of interest, and so on.

Feedback

This book contains a large amount of information on a large variety of subjects. I have tried to be as accurate as possible, but, inevitably, there will be errors. I would appreciate corrections. Please send them to me at GiftOfFire@sdsu.edu or Department of Mathematical and Computer Sciences, San Diego State University, San Diego, CA 92182-7720.

Acknowledgments

The following people assisted in the preparation of this book by providing leads and information, answering questions, and/or reading drafts: Leland Beck (San Diego State University), Jim Bennett (president, Center for Constitutional Issues in Technology), John L. Carroll (San Diego State University), John Ferguson (Disabled Opportunities Center, San Diego), Mike Godwin (staff counsel, Electronic Frontier Foundation), the staff of the Interlibrary Loan Department at San Diego State University, Phil Karn, James McLeod (San Diego Supercomputer Center), Peter G. Neumann (SRI International), Carol Sanders, Jack Sanders (attorney), David Sandwell (Scripps Institution of Oceanography), Milton Sank, Chris Small (Scripps Institution of Oceanography), Robert Ellis Smith (publisher, *Privacy Journal*), Shari Steele (staff attorney, Electronic Frontier Foundation), Duane Steffey (U.S. Census Bureau and San Diego State University), Vernor Vinge (San Diego State University), Jim Warren (AutoDesk, Inc.), the people I interviewed (mentioned in specific endnotes), and many others who answered questions and/or sent material. My students Lynn Okuma and Peggy Brydon Goddard assisted with research.

Joseph S. Fulda, Carol Keene (Colorado Technical University), Wally Roth (Taylor University), and Charlie Welty (University of Southern Maine) reviewed the entire manuscript and provided very helpful comments and encouragement.

Jerry Westby, of West Publishing Company, gave permission to reuse portions of my chapter "Social and Legal Issues" in G. Michael Schneider and Judith L. Gersting, *An Invitation to Computer Science,* published by West, 1995.

Alan Apt and Sondra Chavez, my editors at Prentice Hall, have been very helpful and supportive in the process of creating this book.

I enthusiastically thank you all!

I especially thank my husband, Keith Mayers, for technical help in preparing the manuscript, for his encouragement, knowledge, and editing skills—and for the miraculous accomplishment of getting us married and combining two households without making this book any more behind schedule than it already was.

CONTENTS

1

UNWRAPPING THE GIFT

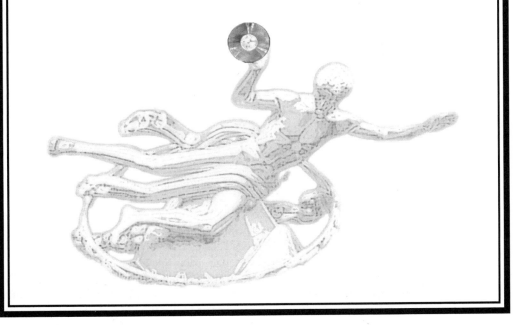

Prometheus, according to Greek myth, brought us the gift of fire. It is an awesome gift. It gives us the power to heat our homes, cook our food, and run the machines that make our lives more comfortable, healthy, and enjoyable. It is also awesomely destructive, both by accident and by arson. The Chicago fire in 1871 left 100,000 people homeless. In 1990 the oil fields of Kuwait were intentionally set ablaze. In 1993 and 1994 wildfires burned a million acres in the western United States and in Australia, destroying homes and killing people. In spite of the risks, in spite of these disasters, few of us would choose to return the gift of fire and live without it. We have learned, gradually, how to use it productively, how to use it safely, and how to respond more effectively to disasters, be they natural, accidental, or intentional.

Computer technology, many would agree, is the most significant new technology since the beginning of the Industrial Revolution. It is an awesome technology, with the power to make routine tasks quick, easy, and accurate, to save lives, and to create large amounts of new wealth. It helps us explore space, improve communications, and do thousands of other tasks. As with fire, the power of computers creates powerful problems: potential loss of privacy, multimillion-dollar thefts, breakdowns of large, complex systems, such as communications networks and banking systems, on which we have come to depend. In this book, we will describe some of the remarkable benefits of computers, some of the problems associated with them, and some of the means for reducing the problems and coping with their effects.

1.1   THE COMPUTER REVOLUTION

Everything that can be invented has been invented.
    –CHARLES H. DUELL, *Director of the U.S. Patent Office, 1899.*[1]

1.1.1   The Ubiquity of Computers and the Rapid Pace of Change

The marvels of recent generations—telephones, automobiles, airplanes, radio, household electrical appliances—were invented in the late 19th and early 20th centuries. They, like computers, led to changes in how we work and play, how we get information, how we interact with our neighbors (even how we define our neighborhood), and how we organize our family lives. But the changes were gradual. One of the most dramatic feats of technology in the past two generations was our entry into space. Sputnik, the first man-made satellite, was launched in 1957. Neil Armstrong walked on the moon in 1969. We still do not have personal spacecraft, vacation trips to the moon, or a large amount of commercial or research activity in space. The moon landing has had little effect on our daily lives.

But have you used a computer in the past two days?

When I asked my computer science students this question, about half the class raised hands. I asked the others if they had used an ATM machine, a CD player, or a VCR. More hands went up until there was only one student whose hand was not raised. As I was about to ask another question, he laughed, put his hand up, and said, "I drove my car."

The point of the question is to remind us that computers are not just the bulky machines we see on desks in homes and offices. Only slightly older than most of today's college students, microprocessors are in hundreds of millions of appliances and devices. They are built into microwave ovens, bread-baking machines, automobile ignition and braking systems, telephones, fax machines, medical instruments, and a large number of other machines we use regularly.

When we speak of computers in this book, we include three categories: the mainframes and PCs that run applications software, embedded chips that control machines, and the "Net," or "cyberspace." Cyberspace is built of computers, control devices, and storage media, but it is more than that. It is the mix of computers, communications systems (wired, wireless, and satellite), commercial services, the Internet, the World Wide Web, bulletin board systems, news and discussion groups, databases, and so on, that are accessible from virtually all over the world.

Computers are almost everywhere now. An estimated 48.5 million desktop and portable PCs were sold worldwide in 1994; roughly one in three U.S. households had a PC, and approximately 7.8 million home computers had CD-ROM players. Millions of Americans use the Internet. Approximately one billion chips are produced worldwide each week.[2]

It was not always this way. New technology replaces older technology. Your university library's catalog system is almost certainly on a computer, accessible from home with a modem. Until recently, library catalogs filled large rooms with racks of trays containing $3'' \times 5''$ index cards. A generation ago, there were no CD players, no VCRs, no cable TV, no ATMs, and no PCs. Computers were large machines, the size of a few refrigerators, kept in air-conditioned rooms. On the 25th anniversary of the first moon landing, a television documentary reported that the lunar landing module used by the Apollo astronauts had less computing power than a 1994 automobile. When your grandparents, and perhaps your parents, were children, there were no computers, not even the old-style business mainframes. The ubiquitousness of computers and the rapid pace of change that has accompanied them are two dramatic aspects of the Computer Revolution.

Although computers are a new development, they had predecessors. In fact, computing and calculating devices have a rich history. We will take a brief look at a few of the highlights of this history before introducing some of the issues raised by the dramatic changes brought about by computers.

1.1.2 A Brief History of Calculating Machines and Computers[3]

Early calculating machines

An abacus consists of beads on rods in a frame. Move the beads along the rods in the right way and you can do arithmetic. The abacus was probably invented about 5000 years ago in Babylonia (now Iraq); its exact origins are uncertain. The slide rule, invented in the 17th century, used John Napier's invention of logarithms to simplify arithmetic operations.

For example, you can multiply two numbers by adding their logarithms. You can add numbers easily with a slide rule by moving a sliding stick between two fixed slats to measure out the sum of the two distances representing the logarithms.

In the 17th century, several people experimented with machines to perform arithmetic. Blaise Pascal, for whom the programming language Pascal is named, began working on his mechanical calculator in 1642 when he was 19 years old. He used wheels to add up numbers. The idea behind its operation is similar to the way a hand on an analog clock moves around to add up time. Because the wheels turned only in one direction, he could not subtract in the natural way. Instead Pascal used a previously known calculating trick called "nines complement" that subtracts by doing addition. If you are familiar with the representation of integers used in today's computers, and the way computers subtract, you may recognize the method Pascal used as a precursor to today's twos complement. Pascal's calculator performed multiplication and division by repeated additions or subtractions, a slow and inelegant method. For this and a variety of other reasons, he was able to sell only about a dozen of his machines. One other reason was that people suspected someone could rig the machines to give dishonest results.

About 30 years after Pascal built his first calculator, Gottfried Wilhelm von Leibniz, known for inventing the calculus, designed his contribution to calculating history: a device he called the Stepped Reckoner. It too used wheels, or gears, to perform its computations. Leibniz designed it to perform multiplication and division quickly and to work on numbers with more digits than Pascal's calculator could handle. The Reckoner was expensive to build, and, unfortunately, although it was based on sound principles, the engineering was faulty. The machine did not work, but subsequent inventors used the same principles in most of the calculating machines built over the next 150 years. Pascal's and Leibniz's calculators worked on decimal numbers. Leibniz was one of the first western mathematicians to study the binary number system. He thought of making a binary calculator, but never did.

The goals of 17th and 18th century calculators were modest: to automate the basic arithmetic operations. Although automating such a simple operation as addition may seem natural to us, it was quite shocking to many people at the time. That a mindless machine could perform tasks associated with human intellectual abilities was disconcerting. Now, centuries later, when computers perform much more sophisticated tasks, people still debate the philosophical and social implications of artificial, or machine, intelligence.

The calculating machines developed in the 17th and 18th centuries had no memory and were not programmable. (Leibniz's machine was not even fully automatic; the operator had to adjust some parts to help it do carries and borrows.) The next major step on the way to modern computers came from the textile industry. In 1801 Joseph-Marie Jacquard invented an automated loom. It was the first device to have a form of memory and program. A sequence of punched cards controlled the loom. A hook could pass through holes in a card and pluck certain vertical threads (the warp threads) so that the horizontal thread (the woof) would go behind the plucked warp threads to create the desired pattern. Thus "expert knowledge" (i.e., the pattern) was stored in machine-readable form. The automated loom could weave faster than an operator thinking about what to do next. Jacquard demonstrated the incredible power of the invention by programming a loom with 10,000 punch cards to weave a detailed portrait of himself in silk.

The innovative ideas of the Jacquard loom were not implemented in calculating devices for about another 90 years. In the meantime, calculating machines advanced in other ways. The first calculating machine to be mass produced, invented in France by Charles Xavier Thomas de Colmar in 1820, used many of Leibniz's ideas. During the next 30 years, insurance companies, banks, and other businesses bought about 1500. Similar machines were in use until the early 20th century.

The Industrial Revolution generated an increase in the use of mathematical tables for navigation, engineering, and business. The tables published at the time contained many errors, from both mistakes in calculation and typographical errors occurring when the tables were set in type. There was a serious need for accurate tables to support booming business and shipping activities. Charles Babbage, a 19th century mathematician and engineer, designed a steam-powered machine he called the Difference Engine to calculate numbers for mathematical tables. It used a technique called "the method of finite differences." In this method, each number is calculated from the previous one, so if the last number is correct, it is likely that the previous ones are correct. This fact would make checking the accuracy of the machine's calculations fairly easy. The Difference Engine was to record its results directly on metal plates for printing the tables, thus eliminating typographical errors. Babbage produced a working model in 1822. A complete Difference Engine would need thousands of precisely tooled gears, axles, and other parts. It would have been ten feet high, ten feet long, and five feet deep. Babbage worked on the project for about ten years, often revising the design when he had new ideas. Because of the design revisions, the very large expense, problems with his chief engineer, and the difficulty at the time of making the parts to the necessary precision, he did not complete the project. However, the machine tools Babbage designed in the course of working on the Difference Engine were a valuable contribution to the British machine tool industry.

While work on the Difference Engine was in progress, Babbage designed a new machine he called the Analytical Engine. There were many new features of this design that made it almost a computer by the modern definition: It had the capability of doing a large variety of mathematical computations; there were parts of the machine that played the roles of memory, a central processing unit, and a control unit; it was programmable. Babbage knew of the Jacquard loom and decided that the programs for the Analytical Engine would be provided on punch cards. The machine had the capability of making simple decisions, thus implementing what we now call conditional branching. It could also be instructed to repeat certain steps a specified number of times; thus it could perform loops. And it could be instructed to perform a subtask, now called a procedure, or subroutine.

Babbage produced thousands of pages of notes and engineering drawings for the new machine, demonstrating fairly well that the concept was valid. The most widely read description of the machine in Babbage's time was written by an amateur mathematician: Lord Byron's daughter, Augusta Ada Byron, Countess of Lovelace, for whom the programming language Ada is named. The Analytical Engine would have been 15 feet tall and 25 feet long—and very expensive to construct. In part because of the failure to complete the Difference Engine, Babbage was unable to get funding to build it.

Across the Atlantic, necessity gave birth to the next significant stage in the development of computers. Between 1870 and 1880, the United States population increased by 26%. It took the government nine years to process all the data from the 1880 census.

During the 1880s the population increased by another 25%. If the same methods were used, the government would not complete processing data from the 1890 census until after the 1900 census was to begin. Herman Hollerith, a Census employee, designed and built punch card processing machines—tabulators, sorters, and keypunch machines—to process census data. Hollerith's machines did the complete 1890 population count in only six weeks, an amazing feat at the time. All the rest of the processing of the 1890 census data was completed in seven years. It could have been done sooner, but the new machines allowed sophisticated and comprehensive analysis of the data, which would have been impossible before. (Here is an early example of computing technology allowing increased processing of data with the potential for good and bad effects: better use of information—or more work done just because it is possible—and invasion of privacy.) Soon other governments and large businesses, like railroads, department stores, and steel companies, were using the machines made by Hollerith's Tabulating Machine Company. In 1924, after a merger and name change to Computing-Tabulating-Recording Company, the company was renamed again by its then-president Thomas J. Watson. His new name is the one we know today: International Business Machines Corporation, or IBM.

The computer era

For 300 years mechanical calculating machines were built with gears, or wheels. In the mid-20th century, the first electronic computing machines were built. The ENIAC,* completed in 1945, is often cited as the first electronic computer, although there are other reasonable contenders for that honor. Today, the definition of a computer would require stored programs. The ENIAC did not have this feature; it was rewired for each program. In any case, the ENIAC provides a good starting point for the modern computer era, and it helps illustrate the enormous development that has occurred in the past 50 years. In this period, computers have become smaller, cheaper, and immensely more powerful at unprecedented rates.

The ENIAC did 333 multiplications or 5000 additions per second. It was eight feet tall, eighty feet long, and weighed thirty tons. It was built of approximately 17,000 vacuum tubes, 70,000 resistors, and thousands of other electrical parts and manual switches. The ENIAC cost approximately $500,000 in 1946 dollars; that would be roughly $5 million to $10 million today. It could not communicate with someone in another room, and untrained people could not communicate with it at all.

In the decades following the ENIAC, transistors replaced vacuum tubes, making computers more reliable. In the 1950s and 1960s, computers were used mostly for business (payroll and inventory), government, and scientific research. In the 1970s, integrated circuits began to make computers smaller and cheaper. The microprocessor was one of the main steps toward providing the power of the ENIAC in a consumer product. The term "personal computer" was used at least as far back as 1974, when inventors began selling kits and instructions for building your own. After selling more than 100 decidedly non-user-friendly small computers to hobbyists, Steve Wozniak and Steve Jobs raised venture capital to sell its successor, the Apple II, to the public in 1977. IBM introduced its personal

---

*ENIAC is an acronym for Electronic Numerical Integrator and Computer.

computer in 1981, and thousands of businesses sprouted to sell clones, peripheral devices, software, and computer magazines.

The software industry grew explosively in the 1980s. Word processors, spreadsheets, games, and database programs filled the shelves of computer stores. Bill Gates and Paul Allen founded Microsoft, the largest software company in the world, in 1975. In 1994 Microsoft's sales were more than $4.6 billion. Software is now written as a consumer product, for nontechnical users. The means of communicating with a computer has evolved from typing arcane commands to pointing and clicking with a mouse.

Today computer speeds are measured in MIPS—millions of instructions per second. Many computers now do 100–1000 MIPS (100,000,000 to a billion instructions per second). A modern personal computer or workstation sits on a desk—or fits in a briefcase. A computer memory chip smaller than a fingernail holds 64 megabytes of data[*] (roughly enough space for the text of more than 50 books). A chip smaller than a fingernail can hold all the logical circuitry of a personal computer. For under $10 we can buy electronic stored-program calculators that work as fast as the ENIAC. For one or two thousand dollars we can buy personal computers that are thousands of times more powerful. Calculators are now built into wristwatches.

Storage media (for programs and data) have been getting smaller and better. In the 1950s and 60s, we kept our programs on decks of punched cards, each card storing up to 80 characters. Since the 1970s, we have used floppy disks, or diskettes. As the diskettes decreased in size, from 8 inches to 5¼ inches to 3½ inches, the storage capacity increased from 180KB to 2.88MB. Personal computer users can store 100 megabytes of software and data on diskettes slightly larger than the common 3½-inch diskettes. Compact disks hold hundreds of megabytes. You can buy the *Encyclopaedia Britannica* on one CD. It is not unusual now for large business systems to have hundreds of gigabytes (billions of bytes) of disk storage.

People have found many metaphors to describe the changes of the past 50 years. As one writer put it, "Since the computer-on-a-chip was invented in 1971, the cost of computing has plunged 10 million-fold. That's like being able to buy a new Boeing 747 for the price of a large pizza."[4]

Early computers worked alone. They were not connected to networks and did not have modems. They were given input, they did some computation, and they produced output. Now, computers commonly have a modem to access other computers, information services, e-mail, and so on. The Internet, originally developed as a military communication system, provided the beginning infrastructure and decentralized design for what is now an inexpensive global communication tool. It was as recently as the late 1980s that interactive information services like Prodigy and CompuServe began, introducing many ordinary users to cyberspace. Virtually all business computers now are connected to other computers in networks. Text, graphics files, binary files, and facsimile documents fly through phone lines, fiber optic cables, and the air (with wireless technologies) at speeds that are regularly increasing. Early modems (in the 1970s) transmitted 300 bits per second (bps).

---

[*]A megabyte, abbreviated "MB," is roughly one million bytes. A byte is the amount of storage used for one character. A kilobyte, abbreviated "KB," is roughly one thousand bytes.

	ENIAC	Today
Speed	5000 additions/sec	More than 100,000,000 instructions/sec
Size	80 feet long, 30 tons	Notebook size to refrigerator size
Cost	$5–10 million (current dollars)	$1000 for a PC
		$5000–20,000 for a workstation
Components	Vacuum tubes, resistors, switches	Integrated circuits, chips
Input media	Punch cards	Keyboard, voice, scanners, handwriting, mouse, touch screens
Output media	Punch cards	On-screen text, graphics, and video; sound; laser printers
Communications	None	Modems, fax; access to e-mail and the World Wide Web
Software	Forget it.	You name it.

FIGURE 1.1: 50 years: Comparing the ENIAC with modern computers.

Now we can access information services at 9600–28,800 bps. Speeds of 2–100 megabits per second are typical among networked computers. The transmission capacity of optical fiber has increased roughly tenfold every four years since 1975. In the mid-1990s, fibers used in long distance transmissions carried 2.4 gigabits (2.4 billion bits) per second. New techniques being developed are expected to enable one fiber to carry 40 gigabits per second before the year 2000. Figure 1.1 summarizes the attributes of the ENIAC and today's computers. In the next decade we are likely to see major advances in both hardware and software for multimedia and communication systems.

The history of computing is full of stories of great innovators such as Pascal, Leibniz, Jacquard, Babbage, Hollerith, and Wozniak. The box on pages 10–11 describes one of the most important computer scientists of the 20th century, Alan M. Turing.

1.2   EXAMINING THE GIFT: AN INTRODUCTION TO SOME ISSUES AND THEMES

Analyzing and evaluating the impact of a new technology can be difficult. Some of the changes are obvious. Some are more subtle. Even when benefits are obvious, their costs and side effects may not be, and vice versa. This section introduces some of the costs, problems, and issues we will study in the rest of the book.

1.2.1   Issues

The automated teller machine (ATM), a common application of computer technology, exemplifies some of the issues we will discuss in more detail throughout the book. Why do we use ATMs? Because they are convenient. They allow us to withdraw cash or make other banking transactions at any time of day or night, at locations that may be closer than our bank branch. But what are the negative aspects of ATMs?

- *Unemployment*
  The automation of the most common teller functions has led to a decline in employment for bank tellers. In 1983, 480,000 people worked as bank tellers. In 1993, there were only 301,000 tellers.[5]

- *Alienation and customer service*
  Automation of teller functions removes the human contact between the customer and a live teller. Instead of talking to a smiling person, we confront a machine. The ATM may be confusing to operate. We may forget our password. We may have a question it cannot answer.

- *Crime*
  People have been robbed after withdrawing cash at ATMs. Stolen and counterfeit ATM cards are used by thieves to steal millions of dollars each year. The anonymity of the machine makes ATM fraud easy. A human teller would notice if the same person made numerous withdrawals, or might know the real cardholder by sight, or might be able to identify a suspect after the theft is discovered.

- *Loss of privacy*
  Because transactions at ATMs are recorded in a database at the bank, the record of a person's transactions at various ATMs can provide information about the person's whereabouts and activities.

- *Errors*
  An error in the computer program that operates the ATMs for a large New York bank caused accounts to be debited twice the amount of the actual withdrawal. In less than one day, more than 150,000 transactions, totaling approximately $15 million, were incorrectly recorded.[6]

Unemployment, alienation, crime, loss of privacy, errors—a lot of serious problems! Are ATMs, on balance, a bad development? Are you going to stop using them? Probably not. Why not? One reason is the benefit we get from them. Convenience may not at first seem like a very important thing. Later we will discuss impressive life-saving and life-enhancing applications of computers. Yet, the example of ATMs suggests that many people do in fact value convenience very highly. For this one benefit, we are willing to accept several negative features. Another reason why we will not give up ATMs is that some of the problems described above are exaggerated, or would occur without ATMs, or have solutions. Let us reconsider them.

- *Unemployment*
  Compared to 10 or 15 years ago, there are now fewer people employed as bank tellers, but there are many more people employed in computer stores. There are many jobs involving the production, sale, and use of computers that did not exist in the early 1980s. Automation causes changes in the kinds of jobs people do. Overall, have computers increased or decreased employment? In Chapter 8 we will consider this question and other issues of computers and work. For example: How do computers change the work environment and the structure of businesses? How do they affect the privacy of workers?

ALAN M. TURING, 1912–1954

Alan Turing was a British mathematician who did some of the most fundamental work in the theory of modern computer science—in the 1930s, before anyone was building computers. Turing defined an elegant and simple mathematical model of a general purpose computer, now called the Turing Machine, and used it to prove theorems about what was possible for computers to do, and what was not possible (no matter how clever the design or advanced the technology). The Turing Machine showed that a computer can be built of very simple components. All the complex things we do with them can be implemented in software. Turing devised a "test," called the Turing Test, to decide when it was reasonable to say that a computer could "think." (His criterion was that it could fool a person conversing with it, through an appropriate interface, into believing that it was a human.) Turing wrote chess-playing programs before there were computers that could run them.[7]

Although primarily a mathematician and theoretician, Turing did valuable practical work too. During World War II the Germans used a very sophisticated (for its time) coding machine to encode its military messages. The machine was called Enigma. It was an electromechanical device that enabled the Germans to use more complicated codes than would have been possible with only human coders. Working in secret for the British government, Turing analyzed the coded messages intercepted by the British and used information known about the structure of the Enigma to work out methods to break the code. It was not a simple matter of figuring out a code one time; the machine configuration was changed often, changing the code. Turing did mathematical analysis, devised algorithms, and designed a machine to implement them. The project required the efforts of a huge staff of clerks. Eventually, the British could regularly read the German messages. The enormous difficulty of the task Turing accomplished is suggested by the German reaction to the British military's obvious knowledge of their secret plans. The Germans assumed their military command was infiltrated by British spies because they considered it impossible to break the Enigma codes.

■ *Alienation and customer service*

Anyone who wants to talk to a human teller can go into a bank during banking hours. No one is required to use an ATM machine; it is a new option. In fact, banks are open more hours now than they were before ATMs existed. In the 1960s, standard bank hours were 10AM to 3PM, Monday through Friday. Now, many banks are open until 5 or 6PM and have Saturday hours.

On the other hand, many services that used to be provided by people are now handled automatically (e.g., telephone information and customer service). Some such systems have the advantage of convenience; some are quite frustrating to use. Some banks now charge a fee for teller transactions that could be done at ATMs. Many banks are closing branches because services are automated. The impact of computers on customer service in banking has been mixed.

■ *Crime*

ATM fraud is a serious problem. We will discuss it, along with other forms of computer fraud, malicious hacking, and other computer crimes, in Chapter 7. Robberies

After the war, Turing designed a general-purpose electronic computer called the Automatic Computing Engine, or ACE. (The word "Engine" in the name was in honor of Charles Babbage.) His design included many clever ideas, some that later became standard. His machine could use binary arithmetic, he recognized the importance of a large memory with low access time, and he suggested the use of cathode ray tubes for internal storage of data. (CRTs were later used in this way in the Manchester Mark I, the first fully electronic stored-program computer, built in 1948.[8]) Turing did not get to build the ACE. One reason, according to Turing's biographer, was that the government laboratory responsible for the project was too stodgy and bureaucratic to act on such innovative work; the lab did not have engineers capable of appreciating or implementing Turing's design. In any case, Turing's report and talks on the ACE design, written when modern computers were in their infancy, are beautiful and brilliant documents describing some of the problems and solutions for building such a machine.

Turing was highly respected and welcomed in the U.S. intelligence and coding community. He was honored in Britain. Then, in 1952, it became publicly known that Turing was homosexual. He was tried and sentenced to medical "treatment." He was no longer trusted; government agents followed him on vacation. He would not be allowed into the United States. In 1954, shortly before his 42nd birthday, Turing killed himself.

In honor of Alan Turing, the Association for Computing Machinery, the professional association of computer scientists, gives an annual award called the Turing Award to computer scientists who have made significant contributions to the field. In the computer science community, the Turing Award is considered similar to a Nobel Prize in the importance of the work for which it is awarded and the honor it bestows on the recipient.

at ATMs, while serious for the victim, are not a significant crime problem. In 1994 there were approximately 8 billion ATM transactions. The rate of attacks on customers at ATMs is one in 3.5 million transactions (and as high as one in a million in some neighborhoods).[9] The banking industry has developed many approaches to reducing fraud and ATM crime.

■ *Loss of privacy*
The records kept of ATM transactions probably are not a serious privacy problem. The time and location of transactions inside a bank may be recorded as well. But this mention of privacy serves to introduce the issues we will consider in Chapter 2. A large portion of our financial transactions, including supermarket purchases, credit card purchases, loan payments, and income are recorded in computer databases. The federal and state governments maintain huge databases with personal information on us. Who should have access to this information, and how should it be protected from abuse and errors?

■ *Errors*

The bank that double-debited ATM accounts corrected the errors quickly. The error rate for ATM transactions is quite small. With billions of transactions each year, we must expect that some errors will be made. Although some errors are tolerable, the potential for damage caused by errors in complex computerized systems is a serious problem. The use of computer systems leads to new kinds of errors that would not have occurred before. We need to study these and learn how to reduce them. Unfortunately, many people do not realize how easy it is for a computer system to do something wrong; they have too much confidence in these (to them) inscrutable machines. Programmers and system designers are often overconfident, too, and do not give enough thought to the potential consequences of errors or poor design. On the other hand, computers can reduce mistakes and increase safety in some cases. In Chapter 4 we will look at a variety of examples and issues related to the reliability and safety of computer systems.

In general, when evaluating computers, we should not compare them to some ideal of perfect service or zero side effects and risk. That is impossible to achieve in most aspects of life. Instead, we should compare computer systems to the alternatives and weigh the problems against the benefits. Of course, as in any endeavor, we continue to seek cost-effective improvements and solutions to problems. The ideal shows us the direction to go.

Throughout this book, when we consider problems related to computers, we will consider solutions of several kinds: technical (sometimes using computer technology itself), managerial, legal, educational, and market mechanisms. Technical solutions involve hardware and software. For example, ATM software used by some banks has checks that would have prevented the double-debit problem we described. We include more than the computer itself as hardware; thus, improved lighting near the ATM to reduce crime is a technical solution. Management solutions are helpful business policies. Legal solutions include effective law enforcement, criminal penalties, lawsuits, legislation, and regulation. For example, there must be appropriate penalties for people who commit computer fraud and appropriate liability laws for cases where system failures occur. Market mechanisms, such as competition and consumer demand, generate many improvements. Customers and computer users must become educated about the tools they use. That includes knowing how and when to use them safely. For example, ATM card counterfeiters get account numbers by collecting receipts left at ATM machines; customers must learn to take their receipts with them. (To protect customers from theft of card numbers, some machines print only the last four digits of the number on the receipt. Some machines have a technical solution for customers who forget to take their ATM cards after a withdrawal: The machine will not release the cash until the customer removes the card.)

The ATM example served well to introduce several of the issues we will study in the rest of this book, but it does not illustrate all of them. Here is a sampling of some of the other issues.

■ *Privacy of communications* (Chapter 3)

As new telecommunications technology and encryption methods make it possible to keep communications secret from others, how should our desire for efficiency, privacy, and competitiveness of communications systems be balanced with the need of law enforcement agencies to intercept and monitor communications of suspected criminals?

- *Intellectual property* (Chapter 5)
  Many millions of dollars of software is illegally copied each year. How should the intellectual property embodied in software be protected? Should it be protected at all, or should software be freely available? Storage in digital form has made other kinds of intellectual property (e.g., books, photographs, and songs) easy to copy without permission of the copyright owner. What is the extent of this problem? What can and should be done about it?

- *Constitutional issues* (Chapter 6)
  How do First Amendment protections of freedom of speech and freedom of the press apply to electronic media? How serious are the problems of pornography, harassment, and libel on the Net? How would censorship affect the Net? Should information service and bulletin board operators be legally responsible for illegal material posted or e-mailed on their systems? How does Fourth Amendment protection against unreasonable search and seizure apply when law enforcement agents want to search files on computers?

- *General social issues* (Chapter 9)
  How does the increasing use of computers and networks affect local community life? Will increasing use of computers increase the separation of rich and poor, creating a two-class society, the information "haves" and "have-nots"? Is there a need for government subsidies for people who cannot afford computers, or for "public spaces" on the Net with kinds of information that commercial services may not provide?
  Both the technological advances brought about by computers and the extraordinary pace of development can cause dramatic impact on people's lives. We must adapt to the prospect of jobs becoming obsolete, to the necessity of learning new skills. Businesses must adapt to the prospect of their products becoming obsolete or not competitive. Our sense of community is changing. Traditional forms of education face competition from software and electronic classrooms. To some, this is frightening and disruptive. They see computers as a dehumanizing tool that reduces the quality of life or as a threat to the status quo and their well-being. Others see challenging and exciting opportunities. To them the development of computer technology is a thrilling and inspiring example of human progress. Do computers have an overall positive or negative impact? We will look at this fundamental controversy.

- *Professional ethics* (Chapter 10)
  The first nine chapters of this book look at the issues from the perspective of any person who lives and works in our highly computerized society and is interested in the impact of computers. The final chapter looks at some of the same topics from the perspective of someone who works as a computer professional who designs or programs computer systems, or a professional in any area who must make decisions and/or set policy about the use of computers. The ACM Code of Ethics and Professional Conduct is included.

1.2.2 Themes

There are a few themes that run through this book. One is:

> Changes in technology usually require adaptive changes in laws, social institutions, business policies, and personal skills and attitudes.

New technology makes possible actions that were not considered when existing laws were written and, hence, are not illegal or criminal. Sometimes it is "obvious" to most of us that the new action should be illegal; sometimes there is controversy.

Another theme is:

> As cyberspace develops, it will have many of the problems, annoyances, and controversies of noncyber life: crime, pornography, pedophiles, hate speech, violent fiction, advertising, copyright infringement, gambling.

Groups that some people find offensive, be they skinheads or gay teenagers, are using the Net. Our reactions to these "cyberspace issues" are likely to depend on our attitudes toward these activities themselves. Many issues and problems that arise from the development of computer technology are not fundamentally different from issues and problems we have confronted before. Thus I often draw analogies from other technologies and other aspects of life. Sometimes we can find a helpful perspective for analysis and even ideas for solutions to new problems by looking at older technologies and other contexts. The emphasis on the fact that similar problems occur in other areas, or outside of cyberspace, is not meant to excuse problems related to computers. It suggests, however, that the root is not always the computer, but may be human nature, ethics, politics, or other factors.

A third theme is diversity:

> Diversity of the quality of computer systems, in their design, user interfaces, reliability, safety, and so on.

> Diversity in the policies adopted by businesses (both producers and users of computer systems).

> Diversity in consumer preferences for products and services, safety, privacy, work environment, and so on.

It is important to remember this diversity when evaluating or generalizing about computers and policies for their use.

A final theme is:

> Differences between personal choices, policies of businesses and organizations, and law.

We can make a personal choice, for example, about whether to put our name on a mailing list, according to our individual values and knowledge. A business policy may be based on many factors, including consumer demand, the goal of making a profit, and the ethics of the business owners or managers. Different businesses adopt different policies. Laws are fundamentally different from personal choices and organizational policies because they impose decisions by force on people who did not make them. Arguments for passing a law should be qualitatively different from reasons for adopting a personal or organizational policy. It may seem odd at first, but arguments on the merits of the proposal—for example, that it is a good idea, or is efficient, or is good for business, or is helpful to consumers—are not good arguments for a law. These arguments can be used to try to convince a person or organization to (voluntarily) adopt a particular policy. Arguments for a law must show why the decision should be enforced against someone who *does not agree* that it is a good idea. It is better to base laws on the notion of rights rather than on personal views about their benefits.

1.3   APPRECIATING THE BENEFITS OF COMPUTERS

Discussions of social issues related to computers often focus on problems, and indeed we will discuss problems in this book. The beneficial uses of computers is an important issue too. Recognizing the beneficial uses is necessary to form a reasonable, balanced view of the impact and value of computers. In this section I will give a sampling of a variety of computer applications. This is not a comprehensive summary of computer applications— that would take several books. Some examples are routine things that you may use frequently; the point is to remind us that a generation ago, those things did not exist. Some are new, perhaps still in development; the point of these is to remind us of the potential for more benefits to come.

Some of the examples described here may spark thoughts about related problems. For example, do the automation applications cause people to lose their jobs? What if a database used by law enforcement to track sexual offenders is expanded to track political dissenters? We will look at such issues in later chapters. Here we look at the aspects that deserve appreciation.

1.3.1   The Common Uses

Probably the first time you used a computer, it was to play a game. Computer games are hardly life-saving, awe-inspiring wonders that profoundly advance the human condition. But they sure are fun. And, if one thinks about it, entertainment and fun are valuable aspects of a happy life.

Aside from games, the computer applications with which most of us are familiar are word processors, spreadsheets, databases, and business applications such as payroll and inventory systems. All of these let us do many tasks more efficiently. Consider word processors. I wrote my first textbook the old-fashioned way: by hand, on paper. The cut-and-paste operation that most word processors provide is named for the way it was done before computers. If I wanted to rearrange paragraphs, I cut the paper into pieces and taped them together in the new order. I drove almost 20 miles to take each chapter to a good technical typist. A week later, I drove the distance again to pick up the chapter. It was expensive and awkward to make changes after a draft was typed. The typed manuscript was entirely retyped by the publisher's typesetter, often introducing typographic errors.

Spreadsheets allow individuals and businesses to manage their finances more easily, quickly consider more options, speed the preparation of financial statements, tax forms, reports, and so on. Databases let us organize and access information more efficiently.

By accomplishing business data processing more quickly and accurately, business software reduces costs to customers and improves service. A restaurant manager reports that computerized inventory and report-generating software frees him from hours of paperwork so that he can spend more time in the restaurant providing service to his customers. Business hours for many stores have expanded as the accounting and inventory paperwork consumes fewer hours per transaction. A medical clinic reported that it could treat more patients when it computerized its record keeping. The ease of storing data on computers allows manufacturers to track the specific batches of parts that go into specific products, so that if a flaw necessitating a recall is discovered, the products affected can be identified precisely.[10]

Customer service from mail order companies, banks, credit card companies, and many other businesses has improved as customer service agents can find a person's order or account information instantly, provide up-to-date information, and make changes. Some businesses, including stock brokerage companies, have automated systems that allow customers to place orders by phone without speaking to a human service agent. Some are beginning to offer services online via the World Wide Web. Among the earliest, United Parcel Service and Federal Express allow customers to check the status of packages they send. The savings in overhead from these automated systems is passed on to the customer in lower costs and commissions.

Computers now play a large role in art and entertainment. Digital technologies have improved the quality of music we can listen to at home. Graphic artists make imaginative use of their new tools. Movies use a variety of high quality computer-generated special effects. Some of the first were the dinosaurs in "Jurassic Park" and the fictional character interacting with past presidents in "Forrest Gump." The charming 1995 hit movie "Toy Story" was the first completely computer-generated movie. Live theater performances use computers also; a computer program controlled the color, direction, and beam size of hundreds of lights to create dazzling effects in the Broadway musical "The Who's Tommy."

Communications and information services

New York to London is only five miles further than New York to Newark via satellite.

–Nicholas Negroponte[11]

The quantity and quality of today's telephone communications would be impossible without computers to design the networks and handle the routing and switching. In the late 1940s, almost all routing and switching was done by human operators plugging wires into boards. The volume of telephone calls in the U.S. has increased so much that, if this work were still done manually instead of with computers, half the adult population of the country would be employed as telephone operators.[12] The cost of international telephone calls may plummet as new software makes it possible to use a PC with speaker and microphone to make calls over the Internet.

Electronic mail has the advantages of telephone calls without the disadvantages. The mail arrives at the recipient's computer as quickly as a phone call, but it does not interrupt important work, dinner, or a shower; the message can be read at the recipient's convenience. The sender does not have the frustration of getting busy signals, nor does he or she have to consider time-zone differences when sending messages to other countries. E-mail was first used largely by computer scientists. As more people and businesses connected to computer networks, its use expanded to scientific researchers, then businesses, then millions of other people. Computer networks now span the globe. I use e-mail to answer questions from a student in a small town in central Mexico as easily as from a student in a computer lab on campus. By the mid-1990s, more than 100 countries were connected to the Internet. The number of frequent users of the World Wide Web in the U.S. more than tripled in 1996.

Using a fax machine or a computer with a fax modem, we can send a document across the country in several seconds instead of several days by mail. Modems and fax machines allow more people to work at home. For many of us, this is simply a convenience. For the elderly, disabled people, or single parents with young children, it is a significant benefit. Not long ago, deaf people were excluded from jobs that required use of a telephone. Now many of them hold such jobs; they use e-mail and fax machines.

Several companies are developing satellite-based international communications systems that by the year 2000 will allow users of mobile telephones to send and receive voice, faxes, and data virtually anywhere.

More than five million people subscribe to information and consumer services, such as CompuServe, Prodigy, America Online, and Microsoft Network. These services give us access to a vast amount and variety of information. *Consumer Reports,* movie reviews, weather reports, news reports, government documents, and so on, are online, available quickly and easily from our home computers. Usenet newsgroups and discussion groups on large commercial services and small bulletin board systems provide forums for information and comment on thousands of subjects. These groups provide opportunities for new social and community interactions, creating "virtual communities." They range from hobbies to political discussions to professional groups to support groups for people with health or personal problems. The World Wide Web includes an enormous variety of information from sites around the world. Documents on one system, with images and sound, are linked to related material on computers at other sites. The user can hop to another site by clicking a mouse and does not need to know where the desired material actually is located. The Web is growing at an astonishing rate. Established in Europe in 1990 for high-energy physicists to share pictures and text with colleagues in other countries, it grew to more than 10,000 sites by 1993 and 33,000 by mid-1995.[13] The Web, and similar innovations, help us not only to find material of interest to us, but also to make available to the world whatever information we want to provide.

Researchers can use several document systems to search newspapers, magazines, and trade journals for articles of interest to them. There are numerous specialized databases and bulletin board systems. Some systems send faxes of articles and documents automatically to the user who selects the appropriate codes from a menu on a touch-tone phone.

Miles of shelves of books in libraries are being replaced by electronic storage. The law school library at Columbia University houses more than 700,000 volumes and a half million sheets of microfilm, the third largest collection of legal materials in the U.S. In 1993, the Columbia Law School canceled plans to build a $20 million building to store new books. Instead, they bought a $1.5 million supercomputer on which to store the contents of tens of thousands of deteriorating old books, freeing shelf space for new ones. One goal of the project is to freeze the number of physical volumes at the current level. That will require converting 10,000–12,000 volumes per year to electronic form. The stored material will be available to researchers anywhere on the Internet. In this and many other digital library projects, books and documents are stored both in text form, to allow full text searches, and in optical images, so the user can see an exact copy of the material on the screen. The University of California CD-ROM Information System stores the equivalent of 260,000 books of federal statistics on 270 CD-ROMs in computer-controlled jukebox changers. Users can access the system through a World Wide Web server and by other Internet services. By 1994 more than 6000 people had used the system. The Library of Congress digitized more than 200,000 items by 1995, including its American history collection, which contains many unique and fragile items. The British Library owns the 11th century manuscript of *Beowulf,* studied by scholars from all over the world. Digitized images of the manuscript are now available to scholars on the Internet. The quality is so good that words erased by the original scribes, fire damage, and changes made in a 19th century restoration are visible. Thousands of works of art from museums around the world are now available on CD-ROM. In addition to the pictures, the disks contain information about the art and artists.[14]

Digital libraries have many advantages. Tasks that used to require transporting people to libraries in motor vehicles can now be done by transporting the information to people through telephone lines and optical fiber—at big savings in time and energy. Scholars who used to travel to view special material like the *Beowulf* manuscript save thousands of dollars. People who could not have paid for such trips now have access to materials worldwide. Digital libraries reduce the demand for paper and for physical space, be it bookshelves or buildings. They provide safe access to old, fragile material. They enable the use of sophisticated search software to find desired material from among thousands of pages, and they allow access to one document or book by many people at the same time, eliminating the problems of the desired book being checked out to someone else. They also eliminate the problem of a book being lost, stolen, or misshelved.

Automobiles

Automobiles now have several microprocessors embedded in various components. Some chips collect information about engine behavior and are used by mechanics to diagnose and fix problems. Anti-lock braking systems (ABS) use sensors and computers to control the pressure on the brakes to prevent skids. The ABS is more expert than human drivers at safely stopping a car.

It may not be long before computers are driving cars. Researchers at the Robotics Institute at Carnegie Mellon University have built a truck, equipped with a TV camera, image processing software, and artificial intelligence software, that drives itself. A closer goal is a warning system that alerts a driver, or even takes over the steering, when the computer determines that the driver is veering off the road or into an obstacle. Such a system could prevent many of the three million accidents that occur every year in the U.S. involving a single car and a sleepy or intoxicated driver. Ford Motor Company and General Motors Corporation are working on radar-based and infrared systems to provide better "night vision" for drivers. (Similar, but much more expensive, systems are used by the military.) Images or diagrams of objects that might cause a collision are projected onto the windshield. Using computer chips, the car engineers hope to reduce the bulky test systems to the size of a coffee can and make them available as an option for passenger cars within a decade.[15]

Education and training

There have been educational computer programs almost since there have been personal computers. Early educational toys like Speak 'n Spell spoke words for the child to spell (by typing on alphabet keys). The toy corrected the child as necessary and had several difficulty levels. Now, multimedia systems and CD-ROMs provide more sophisticated programs and presentations to teach many subjects. Students in rural towns that cannot afford a teacher for specialized subjects take classes offered in nearby cities by interactive television. They receive and submit written assignments by fax. A variety of educational programs are developing on the Internet; good courses and teachers will be available to students far from the teacher's physical location. This phenomenon is called "distance learning."

One of the successful educational applications is teaching illiterate adults to read. Traditional methods fail for many people who may be embarrassed, uninspired by the teaching techniques, or intimidated by a teacher's impatience with their mistakes. Computer programs that teach reading, some with multimedia, are engaging and uncritical. A study at the University of Northern Arizona and observations by people who run remedial reading programs indicate that people using the programs improve dramatically faster than those using traditional methods.[16]

Speech recognition is a useful tool in many educational and training programs. Computer programs that teach foreign languages give instruction in correct pronunciation if they do not understand what the user says. Complex simulation software with graphics and speech recognition is used for sophisticated training systems. Air traffic controllers, for example, are trained in a mockup tower whose "windows" are projection screens. The trainee directs air traffic that is entirely simulated by computer. The computer responds to the trainee's spoken commands to the simulated pilots. Air traffic controllers received training before we had computers, but the simulation allows more intensive training in a safe environment. If the trainee directs two airplanes to land on the same runway at the same time, no one gets hurt.

Crime fighting

The Automated Regional Justice Information System (ARJIS) is an example of the use of computer networks and databases to aid crime fighting. It serves a county of approximately three million people, with 17 cities. The system contains crime reports, arrest reports, field interview records, traffic citations, traffic accident reports, an alias file, and a variety of other kinds of records. It is used to identify suspects, clear suspects, track and identify trends and patterns of crime, and generate reports.[17]

When a crime is committed, police can enter whatever information they may have about the suspect and find potential matches to investigate. With just a "street name" and a description in an attempted murder case, ARJIS helped police narrow down the suspect list to four. The perpetrator was then identified by witnesses. When a suspect with no prior record was arrested for a burglary, police searched unsolved crimes for the same MO* and found several similar burglaries in other cities. Thus ARJIS helped solve the other cases and provided evidence that the suspect was a professional burglar rather than a first-time offender. ARJIS is also used for crime analysis. It helps identify special crime problems and plan allocation of patrols. More than one million data entry and inquiry requests are processed by the system each month.

Readers of detective stories, fans of Scotland Yard, and older police officers know that ingenuity, evidence, investigation, and many scientific tools have been used to solve crimes for centuries. Yet, one detective who has worked with ARJIS for several years said, "I don't know how anyone could do police work before ARJIS came along."[18] Why would he make such a comment? Why does a computerized system like ARJIS seem indispensable now? Increased population and mobility are likely reasons. In the past, a police officer might have personally known most of the people in the neighborhood, and neighbors were more likely to know each other. In Sherlock Holmes' day, criminals were less likely to commit crimes in several different cities. Whether indispensable or not, systems like ARJIS provide, at least, a significant improvement in efficiency: The police chief in one city says he would need almost twice as many detectives for the same level of effectiveness without the system.

Database searching has other applications in crime fighting. For example, insurance fraud is detected by using computers to find patients and doctors who file multiple claims. The FBI's National Crime Information Center (NCIC) is a computer database of arrest warrants and police inquiries.† It was from a query to this database that government agents learned that their suspect in the 1995 bombing of the Oklahoma City federal building had been arrested for a traffic violation shortly after the bombing.

Matching of fingerprints can now be done by computer. Many people think that when fingerprints are found at a crime scene, they are routinely matched against thousands of prints on file to find a suspect. This was not normally done. Fingerprints of a specific suspect could be easily compared, but matching crime-scene fingerprints against those in a card file was slow, painstaking work performed by human specialists. Now that fingerprints can be stored in computer databases and comparisons can be done by computer, the automated fingerprint identification system (AFIS), which can process millions of prints in twenty minutes, can be used to search for a suspect. In a test of the system, prints found at the scene of an unsolved murder that occurred almost 30 years earlier led to a suspect in another state. The computer match was verified by a human fingerprint expert, and the suspect was tried and convicted for the murder. AFIS also helped solve a murder that took place 18 years earlier. In one state, the system helped solve about 200 crimes in its first two years of operation.[19]

Specialized newsgroups on the Internet help solve and deter crimes. Dealers in collectible items post information about stolen art, rare books, and even valuable baseball cards, so that a thief can be caught when he tries to sell them.

---

*MO is an abbreviation for the Latin *modus operendi,* or method of operating.

†Because of errors and misuse, NCIC is the subject of much controversy. We will discuss some of its problems in Chapters 2 and 4.

1.3.2 Computers in Medicine

Computers are now used in virtually all phases of medicine, from research to the operating room to maintaining patient records. We will give a brief overview of some medical applications and their benefits.

Medical devices

Physicians now use a variety of machines, such as CT (computer-aided tomography) scanners and MRI (magnetic resonance imaging) machines, for medical imaging. MRI machines use computers to process the data generated by reflections from a magnetic field around a human body. They produce pictures of internal body organs, muscle, and other soft tissue that X rays cannot "see." These machines use a technique called "scientific visualization." Computers process huge amounts of data and turn them into pictures that people can interpret more easily than hundreds of pages of numbers. Currently, medical imaging is used mostly for diagnosis. However, some brain surgeons use images produced by MRI and biomagnetometers, another kind of scanning machine, in the operating room to reduce damage to critical parts of the brain when removing tumors.

Microprocessors control a variety of medical instruments. One million Americans wear heart pacemakers. Pacemakers contain computer chips that can fine-tune the heartbeat of a person who might otherwise die. People who suffered from episodes of abnormally fast heartbeat had first-year mortality rates of 30% for surgical treatment and 45% for drug treatment. In the mid-1980s, miniature software-controlled defibrillators were developed. They are implanted, like pacemakers, in the patient. When the device senses the start of arrhythmia, or abnormal heartbeat, it gives a low-voltage shock to the heart. The first-year mortality rate for people with these devices is 2–3%.[20] Microprocessors in medical instruments such as intravenous pumps allow patients to use sophisticated equipment at home, eliminating the expense and inconvenience of a hospital visit. Other devices using chips include ultrasound imagers, newborn incubators, and "smart" hospital beds.

A blood glucose scanner is currently under development. This device would shine a light on the patient's finger, then use its chip to analyze the reflected light to determine the amount of glucose in the blood. Anyone with diabetes will recognize the value of this device: It will eliminate the need to prick one's finger several times a day to take blood glucose measurements.

Patient records

Hospitals and medical centers are beginning to replace paper patient records with computerized records. Paper files often contain illegible hand-written notes and are poorly organized. They can be read by only one person at one time, and they are unavailable nearly 50% of the time (e.g., in another doctor's office or misfiled). Computerized records solve these problems. One study of a hospital with computerized patient records showed that patients were released from the hospital almost one day earlier and had bills averaging almost $900 less. Computerized records also make statistical research on diseases and treatments easier.[21]

DESIGNING NEW DRUGS

Drugs to fight diseases do their job by binding to target molecules, usually proteins, and preventing, or inhibiting, them from carrying out their destructive activity. It used to be that drugs were *discovered*—by luck or tedious trial and error. Now it is becoming more common for them to be *designed*—by an approach called "rational drug design," or "structure-based drug design" (SBDD). This approach, determining the detailed three-dimensional atomic structure of the target and designing specific chemical compounds to inhibit it, would be impossible without computer technology and advances in biotechnology.

In structure-based drug design, scientists grow a crystal of the protein, then use X-ray crystallography to map its structure. The crystal is bombarded with a powerful X-ray beam. Computers calculate the structure based on the way the X-rays diffract (i.e., scatter) after hitting the crystal. This work is heavily computational; tens of thousands of measurements of the diffracted radiation are taken and analyzed by computer. After the structure has been determined, graphical software is used to produce a three-dimensional image of the protein.

There are several recent examples of structures discovered by this process. Scientists at the Memorial Sloan-Kettering Cancer Center worked out the details of the structure of a tumor suppressor protein called p53. They report that mutations in p53 are "the most frequently observed genetic alterations in human cancer."[22] Knowing p53's structure can help researchers develop drugs to counter the effects of mutated forms. Researchers at Agouron Pharmaceuticals discovered the atomic structure of an enzyme called rhinovirus 3C protease that is involved in replication of a class of viruses that cause the common cold. Knowledge of the structure will aid the search for drugs to fight the viruses.

Databases and information systems

MedLine is a database of medical journal articles and books. It includes more than 3700 journals and is updated regularly. It is accessed on computer networks or on CD-ROMs, and it enables physicians to easily produce a long list of citations and abstracts of articles related to a specific medical problem. Like other library databases, it makes doing research relatively easy, more efficient and complete. How important is efficient, convenient research? Two studies showed that use of MedLine helped save lives, cure ailments, avoid unnecessary medical procedures, lower costs, and reduce hospital stays. Services like MedLine are particularly helpful in rural areas where a medical library or specialists may not be available. Patients use MedLine too. They investigate their diseases and treatments and take a more informed and active role in their own medical care.[23]

The federal Food and Drug Administration operates a bulletin board system that provides up-to-date information on the uses and side effects of drugs.

Diagnosis

There are many systems designed to aid doctors in diagnosing diseases. Some are databases that can be searched by entering symptoms. Others are specific to particular diseases. The vision field analyzer, a device that tests for glaucoma using computer-generated

The process of developing a potentially useful inhibitor is iterative. The first chemical compound developed may "fit" the protein to a degree and inhibit some of its activity. By varying the design and repeating the X-ray analysis, researchers can improve potency. For example, Agouron scientists went through several design cycles to produce a compound to block the activity of an enzyme involved in growth of tumor cells. The final result is 1500 times as potent as the one developed in the first design cycle. (The compounds developed by these techniques still must be tested for toxicity and other side effects or properties that might make them unsuitable as a drug.)

Previously, development of new drugs involved searching databases containing thousands of compounds, then physically testing those that seemed like good candidates. Attempts to work out the structure of target molecules were made, but took the efforts of many people over many years. The president of Agouron described the importance of computers to drug design as follows: "Through a series of computational steps which historically have sometimes involved a number of post-doctoral careers to complete, but which now move very rapidly with the advent of sophisticated algorithms and perhaps more importantly the availability of supercomputers, we are able to determine, with a very high degree of accuracy and with a net expenditure of less than a year's time, the precise architecture of a particular pharmaceutical target. . . . In the old days when determination of the protein structure was complete . . ., the next step was to build a wire model of the results." He goes on to say that it is difficult to overstate the advantage of using modern computer graphics software to display and manipulate the structure.[24]

images, is more accurate than its noncomputer predecessor used in the 1970s. A new computer program predicts the results of biopsies for prostate cancer with 87% accuracy. Doctors typically can predict the result with 35% accuracy. A computer system for analyzing mammograms does a better job than most doctors. A new ultrasound device uses computers to analyze echoes from sound waves bounced off a lump in a woman's breast. It can determine whether or not the lump is benign and may eliminate the need for 40% of surgical biopsies for breast cancer. Current screening tests for colon cancer are unpleasant and hence avoided by people who may be at risk. A new computed tomography scanning method, using virtual reality techniques, is being developed; it reduces risk, discomfort, and examination time.[25]

Telemedicine, or long-distance medicine

Many rural hospitals cannot afford to have a trained radiologist on staff. They send X-rays to larger hospitals for interpretation by experts. Now, the X-rays can be transmitted by telephone lines instead of being physically carried by couriers. Results are obtained more quickly, benefiting patient care, and the cost of the couriers is eliminated. Radiologists in the U.S. use similar systems to consult on cases in other countries where experts are not available. Some small-town hospitals use two-way video systems to consult with specialists at large medical centers while a local doctor is examining a patient; the specialists can see and hear and participate in the examination, eliminating the expense, time, and possible health risk of transporting the patient to the medical center.[26]

We are beginning to see remote operation of scientific and medical instruments across computer networks. Telemicroscopy is an example. High-voltage electron microscopes are very expensive, specialized instruments used for, among other things, research on Alzheimer's disease and Parkinson's disease. There are four regional high-voltage electron microscope centers in the U.S., funded by the National Institutes of Health. Researchers from around the country and other countries travel to one of the centers with the samples they want to study. Scientists at the San Diego center, the San Diego Supercomputer Center, and the Scripps Research Institution developed computer hardware and software to allow researchers to operate the microscope remotely and view their samples, mailed to the center earlier, in real-time across the computer network. By eliminating the time and expense of travel, telemicroscopy can help get more research done.[27]

The U.S. military is developing a system with which a surgeon can perform surgery miles from the patient on whom he or she is operating. The system combines video and robotic devices controlled by radio waves. The immediate goal is to save lives of soldiers wounded on battlefields far from expert surgeons. It may eventually be used for other emergency situations and to provide specialized surgery for remote patients, perhaps including patients who could not be moved without risks to their health.[28]

Automation

Automation of some hospital processes can provide convenience, cost savings, security, accounting services, and improved morale. For example, some hospitals use an ATM-like machine that dispenses medications and medical supplies. The machines can be placed in numerous convenient locations in the hospital, eliminating the need for long trips to supply rooms. A medical staffer enters a unique identifying number (a password) to use the machine and provides patient information. The transaction is automatically recorded by a central computer for inventory and billing purposes. Security for narcotics in many hospitals is accomplished by use of special keys for narcotics storage areas, sign-out sheets, and manual inventories at the end of each nursing shift. The transaction records made by the computerized system, including the identifier of the person to whom the drugs were dispensed, eliminate the need for those inconveniences and makes discrepancies in narcotics supplies easier to resolve without unnecessary suspicion. These machines free medical staff from tedious chores so that they can spend more time on patient care. By automating several tasks, they also reduce costs of medical care.[29]

1.3.3   Use of Computer Technology by Disabled People

One of the most heartwarming applications of computer technology is the restoration of abilities, productivity, and independence to people with physical disabilities.

There are more than 1000 computer-based devices for the disabled. The purpose of some of these devices is to enable disabled people to use the kinds of computer applications that other people use: word processors, spreadsheets, databases, and communications programs for sending e-mail, accessing bulletin boards, or exploring the information resources on the Internet and commercial systems. The purpose of other devices is to enable disabled people to control household and workplace appliances that most of us operate by hand. For both categories, appropriate input and output devices are needed. We will describe some of them.

Input and output devices

People with poor eyesight can direct a computer display to use a large type size. For people who are blind there are terminals equipped with speech synthesizers to read aloud what a sighted person sees on the screen. Terminals can be set to echo aloud each key the user types, so a blind user can tell if he or she makes a typing mistake. For materials that are not already stored in electronic form, an optical character recognizer combined with a speech synthesizer can read aloud to a blind person. Where noise is a problem (or for a person both blind and deaf), the speech output can be replaced by a grid of buttons raised and lowered by the computer to form Braille characters. Braille printers can be substituted for regular printers to provide a hard copy. For years, books have been available in large type, in Braille, or on tape, but the expense of production for a small market keeps the selection limited. Now any book, article, e-mail message, and so on, that is stored on a computer system, or can be scanned, can be read by a blind or poorly sighted person.

Some people can use their hands, but cannot control them precisely enough to type on a keyboard. They can use specially enlarged keyboards or touch screens, displaying a picture of a keyboard. Various conditions—loss of limbs, quadriplegia (paralysis in both arms and legs, often resulting from an accident), and certain diseases—eliminate all or almost all use of the hands. Speech recognition is an enormously valuable tool for such people. The software and hardware needed are relatively inexpensive, and speech recognition technology is rapidly improving. One such system, DragonDictate, has a 120,000-word vocabulary. The system is used both to give commands to the computer and to dictate documents to a standard word processor. Before computers, people with no use of their hands could operate some devices with a mouth-operated control stick, a tedious process with limited applications.

Speech recognition can also be used to operate environmental control systems. "Environment" in this context means the indoor home or office environment: lighting, temperature, TV, stereo, and appliances. There are several such systems available now. One I saw demonstrated at the Disabled Opportunities Center in San Diego, made by a company called Mastervoice, operates appliances connected to a computer control box through ordinary household wiring. (The original system is in the Smithsonian Institution.) Mastervoice is programmable. For example, when the user says, "I'm home," it can respond by turning on lights (depending on the time of day), opening drapes, turning on heat or air conditioning, and turning on the stereo. "Goodnight" can direct the system to arm a security alarm, turn on hallway and bedroom lights, then turn them off after a predetermined time period. The system can be programmed to turn down the TV when the phone rings, and the user can make telephone calls by simply telling the system whom to call. The system recognizes the owner's voice, so it can be used for security operations, such as locking or unlocking doors. Such a system is a boon to the safety, comfort, and independence of a person with limited mobility and use of hands. Twenty years ago, according to *Business Week,* voice-operated environmental-control systems would have cost $20,000 to

$200,000, and the quality of speech recognition was not good. The user had to repeat commands with the same inflection and tone of voice. Now some of the better systems cost a few thousand dollars and the technology has improved to the point that the Mastervoice system recognized the agitated and weak voice of a person whose breathing apparatus partially failed, and called for help.[30]

A person who cannot speak can use a head mouse, a headset that detects movement of the head and moves the cursor accordingly on the screen. The user can sip or puff into a strawlike device on the headset to "click" the mouse. Another device fits in the mouth like an orthodontic retainer and has buttons that can be operated with the tongue. These devices can be used to operate ordinary computer applications (usually with special software that displays a picture of a keyboard or a menu of control options on the screen), or to operate household appliances. Systems equipped with a small camera aimed at the user's eye can determine what the user is looking at on the screen. Thus someone who can move only one eye can communicate and operate a computer. The impact of such devices on the morale of the user is immense. Think about a person with an active mind, personality, and sense of humor—but without the ability to write, type, or speak. Imagine the difference when the person has the ability to communicate—with family and friends, and with all the people and resources available on the Internet.

Specialized systems are being developed to give disabled people access to activities that would have been merely dreams for them before. The Science Institute for the Disabled at East Carolina University, for example, has developed a system to allow disabled students to operate equipment in chemistry labs so that they can study college chemistry. The laboratory instruments can output their readings directly to a computer that analyzes the data and presents them in a form suitable for the user. A speech synthesizer provides output of instrument readings for a blind student. For experiments that produce a long sequence of readings, the computer produces tones of varying pitch so the user can identify highs and lows. More complex sets of data are presented as musical patterns using a computer-controlled music synthesizer. The system includes speech recognition for students who cannot type.[31]

Impact

Access to the common kinds of software applications and the databases and other information sources now available on computer networks is a tremendous convenience for everyone. The degree of improvement, however, is more dramatic for people who lacked the physical ability to read or write before. One of the results of the availability of computer technology for disabled people is that people who formerly could not work now can. Many disabled people have formed and run their own businesses. The number of disabled entrepreneurs has increased steadily in the last few years. Their businesses include financial services, desktop publishing, billing services, a sportscasting company, law firms, and companies that develop computer tools for the disabled and train people in their use.[32]

"It is with good reason," says David Lunney, the chemist who developed special laboratory equipment for disabled students, "that the personal computer is so widely regarded as the most liberating and empowering device yet developed for people with disabilities." Jim Fruchterman, president of Arkenstone, a company that makes book readers for the blind, says simply that "PCs are the Swiss Army knife for disabled people." Fruchterman's company has developed a portable system using the global positioning system (satellites), geographic information systems (detailed computerized maps), and a voice synthesizer to help blind people walk around and find their way in neighborhoods they were not previously familiar with.[33]

Replacing limbs and organs

Microprocessors are embedded in prosthetic devices, such as artificial arms. These devices use electrodes to pick up the tiny electric fields generated by contractions of the muscles in the upper (natural) arm. The signals are amplified and processed by the microprocessor, which controls tiny motors that move the artificial arm, open and close fingers, and so on. Myoelectric limbs (artificial limbs that use electric signals from the muscles) existed before microprocessors, but they used analog motors and did not have the sensitivity and flexibility of the chip-controlled limbs. Children fitted with the new limbs when they are very young can learn to use the artificial hand and fingers almost as naturally as a natural limb.[34]

In the future, computers may restore some sight to blind people: Researchers are developing a computer chip that will float on the retina of the eye and send visual signals to the brain.[35]

1.3.4 Science, Research, and Engineering

Computers are now essential for science, scientific research, and engineering. They are used for data management, communications, control of instruments, modeling, computation, and creating reports and graphical displays. I will describe one project that illustrates the variety of uses of computers and the improvement they provide over earlier tools and techniques: mapping the ocean floor. See the box on the next page.

1.3.5 Automation

Automation in manufacturing began long ago, but computers have added to the capabilities and flexibility of automated systems. Many factories and warehouses now use computer-controlled automation. An example is the very sophisticated warehouse system (called an Automated Storage and Retrieval System, or ASRS) built in 1987 by Ralphs, a southern California supermarket chain with more than 100 stores. The world's largest computer-controlled ASRS in the grocery industry, the facility is ten stories high. Products are stored on more than 50,000 pallets and retrieved by huge automated cranes. The system keeps track of the location of products and the inventory. Electric eyes check the pallets and direct any with problems to the "pallet hospital." The automated system allowed the company to combine five separate facilities. The new facility reduced land usage and property costs, the number of employees needed, and the number of times each product had to be handled and moved. It is fast and efficient enough to allow deliveries to most of the chain's stores every day, thus improving stock management at the stores. The costs of the system were recovered from the savings it brought about in just a few years.[36]

Automation combined with vision systems produces a variety of machines that are used in production lines. For example, such systems are used to count eggs and hot dog buns on conveyor belts. The software is customized for an application and can determine the orientation of the products, count them, inspect them, and determine which are of

SCIENTIFIC APPLICATION—MAPPING THE ANTARCTIC SEAFLOOR

Mapping the ocean floor has many potential benefits. It may help in navigation, in finding good fishing sites, in understanding the history of the earth, and in studies of continental drift, climate, earthquakes, and hurricanes. Measurements of the depth of the oceans were taken long before computers were invented, but early methods were primitive, slow, and full of inaccuracies (e.g., lowering a heavy weight tied to a long rope over the side of a vessel until it hit bottom). The result was only a very approximate idea of what the seafloor looked like in small areas. With newer methods, using sonar, taking measurements at enough points to map the ocean would take one vessel roughly 300 years. Recently, with the help of satellites, microwaves, and supercomputers, the Scripps Institute of Oceanography and the San Diego Supercomputer Center produced a color video in which we travel, with a fish's eye view, through the peaks and crevices of the Antarctic seafloor. How was this done? With the help of computers at virtually every stage of the project.

For approximately 18 months in the mid-1980s, the Geosat satellite sent microwave radar pulses down to the oceans and measured the pulse reflected back from the ocean surface. Computers were used for the compression and decompression of the radar pulse, to determine the pulse travel time, and to store and then download the data to a tracking facility. Data were transported to a processing facility over a computer network.

Computers were used to add environmental corrections (e.g., applying tide models) to the data, to edit and organize the data, and to calculate the precise positions of the satellite when the measurements were taken. Now the height of the ocean surface could be computed. But we want to map the ocean floor, not the surface. The height of the ocean surface fluctuates with winds, currents, and waves. However, it is also affected by gravitational forces from the ocean floor that depend on its depth and density. Unlike the other factors, the gravitational effect is constant from day to day. Thus the satellite took many measurements over the same area; the readings were averaged to get a value that depends primarily on the mountains and canyons of the ocean floor and not on the variable surface phenomena. Geosat took more than 90,000,000 readings.

Scientists used to examine pages and pages of computer printouts, each containing many columns of numbers, in order to try to understand the results of their experiments. It is said that a picture is worth a thousand words. A picture is also worth a million numbers. Computers were used to produce maps from the data. This is another example of scientific visualization, i.e., turning vast amounts of data into charts, pictures, and videos. Because of the amount of data involved, computer graphics, or visualization, programs take a large amount of computer time and, for scientific applications like the one we are describing, are usually run on supercomputers. The computation needed to produce the images for the three-minute color video of a section of the Antarctic seafloor was done on more than a dozen workstations. By sharing the work, they completed the task in one day.[37]

unacceptable size. If this sounds easy, remember that when we look at something, our brain does a lot of automatic processing. It is not difficult for us to count the hot dog buns even if they are scattered about and not lined up neatly. The computer processes a digital image and must distinguish the product from the background, detect edges of products that are next to each other, distinguish the product from debris on the conveyor belt (e.g., flour dust in a bakery), and so on. Unlike earlier, noncomputerized automated systems for similar applications, the vision system does not come in contact with the product, thus reducing damage. Also, the computer systems have more flexibility.[38]

Robotic arms and other robotic devices are another form of automation. Robot arms are used in factories to assemble products faster and more accurately than people can. A robotic milking machine milks cows at dairy farms while the farmhands sleep; more frequent milking has boosted milk production.[39] Robots can be used in environments that are hazardous to people. They inspect undersea structures and communication cables, and they explore volcanoes. Intelligent robotic systems are being developed for space exploration.

1.3.6   Identification Systems

Technology for identifying people and products, from bar codes to smart cards, has been getting more sophisticated.

Before bar codes and scanners were used on grocery products, grocery store employees put a paper price sticker on each item. The checker read the sticker and punched the amount on the cash register keyboard. With bar codes, the computer system is programmed with the price. Check-out scanners eliminate the need for the stickers and the typing of the price for each unit purchased. The computer system automatically updates inventory records and prepares purchase orders. In the highly competitive grocery industry, anything that reduces costs and provides faster service to customers is important. Many libraries use a similar system to speed the check-out of books. Each book and each customer's library card has a unique bar code. Two quick scans record the transaction in the computer system.

There are numerous other applications of bar codes. I will mention one more. While driving past Benicia, in the San Francisco Bay Area, I saw a startling sight: a three-mile long parking lot, packed bumper-to-bumper with new cars. From a distance it is a colorful mosaic made up of groups of hundreds of identical cars waiting to be shipped to different locations. Each year 150,000 new cars are shipped in and out of this port facility. Each car is worth thousands of dollars, and it is important that none be lost or shipped to the wrong destination. Employees used to manually verify the 17-character vehicle identification number of every car. It took four 10-hour shifts to verify 4000 vehicles. Now an employee uses a bar code reader to scan 4000 vehicles in five hours. The data collected, and information about the car's location, are transmitted by radio to the facility's computer network. When a vehicle enters the facility, and each time it is moved, its location is updated. Thus, vehicles are tracked accurately and efficiently through the whole shipping process.[40]

A newer technology, called touch memory buttons, now competes with bar coding. The memory chip is embedded in a coin-sized disk in a stainless steel casing that can be attached to equipment or carried in a pocket. It can be read by touching the surface with a wand-like device. Touch memory buttons have a few advantages over bar coding. The buttons can hold much more information (currently up to about 8000 bytes, compared to a few bytes in a bar code). Data can be written on the buttons, as well as read, so they can be updated. They are more durable (resistant to weather, tearing, tampering, etc.). Bar codes are fine for supermarket packaging; touch memory buttons have other applications. One is managing a harvest. Large farms employ hundreds or a few thousand workers to pick crops at harvest time. The workers are paid by the box or by the weight of the crops they pick. Farmers used to use punch cards, scratch pads, or tokens to keep track of how many units each worker picked. Later, several office workers would tally up the totals and calculate the pay. Now, workers at dozens of farms carry the touch memory buttons in their pockets or pinned to their shirts. Laptop computers in the field are used to read and write the relevant information. The ease of recording the data speeds up bookkeeping tasks and enables managers to monitor their harvest more accurately and manage it more productively.

Memory buttons are used by Ryder Truck, a company that rents moving vans and commercial trucks. Ryder has a fleet of 130,000 trucks and more than 900 maintenance locations in North America. It is installing a button on each truck that stores the identification number, customer information, maintenance record, and other information. The goals are to reduce manual recording and paperwork, eliminate data entry errors, speed information collection, and thus increase vehicle uptime and improve customer service. The Postal Service is installing touch memory buttons on mailboxes to monitor whether mail is being picked up on time. Memory buttons are also used for identification badges, medical bracelets, security systems, and other applications.[41]

Smart cards are the size of credit cards, but they contain a microprocessor and memory. They can be read by a card-scanning machine and used to access data in a computer network. Hundreds of applications, including uses for financial transactions, health care, credit, and telephone calls are being developed. The cards can use a variety of security techniques to protect data. Because critical medical information can be stored on the card, one advantage could be obtaining proper treatment when traveling or in an emergency. Also, the consumer could have direct access to information not currently easily available, for example, one's credit record.*

1.3.7 Reducing Paper Use and Trash

Electronic storage of text, and the ability to edit and update it, is reducing the need for paper in many businesses—and also the amount of trash produced. A large insurance company reduced its use of paper by 100 million pages in a nine-month period by keeping its manuals on computers instead of printing them. A computerized insurance system for recording insurance claims replaced more than 30 million index cards. A department store chain reported saving $1 million worth of paper per year by keeping sales reports on computer instead of paper.[42] We also reduce trash when, instead of throwing away last month's issue of a magazine, we simply delete it from our disk and download the new issue into the same space. (The electronically distributed newsletter of the Electronic Frontier Foundation ends with the line, "This newsletter is printed on 100% recycled electrons.")

---

*There are numerous potential privacy, security, legal, and constitutional problems related to smart cards.

Some observers have pointed out that fax machines and laser printers make it so easy to print things on paper that we are in fact using more paper now than we did before. Computers give us the ability to use less paper, but they may not give us the incentive to do so. Perhaps the increased paper use will be a temporary phenomenon. Most of us still want a paper copy of a document to read in a comfortable chair or sprawled on the sofa or at the beach. When computers become smaller and documents are stored on credit-card-sized cards instead of diskettes, we may see a substantial decline in paper use. Laptop and notebook computers are helping the transition; many business and professional people now take notes directly on them instead of on paper.

1.3.8 Some Observations

The life-saving and life-enhancing effects of computers are obvious from some of the applications we just described. Sometimes beneficial effects are less obvious. In Chapter 4 we will describe a computer program that has been very helpful in the design of products that must withstand forceful impacts. Safety is the main goal in most of those applications. (Reducing the amount of materials used, thus reducing waste of resources, is another goal.) By the nature of these design and development applications, the people who benefit from them may never know it. A bicycle rider who survives an accident may know that her helmet was an important factor, but she probably would not know that some detail of the design suggested by computer simulations prevented a worse injury. Passengers on an airplane that does not crash after a bird flies into an engine will likely never know that their lives were saved by a design detail inspired by a computer simulation.

For many of us, it would be hard to imagine living without computers. Yet, until very recently, we did. Tolstoy wrote *War and Peace* without a word processor. No one would design a bridge or a large building today without using a computer, but the Brooklyn Bridge, built more than 100 years ago, is both a work of art and a marvelous feat of engineering. The builders of the Statue of Liberty, the Pyramids, the Roman aqueducts, magnificent cathedrals, and countless other complex structures did not wait for computers. We use computers for many tasks that used to be done without them. What are the advantages? Convenience, efficiency, options. Computers allow us to work faster and more accurately than before. For some applications, they reduce the amount of resources, including human effort, required for a task. Access to information on the Net empowers us to make better choices about everything from movies to medical treatments.

Efficiency is sometimes looked down upon as being simply a matter of money, an economic effect, not a social value. That is a mistaken view. If a new drug is discovered 15 years earlier than it would have been without computers, hundreds or thousands of lives may be saved or improved in those 15 years. If computers can help design a safe car that is cheaper than previous designs, more people will be able to afford to ride more safely. Any task that can be done more efficiently frees some of our time and resources for other pursuits, be they work, community, cultural, or leisure activities.

The ability to accomplish a task more efficiently is not a benefit if the task itself has negative consequences. We are ready now to begin to examine problems created or intensified by computers. In the next chapter we consider how efficient information collection and manipulation can threaten our safety, freedom, and privacy.

It is precisely this unique human capacity to transcend the present, to live one's life by purposes stretching into the future—to live not at the mercy of the world, but as a builder and designer of that world—that is the distinction between human and animal behavior, or between the human being and the machine.

—BETTY FRIEDAN[43]

EXERCISES

Review exercises

1. Why was the Jacquard weaving loom important to the history of computing?

2. What was the effect of automated teller machines on the employment of bank tellers?

3. List two jobs that have been made obsolete by computers. List two jobs that would not exist without computers.

4. Some kinds of computer tools are used in both the drug design application (Section 1.3.2) and the Antarctic seafloor mapping application (Section 1.3.4). List them.

5. Describe two applications of speech recognition.

6. List several benefits of having library materials in electronic format.

General exercises

7. List two machines or devices that existed before computers, but that now have computers or microprocessors built in. (Give examples that were not mentioned in the text.)

8. (a) Microwave ovens were first introduced without microprocessors. It is the microwaves, not the computer, that cooks the food. What benefits in microwave ovens come from the computer?

   (b) Choose another device or appliance that existed before microprocessors, but now has a microprocessor in it. What is the benefit obtained from the computer?

9. Try to think of some product (other than slide rules) that has been in use for approximately 100 years or more, but that has recently become obsolete or may become obsolete in the near future because of computer technology.

10. Consider the problem of making a bank deposit but not having the deposit credited to your account. Compare the likelihood of this happening with various ways of making the deposit: going to a teller in a bank, sending the deposit by mail, or using an ATM. What might go wrong? How difficult would it be in each case to convince the bank that you really made the deposit?[44]

11. Think up some computerized device or program that does not yet exist, but that you would be very proud to help develop. Describe it.

12. List three applications of computer technology mentioned in this chapter that reduce the need for transportation. What are some advantages of doing so? For one of the applications you chose, describe a potential weakness or problem that might develop (relative to the old-fashioned way of accomplishing the same objective).

13. One of the advantages of personal computers and information systems is described as "empowerment." List three applications mentioned in this chapter that allow or help ordinary people to do things for which we used to rely on experts.

14. Describe a computer program or application with which you had experience (as a user or a programmer) in medicine, education, or crime fighting.

15. Let's start thinking about Chapter 2. Pick any two applications of computers described in Section 1.3 where the use of computers makes invasion of privacy easier or more likely. Explain how.

16. Thinking ahead to Chapter 4, pick any two applications of computers described in Section 1.3 where an error in the computer system could pose a serious danger to people's lives. Explain how.

Assignments

These exercises require some research or activity that may need to be done during business hours or a few days before the assignment is due.

17. Go around your home and make a list of all the appliances and devices that contain a computer chip.

18. Get a brochure from a car dealer for a new car. Describe the uses of computer chips in the car. For each one, tell if its main purpose is to enhance convenience or safety.

19. Find out when typewriters were first used in the United States. Find out how many are being produced and sold now.

20. Arrange an interview with a disabled student on your campus. Ask the student to describe or demonstrate some of the computer tools he or she uses. (If your campus has a Disabled Student Center, its staff may be able to help you find an interview subject.) Write a report of the interview and/or demonstration.

21. Interview a photographer who has used both manual cameras and automatic cameras with embedded microprocessors. Ask his or her opinions of the advantages and disadvantages of each.

22. When this book was written, smart card applications were in the development or experimental stage. Find out about some current use of smart cards and describe it.

23. If your university or employer has a World Wide Web home page, access and explore it. Write a brief summary of what you found. Mention some links to other sites if there were any. If you are an experienced Web user, find a site with information relevant to any of the issues introduced in Section 1.2.

24. Over the next month or two (whatever is appropriate for the length of your course), collect newspaper or magazine articles on (1) benefits and valuable applications of computers and (2) failures and/or mistakes caused by computer systems. (You may include articles from print or electronic sources.) Collect at least five articles in each group. Mark the source and date on each article. The articles should be current, that is, published or distributed during this time period. Write a brief summary and commentary on two articles in each category indicating how they relate to topics covered in this book.

NOTES

1   Chris Morgan and David Langford, *Facts and Fallacies: A Book of Definitive Mistakes and Misguided Predictions,* St. Martin's Press, 1981, p. 64. Mr. Duell made his comment while urging the President to abolish the Patent Office. (Morgan and Langford refer to Duell only by his title; his name is given in Christopher Cerf and Victor Navasky, *The Definitive Compendium of Authoritative Misinformation,* Pantheon Books, 1984, p. 203.)

2   Jim Carlton, "Study Says Compaq Has Surpassed IBM in Personal Computer Unit Shipments," *Wall Street Journal,* December 23, 1994, p. A3. *Technology in the American Household,* Times Mirror Center for the People and the Press, May 1994, p. 4. The 1994 Harris & Associates survey *Interactive Services, Consumers, and Privacy* found 37% of respondents had a computer at home. The figure for CD-ROM players is from Dataquest, Inc., reported in Frederick Rose and Richard Turner, "The Movie Was a Hit, The CD-ROM a Dud; Software Bites Disney," *Wall Street Journal,* January 23, 1995, p. A1. The number of chips shipped is from Michael Rothschild, "Beyond Repair: The Politics of the Machine Age Are Hopelessly Obsolete," *The New Democrat,* July/August 1995, pp. 8–11.

3   The source for most of the historical information is Stan Augarten, *Bit by Bit: An Illustrated History of Computers,* Ticknor & Fields, 1984. Other sources: Statistical Abstracts of the United States. Emmanuel Desurvire, "Lightwave Communications: The Fifth Generation," *Scientific American,* January 1992, p. 116. Herb Brody, "Internet@Crossroads.$$$," *Technology Review,* May 1995, pp. 24–31.

4   Michael Rothschild, "Beyond Repair: The Politics of the Machine Age Are Hopelessly Obsolete," *The New Democrat,* July/August 1995, pp. 8–11.

5   Joan E. Rigdon, "Technological Gains Are Cutting Costs, And Jobs, in Services," *Wall Street Journal,* February 24, 1994, p. A1.

6   Saul Hansell, "Cash Machines Getting Greedy at a Big Bank," *New York Times,* February 18, 1994, pp. A1, C16.

7   Most of the information about Turing is from Andrew Hodges, *Alan Turing: the Enigma,* Simon & Schuster, 1983.

8   Augarten, *Bit by Bit,* p. 148.

9   ATM transaction data are from Electronic Funds Transfer Association, reported in "Raw Data," *Wired,* January 1996, v. 4.01, p. 66. Crime data are from F. Barry Schreiber, "The Future of ATM Security," *Security Management,* March 1994, 38:3, p. 18A.

10 The comments from the restaurant manager (of a Hungry Hunter restaurant) and the medical clinic were reported in a term paper "Automation: Friend or Foe," by my student Thomas Chhoa. The example of tracking parts (for Land Rovers) is described in Laurie Hays, "Using Computers to Divine Who Might Buy a Gas Grill," *Wall Street Journal,* August 16, 1994, pp. B1, B4.

11 Nicholas Negroponte, "Being Digital," *Wired,* February 1995, p. 182.

12 George F. Gilder, *Microcosm,* Simon & Schuster, 1989, p. 46.

13 Wade Roush, "Spinning a Better Web," *Technology Review,* April 1995, pp. 11–13. John Byczkowski, "Site Seers," *NetGuide,* June 1995, p. 28. Yahoo: A Guide to WWW.

14 The April 1995 issue of *Communications of the ACM* contains a special section with more than 20 articles on digital libraries; it includes all those mentioned here except the Columbia Law Library. Information on that project is from William M. Bulkeley, "Libraries Shift from Books to Computers," *Wall Street Journal,* February 8, 1993, p. B4; news release from Columbia Law School, February 1, 1993; letter from James Hoover, Law Librarian, February 23, 1993.

15 Gautam Naik, "This Robot Drives and May Save Lives," *Wall Street Journal,* April 5, 1994, p. B1. Neal Templin, "Vision Systems in Cars of Future May Ease Drivers' Fear of Dark," *Wall Street Journal,* September 8, 1994, p. B1.

16 William M. Bulkeley, "Illiterates Find Computers Are Patient Mentors," *Wall Street Journal,* November 16, 1992, p. B1.

17 The information on ARJIS is from Donald A. Woodmancy, "Spreading the Word," *Police,* September 1989, pp. 50–52, 87–91; Kathryn Balint, "Upgrade Due for Cops' Computer System,"

San Diego Union, "ComputerLink" section, March 26, 1996, p. 14; and materials provided by San Diego Data Processing Corp.

18 Bill Knight, San Diego Police Department, quoted in Woodmancy, "Spreading the Word."

19 Viveca Novak and Joe Davidson, "Clinton Unveils Measures To Fight U.S. Terrorism," *Wall Street Journal,* April 24, 1995, pp. A3, A4. Andrea Gerlin, "New High-Tech Tools Help Solve Old Murders," *Wall Street Journal,* June 19, 1995, pp. B1, B5.

20 Joseph R. Garber, "Heart Software," *Forbes,* December 20, 1993, p. 248.

21 "Newstrack" ("Rx for Health Care"), *Communications of the ACM,* April 1993, pp. 13–14.

22 Yunje Cho, Svetlana Gorina, Philip D. Jeffrey, and Nikola P. Pavletich, "Crystal Structure of a p53 Tumor Supressor-DNA Complex," *Science,* July 15, 1994, 265:5170 pp. 346–55.

23 Ron Winslow, "More Doctors Are Adding On-Line Tools to Their Kits," *Wall Street Journal,* October 7, 1994, p. B1. The studies mentioned are in *Journal of the American Medical Association* and *Academic Medicine.*

24 Siegfried H. Reich and Stephen E. Webber, "Structure-based Drug Design," *Perspectives in Drug Discovery and Design,* v. 1, 1993, pp. 371–90. "Rational Drug Design," chapter in *Proceedings of the 2nd Annual Paine Webber Biotechnology Conference,* San Diego, CA, October 1989, pp. 305–32. Agouron Pharmaceuticals Inc. Annual Report 1989. Michael Waldholz, "Scientists Unveil a 3-D Portrait of Cancer Gene," *Wall Street Journal,* July 15, 1994, p. B1. Richard Turner, "Agouron Pharmaceuticals Shares Soar after Discovery Linked to Common Cold," *Wall Street Journal,* March 14, 1994. Telephone interview with Dr. Steve Worland, Agouron, July 22, 1994. The quotation is from *Proceedings of the 2nd Annual Paine Webber Biotechnology Conference,* p. 311.

25 Robert Fox, "News Track," *Communications of the ACM,* January 1995, 38:1, p. 9–10. "A Neural Net to Snag Breast Cancer," *Business Week,* March 13, 1995, p. 95. Robert Langreth, "Ultrasound That Trims Need for Biopsy In Breast Cancer Clears FDA Hurdle," *Wall Street Journal,* December 12, 1995, p. B10. "Computer Cuts Risk, Time in Detecting Cancer," *Cancer Researcher Weekly,* May 9, 1994, p. 5.

26 George Anders, "Phone Lines Zip X-Ray Images Cross-Country," *Wall Street Journal,* September 30, 1993, p. B1. Morris Barrett, "Robo-Doc to the Rescue," *Time,* November 13, 1995. Bill Richards, "Many Rural Regions Are Growing Again; A Reason: Technology," *Wall Street Journal,* November 21, 1994, pp. A1, A6.

27 Victoria L. Contie, "Long-Distance Microscopy," *NCRR Reporter,* May/June, 1993, 17:3, p. 3. Telephone interview with Dr. Mark Ellisman, director of the San Diego Microscopy and Imaging Resource, July 18, 1994.

28 Barrett, "Robo-Doc to the Rescue."

29 Pyxis Corporation, San Diego.

30 Disabled Opportunities Center, San Diego, CA. "A Butler in the House," *Electronic House,* March/April 1990. Telephone interview with Christopher Brown, Automated Voice Systems, Inc., Yorba Linda, CA, July 27, 1994.

31 David Lunney, "Adapted Computers as Laboratory Aids for People With Disabilities," 1992.

32 Timothy L. O'Brien, "Aided by Computers, Many of the Disabled Form Own Businesses," *Wall Street Journal,* October 8, 1993, p. A1.

33 The quote from Lunney is in David Lunney, "Adapted Computers as Laboratory Aids for People With Disabilities," 1992. The quote from Fruchterman is from an e-mail message to me. The navigation product for the blind is described in Peter Tyson, "High-Tech Help for the Blind," *Technology Review,* April 1995, pp. 19–21.

34 "New Technology for Artificial Arms," *Exceptional Parent,* November/December 1993, pp. 24–26. Telephone interview with Ed Gosschalk, Southern California Orthotics and Prosthetics, August 15, 1994.

35 Robert Fox, "Newstrack," *Communications of the ACM,* December 1995, pp. 9–10.

36 "High-rise Storage System Combines with Conventional Selection Warehouse for Efficient, Productive Operation," *Grocery Distribution,* 1990. Phone interview with Rick Toneck, Operations Manager, July 12, 1994.

37 Information on the Antarctic seafloor project was provided by James McLeod of the San Diego Supercomputer Center and David Sandwell of Scripps Institution of Oceanography.

38 Tim Blomenberg, "Breaking New Ground in Machine Vision," *Sensors,* August 1994, 11:8, pp. 28–30.

39 Dana Milbank, "Barnyard Breakthrough: Cow Milks Herself," *Wall Street Journal,* May 8, 1995, pp. B1, B6.

40 Dick Hackmeister, "RF/DC Helps New Autos Put to Sea," *IDSystems,* 14:8, August 1994, pp. 21–26.

41 Mark Boslet, "Metal Buttons Carried by Crop Pickers Serve as Mini Databases for Farmers," *Wall Street Journal,* May 31, 1994, p. A11C. Paul Quinn, "How Ya Gonna Beep 'Em Down on the Farm?" *IDSystems,* May, 1994, p. 67. Paul Quinn, "On the Fast Track with Ryder Truck," *IDSystems,* August 1994. Touch Connections catalog. Telephone interview with Michelle McLaren, Dallas Semiconductor, September 29, 1994.

42 William M. Bulkeley, "Information Age," *Wall Street Journal,* August 5, 1993, p. B1. "Newstrack' ("Claims to Fame"), *Communications of the ACM,* February 1993, p. 14.

43 Betty Friedan, *The Feminine Mystique,* W. W. Norton, 1963, p. 312.

44 My thanks to one of the anonymous reviewers for the idea for this exercise.

FOR FURTHER READING

The Alliance for Technical Access, *Computer Resources for People With Disabilities: A Guide to Exploring Today's Assistive Technology,* Hunter House Inc., 1994.

Stan Augarten, *Bit by Bit: An Illustrated History of Computers,* Ticknor & Fields, 1984.

Andrew Hodges, *Alan Turing: the Enigma,* Simon & Schuster, 1983.

The following references include topics that are covered in more than one chapter in this book.

Edward Cavazos and Gavino Morin, *Cyberspace and the Law,* MIT Press, 1994.

Deborah G. Johnson and Helen Nissenbaum, eds., *Computers, Ethics & Social Values,* Prentice Hall, 1995.

Rob Kling, ed., *Computerization and Controversy: Value Conflict and Social Choices,* 2nd ed., Academic Press, 1996.

Lance Rose and Jonathan Wallace, *SysLaw,* PC Information Group, 1992.

Richard S. Rosenberg, *The Social Impact of Computers,* Academic Press, 1992.

Herman T. Tavani, "A Computer Ethics Bibliography," in *Computers and Society,* in four parts, June, September, December 1995, and June 1996.

2

PRIVACY AND INFORMATION

2.1   INTRODUCTION

After the fall of the communist government in East Germany, the people examined the files of Stasi, the secret police. They found that the government had used spies and informers to build detailed dossiers on the opinions and activities of roughly six million people, a third of the population. The informers were neighbors, coworkers, friends, and even family members of the people they reported on. The paper files filled an estimated 125 miles of shelf space. Computers were not used at all.[1]

Personal files, details of purchases, and evidence of romantic affairs can all be found by going through someone's garbage. Surveillance cameras watch shoppers in stores and employees at work.

Computers are not necessary for the invasion of privacy. However, we discuss privacy at length in this book because the use of computers has made new threats possible and old threats more potent. Computers make the collection, analysis, storage, access, and distribution of large amounts of information much easier than before. A sector of data on a disk can be accessed in roughly 10 milliseconds—faster than we can turn a page in a book. Computers have increased both the speed and anonymity with which a person can do searches. Today there are many databases, both government and private, containing personal information* about us. Some of this information, such as our specific purchases in supermarkets, was simply not recorded before. Some, including government documents like divorce and bankruptcy records, were public records, but took a lot of time and effort to access before. In the past, our conversations disappeared when we finished speaking, and our personal communications were normally read only by the sender and recipient. Now that we communicate by e-mail and electronic discussion groups, our words are recorded and can be copied, distributed, and read by others.

Some examples of government and private databases containing personal information are listed in Figure 2.1 and Figure 2.2. This is just a small sample, intended to give you an idea of the variety of information that is stored. The existence and availability of all this personal information in computer databases has generated concern about how the information is collected, protected, and used (sometimes without our permission or knowledge), and how information from different databases is combined to build a detailed picture of our political, medical, financial, legal, and personal affairs.

Some of the risks that arise from the existence of the many government and private databases are the following:

- Unauthorized use by "insiders," the people who maintain the information.
- Inadvertent leakage of information through negligence or carelessness, and access by intruders (e.g., hackers).
- Propagation of errors and the harm caused by them.

---

*The term "personal information" is used in the context of privacy issues to mean any information associated with an individual person's name; it is not restricted solely to what we might think of as sensitive, private information, although it includes that.

■ Intentional uses (marketing, decision making, surveillance) that some people find objectionable.

The boundaries between privacy issues and other issues are sometimes fuzzy. In addition to the many privacy issues we discuss in this chapter, privacy of communications is covered in Chapter 3 (on wiretapping and encryption), with some mention in Chapter 6 (constitutional issues) and Chapter 8 (computers and work). We discuss problems that result from errors in databases in Chapter 4 (bugs, errors, and failures of computer systems). We will address the problem of intruders in Chapter 7 (computer crime), although one of the results of their activities can be invasion of privacy. Monitoring of employees is discussed in Chapter 8.

■ Tax records

■ Bankruptcy records

■ Arrest records

■ Marriage license applications

■ Records of property ownership

■ Motor vehicles records

■ Lists of people with permits to carry firearms

■ Voter registration lists

■ School records, including psychological testing of students

■ Medical records (e.g., those covered by Medicare or the armed services)

■ Welfare records

■ Books checked out of public libraries

FIGURE 2.1: Government databases.

■ Credit histories

■ Medical records

■ Subscription and membership lists

■ Customer lists (including a history of purchases)

■ Video rentals

■ Bank records

■ Telephone records

■ Employment files

■ Airline travel records

■ Personal profiles of online service subscribers

FIGURE 2.2: Private databases.

Awareness of and concern about privacy issues is growing. The 1994 Harris poll on Interactive Services, Consumers, and Privacy found that 82% of the public are concerned about threats to their privacy, up from 64% in 1978 and 79% in 1990.[2] Privacy conferences are held frequently by think tanks, professional associations, advocacy groups, business organizations, government agencies, law schools, and others.

There are three key aspects of privacy:

- Freedom from intrusion, being left alone.
- Control of information about oneself.
- Freedom from surveillance (from being followed, watched, and eavesdropped upon).

We concentrate primarily on the second, and somewhat on the first, in this chapter. It is clear that we cannot expect complete privacy. We usually do not accuse someone who initiates a conversation of invading our privacy. Many friends and slight acquaintances know what you look like, where you work, what kind of car you drive, and whether you are a nice person. They need not get your permission to observe and talk about you. It is often said that if you live in a small town, you have no privacy; everyone knows everything about you. In a big city you are more anonymous. But if people know nothing about you, they may be taking a big risk if they rent you a place to live, hire you, lend you money, sell you automobile or medical insurance, cash your checks, accept your credit card, and so on. We give up some privacy for the benefits of dealing with strangers. Thus privacy involves a balancing act. Privacy scholar Alan Westin describes the factors to be balanced as follows:

(1) Safeguarding personal and group privacy, in order to protect individuality and freedom against unjustified intrusions by authorities;

(2) Collecting relevant personal information essential for rational decision-making in social, commercial, and governmental life; and

(3) Conducting the constitutionally limited government surveillance of people and activities necessary to protect public order and safety.[3]

We will present some philosophical views about privacy after first examining some concrete examples and issues of computer-related privacy problems. Throughout the chapter, we ask questions about how to deal with privacy problems, and we describe many approaches—sometimes conflicting—to answering them.

2.2 GOVERNMENT FILES

When the American Republic was founded, the framers established a libertarian equilibrium among the competing values of privacy, disclosure, and surveillance. This balance was based on technological realities of eighteenth-century life. Since torture and inquisition were the only known means of penetrating the mind, all such measures by government were forbidden by law. Physical entry and eavesdropping were the only means of penetrating private homes and meeting rooms; the framers therefore made eavesdropping by private persons a crime and allowed government to enter private premises only for reasonable searches, under strict warrant controls. Since registration procedures and police dossiers were the means used to control the free movement of "controversial" persons, this European police practice was precluded by American governmental practice and the realities of mobile frontier life.

–ALAN F. WESTIN, *Privacy and Freedom*, 1968[4]

2.2.1 "Big Brother Is Watching You"

In George Orwell's dystopian novel *1984,* Big Brother (the government) watched everyone virtually all the time via "telescreens" in all homes and public places. There was little crime and little political dissent—and no love, and no freedom. Today, the government does not have to physically watch every move we make, because so many of our activities leave data trails in databases available to government agencies. Big Brother is still watching us.

Federal government agencies maintain more than 2000 databases containing personal information. Most of them are computerized. As far back as 1982 it was estimated that federal agencies had approximately 3.5 billion personal files, an average of 15 for every person in the country.[5] Many of the systems are now accessible by computer networks, and the information is used by other government agencies as well as private organizations. Many agencies perform *computer matching* and *computer profiling.* Computer matching means combining and comparing information from different databases (usually using a person's Social Security number to match records). Computer profiling means using data in computer files to determine characteristics of people most likely to engage in certain behavior. A few dozen federal agencies use computer profiling to identify people to watch—people who have committed no crime but may have a "propensity" to do so.[6]

Some of the purposes of the record systems are to help government agencies perform their functions efficiently, to determine eligibility for government jobs and benefits programs, to detect fraud, and to recover payments on delinquent debts (e.g., student loans and child support payments). Fraud in programs such as welfare, Medicare, and worker's compensation and defaults on guaranteed student loans cost billions of dollars each year. Restrictions on the government's ability to use computer matching and other techniques would encourage more fraud and waste. However, because of the scope of the government's activities, the mass of data available to it, and its power to require us to provide information to it whether we want to or not, the use and misuse of government databases pose serious threats to the liberty and personal privacy of all of us. Government files contain sensitive personal and business information. People can suffer embarrassment, fraud, business losses, and other harm, both from authorized government activity and unauthorized release of information.

In addition to the files the government itself maintains, it has access to enormous amounts of sensitive information in business files. Thirty years ago, Supreme Court Justice

Douglas worried about the potential abuse just from government access to the records of someone's checking account:

> In a sense a person is defined by the checks he writes. By examining them agents get to know his doctors, lawyers, creditors, political allies, social connections, religious affiliation, educational interests, the papers and magazines he reads, and so on ad infinitum. These are all tied in to one's social security number, and now that we have the data banks, these other items will enrich that storehouse and make it possible for a bureaucrat—by pushing one button—to get in an instant the names of the 190 million Americans who are subversives or potential and likely candidates.[7]

The irony of the last sentence should not be missed by today's readers: 190 million was the whole population of the U.S. at the time. As Justice Douglas' comments suggest, the issue of privacy from government is entwined with the issue of personal freedom.

To illustrate some problems and issues for privacy and freedom, we will look at some uses of personal information by the Internal Revenue Service (IRS), law-enforcement agencies, and the U.S. Census. Similar problems and issues arise for other federal agencies and numerous state and local agencies. Similar problems and issues also arise with proposals for national identification systems; we will look at those too.

2.2.2   Use of Databases by the IRS and Law Enforcement Agencies

The IRS

The IRS uses computers to match tax data on individuals and small businesses with a variety of federal and state government records. It scans vehicle registration records for people who own expensive cars and boats; it searches professional license records for people who are likely to have large incomes. It searches a database of "suspicious" cash transactions. (Banks and other businesses are required to report all large, or suspicious small, cash transactions to the government.) In 1993, IRS agents examined cash transaction information on two million taxpayers.[8]

In 1994, in an attempt to expand its access to personal information, the IRS announced a database project called Compliance 2000. It planned to build a database of individuals, combining information from federal, state, and commercial sources, including motor vehicle departments, credit bureaus, state and local real estate records, newspapers, boat registration information, federal employment files, federal licensing data, and so on. The Electronic Privacy Information Center (EPIC) reported that although the proposed system would use records that are often inaccurate, such as direct marketing records, taxpayers would not be able to review their records for accuracy.[9] What if the IRS matches tax returns with files of a computerized dating service that include possibly exaggerated information on income? (If this example seems frivolous or unlikely, consider that the Selective Service bought the birthday list from a major ice cream parlor chain that gave free sundaes to customers on their birthdays. The list was used to find 18-year-old men who had not registered for the draft.[10])

Computer matching and database searching have helped the IRS catch people who have not filed tax returns or not reported income accurately. Many of the people investigated, however, had paid their taxes, but had to fight long, expensive legal battles to prove it.[11]

The FBI's National Crime Information Center

The National Crime Information Center (NCIC) has been the object of praise by police officers and criticism by privacy advocates and civil libertarians. NCIC was established in 1967 to help law-enforcement agencies around the country share information to catch criminals. Any agency can enter records and access records entered by others. By the mid-1990s, NCIC grew to roughly 24 million records on wanted felons, stolen property, missing persons, and so on. It includes criminal histories on 17 million people. NCIC handles more than one million transactions a day. Law-enforcement officers use NCIC to find out if there are existing warrants for suspicious people they observe or for suspects they arrest. With travel between states so easy, NCIC can be a very useful tool for catching fugitives and identifying criminals. Unfortunately, the lack of control of entry and use of data in the system, and the easy access by employees of law-enforcement agencies, leave many openings for abuse of police power and privacy, as well as problems of accuracy. Police officers with computer terminals in their cars type in vehicle license numbers at random as they drive. American citizens arriving home from other countries are checked out through NCIC as they go through Customs. Examples of errors in the system that led to repeated arrests and other negative consequences for innocent people will be described in Chapter 4. In the early 1970s the FBI secretly used NCIC to track the movements of thousands of people not wanted for any crime; many of them were opponents of the Vietnam war. Although the original purpose of NCIC was to aid in law enforcement, a large number of requests for criminal history records come from non-criminal justice agencies. The people whose records are accessed are not informed.[12] The growth in uses of NCIC illustrates a common phenomenon: If information is collected, it will probably eventually be used for many purposes that were not intended when the project started.

The FBI, like the IRS, has attempted to expand NCIC to include access to many large private and government databases, including those maintained by credit bureaus, insurance companies, telephone companies, airlines, banks, the IRS, the Social Security Administration, and the Immigration and Naturalization Service. The plan was scaled back because of opposition from people concerned with the potential for privacy and civil liberties violations, but such proposals tend to reappear. A 1996 law allows the FBI to get information from credit reports without a court order.[13] Also in 1996, Congress authorized millions of dollars to expand NCIC and link it to more databases.

Other law-enforcement examples

A few examples illustrate cases in which law-enforcement officials search government and private databases where most of the records examined are clearly those of innocent people. As part of its efforts to enforce drug laws, the federal government maintains a database of people who have legally bought certain prescription medications (e.g., pain relievers containing narcotics). Does the potential value of the database in a criminal investigation justify the invasion of privacy of the vast majority of people honestly using the medication?

In 1991, executives at Proctor & Gamble suspected that an unknown employee was leaking confidential business information to a newspaper reporter. The company convinced a police detective to search telephone records to find out who had telephoned the reporter. Even though there was no evidence that a crime had actually occurred, the telephone records of hundreds of thousands of people were searched. (The search did not turn up calls from any Proctor & Gamble employee.)[14]

Bell Atlantic, one of the regional telephone companies, reported that it received 22,000 requests for telephone records from the FBI, IRS, and other government agencies in one year. In most cases it supplied the records without informing the customer.[15]

Some years ago, the FBI asked libraries to provide lists of people who checked out certain material and lists of material checked out by people of East European background. (Now almost every state has a law against libraries disclosing the books a person has checked out. Librarians have a very strong belief in protecting the privacy of readers.)[16]

2.2.3 Issues

Is the searching of numerous databases by the IRS a legitimate part of its activities or an unreasonable threat to privacy? It is sometimes difficult for people to separate their view of privacy and individual rights from their view of a particular activity or law. In this case, one's views of taxes, tax evaders, and the IRS probably influence one's view on the privacy issue. Some people argue that if anyone is not paying his or her legally required taxes, the rest of us must pay more. Thus, they believe aggressive measures to catch "tax cheats" are necessary. Others point out that innocent people often spend large sums of money on legal fees to defend themselves; many go bankrupt or give up and pay what the IRS demands.

The fundamental political issue behind the discussions above and other topics we discuss in this section concerns the relationship between the individual and the government. How far into our personal lives and personal information should a government be permitted to intrude? How much privacy should we trade for legitimate law enforcement? How much are we trading for the enforcement of bad laws and protection of government power?

As general political issues, these are beyond the main focus of this book. However, here we describe two ways government use of interconnected, computerized databases changes the historic relationship between the individual and the government.

Burden of proof and "fishing expeditions"

As some of the examples we described illustrate, computer matching and profiling are altering the nature of tax, criminal, and other government investigations. Traditionally, law-enforcement officials started with a crime and used a variety of techniques to look for a suspect. Now government agencies can search through huge volumes of information, seeking people who look suspicious for any reason. One result is that, in many cases, the traditional presumption of innocence is replaced by a presumption of guilt. The person whose file is considered suspicious by a computer program may lose benefits or be ordered to pay additional taxes unless he or she can prove innocence. Innocent people are subject to embarrassing and expensive investigations, and sometimes arrest and jail.[17] A second result is a severe weakening of the protections against "unreasonable search and seizure" provided in the Fourth Amendment of the U.S. Constitution. The Fourth Amendment sets limits on the government's rights to legally search our homes and businesses and seize documents. It requires that the government have "probable cause" for the search and seizure; that is, there must be a good reason for the specific search. With so much personal information in government and private databases, rather than safe in our homes, the government can search without a warrant or probable cause. (In Chapter 6 we will discuss other constitutional issues related to computer technology, including other impacts on the Fourth Amendment.)

New computer tools do help catch criminals, but when the government uses databases and sophisticated computer-matching tools to generate investigations of people who were not previously suspected of a crime, is the risk to our privacy and liberty too high? Are the law-enforcement benefits worth the erosion of constitutional safeguards against abuse of power?

2.2.4   The U.S. Census

We saw in Chapter 1 that the U.S. Census played an important role in the history of computing. To solve the problem of processing a huge amount of information from the 1890 census, Herman Hollerith developed programmable punched-card processing machines. Now sophisticated modern computers store and process data on more than 250,000,000 people. In this section, we look at uses of census data that relate to privacy.

The U.S. Constitution authorizes and requires the government to count the people in the United States every ten years, primarily for the purpose of determining the number of Congressional representatives each state will have. Rather than simply counting the people, the Census Bureau now requires information from everyone about their race, national origin, housing, and relationship to people they live with. A sampling of households are required to fill out the "long form," which includes questions about physical and mental health, income, household expenditures, employment, education, and so on. Some of the information is needed for government programs that distribute tax money to the states according to the number of people with low income or other specific characteristics. The information is supposed to be confidential, and federal law says that "in no case shall information furnished . . . be used to the detriment of any respondent or other person to whom such information relates."[18]

The information compiled by the Census Bureau is interesting and useful to marketers, demographers, economists, sociologists, and government agencies. The Bureau issues monthly "product announcements" describing the data available on tape and CD-ROM. It sells to a variety of customers for many purposes. The Bureau does not release the name and address of respondents. It does release data by geographic divisions, some down to individual blocks. The number of people in a block varies substantially, but with seven million blocks, the average is under 40.[19] Release of data in small units allows privacy to be compromised. Computer matching, along with a small sample size, makes it relatively easy to combine summary data with other databases to identify specific people and families.

In 1942 the Census Bureau assisted the Justice Department in using data from the 1940 census to find neighborhoods with high concentrations of U.S. citizens of Japanese ancestry. Knowing how many people to look for in each block, the army rounded up Japanese-Americans and imprisoned them in internment camps. During World War I, the

Census Bureau provided names and addresses of young men to the government to help find and prosecute draft resisters. Computers were not used then, but now that census data are computerized, using them "to the detriment of any respondent" is even easier. Some cities use data from the census to find poor families who violated zoning or other regulations by doubling up in single-family housing. These people were evicted.[20]

2.2.5 Social Security Numbers and National ID Cards

The real danger is the gradual erosion of individual liberties through automation, integration, and interconnection of many small, separate record-keeping systems, each of which alone may seem innocuous, even benevolent, and wholly justifiable.

–U.S. PRIVACY PROTECTION STUDY COMMISSION, 1977[21]

With the advent of smart cards (cards containing a microprocessor and memory), there are increasing proposals for establishment of a computerized national identification card system. In one year alone, there were reports that the U.S. Postal Service, the IRS, the Defense Department, the National Security Agency, and NASA were among the agencies working on ID card plans. We currently use our Social Security number (SSN) for identification for numerous services. Smart cards could reduce some of the problems with the SSN, and they could generate much worse new problems.

Social Security numbers

With varying degrees of ease, someone who knows your name and has your SSN can get access to your work and earnings history, credit report, driving record, bank account, and other personal data. Some banks and brokerage firms that have automated telephone access to accounts use the SSN as the customer's PIN (personal identification number). The potential for both privacy invasion and fraud is clear. Although the SSN gives access to sensitive information, it is rarely treated with appropriate security. SSNs appear on public documents and other openly available forms. It is often required on property deeds, which are public records. It is used as the ID number for students and faculty at many universities, and printed on their ID cards. The state of Virginia included SSNs on published lists of voters until a federal court ruled in 1993 that its policy of requiring the SSN for voter registration was unconstitutional.[22] Some states use the SSN as the driver's license number. The IRS includes the SSN on mailing labels when it sends out tax forms. Some employers use the SSN as an identifier and put it on badges or give it out on request. Some insurance companies, hospitals, department stores (when issuing credit cards), and other organizations routinely ask for your SSN and record it in their files, although they do not actually need it.[23]

The history of the SSN illustrates how the use of a national identification system grows. SSNs were first issued in 1936, to be used only by the Social Security program. The public was assured at the time that the numbers would not be used for other purposes. Only a few years later, in 1943, President Roosevelt signed an executive order requiring federal agencies to use the SSN for new record systems. In 1961, the IRS began using it as the taxpayer ID, so it is now required by employers and others who make payments that must be reported to the IRS. In 1976, state and local tax, welfare, and motor vehicle departments were given authority to use the SSN. A 1988 federal law requires that parents provide their SSN to get a birth certificate for a child. The IRS requires taxpayers to report the SSN for each child over one year old claimed as a dependent (or provide other proof of the existence of the child). Though we were promised otherwise, the SSN has become a general identification number.

Although used as a person's ID number in many databases, SSNs have little known but serious flaws for that role: they are not unique, and they do not identify people. In some cases, Social Security Administration offices in different areas issued the same numbers to different people. In some cases, the same number was issued to different people with the same name. There are a few numbers used by thousands of people because the numbers were on sample cards in new wallets. Social security cards are made of paper. They are easy to forge, but that hardly matters because people are rarely asked for the card, and numbers are rarely verified. The Social Security Administration itself used to issue cards without verification of the information provided by the applicant. In 1991, the agency's commissioner told Congress that more than 60% of SSNs were based on unverified information.[24] While criminals have little trouble creating false identities, innocent, honest people suffer arrest, fraud, destruction of credit rating, and so on, because of problems with the SSN.

Privacy and security experts recommend that people do not give their SSN when requested without first asking if it is legally required or if there is some other good reason to provide it. Businesses are becoming more aware of problems with using SSNs too freely and of the reluctance of some consumers to provide it. When pressed, many businesses will tell a customer that they do not really need it.

National ID cards

The memory on a national ID smart card (perhaps a magnetic strip) would contain a person's name, photo, Social Security number, other identifying information, and health, tax, financial, employment, or other data, depending on the specific proposal and the government agency advocating it. In many proposals, the cards would also access a variety of databases containing such information. The cards would be used when interacting with government agencies and for any other transactions where a person's identity must be verified. This could include banking transactions, credit card purchases, any government payments, and medical treatment.[25]

Advocates of a national ID card describe several benefits. The actual card, not just a number would be needed to verify identity, and the cards would be harder to forge than Social Security cards. A person would need to carry only one card, rather than separate cards for various services, as we do now. The authentication of identity would help reduce fraud both in private credit card transactions and in government benefit programs. Use of ID cards for verifying work eligibility would prevent people from working in the U.S. illegally.

Opponents to these proposals argue that national ID cards are profound threats to freedom and privacy. "Your papers, please" is a demand often associated with police states and dictatorships. In Germany under the Nazis, identification papers included the person's religion, making it easy to enforce restrictions on and imprisonment of Jews. Under the infamous pass laws of South Africa, people carried passes, or identification papers, that categorized them by race and controlled where they could live and work. Smart cards, with the large amount of personal information they can carry or access in national databases, have even more potential for abuse.

Strong anti-immigration sentiment in the U.S. is providing the most support for a national ID card. Legislation has been introduced in Congress to drastically reduce legal immigration quotas and to prevent illegal immigrants (or legal immigrants without work permits) from working. The latter is to be accomplished by requiring that every time any person applies for a job, the prospective employer must verify the person's right to work by checking with the Immigration and Naturalization Service (INS) database. For the scheme to succeed, each person would need a "fraud-proof" ID card. Senator Diane Feinstein supports including each person's fingerprints or voice or retinal pattern on the card. The immediate threat of such a system is the loss of liberty to work. "It is absolutely unprecedented," says congressman Steve Chabot, "to say that the government must grant affirmative permission every time any employee is hired."[26] In a country with an active economy and as large and mobile a population as the U.S., such centralized power over people's freedom to work would not be possible without modern computer and communications networks. In addition to the reduction of freedom, a serious flaw in the INS database illustrates potential practical problems with any ID card linked to a national database: It is riddled with errors. In experiments with the system, approval for 19% of (legal) workers was delayed for several weeks. Approximately 65 million people in the U.S. change jobs or enter the workforce every year, so a 1% error rate would mean denial of work for 650,000 people each year.[27]

In Chapter 4 we will see that a woman could not get her tax refund after she was mistakenly recorded as having died. She would still have been able to get a new job, withdraw money from her bank account, pay her rent, send e-mail, and go to her doctor while she was resolving the problem with the government. What if the tax records were used by the worker verification database? Or what if one ID card was required for all these transactions, and it was canceled? A critic of a proposal for a national identification card in Australia in 1987 described the card as a "license to exist."[28] Is that description literal or metaphor?

2.2.6   Why Worry?

Quis custodiet ipsos custodes? (Who will guard the guards themselves?)

—JUVENAL

Based on my discussions with students and observations of attitudes of the general public, it is clear that people react quite differently to issues of privacy from government. Some are horrified at any mention of national ID cards or government access to the myriad of computerized databases containing personal information. Others are indifferent, whereas others view these changes as expansions of government services and capabilities that are necessary and appropriate to reduce crime, make sure everyone pays their taxes, and enforce various laws. The last group sees no threat to innocent, law-abiding citizens. Many people have a suspicion of businesses and corporations, seeing the profit motive as incentive to dishonest and abusive activity. On the other hand, some people trust the government and public servants (if not the politicians) to carry out government functions in a just, fair, and honest manner. Thus a reasonable question to ask is: How well does the government protect personal data in its databases and obey its own privacy rules?

- Restricts the data the federal government may collect.
- Requires federal agencies to publish a notice of their record systems in the *Federal Register* so that the public may be informed about what databases exist.
- Allows people to access their records and correct inaccurate information.
- Requires procedures to protect the security of the information in databases.
- Prohibits disclosure of information about a person without his or her consent.

FIGURE 2.3: Provisions of the Privacy Act of 1974.

Protecting information

In 1990 the Information Management and Technology Division of the federal government's General Accounting Office (GAO) published a study of how the federal government obtains, verifies, uses, and protects personal data.[29] The Privacy Act of 1974 regulates the federal government's use of personal data. As the GAO report states, this law was passed in part because of concerns in the 1960s and early 1970s about many abuses by the federal government. The abuses included wiretappings, mail openings, burglaries, harassment of individuals for political purposes, and questionable use of personal records. The provisions of the Privacy Act are summarized in Figure 2.3.

Although it was an important step in attempting to protect our privacy from abuse by federal agencies, there are problems with the Privacy Act. It has, to quote one expert on privacy laws, "many loopholes, weak enforcement, and only sporadic oversight."[30] Government agencies simply do not comply with some of the Privacy Act's provisions. The GAO study uses information provided by the agencies themselves; thus, its authors warn that information with negative implications for government agencies is likely to be underreported. The study found that 17% of the record systems reported were exempt. Among the larger systems that are subject to the Act, the GAO found that 15 years after the Act was passed, 35% were not reported in the *Federal Register* as required. Information in 56% of the largest systems can be accessed by other state and federal agencies and by private organizations. Private organizations that provide information to, and get information from, federal databases include health care providers, marketing companies, insurance companies, unions, schools, universities, real estate brokers, banks, and credit bureaus. Although federal agencies are supposed to protect personal privacy, for 8% of their largest systems, they did not know the purpose for which their databases were being used by other government and private organizations. Although agencies are supposed to protect the security of their databases, a significant number reported serious security weaknesses and numerous incidents of employees gaining unauthorized access to personal data.

There are many specific cases of leakage of information from government files. According to another GAO report, abuses of NCIC by employees of law-enforcement agencies include selling information to private investigators, snooping on political opponents, and altering or deleting information. In one case, a former law-enforcement officer used

NCIC to track down his ex-girlfriend; he murdered her. The Los Angeles Police Department found that a significant number of employees illegally snooped for criminal records on people they knew or were considering hiring for such jobs as baby-sitter. Employees of the Social Security Administration and other federal agencies have been arrested for selling data on thousands of people, both to collection agencies and to a credit-card fraud ring. A high-ranking Internal Revenue Service (IRS) official was indicted for selling information from tax files. Hundreds of IRS employees were investigated for unauthorized snooping in people's tax files. It is likely that most of such activity goes undetected. Computer-law scholars report widespread lack of compliance with minimum security standards.[31]

Different solutions in the private sector and in government

We will see in the next several sections that there are many privacy risks from personal information collected and used by businesses for direct marketing and decision making (e.g., for jobs and loans). Proposals to regulate such activities are controversial. Generally speaking, however, many people who study privacy issues believe that more flexibility and diversity is appropriate for policies concerning use and disclosure of personal data in the private sector, whereas for government agencies, it is more important to have consistency and stricter rules. Government must meet a higher standard for privacy protection because it is coercive by nature, and because in the commercial market there is competition. The director of the ACLU Privacy and Technology Project commented, "particularly where the government is involved, consent [to use of personal information] is coerced and meaningless."[32]

Abuse of power and eternal vigilance

The more aggressive or dictatorial a government is, the more it abuses information. But this is the United States, where our rights are protected by a constitution and the democratic system. Why are some people so wary of trusting the government? They know of past abuses. Concern about potential abuse of government power in this country goes back, of course, to the authors of the Declaration of Independence and the Constitution. The quote from Alan Westin at the beginning of Section 2.2 indicates that they did what they could to protect liberty and privacy from intrusions by government based on the technology available at the time. Americans were so distrustful of government that when the question of arming police was considered in the 19th century, they "viewed an armed police with considerable suspicion."[33] Now computers provide a new enormously powerful tool for investigation, surveillance, and intrusion into our personal lives. Thomas Jefferson warned that eternal vigilance is the price of liberty. This vigilance in the context of computerized information systems means giving careful thought to what information we allow the government to collect and how we allow it to be used.

2.3 CONSUMER INFORMATION

2.3.1 Databases and Marketing

According to one estimate, the average consumer is on about 100 mailing lists and in at least 50 databases.[34] If you enter a contest or fill out a warranty questionnaire, information about you may be entered into a database and made available to direct marketers. If you buy a bicycle, you may get a solicitation from a magazine about bicycle touring. If you send a donation to a charity, you are likely to get pleas from other charities of a similar nature. If you buy baby clothes or furniture, you will get many mailings about other baby products. If you frequently read financial news on an online commercial service, you may receive ads for books on investing. If you file a change-of-address notice with the U.S. Postal Service, your name and new address are provided to mailing list managers who sell the lists to mass mailers.[35]

Many companies use some fancy hardware and software to analyze consumer data in a process called *data mining*. American Express mines 500 billion bytes of data on how customers have spent $350 billion since 1991. They send discount coupons and special promotions for the specific stores where customers shop. Blockbuster Entertainment Corporation uses video rental histories in its database of 36 million households to generate specialized lists of recommended movies mailed to customers. Fingerhut Companies stores 600 billion characters of data on mail-order customers; it is upgrading its system to store two trillion characters. Some supermarket chains are storing a year's worth of data on the details of customer purchases. Airlines send incentives to frequent flyers who are flying less frequently. Cruise lines send ads to people who have gone on cruises before. Gamblers who join casino "clubs" for discounts use an electronically coded card for slot machines, food and drink; their activities are recorded. A credit bureau company in Las Vegas maintains records on six million gamblers around the world. Long-distance telephone companies use lists of subscribers to foreign language newspapers to find potential customers for special telephone service deals; they send the ads in the customer's language. A pasta company sends coupons to people who buy its competitor's products.[36]

Businesses use data mining to find potential new customers, as well as to advertise to old ones. The process for locating new customers involves first analyzing huge amounts of data about current customers to form consumer profiles. The information comes from purchases, warranty cards, rebate forms, and so on, and from the many kinds of government records we listed in Section 2.1. Once the desired profile is created, information on a larger group of people is searched, looking for those who match the profile. This kind of marketing was not possible without computers, and was not even possible with the technology of a decade ago. Marketers were limited to studying buying habits of people in broad categories, such as women 25 to 49. Now they can target offers to groups as small as a few dozen people. In 1993, an economist observed that in the previous twenty years, the cost of access to a name on a computerized mailing list dropped to about one thousandth of its earlier cost.[37]

Online services such as CompuServe and America Online are now sources for marketing list information and sites of targeted advertising. They can record all the bulletin boards or other information services accessed by a customer (and must do so for billing purposes in some cases). The online companies and many other online businesses are building consumer profiles based on the particular services used. Access to World Wide Web pages are recorded. A company is selling lists of e-mail addresses of people who post to newsgroups on the Internet; the lists are organized by interest areas, including general interests, hobbies, religion and "adult."[38]

There are many incidents where personal information is collected without the knowledge of the consumer and used in ways that annoy, embarrass, inconvenience, or endanger the person. Consumers who called an 800 telephone number to hear the local pollen count were put on a mailing list to receive a pitch for an asthma drug.[39] The callers were not aware that they had provided any identifying information, but telephone numbers of callers to 900 and some 800 numbers are automatically recorded. Reverse phone directories and other sources are then used to link the phone number to a name and address. (Even unlisted phone numbers can be easily traced to the owner.) The process can be completely automated. The person in whose name the telephone is listed may not be the person who made the call, so someone may be on a list unknowingly and incorrectly, with more potential for embarrassment, denial of insurance, and other problems. In another incident, the wife of an undercover policeman, who made strong efforts to keep their home address secret, found herself on mailing lists after being a patient in a hospital; the hospital sold her name notwithstanding her explicit request that it not do so.[40]

A purchase of pasta or the fact that someone reads an online weather report is not particularly personal or sensitive. Receiving ads in one's native language may be appreciated by the recipient. But would a customer be pleased if he or she were on a list of people considered likely to buy a product for adults who are incontinent? One company compiled such a list and made it available through a commercial list broker—and received negative newspaper publicity and a critical letter from a member of Congress. Would a customer be happy that a store has a record of how many packs of cigarettes, bottles of brandy, or contraceptives he or she buys? The computer-generated receipt from some bookstores lists the specific titles bought. If the purchase is made with a credit card, the buyer's identity is linked to the sale, perhaps of a book about unusual sexual activities or radical politics. A record of a person's online activity could include the fact that the person participates in an online discussion group about herpes or neo-Nazism. Do participants know or approve of this information being stored and distributed?

2.3.2 Privacy and Junk Mail

Do mass mailings invade privacy? Most people do not distinguish between mailings generated by sophisticated computer mining of databases and mailings addressed to "occupant." Both violate the first principle of privacy: being free from intrusion. To many consumers it is a welcome intrusion. They are happy to receive direct mail. Ninety-two million Americans respond by purchasing products or sending contributions.[41] They purchase enough of the products and services offered, and donate enough money, to make the mailings worthwhile to the businesses and organizations that send them. On the other hand, some people refer to such mailings as "junk mail" and dislike them intensely.* The Privacy Rights Clearinghouse reports that no privacy issue "raises more ire among consumers" than junk mail.[42] The recipient has the burden of disposing of the volume of paper received in ads and catalogs.[43] Some critics of direct marketing point out that some people, often elderly, have little self-control; they respond to the ads and spend thousands of dollars they do not have.

Most computer-generated advertising arrives in our mailbox. Another vehicle is telemarketing—those annoying telephone sales pitches. The target lists and the sales pitch it-

---

*The term "junk mail" was invented by newspapers to disparage direct mail because they feared it would reduce their revenue from advertising flyers included in newspapers. (Anne Wells Branscomb, *Who Owns Information?*, Basic Books, 1994, p. 187.)

self may be computer generated. The privacy issues are similar whether the lists are generated by in-store purchases or online activity on a commercial information service, and whether the advertising arrives in our mailbox, over the phone, or on our computer screen.

Marketers argue that finely targeted marketing is likely to be useful to the consumer, and it reduces overhead and, ultimately, the cost of products. A business that sells customer information may be able to charge less than a competitor who does not. A Seagram executive says data mining can eliminate junk mail if junk mail is "anything I didn't ask for and wouldn't be interested in."[44] When people lived in small communities and shopped at local stores, merchants knew the customers and their preferences, and could tell them about new products or special deals that would interest them. Some marketers say that data mining allows them to provide personalized service that was lost as society and shopping became more anonymous. On the other hand, mailings targeted to individuals, or more accurately, the databases from which they are generated, violate the second principle of privacy: control of information about oneself, if the recipient has not given permission for the use of the data. Even the Seagram executive's definition of junk mail includes "anything I didn't ask for."

Care must be taken when assigning blame for problems caused by direct mailings. For example, as an illustration of bad effects of computerized marketing lists, several writers mention the case of a woman who had a miscarriage and continued to receive mailings about baby products.[45] If a woman did not consent to her name being included on the lists, she may object to the misuse of her name and the mailings she receives, whether or not she has a miscarriage. However, many expectant mothers happily and willingly put their names on mailing lists for baby products and services. A miscarriage can cause profound emotional pain. Baby catalogs arriving in the mail, or the sight of another mother with an infant, are reminders of the pain, but it is unreasonable to blame marketers or computerized mailing lists if the woman gave consent to the distribution of her name. Is there anything about computerization of marketing lists that contributes to the woman's pain in such a case? Yes. The ease with which computer files can be copied means that her name may have been sold to a large number of businesses. It would take a huge effort to track down every company that now has her name and ask them to stop sending mail. Consent to distribution of our names and addresses for marketing purposes is a decision that is difficult to revoke.

People have sued mailers for violating their privacy rights by sending unwanted mail, but these suits have failed. There are practical and Constitutional reasons why. If it were illegal to send someone mail without the recipient's consent, how would someone contact the recipient to get consent? If the ban were based on the content of the mailing (e.g., sales pitches and solicitations for contributions), there would be an issue of whether the mailer's First Amendment rights to freedom of speech were violated.

2.3.3   A Dilemma

We often want information about other people (Does the gardener have a police record?), but we often do not want others to have information about us. We do not want "junk mail," but we want to send information about our services and social causes to others. Policies of a few organizations illustrate the dilemma. An article in *Consumer Reports* mentions Metromail, the huge mailing list broker that has files on half the people in the United

States. The article informs us that Consumers Union, the publisher of the magazine, uses Metromail's database to find people who might be interested in its products. However, *Consumer Reports* does not give information on its subscribers to Metromail.[46] A statement from the Audubon Society, a nature organization, explains why it exchanges its mailing list with other groups and does mass mailings. Its arguments are similar to the arguments given by commercial direct marketers: These practices help in recruiting new members, reducing costs, and funding Audubon programs. "It's only 'junk mail' if it goes to the wrong person," the statement says. "Direct mail is one of the most cost effective ways to educate the public, effect social change, and attract new funders."[47] In spite of the clear arguments, the tone of the statement, to the group's conservation-oriented members, is almost apologetic. They know that some members do not approve of direct mail and exchange of lists. (The Audubon Society, like many other organizations, allows members to exclude their names from the distributed list.)

This dilemma presents a problem when thinking about privacy policies, whether for an individual business or when considering potential laws. How can we balance the desire for information exchange with the desire for privacy and reduction of junk mail? Protecting a diversity of options and freedom of choice will be an important element in a good solution.

2.3.4   Consumer Data at Risk

Is the mere existence of the enormous amount of transactional data now stored in databases a risk to our privacy? Yes, unquestionably.

To demonstrate how easy it is to obtain personal information, several television and magazine reporters have compiled dossiers on prominent people in the arts, sports, and politics and ordinary people chosen randomly on the street. They start with just a name, and sometimes an address and Social Security number, and they use only legal methods to demonstrate what is available, within a few hours or days, to anyone who knows where to find it. For those who are willing to break laws, lie, or bribe, more information is available from the so-called information underground. Unscrupulous data dealers provide bank account balances, credit card purchases, unlisted phone numbers, phone numbers recently called, mortgage payments, tax returns, medical history, employer, location of relatives, and a variety of other information. Virtually any information about a person can be bought. Credit card purchases alone can provide a detailed picture of a person's activities and whereabouts. (One of the most aggressive groups wanting phone records and credit records, according to several observers, is divorce lawyers.) A private detective could have obtained a lot of the same information in the past, but not nearly so easily, cheaply, and quickly. In both the public and private sector, strong sanctions are needed against employees who release information without authorization. An example of a good policy is one stated by a vice president of Bell Atlantic: If someone gives out information on a consumer, they are fired.[48]

Frequently, companies involved in litigation subpoena consumer data stored in business databases. Federal Express and American Express, for example, were subpoenaed for package delivery records and charge account records, respectively, for specific customers. The customers were not informed of the subpoenas, although they have a legal right to challenge them. The American Express case received a lot of publicity because the company released the charge account records of about 65 people by mistake, when it was asked for records of one person.[49]

We have already seen that some government agencies are increasing their access to consumer databases. Conversely, marketers make extensive use of the many government databases that are open to the public. Even those records that are supposed to be protected sometimes find their way into marketing databases. For example, many states prohibit the use of voter registration records for commercial purposes, but the records can be used by political and other organizations. Metromail obtained voter files in several states from the AFL-CIO, which allegedly traded the files for other data in Metromail's databases.[50]

Consumer data can leak in ways that may threaten people's safety. A woman, along with many other consumers, filled out a detailed consumer profile form for Metromail, expecting to receive discount coupons and free sample products. The form included hobbies, income, buying habits, health information, investments, and much other personal information. Later, she received a frightening 12-page letter, containing graphic sexual fantasies, from a convicted rapist in a Texas prison who knew everything about her. Prisoners had been contracted to enter the questionnaire data into computers. Parents and privacy advocates, concerned about the safety of children, have criticized Metromail also for providing a service, intended for marketers but available to others, that included names, addresses, and ages of children.[51] These examples illustrate the importance of thinking about possible dangerous uses of personal information and the consequences of making it available to the wrong people.

2.3.5 Key Issues

A person might feel embarrassed or threatened knowing that strangers could get the kinds of consumer information we have described. On the other hand, the person might not care, or might be pleased to get advertising mailings and coupons for related products. Some consumers are startled and uneasy knowing that details of their purchases are recorded at all. The ability to form a detailed profile of a consumer's opinions, preferences, and activities is disturbing. More than one journalist, in describing the phenomenon, has used phrases like data mining "gives some people the creeps."[52]

One issue concerning the collection and use of consumer information is that, in many cases, consumers are not aware that the information is being collected. This is called *invisible information gathering.* When the consumer is not informed that the information is being collected, or how it will be used, he or she has no opportunity to consent or withhold consent for its use.

The second issue for consumer data is *secondary use,* that is, the use of information for a purpose other than the one for which it was supplied. When magazine subscription lists and credit card company records are used for mailing magazines and billing customers, there is no privacy problem. Most consumers do not object when businesses use their own customer lists to send advertisements or special offers to their customers. Privacy can be seriously threatened when information collected by one business or organization is shared with or sold to another, without the knowledge or consent of the person who provided the information.

A third issue, or dilemma, is *balancing risk and benefits.* Computer databases with detailed information on purchases can help both businesses and consumers, but distribution, leakage, and various specific uses of the information by businesses and government agencies can have detrimental effects. How much risk are we willing to accept in exchange for convenience and the availability of useful information? How can we reduce the risks while still getting the benefits?

In the next two sections, we look at special areas of consumer privacy: credit records and medical records. After that, we will have an extensive discussion of a variety of approaches (philosophical, technical, policy, legal, market, etc.) to the privacy problems of consumer data.

2.4 CREDIT BUREAUS

The three major credit bureau companies, TRW, Equifax, and Trans Union* receive and process millions of records daily. The data are supplied by banks, stores, and other businesses. In addition to bill-paying history, a credit report may contain information from public records, such as lawsuits, bankruptcies, and liens. The primary purpose of the credit bureaus is to provide a central storehouse of information to be used to evaluate applicants for credit. They are also used by some employers as part of a background check on job applicants. Approximately 550 million credit reports are sold each year.[53]

The use of credit information, unlike many other kinds of consumer information, is regulated by the federal government. The Fair Credit Reporting Act of 1970 (FCRA) restricts credit bureaus to disclosing credit information only to employers, the government, insurance companies, and others who need it for legitimate business purposes involving the consumer.[54] That last category is vague and easy to circumvent. It is relatively easy to get someone's credit report for other purposes. Credit reports are obtained to embarrass political candidates and to find information about spouses for use in divorce cases.

Credit information is of concern to privacy advocates because a bad credit report can prevent someone from getting a mortgage, a car loan, a job, or other services. (Privacy advocates and business people tend to disagree on the weight given to credit information when making decisions.) Sometimes an applicant is unaware that a credit report has been obtained and is the basis for a negative decision. The FCRA places limits on the age of negative information that may be reported, for example, bankruptcies, criminal convictions, and civil judgments. Some see this as a privacy protection, whereas others see it as an unreasonable restriction on the flow of relevant information.

Many attempts have been made to revise the FCRA. Some proposed changes are the following:†

- Give consumers a legal right to get a copy of their own credit reports for free, including information on who else has requested the person's report. This helps consumers at least to be aware of who is obtaining information about them, and to correct incorrect information. (Credit bureaus generally provide a report to a consumer for a small fee.)

---

*In 1996, TRW sold its credit bureau division to another company.

†The FCRA was amended in 1996, while this book was in production.

- Prohibit employers from obtaining credit reports on employees and applicants without their permission.
- Prohibit employers from obtaining credit reports at all except for specific kinds of jobs.[55]

The credit bureaus have received strong criticism for some of their activities other than compiling and providing credit reports. They used their databases and other sources to produce and sell mailing lists of "elite retail shoppers," "highly affluent consumers," and other specially targeted groups. In fact, credit bureaus had catalogs describing and promoting the variety of lists that were available. Some marketers use summary data on income, credit, and expenditures, available from credit bureaus by zip code, to choose neighborhoods in which to advertise or distribute discount coupons. Some people object to these practices because the consumers did not consent to the use of their credit information for marketing purposes. Interestingly, people in less affluent neighborhoods object that such targeting unfairly discriminates against them because they do not receive the notices and special offers.

The FCRA was written before the widespread use of modern computer technology to generate mailing lists, and there was disagreement about whether the sale of marketing lists was legal. As a result of public criticism and pressure, Equifax decided in 1991 to terminate its marketing mailing-list business. In 1993, the Federal Trade Commission ruled that use of credit information to generate marketing lists violates the law; it ordered TRW and Trans Union to terminate the practice.

Some of the concern about credit bureaus has to do with the other information they collect, in addition to credit records. Equifax, for example, uses its database expertise in many areas of personal records and verification. For example, it provides check guarantee services using a database of payment histories. It performs application verification for insurance companies and keeps records on homeowner, auto, and health insurance policy claims. It provides a medical credential verification service for hospitals hiring medical staff.[56] Although all of these services are important, the potential for combining the various databases to form complete dossiers on consumers, and the serious problems that result from errors, are worrisome.

2.5 MEDICAL RECORDS

Whatsoever things I see or hear concerning the life of men, in my attendance on the sick or even apart therefrom, which ought not to be noised about, I will keep silence thereon, counting such things to be as sacred secrets.

–From the Hippocratic Oath

Our health and medical information is personal. Some is very sensitive: information about alcoholism, sexually transmitted diseases, psychiatric treatment, and suicide attempts. We may strongly desire to keep other health problems private even if they do not have negative social connotations. For example, someone may not wish others to know she had cancer so that they do not feel awkward around her or treat her differently.

2.5.1 The Current Situation

Many people think that the confidentiality of medical records is protected. According to public surveys, they strongly believe it should be.[57] In fact, there is little legal protection for confidentiality, and the collection of laws that exist is described by various legal and privacy writers as "a dizzying array," a "patchwork," and "ambiguous, confusing." Some laws control information about specific diseases, for example AIDS, rather than medical information in general. Some laws require disclosure; some laws prohibit disclosure. In some states, death certificates are public records, that is, available to anyone; in other states, they are not. In some states, only the doctor is covered by a confidentiality requirement; other health care workers and pharmacists are not. Law-enforcement agencies can access medical records. A study by Congress's Office of Technology Assessment says that current laws are "inadequate to guide the health care industry with respect to obligations to protect the privacy of medical information in a computerized environment. It fails to confront the reality that, in a computerized system, information will regularly cross state lines and will therefore be subject to inconsistent legal standards with respect to privacy."[58]

Medical information is used for marketing purposes. Metromail, the mailing-list broker, sells lists of people with specific diseases, such as diabetes and angina, to the pharmaceutical industry. Metromail says that the health information it sells is provided voluntarily in responses to ads and questionnaires. Large drug companies are buying companies that sell prescription drugs to consumers; the purpose is to gain access to the customer lists.[59]

Underground data dealers and other individuals obtain or release medical information for various purposes. There have been incidents where hospital employees released records in an attempt to cause a political candidate to lose an election.

Health maintenance organizations (HMOs), hospitals, and other large medical care providers are developing computerized patient record systems. The trend is clearly toward replacement of paper medical records by computer databases. In Chapter 1 we mentioned some benefits of computerized patient records, but they are vulnerable to the risks we are discussing throughout this chapter. Medical institutions are beginning to recognize the public's concern for privacy of medical information, and they are beginning to adopt and implement privacy policies.

One factor that diminishes our control over our medical records is that most of us do not pay directly for our medical care. We waive confidentiality of our medical records for insurance payments. The insurer needs access to the records to verify eligibility and amounts of payments and to check for fraud (by patients or doctors). The anonymity and impersonal nature of a system of third-party payers (e.g., insurance companies or government) make it an inviting target for fraud. (One father/son team collected $16 million in Medicaid claims for nearly 400,000 phony medical visits.[60]) Preventing and detecting fraud requires access to medical and personal information about patients. Also, because most medical insurance premiums are paid by employers, insurance companies will sometimes provide employee medical records to the employer.[61]

The Medical Information Bureau (MIB), a nonprofit association founded by life insurance companies to detect and deter insurance fraud, collects medical information much as credit bureaus collect credit information. Applicants for life insurance sign an authorization for the insurance company to get a report on their risk factors from MIB. Its database includes information on approximately 15 million people.[62]

Hidden Uses of a Database: An Example

With grants from the federal government, local governments are setting up immunization databases to keep records of all childhood immunizations. The main purpose of the database is to make sure that all children receive the recommended immunizations; county health departments will send reminders to parents when appropriate. Other purposes include improved health of the community and assistance with public health research and statistics. Parents are told that the data on their children will be kept confidential.

The goal of these databases is a fine one. Why would there be concern about it? There are several likely uses of the databases of which parents are not informed when they agree to include their child. A local government agency charged a parent with neglect, in part, for refusing to have the child immunized. Some states permit access to data in local government health files with a subpoena. Some county officials have expressed interest in using the database to find people who are getting benefits from more than one county office. The database may be used to find children of illegal immigrants. Because parents have access to data on their children, the database can be used by an abusive spouse to find the location of a battered mate, with children, in hiding.[63]

The issue is that the database is likely to be used in ways that the parents were not informed about, ways that threaten their privacy, liberty, and safety. Thus, an important question is whether such a database should be developed in the first place. Do the benefits outweigh the risks? Can the main purpose, encouraging childhood immunization, be achieved by other means? The same issue and questions, of course, apply to many other kinds of databases.

Already, because medical records may be available to insurance companies, employers, and government agencies, many people take measures to keep information out of their records. Some pay for certain medical services themselves, even if the treatment would be covered by insurance. They may go to a different physician to keep the record entirely separate from insurance-paid medical care.[64] Psychiatric patients sometimes ask doctors not to keep notes of their sessions. When patients are concerned about the privacy of medical information, the quality of care they receive may suffer. (Of course, the ethical consumer must distinguish between keeping medical information "off the record" to protect privacy and hiding information about relevant health conditions or risky behavior from insurance companies. The latter is fraud.)

A vast amount of medical information is collected by government agencies to plan programs, compile public health statistics, and do medical research.

2.5.2 Privacy and Proposals for Health Care Reform

Many proposals for major reorganization of the health care system in the United States were debated in the 1990s. The proposals vary over a broad political, economic, and philosophical spectrum, and, of course, most people's preference in health care reform depends on other factors, such as cost, patient choice, and universal coverage, as well as privacy. We consider the implications for privacy of some health care reform proposals.

At one extreme on the political scale are plans that give a much larger role in health care regulation and control to government.* Some of the features related to privacy and computer technology from several such proposals are the following:

- Creation of a government or quasi-government national database containing health and personal information on virtually all Americans.
- Requirement that a report on every medical visit be sent to a national health data network, even if the visit is not covered by insurance.
- Requirement for everyone to have a national electronic health ID card. The card would be used to verify a person's eligibility for health care, to store data, and to access personal and medical records.

The benefits of a national database containing everyone's medical record include accessibility when one is traveling or moves to a new area and the ease with which government and medical researchers can get complete data on diseases and health issues they are studying. However, people who disagree profoundly on the political, economic, and health implications of health care reform share concerns about threats to privacy and abuse of medical information made possible or likely by a national database and medical ID cards. Some of the risks, we have seen, already exist, but they are increased by the required centralization, lack of options for consumers, and access by more people, distant from the actual health care provider. Access by law enforcement and other government agencies is easier in such a system. Errors in a centralized system could prevent someone from getting medical care. Other concerns are the possibility that the Social Security number will be used as the health identification number or that the health ID card will become a de facto national ID card. On the other hand, critics of the health care industry and some privacy advocates argue that broad public-sector medical record systems will be cheaper and provide better privacy protection than private health care providers.

At the other extreme in health care reform is the proposal for medical savings accounts. The role of employers and insurers (and government) would be reduced. The employee would pay for most health care directly, or buy insurance if he or she chose to, using funds deposited in a tax-free savings account by the employer. This plan eliminates most of the disclosures of health information to employers and insurance companies that now result from the fact that they pay for it. The proposal does not include a national medical information database or a standardized health care identification card.

Other reform proposals made by various privacy advocates for private or government medical record systems include

1. *Requirement of security measures to prevent unauthorized access and leaks.*
2. *The right of individuals to see and correct their records.*

---

*Examples include the Clinton administration's Health Security Act and the "Single payer" initiative that was on the California ballot in 1994. Both failed.

3. *A prohibition against a medical ID card being used for any other purpose.* Although this is desirable, the history of the Social Security number suggests that it is not likely to be effective. In fact, because many government agencies are aware of the weaknesses of the SSN, if a secure, unique, universal identification system is developed for health care, it would be hard for the government to resist using it as a replacement for the SSN.

4. *A national health board or data protection board to oversee the use of medical records.* Some privacy advocates see this a means of consumer protection. Others see it as a bureaucratic intrusion by government into a sensitive area.

5. *Denial of access to an employee's medical record by the employer.* This is controversial because privacy advocates and employers disagree about what medical information is relevant to employment decisions.

6. *A ban on sale of any lists generated from patient medical information.* This could protect against abuses, but also eliminates an option that some patients might voluntarily consent to.

7. *Criminal penalties for violation of medical privacy regulations.*

2.6   TECHNICAL AND MANAGEMENT PROTECTIONS FOR PRIVACY

If the owner of a database *wants* to protect privacy, there are some technical and management procedures that can be used to do so. We will describe a few here. It is the responsibility of good computer system designers and managers to be familiar with such techniques. Technological and management solutions do not solve policy problems, though. Later we will consider more high-level policy issues about how to control information about ourselves that other people want.

A well-designed database for sensitive information includes several privacy protections. Each person with authorized access to the system should have a unique ID code and a password that he or she must provide to use the system. Users may be restricted from performing certain operations, such as writing or deleting, on some files. User IDs may be coded so that they give access to only specific parts of a record. For example, a billing clerk in a hospital does not need access to the results of a patient's lab tests. The computer system keeps track of each access, including the person looking at a record and the particular information viewed or modified. This is called an *audit trail.* It can be used later to trace unauthorized activity. The knowledge that a system contains such provisions will discourage many privacy violations.

In this chapter we are focusing mostly on how computerized databases threaten privacy. It is worth noting that they can help protect privacy too. Consider, for example, that computerized medical records replace paper records. Studies have shown that when a person is in a hospital, his or her record may be read by approximately 75–80 people (doctors, nurses, lab technicians, billing clerks, etc.). In such an environment, it is easy for unauthorized people to see the record, and it is easy for people to read parts of it that they do not need to see. The techniques described in the previous paragraph can increase a patient's privacy.

A mailing list is a valuable asset. The owner of the list and the people on it have a common interest in preventing unlimited distribution. Often lists are not actually sold; they are "rented." When a list is rented to another organization or business, the renter never actually receives a copy (electronic or otherwise); the mailing is done by a firm that specializes in doing mailings. The risk of unauthorized copying is thus restricted to a small number of firms whose reputation for honesty is important to their business. This idea of using trusted third parties to process confidential data can be used in other applications too. In some states, car rental agencies access a computer service to check the driving record of potential customers. The service examines the motor vehicles department records based on the rental company's criteria (say, a specific number of traffic tickets or accidents) and reports a simple yes or no. The car rental company does not see the driver's record.[65]

Because of the security and identity problems with Social Security numbers, designers of databases with personal information should not use the SSN as the record identifier unless there is a compelling reason to do so. There are techniques that can be used to design an ID number system that distinguishes between valid and invalid numbers, thus reducing fraud and errors.

Encryption, that is, storing information in a coded form, provides privacy protection, reducing some abuses by unauthorized employees and intruders from the outside. New encryption techniques can be used to process transactions on computer networks without providing any information about the customer to the service provider. These techniques, now in the development stage, have the potential for providing an unprecedented amount of privacy and solving many of the privacy problems we are discussing. We will say more about them in the next chapter.

Some libraries have a policy of destroying the checkout record when a book is returned—the best protection against disclosure. This technique cannot be used for most databases, but it is a good reminder of a goal. There is a tendency among people not to throw anything away, including information. Privacy is protected by a policy of destroying records that are old or no longer needed.

One "solution" to privacy intrusions made easier by computerization is simply to not allow the use of computer systems for certain purposes. In a few cases, courts have approved restrictions on the form in which information from government files is provided. For example, in one case a court ruled that a state did not have to give news reporters a criminal's rap sheet (listing his complete record), even though all the information on it was already public and could be found by reporters if they took the time to manually search paper police booking records. This solution is clearly temporary.* Soon virtually all such records will be stored on computer systems instead of on paper, and scanners coupled with character recognition systems make it easy to convert older, printed records to digital formats. Sophisticated search and sorting software enable a user to find and arrange the information as desired. Attempts to solve problems generated by a new technology by preventing its use are not likely to succeed.

---

*And in this case it is controversial because some people do not believe the privacy of a criminal should rank higher than the public's concern for safety, but the issue here is independent of the particular case.

TOLL ROAD TECHNOLOGY: BENEFITS, PROBLEM, SOLUTION

THE BENEFITS

New computer technology at toll roads, bridges, and so on, will save time for drivers and reduce the costs of collection. Vehicles will have a transponder or transmitter that can be read by a sensing device as the vehicle passes a toll station without stopping. The computer system can generate a monthly bill for the customer. The system will also have the flexibility to implement variable charges for different times of the day.

THE PRIVACY PROBLEM

The database used for billing drivers will contain a record of where and when a person traveled (and how fast). There is concern that this information could be used by marketers and by government agencies to track people.

A POTENTIAL SOLUTION

A possible solution is to have an option of buying prepaid toll cards to eliminate the necessity for billing. Identifying information about the driver would not be needed on the card.[66]

2.7 PHILOSOPHICAL, LEGAL, AND ECONOMIC VIEWS OF PRIVACY

Before looking at various approaches to protecting privacy (in the next section), especially legal approaches, it is useful to spend a little time considering underlying issues. In this section we look at some philosophical and legal arguments on the merits of privacy as a value and on whether privacy is a distinct right. We will also look at an economic theory of privacy. There is hardly space here to review all points of view on these topics, or even all criticisms of the views presented. One purpose of this section is to show you the kinds of analyses that are done by philosophers, legal scholars, and economists in trying to elucidate underlying principles in a subject. Another is to emphasize the importance of principles, of working out a theoretical framework in which to make decisions about particular issues and cases.

2.7.1 The Value of Privacy

Privacy, according to its supporters, is necessary to human dignity and individuality.

> The man who is compelled to live every minute of his life among others and whose every need, thought, desire, fancy or gratification is subject to public scrutiny, has been deprived of his individuality and human dignity. [He] merges with the mass. . . . Such a being, although sentient, is fungible; he is not an individual.[67]

It is necessary to liberty and the pursuit of happiness.

Liberty includes the right to live as one will, so long as that will does not interfere with the rights of another or of the public. One may desire to live a life of seclusion; another may desire to live a life of publicity; still another may wish to live a life of privacy as to certain matters and of publicity as to others. . . . Neither an individual nor the public has a right to arbitrarily take away from him his liberty.[68]

Privacy is essential to intimacy.

Intimate relationships have as an important part of their content the exclusive sharing among the intimates of things about themselves that no one else knows.[69]

Critics of privacy argue that it gives cover to deception, hypocrisy, and wrongdoing. It allows fraud. It protects the guilty. Concern for privacy may be regarded with a suspicious "What do you have to hide?" Also, some argue that privacy is expensive to society. Strong privacy restrictions make it more costly to find pertinent information needed for good business and employment decisions, for example.

The arguments in support of the importance of privacy seem persuasive, even if privacy is not absolute. The value of privacy is widely accepted by scholars and the general population, so we will go on to the next question: Is there a *right* to privacy? Is it a distinct right separate from other rights?

2.7.2   The Right to Privacy

Until the late 19th century, legal decisions supporting privacy were based on property rights and contracts. An independent right to privacy was not recognized. In 1890, a crucial article called "The Right of Privacy," by Samuel Warren and Louis Brandeis[70] (later a Supreme Court Justice), argued that privacy was distinct from other rights and needed more protection. Judith Jarvis Thomson, an MIT philosopher, argued in a 1975 essay that the old view was more accurate, that in all cases where a violation of privacy is a violation of someone's rights, another right is violated.[71] We will present some of the claims and arguments of these papers.

Warren and Brandeis: The inviolate personality

The main target of criticism in the Warren and Brandeis article is newspapers, especially the gossip columns. They vehemently criticize the press for "overstepping . . . obvious bounds of propriety and decency." The kinds of information of most concern to them are personal appearance, statements, acts, and interpersonal relationships (marital, family, and others).[72] Warren and Brandeis take the position that people have the right to prohibit publication of facts about themselves and photographs of themselves. This claim is not based on any property right or other rights besides privacy; rather, it is part of the right to be left alone. Warren and Brandeis base their defense of privacy rights on, in their often-quoted phrase, the principle of "an inviolate personality."

Privacy violations have similarities to other wrongs, say Warren and Brandeis, so they explicitly mention related issues and argue that privacy is distinct from them. Here, briefly, are their arguments.

1. Slander, libel, or defamation are concerned with damage to one's reputation or standing in the community, whereas violation of privacy includes the hurt feelings of the person violated.

2. Copyright controls the use of written materials (or art and photographs) after publication. Privacy includes the right to control whether or not, and in what context, they are published.

3. Prepublication control of literary materials, but not of facts, could be seen as a property right, and, by 1890, there was already legal precedent that letters could not be published without consent of the writer. But Warren and Brandeis argue that, for example, if someone writes a letter in which he says he had a fierce argument with his wife, that fact itself is protected and cannot be published by the recipient of the letter.

4. In many cases, publication of personal or business information constitutes a breach of trust or a violation of a contract (explicit or implied). These charges cannot be brought against someone who has no contract or relationship of trust with the victim. Warren and Brandeis cite photographers who could quickly snap a picture of someone on the street. A modern example is a person who cracks a computer system and copies records.

Thus, according to Warren and Brandeis, there are important aspects of privacy that are not protected by slander, libel, and defamation laws; copyright; property rights; or contracts. Privacy is distinct and needs its own protection.

Warren and Brandeis allow exceptions for publication of information of general interest (news), use in limited situations when the information concerns another person's interests, and oral publication. (They were writing before radio and television, so oral publication meant a quite limited audience.)

Judith Jarvis Thomson: Is there a right to privacy?

Judith Jarvis Thomson argues the opposite point of view. She gets to her point after examining a few scenarios.

Suppose you own a magazine. Your ownership rights include the rights to destroy, read, sell, or give away the magazine. You also have the right to refuse to allow others to destroy, read, sell, give away, or even see your magazine. These are all parts of your property rights to the magazine. If someone does anything to your magazine that you did not allow, that person is violating your property rights. For example, if someone uses binoculars to see your magazine from a neighboring building, that person is violating your right to exclude others from seeing it. If the magazine is an ordinary news magazine, the person is violating your property right; privacy is not at issue. If it is a pornographic magazine, or any magazine you do not want others to know you read, your privacy is compromised, but the right violated is your property right.

You may waive your property rights, intentionally or inadvertently. If you absentmindedly leave the magazine on a park bench, someone may take it. If you leave it on the coffee table when you have guests at your home, someone may see it. A person is not violating your property right, or your privacy, by looking at something you place in front of him or her. If you read the magazine on a bus, and someone sees you and tells other people that you read dirty magazines, your rights are not violated. The person may be doing something impolite, unfriendly, and cruel, but not something that violates a right.

Our rights to our person and our body include the right to decide to whom to show various parts of our bodies. By walking around in public, most of us waive our rights to prevent others from seeing faces. If we wear shorts, we expose our knees. Some people, Moslem women for example, cover their faces, exercising their right to keep others from viewing them. If someone uses binoculars to spy on us when we are at home and view parts of our bodies that we choose to exclude from view, they are violating our rights to our person and our privacy. If we wear skimpy bathing suits at the beach and someone stares at us, that person may be rude, but is not violating our rights. Similarly, according to Thomson, our right to our person includes the right to decide who may listen to us. If we sing in the shower or have an intimate conversation at home, no one has the right to eavesdrop, but if we sing or speak in public, we waive the right, and people may listen. In these cases, our privacy is violated if someone sees or hears something sensitive that we wish to keep private, but the *right* violated is our right to our person.

If someone beats you to get some information, the beater is violating your right to be free from physical harm done by others. If the information is the time of day, or the location of your car keys, privacy is not at issue. If the information is more personal, then both your right to be free from attack and your privacy are violated. On the other hand, if a person simply asks you where your car keys are, or asks whom you live with, then no rights are violated. Also, if you answer and do not make a confidentiality agreement, the person may be acting inconsiderately by repeating the information to someone else, but is not violating your rights by doing so. However, if the person agreed not to repeat the information, but then does, it does not matter whether the information was personal or not; the confidentiality agreement has been violated.

In these examples, whether or not privacy is violated depends on the kind of information. But in each case, there is no violation of a privacy *right* without violation of some other right, such as the right to control our property or our person, the right to be free from violent attack, or the right to form contracts (and expect them to be enforced). Thomson's arguments lead her to the view that "every right in the right to privacy cluster is also in some other right cluster." Thus it is not necessary to precisely define the boundaries of the cluster of privacy rights. "The wrongness of every violation of the right to privacy can be explained without ever once mentioning it [i.e., privacy]." Thomson concludes, "I suggest it is a useful heuristic device in the case of any purported violation of the right to privacy to ask whether or not the act is a violation of any other right, and if not whether the act *really* violates a right at all."[73]

Criticisms of Warren and Brandeis and Thomson

Critics of the Warren and Brandeis position argue that their arguments do not provide a workable principle or definition to determine when a privacy right violation occurs. Their notion of privacy is too broad; it conflicts with freedom of the press; it appears to make any unauthorized mention of a person a violation of the person's right.[74] Some critics present theories and examples, in addition to Thomson's, to show that privacy violations are encompassed by existing legal wrongs, for example, trespass and appropriation of a person's likeness.[75]

Critics of Thomson present examples where they see a right to privacy (not just a desire for privacy) violated, but no other right is violated. Thomson's notion of the right to our person may be seen as vague or too broad. Her examples may (or may not) be a convincing argument for the thesis that all privacy rights questions can be resolved by considering other rights, but no finite number of examples can *prove* such a thesis.

Neither article directly refutes the other. Their emphases are different. Warren and Brandeis focus on how information is used (publication); Thomson focuses on how it is obtained.

2.7.3 Applying the Theory to Databases

How do the theoretical arguments we have presented apply to the privacy issues related to the vast amount of personal data in computerized databases? What do legal precedents, developed during the past century contribute to the current debate?

First, throughout Warren and Brandeis, the objectionable action is *publication* of personal information, which means widespread, public distribution. Many court decisions since the appearance of their article, have taken this point of view.[76] If information in consumer databases were published (in print or electronically, say on bulletin boards), that would violate the Warren and Brandeis notion of privacy. A plaintiff might well win a case if his or her consumer profile were published or if he or she were on a published list of people who bought condoms or did not pay their debts. But publication is not the main concern of privacy advocates in the current context of databases. Warren and Brandeis and various court decisions allow disclosure of personal information to people who have an interest in it. By implication, they do not preclude, for example, disclosure of a person's driving record to a car rental company from which he or she wants to rent a car or disclosure of information about whether or not someone smokes cigarettes to a life insurance company from whom the person is trying to buy insurance. They do not preclude use of consumer information to generate targeted mailing lists if the lists are not published. (If disclosure of the information violates a trust or confidence or contract, then it is not permissible, independent of privacy considerations.)

An important aspect of both papers we have reviewed is that of *consent*. There is no privacy violation if information is obtained or published with the person's consent.

2.7.4 An Economic Viewpoint

Federal judge Richard Posner's article "An Economic Theory of Privacy,"[77] gives economic arguments about how to allocate property rights to information. Posner says that his economic analysis of privacy is consistent with the common law, the body of legal principles evolved by English and American judges in civil cases over hundreds of years. Here is a summary of his arguments.

Information has value, both economic and personal. It is of value to us to determine if a business, customer, client, employer, employee, and so on, is reliable, honest, and so on. It is a personal value to us to learn if potential friends are selfish, discreet, and so on. Even gossip columns—the terrible target of Warren and Brandeis—according to Posner, have personal and social value. They can provide role models for people aspiring to a high position in "society," and they provide "morality plays," teaching lessons about the social costs of inappropriate behavior. But personal and business interactions have many opportunities for misrepresentation and therefore exploitation of others. Keeping certain information secret has value to the person whom the information concerns. The goal of an economic theory of allocation of property rights in information is to maximize production of socially valuable information.

Posner's analysis leads to the conclusion that, in some cases, individuals or organizations should have a property right to information, while in other cases, they should not (i.e., the information should be in the public domain). If information is expensive to discover, create, or collect, then lack of rights to the information means that the person or business that made the investment will not profit from it. The result is that less of this kind of information will be produced, to the detriment of society. Thus, for example, trade secrets, the result of much expenditure and effort by a business, should be protected. Personal information, such as the appearance of one's naked body, is not expensive for that person to obtain, but virtually all of us place value on protecting it, and concealment is not costly to society. So it makes sense to assign the property right in this information to the individual.

A third area where property rights should protect privacy is in conversations and communications. If people know that their conversations and communications are not protected, they will speak less frankly. More "reading between the lines" will become necessary; it will be more difficult and costly for people involved in the communications to get clear and accurate information. Posner mentions as an example the law giving college students access to letters of recommendation written about them, violating the privacy of the people who write the letters. He says that virtually all students sign a waiver of access because they know that nonconfidential letters are worthless. Confidentiality of communications between doctors and patients, lawyers and clients, and priests and parishioners is valuable for similar reasons. We have already mentioned that lack of privacy protection provides incentives for patients to withhold medical information from doctors, raising the social and personal cost of maintaining good health.

Posner argues that a person should not have a property right to "discreditable" personal information (e.g., one's criminal history or credit history) or other information whose concealment aids people in misrepresentation, fraud, or manipulation. Such information should be in the public domain. That means a person should not have the right to prohibit others from collecting it, using it, and passing it on, as long as they are not violating a contract or confidentiality and do not obtain the information by eavesdropping on private communications or other prohibited means.

In recent decades the trend in legislation has not followed Posner's position (or the common law, according to Posner). Recent legislation gives individuals more privacy protection for both facts and communications,* and gives organizations (business, government, and others) less protection in both areas. Posner, who disagrees with this trend, gives the extreme example that various business activities of a corporation have less privacy protection than the criminal record of a rapist.

Critics of Posner's point of view include people who use the same method of analysis but come to different conclusions, and others who believe that property rights should be derived from moral theory, not economic principles.

---

*With some exceptions, discussed in the next chapter.

2.7.5   Privacy and Transactions

No matter which of the views presented so far in this section you find convincing or weak, we have another puzzle to consider: how to apply philosophical, legal, and economic notions of privacy to transactions, which involve more than one person. The following scenario will illustrate the problem.

One day in the small farm community of Friendlyville, Joe buys five pounds of potatoes from Maria, and Maria sells five pounds of potatoes to Joe. (I describe the transaction in this repetitious manner to emphasize that there are two people involved and two sides to the transaction.)

Either Maria or Joe might prefer the transaction to remain secret. Joe may be embarrassed that his own potato crop failed. Or Joe may be unpopular in Friendlyville, and Maria fears the townspeople will be angry at her for selling to him. Either way, we are not likely to consider it a violation of the other's rights if Maria or Joe talks about the purchase or sale of the potatoes to other people in town. But suppose Joe asks for confidentiality as part of the transaction. Maria has three options. (1) She can say OK. (2) She can say no; she loves to chat with friends and it would be difficult for her to remember that she should not mention this one transaction. (3) She can agree to keep the sale confidential if Joe pays a higher price. In the latter two cases, Joe can decide whether or not to buy the potatoes. On the other hand, if Maria asks for confidentiality as part of the transaction, Joe has three options. (1) He can say OK. (2) He can say no; he loves to chat with friends and it would be difficult for him to remember that he should not mention this one transaction. (3) He can agree to keep the purchase confidential if Maria charges a lower price. In the latter two cases, Maria can decide whether or not to sell the potatoes.

Privacy includes control of information about oneself, but the point here is that there is no clear reason why either party to the transaction has more right than the other to control information about the transaction. If a confidentiality agreement *is* made, then the parties are obliged to respect it.

If a property right or other privacy rights in the information about the transaction are to be assigned to one of the parties, we need a firm philosophical foundation for choosing which party gets the rights. Warren and Brandeis are not of much help. They say we should have control of publication of facts about ourselves. Even if we consider discussion of the transaction in the town square to be publication, we still have the question: Is the transaction a fact about Maria or a fact about Joe? There does not appear to be a convincing reason to favor one over the other, yet this problem is critical to legal policy decisions about consumer information in computer databases.

2.7.6   Changing Views

Proposals from some privacy advocates today depart from the principles and precedents we discussed here in several ways. There are proposals (and some existing laws) that restrict a person's right to consent to certain contracts with respect to personal information; that is, some collections and uses of information are prohibited. There are proposals (and some existing laws) to prohibit disclosure of certain kinds of information to, or use of it by, people to whom it is relevant. One example is the question of whether an insurance company can request or use the knowledge that an applicant has AIDS. Other examples include prohibition on disclosure of tenant history to prospective landlords and use of information by prospective employers about an applicant's history of workers compensation claims. Another area of departure from Warren and Brandeis and past legal history are proposals for criminal, rather than civil, penalties for violations of regulations about collection and use of personal information.

Philosophers and economists often use simple two-person transactions or relationships, like the Maria/Joe scenario, to try to clarify the principles involved in an issue. Do the observations and conclusions about Maria and Joe generalize to large, complex societies and a global economy, where one party to a transaction is often a business? All transactions are really between people, even if indirectly. So if a property right or other privacy rights in the information about a transaction are to be assigned to one of the parties, we need an argument why the transaction in a modern economy is different from the one in Friendlyville. In the next section we will discuss two viewpoints on the regulation of information about consumer transactions: the free market view and the consumer protection view. The free market view treats both parties equally, whereas the consumer protection view includes arguments for treating the parties differently.

2.8   POLICY, LEGAL, AND MARKET PROTECTIONS FOR PRIVACY

2.8.1   Guidelines for Information Usage

Public awareness and concern about the uses of consumer data, medical information, and so on, have led government bodies, industry organizations, individual businesses, scholars, and privacy organizations to develop sets of guidelines for handling personal information. Some are presented as policy recommendations for responsible businesses to follow. Others are implemented as law. (By 1993 there were more than 800 federal and state laws concerning confidentiality of personal information.[78])

One example of privacy guidelines is the "Code of Fair Information Practices," which was recommended in 1973 by a government advisory committee on automated personal data systems. Its provisions are listed in Figure 2.4.

The Code has been adopted as policy by several companies. Some of its provisions appear in the Privacy Act of 1974 and other federal and state legislation governing a variety of databases. Experience with databases in the decades since the Code was written has generated suggestions for revisions and additional provisions. Many privacy advocates consider the first and second points to be out-of-date. The myriad of databases that now pose threats to privacy are not secret, but most people do not know of their existence. Hence, even if there is a way to find out what is in a particular database, people do not know to ask. Thus, some propose a new "disclosure" guideline: All organizations maintaining databases with personal information should periodically send each person in the database a notice telling what information about him or her is stored. For some businesses and organizations, this would be a good policy. For others, it would be an enormous financial burden. It would generate a huge amount of what some would consider junk mail. Another guideline that is widely recommended now is that information that is not needed not be collected (e.g., Social Security numbers, in many cases). Of course, people sometimes disagree about what is needed.

1. There should be no systems whose existence is secret.

2. There should be a way for a person to find out what data about him or her are in the system and how they are used.

3. Information obtained for one purpose should not be used for another purpose without the person's consent.

4. There should be a way for a person to correct errors in his or her files.

5. Any organization creating, maintaining, using, or distributing personal data is responsible for the reliability and security of the data.

FIGURE 2.4: The Code of Fair Information Practices.

The principles of the Code, along with some of the updates mentioned, are fairly general and would probably be accepted by many people as reasonable guidelines. Controversies arise when *specific* implementations are considered, particularly when they are to be enforced by law. In Section 1.2 we suggested that, when the question is whether or not to pass a law, personal preferences and practical arguments should be given less weight than rights. Some privacy advocates propose the disclosure guideline as a legal requirement. Does the desire of some people to know what others know about them justify imposing a legal requirement on anyone who collects information? Those who believe legal burdens should be imposed only on people who are violating someone's rights would say no. Some privacy advocates argue that the risks to privacy and the potential of problems caused by errors in the records justify the requirement.

As an illustration of the variety of options for implementing privacy protections, we will briefly consider several options for the third point of the Code of Fair Information Practices. When considering these, think about situations where they might be good policy and situations where you think they should be required by law.

Informed consent: A business or organization informs consumers* about what information is being collected and how it will be used; then the consumer decides whether or not to interact with that organization.

Many businesses and organizations have become more aware of the public's interest in how personal information is used. It is becoming common for credit card companies, online services, cable companies, health companies, magazines, and so on, to have explicit policy statements about how they use the information collected from their subscribers and customers. The statements vary in clarity, completeness, and prominence among all the small-print details in the contract. The policies also vary quite a bit in content. American Express explains the sources of information used and informs members that the company profiles a consumer's "preferences and lifestyle."[79] America Online states that "AOL, Inc. may use or disclose information regarding Member for any purpose" (with a few exceptions), whereas Prodigy promises, "We do not rent, sell, barter, or give away our member list for use by any outside party."[80] (American Express and America Online allow the opt-out option we describe next.)

---

*When I use the term "consumers," I include members, contributors, and others who would be on the mailing lists of various businesses and organizations.

Opt out: Consumers are given an opportunity to "opt out" from mailing lists and other uses of information about them. To opt out, one must check a box on a contract, membership form, or agreement, or call or write to the organization to request removal from distribution lists. American Express, which sends a copy of its privacy statement to cardholders each year with clear instructions for members to opt out of its marketing lists, reports that approximately 5% of their cardholders choose to do so.[81] The U.S. Direct Marketing Association operates a service through which people can specify that they do not want to receive unsolicited mail or telephone advertising. Many member businesses will eliminate those people from their lists, but are not required to do so.

Opt in: Personal information is not distributed to other businesses or organizations unless the consumer has explicitly "opted in" by checking a box or signing a form permitting disclosure. This reverses the presumption of consent and is advocated by people who believe the opt out option may not be obvious or easy enough for consumers who would prefer it.

Opt in for each use: Consumer consent is required for each use and each disclosure of information. This is recommended by some privacy advocates who think blanket consent agreements are too broad; consumers do not realize all the ways the information may be used. However, this option has an attribute economists call "high transaction costs." It could be so expensive and difficult to implement that it would eliminate most secondary uses of information, including those many consumers find desirable.

2.8.2   More Mechanisms for Protecting Privacy

Ownership of data

Some economists, legal scholars, and privacy advocates discuss the idea of giving people property rights in information about themselves. The concept of property rights can be very useful even when applied to intangible property (computer programs, for example), but there are problems in trying to use this concept for information. First, as we have seen, activities and transactions often involve at least two people, each of whom would have reasonable but conflicting claims to own the information about the transaction. Some personal information does not appear to be about a transaction, but there still may be problems in assigning ownership. For example, your birthday is recorded in some databases. Do you own your birthday? Or does your mother own it? After all, she was a more active participant in the event!

The second problem with assigning ownership of personal information arises from the notion of owning facts. Information is stored on computers, but it is also stored in our minds. Can we own information about ourselves without violating the freedom of thought and freedom of speech of others? These questions are being tested in a suit brought by a consumer against a magazine that sold his name to another magazine. Rather than suing the second magazine for violating his privacy by sending "junk mail,' he is suing the first one for selling his name, which he claims is his property.[82]

Although it may be unreasonable to assign ownership in individual facts, another issue is whether we can own our "profiles," that is, a collection of data describing our activities, purchases, interests, and so on. We cannot own the fact that our eyes are blue, but we do have the legal right to control some uses of our photographic image. In almost all states a person's photograph cannot be used for commercial purposes without the person's consent. Should our consumer profiles be treated the same way?

Consumer awareness and action

Public opinion and consumer preferences have a strong impact on decisions made by businesses—and the success or failure of specific products, as well as whole businesses. A strong negative reaction by the public terminated Lotus Development Corporation's plans for a product called "Marketplace: Households." Lotus planned to sell a database including information on nearly half the population of the United States along with software that would permit the user to generate mailing lists based on a variety of marketing criteria (e.g., income categories, shopping habits). The intended customers for the low-priced product were thousands of small businesses. Very little specific information about specific individuals was included; information was provided about neighborhoods. The information in the database was already available to clients of the large credit bureaus, and some of it is available to anyone from a variety of government agencies. Nonetheless, many people were horrified by Lotus's plans. Lotus received more than 30,000 letters, phone calls, and e-mail messages objecting to it. It dropped the project. There are many examples of the power of consumer preference: for example, the failure of New Coke in spite of a big promotional campaign; and the increase in smoke-free restaurants (where not required by law), decaffeinated coffee and espresso, low-fat meals on restaurant menus, and, in the privacy area, businesses and organizations that do not release personal data at all or offer an opt-out option.

Consumer advocates recommend that people read the medical information waivers they sign and make changes on the form to limit the waiver to relevant material, time periods, and recipients.

Through articles in national news magazines, television reports, and chapters like this, consumers are learning that information we provide on contest entries and product questionnaires goes into marketing databases. You can make your own decision about which questions you are willing to answer and which you are not.

Consumers are becoming more assertive: In a 1994 Harris survey, 70% said they have refused to give information to a business or company because they thought it was not really needed or was too personal. In 1990, only 42% reported ever refusing to give information.[83]

2.8.3 Contrasting Viewpoints

The political, philosophical, and economic views of many scholars and advocates who write about privacy differ. As a result, their interpretations of various privacy problems and their approaches to solutions often differ. We will contrast two perspectives on personal information issues. I call them the free market view and the consumer protection view. Many people use a mix of the two, applying them in different situations.

The free market view

People who prefer market and contractual solutions for privacy problems tend to emphasize the diversity of individual tastes and values, the response of markets to consumer preferences, and the flaws of detailed or restrictive legislation and regulatory solutions. It is impossible to calculate in advance how much money, convenience, or other benefits people will want to trade for more or less privacy. Just as some people buy Chevrolets and others buy Hondas, different levels of privacy can be offered by different companies, satisfying different consumers. We cannot always expect to get exactly the mix of attributes we may want in any product, service, or job if no seller or employer chooses to offer that combination. For example, we may not get both privacy and special discounts; we may not get information services—or magazines—without advertising, or a specific job without agreeing to provide certain personal information to the employer, just as we may not find a car with the exact set of features we want.

Figure 2.5 shows a set of guidelines that apply a free market/freedom of contract viewpoint to use of personal information.[84]

The first point incorporates the idea of informed consent. Some businesses might argue that they can use information in any way they choose unless there is an explicit statement to the contrary. The guidelines presented here make a presumption of privacy.

The second supports freedom of contract. Contracts—including freedom to form them and enforcement of their terms by the legal system—are a mechanism for implementing flexible and diverse economic transactions that take place over time and between people who do not know each other well or at all. Achieving the advantages of contracts requires that consumers exercise responsibility to be informed and make tradeoffs, rather than depending on a standard set of rules. The policy concerning distribution of membership lists, use of consumer information, and so on, is one of the many factors a person can consider when deciding whether to join an organization or patronize a business. The policy is often part of the contract between the business and the customer.

The third point indicates opposition to legal prohibitions on collection, use, or disclosure of whole classes of information, or other very restrictive regulations.

One basic market mechanism is price setting. Some economists speculate about new ways to allow people to set their own price on their privacy. For example, new telecommunications technology may allow our phones to automatically screen calls, letting through those we want and announcing a fee to listen to those identified as sales pitches. Some companies that want to advertise on online information services are exper-

---

1. *Truth in information gathering.* Organizations collecting personal data (including government agencies and businesses) should clearly inform the person providing the information if it will not be kept confidential (from other businesses, individuals, and government agencies). They should be liable for violations.

2. *Freedom in information contracting.* People should be free to enter agreements to disclose personal information in exchange for a fee or for services according to their own judgment.

3. *Freedom of speech and commerce.* People (as well as businesses and organizations) should not be prevented by law from disclosing facts independently and unintrusively discovered (e.g., without theft, trespass, or violation of contractual obligations).

FIGURE 2.5: Freedom of Information Use Guidelines.

imenting with the idea of paying subscribers for the time spent viewing the advertising material.

Market supporters prefer to avoid restrictive legislation and detailed regulation for many reasons. They argue that (1) the actual laws that get passed often depend more on the current focus of media attention and special-interest pressure than on well thought out principles. Lobbying pressure can come from both sides of an issue. Businesses may lobby for a legal right to use consumer information without consent, and privacy advocates may argue for regulations more stringent than consumers want. (2) Business response to customer desires is sometimes uneven, haphazard, and incomplete, but businesses respond over time to the preferences of millions of consumers expressed through their purchases. (3) When laws are not written carefully, they often have unintended effects or interpretations.[85] They may apply where they do not make sense or where people simply do not want them. (4) Laws that include very specific regulations prevent other options from being tried. (5) Regulatory laws violate the freedom of choice of both consumers and businesses.

Market supporters argue that private firms are owned by individuals or groups of individuals who have invested their own resources in the business. In a free society, they may offer a variety of products and services as they choose. In a competitive market, the buying decisions of consumers will reward those who best provide what consumers value.

The consumer protection view

As we have mentioned in various places, some privacy advocates argue for the more stringent consent requirements described in Section 2.8.1, for legal restrictions on consumer profiling, and for prohibitions on certain types of contracts or agreements to disclose data. These advocates would argue that the Joe/Maria scenario in Friendlyville, described in Section 2.7, is not relevant in a complex society. The imbalance of power between the individual and a large corporation is one reason. Another is that in Friendlyville, the information about the transaction circulates only to a small group of people, whom Joe and Maria know. If someone draws inaccurate or unfair conclusions, Joe or Maria can talk to the person and present his or her explanations. In a larger society, information circulates among many strangers, and we often do not know who has it and what decisions about us are being based on it.

Where a market supporter would point to changes in policies by businesses over time, consumer protection advocates point to the fact that a consumer cannot realistically negotiate contract terms with a business; at any specific time, the consumer can only accept or reject what the business offers. And the consumer is often not in a position to reject it. If we need a loan for a house or car, we have to accept whatever terms the lender offers. If we need a job, we are likely to agree to disclose personal information against our true preference because of the economic necessity of working. A person in need of medical care may be pressured to sign a waiver of confidentiality. Supporters of this viewpoint might say that the second point in the Freedom of Information Use Guidelines sounds good in theory but is not practical. The former director of the American Civil Liberties Union's Privacy and Technology Project urged a Senate committee studying confidentiality of health records to "re-examine the traditional reliance on individual consent as the linchpin of privacy laws."[86]

Those who take the consumer protection viewpoint tend to see privacy as a right rather than something to be bargained about. They emphasize all the unsettling uses of personal information we have mentioned throughout this chapter. They argue that the improvements that have occurred resulted from government action or the threat of it, not from business response to consumer preferences. Because consumer protection advocates do not believe a free market provides enough protection for consumers and employees, they want Congress and state legislators to override some decisions by individuals and businesses about use of personal information.

The suggestion of a legal ban on the sale of all personal medical information, made by some privacy advocates, illustrates the trade-offs made in this approach.[87] As with other kinds of consumer data and marketing lists, some patients might be willing to have their names on mailing lists for products related to their medical condition. The sale of such lists can provide income to the medical facility and allow its prices to be lower than they would be otherwise. On the other hand, abuse is easy, and unwanted release of medical information can have devastating effects. Free market supporters would leave the decisions to individual patients and medical organizations. Those who support a ban believe that is too risky.

Longtime consumer advocate and privacy "absolutist" Mary Gardiner Jones, is concerned about the vast amount of highly personal information collected by online information services and the potential use of personal information to be collected by telecommunications companies on the information superhighway. She does not accept the idea of consumers consenting to dissemination of personal data. She says, "You can't expect an ordinary consumer who is very busy trying to earn a living to sit down and understand what [consent] means. They don't understand the implications of what use of their data can mean to them." She considers the idea that some consumers like having their names on mailing and telemarketing lists to be a myth created by industry.[88]

EXERCISES

Review exercises

1. Add two examples to the list in Figure 2.1 and to the list in Figure 2.2.

2. What was one database or list used by the Selective Service to find 18-year-old men who had not registered for the draft?

3. Describe one benefit and one problem related to the FBI's NCIC database.

4. What does the term "data mining" mean?

5. Describe one case of release of personal information by a business that caused a problem for the person whom the information concerned.

6. What is one government database or record system from which information has been illegally sold?

7. List three techniques that can be designed into computer systems to protect privacy.

8. Give an example of "invisible information gathering."

9. Which of the following believe there is a distinct right to privacy: Samuel Warren and Louis Brandeis, Judith Jarvis Thomson, Richard Posner?

10. Explain the difference between "opt in" and "opt out" policies for distribution of a customer's name and address to other businesses.

General exercises

11. List two government databases that probably have information about you. For each one, tell what service or benefit, if any, you got in exchange for providing information about yourself.

12. List two private databases that probably have information about you. For each one, tell what service or benefit, if any, you got in exchange for providing information about yourself.

13. Consider the three aspects of privacy listed near the end of Section 2.1. Give examples of situations where they would not be absolute.

14. A city government wants to track down people who run small businesses and do not pay the city's $125 business license fee. The city has hired a private detective to obtain IRS tax records of city residents and determine who has reported small business income to the IRS but not paid for a license.[89]

(a) List all the arguments you can think of that the city government might give in support of this action.

(b) List all the arguments you can think of that privacy advocates might give against it.

(c) Do you think this kind of "information sharing" between the IRS and a city government should be permitted or prohibited? Give your reasons.

15. Suppose a small political party strongly opposes an existing law, for example, the income tax or the law against smoking marijuana. Consider the possibility of allowing government agencies like the IRS and the FBI to use the voter registration database (which includes a person's party affiliation in some states) to initiate investigations of party members to see if they comply with the existing laws. Give arguments in favor of this; give arguments in opposition. Which side do you think is stronger? Why?

16. Some IRS employees are authorized to obtain credit reports from credit bureaus (for official use by the agency). The IRS found that the employees were illegally accessing people's credit reports for their own purposes at a significant rate. Suggest some procedural measures to reduce this problem. Suggest appropriate penalties for violations.

17. Many states sell voter registration records on tape or disk. In some states, the records include the political party each registrant belongs to and the elections in which he or she voted. Which of the disclosure options described in Section 2.8.1 do you think should apply? Why?

18. When formulating a policy on whether certain government records should be open to the public, we should distinguish between personal preferences and general principles. Consider motor vehicle records. Try to formulate a policy about access to the database by the news media that covers both a newspaper trying to get home addresses from vehicle license plate numbers for cars parked at an abortion clinic and a newspaper trying to get home addresses from vehicle license plate numbers for cars parked at a Ku Klux Klan rally.

19. Computer chips are being implanted into pets and farm animals so they can be identified if they get lost. Some people suggest using the same technology for children. Discuss the privacy implications of such proposals. What are the risks? Do the benefits outweigh the risks? If there were a bill in Congress to require ID chips in children, would you support it? Why?

20. We noted that that Consumers Union, publisher of *Consumer Reports,* uses a huge mailing list broker to find potential customers, but *Consumer Reports* does not give information on its subscribers to the list broker. First take the position that their behavior is inconsistent and hypocritical. Give all the arguments you can think of for this position. Then take the position that the policy is reasonable. Give arguments for this position. Finally, tell which side you think is more persuasive. Which principles or points are most important?

21. Give arguments in favor of and opposed to a law to require that credit bureaus send a copy of each person's credit report to the person once a year (without charge).

22. A business maintains a database containing the names of shoplifters. It distributes the list to stores that subscribe. On the question of whether this should be made illegal, describe the likely position of each of Warren and Brandeis, Thomson, and Posner (with their reasons).

23. Current telephone technology makes it possible for the phone number of a person placing a call to be displayed on the telephone of the recipient of the call. This is commonly called Caller ID.

   (a) In what ways is this a protection of privacy for the recipient of the call (freedom from intrusion)? In what ways is it a violation of privacy for the caller (control of information about him- or herself)? What are some good reasons why a nonbusiness, noncriminal caller might not want his or her number displayed?

   (b) What are some of the positive and negative business uses of Caller ID?

   (c) What policies do you think the telephone companies should have concerning Caller ID? Give reasons.

   (d) Different states have passed laws specifying different policies for Caller ID. What do you think the law should say about it? Give your reasons.

24. Suppose students who live in a dormitory on a college campus are given cards with a magnetic strip that opens the front door of the dorm. Students are not told that each card contains the individual student identifier and that a record of each use of the card is kept. What are possible good purposes of such record keeping? What are some problems with it? Is it right? Is it okay if students are told? Give arguments and examples to support your answers.

25. Various approaches to protecting privacy of personal information tend to put different amounts of emphasis on each of the following factors.

   ■ How the data were obtained (e.g., by voluntary agreement, by theft, by independent discovery).

   ■ The specific kind of information (e.g., customer names, specific purchases made, personal medical information).

   ■ The nature of the prospective user of the data (government, business, or individual) and the intended purpose.

   (a) Which factor(s) is (are) emphasized most in the Freedom of Information Use Guidelines (see Figure 2.5). Justify your answer.

   (b) Which factor(s) is (are) emphasized most in the consumer protection view? Justify your answer.

26. (a) Consider a company that specializes in information services or manages databases with personal information (e.g., a credit bureau, a large retailing chain, a credit card company). The managers of the company are considering a policy of requiring that the staff prepare a privacy impact study for any new information service or database the company develops, and that the study be used in deciding whether to proceed with the new service and how to design it. Give some arguments the managers should consider for and against this policy.

   (b) A privacy advocacy group recommends that privacy impact studies be required by law, like environmental impact studies, to assess the implications of new information systems on consumer privacy. The study would have to be prepared by a licensed privacy analyst and submitted to a government agency for approval before a company could use or market the new system. Give arguments for and against such a law.

27. Many privacy activists propose that the United States establish an office or position at the federal government level to oversee and regulate privacy issues. (Several European countries have such an office.) Give some arguments for and against this proposal.

Assignments

These exercises require some research or activity that may need to be done during business hours or a few days before the assignment is due.

28. Find out what policy your university has about releasing the names, addresses, and telephone numbers of students either individually or as a computerized list.

29. Get an application from a local supermarket or discount store for a check-cashing card or store club membership card. Does it say anything about how information on a card holder's purchases will be used? If so, summarize the statement.

30. Get a copy of the current privacy policy statements from two large online information services or Internet service providers. Summarize the policies about disclosure of member names and addresses, e-mail usage, and information about specific services used by members.

31. The Telephone Consumer Protection Act of 1991 regulates telemarketing. Find this law and summarize its main provisions.

32. Find any medical privacy bill currently in Congress or passed in the past three years. Summarize the provisions related to computerized medical records or a national medical database.

Class exercises

1. Students should do this exercise in groups. Each group presents its results in class.

    Develop a privacy policy for Vic's Video, a video rental chain. The policy should cover what information, if any, about customers will be sold, opt in or opt out provisions, how long data will be kept, and any other issues you consider relevant. Consider that the store will probably have the following information about each customer: name, address, phone number, credit card number, driver's license number, history of rentals. Write the policy in a form that would be appropriate for posting in the store. Do not consider current laws about video rental information; write what you think is reasonable.

    If the policies presented by different groups differ in significant ways, discuss whether one policy should be set by law or if variation among different vendor policies should be allowed.

2. This is a two-part exercise. First, students, working individually or in groups, write one or two scenarios where there is a good argument that a right to privacy is violated, but no property right, right to our person, or contract is violated. These are to be given to the instructor prior to the class meeting where the second part of the exercise is done. The instructor selects five of the best scenarios. In class, divide students into groups, one for each scenario. Give the groups time to privately discuss their case and try to find some well-accepted, nonprivacy right that is violated in the scenario. If they cannot find such a right, they can conclude that the violation in the scenario is not one that should be prohibited by law; on the other hand, they may conclude that this is a case where a right to privacy deserves legal protection in the absence of a violation of another right. Each group of students then presents its conclusions to the class. Allow time for class discussion after each presentation.

NOTES

1   James O. Jackson, "Fear and Betrayal in the Stasi State," *Time,* February 3, 1992, pp. 32–33.

2   Louis Harris and Associates, Inc., *Interactive Services, Consumers, and Privacy,* Study No. 943007.

3 Alan F. Westin, "Consumer Privacy Issues in the Nineties," from *The Equifax Report on Consumers in the Information Age,* Harris survey, 1990.

4 Alan F. Westin, *Privacy and Freedom,* Atheneum, 1968, p. 67.

5 David F. Linowes, *Privacy in America,* University of Illinois Press, 1989, p. 82.

6 Jeffrey Rothfeder, *Privacy for Sale,* Simon & Schuster, 1992, p. 25. Rothfeder mentions specifically the Social Security Administration, the IRS, and the Secret Service.

7 *Marchetti v. United States* 390 U.S. 39 (1968), quoted in Steven A. Bercu, "Smart Card Privacy Issues: An Overview," BOD-T-001, July 1994, Smart Card Forum.

8 Janet Novack, "'You Know Who You are, and So Do We'," *Forbes,* April 11, 1994, 153:8, pp. 88–92.

9 From *EPIC Alert:* "IRS Initiates Massive New Database," January 18, 1995, v. 2.01; "IRS Backing Off of Compliance 2000 Program," February 6, 1995, v. 2.02; "IRS Issues 'Clarification' on Compliance 2000 Program Notice," March 9, 1995, v. 2.04.

10 Rothfeder, *Privacy for Sale,* p. 142.

11 Novak, "You Know Who You Are, and So Do We."

12 "A Review of NCIC 2000," Computer Professionals for Social Responsibility, February 1989 (a report prepared for the Subcommittee on Civil and Constitutional Rights, House of Representatives Committee on the Judiciary). John Hanchette, "Some Computer Data Bases Dangerous to Your Privacy," Gannett News Service, September 1, 1994.

13 Intelligence Authorization Act of 1996, reported in Vanessa O'Connell, "Wider FBI Access To Credit Files Stirs Privacy Concerns," *Wall Street Journal,* March 21, 1996, p. A4.

14 Rothfeder, *Privacy for Sale,* p. 72.

15 Rick Henderson, "Balance Sheet," *Reason,* November 1992, p. 16.

16 Statement from a representative of a librarians' organization, Computers, Freedom, and Privacy Conference, March 1993, San Francisco.

17 This observation is made in John Shattuck, "Computer Matching Is a Serious Threat to Individual Rights," *Communications of the ACM,* June, 1984, 27:6, pp. 537–545, and in "A Review of NCIC 2000," Computer Professionals for Social Responsibility.

18 U.S. Code, Title 13.

19 "Factfinder for the Nation," Census Bureau newsletter, March 1991.

20 Letter from Vincent Barabba, director of Census Bureau under Presidents Nixon and Carter, and comments from Tom Clark, Justice Department coordinator of alien control, quoted in David Burnham, *The Rise of the Computer State,* Random House, 1983, pp. 23–26. Margo Anderson, *The American Census: A Social History,* Yale University Press, 1988. James Bovard, "Honesty May Not Be Your Best Census Policy," *Wall Street Journal,* August 8, 1989.

21 Quoted in a Privacy Rights Clearinghouse flyer.

22 Greidinger v. Davis, U.S. Court of Appeals, Fourth Circuit.

23 Most of the information in this section is from Chris Hibbert, "What to do when they ask for your Social Security Number," available by anonymous ftp from rtfm.mit.edu in the file /pub/usenet/news.answers/ssn-privacy or from www.cpsr.org/cpsr/privacy/ssn/ssn.faq.html.

24 Gwendolyn King, as reported in Glenn Garvin, "Bringing the Border War Home," *Reason,* October 1995, pp. 18–28.

25 Mitch Ratcliffe, "Feel Like You're Being Watched? You Will . . .," *EFFector Online,* May 6, 1994.

26 Quoted in Joe Davidson, "House Panel Backs Telephone Process To Verify Authorization of New Hires," *Wall Street Journal,* September 22, 1995, pp. A2, A14.

27 The figures are from Glenn Garvin, "Bringing the Border War Home," *Reason,* October 1995, pp. 18–28.

28 Quoted in Jane Howard, "ID Card Signals 'End of Democracy'," *The Australian,* September 7, 1987, p. 3.

29 "Computers and Privacy: How the Government Obtains, Verifies, Uses, and Protects Personal Data," U.S. General Accounting Office, 1990, GAO/IMTEC-90-70BR.

30 Steven A. Bercu, "Smart Card Privacy Issues: An Overview," BOD-T-001, July 1994, Smart Card Forum.

31 The GAO report on NCIC abuses is reported in Hanchette, "Some Computer Data Bases Dangerous to Your Privacy," and Winn Schwartau, "AFIS and the NCIC—Privacy Please!" *Security Technology News,* June 17, 1994. Other cases are from the following sources: Rothfeder, *Privacy for Sale,* p. 25. *Privacy Journal,* May 1992, p. 3, and January 1992, p. 1. "Tax Report," *Wall Street Journal,* September 8, 1993, p. 1. Saul Hansell, "U.S. Workers Stole Data On 11,000, Agency Says," *New York Times,* April 6, 1996, p. 6. "Other Executive Branch Activity," *Privacy and American Business,* 1:4, 1994, p. 14. *Privacy Journal,* December 1992, p. 2. James J. Vergari and Virginia V. Shue, *Fundamentals of Computer-High Technology Law,* American Law Institute, 1992, p. 277.

32 Janlori Goldman, statement to the Senate Judiciary Subcommittee on Technology and the Law, January 27, 1994.

33 David R. Johnson, *American Law Enforcement: A History,* Forum Press, 1981.

34 Susan E. Fisher, "What Do Computers Know About You?" *PC Week,* February 11, 1991, 8:6, p. 156.

35 *Privacy Journal,* December 1992, February 1993. Anne Wells Branscomb, *Who Owns Information?,* Basic Books, 1994, pp. 9–10.

36 Jonathan Berry et al, "Database Marketing," pp. 56–62, and John Verity, "Silicon and Software That Mine for Gold," p. 62, both in *Business Week,* September 5, 1994. Laurie Hays, "Using Computers to Divine Who Might Buy a Gas Grill," *Wall Street Journal,* August 16, 1994, pp. B1, B4. "An Eye on High Rollers," *Privacy Journal,* July 1994, p. 6. Bruce Orwall, "Like Playing Slots? Casinos Know All About You," *Wall Street Journal,* December 20, 1995, pp. B1, B4.

37 Eli M. Noam, "Privacy in Telecommunications: Markets, Rights, and Regulations," April 1994.

38 Jared Sandberg, "Purists Beware: Ads Have Invaded On-Line Services," *Wall Street Journal,* August 23, 1994, pp. B1, B5. "Your Net Activities for Sale," *EPIC Alert,* October 16, 1995, v. 2.11.

39 Rothfeder, *Privacy for Sale,* p. 92.

40 Second Annual Report of the Privacy Rights Clearinghouse, Center for Public Interest Law, University of San Diego, January 1995, p. 39.

41 Branscomb, *Who Owns Information?,* p. 11.

42 Second Annual Report of the Privacy Rights Clearinghouse, p. 17.

43 One popular argument against mass mailings, that they destroy forests, seems to be weak. Most paper is made from recycled ingredients or from trees grown specifically for that purpose, as a crop. Using less paper to save trees is like eating less bread to save wheat. But, there is no good reason to buy a loaf of bread if you are just going to throw it in the trash.

44 Richard P. Shaw, quoted in Berry, "Database Marketing," p. 58.

45 Second Annual Report of the Privacy Rights Clearinghouse, p. 24. Branscomb, *Who Owns Information?* p. 20.

46 "Who's Reading Your Medical Records?" *Consumer Reports,* October 1994, pp. 628–632.

47 Statement provided by the Audubon Society.

48 Ed Young, vice president of Bell Atlantic, at Privacy and American Business conference, Washington, DC, October 5, 1994.

49 G. Bruce Knecht, "A New Casualty in Legal Battles: Your Privacy," *Wall Street Journal,* April 11, 1995, p. B1.

50 Rick Wartzman, "A Research Company Got Consumer Data from Voting Rolls," *Wall Street Journal,* December 23, 1994, pp. A1, A6.

51 "The Quintessential Abuse of Privacy," *Privacy Journal,* May 1996, 22:7, pp. 1,4. Jill Goldsmith, "Donnelley Under Attack on Child Data," *Wall Street Journal,* June 14, 1996, p. B7D.

52 Berry, "Database Marketing."

53 Simson Garfinkel, "Separating Equifax from Fiction," *Wired,* September 1995, pp. 96–107.

54 Fair Credit Reporting Act of 1970, 15 U.S. Code Section 1681, quoted in Branscomb, *Who Owns Information?* p. 21.

55 "In Congress—FCRA," *Privacy Journal,* June 1994, 20:8, p. 6. "Fair Credit Reporting Act," *Privacy and American Business,* 1:4, 1994, p. 11.

56 Garfinkel, "Separating Equifax from Fiction."

57 Louis Harris & Associates surveys for Equifax, 1993, and *Privacy and American Business,* January 1994.

58 Branscomb, *Who Owns Information?* p. 65. U. S. Congress, Office of Technology Assessment, "Protecting Privacy in Computerized Medical Information," September 1993, p. 15.

59 "Who's Reading Your Medical Records?" *Consumer Reports,* October 1994, pp. 628–32.

60 Branscomb, *Who Owns Information?* p. 71.

61 The more natural alternative of the employer simply paying the amount of the insurance premium to the employee as part of the salary, and the employee shopping for medical services or insurance, is not done because of tax policy and a side-effect of wage controls imposed by the government 50 years ago.

62 "How Private Is My Medical Information?" Fact Sheet No. 8, Privacy Rights Clearinghouse, Center for Public Interest Law, University of San Diego.

63 Benefits and potential problems of the immunization databases are described in Linda Berez, "All Kids Count: San Diego County's Child Immunization Registry," term paper for CS 440, San Diego State University, Spring 1996. Sources for some of the problems include Lawrence O. Gostin et al, "Childhood Immunization Registries: A National Review of Public Health Information Systems and Protection of Privacy," *JAMA (Journal of the American Medical Association),* December 13, 1995, pp. 1793–99; Lawrence O. Gostin et al, "Legislative Survey of State Confidentiality Laws, with Specific Emphasis on HIV and Immunization."

64 The Privacy Rights Clearinghouse (Center for Public Interest Law, University of San Diego) makes these suggestions in its Fact Sheet No. 8, "How Private Is My Medical Information?"

65 R. J. Ignelzi, "Road Blocks," *The San Diego Union-Tribune,* July 19, 1994, pp. E1, E3.

66 Thad Dunning, "The Information Highway Isn't the Only One Wired," *Privacy Journal,* June, 1994, 20:8, p. 3.

67 Edward J. Bloustein, "Privacy as an Aspect of Human Dignity," in Ferdinand David Schoeman, ed., *Philosophical Dimensions of Privacy: An Anthology,* Cambridge University Press, 1984, pp. 156–203, quote on p. 188.

68 From a 1905 court decision, quoted in Bloustein, "Privacy as an Aspect of Human Dignity."

69 Robert S. Gerstein, "Intimacy and Privacy," in Schoeman, *Philosophical Dimensions of Privacy: An Anthology,* p. 265.

70 Samuel D. Warren and Louis D. Brandeis, "The Right to Privacy," *Harvard Law Review,* 1890, v. 4, p. 193.

71 Judith Jarvis Thomson, "The Right to Privacy," in Schoeman, *Philosophical Dimensions of Privacy: An Anthology,* pp. 272–89.

72 The inspiration for the Warren and Brandeis article, not mentioned in it, was gossip columnists writing about extravagant parties in Warren's home and particularly newspaper coverage of his daughter's wedding. The background of the article is described in a biography of Brandeis and summarized in the critical response to the Warren and Brandeis article by William L. Prosser ("Privacy," in Schoeman, *Philosophical Dimensions of Privacy: An Anthology,* pp. 104–55).

73 All quotations from Thomson, "The Right to Privacy," p. 287.

74 Schoeman, *Philosophical Dimensions of Privacy: An Anthology,* p. 15.

75 See, for example, Prosser, "Privacy," in Schoeman, *Philosophical Dimensions of Privacy: An Anthology,* pp. 104–55.

76 Cases are cited in Prosser, *ibid.*

77 Richard Posner, "An Economic Theory of Privacy," in Schoeman, *Philosophical Dimensions of Privacy: An Anthology,* pp. 333–345.

78 Robert Ellis Smith, *The Law of Privacy in a Nutshell,* Privacy Journal, 1993, p. 5. *Privacy and American Business,* May/June 1995, p. 1.

79 The complete text of the statement is in Branscomb, *Who Owns Information?* pp. 193–94.

80 *Handbook of Company Privacy Codes,* Privacy and American Business, October 1994, pp. 81, 86. (These policies may have changed.)

81 Patricia Patterson, American Express, Privacy and American Business conference, October 1994.

82 The suit was filed in 1995 by Ram Avrahami against *U.S. News & World Report* and is supported by the Electronic Privacy Information Center. Ironically, Avrahami is a marketing manager for a telecommunications company. ("Landmark Privacy Case," *EPIC Alert,* October 16, 1995, v. 2.11.) He lost, but the case may be under appeal. See EPIC's Web page (www.epic.org/privacy/junk_mail/) for updates.

83 Louis Harris and Associates, Inc., "Interactive Services, Consumers, and Privacy (A National Survey)," 1994, Study No. 943007.

84 These guidelines show up in some form in the writings of various market-oriented writers. The presentation here closely follows Phil Salin, "Notes on Freedom of Electronic Assembly and Privacy," November 27, 1990.

85 Recall that the Privacy Act of 1974 prohibits disclosure of government files about a person without his or her consent, a sensible rule in many cases. A news reporter who was held hostage in the Middle East for more than a year decided to write a book about his ordeal. His requests for relevant government files were denied by several federal agencies; he was told that to protect the privacy of his captors, he would need their permission to see the files. ("Held Hostage Again," *Privacy Journal,* December 1992, p. 6. "In the Courts," *Privacy Journal,* November 1994, p. 7.)

86 Janlori Goldman, statement to the Senate Judiciary Subcommittee on Technology and the Law, January 27, 1994.

87 For example, Mary Gardiner Jones, head of the Consumer Interest Research Institute.

88 Dan Freedman, "Privacy Profile: Mary Gardiner Jones," *Privacy and American Business,* 1:4, 1994, pp. 15, 17.

89 Melinda Powelson, "Faced with Cash Crunch, City Turns to Allegedly Big-brother Tactics," *Reader,* January 21, 1993, p. 4.

FOR FURTHER READING

Published material

Anne Wells Branscomb, *Who Owns Information?*, Basic Books, 1994.

Center for Social and Legal Research, publisher, *Privacy & American Business* (newsletter).

Simson Garfinkel, "Separating Equifax from Fiction," *Wired,* September 1995, pp. 96–107. An article on the history and wide-ranging data collection activities of Equifax.

Richard P. Kusserow, "The Government Needs Computer Matching to Root Out Waste and Fraud," *Communications of the ACM,* June 1984, 27:6, pp. 446–52. The government's side of the computer matching controversy. See Shattuck below for the opposing side.

National Research Council/Social Science Research Council, *Private Lives and Public Policies: Confidentiality and Accessibility of Government Statistics,* National Academy Press, 1993.

Eli M. Noam, "Privacy in Telecommunications: Markets, Rights, and Regulations," April 1994. A good overview of issues and laws related to telecommunications privacy.

Privacy & American Business, *Handbook of Company Privacy Codes,* October 1994.

Privacy Forum Digest, an online digest available from vortex.com.

Jeffrey Rothfeder, *Privacy for Sale,* Simon & Schuster, 1992.

Ferdinand David Schoeman, *Philosophical Dimensions of Privacy: An Anthology,* Cambridge University Press, 1984.

John Shattuck, "Computer Matching Is a Serious Threat to Individual Rights," *Communications of the ACM,* June 1984, 27:6, pp. 537–45. See Kusserow above for the government's arguments in favor of computer matching.

Robert Ellis Smith, publisher, *Privacy Journal* (newsletter).

Alan F. Westin, *Privacy and Freedom,* Atheneum, 1968.

Organizations

These organizations make extensive materials available to the public in hardcopy and via the World Wide Web, gopher, and ftp.

Electronic Frontier Foundation (www.eff.org). EFF has an online newsletter.

Electronic Privacy Information Center (www.epic.org). EPIC has an online newsletter and publishes "An Online Guide to Privacy Resources."

The Privacy Rights Clearinghouse (www.privacyrights.org).

3

WIRETAPPING AND ENCRYPTION

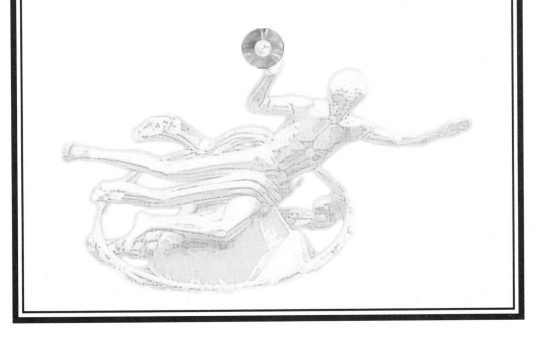

3.1   INTRODUCTION

In this chapter we study two closely related issues that profoundly affect communications privacy: wiretapping by government agencies and the government's attempts to restrict the use of secure encryption. We begin with a brief history of the use and legal status of wiretapping and cryptography. Although most of the chapter is a discussion of the wiretapping and encryption controversies, I will also describe some intriguing applications of cryptography that have the potential for making possible business and financial transactions over computer networks that are both secure and anonymous, thus avoiding many of the privacy problems we discussed in the previous chapter.

3.1.1   Background on Wiretapping

Within ten years of the invention of the telephone, people (in and out of government) were wiretapping them.[1] Throughout the years when telephone connections were made by human operators and most people had party lines (one telephone line shared by several households), operators and nosy neighbors sometimes listened in on telephone conversations.

Increased wealth and new technology eliminated party lines and human operators, but telephones continue to be vulnerable to wiretapping. The legal status of wiretapping was debated throughout most of the 20th century. Wiretapping was widely used by federal and state law-enforcement agencies, businesses, private detectives, political candidates, and others. In 1928 the Supreme Court ruled that wiretapping was not unconstitutional, but it could be banned by Congress. In 1934 Congress passed the Federal Communications Act. This law states that no person not authorized by the sender could intercept and divulge a message; there is no exception for law-enforcement agencies. A 1937 Supreme Court decision ruled that wiretapping violated the law. Federal and state law-enforcement agencies and local police ignored the ruling and continued to wiretap regularly for decades, sometimes with the approval of the Attorney General. In one well-publicized case, the FBI monitored the telephone calls between a defendant and her attorneys during her trial. Evidence obtained by illegal wiretapping could not be used in court, so the FBI kept a separate, secret file system. The FBI bugged and wiretapped members of Congress and the Supreme Court. Most states had their own laws prohibiting wiretapping, but although there was publicity about extensive use of wiretapping by police, none was prosecuted. In many cases, of course, law-enforcement agencies were wiretapping people suspected of crimes. But in many other cases, they tapped people with unconventional views, members of civil rights groups, and political opponents of powerful government officials. The wiretap issue continued to be debated fiercely in Congress, state legislatures, the courts, books, and the news media. Congress repeatedly rejected proposals to allow wiretapping and electronic surveillance. In 1968, as part of the Omnibus Crime Control and Safe Streets Act, Congress explicitly allowed wiretapping and electronic surveillance by law-enforcement agencies for the first time in U.S. history. The main argument given for this change was the necessity to combat organized crime. (The racial riots, assassinations of President John F. Kennedy, Martin Luther King, Jr., and Robert Kennedy, and antiwar demonstrations in the five years leading up to passage of the crime law probably contributed to its passage.) The law provides that the government needs a court order to monitor or record the content of a telephone call. However, a device called a pen register can be used to determine the number called (it can record the touch tones). Because pen registers are not covered by the Federal Communications Act of 1934 or the Crime Act of 1968, the government still did not need a court order to obtain so-called "transaction information," such as numbers called.

Senator Sam Ervin commented, "The mere fact of passing a law never resolves a controversy as fierce as this one."[2] He was right. Debate continued about whether the privacy protections in the law were strong enough to be constitutional; Supreme Court justices disagreed vehemently. Wiretapping by government and politicians that was illegal or of questionable legality continued after the law was passed, most notably during the Vietnam war, the Watergate scandal, and the Pentagon Papers case. Several high-ranking members of the Clinton administration were victims of unconstitutional wiretaps when they worked for the government during the Nixon administration. Journalists were also wiretap targets at that time. One legal scholar wrote that there is no clear evidence that the law made a significant difference in either increasing or reducing illegal eavesdropping.

Now telephone, fax transmissions, e-mail, voice mail, and computer networks carry a vast amount of personal and business information, vulnerable to interception. The Electronic Communications Privacy Act of 1986 extended the 1968 wiretapping regulations to electronic communication, including electronic mail, cordless and cellular telephones, and paging devices. This was a significant step toward protecting privacy in cyberspace: The government now needs a court order to legally intercept and read e-mail.

The nature and scope of information the government can collect about a person via wiretapping have fundamentally changed. With the introduction of new information and consumer services on computer networks, we now shop, use bulletin boards, and send e-mail over telephone lines. The government can learn a lot more about our habits, activities, and interests just from transaction information (without tapping content) than they could before such services were so widely used. If they can capture touch tones, they can learn account numbers, passwords, and PINs. For cellular telephones to work, the telephone system must know approximately where we are. The use of portable telephones is increasing. The information in the system could be used to track people's movements.

At the same time that computer technology increases the amount and sensitivity of information available via wiretap, some of the new communications features, such as optical fiber, call forwarding, and speed dialing, make wiretapping* more difficult. The FBI's concern about this problem reignited the debate on wiretapping by law-enforcement agencies in the 1990s. In Section 3.2 we will examine the controversial wiretap law passed in 1994.

3.1.2 What Is Cryptography?

Simply put, cryptography is making and breaking secret codes. More elegantly, it is "the art and science of hiding data in plain sight."[3] The point is to transform a message or data, called the *plaintext,* into a form that is meaningless to anyone who might intercept it. (The

---

*For simplicity, I will sometimes use the word "wiretap" in contexts where there are no wires. Consider it to mean interception of a communication in a telephone or computer network.

German Enigma machine mentioned in Chapter 1 was an encryption device.) The message could be battle plans carried by a runner through territory occupied by an opposition army, or it could be business plans sent by e-mail over a computer network. The coded text is called *ciphertext*. The recipient of the ciphertext decodes it (this process is called *decryption*) and reads the plaintext message.

Encryption generally includes a coding scheme, or cryptographic algorithm, and a specific sequence of characters (e.g., digits or letters), called a *key,* used by the algorithm. For example, a coding scheme many children learn is one where each letter of the alphabet is replaced by another specific letter. A key would be a scrambled alphabet, for example, qwertyuiopasdfghjklzxcvbnm. With this key, each *a* in the message is replaced by *q*, each *b* is replaced by *w,* each *c* by an *e,* and so on. (This is not a good encryption scheme; it is easy to break.)

Encryption is used because someone else wants the information in the message. Thus, while some people are busy trying to develop good encryption algorithms, others are busy trying to develop methods to decode ciphertext. The latter endeavor is called *cryptanalysis.*

For all encryption methods until recently, both the sender and the recipient of an encrypted message must know the key—and keep it secret from everyone else. This presents a problem. If the key could be safely sent by the same communication method as the message, encryption would not be needed. Generally the key must be transmitted by a more expensive or difficult method, perhaps an in-person meeting of the parties. A new development in cryptography, called *public key cryptography,* eliminates the need for secure transmission of keys and has a variety of other fascinating applications. We will describe public key cryptography in Section 3.3.1.

3.1.3   Uses of Encryption

Codes have been used by businesses, church officials, and lovers; but, for centuries, the most serious users were governments, their military agencies, and their spies. Most of us, children and adults alike, have merely played with codes found on cereal boxes and with cryptograms and similar puzzles that appear in magazines and newspapers.

Now, that is changing. Data transmitted by satellite can be "seen" by anyone with a satellite dish. E-mail that goes through several computers on its way to its destination may be read on any of those intermediate systems. Messages and data in transit can be read by wiretaps. Industrial espionage has a whole bag of new techniques. Driving around Silicon Valley eavesdropping on cellular phone conversations was, reportedly, a popular form of industrial spying. The French government admits to eavesdropping on the communications of American business people and providing valuable commercial information to French companies.[4] The need to maintain the security and secrecy of communications is increasing. Encryption is one of the tools for doing so.

A few examples of private-sector applications of encryption are listed in Figure 3.1. With the huge number of financial transactions that occur over computer networks, the first three examples alone show the importance of encryption. The Clearinghouse Interbank Payment System transmits approximately one trillion dollars per day over wire and by satellite.[5] Encryption is essential to the integrity of the financial system. Note that in addi-

- Electronic transfer of funds between financial institutions.
- Passwords and personal identification numbers for consumer transactions, automated teller machines, and so on.
- Credit card numbers, for purchases on the Internet.
- Bank records and other financial data—to protect privacy and to protect against theft of funds.
- Sensitive business communications.
- Research and product development files—to protect trade secrets.
- Cable television signals—to prevent reception by people who have not paid.
- Any sensitive data stored in databases, for example, medical records.
- Personal e-mail and telephone communications.
- Personal files on home computers.
- Tests and student grade files kept by teachers.

FIGURE 3.1: Uses of encryption.

tion to communications applications, encryption can be used on stored material to protect it from unauthorized access, modification, or theft by outsiders. Several of the examples in Figure 3.1 are of this type. Surveys of businesses show a high rate of unauthorized access to their computer systems; intruders include competing businesses and hackers. Shortly before his arrest in 1995, fugitive hacker Kevin Mitnick allegedly stole thousands of customer credit card numbers from a national Internet service provider.[6] The numbers would have been useless to a thief if they had been encrypted. It may soon come to be expected as a routine security measure that sensitive information be encrypted in storage as well as during transmission to protect against leaks and intruders.

A company that provides encryption for cellular phone calls reports that the biggest and fastest growing segment of his customers consists of lawyers. Lawyers are concerned about the ease with which they can be overheard, perhaps compromising attorney-client confidentiality and leaking information about negotiations or courtroom strategies. Football teams use radio helmets to transmit instructions to quarterbacks on the field; the transmissions are encrypted to protect them from the opposing team. Researchers and writers who now collaborate over computer networks may encrypt their discussions and drafts of papers to protect their ideas before publication. Sometimes, users are not even aware that they are using encryption. For example, users of Lotus Notes send one million encrypted messages a day; the software handles the encryption and decryption automatically.[7]

Eavesdropping by private citizens and unauthorized access to computer systems are prohibited by law, but that is not sufficient protection. Burglary is illegal, but we put deadbolt locks on our doors, and some people install alarm systems in their homes. The law provides for punishment of offenders who are caught and convicted, but we use technology to protect ourselves. And we have seen that laws are sometimes ignored even by the people who are supposed to enforce them. Encryption is widely viewed as the most important technical method for ensuring the privacy and authenticity of messages sent through computer networks. A Microsoft vice president commented that "Public-key cryptography is a cornerstone of the Information Superhighway."[8]

3.1.4 The New Controversies

The current controversies about wiretapping and encryption began in 1991 when the following statement appeared in a bill in the U.S. Senate.

> It is the sense of Congress that providers of electronic communications services and manufacturers of electronic communications service equipment shall ensure that communications systems permit the government to obtain the plain text contents of voice, data, and other communications when appropriately authorized by law.[9]

In this statement, the government was attempting to give telecommunications service and equipment providers the responsibility to ensure that the government could both intercept any message and decode it if it were encrypted. One critic compared this to requiring building contractors to provide the government with master keys for all buildings in the U.S.[10] The statement of intent did not pass in 1991, but the government has undertaken an intensive campaign to implement it since then. In 1992, arguing that new technology was making wiretapping more difficult, the FBI launched the first of a series of bills, called the digital telephony bills, or the wiretap bills, requiring that the technology used in communications systems be redesigned, and existing equipment modified, to ensure the ability of law-enforcement agencies to intercept all telephone calls, e-mail, and other computer network communications. (*Privacy Journal* reports that the FBI's internal name for the telephony proposal was "Operation Root Canal."[11]) Prior to that, and throughout the ensuing debate, existing laws required that the communications industry cooperate with lawful wiretap requests, and the industry has generally done so. The government used its own sophisticated equipment and usually bore most of the cost of its interception operations.

The wiretap bills addressed only one part of the government's problem. If the intercepted messages are encrypted, law-enforcement agents cannot read them. In 1993 the government introduced an encryption scheme, known as the Clipper Chip, for telephones. The central and controversial aspect of the Clipper Chip was that the government would hold the keys for the codes used in the chips and thus would be able to decode intercepted conversations. Related chips for computers, for electronic communications (data, e-mail, etc.), were also announced.

The purpose of both proposals, according to the government, is to aid law enforcement in protecting us from terrorists and criminals. The problems with both, according to critics, include threats to privacy, global competitiveness, and civil liberties.

The wiretap act, called the Communications Assistance for Law Enforcement Act, passed in 1994. This law faced intense opposition and was scaled back somewhat from the earlier versions. The Clipper Chip also faced intense opposition, and the government abandoned its goal of having the chip in all phones. However, the government is continuing its efforts to assure its access to all communications and may try to ban encryption for which it does not have access to the keys.

In Section 3.2 we will look at the new wiretap law and the arguments raised in the debate about it. In Section 3.3 we will look at the government's efforts to control encryption.

3.2 DESIGNING COMMUNICATIONS SYSTEMS FOR INTERCEPTION

3.2.1   The Communications Assistance for Law Enforcement Act of 1994

The Communications Assistance for Law Enforcement Act of 1994 (CALEA) requires that telecommunications equipment be designed so that the government* (with a court order or other authorization) can

- Intercept all wire and electronic communications originating from or coming to a particular subscriber.
- Intercept communications to and from mobile users, for example, people using portable phones or portable computers.
- Obtain call-identifying information, including the phone number from which a call originates and the phone number of the destination.
- Have the intercepted communications and call-identifying information transmitted to a location specified by the government.

CALEA authorizes $500,000,000 for hardware and software modifications to current telecommunications equipment and gives the industry a few years to make the changes. It provides for fines of $10,000 a day for carriers that are not in compliance.

Opposition to the wiretap bills came from computer and telecommunications companies (including IBM, AT&T, and Microsoft), industry organizations, privacy advocates, civil libertarians, and organizations such as the Electronic Frontier Foundation and Computer Professionals for Social Responsibility. In 1994 the FBI made a determined effort to pass a bill. Recognizing that it was likely to pass, some opponents worked with members of Congress to modify the draft to limit its scope and add some privacy protections. One major change in CALEA over earlier versions is that information services (e.g., CompuServe, America Online, Prodigy, bulletin boards, Internet services) are exempt from the requirement that their systems be *designed for* government interception. Government agencies may continue to use wiretap orders to intercept transmissions on information networks. (The first several bills were broad enough to apply the "design for interception" requirements to consumer information services and virtually all computer networks, including the Internet and local area networks used by businesses, universities, etc.) Currently, of course, most people use telephones to connect to information services and BBSs. As more business and communications occur on computer networks, criminals and terrorists will use them routinely, like everyone else. Thus, the FBI probably considers CALEA only a

---

*In this context "government" includes the federal government and its agencies, state governments, and various other government subdivisions.

first step and will try to extend it. Another major change from earlier drafts is the authorization of $500,000,000 for modification of the telephone system. Earlier versions of the bill left the expenses to the telecommunications companies.

Although the history of illegal wiretapping by law-enforcement agencies was rarely mentioned in the debate on the digital telephony bills, concern about illegal wiretaps may be the reason for one of the provisions in CALEA: the requirement that taps be initiated at the communications company's premises. This may reduce the likelihood of law enforcement initiating taps secretly. Another purpose of this provision may be to make it more difficult for others (e.g., hackers, industrial spies) to initiate illegal interceptions.

The arguments below, raised in the two-year debate on the various versions of the FBI wiretap bills, are relevant to the bill that passed and to potential future extensions to computer networks.

3.2.2 The Arguments

Protection from terrorists and criminals

The essential argument in favor of ensuring the ability of law-enforcement agencies to intercept communications is that they need this ability to protect us from drug dealers, organized crime, other criminals, and terrorists. After the bombing of the New York World Trade Center in 1993 and the Oklahoma City federal building in 1995, many people may find the terrorist threat a more compelling argument.

After the first of the digital telephony bills was proposed in 1992, FBI Director William Sessions wrote in a letter to the *Wall Street Journal* that the purpose of the proposal was "to ensure that as telecommunications technology advances, the ability of law enforcement to conduct court-ordered electronic surveillance is not lost." He continued:

> In 1968, Congress carefully considered and passed legislation setting forth the exacting procedure by which court authorization to conduct electronic surveillance can be obtained. Since that time it has become an invaluable investigative tool in combating serious and often life-threatening crimes such as terrorism, kidnapping, drugs and organized crime. The 1968 law contemplates cooperation by the telecommunications service providers in implementing these court orders. The proposed legislation only clarifies that responsibility by making it clearly applicable regardless of the technology deployed.[12]

The FBI argued that it is not asking for any new powers; it is just maintaining the status quo. Sessions says in the letter, "No new authority is needed or requested. All the legislation would do if enacted is ensure that the status quo is maintained and the ability granted by Congress in 1968 preserved." Opponents of the wiretap bills, however, argued that the bills do include significant changes from the past thirty years (not to mention the long history of opposition to wiretapping that preceded the 1968 law). In the past, communications equipment was designed for its communications purpose; the FBI developed its tools for interception. The government has a legal right to wiretap with a court order, and the communications provider was required to assist, but there was never a legal guarantee of success in the interception. The government never before could require that equipment be designed and modified to meet the interception needs of law enforcement.*

The value of wiretaps to law enforcement is accepted by many opponents of CALEA. The analysis of the 1992 bill by the Electronic Frontier Foundation includes the following comments:

> There is no doubt that authorized wiretapping is an important weapon properly used by the FBI to fight serious crime. And there is general agreement among communications service providers, and the makers of communications and computing equipment, that the FBI is entitled to full cooperation in its efforts to exercise the powers granted to it in the [1968] wiretap statute. If new technologies require changes in police tactics, then accommodations may be needed on all sides to make sure that new tactics that do not threaten the effectiveness or safety of law enforcement (or unreasonably threaten privacy interests) are available.[13]

Opponents argued that the necessity for CALEA has not been justified, and the expense and other potential problems outweigh the benefits.

Is it needed?

In the mid-1990s, approximately 500 wiretaps were authorized by federal courts each year, up from about 300 per year in the late 1980s. (State agencies obtain a total of 500–600 wiretap orders each year.) Half of all wiretaps are conducted in the New York City area. Critics claim that wiretaps are a less useful law-enforcement tool than informants, detective work, witnesses, and so on. They point out that the World Trade Center bombing, for example, was solved by means other than wiretaps. On the other hand, government officials argue that in the cases where wiretaps are used, they are essential for catching and/or convicting dangerous criminals. Wiretaps are used in 90% of terrorism cases that went to trial.[14]

The FBI offered no evidence for its claim that new technologies make intercepting communications more difficult. Several organizations have used the Freedom of Information Act (FOIA) to obtain internal government memos about wiretapping difficulties. *Privacy Journal* reports that an FBI survey of its field offices apparently showed no need for the bill. Memos from a variety of law enforcement and other government agencies, such as the Drug Enforcement Agency and the IRS, reported no problems with intercepting communications using advanced telephone technology.[15] According to the Electronic Privacy Information Center (EPIC), the telecommunications industry says it is unaware of any case where a company has not been able to provide the interception or information required by a law-enforcement agency. However, FBI Director Louis Freeh testified in Congress that the FBI was unable to fully implement some court-ordered wiretaps; he cited surveys conducted by the FBI about technical problems that hamper wiretapping. EPIC requested the surveys under the FOIA, but the FBI took legal action to delay their release until after

---

*Also, soon after CALEA passed, the FBI supported bills in Congress to expand the government's wiretapping authority, for example, to allow "emergency" wiretaps without court orders.

passage of the bill.[16] It could be that the FBI knows the memos do not support their argument, or they may be concerned that releasing details about their ability or inability to intercept calls would benefit criminals. Either way, opponents argue that the FBI has not shown that, with continuing cooperation from the communications industry, current or future law-enforcement activities would be weakened. The FBI argued that it cannot depend on continued industry cooperation. There are approximately 2000 service providers; the diversity of the industry means that there will be different equipment and algorithms in use. "The prospect of trying to enforce laws without a nationwide standard for surveillance would turn enforcement into a nightmare," according to the FBI.[17] The idea of a "nationwide standard for surveillance" is a nightmare to those who place high value on privacy and civil liberties.

Cost

Given the small number of legal wiretaps, $500,000,000 is a high law-enforcement cost. Critics argue that this figure, authorized in CALEA, is not sufficient. A telephone industry spokesman testified at a Congressional hearing that just modifying call forwarding would cost $1.8 billion.[18] Whether half a billion or two billion, and whether we pay on our telephone bill or our tax bill, it is clear that the changes will be very expensive.

Documents obtained by Computer Professionals for Social Responsibility under FOIA cast doubt on the FBI's cost/benefit analysis. The FBI argued that wiretaps have an economic benefit of several billion dollars a year in fines, forfeitures, prevented economic losses, and so on.[19] Memos from the White House and the Treasury Department criticized the FBI analysis. A White House memo says:

> The analysis should make consistent assumptions with respect to both costs and benefits. The benefits analysis should reflect clearly that only some cases involve electronic surveillance; that some surveillance could continue in the absence of this legislation (at least for some period of years); and that some convictions could probably still be obtained absent surveillance.

> The analysis does not consider the existence of or the potential for other forms of surveillance that might compensate for the reduction in telephone wiretapping capabilities.[20]

Economists point out that anything subsidized is likely to be overused, thus wasting resources. Rather than requiring taxpayers to spend billions to subsidize wiretapping, one economist recommends that law-enforcement agencies be given a reasonable budget and then be permitted to decide on the most effective means of using it. Just as police departments weigh the costs and benefits of patrol cars versus helicopters, investigators can weigh increased expenditures to improve their wiretapping capabilities against spending on other techniques, such as informers, bugs, undercover agents, and so on.[21]

Innovation and global competitiveness

A memo from the Vice President's staff expressed concern that the standards imposed by the FBI would stifle or delay new technologies, such as personal communications services.[22] Such delays have economic costs not considered by the FBI. Worse than delay, the requirements could prevent some potential improvements in communications technology from being implemented. The wiretap law could damage U.S. competitiveness in global markets. The reduced security and privacy resulting from the designed-in tapping capability, as well as the additional expense, would make U.S. communications products less competitive in other countries.

3.3 ENCRYPTION POLICY AND THE KEY-ESCROW CONTROVERSY

3.3.1 Public Key Cryptography

Public keys

Recall that in the general encryption scenario we described in Section 3.1.2, there is one (secret) key for each pair of parties who wish to communicate privately. The key must be passed between the parties by a method more secure than the communications method used for sending messages. The military can afford the expense of couriers, armed guards, and other means of getting keys to a relatively small number of officers, but for businesses that communicate with a large number of people and other businesses, this is impractical.

In the 1970s, a revolution in cryptography took place. Whitfield Diffie and Martin Hellman developed a completely new encryption scheme called public key cryptography. Soon after, Ronald Rivest, Adi Shamir, and Leonard Adleman developed RSA, a practical implementation of the Diffie and Hellman method. In this scheme there are two mathematically related keys. One is used to encrypt a message, the other to decrypt it. The feature that makes public key encryption so remarkable is that knowing the key used to encrypt the message provides no help at all in decrypting it. Thus, each person can have his or her own key pair, and the encrypting key can be public; it is called the person's *public key*. The decrypting key is the person's private key. Public keys can be made widely available in directories. Anyone who wants to send someone a secret message can encrypt the message with the recipient's public key. Even if the ciphertext and the recipient's public key are known by an outsider, the outsider cannot decrypt the message. Only the recipient, using the private key, can do that. It is extremely difficult to decode a message without the proper key, even with the government's fastest computers.

One major advantage of public key cryptography is that it eliminates the need to transmit a secret encryption key between the two parties. Indeed, it eliminates the need for any prior planning or communication between the parties. All that is needed is the recipient's public key.

Worried about the government's moves to limit cryptography, a programmer named Philip Zimmermann developed a program using public key cryptography for e-mail. He called it PGP (for Pretty Good Privacy). Believing that it was essential to provide people with a secure means of protecting their privacy, Zimmermann gave away his program for free. PGP was widely distributed on the Internet. It is now the most popular program for e-mail encryption and is used around the world.*

---

*RSA Data Security, the company founded by the developers of RSA, accused Zimmermann of violating its patents. Zimmermann signed an agreement to stop distributing PGP, although he still helps others use and update it. PGP is still available on the Internet for free, but it is also sold by a company that licenses RSA's technology.

Digital signatures

Currently we put our signature on paper documents such as contracts and checks to formalize a legal agreement or transaction. The signature binds us to terms of a contract, authorizes sale of property, releases assets or funds to others, and so on. Of course, signatures can be forged, but our financial and legal systems rely on them. We can discuss a deal, negotiate terms, and discuss drafts of contracts all by e-mail, but we still sign a paper copy. One of the remarkable features of some public key cryptography schemes, including RSA, lets us "sign" an electronic copy: The roles of the two keys can be reversed. That is, if a message is encrypted with the private key, it can be decrypted with the public key from that key pair. If a message is encrypted with any other key, applying the public key will produce gibberish. This feature provides *digital signatures*. A person who wishes to sign an electronic document can add a statement of acceptance to it and then encrypt it with his or her private key. The ciphertext can be decrypted with the person's public key. Applying any other key to the ciphertext produces gibberish. The document can be decrypted and read by the other parties to the contract, or by a court. The encrypted version is a signed contract because it could have been encrypted only by using the signer's private key.

Many computer science students and hackers know that on some computer systems, it is easy to fake e-mail return addresses. One can send a message purporting to be from someone else, causing mischief or worse problems. In situations where authentication of the sender is important, the honest sender can send the message encrypted with his or her private key.

Suppose we want to send a private (secret), signed message. The digital signature technique described so far has the flaw that the message can be read by anyone who has a copy of it because it can be decrypted with a public key. To send a private, signed message, the sender first encrypts the message with his or her private key, thus "signing" it, then encrypts the ciphertext with the recipient's public key, generating ciphertext of the ciphertext. The recipient first applies his or her private key, then the sender's public key, and recovers the original plaintext message. Because the first stage of recovery requires the recipient's private key, no one else can decrypt the message.

Protection from the "dossier society"

Money is coined liberty.

–Fyodor Dostoevsky[23]

Computer scientist David Chaum developed a set of techniques using RSA public key cryptography that make possible "digital cash" and other privacy-protected transactions.[24] Digital cash is being developed by several companies (including Chaum's, which calls it "e-cash"). It can let us do secure financial transactions electronically without the seller acquiring a credit card or a checking account number from the buyer. The technique also ensures that bank records contain no information linking the payer and recipient of the funds. This provides the convenience of credit card purchases with the anonymity of cash. Because a unit of digital cash is simply a file, it can be stored on one's hard disk at home and used for transactions on the Internet, or it can be stored on a Smart Card and used for ordinary shopping. Digital cash carried on a card can be backed up at home, so if the card is lost or stolen, the owner does not lose the cash. There are ways to prevent the same file from being spent twice, so duplicating a digital cash file is not a problem.

Another kind of transaction made possible by Chaum's techniques is secure and private electronic transfer of what he calls "credentials" (good ones like a diploma and bad ones like a bad credit report).

With such schemes, records of different transactions cannot be easily linked to form a consumer profile or dossier. These techniques provide privacy protection for the consumer with respect to the organizations he or she interacts with, and protection for organizations against forgery, bad checks, and credit card fraud. They can help us keep our names off marketing lists, if we choose, and provide more control over personal information than many proposed laws for privacy protection. Easy-to-use commercial software tools for implementing these techniques are being developed.

Cash transactions make it harder for the government to detect and prosecute people who are "laundering" money earned in illegal activities, earning money they are not reporting to the IRS, or hiding stolen money. Thus, a truly anonymous digital cash system would be opposed and probably prohibited by most governments. Some systems being developed include provisions for law enforcement and tax collection. The potential illegal uses of digital cash have long been possible with real cash. It is only in recent decades, as we have increased our use of checks and credit cards, that we have lost the privacy we had from marketers and government when we used cash for most transactions. As with communications and wiretapping, the government will try to ensure that new technology does not reverse its current access to financial information, although it did not have such access in the past.

3.3.2   Encryption Policy Before the Mid-1990s

Secrecy

Until recently, the main characteristic of U.S. government policy about cryptography was secrecy. Most of the cryptographers in the country worked for an agency whose existence was secret and whose budget still is, although it is larger than the CIA.[25] The agency is the National Security Agency (NSA), formed in 1952 by a secret presidential order. The agency began to get public attention in the late 1970s when it started to lose control of cryptography. According to James Bamford, author of the first book on the NSA's history and activities,[26] no law has been enacted that defines the scope of responsibilities of the NSA or prohibits it from engaging in any activity. The NSA owns and uses the most powerful computers available to break codes. It almost certainly could break virtually any that were in use before the 1980s. It monitors all communications between the U.S. and other countries, and a lot of communications within other countries.[27] One apparent goal of the NSA has been to design codes for the government that no other governments could break; another is to break everyone else's codes.

One tool for keeping information about strong cryptography out of the hands of enemies, terrorists, and private citizens is to classify such information as secret or confidential. It is a crime to give classified material to anyone who does not have government authorization to receive it. In the late 70s, researchers in universities were developing public key cryptography, and inventors were inventing scrambling devices. George Davida, an electrical engineer and computer scientist specializing in data security and cryptography, applied for a patent and instead received a "secrecy order" in the mail telling him he would be breaking the law if he told anyone about his work. The NSA tried to discourage cryptography researchers from publishing their work, threatening to classify it. The inventors and researchers fought back, and the NSA backed down. Next the NSA argued for a law either prohibiting distribution of cryptographic information completely or requiring that all such work be submitted to a government agency (presumably NSA) for approval prior to dissemination. An advisory group of academics approved a voluntary scheme whereby the NSA would ask that a specific work not be published. George Davida, the only member of the advisory group to vote against the plan, argued that such censorship was a dangerous precedent allowing the government to control the publication of scientific research. He said:

> It would be only too easy for us to lose our constitutional freedoms in bits and pieces. . . . One gets the impression that the NSA is struggling to stand still, and to keep American research standing still with it, while the rest of the world races ahead. . . . The NSA can best perform its mission in the old-fashioned way: Stay ahead of others.

Another tactic tried by the NSA was to take over funding for cryptography research from the National Science Foundation so that it could control the researchers.[28]

The NSA's attempts to prevent publication raise First Amendment issues. We will discuss some constitutional issues related to cryptography in Chapter 6.

Standards

Since the 1970s, the government and business leaders have tried to adopt an encryption standard for business and financial communications that must be protected from criminals, competitors, and hackers. The Data Encryption Standard (DES), developed by IBM and the NSA and announced as a standard in 1976, has been a source of continuous controversy. Suspicion of the NSA ran high enough that some cryptography experts suspected that it had secretly installed "trap doors" to allow them to decrypt messages without a key. (Now many think this did not actually happen.) There was debate about whether DES was secure enough. It could be broken with perhaps a few million dollars of computer equipment and time. That meant it was secure from nosy neighbors and most business competitors, but not from foreign governments and the NSA. It is widely believed that the government opposed a stronger standard advocated by many security experts because even the NSA's powerful computers would have trouble decrypting messages encoded with the stronger standard.

Export restrictions

Because of the traditional military applications, the government classifies coding machines and encryption software as "munitions," like tanks and bombs, subject to export control. The NSA decides what exports to approve; it does not approve the more secure systems. It is believed that it approves only those it has the computing power to break. This means that U.S. manufacturers must go to the extra expense of making two versions of each product, one for the domestic market and one for export, or sell the weaker versions in the U.S. as well, or give up their export business. Most U.S. software makers who include encryption software in their products cannot efficiently distribute two versions of the products, so they use the weaker, exportable version for all customers. It is convenient for international businesses to use one system to communicate between domestic and foreign offices. If they use commercial software made by a U.S. software company with embedded encryption, even if a stronger version were available in the U.S., the company would need to use the weaker version that can be exported to its overseas offices. Thus, for several reasons, the export restrictions result in weaker encryption being used by American businesses and individuals.

Products produced for export are less competitive with those of foreign companies that use the better encryption techniques. One data security expert reported that a $100 million contract for financial computer terminals went to a European company after U.S. companies were prohibited by the government from exporting a truly secure system.[29] The vulnerability of exportable encryption was highlighted in 1995 when a French student decoded a message encrypted by the foreign version of Netscape's Internet navigation software. Secure encryption is needed for commerce on the Internet (e.g., to protect credit card numbers). Internet businesses complain that the export restrictions are slowing the growth of international electronic commerce.

The export restrictions have consequences for individual businesspeople, not just system and software developers. It is now common for people to travel with laptop computers. Someone on a business trip to another country, carrying software routinely used on a laptop, may be breaking the export laws.

The U.S. policy is strangely outdated. The better encryption schemes are available in other countries, and the algorithms appear in technical publications available around the world. The Software Publishers Association (SPA), an organization of more than 1000 leading software publishers, studied the availability of cryptography worldwide. They found several hundred foreign cryptographic products available in the global marketplace. More than half of them use encryption methods that could not be exported by U.S. companies. Many of the products are software, installed by the user from a floppy disk; they are easy to install and use. Implementations of DES, RSA, and PGP are available on Internet sites all over the world. SPA mentions that even the strong U.S. products are widely available—in illegal, pirated copies, for which the U.S. programmers and publishers receive no income. SPA concludes that "unilateral US export controls keep US firms from competing in the global marketplace. . . . The US government is succeeding only in crippling a vital American industry's exporting ability."[30] The federal government's Computer Systems Security and Privacy Advisory Board, made up of government and industry representatives, also states that "current controls are negatively impacting U.S. competitiveness in the world market and are not inhibiting the foreign production and use of cryptography."[31] Global sales of encryption products were expected to be close to $2 billion in 1996. The effect of export restrictions can be estimated by comparing the U.S. share of the global market for encryption products with U.S. share for other computer products. The U.S. has approximately 75% of the world market for software and hardware, but only about 50% of the encryption market. Government officials continue to argue that the export restrictions keep strong encryption from many international terrorists, criminals, and unfriendly foreign powers.[32]

Because of the wide availability of encryption software both in and outside the U.S., the government has tried a new approach to thwarting the use of strong encryption: It began threatening prosecution of companies that export software designed so that encryption programs like PGP can be used with it, even though the software does not actually include the encryption programs.[33]

The case of Philip Zimmermann illustrates the chilling effect of the export restrictions on the distribution of strong cryptography within the United States. In 1991, copies of PGP appeared on numerous domestic Internet sites. They reportedly were posted by an acquaintance of Zimmermann's to make strong encryption available to Americans before it might be outlawed. Copies of PGP were downloaded from the Internet in other countries. The government began an investigation of Zimmermann. For more than two years he was under threat of indictment for exporting encryption in violation of the export control laws and could have been sent to jail for several years. In 1995, while the investigation was underway, Zimmermann developed a version of PGP for use with a personal computer equipped with a sound card and modem; the computer can be used as a secure telephone. This is not illegal, but Zimmermann said the hard part of the project was determining how to release it without being put in jail. He said that his political speaking was subdued because of the investigation. Eventually, the government closed the investigation without bringing charges against Zimmermann. Ironically, a law-enforcement expert recommends PGP to police departments and estimates that hundreds of law-enforcement officers use it.[34]

Banning information

When trying to measure the depth of the government's concern about information passed secretly to or among enemies, it may help to consider some of the restrictions placed on communications in wartime. During World War II, the government employed almost 15,000 people to open mail going overseas to eliminate any that contained military information of use to Germany or Japan. The censors read a million pieces of mail per day. They also listened to telephone conversations and read magazines and movie scripts. The drawings of children were suspect; they could mask a map of some sort. Crossword puzzles could contain hidden messages. And so could knitting instructions, moves in a chess game played by mail, orders of flowers that specified the particular types of flowers to be included, and phoned-in requests to radio stations to play specific songs. Any of these normally innocent things could be a form of code, giving vital information to an enemy. Many of these activities were simply banned during the war. During the Persian Gulf War, military censors refused to allow Navajos at home to broadcast greetings on Armed Forces Radio to their relatives and friends stationed overseas. They feared that the Navajos could be transmitting secret information. (During World War II, the Marines used Navajos to do exactly that; a military code was developed using the complexity of the spoken Navajo language. Because of the Navajo contribution to that war, public attention shamed the censors into lifting the ban in the Gulf War.)[35]

In wartime, the highest priority of the government is to win the war. The fear that there might be one secret enemy message hidden in the thousands of innocent drawings, songs, flower arrangements, or Navajo greetings was enough to restrict the freedom and peaceful activities of everyone. Two questions arise from this history. Were these actions paranoia on the government's part or a reasonable precaution to protect the lives and freedom of Americans? How relevant are the government's wartime restrictions to times of peace, or "cold war," or wars on drugs?

3.3.3   Key Escrow Encryption

The government had tried to keep cryptography itself secret, and that worked well when few individuals or businesses had much interest in using it. As computer technology and telecommunications led to increasing use of encryption in the financial industry and by other large businesses, the government used export control and its influence in setting an encryption standard to pressure industry to adopt encryption schemes the NSA could break. Then public key cryptography, RSA, and PGP made encryption cheap and easy. Everyone—individuals, businesses, and criminals and terrorists—can, if they choose, encode their messages so that the government cannot read them. A journalist described this situation as "the NSA's worst nightmare." In 1993, the government announced plans for the Clipper Chip and created a storm of controversy.

The Clipper Chip

Accepting the need for strong encryption for business and the desire for privacy of many Americans, the government came up with a plan to provide both, while giving the government a "back door," a way to decrypt any message. The NSA developed the encryption algorithm called Skipjack. It was implemented on a chip, called the Clipper Chip, for telephones. Skipjack was also implemented on other chips, called Capstone and Tessera, for computers.[36] Each chip includes an identification field, called the Law Enforcement Access Field (LEAF), with every coded message it sends. When law-enforcement agencies intercept an encrypted message, the LEAF tells them which key will decrypt the message.

Several aspects of the plan were intended to protect against abuse by the government and decryption of messages by outsiders. It uses a "key escrow" scheme. Each key is split in two parts. Neither part alone is sufficient to decrypt a message. The two parts are held by two different government agencies, called escrow agents, so no one agency could use a key secretly. Law-enforcement agencies would not themselves have the keys. The escrow agents would not release the keys to law-enforcement agencies without a court order. The hardware used by law-enforcement agencies to receive the keys and decrypt messages would be sold only to law-enforcement agencies and would be registered.

The proposal announced in 1993 was for the government to adopt Clipper as a standard for use by the government (for unclassified communications). It would also be used by businesses that deal with the government. The government emphasized that use of Clipper would be voluntary, but made it clear that it wanted the system to become standard for all telephone and computer communications.

There were many practical and economic objections to the Clipper Chip. More fundamentally, many objections have to do with our right to privacy—including privacy from the government. Specific problems with Clipper led the government to drop its plan to promote Clipper and its sister chips as the standard for all communications. Instead, the government is trying to work out an alternative "key escrow" plan where other encryption methods could be used, but the government would still have access to the keys (with an appropriate court order). Many of the arguments for and against the Clipper Chip apply as well to any compulsory key escrow plan. We will examine those after looking at some problems specific to Clipper.

Secrecy and security of Clipper

The algorithm used in the government-designed chips is secret. It must be kept secret so that people (in the U.S. and in other countries) cannot use it in other devices without providing the keys to the government's escrow agents. The NSA, quite sensibly, does not want the results of its work in developing a strong encryption algorithm to be available to foreign individuals and foreign governments—the very people whose communications the NSA monitors. There are two problems with secrecy, however.

First, computer scientists cannot evaluate the protection the chip would provide from hackers or industrial spies. The quality of the encryption algorithm is quite important. More than one expert has suggested that the security of our vast communications and financial systems, and the economic health of our technology export business, may be more important to our national security than being able to read secret messages of potential enemies.[37] To reassure the technical community and the public, the government allowed a panel of cryptography experts to examine the algorithm after agreeing not to disclose any details. They concluded that there was no significant risk that Skipjack could be broken. A few months later a scientist at AT&T found a flaw in the design. A user could circumvent the LEAF mechanism that attaches to each encrypted message the information the government needs to get the proper key for decoding the message. The government responded that the method of circumventing the LEAF would take too long to work in practice when using the chip. Although the flaw was not one that compromised the encryption itself, the finding illustrates that a small panel of experts can miss something. New techniques and technologies are more robust and reliable if they are exposed to testing and experimentation by many researchers and engineers.[38]

A second problem with secrecy of the algorithm is the possibility, or the concern about the possibility, that the NSA has built in a trapdoor that lets it decrypt messages without getting the keys from the escrow agents.

Another issue is the security of keys stored by government escrow agents. We have seen that government employees in the IRS and Social Security Administration illegally sold data from government records. How confident should we be that the keys would be well protected?

Commercial key escrow

There are good business and personal reasons for using some sort of key escrow system. If a company employee is not available and someone else in the company must read files that were encrypted by the employee, there is a problem. If someone loses an encryption key, encrypted files cannot be decrypted. A number of businesses are working on key escrow plans. One proposal is that large companies and organizations establish their own escrow office for their employees. Another is that bonded companies, like escrow companies that process real estate purchases, offer key escrow service to businesses and individuals. A company is developing a method for key escrow in which the escrow agent would not actually keep copies of the keys, thus reducing the chances of abuse or leaks. Under this scheme, when you encrypt a file, the key would be automatically included in the encrypted file, but the key would be encrypted using the escrow agent's public key. Thus the escrow agent could decode the customer's key only when presented with a copy of the file, and no one else could. Law-enforcement agencies would be able to obtain messages and have them decoded by escrow agents by using search warrants and court orders without any fundamental change in current powers or procedures.[39]

If commercial key escrow develops as a voluntary alternative available in the market, there are no major political issues. However, some possibilities being considered by the government include licensing of escrow agents, requiring that all users of encryption use a licensed agent, and banning nonescrowed encryption. Such requirements and restrictions raise the issue of freedom to protect one's own privacy. As we shall see, government statements about its intentions concerning mandatory key escrow have been inconsistent.

Arguments about key escrow schemes

The government position: privacy and protection. The essential argument in favor of mandatory key escrow encryption is the same argument for ensuring the ability of law-enforcement agencies to intercept communications in the first place: to protect us from drug dealers, organized crime, other criminals, and terrorists. The government's argument is presented well in a statement by John Podesta, assistant to President Clinton:

> The development of key escrow encryption technology was born out of a recognition on the part of the U.S. Government of the public's growing desire for high quality encryption capability for commercial and private use. At the same time, the Government was concerned that the widespread use of this technology could make lawfully authorized electronic surveillance much more difficult. Historically, law enforcement encountered very little encryption, owing largely to the expense and difficulty in using such technology. With growing availability of lower cost, commercial encryption technology for use by U.S. industry and private citizens, it became clear that a strategy was needed that could accommodate the needs of the private sector for top notch communications security; of U.S. industry to remain competitive in the world's secure communications market; and of U.S. law enforcement to conduct lawfully-authorized electronic surveillance.[40]

Vice President Al Gore said, "Our policy is designed to provide better encryption to individuals and businesses while ensuring that the needs of law enforcement and national security are met. Encryption is a law and order issue since it can be used by criminals to thwart wiretaps and avoid detection and prosecution." The White House Press Secretary's statement says, "Unfortunately, the same encryption technology that can help Americans protect business secrets and personal privacy can also be used by terrorists, drug dealers, and other criminals.[41]

To illustrate the danger of strong encryption in the hands of criminals, supporters of key escrow cite the case of a pedophile who kept information about his young victims on his computer, encrypted with PGP. They provide little concrete information to illustrate the danger to national security from secure encryption; the NSA would not provide information in a public congressional hearing. In another often-cited example of negative use of encryption, a group of neo-Nazis in Germany used PGP to encrypt messages on their bulletin board network, used to plan illegal activities.[42]

In addition to the law-enforcement goal of helping to catch criminals, the government presents Clipper and key escrow as tools to improve privacy. Currently, most telephone conversations and e-mail are not encrypted at all, so key escrow encryption would give us more privacy than many communications have now. Opponents argue that this is disingenuous. The government is comparing the level of privacy using key escrow with the current situation when use of encryption is just beginning and is not yet widespread among individuals. The motivation for the government's proposals came from worries about the likely future of private, fully secure encryption. They are trying to *reduce* the level of privacy that would otherwise be available in the near future.

Will It Be Voluntary? The government's justification for the Clipper Chip was illegal activities of terrorists and criminals. Opponents pointed out that even if the Clipper Chip and its computer network cousins were installed in virtually all telephones and computer networks, drug dealers and terrorists could use other devices and software to encrypt their messages before they go through the NSA's chips. Similarly, if key escrow is available, criminals would not use it, or, again, could encrypt their messages first with nonescrowed encryption. Government officials argue that even if criminals and terrorists use another form of encryption when communicating among themselves, they would be using escrowed encryption when communicating with legitimate businesses, and those communications can be helpful to law enforcement. However, the obvious "loophole" in any voluntary scheme led many observers to believe the government's goal was to outlaw other encryption methods. The government frequently claimed that use of the Clipper Chip or other key escrow encryption would be voluntary. For example, in 1994 an administration official told a Congressional committee:

> As the Administration has made clear on a number of occasions, the key-escrow encryption initiative is a voluntary one; we have absolutely no intention of mandating private use of a particular kind of cryptography, nor of criminalizing the private use of certain kinds of cryptography.[43]

However, in a 1993 document obtained by the Electronic Privacy Information Center from the FBI under the Freedom of Information Act (FOIA) in 1995, the FBI, NSA, and Department of Justice concluded that

> Technical solutions, such as they are, will only work if they are incorporated into *all* encryption products. To ensure that this occurs, legislation mandating the use of Government-approved encryption products or adherence to Government encryption criteria is required.[44]

Another FBI document[45] advocates legislation prohibiting cryptography that does not meet the government standard. Statements by FBI director Louis Freeh strongly suggest a desire to ban unescrowed encryption of telephone and e-mail conversations: "Unless the issue of encryption is resolved soon, criminal conversations over the telephone and other communications devices will become indecipherable by law enforcement." "The objective is for us to get those conversations. . . . Wherever they are, whatever they are, I need them."[46] A bill introduced in Congress in 1995 would make it illegal to distribute any encryption software on the Internet unless the government was given the tools to decrypt all messages prior to distribution of the software.[47]

Freedom and trade-offs. Secure encryption, its supporters point out, can protect against terrorists too, especially when the terrorists are in power. Philip Zimmermann, author of PGP, has widely publicized a message he received from Latvia telling him that PGP was very popular among the anti-Soviet underground. The message goes on to say. "Let it never be, but if dictatorship takes over Russia, your PGP is widespread from Baltic to Far East now and will help democratic people if necessary." A human rights worker in a third world country told Zimmermann he uses PGP to encrypt his interviews. If the country's death squads found and could read his notes, they would kill the witnesses he interviewed.

The seriousness of the crimes that might be protected by secure encryption is not ignored by privacy advocates. The problem is one of trade-offs. Zimmermann says, "There are some really bad criminals that need to be caught. I don't think putting a bugging device in every phone in America is the way to do it." Speaking of the neo-Nazis who use PGP, he said, "I'm sorry to see people like that use my software, but if people like that ever came to power, we'd be glad that my software is available." He says Americans do not understand why he is so paranoid about the government, "but people in police states, you don't have to explain it to them. They already get it, and they don't understand why we don't."[48]

Another perspective on the concern about criminal use of secure encryption is offered by James Bidzos, president of RSA Data Security. He suggests that law-enforcement agencies could have made similar arguments against the building of the interstate highway system. Criminals could flee to different states or transport stolen goods across state lines. We recognize that, yes, these are indeed problems, but the economic and personal benefits from such a safe, convenient, efficient transportation system far outweigh the problems.[49]

The NSA's role. In the discussions about encryption standards in the 1970s and 80s, the National Institute of Standards and Technology (NIST) was the public participant, although people in the industry and others believed that the NSA was directing the government's positions and decisions. With the Clipper Chip, the NSA apparently gave up its attempts to stay in the background. Documents released to Computer Professionals for Social Responsibility under the FOIA indicate that the NSA was also involved in devising the FBI's wiretap bills.[50] Some people see the involvement of the NSA in domestic communications policy as sinister in and of itself. Spy agencies are not known for their adherence to constitutional rights. Spokesmen for the Electronic Frontier Foundation wrote:

> Inasmuch as digital privacy policy has broad implications for constitutional rights of free speech and privacy, these issues must be explored and resolved in an open, civilian policy context. This principle is clearly articulated in the Computer Security Act of 1987. . . . The structure of the Act arose, in significant part, from the concern that the national security establishment was exercising undue control over the flow of public information and the use of information technology. When considering the law in 1986, the Congress asked the question, 'Whether it is proper for a super-secret agency [the NSA] that operates without public scrutiny to involve itself in domestic activities. . . ?' The answer was a clear no, and the authority for establishing computer security policy was vested in NIST (then the National Bureau of Standards).[51]

An NSA spokesman says, on the other hand, that by continually developing better key escrow encryption techniques, it is contributing to solutions for the difficult problem of balancing privacy with law enforcement and national security.

Global trade. To increase support for the Clipper Chip, the government announced that communication equipment using it could be exported. After the failure of Clipper to win acceptance, the government announced that it will permit export of encryption schemes using longer keys than it previously permitted—if the keys were escrowed. Critics (in the U.S. and outside) say few customers in other countries will buy equipment or software that makes their communications vulnerable to the U.S. government via key escrow. The U.S. communications industry will continue to be at a disadvantage in the global market.

Proponents and opponents. Support for compulsory key escrow encryption and the wiretap bill comes from the government, in particular the NSA, the FBI, and the White House. Two notable nongovernment supporters are computer scientists Dorothy Denning and David Gelernter. Denning, highly respected for her expertise in computer security, says that the threats of organized crime and terrorism swayed her to the government's side. In 1993, a letter bomb mailed to Gelernter by the Unabomber exploded and seriously injured him. Gelernter argues that without the wiretap act, crime, particularly terrorist crime, would increase. About Clipper he said, "Clipper chips will make computer-based communication routinely safe and private, in a way that gives us a fighting chance of keeping our ability to spy on criminals."[52]

The opposition ranges across the political spectrum, including civil libertarians, conservative talk show host Rush Limbaugh, industry groups, privacy advocates, and a colorful group of people called cypherpunks. One writer describes the cypherpunks as a "loose-knit band of scrappy, libertarian-leaning computer jockeys who have dedicated themselves to perfecting and promoting the art of disappearing into the virtual hinterlands."[53] Some wear long hair and sandals, some earned millions of dollars from their pioneering work in computer technologies, and all of them believe that privacy from government and large business institutions must be protected.

Is the genie out of the bottle? Cypherpunks and others who support our right to use whatever technical means we choose to protect our privacy are fond of saying, "The genie is out of the bottle." They mean that strong encryption, such as PGP, is so widely available that governments cannot stop its use. This argument misses some serious consequences of making unescrowed encryption illegal. Consider the analogy of drug laws. They have not stopped the use of drugs, but the drug laws force users into criminal society, contribute to corruption of law-enforcement personnel, and justify violations of civil liberties, (e.g., seizure of property of people suspected, but not convicted, of violating the law). Forcing secure encryption underground would jeopardize the freedom of noncriminal, honest people who simply believe in protecting privacy. If the mere distribution or use of unescrowed encryption is a crime, the government can put its critics, or people with unpopular views, in jail without proving that they have done anything that is otherwise illegal.

The National Research Council report

In the midst of the encryption controversy, Congress requested that the National Research Council (NRC), the research affiliate of the National Academy of Sciences, do a thorough study of U.S. encryption policy and make recommendations. The NRC report, prepared by a panel of experts from business, government, and academia, was completed in 1996. It strongly supports the use of powerful encryption and loosening of export controls, citing many of the arguments we presented. The report states that there should be no law barring manufacture, sale, or use of any form of encryption in the United States. It argues that strong encryption provides increased protection against hackers, thieves, and terrorists who may threaten our economic, electric power, and transportation infrastructure. It argues that the free market and business needs for data protection would do a better job than the National Security Agency and the FBI. It says that plans that rely on government escrow of keys would have security and liability risks.[54] The Clinton administration disagreed with some of the panel's major recommendations. It continued to make new proposals for key escrow requirements.

3.4 FUNDAMENTAL ISSUES

The conflict between private and secure communications, on the one hand, and access by the government, on the other, will continue to generate controversy. Both the wiretapping and key escrow issues, like the issues in Chapter 2 related to government use of personal data, raise questions about the fundamental relationship between the people and the government.

What surveillance and interception policies are appropriate for the government when we use computer networks for casual e-mail, purchases, access to discussion groups and information services, and sensitive business and financial communications? Should communications systems be designed to meet "a nationwide standard for surveillance," or should they use the best technology available for achieving speed, convenience, low cost, and privacy? How much should the freedom and privacy of honest and peaceful people be weakened to aid the government's law-enforcement activities? How far can we trust the government not to abuse its power?

There are very strong emotions on both sides of the wiretap and key escrow debates. To some people it seems so obvious that legitimate law-enforcement needs require that the government have access to any communication (with a court order). To others the potential for abuse is the overriding concern. I have puzzled over the question of why "gut reactions" differ so much. Perhaps it is because the same agency that deals with the horrors of kidnapped children and terrorist bombings also infiltrates and wiretaps groups whose religious or political views differ from the mainstream or are simply opponents of powerful people. Tension about the powers of law enforcement arises from laws that are unpopular with large segments of the peaceful, normally law-abiding public, both on the left and right (e.g., laws against use of recreational drugs and laws against ownership of certain guns). This tension will probably not diminish as long as the same law-enforcement agencies protect us from violent criminals and terrorists and also suppress contrary ideas and unconventional activities.

EXERCISES

Review exercises

1. Describe at least three different kinds of uses of encryption that have social value. (Indicate why they are valuable.)

2. What is an important difference between public key cryptography and secret key cryptography?

3. Explain how public key cryptography provides a mechanism for digitally "signing" a document.

4. What were some of the communications prohibited by the government during World War II?

5. What is the main difference between the Communications Assistance for Law Enforcement Act of 1994 and the wiretapping capability the government had before?

6. Give an example where encryption was used by a criminal.

7. What are some reasons why a business might choose to use a private system to escrow encryption keys?

General exercises

8. Among the threats from which the Communications Assistance for Law Enforcement Act and mandatory escrow of encryption keys are designed to protect us, which two do you think are the most serious? Which two arguments against the Communications Assistance for Law Enforcement Act do you think are the strongest? Which two arguments against mandatory escrow of encryption keys do you think are the strongest?

9. Two examples of use of PGP mentioned in the text are (1) neo-Nazi bulletin boards with information about illegal activities, and (2) interviews with victims and/or witnesses of death squad activities, presumably sanctioned by the government, in a third world country. Do these examples balance each other out when considering whether the government should have the keys, or does one case give a more compelling argument for one side?

10. (a) In what ways do restrictions on export of strong encryption systems make it more difficult and costly for Americans to use strong encryption within the U.S.?

    (b) Some critics of U.S. encryption policy believe that a major reason why the government wants to maintain export restrictions is to reduce the use of strong encryption by U.S. citizens. What evidence is there for or against this interpretation of the government's motives?

    (c) What restrictions, if any, do you think there should be on export of encryption hardware and software? Give your reasons.

11. Digital cash can be designed to allow transactions to be made securely and anonymously. Considering the privacy benefits and the potential for use by tax evaders and criminals, do you think fully anonymous digital cash should be made illegal? Give your reasons.

12. Consider commercial key escrow, described in Section 3.3.3. Give some arguments in favor of requiring by law that all users of encryption use a key escrow agent licensed by the government. Give some arguments against such a requirement.

Assignments
These exercises require some research or activity that may need to be done during business hours or a few days before the assignment is due.

13. Get a copy of the Communications Assistance for Law Enforcement Act of 1994 and find answers to the following questions. (Use your own words, not the legal jargon of the law.)

    (a) Section 103 (Assistance capability requirements) is the main part of the law. Summarize the requirements in part (a) of this section and the limitations in part (b).

    (b) What is the meaning of "telecommunications carrier"? (See Section 102 Definitions.)

    (c) What are the telecommunications carrier's responsibilities if the communication intercepted by law enforcement is encrypted?

    (d) How soon must telecommunications carriers be in compliance with the requirements of the Act? (See Section 104.)

(e) What requirements and possible penalties does the law impose on manufacturers of telecommunications switching and transmission equipment? (See Section 201.)

14. Contact police departments in your area and ask if they can describe a case where they used wiretapping to catch or convict a criminal. Write a summary of such a case.

15. Find a copy of PGP on the Internet.

16. Access the World Wide Web home page of a company making software for digital cash and report on any one of its products. What are some advantages and some disadvantages of using the product?

17. Several bills about encryption policy were introduced in Congress in 1996. Some would loosen controls on encryption and some would tighten controls. Find out the current status of at least one such bill. Has important legislation about encryption been passed since this book was published?

Class exercises

1. Hold a debate in class on the question of whether there should be a legal requirement that all encryption keys be escrowed.

NOTES

1 The historic information in this section is from Alan F. Westin, *Privacy and Freedom,* Atheneum, 1968; Alexander Charns, *Cloak and Gavel: FBI Wiretaps, Bugs, Informers, and the Supreme Court,* University of Illinois Press, 1992 (Chapter 8); Edith Lapidus, *Eavesdropping on Trial,* Hayden Book Co., 1974; and Walter Isaacson, *Kissinger: A Biography,* Simon and Schuster, 1992.

2 The quote is in the foreword of Lapidus, *Eavesdropping on Trial.*

3 Larry Loen, "Hiding Data in Plain Sight," *EFFector Online,* January 7, 1993, v. 4.05.

4 Mary Eisenhart, "Encryption, Privacy & Data Security," *MicroTimes,* March 8, 1993, pp. 111–122.

5 Lance J. Hoffman, Faraz A. Ali, Steven L. Heckler, Ann Huybrechts, "Cryptography Policy," *Communications of the ACM,* September 1994, 37:9, pp. 109–117.

6 John Markoff, "Hacker Case Underscores Internet's Vulnerability," *New York Times,* February 17, 1995, p. D1.

7 Milo Geyelin, "Cellular Phones May Betray Client Confidences," *Wall Street Journal,* September 1, 1994, p. B1. James Bidzos, quoted in Eisenhart, "Encryption, Privacy & Data Security."

8 Nathan P. Myhrvold, quoted in Russell Mitchell, "The Key to Safe Business on the Net," *Business Week,* February 27, 1995, p. 86.

9 Senate Bill 266, Senators Biden and DeConcini.

10 John Perry Barlow, "Decrypting the Puzzle Palace," *Communications of the ACM,* July 1992, 35:7, pp. 25–31.

11 "Overkill By the FBI For New Tapping Authority," *Privacy Journal,* December 1993, p. 3.

12 William Sessions, "FBI Must Keep Up With Wonks and Hackers," Letters to the Editor, *Wall Street Journal,* August 4, 1992, p. A15.

13 "An Analysis of the FBI Digital Telephony Proposal," Electronic Frontier Foundation, September 18, 1992.

14 "Federal Wiretaps Stay at High Level," *Privacy Journal,* June 1996, p.6. Robert Fox, "Newstrack," *Communications of the ACM,* July 1994, 37:7, p. 9. "In Congress: FBI Wiretapping Proposal on a Fast Track," *Privacy Journal,* September 1994, p. 3. Hoffman et al, p. 115.

15 "Overkill By the FBI For New Tapping Authority," *Privacy Journal,* December 1993, p. 3.

16 Mary Lu Carnevale, "Bill Would Ensure Law Enforcement Is Able to Tap Wires," *Wall Street Journal,* September 30, 1994, p. B7. "Judge Rejects Delay on FBI Wiretap Data; 'Stunned' by Bureau's Request," EPIC Press Release, October 3, 1994.

17 John Schwartz, "Industry Fights Wiretap Proposal," *Washington Post,* March 12, 1994, pp. C1, C7.

18 *CPSR Alert,* April 14, 1994, v. 3.06.

19 Brock Meeks, "Jacking in from the 'We Doubt It' Port," *Cyberwire Dispatch,* 1994.

20 May 22, 1992, White House memo, quoted in *CPSR Alert,* April 14, 1994, v. 3.06.

21 Robin Hanson, "Can Wiretaps Remain Cost Effective?" *Communications of the ACM,* December 1994, 37:12, pp. 13–15.

22 Meeks, "Jacking in from the 'We Doubt It' Port."

23 Fyodor Dostoevsky, *The House of the Dead,* 1862; translation by Constance Garnett, 1915.

24 David Chaum, "Achieving Electronic Privacy," *Scientific American,* August 1992, pp. 96–101. David Chaum, "A New Paradigm for Individuals Living in the Information Age," in Deborah G. Johnson and Helen Nissenbaum, *Computers, Ethics & Social Values,* Prentice Hall, 1995, pp. 366–73. Julian Dibbell, "Building a Better Monkey Wrench," *Voice,* August 3, 1993, p. 34.

25 Philip Elmer-Dewitt, "Who Should Keep the Keys?" *Time,* March 14, 1994, pp. 90–91. Julian Dibbell, "Code Warriors Battling for the Keys to Privacy in the Info Age," *Voice,* August 3, 1993, pp. 33–37.

26 James Bamford, *The Puzzle Palace: A Report on NSA, America's Most Secret Agency,* Houghton Mifflin, 1982.

27 Bamford, *The Puzzle Palace,* p. 4. In 1920, the federal government's Black Chamber, a secret group of code experts and a precursor to the National Security Agency, successfully pressured the main cable (telegram) companies to let the government routinely see foreign cables, in violation of the federal Radio Communication Act of 1912, which made it illegal for a cable company employee to divulge a message to anyone except the addressee without a court order. (Bamford, p. 12.)

28 Bamford, *The Puzzle Palace,* pp. 356–57, 361–62. The Davida quote is on p. 361.

29 James Bidzos, president of RSA Data Security, quoted in John Perry Barlow, "Decrypting the Puzzle Palace," p. 27.

30 Lance Hoffman, "SPA Study of Foreign Availability of Cryptography," *SPA News,* March, 1994, pp. U1, U4.

31 Hoffman et al, "Cryptography Policy," pg. 113.

32 Hoffman et al, "Cryptography Policy," pg. 111.

33 Loring Wirbel, "State Dept. Tries to Quash APIs for PGP Cryptography," *Electronic Engineering Times,* April 29, 1996, p. 4.

34 William Sternow, quoted in Eric Dexheimer, "Police Uneasy with This Cure for the Common Code," *San Diego Union Tribune,* Computer Link section, March 1, 1994, p. 1ff.

35 David Kahn, *The Codebreakers,* Macmillan, 1967, pp. 515–17. Julian Dibbell, "Tale From the Crypto Wars," *Voice,* August 3, 1993, p. 36. Nathan Aaseng, *Navajo Code Talkers,* Walker & Co., 1992.

36 Bob Davis, "Clipper Chip Is Your Friend, NSA Contends," *Wall Street Journal,* March 22, 1994. See also S. Kent et al, "Codes, Keys and Conflicts: Issues in US Crypto Policy, Report of a Spe-

cial Panel of the ACM US Public Policy Committee," June 1994 (http://info.acm.org/reports/acm_crypto_study.html).

37 James Bidzos, in Eisenhart, "Encryption, Privacy & Data Security." James Chandler, George Washington University National Law Center, mentioned in Hoffman et al, "Cryptography Policy," p. 115.

38 Brickell et al, "SKIPJACK Review, Interim Report," July 28, 1993, in *EFFector Online,* 5:14, August 5, 1993. Don Clark, "Clipper Chip's Flaw May Force Change In Encryption Design for Computers," *Wall Street Journal,* June 3, 1994.

39 Stephen Walker, Trusted Information Systems, Inc., "Commercial Key Escrow: Something For Everyone," The Fifth Conference on Computers, Freedom and Privacy, San Francisco, March 28–31, 1995, pp. 158–65.

40 "Answers to Clipper Questions," *EFFector Online,* 5:14, August 5, 1993.

41 *EFFector Online,* 7:3, February 9, 1994.

42 Dexheimer, "Police Uneasy with This Cure for the Common Code," p. 18. Steven Levy, "Battle of the Clipper Chip," *New York Times Magazine,* June 12, 1994, pp. 44–70. During hearings on encryption, an NSA representative spoke only in a classified meeting.

43 Assistant Attorney General Jo Ann Harris, before a Senate Judiciary Subcommittee, May 3, 1994.

44 The report is titled "Encryption: The Threat, Applications and Potential Solutions." It is quoted in "Documents: FBI & NSA Want to Ban Non-Escrowed Encryption," *EPIC Alert,* August 21, 1995, v. 2.09.

45 "Impact of Emerging Telecommunications Technologies on Law Enforcement," also quoted in *EPIC Alert,* ibid.

46 FBI director Louis Freeh, testimony before the House Committee on the Judiciary Subcommittee on Crime, March 30, 1995, reported in *EFFector Online,* December 15, 1994, 7:15, and at a conference on cryptography, October 1994, reported in *EPIC Alert,* October 28, 1994, v. 1.06.

47 The Anti-Electronic Racketeering Act of 1995, introduced by Sen. Charles Grassley.

48 Zimmermann quotes from conversation and Dexheimer, "Police Uneasy with This Cure for the Common Code," p. 12.

49 Eisenhart, "Encryption, Privacy & Data Security," p. 118.

50 "Overkill by the FBI for New Tapping Authority," *Privacy Journal,* December 1993, p. 3.

51 Jerry Berman and Daniel J. Weitzner, *EFFector Online,* 5:5, April 2, 1993.

52 David Gelernter, "Wiretaps for a Wireless Age," *New York Times,* May 8, 1994, Sec. 4, p. 17.

53 Dibbell, "Tale From the Crypto Wars."

54 National Research Council, *Cryptography's Role in Securing the Information Society,* National Academy Press, 1996 (www2.nas.edu/cstbweb).

FOR FURTHER READING

James Bamford, *The Puzzle Palace: A Report on NSA, America's Most Secret Agency,* Houghton Mifflin, 1982.

John Perry Barlow, "A Plain Text on Crypto Policy," *Communications of the ACM,* November 1993, 36:11, pp. 21–26.

Jerry Berman and Daniel J. Weitzner, "Keys to Privacy in the Digital Information Age," *EFFector Online,* 5:5, April 2, 1993.

Alexander Charns, *Cloak and Gavel: FBI Wiretaps, Bugs, Informers, and the Supreme Court,* University of Illinois Press, 1992.

David Chaum, "Achieving Electronic Privacy," *Scientific American,* August 1992, pp. 96–101.

Dorothy E. Denning, "The Case for 'Clipper'," *Technology Review,* July 1995, pp. 48–55. Denning makes the case in favor of the Clipper Chip. For another article by Denning see www.cosc.georgetown.edu/~denning/crypto/Future.html.

Dorothy E. Denning et al, "To Tap or Not To Tap," *Communications of the ACM,* March 1993, 36:3, pp. 25–44. This debate on wiretapping and encryption policy includes an article by Denning and responses from a variety of points of view.

David Flaherty, *Protecting Privacy in Surveillance Societies,* University of North Carolina Press, 1989.

Robin Hanson, "Can Wiretaps Remain Cost Effective?" *Communications of the ACM,* December 1994, 37:12, pp. 13–15. An economic analysis of the costs and benefits of the wiretap act.

Lance J. Hoffman, editor, *Building In Big Brother: The Cryptographic Policy Debate,* Springer Verlag, 1995.

Lance J. Hoffman, Faraz A. Ali, Steven L. Heckler, Ann Huybrechts, "Cryptography Policy," *Communications of the ACM,* September 1994, 37:9, pp. 109–17.

S. Kent et al, "Codes, Keys and Conflicts: Issues in US Crypto Policy, Report of a Special Panel of the ACM US Public Policy Committee," June 1994 (http://info.acm.org/reports/acm_crypto_study.html).

Edith Lapidus, *Eavesdropping on Trial,* Hayden Book Co., 1974. Contains history of wiretapping and the relevant sections of the Omnibus Crime Control and Safe Streets Act of 1968.

National Research Council, *Cryptography's Role in Securing the Information Society,* National Academy Press, 1996 (www2.nas.edu/cstbweb).

Bruce Schneier, *Applied Cryptography: Protocols, Algorithms, and Source Code in C,* John Wiley & Sons, Inc., 1994.

Alan F. Westin, *Privacy and Freedom,* Atheneum, 1968. Contains history of wiretapping and other means of surveillance.

Philip R. Zimmermann, *The Official PGP User's Guide,* MIT Press, 1995. Includes discussion of the legal, ethical, and political issues surrounding PGP.

Philip R. Zimmermann, *PGP Source Code and Internals,* MIT Press, 1995.

4

CAN WE TRUST THE COMPUTER?

4.1   WHAT CAN GO WRONG?

4.1.1   Questions About Reliability and Safety

"Data Entry Typo Mutes Millions of U.S. Pagers"

"Software Errors Cause Radiation Overdose"

"IRS Computer Sends Bill For $68 Billion in Penalties"

"Software Glitch Clogs AT&T Telephone Lines"

"Robot Kills Worker"

"DMV Spent $44 Million on Failed Computer Project"

"Man Arrested Five Times Due to Faulty FBI Computer Data"

"High-Tech Baggage System 'Eats' Luggage"

"Computer Predicts We Will Run Out of Copper by 1985"

What can go wrong when we use computers? Almost anything. Most computer applications, from consumer software to systems that control airplanes and telephone networks, are so complex that it is virtually impossible to produce a program with no errors. In this chapter, we will describe a variety of mistakes, problems, and failures involving computers—and some of the factors responsible for them. Some errors are minor; for example, a word processor might incorrectly hyphenate a word that does not fit at the end of a line. (The system I used for this book broke the word "robots" into "robot" and "s.") Some form letter systems begin letters with "Dear Mr. Association" because "Association" is the last word in the first line of an address on a mailing list. Some incidents are funny; some are tragic; some cost millions of dollars. All of the examples can teach us something. We will look at one case in depth (in Section 4.2): the Therac-25. This computer-controlled radiation treatment machine had a large number of flaws that resulted in the deaths of several patients. Section 4.3 looks at a few factors related to computer failures in more depth and describes some approaches to reducing problems. Section 4.4 puts the risks of computer systems in perspective by considering risks (and ways to reduce them) in other systems. In Sections 4.5–4.7 we consider the reliability of complex analysis and predictions made by computers based on mathematical models.

The headlines above and the examples we will describe raise many questions. Are we risking major disasters from breakdowns in computerized banking and communication systems? Are computer-controlled medical devices, factory automation systems, and airplanes too unsafe to use? Are we too dependent on computers?

Or, like many stories on the evening news, do the headlines and horror stories emphasize the dramatic and unusual events—the bad news? Car crashes are reported on the news, but we do not hear that 200,000 car trips were completed safely in our city today. Although most car trips *are* safe, there is a good purpose for reporting crashes on the news: It teaches us what the risks are (e.g., driving in heavy fog), and it reminds us to be responsible and careful drivers.

Just as car crashes can be caused by many factors (faulty design, sloppy manufacturing or servicing, bad road conditions, a careless or poorly trained driver, confusing road signs, etc.), computer glitches and system failures also have a myriad of causes, including faulty design, sloppy implementation, careless or insufficiently trained users, and poor user interfaces. Often more than one factor is involved. Sometimes, no one did anything clearly wrong, but an accident occurs. Occasionally, the irresponsibility of software developers is comparable to driving while very drunk.

Although millions of computers and software programs are working fine every day, it is crucial that we understand the risks and reasons for computer failures. How much risk must or should we accept? If the inherent complexity of computer systems means they will not be perfect, how can we distinguish between errors to accept as trade-offs for the benefits of the system and errors that are due to inexcusable carelessness, incompetence, or dishonesty? How good is good enough? When should we, or the government, or a business decide that a computer is too risky to use? We cannot answer these questions completely, but this chapter provides some background and discussion that can help you in forming conclusions.

This chapter should help us understand computer-related problems from the perspective of several of the roles we play, specifically,

- **A computer user.** Whether we use a personal computer at home or a sophisticated, specialized system at work, we should understand the limitations of computers and the need for proper training and responsible use. We must recognize that, as in other areas, there are good products and bad products.

- **A computer professional.** Automotive engineers study car crashes to determine their cause and build safer cars in the future. Studying computer failures should help you become a better computer professional (system designer, programmer, or quality assurance manager, e.g.) if that is your career direction. (In Chapter 10, we discuss aspects of professional ethics that relate to the quality and safety of computer systems.)

- **An educated member of society.** There are many personal decisions and social, legal, and political decisions that depend on our understanding of the risks of computer system failures. We may be on a jury. We may be an active member of an organization lobbying for legislation. We may be deciding whether or not to try an experimental computer-controlled medical device or whether to fly in a new computer-controlled airplane. One goal of this chapter is to provide some perspective and analysis to help us evaluate the reliability and safety of various computer applications and of computer technology in general.

Computer errors and failures can be categorized in several ways, for example, by the cause, by the seriousness of the effects, or by the application area. In any scheme used to organize the discussion, there will be overlap in some categories and mixing of diverse examples in some. For the remainder of this section I will use three categories: problems for individuals, usually in their roles as consumers; system failures that affect large numbers of people and/or cost large amounts of money; and problems in safety-critical applications where people may be injured or killed.

The incidents described here are a sampling of the many that occur. In most cases, by mentioning specific companies or products, I do not mean to single those out as unusual offenders. One can find many similar stories in newspapers and magazines—and espe-cially in the Risks Forum (the comp.risks newsgroup on Usenet) organized by Peter Neu-mann. Neumann has collected thousands of reports describing a wide range of computer-related problems.

4.1.2 Problems for Individuals

Many people are inconvenienced and/or suffer losses from errors in billing systems and in databases containing personal data. Users of home computers confront frustrating bugs in operating systems and applications software.

Billing errors

    The first few errors we look at are relatively simple ones whose negative conse-quences were relatively easily undone.[1]

- A woman was billed $6.3 million for electricity; the correct amount was $63. The cause was an input error made by someone using a new computer system.
- In 1993, the IRS modified their programs with the intent of not billing Midwest flood victims. Instead, the computer generated erroneous bills for almost 5000 people. One Illinois couple received a bill for a few thousand dollars in taxes—and $68 bil-lion in penalties.
- The auto insurance rate of a 101-year-old man suddenly tripled. Rates depend on age, but the program was written to handle ages only up to 100. It mistakenly classi-fied the man as a teenager.
- Hundreds of Chicago cat owners were billed by the city for failure to register dachs-hunds, which they did not own. The city was using computer matching with two databases to try to find unlicensed pets. One database used DHC as the code for do-mestic house cat, and the other used the same code for dachshund.

The first three problems came from errors in the design and/or implementation of the pro-grams. Some errors could have been avoided with more care. Some problems resulting from the errors could have been avoided if the programs had included tests to determine if the amount was outside some reasonable range or changed significantly from previous bills. In other words, because programs may contain errors, good systems have provisions for checking their results. If you have some programming experience, you know how easy it would be to include such tests and make a list of cases for someone to review. These er-rors are perhaps more humorous than serious. When mistakes are as big as these, they are obvious, and the bills are corrected. They are still worth studying because the same kinds of design and programming errors can have more serious consequences in different appli-cations. In the Therac-25 case (Section 4.2) we will see that including tests for inconsistent or inappropriate input could have saved lives.

    In the fourth example above, it was not errors in the software or the databases that caused the incident; the city staff did not know enough about the systems they used.

Database accuracy problems

In Chapter 2, we discussed privacy issues related to large government and private databases containing personal information. We deferred the problem of accuracy to this chapter. If the information in a database is not accurate, we can suffer inconvenience or serious harm. When information is entered automatically by other computer systems, mistakes that might be obvious to a human can be overlooked. Even if an error is corrected, the problems may not be over for the person affected. Computer records are copied easily and often; copies of the incorrect data may remain in other systems.

When interest rates dropped in the early 1990s, hundreds of people applying for new mortgages discovered that their credit reports mistakenly listed a late payment for their current mortgage. The error had occurred when one bank, call it Bank A, bought another, Bank B. It took more than a month for Bank A to transfer all the old Bank B mortgage accounts to Bank A's system. Payments made by thousands of Bank B customers were recorded as being paid when the transfer was completed—more than a month after they were actually paid. The "late" payments were automatically reported to the credit bureaus. This error did not have serious consequences. Bank A quickly realized what had caused the problem and sent correction letters to all three credit bureaus. Cases of errors in credit bureau files do not always end this well. Credit bureaus have received heavy criticism for incidents where incorrect information has caused people to lose their homes, cars, jobs, or insurance. Thousands of residents of New England were listed incorrectly in TRW records as not having paid their local property taxes. The problem was attributed to an input error. People were denied loans before the scope of the problem was identified and it was corrected. (TRW paid damages to many of the people affected.)[2]

A county agency used the wrong middle name in a report to a credit bureau about a father who did not make his child support payments. Another man in the same county had the exact name reported; he could not get credit to buy a car or a house. A woman in Canada could not get her tax refund because the tax agency insisted she was dead. Her identification number had been mistakenly reported in place of her mother's when her mother died. Note that although computerized records were used in these cases, computers did not cause the problem. The source of the problems was incorrect data being entered into records; they might have been as likely to occur with paper forms.

A 14-year-old boy in his first year of high school was excluded from football and some classes without explanation. He eventually learned, almost by accident, that school officials thought he had been using drugs while in junior high school. The two schools used different disciplinary codes in their computerized records. The boy had been guilty of chewing gum and being late.[3] This case is very similar to the case of the dachshund/cat confusion described earlier—except that the consequences were more significant. Both cases illustrate the problems of relying on computer systems without taking responsibility to learn enough about them to use them properly.

The Medical Information Bureau (MIB) maintains records on roughly half a million people; it estimates that 3–4% of its records contain errors. Some may be minor and not have serious consequences, but people have charged that their records contained incorrect reports of Alzheimer's disease, heart attacks, and drug and alcohol abuse. Such information can result in denial of jobs or insurance. (According to MIB rules, companies are not supposed to make decisions solely based on the MIB report, but privacy advocates believe that some do.)[4]

Some of the cases we mentioned can be extremely disruptive and damaging to people's lives and financial situations. When the errors are in databases used by law enforcement agencies, the consequences can include arrest at gunpoint, strip searches, and being jailed, often with violent criminals. Studies of the FBI's National Crime Information Center (NCIC) database in the 1980s found that roughly 11% of the arrest warrants listed in it were inaccurate or no longer valid. People are arrested when a check of the database shows a warrant for them—or for someone with a similar name. I will mention a few NCIC cases; the news media and government studies have reported many more.

An adoption agency ran a routine check on an applicant and found that he had been convicted of grand larceny. In fact, he had been involved in a college prank, stealing a restaurant sign, years before, and the charges had been dropped after he apologized and paid for the damage. The error could have caused the agency to deny the adoption. A Michigan man was arrested for several crimes, including murders, committed in Los Angeles. Another man had assumed his identity after finding his lost wallet (or a discarded birth certificate; reports varied). It is understandable that the innocent man was listed in NCIC as wanted. However, he was arrested four more times within 14 months. (After repeatedly asking the city of Los Angeles to correct the records, he sued and won a judgment against the city.) A man was imprisoned at a military base for five months because NCIC mistakenly reported that he was AWOL. A college professor returning from London was arrested and jailed for two days after a routine check with NCIC at Customs showed that he was a wanted fugitive. NCIC was wrong—for the third time about this particular man. Similar problems occur with local police systems: An innocent driver was stopped by police and frisked because his license plate number was incorrectly listed as the license number of a man who had killed a state trooper. The computer record did not include a description of the car.[5]

There are several factors in causing the severity of the problems that result from errors in databases: a large population (where many people have identical or similar names); the fact that most of our financial interactions are with strangers; automated processing without human common sense or the ability to recognize special cases; overconfidence in the accuracy of data stored on computers; and a lack of accountability for failure to update information and correct errors.

Consumer hardware and software

Why did Intel name its new chip the Pentium? –Because when it added 100 to 486, it got 585.994257.

–One of many jokes about the Pentium chip flaw.

Several major operating systems and applications software packages for personal computers have had serious errors in their first releases. Computer scientists and cypherpunks (computer users with expertise in cryptography) discovered significant security flaws in Netscape, the popular World Wide Web browser program. Software is routinely sold with known bugs. Bugs in popular tax preparation programs sold by Intuit caused the wrong tax to be computed. The company was aware of at least one bug but shipped the program without warning customers. After the problems were publicized, Intuit promised to pay interest and penalties caused by the errors.[6] The calculator in some versions of Microsoft Windows shows the result of 2.01–2 as 0.00.*

Personal computer hardware also has flaws. Computer chips are increasingly complex. Sophisticated algorithms, some that used to be implemented in software, are now implemented on chips. Intel received a flurry of intensely negative publicity when a mathematician discovered that the Pentium chip had a bug in the process used for division of numbers represented in floating-point format.† Intel was "flamed" on the Internet, criticized by competitors, and ridiculed by numerous widely circulated jokes about the Pentium. The bug was of most concern in scientific applications, which use floating-point computations extensively. Home users of PCs were not likely to experience a problem, and sales of Pentium machines were strong during and after the controversy. What is interesting about the Pentium incident is that a flaw in a chip is not unusual. Intel's 386 and 486 chips had math flaws. The floating-point unit in some of Motorola's PowerPC chips did not work as specified. During the Pentium controversy, Compaq was recalling notebook computers that had memory problems and were described as "plagued by bugs." Some Hewlett-Packard workstations crashed and corrupted data because of a chip flaw. What angered so many people about the Pentium was that Intel knew of the problem but did not tell customers. Intel's response, after the bug was disclosed, was perceived by many people as being customer-hostile, and led to more negative publicity. Eventually the negative publicity prompted an apology from the company and a new policy of replacing the chip for any customer who asked.[7]

The mathematician who disclosed the Pentium flaw stated that "microprocessors [have] become so complex that it is no longer possible to completely debug them, or even to determine every bug that exists in one."[8] The same, of course, is true for software. Manufacturers make trade-offs between additional debugging and getting a product to market sooner. Technically oriented customers grumble but make do. Software sellers say that as more ordinary people begin using computers, they will be less tolerant of problems and glitches. Bugs in Walt Disney Co.'s "Lion King" CD-ROM, for example, led to thousands of complaints from parents of disappointed children. (As in the Pentium case, consumer anger was increased by Disney's initial unhelpful response to the problems.) Consumers are angered by dishonesty (i.e., by companies selling products with known serious flaws without telling customers about them) and by denials of problems and lack of adequate response to complaints. Some businesses will continue to try to hide problems, whereas others are recognizing that honesty and customer service are good business. Software producers expect market pressure to force improvement in consumer software. One commented, "As the consumer starts discriminating on what they'll buy, you have to get better."[9]

---

*The bug is apparently in the display, not the internal result; subsequent calculations using the result treat it as 0.01.

†Floating point format is used for very large numbers and for numbers with a fractional, or decimal part, for example, 1.5.

4.1.3 System Failures

> *No matter how carefully designed and operated a system is, it can still fail grotesquely.*
>
> –PETER G. NEUMANN, *Software Engineering Notes*[10]

Modern communications, banking, and financial systems depend heavily on computers. The computers do not always function as planned. The costs of failures can include millions of dollars and virtually complete shutdown of basic services.

Communications

Nationwide AT&T telephone service for voice and data was disrupted for nine hours in January 1990 because of a software error in a four-million line program. The disruption was variously described as a "slowdown," a "shutdown," and a "virtual paralysis." It prevented roughly 50 million calls from getting through. AT&T's official report stated, "While the software had been rigorously tested in laboratory environments before it was introduced, the unique combination of events that led to this problem couldn't be predicted."[11] In June and July 1991, telephone networks in several major east coast and west coast cities failed. The cause was a three-line change in a two-million line telecommunications switching program. The program had been tested for 13 weeks, but was not retested after the change—which contained a typo. In November 1991, a four-hour telephone outage in New England occurred when a technician changed a piece of disk equipment. Flights at Logan Airport in Boston were delayed or canceled because the communication systems used by the controllers and the pilots is connected to the AT&T system that failed. Commenting on the failure of millions of pagers, alluded to in one of the headlines at the beginning of this chapter, a company official said, "We designed our system architecture expressly so this couldn't happen. Of course, we *thought* it couldn't happen." The problem occurred when someone typing codes into a database forgot to hit the enter key in a line of data.[12]

Business and financial systems

The NASDAQ stock exchange was virtually shut down for two and a half hours in July 1994 because of a problem with new communications software that had been installed earlier in the week. A backup system also failed. Another computer failure caused an hourlong shutdown a year later. More than 5000 stocks are traded on NASDAQ, which operates over 200,000 terminals around the country. In a few incidents, large investment firms and newspapers reported incorrect or out-of-date stock prices; they blamed computer errors.[13] Other stock and commodities exchanges have halted trading because of computer problems. So far, the costs of these kinds of errors have been primarily lost business to the stock exchanges and losses for individual investors (both of which can be substantial). There is concern that future errors in stock, banking, or other financial systems could trigger a recession or a serious world-wide economic disruption.

In Chapter 1 we mentioned the ATM system that doubled the amount withdrawn from customer accounts. At another major bank a software error disrupted processing of transactions; the bank had to borrow almost $24 billion overnight to cover its shortfall—and pay about $5 million in interest.[14]

A computer error in a contest sponsored by Pepsi Cola in the Philippines caused 800,000 winning numbers to be generated instead of the intended 18. The face value of the winnings would have been $32 billion. Pepsi paid nearly $10 million to customers with winning numbers to maintain "good will," but still faced hundreds of lawsuits and criminal complaints.[15] Pepsi Cola is large enough to absorb a $10 million expense; smaller companies have been destroyed by computer errors.

Destroying businesses

Once the fourth largest carpet distributor in the U.S., Kane Carpet Company went out of business 17 months after installing a new computerized inventory control system. The company estimated its losses at $37 million and blamed it all on the inventory system. A few dozen companies that bought another inventory system called Warehouse Manager blame the system for disastrous losses; one previously successful company saw its income decline by about half and laid off half its employees. The specific complaints were numerous. One company could not get the system to place a purchase order for several weeks; it claimed the backlog in orders cost $2000 per day. Processes that were supposed to take seconds, such as printing invoices, took several minutes while customers waited in long lines. Both systems gave incorrect information about inventory. Clerks were told that products were in stock when they were not, and *vice versa*. Both errors led to dissatisfied customers and lost sales. According to users of Warehouse Manager, the system reported incorrect prices to clerks. A part that cost $114 was listed for sale at 54 cents. A $17 part was listed for sale at $30. One error means lost money for the company; the other means lost customers who find a better price elsewhere. When two clerks tried to access the computer from their terminals simultaneously, the terminals locked up. Some companies said the system erased information needed for accounting and tax reports.[16]

What was responsible for the problems in Warehouse Manager? The program was sold by NCR Corporation, but it was developed by another company. It was originally designed for and implemented on a different computer and operating system. It appears that there were unexpected problems when the program was rewritten for NCR's machines and its ITX operating system. According to the *Wall Street Journal,* internal memos at NCR reported that the system had been inadequately tested and was performing badly in real business settings. NCR salespeople told prospective customers that Warehouse Manager was running successfully at 200 installations, but most of them were installations using the machine for which the program was originally designed. Several users claim that although NCR was receiving complaints of serious problems from many customers, the company told them the problems they were having were unique.

NCR blamed the problems on the company that wrote Warehouse Manager and modified it for ITX. Eventually NCR agreed it "did not service customers well" and the program should have been tested more. The company settled most of the few dozen lawsuits out of court, with confidentiality agreements about the terms.

The sources of the problems in this case included technical difficulties (converting software to a different system), poor management decisions (inadequate testing), and, according to the customers, dishonesty in promoting the system and responding to the problems.

Delayed and abandoned systems

Software glitches delayed the opening of a highly automated packing plant for Ben & Jerry's ice cream company. A bug in a new checkout scanner program developed for Walgreen, a supermarket chain, occasionally caused an incorrect price to be used. Walgreen delayed introduction of a new inventory control system for six months while the problem was solved. An $810 million project to upgrade the radar systems at Canada's major airports was delayed because of software errors. Among other problems, the program showed some airplanes flying backwards.[17]

Many systems are so fundamentally flawed that they are junked after wasting millions of dollars. The California Department of Motor Vehicles, for example, abandoned a $44 million computer system that never worked properly. A consortium of hotels and a rental car business spent $125 million on a comprehensive travel industry reservation system, then canceled the project because it did not work.[18]

There are many more such examples. One infamous case of a delay caused by a faulty computer system is the Denver International Airport.

The Denver Airport baggage system

What is the difference between the new Denver Airport and the White House?
—You can land a plane at the White House.

—A joke about the delays in opening the Denver International Airport*

I saw an odd sight when I flew past the huge new Denver International Airport and the miles of wide highway leading to it. The airport covers 53 square miles, roughly twice the size of Manhattan. I saw nothing moving at the airport and no cars on the road—10 months after the $3.2 billion airport was to have opened in October 1993. The opening was rescheduled at least four times until the actual opening in 1995. The delay cost more than $30 million per month, or over one million dollars a day, in bond interest and operating costs. Most of the delay has been attributed to the now infamous computer-controlled baggage-handling system, which cost $193 million.[19]

The plan for the baggage system was quite ambitious. Outbound luggage checked at ticket counters or curbside counters was to be delivered to any part of the airport in less than 10 minutes via an automated system of cars traveling up to 19 miles per hour on 22 miles of underground tracks. Similarly, inbound luggage was to be delivered to terminals or transferred directly to connecting flights anywhere in the airport. Each bag is put into a car bar-coded for its destination. Laser scanners throughout the system track the 4000 cars and send information about their locations to computers. The computers use a database of flights, gates, and routing information to control motors and track switches to route the cars to their destinations. The complete system includes about 100 computers.

It did not work as planned. During tests of the system over several months, cars crashed into each other at track intersections; luggage was misrouted, dumped, and flung

---

*In 1994 a pilot crashed a small plane on the White House lawn.

about; and cars that were needed to move luggage were mistakenly routed to waiting pens.

Both the specific problems and the general underlying causes are instructive. Some of the specific problems were as follows:

- **Real-world problems.** Some of the scanners got dirty or were knocked out of alignment and could not detect cars going by. This was related to the car crashes.
- **Problems in other systems.** The airport's electrical system could not handle the power surges associated with the baggage system; the first full-scale test blew so many circuits that the test had to be halted. Faulty latches on the cars caused luggage to be dumped on the tracks between stops.
- **Software errors.** For example, the routing of cars to waiting pens when they were actually needed was attributed to a software error.

No one expects software and hardware of this complexity to work perfectly the first time it is tested. In real-time systems,* especially, there are numerous interactions and conditions that may not be anticipated. It is not surprising that problems would be encountered during development. Mangling a suitcase is not embarrassing if it occurs during an early test and if the problem is fixed. It is embarrassing if it occurs after the system is in operation or if it takes a year to fix the problems. What led to the extraordinary delay in the Denver baggage system? There seem to have been two main problems:

- **The time allowed for development and testing of the system was insufficient.** The only other baggage system of comparable size is at Frankfurt Airport in Germany. The company that built that system spent six years on development and two years testing and debugging. BAE Automated Systems, the company that built the Denver system, was asked to do it in two years. Some reports indicate that because of the electrical problems at the airport, there were only six weeks for testing.
- **Significant changes in specifications were made after the project began.** Originally, the automated system was to serve United Airlines, but Denver officials decided to expand it to include the entire airport, making the system 14 times as large as the automated baggage system BAE had installed for United at San Francisco International Airport.

PC Week's reporter said, "The bottom-line lesson is that system designers must build in plenty of test and debugging time when scaling up proven technology into a much more complicated environment."[20] Some observers criticize BAE for taking on the job when the company should have known that there was not enough time to complete it. Others blame the city government for poor management, politically motivated decisions, and proceeding with a grandiose but unrealistic plan.

---

*Real-time systems are systems that must detect and control activities of objects in the real world within time constraints.

4.1.4 Safety-Critical Applications

There are many examples of problems in safety-critical computer systems in military applications, power plants, aircraft, trains, automated factories, medical applications, and so on. Most of the deaths that have occurred because of computer-related problems were in aviation and medical applications.[21] We will look briefly at a few aviation cases, then at one medical instrument case in depth in the next section.

Computers in the air

The A320 Airbus airplane was the first fully "fly-by-wire" airplane. The pilots do not directly control the plane; their actions are inputs to computers that control the aircraft systems. Between 1988 and 1993, four A320s crashed. Although the official cause for some of the crashes was ruled "pilot error," pilots and some observers fault the fly-by-wire system. Pilots have complained that the airplane does not respond as expected, that it seems to have "a mind of its own" and may suddenly behave in unexpected and inappropriate ways. In the 1992 crash, the pilots specified a rate of descent of 3300 feet per minute instead of the normal 800 feet per minute. The official report on the crash indicated that reasons for the error probably included the pilots' lack of familiarity with the A320 automation equipment and confusing design of the controls and displays. The crew left the "vertical navigation" entirely to the automatic systems although there were indications that the descent rate was too high. Perhaps they had too much confidence in the computer's ability to detect and correct mistakes. In the 1993 crash, the computer did not recognize that the plane had landed; it prevented the pilot from reversing engine thrust to brake the airplane. Pilots and human-factors specialists emphasize the need for an easy way to override the computer and easy transfer between automatic and manual control.[22]

While there has been much concern about the possibility of crashes caused by computerizing pilot functions, the lack of computer automation was considered a factor in a 1995 crash that killed 160 people. According to an FAA official, computer automation has reduced or eliminated some types of pilot errors while introducing new ones.[23]

The Traffic Collision Avoidance System (TCAS) is intended to detect a potential in-air collision and direct the airplanes to avoid it. The first version of the system had so many false alarms that it was unusable. TCAS II still has a high rate of false alarms in some situations; more improvements are being made in the software. Some pilots complained that the system directed them to fly toward a nearby airplane rather than away from it, potentially causing a collision rather than avoiding one. (To its credit, TCAS has helped avoid some collisions.)[24]

Several crashes of U.S. Air Force Blackhawk helicopters, killing nearly two dozen people, were eventually attributed to radio interference with the computer system that controlled the helicopter.[25]

Air traffic control

There were more than a dozen computer breakdowns at the air traffic control center for the Chicago area in 1995. The result was long delays in flights and increased risk of collisions. The problem is that the system uses computers that are 25–30 years old, so old that spare parts and service are not available from the manufacturers any longer. The Federal Aviation Administration, which operates the air traffic control system, is cutting hiring and training of technicians who repair and maintain the equipment. The problem here, though a "computer breakdown," has little to do with any inherent weakness in computers. Equipment ages, and the number of aircraft miles flown has almost doubled in the past 25 years. The source of the problem is political: The federal government funds many foolish, unimportant, or special-interest programs, but it has not made a priority of the safety of the millions of people who fly.

4.2 CASE STUDY: THE THERAC-25

4.2.1 Therac-25 Radiation Overdoses

The Therac-25 was a software-controlled radiation therapy machine used to treat people with cancer. Between 1985 and 1987, Therac-25 machines at four medical centers gave massive overdoses of radiation to six patients. In some cases, the operator repeated an overdose because the machine's display said that no dose had been given. Medical personnel later estimated that some patients received between 13,000 and 25,000 rads,* where the intended dose was in the 100–200 rad range. These incidents caused severe injuries and the deaths of three patients.

What went wrong?

Studies of the Therac-25 incidents showed that many factors were involved in causing the injuries and deaths. The factors include lapses in good safety design, insufficient testing, bugs in the software that controlled the machines, and an inadequate system of reporting and investigating the accidents. (Articles by computer scientists Nancy Leveson, Clark Turner, and Jonathan Jacky are the main sources for this discussion.[26])

To understand the discussion of the problems, it will help to know a little about the machine. The Therac-25 is a dual-mode machine; that is, it can generate an electron beam or an X-ray photon beam. The type of beam to be used depends on the tumor being treated. The machine's linear accelerator produces a high-energy electron beam (25 million electron volts) that is dangerous. Patients are not to be exposed to the raw beam. The computer monitors and controls movement of a turntable on which three sets of devices are mounted. Depending on whether the treatment is electron or X-ray, a different set of devices is rotated in front of the beam to spread it and make it safe. It is essential that the proper protective device be in place when the electron beam is on. A third position of the turntable may be used with the electron beam off, and a light beam on instead, to help the operator position the beam in precisely the correct place on the patient's body. There were several weaknesses in the design of the Therac-25 that contributed to the accidents (including some in the physical design that we will not mention here).

4.2.2 Software and Design Problems

Design flaws

The Therac-25, developed in the late 1970s, followed earlier machines called the Therac-6 and Therac-20. It differed from them in that it was designed to be fully computer

---

*A rad is the unit used to quantify radiation doses. It stands for "radiation absorbed dose."

controlled. The older machines had hardware safety interlock mechanisms, independent of the computer, that prevented the beam from firing in unsafe conditions, for example, if the beam-attenuating devices were not in the correct position. Many of these hardware safety features were eliminated in the design of the Therac-25. Some software from the Therac-20 and Therac-6 was reused in the Therac-25. This software was apparently assumed to be functioning correctly. This assumption was wrong. When new operators used the Therac-20, there were frequent shutdowns and blown fuses, but no overdoses. The Therac-20 software had bugs, but the hardware safety mechanisms were doing their job. Either the manufacturers did not know of the problems with the Therac-20, or they completely missed their serious implications.

The Therac-25 malfunctioned frequently. One facility said there were sometimes 40 dose rate malfunctions in a day, generally underdoses. Thus operators became used to error messages appearing often, with no indication that there might be safety hazards.

There were a number of weaknesses in the design of the operator interface. The error messages that appeared on the display were simply error numbers or obscure messages ("Malfunction 54" or "H-tilt"). This was not unusual for computer programs in the 1970s when computers had much less memory and mass storage than they have now. One had to look up each error number in a manual for more explanation. The operator's manual for the Therac-25, however, did not include any explanation of the error messages. Even the maintenance manual did not explain them. The machine distinguished between the severity of errors by the amount of effort needed to continue operation. For certain error conditions, the machine paused, and the operator could proceed (turn on the electron beam) by pressing one key. For other kinds of errors, the machine suspended operation and had to be completely reset. One would presume that the one-key resumption would be allowed only after minor, not safety-related, errors. Yet this was the situation that occurred in some of the accidents in which patients received multiple overdoses.

Investigators studying the accidents found that there was very little documentation produced during development of the program concerning the software specifications or the testing plan. Although the manufacturer of the machine, Atomic Energy of Canada, Ltd. (AECL), a Canadian government corporation, claimed that it was tested extensively, it appeared that the test plan was inadequate.

Bugs

Investigators were able to trace some of the overdoses to two specific software errors. Because many readers of this book are computer science students, I will describe the bugs. These descriptions illustrate the importance of using good programming techniques. However, some readers have little or no programming knowledge, so I will simplify the descriptions.

After treatment parameters are entered by the operator at a control console, a software procedure, Set-Up Test, is called to perform a variety of checks to be sure the machine is positioned correctly, and so on. If anything is not ready, the routine schedules itself to be executed again so that the checks are done again after the problem is resolved. (It may simply have to wait for the turntable to move into place.) The Set-Up Test routine may be called several hundred times while setting up for one treatment. When a particular flag variable is zero, it indicates that a specific device on the machine is positioned correctly. To ensure that the device is checked, each time the Set-Up Test routine runs, it increments the variable to make it nonzero. The problem was that the flag variable was stored in one byte. When the routine was called the 256th time, the flag overflowed and showed a value of zero. (If you are not familiar with programming, think of this as an odometer rolling over to zero after reaching the highest number it can show.) If everything else happened to be ready at that point, the device position was not checked, and the treatment could proceed. Investigators believe that in some of the accidents, this bug allowed the electron beam to be turned on when the turntable was positioned for use of the light beam, and there was no protective device in place to attenuate the beam.

Part of the tragedy in this case is that the error was such a simple one, with a simple correction. No good student programmer should have made this error. The solution is to set the flag variable to a fixed value, say 1, when entering Set-Up Test, rather than incrementing it.

In a real-time system where physical machinery is controlled, status is determined, and an operator enters—and may modify—input (a multitasking system), there are many complex factors that can contribute to subtle, intermittent, and hard-to-detect bugs. Programmers working on such systems must learn to be aware of the potential problems and to program using good techniques to avoid them. In some of the accidents, a set of bugs allowed the machine to ignore changes or corrections made by the operator at the console. When the operator typed in all the necessary information for a treatment, the program began moving various devices into place. This process could take several seconds. The software was written to check for editing of the input by the operator during this time and to restart the set-up if editing was detected. However, because of bugs in this section of the program, some parts of the program learned of the edited information while others did not. This led to machine settings that were incorrect and inconsistent with safe treatment. According to the later investigation by the Food and Drug Administration (FDA), there appeared to be no consistency checks in the program. The error was most likely to occur if the operator was experienced and quick at editing input.

4.2.3 Why So Many Incidents?

There were six known Therac-25 overdoses. You may wonder why the machine continued to be used after the first one.

The Therac-25 had been in service for up to two years at some clinics. It was not pulled from service after the first few accidents because it was not known immediately that it was the cause of the injuries. Medical staff members considered various other explanations. The staff at the site of the first incident said that one reason they were not certain of the source of the patient's injuries was that they had never seen such a massive radiation overdose before. The manufacturer was questioned about the possibility of overdoses, but responded (after the first, third, and fourth accidents) that the patient injuries could not have been caused by the machine. According to the Leveson and Turner investigative report, they also told the facilities that there had been no similar cases of injuries.

After the second accident, AECL investigated and found several problems related to the turntable (not including any of the ones we described). They made some changes in the system and recommended operational changes. They declared that the safety of the machine had been improved by five orders of magnitude, although they told the FDA that they were not certain of the exact cause of the accident; that is, they did not know if they had found the problem that caused the accident or if they had just found other problems. In making decisions about continued use of the machines, the hospitals and clinics had to consider the costs of removing the expensive machine from service (in lost income and loss of treatment for patients who needed it), the uncertainty about whether the machine was the cause of the injuries, and later, when that was clear, the manufacturer's assurances that the problem had been solved. After some of the later accidents, machines were removed from service. They were returned to service after modifications by the manufacturer, but the modifications had not fixed all the bugs.

A Canadian government agency and some hospitals using the Therac-25 made recommendations for many more changes to enhance safety; they were not implemented. After the fifth accident, the FDA declared the machine defective and ordered AECL to inform users of the problems. The FDA and AECL spent about a year (during which the sixth accident occurred) negotiating about changes to be made in the machine. The final plan included more than two dozen changes. The critical hardware safety interlocks were eventually installed, and most of the machines remain in use with no new incidents of overdoses since 1987.[27]

4.2.4 Overconfidence

In the first overdose incident, when the patient told the machine operator that she had been "burned," the operator told her that was impossible. This was one of many indications that the makers and some users of the Therac-25 were overconfident about the safety of the system. The most obvious and critical indication of overconfidence in software was the decision to eliminate the hardware safety mechanisms. A safety analysis of the machine done by AECL years before the accidents suggests that they did not expect significant problems from software errors. In one case where a clinic added its own hardware safety features to the machine, AECL told them it was not necessary. (None of the accidents occurred at that facility.)

The hospitals using the machine assumed that it worked safely, an understandable assumption. Some of their actions, though, suggest overconfidence, or at least practices that should be avoided, for example, ignoring error messages because the machine produced so many of them. A camera in the treatment room and an intercom system enabled the operator to monitor the treatment and communicate with the patient. (The treatment room is shielded, and the console used by the operator is outside the room.) On the day of an accident at one facility, neither the video monitor nor the intercom was functioning. The operator did not see or hear the patient try to get up after an overdose; he received a second overdose before he reached the door and pounded on it. This facility had successfully treated more than 500 patients with the machine before the accident.

4.2.5 Conclusion and Perspective

From design decisions all the way to responding to the overdose accidents, the manufacturer of the Therac-25 did a poor job. Minor design and implementation errors might be expected in any complex system, but the number and pattern of problems in this case, and the way they were handled, suggests irresponsibility that merits high awards to the families of the victims and possibly, some observers believe, criminal charges. This case illustrates many of the things that a responsible, ethical software developer should not do. It illustrates the importance of following good procedures in software development. It is a stark reminder of the consequences of carelessness, cutting corners, unprofessional work, and attempts to avoid responsibility. It reminds us that a complex system may work correctly hundreds of times with a bug that shows up only in unusual circumstances, hence, the importance of always following good safety procedures in operation of potentially dangerous equipment. This case also illustrates the importance of individual initiative and responsibility. Recall that some facilities installed hardware safety devices on their Therac-25 machines. They recognized the risks and took action to reduce them. The hospital physicist at one of the facilities where the Therac-25 overdosed patients spent many hours working with the machine to try to reproduce the conditions under which the overdoses occurred. With little support or information from the manufacturer, he was able to figure out the cause of some of the malfunctions.

Even if the Therac-25 case was unusual,* we must deal with the fact that the machine was built and used, and it killed people. There have been enough accidents in safety-critical applications to indicate that significant improvement is needed. Should we not trust computers for such applications at all? Or, if we continue to use computers for safety-critical applications, what can be done to reduce the incidence of failures? We will discuss some approaches in the next section.

To put the Therac-25 in some perspective, it is helpful to remember that failures and other accidents have always occurred and continue to occur in systems that do not use computers. Two other linear accelerator radiation-treatment machines seriously overdosed patients. Three patients received overdoses in one day at a London hospital in 1966 when safety controls failed. Twenty-four patients received overdoses from a malfunctioning machine at a Spanish hospital in 1991; three patients died. Neither of these machines had computer controls. Two news reporters reviewed more than 4000 cases of radiation overdoses reported to the U.S. government. The Therac-25 incidents were included, but most of the cases did not involve computers. Here are a few of the overdose incidents they describe. A technician started a treatment, then left the patient for 10–15 minutes to attend an office party. A technician failed to carefully check the prescribed treatment time. A technician failed to measure the radioactive drugs administered; she just used what looked like the right amount. In at least two cases, technicians confused microcuries and millicuries.† The general problems were carelessness, lack of appreciation for the risk involved, poor training, and lack of sufficient penalty to encourage better practices. In most cases, the medical facilities paid small fines or were not fined at all. (One radiation oncologist severely injured five women. He was eventually sued.)[28]

Some of these problems might have been prevented by good computer systems. Many could have occurred even if a computer were in use. None excuse the Therac-25. They suggest, however, that individual and management responsibility, good training, and accountability are more important factors than whether or not a computer is used.

---

*Sadly, some software safety experts say the poor design and lack of attention to safety in this case are *not* unusual.

†A curie is a measure of radioactivity. A milicurie is one thousand times as much as a microcurie.

4.3   INCREASING RELIABILITY AND SAFETY

4.3.1   What Goes Wrong?

Computer programs have tens of thousands, hundreds of thousands, or millions of lines of code. (Microsoft's Windows 95 has more than 11 million lines.) There is plenty of room for errors. Figure 4.1 lists common factors in computer errors and system failures. Most of them are illustrated in examples we have described. Some are technical issues, and some are managerial, social, legal, and ethical issues.

Overconfidence

Overconfidence, or an unrealistic or inadequate understanding of the risks in a complex computer system, is a core issue. When system developers and users appreciate the risks, they will then be more motivated to use the techniques that are available to build more reliable and safer systems and to be responsible users. How many PC users never backed up their files until after they had a disk crash and lost critical data or months of work?

- The complexity of real-time, multitasking systems.
- "Non-linearity" of computer software. This means that, whereas a small error in an engineering project may cause a small degradation in performance, a single typo in a computer program can cause a dramatic difference in behavior.
- Failing to plan and design for unexpected inputs or circumstances.
- Interaction with physical devices that do not work as expected.
- Incompatibility of software and hardware, or of application software and the operating system.
- Inadequate management.
- Insufficient testing.
- Carelessness.
- Business and/or political pressure to get a product out quickly.
- Misrepresentation, hiding problems.
- Inadequate response when problems are reported.
- Inadequate attention to potential safety risks.
- Data-entry errors.
- Inadequate training of users.
- Errors in interpreting results or output.
- Overconfidence in software.
- Lack of market or legal incentives to do a better job.

Figure 4.1: Some factors in computer system errors and failures.

Some safety-critical systems that failed (e.g., systems that control airplanes and trains) had supposedly "fail-safe" computer controls. In some cases the logic of the program was fine, but the failure resulted from not considering how the system interacts with real users (such as pilots) or real-world problems (such as loose wires or fallen leaves on train tracks).

Can the risks of failure in a system be analyzed and quantified? Yes, but the techniques for developing estimates of failure rates must be used carefully. For example, the computers on the A320 airplane each have redundant software systems designed by separate teams of programmers. The redundancy is a safety feature, but how much safety does it provide? The failure rate was supposed to be less than one failure per billion flight hours. It was calculated by multiplying the estimated failure rates of the two systems, one in 100,000 hours. The calculation is reasonable if the systems are independent. But safety experts say that even when programmers work separately, they tend to make the same kinds of errors, especially if there is an error, ambiguity, or omission in the program specifications.[29]

Unrealistic reliability or safety estimates can come from genuine lack of understanding, or carelessness, or intentional misrepresentation. People without a high regard for honesty sometimes give in to business or political pressure to exaggerate or to hide flaws, avoid unfavorable publicity, and avoid the expense of corrections or lawsuits. The manufacturer of the Therac-25 declared that changes in the system increased safety by five orders of magnitude (a factor of 100,000). It is hard to guess how they arrived at that figure.

Political pressure to produce inflated safety predictions is, of course, not restricted to computer systems. In 1986 the Challenger space shuttle broke apart, killing the seven people aboard. The investigation by Nobel Prize winner Richard Feynman sheds interesting light on how some risk estimates are made. Feynman found that NASA engineers estimated the chance that an engine failure would terminate a flight to be about one in 200–300. Their boss gave the official NASA estimate of the risk: one in 100,000. The document that justified this unbelievable (in Feynman's judgment) estimate, calculated it from failure estimates for various components. Feynman concluded that the failure rates for the components were chosen to yield the prechosen result of one in 100,000.[30] One lesson from the Therac-25 and Challenger is to be skeptical about numbers whose magnitude may seem unreasonable to common sense.

4.3.2 Professional Techniques

Software engineering and professional responsibility

The many examples of computer system errors and failures suggest the importance of using good software engineering techniques at all stages of development, including specifications, design, implementation, documentation, and testing. Although complex systems will not be perfect, there is a wide range between poor work and good work, as there is in virtually any field. Professionals, both programmers and managers, have the responsibility to study and use the techniques and tools that are available. Professional responsibility includes knowing or learning enough about the application field and the software or systems being used to understand potential problems and to do a good job. Obviously, this is especially important in safety-critical applications. (There was a case where a programmer at a medical facility discovered that on the system he was using a process could fail to execute on time while a window was being moved on the screen. The system controlled a patient's respirator.[31])

The programming team for the Clearinghouse Interbank Payment System, which transfers about one trillion dollars a day among various banks, spent years working on the specifications for upgrading an earlier program; then they spent six months on the programming. They developed and carried out a realistic and extensive set of tests simulating a day with a trillion dollars of transactions. Clearly this is a system where reliability is crucial, both to individual customers and to the functioning of the economy.[32] Unfortunately, many software developers tend to skimp on the planning, specification, and design phases of a project; get quickly to the programming; then deliver the product with minimal testing. In fact, programming, or coding, is a relatively small part of a well-designed system.

A subfield of computer science focusing on design and development of safety-critical software is growing. Safety specialists emphasize that safety must be "designed in" from the start. There are techniques of hazard analysis that help system designers identify risks and protect against them. Software engineers who work on safety-critical applications should have special training. Software safety expert Nancy Leveson emphasizes that we can learn much from the experience of engineers in building safe electromechanical systems. "One lesson is that most accidents are not the result of unknown scientific principles but rather of a failure to apply well-known, standard engineering practices. A second lesson is that accidents will not be prevented by technological fixes alone, but will require control of all aspects of the development and operation of the system."[33]

Software developers need to recognize the limitations of software. As computers have become more capable, software monitoring and control of machinery have become more common. In Chapter 1 we mentioned several computer systems being developed to take over some of the tasks involved in driving a car. The risks of turning control over to computers must be weighed carefully. Most software today is simply not safe enough for safety-critical applications. Hardware safety mechanisms, as used by engineers in pre-computer systems, still have an important role; they should not be omitted without extremely strong justification.

User interfaces and human factors

Well-designed user interfaces can help avoid many computer-related problems. Principles and practices for doing a good job are known.[34] System designers and programmers need to learn from psychologists and human factors experts. As an illustration of some principles that can help build safer systems, consider automated flight systems. An expert in this area emphasizes the following points:[35]

- **The pilot needs feedback to understand what the automated system is doing at any time.** This is critical when the pilot must suddenly take over if the automation fails or must be turned off for any reason. One example is having the throttle move as a manually operated throttle would, even though movement is not necessary when the automated system is operating.

- **The system should behave as the pilot (or, in general, experienced user) expects.** Pilots tend to reduce their rate of climb as they get close to their desired altitude. On the McDonnell Douglas MD-80, the automated system maintains a climb rate that is up to eight times as fast as pilots typically choose. Pilots, concerned that the plane might overshoot its target altitude, made adjustments, not realizing that their intervention turned off the automated function that causes the plane to level out when it reaches the desired altitude. Thus because the automation behaved in an unexpected way, the airplane climbed too high—exactly what the pilot was trying to prevent. (The incidence of the problem was reduced with more training, but the human factors approach is to design the automation to suit the human, not *vice versa.*)

- **A workload that is too low can be dangerous.** Clearly, if an operator is overworked, mistakes are more likely. One of the goals of automation is to reduce the human workload. However, a workload that is too low can lead to boredom, inattention, or lack of awareness of current status information that might be needed in a hurry when the pilot must take over.

Redundancy and self-checking

Redundancy and self-checking are two techniques important in systems on which lives and fortunes depend. We already mentioned redundancy in the A320 airplane. Similarly, the space shuttle uses four identical but independent computer systems that receive input from multiple sensors and check their results against each other. If one computer disagrees with the other three, it is taken out of service. If one of the three remaining is judged by the other two to be faulty, it is taken out of service, and the rest of the flight is canceled. In case of a more serious problem, perhaps caused by a common flaw in the software, there is a fifth computer, made by another manufacturer and programmed by different programmers, that can control the descent of the shuttle.[36] This degree of redundancy is expensive and is not used in many applications, but it illustrates the kinds of precautions that can be taken for systems that operate in dangerous physical environments where human lives are at stake.

Complex systems can collect information on their own activity for use in diagnosing and correcting errors. After Chemical Bank's ATMs mistakenly doubled the amount of customers' withdrawals, the bank was able to correct the balances in the affected accounts. In Section 2.6 we mentioned that an audit trail (i.e., a record of access and modifications to a database) can help detect and discourage privacy violations. Audit trails are vital in financial systems. A detailed record of transactions helps protect against theft as well, and, as in this case, it helps trace and correct errors. The bank was able to prevent an inconvenience caused by a software bug from becoming a huge problem that could have cost customers and the bank (in lawsuits) millions of dollars.

AT&T's telephone system handles roughly 100 million calls a day. The very complex software for the system is developed and extensively tested by experienced programmers. The system is designed to constantly monitor itself and correct problems automatically. Half of the computing power of the system is devoted to checking the rest for errors. When a problem is detected in a switching component, the component automatically suspends use of the switch, informs the rest of the network that it is out of service temporarily and should not receive calls, activates recovery routines that take a few seconds to correct the problem, then informs the network that the component is functioning again. But wait a minute! This is the same system that failed a few years ago, disrupting phone service for hours. In fact, it was this very part of the system that caused the breakdown. There was a bug in the routine that processed recovery messages from switches that had failed and recovered. The same software operated in each switch. Thus, each switch that received the message failed, then recovered and sent a recovery message. A chain reaction of failures occurred. The bug was in a software upgrade that had been running for about a month.[37] Even when the best professional practices are followed, even with extensive testing, we cannot be guaranteed that such complex systems do not have bugs.

Testing

It is difficult to overemphasize the importance of adequate, well-planned testing of software. Testing is not arbitrary; there are principles and techniques for doing a good job. Unfortunately, many programmers and software developers see testing as a dispensable luxury, a step to be skimped on to meet a deadline or to save money. This is a common, but foolish, risky, and often irresponsible attitude.

In his Challenger investigation, Richard Feynman concluded that the computer systems used on board the shuttle were developed with good safety criteria and testing plans. Ironically, he was told that because the shuttle software usually passed its tests, NASA management planned to reduce testing to save money. Fortunately, instead, as a result of studies done after the loss of the Challenger, NASA instituted a practice called independent verification and validation (IV&V).* That means that the software is tested and validated by a company other than the one that developed the program and other than the customer. (Testing and verification by an independent organization is not practical for all projects, but many software developers have their own testing teams that are independent of the programmers who develop a system.) The IV&V team acts as "adversaries" and tries to find flaws. After a few years, NASA planned to eliminate IV&V, but switched direction again. In response to several studies, including an extensive one done by software safety experts in 1992, NASA decided to make IV&V a permanent part of the program.[38] This example illustrates a common ambivalence about testing.

4.3.3   Law and Regulation

Criminal and civil penalties

Legal remedies for faulty systems include suits against the company that developed or sold the system and criminal charges when fraud or criminal negligence occurs. Families of Therac-25 victims sued; the suits were settled out of court. A bank won an $818,000 judgment against a software company for a faulty financial system that caused problems described as "catastrophic" by a user. A company that supplied critical parts for the Navy's F-18 jets pleaded guilty to routinely failing to perform required tests and falsifying test reports. The company was fined $18.5 million and may have to pay millions more in civil penalties.[39] The latter is not a computer-related case, but the issues and potential penalty would be similar if tests of a safety-critical computer system were falsified.

---

*The destruction of the Challenger was caused by seals that failed because of the cold weather, not by software error. Studies were done on many aspects of safety afterwards.

Many contracts for business computer systems limit the amount the customer can recover to the actual amount spent on the computer system. Customers know, when they sign the contract, that losses incurred because the system did not meet their needs for any reason are generally not covered. Such contract limitations have been upheld in court, and they should be. If people and businesses cannot count on the terms of a contract being upheld by the legal system, contracts would be almost useless; millions of business interactions that take place daily would become more risky and therefore more expensive. Because fraud and misrepresentation are not, or course, part of a contract, some companies that suffer large losses allege fraud and misrepresentation by the seller in an attempt to recover some of the losses, whether or not the allegations are firmly grounded.

Well-designed liability laws and criminal laws—not so extreme that they discourage innovation, but clear and strong enough to provide incentives to produce safe systems—are important legal tools for increasing reliability and safety of computer systems, as they are for other industries. After-the-fact penalties do not undo the injuries that occurred, but paying for mistakes and sloppiness is incentive to be responsible and careful. It compensates the victim and provides some justice. An individual, business, or government that does not have to pay for its mistakes and irresponsible actions will make more of them.

Unfortunately, liability law in the U.S. is very flawed. Multimillion dollar suits are often won when there is no scientific evidence or sensible reason to hold the manufacturer or seller responsible for accidents that occur with use of a product. Abuse of the liability lawsuit system virtually shut down the small airplane manufacturing industry in the U.S. It is difficult enough for jurors to evaluate the scientific evidence relating to silicone breast implants, for example. It will be at least as difficult for jurors to decide whether a bug in a computer program should have been detected, or whether it was responsible for an accident, or whether the damage was a risk the buyer must reasonably take. The newness and complexity of large computer systems make designing liability standards difficult, but this task needs to be done.

Regulation

Is there legislation or regulation that can *prevent* life-threatening computer failures? A law saying that a radiation machine should not overdose a patient would be silly. We know that it should not do that. No legislator or regulator knew in advance that that particular computer application would cause harm. We could ban the use of computer control for applications where an error could be fatal, but such a ban is ill advised. In many applications the benefits of using computers are well worth the risks.

A widely accepted option is regulation, possibly including specific testing requirements and requirement for approval by a government agency before a new product can be sold. The FDA has regulated drugs and medical devices for decades. Extensive testing, huge quantities of documentation, and government approval are required before new drugs and some medical devices can be sold. Arguments for such regulation, for both drugs and for safety-critical computer systems are the following:

- The profit motive may encourage businesses to skimp on safety; the government has a responsibility to prevent that from happening.

- It is better to prevent a bad product from being used than to rely on after-the-calamity remedies.

- Most potential customers and people who would be at risk (patients, airplane passengers) do not have the expertise to judge the safety or reliability of a system.

- It is too difficult and expensive for ordinary people to successfully sue large companies.

If the FDA had thoroughly examined the Therac-25 before it was put into operation, the flaws might have been found before any patients were injured. However, the weaknesses and trade-offs in the regulatory approach should be noted.[40]

- The approval process is extremely expensive and time-consuming. The delays caused by the regulation and requirements for government review cost many lives. In some cases companies abandon useful products because the expense of meeting FDA requirements is too high.

- Regulations that require specific procedures or materials discourage or prevent the use of newer and better ones that were not thought of by the people who wrote the rules.

- The goal of the regulation, be it safety, privacy, accuracy, less pollution, or whatever, tends to get lost in the details of the paperwork required. One writer on software safety commented, "The whole purpose of [following good software development techniques and documenting the steps] is to ensure that the necessary planning and design is performed, but regulatory agencies tend to focus on the visible products of the effort: the documents."[41]

- The approval process is affected by political concerns, including influence by competitors and the incentive to be overcautious. (Damage caused by an approved product results in bad publicity and possible firing for the regulator who approved it. Deaths or losses caused by the delay or failure to approve a good new product get little publicity.)

Leveson and Turner, in their Therac-25 article, summarize some of these dilemmas:

> The issues involved in regulation of risky technology are complex. Overly strict standards can inhibit progress, require techniques behind the state of the art, and transfer responsibility from the manufacturer to the government. The fixing of responsibility requires a delicate balance. Someone must represent the public's needs, which may be subsumed by a company's desire for profits. On the other hand, standards can have the undesirable effect of limiting the safety efforts and investment of companies that feel their legal and moral responsibilities are fulfilled if they follow the standards. Some of the most effective standards and efforts for safety come from users. Manufacturers have more incentive to satisfy customers than to satisfy government agencies.[42]

We have focused so far on legal approaches to protecting against business system failures and dangers in safety-critical applications. What about the problem of accuracy of information in databases maintained by businesses and government agencies? Detailed regulation of private databases is recommended by some privacy advocates. Most of the discussion above about liability, criminal negligence, and regulation applies as well to accuracy of private (business) databases. Achieving and maintaining accuracy in government databases is made difficult by the lack of market incentives for accuracy and the fact that the government can refuse to be sued. The government argues that it should not have to pay for mistakes, such as drug raids on the wrong house or problems caused by errors in government databases. Outside of government, we pay for carelessness. If you are playing ball in your backyard and accidentally throw the ball through a neighbor's window, you pay for the window.

Professional licensing

Another very controversial approach to improving software quality is licensing of software development professionals. Licenses are required by law for hundreds of trades and professions. Licensing requirements typically include specific training, passing competency exams, ethical requirements, and continuing education. The desired effect is to protect the public from poor quality and unethical behavior. The history of licensing in many fields shows that the actual goals and the effects were and are not always very noble. In some trades, particularly plumbing, the licensing requirements were devised to keep black people out. Economic analysis shows that the effect of licensing is to reduce the number of practitioners in the field and keep prices and income for licensees higher than they would otherwise be, in some cases without any improvement in quality. Some people consider licensing to be a fundamental violation of the freedom to work, that is, to offer one's services without needing the government's permission. These objections do not apply to voluntary approaches to measuring qualifications of software personnel. A diploma from a respected school is one measure. Certification programs by professional organizations, particularly for advanced training in specialized areas, can be useful.[43]

4.3.4 Taking Responsibility

Businesses

In some of the cases we mentioned, businesses made large payments to customers in compensation for problems or damages caused by computer programs. For example, Intuit offered to pay interest and penalties that resulted from the errors in its flawed income tax programs. Pepsi paid $10 million to customers who thought they had won its contest. A quick and voluntary decision to pay for damages is nothing new with computers of course. In the spring of 1994, jet fuel was accidentally mixed with fuel for propeller airplanes at several California airports. The improper fuel can cause engines to fail. Within weeks, the fuel company agreed to pay for overhaul of the affected engines. The cost of rectifying their mistake was estimated at $40–50 million. Their motivation may have been partly to reduce losses that would result from the inevitable liability suits or government fines. Other factors include recognition of the importance of customer satisfaction and the reputation of the business. We noted that business pressures are often a reason for cutting corners and releasing defective products. Business pressure can also be a cause for insistence on quality and maintaining good customer relations. Also, some businesses have an ethical policy of behaving responsibly and paying for mistakes, just like the person who pays for breaking a neighbor's window.

Customer awareness

How can customers protect themselves from faulty software? How can a business avoid buying a seriously flawed program? How can a hospital protect its patients from dangerous systems?

The first step is to recognize and accept that complex computer systems are difficult to design and develop, and many will have flaws. For high-volume, consumer software, one can consult the many magazines that review new programs. Specialized systems with a small market are more difficult to evaluate before purchase. We can use a hint from another field where there seem to be some reliable and some questionable practitioners: home remodeling. We can check the company's reputation with the Better Business Bureau. We can get references (i.e., names of previous customers) and ask them how well the job was done. Online user groups for specific software products are excellent sources of information for prospective customers. In the case of the Therac-25, the users eventually spread information among themselves. If there had been an online Therac-25 user group at the time of the accidents, it is likely that the problems would have been identified sooner and some of the accidents would have been avoided.

4.4   PERSPECTIVES ON DEPENDENCE, RISK, AND PROGRESS

4.4.1   Are We Too Dependent on Computers?

A fire in March 1994 at a telephone switching facility in Los Angeles disrupted telephone service for half a day. Here are some of the effects on computer users, as reported in a newspaper article.[44]

- "More than 150,000 customers, cut off from the outside world, could barely function without their phones and modem-equipped computers."
- Fax machines were idled.
- Drivers could not buy gasoline with their credit cards. "Customers were really angry," said a gas station manager.
- Stockbrokers could not connect to New York by phone or computer.
- More than 1000 automated teller machines did not function; they use phone lines to connect to central computers.
- A travel agent said, "I can't get in to make reservations for our clients." The agency no longer uses printed airline schedules; it is "computer- and phone-dependent."
- "A California lottery spokesman said that 1200 of the state's 22,000 terminals were down." "The fire made it difficult for many to buy tickets or get their winnings."

The underlying problem here was the phone network. Redundancy and separate dedicated networks for certain applications might have reduced the problems, but the incident serves as a good reminder about how many ordinary daily activities are dependent on computer networks. A physician who specializes in medical information systems commented that "modern hospitals and clinics cannot function efficiently without them."[45] Modern crime fighting depends on computers. Some military jets cannot fly without the assistance of computers. Because of their usefulness and flexibility, computers are now virtually everywhere. Is this good or bad? Or neutral?

Are criticisms of "dependence on computers" fair?

Comments about our dependence on computers appear in many discussions of the social impact of computers. What do they mean? Often the word "dependence" has a negative connotation. "Dependence on computers" suggests a criticism of our society or of our use of computers. Is it appropriate? Several aspects of these criticisms are wrong and some are valid. Some misconceptions about dependence on computers come from a poor understanding of the role of risk, confusion of "dependence" with "use," and blaming computers for failures where they were only innocent bystanders. On the other hand, abdication of responsibility that comes from overconfidence or ignorance is a serious problem. Also, there are valid technical criticisms of dependence when a system is designed so that a failure in one component can cause a major breakdown.

"Dependence" or "use"?

> *Electricity lets us heat our homes, cook our food, and enjoy security and entertainment. It also can kill you if you're not careful.*
>
> –"Energy Notes," May 1994. (Flyer sent with San Diego Gas & Electric utility bills)

Hospitals and clinics cannot operate without electricity. We use electricity for lighting, entertainment, manufacturing—just about everything. In the early 1990s there were several disruptions of telephone systems and air traffic because of computer problems. In those same years there were several disruptions of telephone systems and air traffic because of electric power problems. The four-hour disruption of AT&T phone service and air traffic at the three major New York area airports in September 1991 was the result of batteries running down because a backup power generator was not properly connected. In January 1995, one of the New York area airports had to be closed after workers accidentally cut electrical cables, causing a power blackout.[46]

Is our "dependence" on computers different from our dependence on electricity. Is it different from a farmer's dependence on a plow? The Sioux people's dependence on their bows and arrows? Modern surgery's dependence on anesthesia? Computers and plows are tools. We use tools because we are better off with them than without them. They reduce the need for hard physical labor and tedious routine mental labor; they help us be more productive, or safer, or more comfortable. When we have a good tool, we may forget or no longer even learn the older method of performing a task. If the tool breaks down, we are stuck; we cannot perform the task until the tool is fixed. That may mean that no telephone calls get through for several hours. It may mean that a large amount of money is lost, and it may mean that people are endangered or die. But the negative effects of a breakdown do not condemn the tool. To the contrary, for many computer applications (not all), the inconveniences or dangers of a breakdown are a reminder of the convenience and productivity provided by the tool when it is working, for example, of the billions of telephone calls (carrying voice, e-mail, files, and data) that are completed—that are made possible or more convenient or cheaper because of computers—each year. We saw that a bad computerized inventory system devastated some small businesses. On the other hand, thousands of businesses now use computerized inventory systems successfully.

We could avoid the risk of a broken plow by plowing with our hands. We could avoid the risk of losing a document file on a disk by doing all our writing by hand on paper. Even ignoring the possibility of a fire destroying our paper records, it should be clear that we do not choose the "safe," or nondependent option because, most of the time, it is less convenient and less productive. If one enjoys wilderness camping, as I do, one can observe how "dependent" we normally are on electric lights, refrigeration, and plumbing. That does not mean we should cook on camp stoves and read by firelight at home.

Risk

Things we thought were absolutely OK collapsed.
   –An earthquake analyst, after the devastating Kobe Japan quake in 1995[47]

We trust our lives to technology every day. We trust older, noncomputer technologies every time we step into an elevator, a car, or a building. As the tools and technologies we use become larger, more complex, and more interconnected, the amount of damage that results from an individual disruption or failure increases, and the costs may be paid in dramatic and tragic events. If a person out for a walk bumps into another person, neither is likely to be hurt. If both are driving cars at 60 miles per hour, they may be killed. If two jets collide, or one loses an engine, several hundred people may be killed. However, the death rate per mile traveled is about the same for air travel as for cars.[48]

Most new technologies were not very safe when they were first developed. If the death rate from commercial airline accidents in the U.S. were the same now as it was 40 years ago, 8,000 people would die in plane crashes each year (instead of fewer than 200). Some early polio vaccines, in which the virus was not totally inactivated, caused polio in some children. We learn how to make improvements; problems are discovered and solved; scientists and engineers study disasters and learn how to prevent them. What has happened to the safety record in other technologies? The number of deaths from automobile accidents declined from 54,633 in 1970 to 43,536 in 1991 (while population, of course, increased). Why? Some significant reasons are increased education about responsible use (i.e., the campaign against drunk driving), devices that protect people when the system fails (seat belts and airbags), and improvements in technology, many of which use computers.* In the same period the rate of death from commercial airplane accidents declined from 0.8 per 100,000 people to 0.4 per 100,000—while the use of computers in airplanes increased.[49]

Risk is not restricted to technology and machines. It is a part of life. Sharp tools are risky. Someone living in a jungle faces danger from animals. A desert hiker faces rattlesnakes. Just as with complex technological systems, a person will be safer if he or she

---

*The 55 mph speed limit was not a significant factor, as it was widely ignored.

knows the risks and takes reasonable precautions. Just as with complex technological systems, the precautions are sometimes not enough.

We mentioned a few cases where delays in implementing computer systems cost millions of dollars. Delays in large construction and engineering projects (before the use of computers) were not uncommon either. Ask anyone who has written a book if it was completed on schedule!

Software safety expert Nancy Leveson says that the mistakes made in software are the same as those that used to be common in engineering. Over many years engineers have developed techniques and procedures to increase safety. Software developers need to learn from engineers and adapt their methods to software.

There are some important differences between computers and other technologies. Computers make decisions; electricity does not. The power and flexibility of computers encourages us to build more complex systems—where failures have more serious consequences. The pace of change in computer technology is much higher than for other technologies. Software is not built from standard, trusted parts as is the case in many engineering fields. The software industry is still going through its "growing pains"; it has not yet developed into a mature, fully developed discipline.

False charges—or, blaming the stove for a poorly cooked meal

As we have said several times already, computers are virtually everywhere. That means that when anything goes wrong, there is probably a computer that can be blamed, sometimes unfairly. I will mention just a few such examples that have appeared in other books.

In Holland, the body of a reclusive, elderly man who died in his apartment was not discovered until six months after his death, when someone noticed that he had a large accumulation of mail. This incident was described as a "particularly disturbing example of computer dependency." Many of the man's bills, including rent and utilities, were paid automatically, and his pension check was automatically deposited in his bank account. Thus "all the relevant authorities assumed that he was still alive."[50] But who expects the local gas company or other "relevant authorities" to discover a death? The problem here clearly was the lack of concerned family, friends, and neighbors. I happened to be present in a similar situation. An elderly, reclusive woman died in her home. Within *two days,* not six months, the mailman noticed that she had not taken in her mail. He informed a neighbor, and together they checked the house. I do not know if her utility bills were paid by computer; it is irrelevant.

Published collections of computer-related risks involving trains include cases of faulty brakes, operators disabling safety controls, a loose wire, and a confused driver who drove his train in the wrong direction during rush hour. Many of the cases involved human errors. We have seen that some human errors are the result of confusing or poorly designed computer systems, but that was not apparently the case in several of the reported incidents. An incident where a computer reportedly fell on a man's foot was listed as a health risk of computers.[51]

I mention these cases because accurate identification of the source of a problem is an important step to solving it. Including such incidents as risks of computers obscures the distinction between them and cases where computer systems *are* at fault—and where we must focus our attention to make improvements.

4.4.2   Making Trade-offs When Perfection Is Not an Option

We have emphasized through a number of examples that software is complex. We cannot be sure that all possible situations have been considered or that all bugs have been found and corrected. In fact, we can be more certain that flaws do exist in the system.

How close to perfection should we expect our systems to be? A water utility company sent a customer an incorrect bill for $22,000. A spokesman for the company pointed out that one incorrect bill out of 275,000 monthly bills is a good error rate. Is that reasonable? How accurate should the software for ATMs be? The double withdrawal incident mentioned in Chapter 1 affected roughly 150,000 accounts. With approximately eight billion ATM transactions each year, that is one error in roughly 45,000 transactions. Is that an acceptable rate? (There were probably other ATM errors in that year, but the publicity given this case suggests that it affected far more transactions than others.) How accurate should software for check processing be? 99%? 99.9%? Bank of America processes 17 million checks per day. Even if it made errors on 1000 checks every day, that would be an accuracy rate of better than 99.99%.[52]

At some point, the expense of improving a system is not worth the gain, especially for applications where errors can be detected and corrected at lower cost than it would take to try to eliminate them. How should the decision be made about how much to invest to make a system more reliable? For many applications, the decision is probably best left to the people responsible for the costs of the improvements and the costs of a failure (in liability and customer dissatisfaction).

For many applications that involve health and safety (with or without computers), though we may be more reluctant to accept it, there is also a point at which improvements to reduce risk are not worth the cost.[53] At this point, however, there are probably few, if any, safety-critical computer systems developers who are wasting money on "too much" safety.

4.4.3   Conclusions

We have made several points:

1. Many of the issues related to reliability for computers have arisen before with other technologies.
2. Perfection is not an option. The complexity of computer systems makes errors, oversights, and so on, a near certainty.
3. There is a "learning curve" for new technologies. By studying failures, we can reduce their occurrence.
4. Risks of using computers should be compared with risks of other methods and with benefits obtained.

This does not mean that computer errors and failures should be excused or ignored because failures occur in other technologies. It does not mean that carelessness or negligence should be tolerated because perfection is not possible. It does not mean that accidents should be excused as part of the learning process, and it does not mean that accidents should be excused because, on balance, the contribution of computers is positive.

I emphasize the similarities with failures and delays in other technologies (and non-technological activities) to provide some perspective. Some critics of computers speak as if risks and system failures are new phenomena. I am not arguing that computer failures are less serious because other systems have problems too. The potential for serious disruption of normal activities and danger to people's lives and health because of flaws in computer systems should always remind the computer professional of the importance of doing his or her job responsibly. Computer system developers and other professionals responsible for planning and choosing systems must assess risks carefully and honestly, and include safety protections, appropriate plans for shutdown of a system when it fails, for backup systems where appropriate, and for recovery.

Knowing that one will be liable for the damages one causes is strong incentive to find improvements and increase safety. When evaluating a specific instance of a failure, we can look for those responsible and try to ensure that they bear the costs of the damage they caused. It is when evaluating computer use in a particular application area or when evaluating the technology as a whole that we should look at the balance between risks and benefits and compare the risks and benefits with those of noncomputerized alternatives.

4.5   EVALUATING COMPUTER MODELS

4.5.1   Models and Social Policy

Computer-generated predictions and conclusions about subjects of important social interest frequently appear in the news. Figure 4.2 lists a few examples.

Predictions that come from complex computer programs and expensive computers impress people. But the programs vary enormously in quality. Some are worthless, whereas others are very reliable. Predictions about problems like those in Figure 4.2 are used to justify multibillion-dollar government programs, restrictions on people's freedom of action, and regulations with significant impact on the economy and the standard of living of hundreds of millions of people. It is important for both computer professionals and the general public to have some idea of what is in such computer programs, where their uncertainties and weaknesses may lie, and how to evaluate their claims.

> - When we will run out of a critical natural resource.
> - Population growth.
> - The cost of a proposed government program.
> - The cost of waste disposal for juice boxes.
> - The effects of second-hand smoke.
> - The effects of a tax cut on the economy.
> - The threat of global warming.
> - When a big earthquake is likely to occur.

FIGURE 4.2: Some problems studied with computer models.

What are computer models?

A mathematical model is a collection of data and equations describing, or simulating, characteristics and behavior of the thing being studied. The models and simulations of interest to us here require so much data and/or computation that computers are needed to do the required computations. Computers are used extensively to model and simulate both physical systems, such as the design for a new airplane or the flow of water in a river, and abstract systems, such as parts of the economy.

Models allow us to investigate the possible effects of different designs, scenarios, and policies. They have obvious social and economic benefits: They enable us to consider alternatives and make better decisions, reducing waste, cost, and risk.

Although these models are abstract (i.e., mathematical), the meaning of the word "model" here is similar to its meaning in "model airplane." Models are simplifications. Model airplanes generally do not have an engine, and the wing flaps may not move. Models are not necessarily toys. In a chemistry class, we may use sticks and balls to build models of molecules, to help us understand their properties. A model of a molecule may not show the components of the individual atoms. Similarly, mathematical models do not include equations for every factor that may influence the outcome, or they may include equations that are simplified because the correct ones are unknown or too complicated. For example, a constant known as the acceleration of gravity can be used in equations to determine when an object dropped from a high place will hit the ground. The effect of wind may not be included in the equations, but on some days, wind could make a difference.

Physical models are not the same size as the real thing. Model planes are smaller; the molecule model is larger. In mathematical models, it is time rather than physical size that often differs from reality. Computations done on a computer to model a complex physical process in detail may take more time than the actual process takes. For models of long-range social phenomena, such as population growth, the computation must take less time than the real phenomenon for the results to be useful.

4.5.2 Evaluating models

Among three models developed to predict the change in health care costs that would result if the U.S. adopted a Canadian style national health plan, the predictions varied by $279 billion. Two of the models predicted large increases and one predicted a drastic decrease.[54] Why was there such a difference? There are both political and technical reasons why models may not be accurate. Political reasons, especially for this example, are probably obvious. Among the technical reasons,

- We may not have complete knowledge of the system being modeled. In other words, the basic physical or social science involved may not be fully understood.
- The data describing current conditions or characteristics may be incomplete or inaccurate.
- Computing power may be inadequate for the number of computations that would be needed if the full complexity of the system were modeled.

■ It is difficult, if not impossible, to numerically quantify variables that represent human values and choices.

The people who design models decide what simplifications and assumptions to make.

Are reusable (washable cloth) diapers better for the environment than disposable diapers? When bans and taxes on disposable diapers were proposed, this controversy consumed almost as much energy as diaper manufacturing. Several computer models were developed to study the question. The particular kind of model used is called a life-cycle analysis; it attempts to consider the resource use and environmental effects of all aspects of the product, including manufacture, use, and disposal. To illustrate how difficult such a study may be, Figure 4.3 lists a few of the questions where assumptions were made by the modelers. Depending on the assumptions, the conclusions differed.[55]

■ How many times is a cloth diaper used before it is discarded? (Values ranged from 90 to 167.)

■ Should credit be given for energy recovered when waste is incinerated, or does pollution from incineration counterbalance the benefit?

■ What value should be assigned for the labor cost of washing diapers?

■ How many cloth diapers are used each time a baby is changed? (Many parents use two at once for increased protection.) The models used values ranging from 1.72 to 1.9.

■ How should the pesticides used in growing cotton be counted?

FIGURE 4.3: Factors in diaper life-cycle modeling.

There are examples of highly publicized models where the simplifications and assumptions were questionable. Their impact on the results can be decisive. The TAPPS computer model for nuclear winter, popularized by Carl Sagan in the 1980s, predicted that millions of tons of smoke from a nuclear war would stay in the sky for months blocking sunlight, causing temperatures on earth to drop 15°C–25°C, causing crops and people to freeze. A critic of the model pointed out that it represented the earth as a smooth, oceanless ball, did not distinguish day and night, and did not include wind.[56]

For many scientific models, experiments can be done to test the model, or significant parts of it. For many of the issues of social and political interest, experiments are not possible or are limited to small parts of the model. Especially in such cases, and especially when a model is being used as an argument in a debate about government policy, it is helpful to know the state of knowledge about the subject and the assumptions made by the modelers.

The following three questions help us determine the validity and accuracy of a model.

1. How well do the modelers understand the underlying science or theory (be it physics, chemistry, economics, or whatever) of the system being studied? How well understood are the relevant properties of the materials involved? How accurate and complete are the data used?

2. Models necessarily involve simplifications of reality. What are the simplifications in the model?

3. How closely do the results or predictions of the model correspond with results from physical experiments?

The case studies in the next two sections illustrate our discussion of evaluating computer models and simulations. The topics are crash-analysis models used in the design of cars and climate models used to study global warming.

4.6   CASE STUDY: CAR CRASH-ANALYSIS PROGRAMS*

4.6.1   Background

Car crash-analysis programs gained wide usage by the late 1980s. One of the major programs, DYNA3D, was developed at Lawrence Livermore National Laboratory for military applications, but is now used in product design. The program models the interactions of physical objects on impact. DYNA3D is especially designed for high-speed collisions. It uses a technique called the finite-element method. A grid is superimposed on the frame of a car, dividing the car into a finite number of small pieces, or elements. The grid is entered into the program, along with data describing the specifications of the materials making up each element (e.g., density, strength, elasticity, etc.). Suppose we are studying the effects on the structure of the car from a head-on collision. Data can be initialized to represent a crash into a wall at a specified speed. The program computes the force, acceleration, and displacement at each grid point and the stress and strain within each element. These calculations are repeated to show what happens as time passes in small increments. Using graphics programs, the simulation produces a picture of the car at intervals after impact, as illustrated in Figure 4.4. To simulate 40–100 milliseconds of real time from the impact takes up to 35 hours of computer time on a supercomputer. Clearly, these programs require intensive computation.[57]

The cost of a real crash test can range from $50,000 to $800,000. The high figure is for building and testing a unique prototype for a new car design. The crash-analysis programs allow engineers to vary the thickness of steel used for selected components, or change materials altogether, and find out what the effect would be without building another prototype for each alternative. But how good are the programs?

4.6.2   Evaluating the Models

How well is the physics of car crashes understood?

Force and acceleration are basic principles; the physics involved in these programs would be considered fairly easy. The relevant properties of steel, plastics, aluminum, glass, and other materials in a car are fairly well known. However, although the behavior of the materials when force is applied gradually is well known, the behavior of some materials

---

*This section appeared in my chapter, "Social and Legal Issues," in *An Invitation to Computer Science* by G. Michael Schneider and Judith L. Gersting, West Publishing Co., 1995. (Used with permission.)

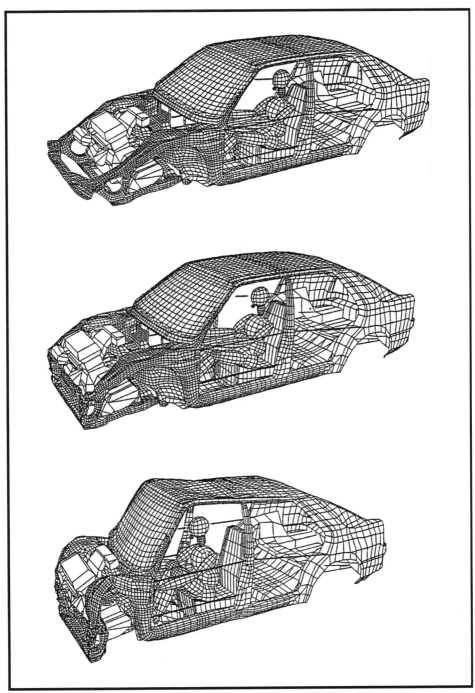

FIGURE 4.4: LS-DYNA3D simulation of a frontal Crash (35 mph before impact; 20 and 70 milliseconds after). (Reproduced by the permission of Livermore Software Technology Corporation.)

under abrupt acceleration, as in a high-speed impact, and their behavior near or at their breaking point are less understood. There are good data on the density, elasticity, and other characteristics of materials used in the model.

What simplifications are made in the programs?

The grid pattern is the most obvious; a car is smooth, not made up of little blocks. Also, time is continuous; it does not occur in steps. The accuracy of the simulation will depend in part on how fine the grid is and how small the time intervals are. As computer speeds increase, we can do more precise computation. In the early 1990s, crash-analysis programs used roughly 10,000–50,000 elements and updated the calculations for time intervals of one millionth of a second.

How do the computed results compare to actual crash tests on real cars?

How are such comparisons performed? The real tests are taped by high-speed cameras. Various kinds of sensors, such as strain gauges, are attached to the car, and reference points are marked on the frame. The tapes can be visually compared with the computer output. The values recorded by the sensors are compared with values computed by the program, and the distortion or displacement of the reference points can be physically measured and compared to the computed positions. From the results of the physical crash, elementary physics can be used to calculate backward and determine the deceleration and other forces acting on the car. These can be compared to the values computed in the simulation. The conclusion? The crash-analysis programs do an extremely good job. Results from the program correspond very closely to data collected in actual test crashes.[58]

Once we know that the models are reasonably accurate, we can conclude that the computer programs provide some benefits we cannot get from physical testing. The computer can provide more data than the sensors and can compute what is happening in areas of the car that the cameras cannot see. The simulation can provide more information than a real crash if there is unexpected damage in a position where few sensors were placed.

4.6.3   Uses of the Crash-analysis Models

Car crash-analysis programs are replacing physical crash testing as a design tool for new cars. The crash test is used as confirmation and is required by the federal government. Should the simulation results replace the physical crash? There can be many answers to this question, depending on its context. Suppose the government did not require a physical crash test. Would you buy a car that had been certified crashworthy only by a computer? To decide whether or not to do physical crash tests, a car manufacturer would probably consider the accuracy of the models, the costs of physical testing, liability laws, and public relations. A company that provides liability insurance for car manufacturers would consider whether the simulations are reliable enough for them to do accurate risk analysis. A legal scholar or an economist might consider whether the law should specify a specific test or focus on rules for liability—letting the manufacturer decide on the best way to ensure that its cars are safe. A legislator may consider the reliability of the simulations, public attitudes about computers, and the arguments of lobbyists. In fact, engineers who work with the crash-analysis programs do not believe that physical crashes will or should be eliminated. They remind us that the simulation is an implementation of theory. The program may give poor results if it is used by someone who does not understand it well. Results may be poor if something happens that the program simply was not designed to consider. Overall, the crash-analysis programs are excellent design tools that enable increases in safety with far less development cost. But the real crash is the proof.

The DYNA3D program, and some variations of it, are used in a large variety of other impact applications. Some are listed in Figure 4.5. One reason for its wide use is the increase in computing power and the declining cost. In the late 1970s serious engineering applications of DYNA3D were run on $10 million computers. Now, many applications can be run on workstations in the $20,000–$60,000 range. Another reason is the confidence that has developed over time in the validity of the results.

- To predict damage to a hazardous waste container if dropped.
- To predict damage to an airplane windshield or nacelle (engine covering) if hit by a bird.
- To determine whether beer cans would get dented if an assembly line were speeded up.
- To simulate a medical procedure called balloon angioplasty, where a balloon is inserted in a blocked artery and inflated to open the artery. The computer program helps researchers determine how to perform the procedure with less damage to the arterial wall.
- To predict the action of airbags and the proper location for sensors that inflate them.
- To design interior parts of cars to reduce injuries during crashes (e.g., the impact of a steering wheel on a human chest).
- To design bicycle and motorcycle helmets to reduce head injuries.
- To design cameras to reduce damage if dropped.
- To forecast effects of earthquakes on bridges and buildings.

FIGURE 4.5: Other uses of DYNA3D and related programs.

4.7 CASE STUDY: CLIMATE MODELS AND GLOBAL WARMING*

4.7.1 Background

In the late 1980s, the news was full of reports of impending global warming caused by the human-induced increase of carbon dioxide (CO_2) and other greenhouse gases in the atmosphere. Some scientists predicted that we might see the warming within a decade. Global warming predictions are based on computer models of climate. In this section we will look at the computerized models. First we need a little background.

---

*This section appeared in my chapter, "Social and Legal Issues," in *An Invitation to Computer Science* by G. Michael Schneider and Judith L. Gersting, West Publishing Co., 1995. (It has been slightly revised. Used with permission.)

The earth is warmed by solar radiation. Some of the heat is reflected back; some is trapped by gases in the atmosphere. The latter phenomenon is known as the greenhouse effect. Without it, the temperature on the earth would be too cold to support life. The main "greenhouse gases" are water vapor, carbon dioxide (CO_2), methane, chlorofluorocarbons (CFCs), and ozone. Among those whose concentration has been increased by human activity, CO_2 is the most important. The problem of concern now is that this increase may enhance the greenhouse effect significantly, increasing temperatures and causing other major climate changes.

CO_2 currently makes up roughly one-thirtieth of one percent of the atmosphere, or 355 parts per million (ppm) by volume. This is substantially higher than for most of the past 160,000 years.* An upward trend of both CO_2 and methane began roughly 16,000 years ago. However, since the beginning of the Industrial Revolution, concentrations have been increasing at a faster rate. Since 1950 the climb has been very steep. The main source of increased CO_2 is the burning of fossil fuels (e.g., oil and coal).

The computer models used to study climate are called general circulation models (GCMs). GCMs were developed from atmospheric models that have been used for a long time for weather prediction. They are quite complex. They contain information about the sun's energy output; the orbit, inclination, and rotation of the earth; geography (a map of land masses); topography (mountains, etc.); clouds; sea and polar ice; soil and air moisture; and a large number of other factors. Like the crash-analysis models, the GCMs use a grid. The grid circles the earth and rises through the atmosphere. The computer programs solve equations for each grid point and element (grid box) for specified time intervals. The equations simulate factors such as atmospheric pressure, temperature, incoming solar energy, outgoing radiant energy, wind speed and direction, moisture, and precipitation. For global warming studies, the atmospheric models are combined with models of the oceans that include temperature, currents, and other factors. The modeling programs are generally run to compute the effects of doubling CO_2 concentration from its approximate level at the beginning of the 20th century. (Current trends suggest that CO_2 concentration will double sometime in the 21st century.) More recent studies include other greenhouse gases as well.

Because of the global importance of potential climate changes, the Intergovernmental Panel on Climate Change (IPCC), sponsored by the United Nations and the World Meteorological Organization, published several major reports on the scientific assessment of climate change. The reports were prepared and reviewed by several hundred scientists worldwide. They are considered an authoritative review of the state of scientific knowledge about climate change. They are the main references used for this discussion.[59]

4.7.2   Evaluating the Models

How well is the science of climate activity understood? How complete and accurate are the data?

The climate system is composed of five subsystems: atmosphere, oceans, cryosphere (ice packs, snow), geosphere (land, soil), and biosphere (vegetation). Effects in the air (such as changes in temperature, wind speed and direction, etc.) can be computed using

---

*The past data come from measurements of gases trapped in ice cores drilled in Antarctica and Greenland.

well-understood principles of physics. The laws of physics are used to compute temperature and other effects in the oceans as well. However, there is still a large amount of scientific uncertainty about each component.

The oceans have a large capacity to absorb heat. The circulation of water in the oceans, due to currents, affects heat absorption. Surface currents are fairly well known; deep currents are less well known. Not enough is known about the exchange of energy between the oceans and the atmosphere.

Clouds are extremely important to climate. Many processes involved with the formation, effects, and dissipation of clouds are not particularly well understood.

Some greenhouse gases have cooling effects as well as warming effects. Although the IPCC tried to quantify these effects in 1990, by 1992, IPCC scientists decided the figures published in 1990 were likely to be in substantial error, and they did not yet know enough to give new numerical values.[60]

If temperatures rise, natural wetlands give off more methane, contributing to more warming. This is called positive, or destabilizing, feedback: An output or side effect of the process amplifies the original effect. There are negative, or stabilizing, feedbacks too. When the earth warms, more water evaporates and forms clouds; the clouds reflect some of the sun's heat back up away from the earth. (Clouds have positive feedback effects also.) There are many such feedback mechanisms affecting climate. For some, it is not known if the feedback is positive or negative. Many uncertainties in the models are attributed to lack of knowledge or lack of full representation of feedback mechanisms.

Another area of uncertainty is natural climate variation. The earth has experienced ice ages and warm periods. There is also a lot of year-to-year fluctuation. We do not know all the causes of the changes, and we do not know the current natural temperature trend.

The IPCC reports make several references to the need for more data on many climate factors including clouds, ocean currents, and the ozone layer. Research programs costing millions of dollars are in progress to collect such data and data on other factors that are not considered in current models.[61]

What simplifications are made in the models?

There are about half a dozen major climate modeling centers in the world. The models vary in many ways, and they are being modified and improved as time passes. Many of our comments are about the models used in the 1980s—those on which fears of catastrophic global warming were based. Some of our comments are generalizations; they may not all be true of all the models at any one time.

The grid points in the models are typically spaced about 500 kilometers (roughly 300 miles) apart. The state of California, for example, may be represented by half a dozen grid points. Islands as small as Japan and England may not appear on the "map" at all, as they may lie between grid points in an ocean or sea. See Figure 4.6 for a sample map. The grid is coarse because the computing time required to run the programs depends on the number of points. Recall that it takes up to 35 hours of computer time to simulate 40–100 milliseconds of a car crash. To be useful, climate studies must be done faster than real time. A 500-kilometer grid, rising ten layers in the atmosphere, has roughly 20,000 points. Because of the grid size, small storms and other small phenomena fall between the grid points and either are not fully represented or are expanded to fill a cell of the grid.

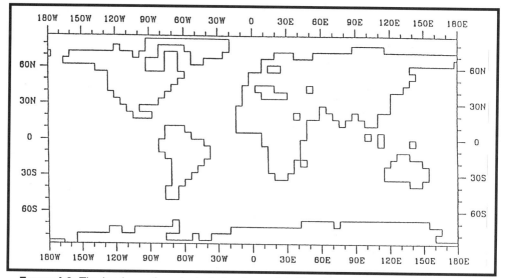

FIGURE 4.6: The land map for a typical climate model. (Reprinted with the permission of Dr. Ulrich Cubasch [Deutsches Klimarechenzentrum].)

Some models do not distinguish between day and night. This simplification is significant because temperature records for some areas of the northern hemisphere show increases in the nighttime winter lows and decreases in the daytime summer highs, which could be a benign or even beneficial form for an average warming to take.[62] The models include many other simplifications, for example, representing only the top layer of the oceans.

Ideally, all of the processes that affect climate would be represented in the GCMs by equations derived from the underlying science (generally, physics and some chemistry). This is not possible because it would require too much computation time and because all the underlying science is not known. Values of some variables are selected to make the models predict present conditions with reasonable accuracy. The process of modifying the values until the desired result is achieved is called "tuning" the model. Although models can be tuned by balancing the values for several variables so that the model accurately describes present conditions, it is not known if that choice of values will predict future conditions accurately.

How closely do the results of the computer programs correspond to results from physical experiments?

We cannot do physical experiments for global warming. Thus we need to consider other ways to assess the results of the computer simulations.

Predictions from the models for average global temperature increase range from a little more than 1°C to a little more than 5°C. The wide variation in the predictions of the models, by itself, suggests that we are far from having a clear understanding of climate behavior and the impact of the greenhouse gases. For a well-understood phenomenon, the predictions of good models would show more agreement.

Scientists gain confidence in the models because they predict seasonal variations and other broad-scale phenomena. The general patterns of predictions by different models are similar. For example, they all predict warming, and they all predict that more of the warming would take place near the poles and in winter.

The most obvious test that could be done to validate the models is to run them for conditions of the past century, including the increase in greenhouse gases that has occurred so far, to see if they predict the current temperature. Unfortunately, because of insufficient data about past conditions and for other technical reasons, the validity of the experiments that have been done is not clear. We will describe and analyze the results briefly.

As we mentioned earlier, concentrations of greenhouse gases in the atmosphere have increased very steeply since about 1950. Between the late 19th century and 1990, the average temperature rose by $0.3°C–0.6°C$. Most of the warming occurred before 1950. Some of the climate models predicted temperature increases three to five times as high as actually occurred. Evaluating these results is not a simple task. There are many factors that affect temperature. An increase in aerosols (airborne particles) in the atmosphere, from volcanic eruptions and industrial activities, contribute to cooling. Urbanization, and other human activities besides emission of greenhouse gases, caused some warming. Still other factors, such as variation in solar output and other natural phenomena, could have affected the temperature in either direction. Thus, it is not known how much of the warming over the past century is attributable to greenhouse gases. The magnitude and rate of the temperature change in the past century may not be unusual; it is possible that all of it is within the range of natural fluctuation. Considering all the uncertainties and the overly high predictions of the models, IPCC scientists estimate that if all the warming that occurred was due to greenhouse gases, then the likely future warming would be $1°C–2°C$, that is, at the lower end of the range predicted by the GCMs.

The IPCC report predicts a global mean temperature increase of $0.2°C–0.5°C$ per decade. Satellite data show an average global temperature rise of only $0.06°C$ for the decade of the 1980s. Although the models predict very high warming near the poles, arctic temperatures in some regions have gone down over the past 50 years.

Another way to try to understand the accuracy of GCM predictions is to consider how sensitive they are to modifications and improvements. There is very much scientific uncertainty about the behavior of clouds and their feedback properties. One modeling center did an experiment where they ran the same model except that clouds were treated differently each time. Their predictions for temperature increase ranged from $1.9°C$ to $5.2°C$, more than a 170% difference between the lowest and highest predictions.

Newer models, using more complete representations of the oceans, and/or including some of the cooling effects of industrial activity, show substantially reduced or slower warming. In 1995, as a result of improvements in the models, the IPCC reduced its prediction of the global average temperature increase.[63]

Conclusions

GCMs have improved dramatically in the few decades that scientists have been developing and working with them. Increased computer power allows more experiments, better calibration, and increased resolution (smaller grid size). Increased data collection and basic science research improve our understanding of the behavior and interactions of climate system components. But given results so far and the complexity of climate phenomena, it seems fair to conclude, as an IPCC report comments, that "climate models are still in an early stage of development."[64] They seem to overestimate the amount of warming that will occur. The 1992 IPCC update says, "Since the 1990 report there has been a greater appreciation of many of the uncertainties which affect our predictions of the timing, magnitude and regional patterns of climate change."[65] The models are a tool for understanding climate change, but are not yet at a stage where we can have a lot of confidence in the precision of their results. Certainly they have not achieved the level of reliability of the car crash-analysis models.

EXERCISES

Review exercises

1. List several cases described in Sections 4.1–4.4 where insufficient testing was a factor in a program error or failure.

2. List several cases described in Sections 4.1–4.4 where the provider did an inadequate job of informing customers about flaws in the system.

3. The Therac-25 radiation machine involved errors in software, overall design, and management or operations. Describe one error of each type.

4. List the three questions we used to evaluate computer models.

5. What is one simplification in the car crash models? In the climate models?

General exercises

6. Describe two or three computer errors or system failures you had heard about before reading this chapter (preferably ones that are not in the chapter).

7. Many records stored on computers include a date, and some older software systems use two digits to represent the year (e.g., 78, 95). Pick any two applications (e.g., billing for telephones, driver's license renewal), and describe problems that might occur in the year 2000.

8. (a) Suppose you write a program to add two integers. Assume that both integers and their sum will fit in the standard memory unit used by the computer for integers. How likely do you think it is that the sum will be correct? (If you used the program a million times on different pairs of integers, how many times do you think it would give the correct answer?)

   (b) Suppose a utility company has a million customers and it runs a program to determine if any customers have overdue bills. How likely do you think it is that the results of the program will be correct?

   (c) Probably your answers to parts (a) and (b) were different. (They should be!) Give some reasons why the likely number of errors would be different in these two examples.

9. If you have access to Usenet, read a few recent postings in comp.risks, the Risks Forum news group. Write a summary of two items.

10. Consider the case described in Section 4.1.2, in which a boy was assumed to be a drug abuser because two schools used different disciplinary codes in their computerized records.

   (a) Is this kind of problem more likely to occur with computerized records than with paper records? Why, or why not?

   (b) Describe some policies or practices that can help prevent such problems.

11. In order to keep illegal immigrants and foreign visitors from working in the U.S., the federal government is considering requiring that that every job applicant be checked against a national database before being hired. One U.S. senator commented, "Over the years we've heard many complaints about the accuracy of the INS [Immigration and Naturalization Service] database. Isn't it problematic to rely on a faulty database for verification of employment authorization?" Another replied, "I do not think it is problematical to come up with a registry that is going to have the verifiable information that we're looking for" if the government is willing to spend the money to improve it.[66]

    Discuss the strength of both arguments concerning the probable reliability of the database. Describe some potential consequences of inaccuracies.

12. For a long time, it has been possible to make airplane reservations by phone; tickets were mailed to the customer. Now, several airlines have a new system that does not use paper tickets. A customer makes a reservation by phone, gets a confirmation number, and just shows a picture ID, such as a driver's license, at the airport gate to board the plane.

    (a) What is the role of computers in making ticketless service possible?

    (b) What is one advantage of this service to the customer? To the airline? To society in general?

    (c) Describe two potential problems that could occur with this service.

13. Suppose you are responsible for the design and development of a computer system to control an amusement park ride. The operator will enter the number of people on the ride and what seats they occupy, so the software can consider weight and balance. The system will control the speed and time of the ride. The amusement park wants a system where, once the ride starts, a person is not needed to operate it.

    List some important things that can or should be done to ensure the safety of the system. Consider all aspects of development, technical issues, operating instructions, and so on.[67]

14. The Strategic Defense Initiative of the 1980s was a proposal for a computer system to detect a nuclear attack and automatically launch weapons to destroy the incoming missiles. Discuss some potential risks of such a system.

15. Who are the "good guys"? Pick two people or organizations mentioned in this chapter whose work helped make computer systems safer or reduced the negative consequences of errors. Tell why you picked them.

16. Most consumer and business software packages are sold with a statement that the seller is not liable for damages caused by the use of the software. Some people advocate a law requiring software vendors to provide stronger warranties. Discuss the pros and cons of such a requirement. Consider the likely effects on and/or relevance of quality, price, competition, and freedom of contract.

17. There is a story that a major retail company "lost" a warehouse from its inventory computer system for three years. No goods were shipped to or from the warehouse. Payroll was handled by a separate system, so the employees continued to be paid. To what extent is this a computer failure? What other important factors are involved? Why would such an incident be less likely without computers? Is this incident a strong argument against using computerized inventory systems?

18. Theft of expensive home appliances (e.g., TVs, stereo systems) is not new. In what ways is the impact on the victim of the theft of a home computer more serious?

19. During the Gulf War, a commander in the Royal Air Force left disks containing military plans for Desert Storm in his car. They were stolen—apparently by ordinary thieves who took his computer, not by spies. One book describes this as a "particularly disturbing example of computer dependency."[68] The point of this exercise is to analyze how much difference it would

have made if the plans were in a paper file folder. Give reasons for your answers to each of the questions.

Do you think the commander would have been more likely or less likely to leave paper files in his car? Would the thieves have been more or less likely to recognize what the files contained if they had been on paper? Would the thieves have been likely to panic and discard the files, return them, or sell them to Iraq? Was the commander more or less likely to face a court martial if the files were on paper? Overall, how much do you think computers have to do with the essential issues in this case?

20. The robot cow-milking machines mentioned in Chapter 1 have some problems. The machines are twice as expensive as conventional milking machines that must be attached by hand. They have software glitches. The system alerts the farmer by beeper when there is a problem. He is beeped several times a day, often for false alarms. The machines have trouble milking cows with unusual-sized udders. Some cows kick the machines. About 10% of the cows can't use the machine. In the summer, when cows are at pasture, they must be herded into the barn to use the machine.[69]

Evaluate these problems. Which are serious? Which are likely to be solved? Which are not really problems caused by the machine?

21. Write five questions whose answers would be needed in a life-cycle analysis model comparing the environmental impact of juice boxes with the environmental impact of juice in bottles. (Use the questions for diapers in Figure 4.3 as a guide.) Consider manufacture, transportation, use, and disposal.

22. Suppose the government no longer required physical crash tests for new cars. What factors would you consider in deciding whether or not to buy a car that was crash tested only by computer simulation? What magazines or technical literature would you consult, if any, in making your decision?

23. We suggested that different people and institutions would consider different factors when deciding whether to require physical crash testing of cars. Which group do you think would rely most heavily on technical information about the quality of the computer simulation programs: customers, car manufacturers, companies that insure the manufacturers, legal scholars, or legislators? Why?

24. An article in the magazine *Audubon*[70] states that "Since the 1960s more than 100 separate studies have confirmed that a doubling of the CO_2 concentration would raise average surface temperatures by one to four degrees centigrade." Is this an accurate statement? Explain your answer.

25. Suppose there are three companies that make a similar product. One does physical tests to check the safety of the product. One uses only computer simulations. The third will not disclose the testing methods it uses. Suppose you are on a jury for a case where someone is suing one of the companies because of an injury received from the product.

(a) Would your decision about awarding money to the plaintiff be affected by the company's policy about testing? If so, how? If not, what factors are more important to you?

(b) Suppose reliable data show that the injury rate for the product is almost identical for all three companies. With that additional information, would your decision be affected by the company's testing policy?

26. Which of the following models do you think produce very accurate results? Which do you think are less reliable? Give your reasons.

- Models that predict the effect of an income tax change on government revenue.
- Models that predict the position of the moon.

■ Models that predict the speed of a new racing boat hull design under specified wind conditions.*

Assignments

These exercises require some research or activity that may need to be done during business hours or a few days before the assignment is due.

27. Find newspaper or magazine articles about the more than 500-point drop in the stock market that occurred in October 1987. What was the role of computer programs in this incident?

28. Suppose you have the following data:

    ■ The number of tons in the known reserves of an important natural resource like, say, copper.

    ■ The average amount of the resource used per person (worldwide) per year.

    ■ The total population of the world.

    (a) Write a program, using a programming language or a spreadsheet, to determine in how many years the resource will run out. The program's input should be the three data described above.

    (b) One obvious flaw in the program is that it assumes the population is constant. Include the rate of population increase per year as another input.

    (c) Suppose your program is correct and the input data are reliable. List all the reasons you can think of why this program is really not a good predictor of when we will run out of the resource.

    (d) In 1972, a group called the Club of Rome received a lot of attention when it published a study using computer models that implied that the world would run out of several important natural resources in the 1980s. Today, many of those resources are cheaper than they were then, indicating that they are now less scarce. Why do you think so many people accepted the predictions in the study?

28. Find two articles about the TAPPS nuclear winter model from newspapers or magazines in the mid-1980s (try 1984–1986). (Do not use either of the two mentioned in the endnotes for Section 4.5.) What information, if any, do they provide about the assumptions, simplifications, and limitations of the model?

Class exercises

1. Assume that the family of one of the victims of the Therac-25 is suing the hospital where the machine was used, AECL (the maker of the machine), and the programmer who wrote the Therac-25 software. Divide students into six groups: attorneys for the family against each of the three respondents and attorneys for each of the three respondents. Each group is to present a five-minute summation of arguments for its case. Then, let the class discuss all aspects of the case and vote concerning which if any of the respondents should pay the family and whether any should be charged with a criminal offense.

2. Consider the following scenario. A state's highway patrol keeps records of stolen cars in its computer system. A car can be checked by typing in the license plate number. The records are not routinely updated when stolen cars are recovered. A car was still listed as stolen a few years after it had been recovered and later sold. The new owner of the car was shot and killed by a police officer during a traffic stop; the officer thought the car was stolen and that the driver was acting suspiciously. An investigation concluded that the officer "acted in good faith." The family

---

*Extensive computer modeling is used to design boats for the America's Cup races.

has filed a wrongful death suit against the highway patrol and the police officer. Divide the class into teams of attorneys for the family, the highway patrol, and the officer. Each team is to present a five-minute summation of arguments for its case. Then, let the class vote concerning which, if any, of the respondents should pay the family and whether anyone should be charged with a criminal offense.*

3. Poll the class and find out how many students have tried hang gliding or bungee jumping. How many say "No way!"? How many would like to be one of the first people to buy a new pocket-sized computer that has novel new features (say, the user communicates with it by speaking to it in normal conversational English)? How many would wait six months or so to see how well it really works? How many would ride on a computer-controlled subway train that had no human driver?

Generate a discussion of personal differences in risk-taking. Is there one correct level of risk?

NOTES

1   Sources for some of the billing error cases include Philip E. Ross, "The Day the Software Crashed," *Forbes,* April 25, 1994, 153:9, pp. 142–56; and Peter G. Neumann, "Inside Risks," *Communications of the ACM,* July 1992, p. 122.

2   I learned of the mortgage problem because I was one of the victims. Sources for the other credit database accuracy cases include Jeffrey Rothfeder, *Privacy For Sale,* Simon & Schuster, 1992, p. 34 and pp. 130–31; "A Case of Mistaken Identity," *Privacy Journal,* December 1992, p. 7; "In the States," *Privacy Journal,* January 1993, p. 3; Neumann, "Inside Risks," *Communications of the ACM,* January 1992, p. 186, and July 1992, p. 122.

3   Associated Press, "Teen 'Convicted' by Computer," *San Jose Mercury,* March 7, 1996, p. 3B.

4   "Who's Reading Your Medical Records?" *Consumer Reports,* October 1994, pp. 628–32. "How Private Is My Medical Information?" Fact Sheet No. 8, Privacy Rights Clearinghouse, Center for Public Interest Law, University of San Diego.

5   Dan Joyce, e-mail correspondence, May 17, 1996 (the adoption case). Study by the Office of Technology Assessment, reported in Rothfeder, *Privacy For Sale.* "Jailing the Wrong Man," *Time,* February 25, 1985, p. 25. David Burnham, "Tales of a Computer State," *The Nation,* April 1983, p. 527. Evelyn Richards, "Proposed FBI Crime Computer System Raises Questions on Accuracy, Privacy," *Washington Post,* February 13, 1989, p. A6. "Wrong Suspect Settles His Case for $55,000," *New York Times,* March 6, 1998, p. 30. Peter G. Neumann, "Risks to the Public in Computer and Related Systems," *Software Engineering Notes,* April 1988, 13:2, p.11. Several similar cases are reported by Peter G. Neumann in "Inside Risks," *Communications of the ACM,* January 1992, p. 186.

6   Joan E. Rigdon, "Buggy PC Software Is Botching Tax Returns," *Wall Street Journal,* March 3, 1995, pp. B1, B4.

7   Sources about the Pentium chip and other bugs include various Internet postings and the following articles, all from the *Wall Street Journal:* Don Clark, "Some Scientists Are Angry over Flaw in Pentium Chip, and Intel's Response," November 25, 1994, p. B6; Don Clark, "Intel's Grove Airs Apology for Pentium over the Internet," November 29, 1994, p. B6; Jim Carlton and Stephen

---

*I have changed some details, but this scenario was suggested by a real case.

Kreider Yoder, "Humble Pie: Intel to Replace Its Pentium Chips," December 21, 1994, pp. B1, B8; Scott McCartney, "Compaq Recalling Notebook Computer From Dealers in Europe to Repair Bug," December 22, 1994, p. B2.

8   Thomas Nicely, quoted in Carlton and Kreider Yoder, "Humble Pie."

9   Frederick Rose and Richard Turner, "The Movie Was a Hit, The CD-ROM a Dud; Software Bites Disney," *Wall Street Journal,* January 23, 1995 pp. A1, A6. The comments are from Mike Maples, Microsoft, in Joan E. Rigdon, "Frequent Glitches in New Software Bug Users," *Wall Street Journal,* January 18, 1995, pp. B1, B5.

10 "AT&T Phone Failure Downs Three New York Airports for Four Hours," *Software Engineering Notes,* October 1991, 16:4, p. 6–7.

11 "AT&T Crash, 15 Jan 90: The Official Report," in "Subsection on Telephone Systems," *Software Engineering Notes,* April 1990, 15:2, p. 11–14.

12 "Subsection on Telephone Systems," *Software Engineering Notes,* April 1990, 15:2, pp. 11–14. Philip E. Ross, "The Day the Software Crashed," *Forbes,* April 25, 1994, 153:9, pp. 142–56. Ann Lindstrom, "Outage Hits AT&T in New England," *Telephony,* November 11, 1991, 221:20, p. 10. "Data Entry Typo Mutes Millions of U.S. Pagers," *Wall Street Journal,* September 27, 1995, p. A11.

13 David Craig, "NASDAQ Blackout Rattles Investors," *USA Today,* July 18, 1994, p. 2B. Associated Press, "NASDAQ Defends Its System after Stock-Pricing Errors," *New York Times,* September 13, 1994, p. D19. "Note to Readers," *Boston Globe,* October 25, 1994, p. 52.

14 *Science News,* September 13, 1986, p. 172. Philip E. Ross, "The Day the Software Crashed," *Forbes,* April 25, 1994, 153:9, pp. 142–56.

15 Tamala M. Edwards, "Numbers Nightmare," *Time,* August 9, 1993, p. 53.

16 Sources for the inventory program problems include Thomas Hoffman, "NCR Users Cry Foul over I series Glitch," *Computerworld,* February 15, 1993, p. 72; Milo Geyelin, "Faulty Software Means Business for Litigators," *Wall Street Journal,* January 21, 1994, p. B1; Milo Geyelin, "How an NCR System for Inventory Control Turned into a Virtual Saboteur," *Wall Street Journal,* August 8, 1994, p. A1; Mary Brandel and Thomas Hoffman, "User Lawsuits Drag On for NCR," *Computerworld,* August 15, 1994, p. 1.

17 William M. Bulkeley and Joann S. Lublin, "Ben & Jerry's New CEO Will Face Shrinking Sales and Growing Fears of Fat," *Wall Street Journal,* January 10, 1995, p. B1. The Walgreen case is in Ross, "The Day the Software Crashed," p. 146. Bruce Campion-Smith, "Glitches Stalling Updated Airport Radar," *Toronto Star,* August 3, 1992, p. A1. David Hughes, "ATC, Airport Upgrades Poised for New Growth," *Aviation Week and Space Technology,* April 5, 1993, 138:14, p. 40.

18 Carl Ingram, "DMV Spent $44 Million on Failed Project," *Los Angeles Times,* April 27, 1994, p. A3. Effy Oz, "When Professional Standards Are Lax: The CONFIRM Failure and its Lessons," *Communications of the ACM,* October 1994, 37:10, pp. 29–36.

19 The DIA delay was widely reported in the news media. A few of the articles used as sources for the discussion here are W. Wayt Gibbs, "Software's Chronic Crisis," *Scientific American,* September 1994, 271:3, pp. 86–95. Robert L. Scheier, "Software Snafu Grounds Denver's High-Tech Airport," *PC Week,* 11:19, May 16, 1994, p. 1. Price Colman, "Software Glitch Could Be the Hitch. Misplaced Comma Might Dull Baggage System's Cutting Edge," *Rocky Mountain News,* April 30, 1994, p. 9A. Steve Higgins, "Denver Airport: Another Tale of Government High-Tech Run Amok" *Investor's Business Daily,* May 23, 1994, p. A4. Julie Schmit, "Tiny Company Is Blamed for Denver Delays," USA Today, May 5, 1994, pp. 1B, 2B.

20 Scheier, "Software Snafu Grounds Denver's High-tech Airport."

21 Data compiled by Peter Mellor, Centre for Software Reliability, England, reprinted in Peter G. Neumann, *Computer-Related Risks,* Addison Wesley, 1995, p. 309.

22 "Airbus Safety Claim 'Cannot Be Proved'," *New Scientist,* September 7, 1991, 131:1785, p. 30. Robert Morrell Jr., Risks Forum Digest, July 6, 1994, 16:20. "Training 'Inadequate' Says A320 Crash Report," *Flight International,* December 22, 1993, p. 11 (on the January 1992 Strasbourg A320 crash, excerpted by Peter B. Ladkin in Risks Forum Digest, January 2, 1994). Ross, "The Day the Software Crashed," p. 156, on the 1993 Warsaw crash. David Learmont, "Lessons from the Cockpit," *Flight International,* January 11, 1994.

23 William M. Carley, "Could a Minor Change in Design Have Saved American Flight 965?" *Wall Street Journal,* January 8, 1995, pp. A1, A8.

24 Barry H. Kantowitz, "Pilot Workload and Flightdeck Automation," in M. Mouloua and R. Parasuraman, eds., *Human Performance in Automated Systems: Current Research and Trends,* pp. 212–23. The TCAS problems are mentioned on p. 214. Tom Forester and Perry Morrison, *Computer Ethics: Cautionary Tales and Ethical Dilemmas in Computing,* second edition, MIT Press, 1994, mentions avoidance of a collision, p. 113.

25 Peter G. Neumann, *Computer-Related Risks,* p. 158.

26 Nancy G. Leveson and Clark S. Turner, "An Investigation of the Therac-25 Accidents," *IEEE Computer,* July 1993, 26:7, pp. 18–41. Jonathan Jacky, "Safety-Critical Computing: Hazards, Practices, Standards, and Regulation," in Charles Dunlop and Rob Kling, eds., *Computerization and Controversy,* Academic Press, 1991. Most of the factual information about the Therac-25 incidents in this chapter is from Leveson and Turner.

27 Conversation with Nancy Leveson, January 19, 1995.

28 Jonathan Jacky, "Safety-Critical Computing: Hazards, Practices, Standards, and Regulation," in Charles Dunlop and Rob Kling, eds., *Computerization and Controversy,* Academic Press, 1991, p. 615. Peter G. Neumann, "Risks to the Public in Computers and Related Systems," *Software Engineering Notes,* April 1991, 16:2, p. 4. Ted Wendling, "Lethal Doses: Radiation That Kills," *Plain Dealer,* December 16, 1992, p. 12A. (I thank my student Irene Radomyshelsky for bringing the last reference to my attention.)

29 "Airbus Safety Claim 'Cannot Be Proved'," *New Scientist,* September 7, 1991, 131:1785, p. 30.

30 Richard P. Feynman, *What Do You Care What Other People Think?,* W. W. Norton & Co., 1988, pp. 182–183.

31 Govinda Rajan and Mathew Lodge, "X Windows Makes Patient Breathless ," Risks Forum, March 10, 1994, 15:64.

32 Ross, "The Day the Software Crashed," p. 146. A colleague warned me not to describe this or any other example in my book as "well done." The day the book is published there could be a headline saying "U.S. Banking System Crashes Due to CIPS Software Error." That would be a reminder that certainty and perfection in complex software systems are not possible. Professional expertise, responsibility, good planning, sensible testing, and so on, are.

33 From an e-mail advertisement for Nancy G. Leveson, *Safeware: System Safety and Computers* (Addison Wesley, 1995).

34 See, for example, the Shneiderman book in the list of references below.

35 Kantowitz, "Pilot Workload and Flightdeck Automation."

36 Feynman, *What Do You Care What Other People Think?* Feynman also mentions that the Challenger used obsolete hardware. Part of the reason was the recognition of the difficulty and expense of developing a completely new system from scratch for modern hardware that would meet the safety requirements of the shuttle. But using the old equipment had safety risks, for example, from the difficulty of getting high quality parts. Feynman thought it was time to make the change.

The shuttle, like other systems, is not immune from problems. The Risks Forum includes reports of computer failures caused by a loose piece of solder, subtle timing errors, and other factors.

37 "AT&T Crash, 15 January 90: The Official Report."

38 Feynman, *What Do You Care What Other People Think?*, pp. 190–94 and 232–36. Aeronautics and Space Engineering Board, National Research Council, *An Assessment of Space Shuttle Flight Software Development Processes*, National Academy Press, 1993.

39 Mary Brandel and Thomas Hoffman, "User Lawsuits Drag on for NCR," *Computerworld*, August 15, 1994, p. 1. Andy Pasztor, "Lucas's $18.5 Million Fine for Work on Navy Jet Underscores Safety Fears," *Wall Street Journal*, January 1995, p. A4.

40 These problems and trade-offs occur often with regulation of new drugs and medical devices, regulation of pollution, and various kinds of safety regulation. They are discussed primarily in journals on the economics of regulation, but some received general publicity when AIDS activists encountered and fought the FDA bureaucracy. Several medical devices that doctors and surgeons believe could save thousands of lives are available in other countries but cannot be used in the U.S.

41 Jacky, "Safety-Critical Computing: Hazards, Practices, Standards, and Regulation," p. 624.

42 Leveson and Turner, "An Investigation of the Therac-25 Accidents," p. 40.

43 See, for example, Walter Williams, *The State Against Blacks*, McGraw-Hill, 1982, Chapters 5–7. One year during a construction lull, a state failed everyone who took the contractor's license exam. It is illegal in 48 states for most software engineers to call themselves software engineers because of licensing laws for engineers. One company was forced to spend thousands of dollars changing job titles, business cards, and marketing literature to remove the word "engineer." (Julia King, "Engineers to IS: Drop That Title!" *Computerworld*, May 30, 1994, 28:22, pp. 1, 119.)

44 Miles Corwin and John L. Mitchell, "Fire Disrupts L.A. Phones, Services," *Los Angeles Times*, March 16, 1994, p. A1.

45 William R. Hersh, "Informatics: Development and Evaluation of Information Technology in Medicine," *Journal of the American Medical Association*, January 1, 1992, p. 167.

46 "AT&T Phone Failure Downs Three New York Airports for Four Hours," *Software Engineering Notes*, October 1991, 16:4, pp. 6–7. "What's News," *Wall Street Journal*, January 10, 1995, p. A1.

47 Yoichiro Fujiyoshi, quoted in Craig Forman et al, "Quake's Aftershocks Will Rattle Segments of Japan's Economy," *Wall Street Journal*, January 18, 1995, p. A1.

48 National Transportation Statistics, Annual Report, September 1993, Historical Compendium, 1960–1992, U.S. Dept. of Transportation, p. 74 and p. 95.

49 Data from the National Air Transportation Safety Board and the U. S. Bureau of the Census, *Statistical Abstract of the United States: 1994*, Tables 134 and 996. Deaths in railroad accidents have also declined.

50 Forester and Morrison, *Computer Ethics*, p. 4.

51 Peter G. Neumann, "Inside Risks: Risks on the Rails," *Communications of the ACM*, July 1993, 36:7, p. 130, and *Computer-Related Risks*, p. 71. Although I take issue with some particulars, Neumann's Risks Forum, articles, and book are invaluable sources of information and analysis about risks of computer systems.

52 "More Risks of Computer Billing—$22,000 Water Bill," *Software Engineering Notes*, October 1991, 16:4, p. 6. Richard M. Rosenberg, "Success Components for the 21st Century," *The Magazine of Bank Management*, January/February 1994.

53 Here is a non-computer-related example. A study by the Harvard Center for Risk Analysis of the cost of various medical procedures and techniques for accident prevention and pollution control

found that control of benzene emissions at tire manufacturing plants costs almost $20 billion per life-year saved. Most other techniques studied cost far less per life-year saved. Overall safety could be improved if resources were directed at the more cost-effective techniques. (Tammy O. Tengs et al, "Five Hundred Life-Saving Interventions and Their Cost-Effectiveness," Center for Risk Analysis, Harvard School of Public Health. Some safety experts and consumer advocates object to such analyses because they can be manipulated to justify reductions in safety or to shirk responsibility for unsafe systems. Risk experts considered the Harvard study to be thorough and rigorously done.)

54 Amanda Bennett, "Strange 'Science': Predicting Health-Care Costs," *Wall Street Journal,* February 7, 1994, p. B1.

55 Cynthia Crossen, "How 'Tactical Research' Muddied Diaper Debate," *Wall Street Journal,* May 17, 1994, pp. B1, B9.

56 Richard P. Turco, Owen Toon, Thomas Ackerman, James Pollack, and Carl Sagan, "Nuclear Winter: Global Consequences of Multiple Nuclear Explosions," *Science,* December 23, 1984, p. 1284. Russell Seitz, "In From the Cold: 'Nuclear Winter' Melts Down," *The National Interest,* Fall 1986.

57 The main sources for this section include J. O. Hallquist and D. J. Benson, "DYNA3D—An Explicit Finite Element Program for Impact Calculations," in *Crashworthiness and Occupant Protection in Transportation Systems,* T. B. Khalil and A. I. King, eds., American Society of Mechanical Engineers, v. 106, p. 1. William H. Allen, "How To Build a Better Beer Can," pp. 32–36, and "DYNA Gets to the Heart of the Matter," p. 36, both in *Supercomputing Review,* March 1991. Steve Wampler, "DYNA3D: This Computer Code Seems to Offer Something for Everyone," *The Quarterly,* Lawrence Livermore National Laboratory, September 1989, 20:2, pp. 7–11. "Motorists, Pedestrians May Find LLNL Computer Code a Life-Saver" and "LLNL Computer Code Makes the Jump from Modeling Machines to Man," news releases from Lawrence Livermore National Laboratories, March 7, 1991 (NR-91-03-01 and NR-91-03-02).

58 Thomas Frank and Karl Gruber, "Numerical Simulation of Frontal Impact and Frontal Offset Collisions," *Cray Channels,* Winter 1992, pp. 2–6.

59 J. T. Houghton, G. J. Jenkins, and J. J. Ephraums, eds., *Climate Change: The IPCC Scientific Assessment,* Cambridge University Press, 1990. J. T. Houghton, B. A. Callander, and S. K. Varney, eds., *Climate Change 1992: The Supplementary Report to the IPCC Scientific Assessment,* Cambridge University Press, 1992. Most of the information in this section, including strengths and weaknesses of the models, comes from these reports. I also used a large variety of other books and articles for background. One book by a climatologist critical of the models is included in the references at the end of the chapter.

60 Houghton et al, *Climate Change 1992,* p. 14.

61 Andrew Lacis, *R & D,* June 1992, 34:7, p. 22.

62 Houghton et al, *Climate Change 1992,* pp. 17, 139. Patrick J. Michaels, *Sound and Fury: The Science and Politics of Global Warming,* Cato Institute, 1992, pp. 114–118.

63 Houghton et al, *Climate Change 1992,* p. 103. Carl Zimmer, "Verdict (Almost) In," *Discover,* January 1996, pp. 78–79. "Report on Global Warming Makes Dire Predictions," *Wall Street Journal,* October 25, 1995, p. B5. (In spite of the headline, this article reports that the new IPCC prediction for global temperature increase in the next century is 1°C-3.5°C, which is lower than its prediction of a few years earlier.)

64 Houghton et al, *Climate Change: The IPCC Scientific Assessment,* p. 243.

65 Houghton et al, *Climate Change 1992,* p. 19.

66 The quotes are from Edward Kennedy and Barbara Jordan, in David Lawsky, "New Job Checks on Immigration Status Proposed," Reuters World Service, August 3, 1994.

67 A crash of a computer-controlled roller coaster in Missouri in 1990 injured 28 people. Peter G. Neumann, "Inside Risks: Risks on the Rails," *Communications of the ACM,* July 1993, 36:7, p. 130.

68 Forester and Morrison, *Computer Ethics,* pp. 4–5.

69 Dana Milbank, "Barnyard Breakthrough: Cow Milks Herself," *Wall Street Journal,* May 8, 1995, pp. B1, B6.

70 Bruce Stutz, "The Landscape of Hunger," *Audubon,* March/April 1993, pp. 54–63 (quotation on p. 62).

FOR FURTHER READING

W. Robert Collins, Keith W. Miller, Bethany J. Spielman, and Phillip Wherry, "How Good Is Good Enough?" *Communications of the ACM,* January 1994, 37:1, pp. 81–91. A discussion of ethical issues about quality for software developers.

Richard Epstein, *The Case of the Killer Robot,* John Wiley and Sons, 1996.

Richard P. Feynman, *What Do You Care What Other People Think?,* W. W. Norton & Co., 1988. Includes Feynman's report on the investigation of the destruction of the Challenger space shuttle, with many insights about how to, and how not to, investigate a system failure.

J. T. Houghton, G. J. Jenkins, and J. J. Ephraums, eds., *Climate Change: The IPCC Scientific Assessment,* Cambridge University Press, 1990.

J. T. Houghton, B. A. Callander, and S. K. Varney, eds., *Climate Change 1992: The Supplementary Report to the IPCC Scientific Assessment,* Cambridge University Press, 1992.

Jonathan Jacky, "Safety-Critical Computing: Hazards, Practices, Standards, and Regulation," in Charles Dunlop and Rob Kling, eds., *Computerization and Controversy,* Academic Press, 1991.

Thomas K. Landauer, *The Trouble With Computers: Usefulness, Usability, and Productivity,* MIT Press, 1995.

Nancy G. Leveson, *Safeware: System Safety and the Computer Age,* Addison Wesley, 1995.

Nancy G. Leveson and Clark S. Turner, "An Investigation of the Therac-25 Accidents," *IEEE Computer,* July 1993, 26:7, pp. 18–41.

Patrick J. Michaels, *Sound and Fury: The Science and Politics of Global Warming,* Cato Institute, 1992. Michaels is a climatologist critical of the climate models.

Peter G. Neumann, moderator, Risks Forum, Usenet (comp.risks).

Peter G. Neumann, *Computer-Related Risks,* Addison-Wesley, 1995.

Peter G. Neumann et al., "Inside Risks," *Communications of the ACM,* regular column, on the last page of each issue.

Donald Norman, *The Psychology of Everyday Things,* Basic Books, 1988. A study of good and bad user interfaces on many everyday devices and appliances.

Effy Oz, "When Professional Standards Are Lax: The CONFIRM Failure and its Lessons," *Communications of the ACM,* October 1994, 37:10, pp. 29–36. A study of a $125-million-dollar project that was canceled.

David Parnas, "SDI: Violation of Professional Responsibility," *Abacus,* Winter 1987, pp. 46–52.

Ivars Peterson, *Fatal Defect: Chasing Killer Computer Bugs,* Times Books (Random House), 1995.

Henry Petroski, *To Engineer Is Human: The Role of Failure in Successful Design,* St. Martin's Press, 1985.

Jeffrey Rothfeder, *Privacy for Sale,* Simon & Schuster, 1992. Although the main focus of this book is privacy, it contains many examples of problems that resulted from errors in databases.

Ben Shneiderman, *Designing the User Interface,* Addison-Wesley, 1987.

Aaron Wildavsky, *Searching for Safety,* Transaction Books, 1988. On the role of risk in making us safer.

5 PROTECTING SOFTWARE AND OTHER INTELLECTUAL PROPERTY

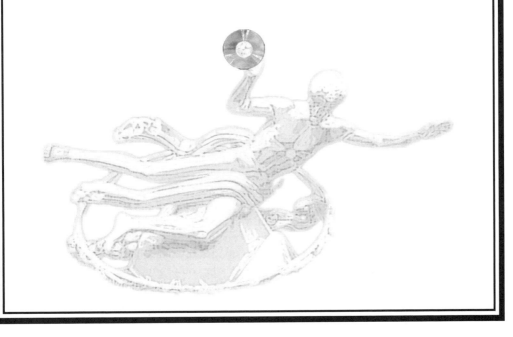

> *The Congress shall have Power To . . . promote the Progress of Science and useful Arts, by securing for limited Times to Authors and Inventors the exclusive Right to their respective Writings and Discoveries. . . .*
>
> –U.S. Constitution, Article I, Section 8

5.1   INTELLECTUAL PROPERTY ISSUES

5.1.1   What Is Intellectual Property?

Have you ever given a floppy disk to a friend that contained a word processor or spreadsheet program? Have you taped a movie on your VCR to watch later in the week? Have you posted a copy of a newspaper or magazine article on a computer bulletin board system? Have you uploaded or downloaded software on a bulletin board? More importantly, do you know which of these actions are legal and which are illegal, and why?

Books, articles, plays, songs, works of art, movies, and software are protected by copyright, a legal concept that defines rights to intellectual property. Some software is protected by patent, another legal concept that defines rights to intellectual property.

Why is intellectual property given legal protection? The value of a book or a song or a computer program is much more than the cost of the effort and materials used to print it or put it on disk. The value of a painting is higher than the cost of the canvas and paint used to create it. In general, the value of intellectual and artistic works comes from the creativity, ideas, research, skills, labor, and other nonmaterial efforts and attributes provided by their creators. Designing and developing a program can take months or years of work and cost thousands or millions of dollars. Our property rights to the physical property we create or buy include the rights to use it, to prevent others from using it, and to set the (asking) price for selling it. We would be reluctant to make the effort to earn or produce physical things if anyone else could just take them away. If anyone could copy a novel or a computer program for the small price of the copying itself, the creator of the work would receive very little income from the creative effort, and some of the incentive for producing it would be gone.

The key to understanding intellectual property is to understand that the thing protected is the intangible creative work—which is embodied in a physical form. When one buys a novel, one is buying the physical collection of paper and ink that contains a copy of the book's contents, but one is not buying the plot, the organization of ideas, the presentation, the characters and events that form the abstraction that is the intangible "book."[1] The owner of the physical book may give away, lend, or resell the one physical book he or she bought, but not make copies (with some exceptions). The right to make copies still belongs to the owner of the intangible "book," that is, the owner of the copyright. The principle is similar for software. The buyer of a software package is not buying the program, but only one copy of it. The program itself, in the abstract, is still owned by the copyright owner.

Protection of intellectual property has both individual and social benefits: It protects the right of the creator of something of value to be compensated for what he or she has created, and, by so doing, it encourages production of valuable, intangible, easily copied creative work.

Some people reject the whole notion of copyrights and patents. They see these mechanisms as providing government-granted monopolies, violating freedom of speech, and limiting productive efforts. Intellectual property differs from physical property in that making a copy does not deprive its creator of its use; thus "theft" of intellectual property by copying is quite different from theft of physical property. We will elaborate on these views in Section 5.3.3. Copyright and patent are well-established in Western countries, but not in all areas of the world (not in some Asian countries, for example). Most of the issues in this chapter are within a context that accepts the legitimacy of copyright and patent. A few of the controversies we discuss revolve around the legitimacy and extent of copyright.

5.1.2 Copyrights and Patents

U.S. copyright law (Title 17 of the U.S. Code) gives the copyright holder the following exclusive rights, with some exceptions:

- To make copies of the work;
- To produce derivative works, such as translations into other languages or movies based on books;
- To distribute copies;
- To perform the work in public (e.g., music, plays); and
- To display the work in public (e.g., artwork, movies).

There are several exceptions for libraries. Another very important exception is the "fair use" doctrine, which we discuss in Section 5.2.2. A specific exception for software allows the owner of a copy of a program to make a backup ("archival") copy. The copyright owner may give, rent, license, or sell rights to others, but uses of copyrighted material that are not authorized by the copyright owner or permitted by one of the exceptions in the law are infringements of the copyright and are subject to civil or criminal penalties.[*]

What kind of intellectual property is protected by copyright? Facts, ideas, concepts, processes, and methods of operation are not copyrightable.[†] Copyright protects creative expression, that is, the expression, selection, and arrangement of ideas. The boundary between an idea and the expression of an idea is often not clear. Hence, many cases of alleged copyright infringement go to court. Also, it is often not clear what constitutes a "fair use" of a copyrighted work; the guidelines (which we describe later) are interpreted and applied by courts in specific cases.

Patents (covered in Title 35 of the U.S. Code) are granted for inventions of new things or processes. They protect new ideas by giving the inventor a monopoly on the invention for a specified period of time (currently 20 years). The purposes of patents are similar to those of copyrights: to reward the inventor and encourage disclosure and use of

---

[*]Copyrights are granted for a limited, but long, time, for example, the lifetime of the author plus 50 years.

[†]Recall from Chapter 2 that some privacy advocates suggest giving people property rights in facts about themselves, whereas copyright law has always recognized that copyrighting facts would be an unreasonable infringement on the flow of information.

the invention so others benefit from it too. Patents differ from copyrights in that they protect the underlying idea of an invention, not just a particular expression or implementation of it, and they prohibit anyone else from using the idea without authorization of the patent holder, even if another person independently came up with the same idea or invention. Thus, if the invention of a word processor were patentable, all companies that sell word processors would have to make agreements with, and pay royalties to, the patent holder.

There is significant debate about whether copyright or patent is the more appropriate protection for software. There are two aspects to the debate. First, what is the nature of a new program, or a new kind of program? Is it an invention, a new idea? Or is it a "writing," an expression of ideas, algorithms, techniques? Second, what are the practical consequences of each choice in terms of encouraging innovation and production of new products?

Software is so broad a field and so varied that specific programs can fit in either category—invention or writing. The first spreadsheet program, VisiCalc, introduced in 1979, was a remarkable innovation that had enormous impact on ways of doing business planning and on the sales of computer software and hardware. If the government had been willing to grant patents on software at that time, VisiCalc might have qualified for one. Similarly, the first hypertext system might be seen as a patentable invention. On the other hand, a particular computer game may have more in common with a literary work, like a novel.

For many years, the U.S. Patent Office was reluctant to give patents for software. When it began to do so more often, it made mistakes. The Patent Office had no software experts and granted some patents for techniques that were considered obvious and/or were already widely used. In one such case, the Patent Office reversed itself and withdrew a patent it had granted to Compton's New Media for a search system for multimedia databases. In the late 1980s the number of patents granted for software began a significant increase.[2]

The financial impact of patent decisions can be huge, and the complexity of the issues can make decisions difficult. For example, the jury in the Stac Electronics patent infringement suit against Microsoft decided on a $120 million award for Stac. A jury decided that Nintendo should pay more than $208 million for infringing a patent for a technique to display computerized images on a television screen. Nintendo claimed that it used a different technology, but that the highly technical details were not understood by the jury.[3]

5.1.3 New Issues

What new issues and problems related to intellectual property have arisen because of computers?

Software is a new form of intellectual property. Definitions and rules are developing gradually to extend the notion of intellectual property to software. The rules are still changing, as problems and new situations arise. We will look at current copyright law for software and some of the emerging issues and resolutions. Finding good solutions to the problems is important because of the size and impact of the U.S. software industry. (It generates more than $100 billion a year in income.)

Billions of dollars of software is copied illegally worldwide every year. Yes, billions. We will look at the problem of "software piracy," the copying of software (and documentation) in large quantities for resale and illegal copying by businesses and individuals for their own use.

Copying of older forms of copyrighted works, as well as software, has become much easier because of new computer technology. The explosively increasing use of computer networks, information services, the World Wide Web, and computer bulletin boards (BBSs) has created huge new problems for protection of copyrighted material. Finding solutions is difficult; some proposals (including those proposed by the federal government and included in proposed legislation) are very controversial.

There are complex questions about how similar one software developer's program may legally be to another's. Many lawsuits about software copyrights arise in this area, that is, from software companies suing other software companies whose products have a similar "look and feel" or other similarities.

There is disagreement about whether copyright is the appropriate protection mechanism for software. Some argue for patents, some for completely new rules designed specifically for software. Some argue that there should be no restrictions on copying software.

We will discuss these issues and others and consider a variety of approaches to resolving the new problems that arise from computer technologies.

The copyright for a particular software program may be held by the author of the program, a large software company whose employees developed the program, or another entity to which the copyright was transferred. Copyrights on books and other literary works are often held by publishers. For simplicity, we will use the phrase "software publisher" to refer to an owner of a software copyright.

5.2 COPYRIGHT LAW

5.2.1 A Bit of History

A brief history of copyright law will help illustrate how new technologies require changes or clarifications in law.[4]

The first U.S. copyright law, passed in 1790, covered books, maps, and charts. Movies, sound recording, and photography did not exist then. The law was later extended to cover them. The definition of an unauthorized copy in the Copyright Act of 1909 specified that it had to be in a form that could be seen and read visually. Even with the technologies of the early 20th century, this requirement was a problem. It was based on a court decision in a 1908 case where a song was copied onto a perforated piano music roll. (Such rolls were played on automatic pianos.) The music could not be read visually from the piano roll, so the copy was not considered a violation of the song's copyright.[5] It is easy to imagine other kinds of copying, even before computers, that result in nonvisual copies, but do violate the spirit and purpose of copyright.

The government began recognizing copyrights for software and databases in the 1960s, although copyright law at the time did not mention them. The old law was not good enough for the new technology. In the 1970s a company sued for protection of its chess program, which was implemented on a read-only-memory (ROM) chip in its hand-held computer chess game. Another company sold a game with the identical program; it was assumed they copied the ROM. But because the ROM could not be read visually, a court held that the copy was not an infringement of the program's copyright.[6] Again, the purpose of copyright was not served well. The creative work of the programmers was not protected; they received no compensation from a competitor's sales of their work.

In 1976 and 1980, the copyright law was revised to cover software. "Literary works" protected by copyright include computer databases and computer programs that exhibit "authorship," that is, contain original expression of ideas, not just the ideas themselves. Recognizing that technology was changing rapidly, the revised law specifies that appropriate literary works could be copyrighted "regardless of the nature of the material objects . . . in which they are embodied. A copy is in violation of a copyright if the original can be "perceived, reproduced, or otherwise communicated by or from the copy, directly or indirectly." Film, tapes, discs, and cards are mentioned as examples of forms in which protected material can be embodied.* During the 1980s many other countries extended their copyright laws to cover software; the details vary.[7]

One significant theme in the development of copyright law, illustrated by the examples above, has been devising good definitions to broaden the scope of protection to new technologies. As copying technologies improved, another problem needed to be addressed: A lot of people will break a law if it is easy and the penalties are weak. In the 1960s, the growth of the music industry was accompanied by high growth in illegal sales of unauthorized copies of recorded music (e.g., tapes). In 1982 high-volume copying of records and movies was made a felony. In the 1980s the enormous growth of the software industry was accompanied by a large amount of copying of software. The industry responded by pressing for explicit legal limitations on copying and for stiffer penalties for software copyright infringement. In 1992, making multiple copies of copyrighted work "willfully and for purposes of commercial advantage or private gain" became a felony offense. Making or distributing ten or more copies with retail value of more than $2500 within six months is punishable by up to five years in jail. The copies can be of different programs (e.g., one copy each of ten programs). Repeat offenders can get up to a ten-year jail sentence. Lesser offenses (e.g., making fewer than ten copies) are punishable by up to a year in jail. Fines under some circumstances can be as high as $250,000.[8] Companies can be sued or prosecuted if ten employees out of hundreds or thousands have an illegal copy of a program on their computers. Many software users and attorneys believe that the 1992 law went too far, that making ten copies worth $2500 is too small an offense to merit such severe penalties.

What copying is permissible? Under copyright law, the buyer has the right to make a copy necessary to install the software on a computer and to make one "archival" copy.[9] Licensing agreements for business software may grant other copying rights. The licensing agreements that come packaged with some personal computer software indicate that making a copy for a second computer, such as a portable or laptop, is acceptable if only one copy is in use at a time. Certain other uses are permissible under the fair use doctrine.

---

*Already, the punch cards, used for input of programs and data for decades, are obsolete.

5.2.2   The Fair Use Doctrine

As the Constitution indicates, the purpose of copyright is to encourage production of useful work. Copyright law and court decisions have attempted to define the rights of authors and publishers consistent with this goal and the goal of encouraging the use and flow of information. The fair use doctrine allows uses of copyrighted material that contribute to the creation of new work (such as reviews that quote part of a copyrighted work) and uses that are not likely to deprive authors or publishers of income for their work. Fair uses do not require the permission of the copyright holder.

The notion of fair use (for literary and artistic works) grew from judicial decisions; it was included explicitly in U.S. copyright law in 1976 and applies to software also. Fair use policies differ in other countries. Laws in some countries explicitly allow private, noncommercial copying. In Europe, fair use for software appears to be very restricted. The World Intellectual Property Association is attempting to get an international agreement to reject even private, noncommercial use without authorization.[10]

The 1976 copyright law was written before the widespread use of personal computers and before computer networks and online services. The software issues addressed pertained mainly to large business systems. Thus, many of the situations where questions of fair use of software arise now were not considered. The examples in the law that might be accepted as fair use are "criticism, comment, news reporting, teaching (including multiple copies for classroom use), scholarship, or research."[11] The law lists four factors to be considered in determining if a particular use is fair. They must be interpreted for software in court cases and may need to be rewritten to clarify fair use for modern digital technology. The factors in the law are as follows:

1. The purpose and nature of the use, including whether it is for commercial purposes or nonprofit educational purposes. (Copying for commercial purposes is less likely to be considered fair use.)
2. The nature of the copyrighted work. (Creative work, such as a novel, has more protection than factual work.)
3. The amount and significance of the portion used.
4. The effect of the use on the potential market for or value of the copyrighted work. (Uses that reduce sales of the original work are less likely to be considered fair.)

No one of the factors alone determines whether a particular use is fair, but the last one is given more weight than the others.

5.2.3   Fair Use Cases

The fair use doctrine is important for two quite different applications. First, it helps us figure out under what circumstances we as consumers can legally copy software (and other copyrighted material). Second, software developers often must copy some or all of another company's program as part of the process of developing their own products, which may compete with the other company's work. Is such copying a fair use? Here we will look at two real cases and a hypothetical one that address the first situation: What consumer uses are fair? We discuss the second situation in Section 5.5, along with other copyright issues for software developers.

Sony vs. Universal City Studios

The Sony case is the first case about private, noncommercial copying of copyrighted work to be decided by the Supreme Court.[12] It is not about software directly, but the decision has implications for fair use of software and has been cited in later software cases. Two movie studios sued Sony for contributing to copyright infringement because its Betamax machines were used by some customers to record copyrighted movies that were shown on television. Thus, one important issue raised in this case is whether makers of copying equipment can be sued because some users will use the equipment to infringe copyrights. Some publishers advocate banning or restricting various copying technology, for example, digital tapes and CD writers. We will discuss this issue later. Here we focus on the other issue the Supreme Court decided in the Sony case: whether recording a movie for personal use was a copyright infringement or a fair use. The entire movie was copied, and movies are creative, not factual, works. Thus it appears that interpretation of factors (2) and (3) of the fair use guidelines argues against fair use. The main purpose of recording the movie was to view it at a later time. Normally the tape was reused after the consumer viewed the movie, making it an "ephemeral copy." The copy was made for a private, noncommercial purpose, and no harm to the movie studios had been demonstrated. The Court interpreted factor (2), the nature of the copyrighted work, to include not simply whether it was creative or factual, but also the fact that the studios receive a large fee for broadcasting movies on television, and the fee depends on having a large audience that views the movies for free. So factors (1), (2), and (4) argue for fair use. The Court ruled, in a 5–4 decision, that recording a movie for viewing at a later time was a fair use.

The fact that the entire work was copied did not necessitate a ruling against fair use, although in many of the examples of fair use, only small excerpts are used. The fact that the copying was a private, noncommercial use was significant. The court ruled that private, noncommercial uses should be presumed fair unless there was realistic likelihood of economic harm to the copyright holder. Publishers generally are not happy with this presumption.

An Internet Case: The Church of Scientology

In 1995 the Church of Scientology filed suits against several former members and critics charging that they had posted copyrighted documents containing sacred teachings of the church on the Internet.* These cases raise many issues about the First and Fourth Amendments to the U.S. Constitution because the church took a number of actions that appeared to be attempts to intimidate critics, system administrators of BBSs where the church was discussed critically, and others who assisted the critics. They sued the *Washington Post,* among others. We will discuss some aspects of the cases related to constitutional issues in Chapter 6. Here we focus on the copyright issue.

---

*The legal actions were taken by auxiliary organizations, the Religious Technology Center and Bridge Publications.

The church critics who posted the documents argue that the postings were fair use. Entire copies of documents were made, but not for commercial gain. The postings were part of discussions of alleged abuses by the church. Many Net observers considered the fair use argument to be strong and the freedom of speech implications of the cases to be significant. In early stages of several of the cases, judges expressed the opinion that the Church would lose. However, there has been one case so far in which a judge ruled that the man who posted the church documents, a former member and longtime critic, had violated copyright law. The copying in this case differs from the Sony case (and the Sega case that we discuss in Section 5.5.1) in that the copying was not done for a limited, private use. Here the copies were posted publicly where they could be seen by many people and easily copied again. This, of course, is true of anything posted to a BBS or the Internet.[13]

Ricky Realtor vs. Software, Inc.—A Hypothetical Case

There are many situations where we want to make a copy of a computer program. Most consumers are not aware of details of copyright law or the intricacies of the fair use doctrine. The public views private, noncommercial copying as acceptable, although many people realize the issue gets fuzzy when the copying saves them the price of purchasing the software. Publishers try to give the impression that any copying not explicitly authorized is a copyright infringement; they sometimes argue as though fair use did not exist. In the exercises at the end of the chapter, we give a few common copying situations to evaluate. We consider one here.

Suppose Ricky Realtor uses software on a desktop computer at work, but sometimes works in the field or travels with a laptop. Is copying the software to the laptop a fair use, or must Ricky buy another copy? We cannot say for sure, because we do not know what arguments might be made in court and we do not know how the court would react to them. Here are some points to consider.

- The purpose of the copying is convenience. It would be legal to carry the desktop computer to another location, but that would be very inconvenient.
- The software would be in use on only one computer at a time. If necessary, Ricky could delete the program from the desktop machine each time it is copied to the laptop and later delete it from the laptop when it is copied back to the desktop machine. Thus there would be only one copy on any machine at one time. But repeatedly copying and deleting the program would be a purposeless waste of time.
- The purpose of the copy is not commercial in the sense that it would be sold. However, it is being used to accomplish a business purpose.
- The entire work is being copied.
- How much harm is done to the software publisher? Suppose Ricky had to choose between buying another copy, on the one hand, and repeatedly copying and deleting the program to ensure that there was only one copy on any machine at one time, on the other hand. Ricky might choose to copy and delete rather than pay. People who often switch back and forth between the laptop and the desktop might buy the extra copy.

Can you think of any additional arguments that the software company or Ricky would make? Do you think keeping a copy on the laptop is a fair use?

5.3   SOFTWARE COPYRIGHT: PIRACY, PROTECTION, REJECTION

5.3.1   What Is Software Piracy? What Does It Cost?

There are three main categories of software copyright infringement, colorfully called "software piracy" by software publishers:

- Some businesses produce and sell unauthorized copies of popular software packages.
- Many businesses, organizations, and schools buy one or a few copies of a software package and install it on dozens or hundreds of computers.
- People intentionally put copyrighted software on computers accessible by modem for others to download. Some computer bulletin board systems exist almost exclusively for this purpose.

Many of the issues about software piracy on BBSs are the same as for infringement of copyright of other kinds of work in cyberspace, so we will discuss the third problem in Section 5.4.

The Software Publishers Association (SPA) estimated that, in 1994, the value of business software produced by U.S. companies that was pirated worldwide was $8.08 billion.* Obviously, it is difficult to get accurate figures for illegal activities. To make its estimates, the SPA used survey data to determine the average number of software applications installed on each business computer. They used computer and software sales information to calculate the average number of applications purchased for each. The gap between the number purchased and the number installed is attributed to piracy. In several countries (e.g., Korea, Brazil, India, and Pakistan), the average number of legally purchased applications per computer is less than one, a strong indication of large-scale piracy. According to the SPA, the Chinese have bought more than one million computers, but in 1993 and 1994, they bought only $1 million of software legally. Figure 5.1 shows the SPA estimates of the software piracy rates in various countries. Although these figures cannot be precisely accurate, they show that the problem is significant.[14]

In the United States, there are on average 5.4 legal applications purchased per computer. The piracy percentage in the U.S. is lower than in most other countries, but the total amount of software used is high. The SPA estimates that $1.5 billion of software was pirated in the U.S. in 1993.[15]

Software theft has two social costs. One, it results in higher prices for legally sold copies of software because the number of copies from which the software seller gets any return is reduced. Shoplifting and other forms of theft have the same result: If they are widespread, honest customers suffer from higher prices because of the increased cost of security and the smaller number of people paying for the goods or services. It is in the best

---

*Some reports describe the $8.08 billion as "losses to software publishers" from piracy. It is impossible to accurately estimate how many people using pirated software would buy full-price legal copies if the pirated copies were not available. It is reasonable to say that many would not, so the loss to publishers is significantly smaller than the total value of pirated software.

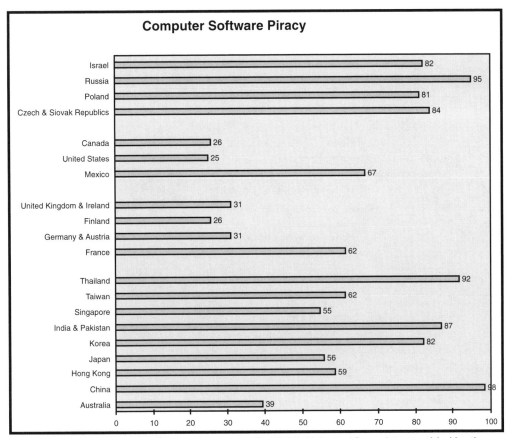

FIGURE 5.1: Estimated software piracy rates for 1994. (Adapted from data provided by the Software Publishers Association. Used with permission.)

interests of honest people to discourage theft. Two, widespread software theft ultimately leads to less development of good software because it reduces the return to software developers on their investment of time, creativity, and labor.

Copying for resale

Whole illegal businesses exist to produce, transport, and sell copies of the diskettes, documentation, and sometimes identical packaging for popular business and personal computer software. This form of software piracy is called counterfeiting. In some raids by law enforcement agencies, thousands of packages have been found. Raids in California and New Jersey in 1992 uncovered 150,000 unauthorized copies of Microsoft's MS-DOS operating system. A 1995 raid in Los Angeles yielded an estimated $1 million in software. The man arrested for counterfeiting in that case allegedly ran a mail-order business and advertised in trade publications. In China, more than two dozen factories allegedly produce millions of pirated compact disks (both software and music CDs), mostly for export to other countries (including the U.S.). In a 1996 raid, more than 5000 counterfeit Microsoft

CDs, with labels in Russian, were found in a Chinese factory with several production lines working day and night.[16]

Counterfeiters sell software for lower prices than legal copies, but they profit because they do not pay the designers, developers, programmers, managers, clerical staff, and so on, of the companies that developed the software. The difference between the legal and the pirate price can be extreme. In China, for example, one can buy a software package with a legal value of $6000 for just $105.[17]

Some businesses produce copies of software packages "to order." In some countries, one can walk into a store, request a particular program, and wait while the storekeeper goes into the back room to make a copy on a diskette. Hardware vendors sometimes load unauthorized copies of software onto a machine they are selling and charge the buyer a price far below the price of legal copies. Some software resellers sell unlicensed copies of expensive business packages to business customers. Sometimes the customer is unaware that the software is not legitimate.

Some countries traditionally do not recognize or protect intellectual property, including copyrights, patents, and trademarks, although most countries now are parties to international agreements to respect intellectual property and enforce laws to do so. Ignoring foreign copyrights has long been common practice in some countries, especially in Asia. I have on my bookshelf a copy of my *Computer Algorithms* textbook—in Chinese. It was produced in China without permission from (or payment to) the publisher or me. Counterfeiting of brand name products, from blue jeans to expensive watches, is also very common in Asia. Thus, software piracy is a variant of an old phenomenon.

Under pressure from the U.S. in 1991, China passed laws to protect intellectual property rights, and particularly rights for foreign works, but the laws were not enforced. Some of the copying of software was reportedly done in government factories. In 1995, with encouragement from the software and entertainment industries, the U.S. government again pressured the Chinese government to enforce copyrights. They urged the shutdown of factories producing pirated compact disks. The form of the pressure applied by the U.S. government was a threat of high tariffs on Chinese products. Unfortunately, in international negotiations, the offenders are not necessarily those who are threatened with punishment. In this case, legitimate Chinese businesses that produce export products, and American consumers who buy them, would be punished. The two governments signed a major agreement under which the Chinese would crack down on pirating of software, compact disks, and videotapes and train judges and government officials about intellectual property. It is not clear how effective the agreement will be. Only a few months after it was signed, Hong Kong officials reported that Chinese factories were turning out unauthorized copies of Microsoft's Windows 95 before its official release date. In 1996 the Chinese government took a number of significant steps toward reducing piracy. However, some involve controls that would be considered unacceptable threats to freedom of expression in the U.S., for example, prohibiting import of CD production equipment without government approval and requiring that all CDs produced be registered with the government.[18]

Why is software piracy (and other product piracy) more common outside the U.S.? We have already mentioned the general lack of a tradition of legal recognition and protection of intellectual property in some countries. There are other factors as well. Many countries with high piracy rates do not have a significant personal computer software industry.

Thus they do not have domestic programmers and software companies to lobby for protection of software. (The lack of a domestic software industry may be an effect, as well as a contributing cause; it is difficult for such an industry to develop when it cannot recover its investment in software development.) The fact that the victims of piracy are from another country, and a rich one, may make both the people and the governments less inclined to take action to reduce software theft. In the U.S., where in most cities there are legitimate software stores with aisles full of fancy boxed software, a customer is likely to know that back-room copying is illegal. In countries with few legitimate dealers and where it is not unusual to purchase food unpackaged in outdoor markets, customers may not think there is anything unusual (or wrong) about the way software is sold. Another possible reason for software piracy in other countries is that the people are poorer; they cannot afford the high legal price of software. However, although some countries with high piracy rates are poor, others, such as the Nordic countries, are not. Many individuals and businesses who buy pirated software would probably not steal clothes, food, or office furniture. Thus, although the economic savings are a factor, the cultural and political factors, and the lack of enforcement, are probably more important.

In-house copying by organizations

Employees of many businesses and organizations make unauthorized copies of software for large numbers of computers, and they allow an unauthorized number of users to share software on networks. This occurs at large newspaper companies, architectural firms, consulting firms, manufacturing companies, government agencies, and schools and universities. It happens in the U.S. and is very common in Asia, the Middle East, and Eastern Europe.

In some companies, employees and managers know copying is illegal, but management encourages or tolerates it to keep costs down. They see the chance of getting caught as small and are not concerned with the ethical issues.

Most U.S. information systems managers know that copying is illegal, but many believe that complying with legal requirements is difficult and unfair. They complain that licensing agreements are unclear and confusing. Software can be licensed for a machine, a user, a file server, or a whole site (to name a few options). Particularly on networks, there is confusion about how many users may use the software, or the restrictions may be difficult to enforce. Before personal computers became the norm, employees used terminals connected to mainframe computers; only one license was needed. Some businesses have been slow to adapt to the licensing structure for multiple machines. Some managers feel that requiring a license for each machine is unreasonable; although the software must be installed on each machine for perhaps a few hundred employees, a much smaller number is actually using the software at any one time.

Freebies for friends

Many people make copies of commercial software for friends who do not want to pay the price of buying one. Many people accept copies from friends. Sometimes they charge or pay a small fee. Although these activities, in most cases, are copyright infringement, the people involved are not likely to be caught or prosecuted. Thus the issue to deal with here is the ethical one. Should people do this? Would *you* do this?

Some of the arguments people make in support of personal copying include the following:

- They cannot afford to buy the software at the commercial price. The company is not really losing a sale. Besides, the company is a large corporation, and it would not be hurt by losing a few sales.
- This violation is insignificant compared to the billions of dollars lost to piracy by dishonest resellers making big profits.
- Everyone does it. You would be foolish not to.

Some arguments on the other side are

- Not being able to afford something is not an excuse for stealing it.
- One person making a copy would not cause a significant loss to the software company, but if the practice is widespread, software publishers and programmers do lose.
- Copyright infringement unfairly deprives programmers of income from their efforts. To the extent that software theft reduces the incentive to invest in software development, it also means less employment for programmers. (This argument may be particularly persuasive for students who are studying computer science and planning to become software developers.)

The weight and elaboration of these arguments may vary in different circumstances. We may find that in some cases, copying is ethically justified, whereas in others it is not. Helen Nissenbaum considers a scenario in which one character, Millie, wants to give a copy of a software package to a friend, Max, who cannot afford to buy one.[19] Nissenbaum considers several practical and ethical arguments. One of her arguments is that Millie has a countervailing claim against the programmer's right to prohibit making the copy: her "freedom to pursue the virtue of generosity." Although it is clear that it would be an act of generosity for Millie to buy a copy of the program for her friend, it is less clear whether copying the software is an act of generosity on Millie's part or an act that compels involuntary generosity from the programmer.

5.3.2 Protecting Software Copyrights

Overview

Software publishers and vendors have tried a number of approaches to reduce software copyright infringement. They include the following:

- Technical devices to prevent or deter copying.
- Enforcement and revision of copyright law.
- Education about the reasons for copyright protection and the social costs (higher prices and reduced innovation) of piracy.
- Marketing and contractual changes from software publishers that reduce the incentive to copy illegally.

Technical solutions

A variety of techniques for protecting software have been tried with varying success. For a while software publishers used "copy protection" on diskettes; tricks were used so that the diskette could not be copied or the copy could not run. Copy protection is no longer widely used, largely because consumers rejected it. Customers did not like the inconvenience of replacing a diskette if something went wrong. Some customers refused to buy copy-protected software if there were a nonprotected competitor. Hackers figured out how to thwart protection mechanisms. Some companies sold programs that deactivated the built-in copy protection on other programs. In an important case where a software vendor sued a company selling a program to thwart its copy protection, the court ruled that, because the program could be used for lawful purposes (e.g., enabling someone to make backup copies), it could be sold.[20]

A serial number encoded in software can be used to determine the original of an unauthorized copy (if the original copy is registered, more likely with large business software packages). Expiration dates are encoded in sample versions of software; the software can be programmed to destroy itself after that date. Some companies are developing digital "watermarks" using encryption to encode information about the ownership of digital works. The packages of some popular consumer software have holograms on them to distinguish them from look-alike counterfeits.

Performix Inc. developed a program used by major computer manufacturers to test performance of their systems. Performix discovered that an unauthorized copy of the program was being installed on its competitor's computers when the program automatically sent e-mail to Performix.[21] Some people find it objectionable that a program would secretly send e-mail to the software company when the program is installed. The publishing industry is considering similar techniques for protecting copyrights on other (nonsoftware) intellectual property. Privacy advocates are concerned that these techniques can be extended to search someone's computer and report on its contents—without a search warrant or the knowledge of the computer's owner.

Enforcement and education

Don't copy that floppy.

—The slogan on SPA advertisements

People ignore laws they consider unreasonable, especially if many others do so as well, if it is considered socially acceptable, and if the law is not enforced. (The 55-mph speed limit was one example.) Copying software used to be common practice. As one writer said, it was "once considered a standard and acceptable practice (if it were considered at all)."[22]

Since 1988 the Software Publishers Association (SPA) has been conducting both an educational and an enforcement campaign to reduce software theft. (See Figure 5.2.) The Business Software Alliance (BSA) has been engaged in similar activities, mostly in Europe. The SPA has a toll-free phone number that can be called with tips about illegal copying. Callers are usually current or former employees of the offending organizations—or competitors. They are motivated by ethical and legal concerns, by spite, and, in the case of

FIGURE 5.2: An advertisement from the Software Publishers Association.

competitors who pay for their software, by their dislike of unfair competition. In several countries (not including the U.S.), the BSA pays large rewards for tips leading to successful legal action against software pirates. Individual software companies, including Microsoft, have offered large rewards for information leading to the arrest and conviction of hackers who put the companies' programs on the Internet.[23]

The SPA responds to tips about business violators by sending warning letters and arranging to conduct voluntary audits of the organization's software. In some cases, they get a court order and conduct a surprise raid accompanied by law-enforcement officers. In most cases the violation of the law is so clear that the business or organization agrees to pay for the copied software and to pay fines rather than go to trial. An environmental and engineering firm paid a fine of $350,000, one of the highest. A junior college in Florida paid a fine of $135,000. In 1993, the SPA collected a total of $3.7 million in fines. The raids and fines are highly publicized to remind other businesses and organizations that software copyrights will be enforced.[24] The SPA's "software police" are active in cyberspace as well as in business offices. They regularly check bulletin boards for copyrighted software, and they provide information and evidence to the FBI.

The SPA's high-profile attack on software piracy has been criticized by some information service managers. A column in *PC Week* argues that "the idea of using embarrassment, negative publicity and CIA-like covert tactics to get end users and their employers to 'comply' with license agreements is petty, childish and counterproductive." A service bureau manager commented that "what the SPA does is like a mob shakedown."[25] Others accept the enforcement as legitimate. Whether fair or not, it appears to be working. An executive at a large publishing company says, "We are proactive in ensuring compliance, especially since SPA actively seeks out folks who aren't in compliance."[26] SPA reports that software copying by businesses is declining, especially in large companies, which are adopting policies and practices to assure compliance with copyright law and the license agreements they sign. Reasons for increased compliance among businesses include both a better understanding of the ethical issues involved and fear of fines and exposure in a social climate that is gradually coming to view copyright violation as not acceptable.

Markets and management

Solutions to some problems concerning licensing of software for businesses need cooperation, flexibility, and innovative contracting terms from software vendors. Publishers of scientific journals set subscription rates for libraries higher than for individuals because library copies will be used by more people. Software publishers can experiment with different pricing policies that may more accurately reflect the usage of a program. One tool that is beginning to be used for software on networks is metering. A business can pay for usage instead of for users, and the management of the software is automatic. Academic discounts are a good public relations and antitheft tool for educational users. Quantity discounts can reduce infringement in large businesses.

Employees (and software publishers) emphasize the importance of management setting a clear policy against in-house copying of software, and showing that they truly support it.

Free demo copies, provided by some software companies, remove some of the incentive for unauthorized copying by consumers. One company, Oracle Corp., allows potential customers to download software from the Internet for a free 90-day trial period. After the trial period, people are supposed to erase the program or pay for it. Oracle is relying on a combination of incentives for compliance: trust, reminders when the trial period expires (customers are asked for name and phone number), and fear of prosecution for violation of copyright law. Depending on how many people eventually pay, Oracle may build into the software passwords that expire at the end of the trial period. The president of another company that distributes software on the Internet commented, "You have to surrender your desire to make the immediate sale in the belief that it will yield a much bigger harvest. It's like a Zen thing."[27]

5.3.3   Abandon Software Copyright?

There are some people who do not believe that software should be copyrighted at all. Richard Stallman is one. Stallman developed GNU Emacs, a system including a sophisticated text editor and many UNIX-like utilities, that is freely available and very popular. To develop and distribute Emacs and to promote his ideas, Stallman founded the Free Software Foundation and the League for Programming Freedom. He advocates allowing unrestricted copying of programs and making the source code* of all software available to everyone. Under this copying policy, more people can use and benefit from the program, users and programmers can adapt and improve programs, and programmers can use existing programs to create new and better ones. Stallman compares software to a recipe; we can all decide to add a little garlic or take out some salt without paying a royalty to the person who developed it. Stallman argues that the primary purpose of copyright, as stated in the U.S. Constitution, is to promote progress in arts and sciences, not to compensate writers.[28]

How would software developers be paid if there were no restrictions on copying and distributing software? Stallman's Foundation is supported by contributions, some from computer manufacturers. A lot of software he distributes is developed by programmers who donate their work because they share his vision and enjoy doing what they do. Several of the first World Wide Web browser programs, including Netscape, were made available for free (by their authors) on the Internet. Stallman believes that many good programmers would work like artists for low pay because they are committed to their craft. Many companies now give away free software to encourage prospective customers to buy other software and services. However, it seems likely that only a small percentage of software will be produced as a charitable endeavor or be provided free by companies. Other ways of funding software, according to Stallman, might include government grants to universities.

Other writers have suggested explicitly that software be recognized as a "public good," like public schools and national defense, that anyone be allowed to copy it, and that the federal government subsidize it. The amount of the subsidy to software companies would be based on how many people use their software and how much the users think it is worth, with these amounts determined by surveys.[29]

---

*Source code is the human-readable form of a program. Commercial programs are normally distributed in object code, the code run by the computer, but not intelligible to people.

5.4 COPYRIGHT IN CYBERSPACE

5.4.1 Problems from New Technologies

The increasing use of electronic media and computer networks has created new problems for protection of literary, artistic, and musical works—as well as computer software. Some of the technological sources of the problems are the following:

- High-volume, relatively inexpensive digital storage media, such as hard disks and CD-ROMs.
- Storage of all sorts of information (text, sound, graphics) in standard digitized forms.
- Character scanners and photo scanners, which simplify converting printed text, photos, and artwork to electronic form.
- The ease of copying digitized material onto diskettes.
- The ease of distributing digitized material over computer networks.

Although photocopiers, by making copying of printed material easy, threatened copyright protection, they were not nearly as serious a threat as modern digital technology. A complete photocopy of a book is bulky, sometimes of lower print quality, awkward to read, and more expensive than a paperback. New computer, storage, and communications technologies have made copying extremely easy and cheap. And unlike other copying technologies, the copy of a digital file is indistinguishable from the original. Enforcement of copyright is becoming much more difficult; some say impossible. As more and more creative work, including novels, essays, and movies, are distributed digitally instead of in physical books, magazines, and tapes, there is potential that widespread copying will eliminate any reasonable return to authors and publishers. Solving this problem in a way that maintains a reasonable balance between the interests of publishers and the interests of the public will not be easy.

We will look first at the problem of software piracy in cyberspace, then at other copyright infringement problems.

5.4.2 Illegal Software Distribution in Cyberspace

Pirated software can show up in surprising places. Hackers broke into the National High Magnetic Field Laboratory at Florida State University and set up a hidden cache of copyrighted software. In one day about 200 people, most with overseas Internet addresses, logged on to download the programs. Someone broke into a restricted computer system at Lawrence Berkeley Laboratory and loaded thousands of dollars worth of stolen software. The locations and access methods for these secret depositories of software on legitimate systems are disclosed in online chat sessions for users who want to acquire the programs without paying for them. The software in these caches included word processors, spreadsheet programs, operating systems, utilities, and games—just about anything one might find in a large software store. Some, like Microsoft's Windows 95 and a new version of the game Doom, were pirated before they were available in stores.[30] Of course, it is difficult for law-enforcement agents and software publishers to find the illegal caches at legitimate sites and catch the people who set them up.

Computer bulletin board systems are another arena for software piracy. Most BBSs are legitimate forums for information exchanges of all sorts. On some BBSs, software called freeware or shareware is available from programmers who choose to make their work available for free or on a pay-as-you-will basis. There are no problems with this; the author, or copyright holder, is permitting other people to make copies. Some bulletin boards, on the other hand, are set up for the purpose of trading commercial, copyrighted software without the knowledge or permission of the copyright holders. On other BBSs, this is one of many activities, and it may occur without the knowledge of the operator.

In Massachusetts in 1994, Richard Kenadek became the first BBS operator to be indicted for criminal copyright infringement. Subscribers paid $99 a year to copy from approximately 200 commercial programs on his BBS, called Davy Jones Locker. The government claimed he received approximately $40,000. Kenadek pleaded guilty and was sentenced to six months of home confinement and two years' probation.[31]

David LaMacchia, an MIT student, was accused of running a bulletin board on a university computer on which, according to prosecutors, over a million dollars' worth of copyrighted software was distributed (during less than two months of operation). The indictment said that LaMacchia, using an alias, posted messages on the board asking for specific software. Users uploaded popular applications packages, for example, WordPerfect 6.0, and games. Programs were sent and retrieved through an anonymous remailer (i.e., a service that replaces return addresses with code names so that the senders and recipients of the software are not identified at the BBS). Mr. LaMacchia was not accused of copying or distributing software himself, and he did not charge anyone to use the bulletin board. To be guilty of criminal copyright infringement, a person must act "for purposes of commercial advantage or private financial gain." Thus LaMacchia was not charged under copyright law; he was indicted for committing wire fraud (fraud using the telephone).[32] The indictment against LaMacchia was dismissed because, for various reasons, the wire fraud laws did not apply. The judge's comments illustrate some of the problems of current software copyright law:

> What the government is seeking to do is to punish conduct that reasonable people might agree deserves the sanctions of the criminal law. . . .

> While the government's objective is a laudable one, particularly when the facts alleged in this case are considered, its interpretation of the wire fraud statute would serve to criminalize the conduct of not only persons like LaMacchia, but also the myriad of home computer users who succumb to the temptation to copy even a single software program for private use. It is not clear that making criminals of a large number of consumers of computer software is a result that even the software industry would consider desirable. . . .

> If the indictment is to be believed, one might at best describe his actions as heedlessly irresponsible, and at worst as nihilistic, self-indulgent, and lacking in any fundamental sense of values. Criminal as well as civil penalties should probably attach to willful, multiple infringements of copyrighted software even absent a commercial motive on the part of the infringer. One can envision ways that the copyright law

could be modified to permit such prosecution. But, "[i]t is the legislature, not the Court, which is to define a crime, and ordain its punishment."[33]

Issues

One question suggested by the LaMacchia case is: Should someone who sets up and operates a BBS for illegal purposes be considered criminally involved in the activities that occur on the BBS, even if he or she does not commit the illegal actions? The driver of a getaway car for a bank robbery is committing a crime, even if he or she does not enter the bank, carry a gun, or demand money from anyone. Is this an appropriate analogy? If a BBS operator is to be held legally liable for actions taken by subscribers, the law must be written to clearly and fairly distinguish three cases:

- The BBS operator knowingly and willfully operates the board for illegal purposes;
- The operator is aware of infringing material on the BBS but does nothing to eliminate or discourage it;
- The operator runs a large BBS for legitimate purposes, but some users or subscribers upload and trade copyrighted software.

The problem of liability of service providers (both operators of BBSs and operators of commercial services like CompuServe and America Online) for content posted by subscribers is complex and arises for control of pornography and other content that governments outlaw. We will return to this issue in this and other chapters.

A second question suggested by the LaMacchia case is: How relevant is the fact that LaMacchia did not charge users of the BBS, that he did not profit financially from it? Harvard law professor Lawrence Tribe warns that to avoid threats to open transmission of information in cyberspace, prosecutions should be avoided in cases that lack a profit motive.[34] In some contexts, a profit motive, or financial gain, is essential in determining if an activity is a crime. In other contexts, it is irrelevant. A profit motive is not a significant factor in determining where freedom of speech is to be protected; virtually all book and newspaper publishers are in business to make a profit, yet they have strong freedom of speech protection. Vandals do not profit financially from their action, but vandalism is a crime because it destroys—or reduces the value of—someone's property. When software is widely copied without permission, the software publisher loses potential revenue; the value of the software as an asset to the owner is diminished. However, there is an important point to Tribe's warning. Writing fair and workable laws regarding responsibilities of operators of small BBSs and large commercial online services like CompuServe for copyright infringement will be quite difficult. If the laws are too broad or too vague, operating a BBS will become legally risky. Some will shut down, and many will be more expensive. In Section 5.4.5 we will look at some problems with specific legislative proposals made by the federal government.

5.4.3   Literary and Artistic Material in Cyberspace

What (potentially) copyright-infringing material can we find in cyberspace? Just a few examples include columns by humorist Dave Barry, pictures of Winnie the Pooh and Walt Disney Co. characters, scenes from Disney movies, Playboy pinups, and a myriad of Star

Trek items. "Derivative works" include modified pictures showing Disney characters in "indiscreet" poses—not only a possible copyright infringement, but one that the company may find harmful to its image. Digital cable music companies provide subscribers with compact-disk quality music that can be recorded at home, threatening the income of recording artists and CD companies. The rapid growth in development of digital libraries, described in Section 1.3, means that copyright will be challenged for virtually all kinds of literary work.[35]

There are several aspects to the problem of distribution of intellectual property over computer networks. One is how to deal with the already widespread copyright infringement of traditional material. Another is how to develop new laws, rules, and/or guidelines for cyberspace. And another is how to manage distribution of material in a way that easily allows for payment of fees by honest users who are willing to pay. A number of technical, managerial, and legal solutions are being developed to address these problems. We will describe a few of them here and in the next section.

Publishers, movie studios, and other copyright owners have begun aggressively monitoring cyberspace. They obtain court orders to shut down BBSs, pressure operators of BBSs and information services to delete infringing files, and file civil suits. A large music-rights licensing company, for example, sued CompuServe because copyrighted songs were being distributed by subscribers. Playboy won a court order against a BBS operator who argued that he was unaware that subscribers on his system were posting digitized Playboy photos. The issue of how much liability the operators should have for infringing copyrights on literary and visual works is, of course, the same as the issue of liability for infringing software copyrights. We made the point in the discussion of software that designing fair and effective laws or rules for liability of operators is tricky. It is much easier for law enforcement to find and indict the system operator, or for publishers to sue the system operator, than it is to find the individuals who actually make the copies. Should the system operator be held responsible? Clearly, the size of the system and the percentage of its activity that is illegal are relevant criteria.

Some BBS operators are devising contracts for their subscribers in which the subscribers promise not to violate copyright (and other) laws. Operators hope that, along with occasional on-screen reminders and warnings, such contracts will give them some legal protection from prosecution for actions of subscribers. In addition, the explicit statements in the contracts "would raise the consciousness of a subscriber to know what the rules are," according to a vice president of Delphi.[36]

For people willing to pay copyright or other usage fees, some solutions devised by publishers for nonelectronic material may be extendible to cyberspace. Organizations representing copyright holders for music, journals, and magazines negotiate with users of such works to collect fees. For example, the American Society for Composers, Authors, and Publishers (ASCAP) and Broadcast Music, Inc. (BMI) collect about $600 million a year in fees for live performances and recordings of copyrighted songs played in commercial places. After photocopying machines, whose widespread use began in the 1960s, made copying books and magazines easier and led to increased copyright infringement, journal publishers formed the Copyright Clearance Center. The Center negotiates yearly fees with large companies whose employees frequently make copies of journal articles. There are now services that do the same for digitized photographs. These organizations make it feasible for the users of copyrighted material to pay reasonable fees without having to go to the large expense of finding the copyright holder for each item they wish to copy and negotiating with each one individually. The organizations distribute the collected fees to authors and publishers either in accordance with the number of times a particular author's work is used, or, where that is difficult to determine, by other formulas worked out by the organizations and members. Schemes for paying copyright fees for the use of creative work in online systems are being developed by various groups. The National Writers Union and UnCover, a large database of magazines and academic journals, established the Publication Rights Clearinghouse to provide for collection of license fees for freelance writers whose articles are distributed by UnCover. To settle the suit by a music-rights licensing company over copyrighted songs being distributed by subscribers, CompuServe agreed to establish a system through which content providers could electronically license rights to music. In some online licensing schemes, the same accounting system used for regular billing can process copyright fees.[37]

The New York Public Library and the Smithsonian Institution deliberately lower the image quality of the collections of photographs and paintings they put online so that the images can be used for research, but are not good enough for commercial uses.[38] It seems unlikely that this approach will last; customers will probably demand, through the market, high-quality images. Other methods we have mentioned will probably replace this one.

5.4.4   The Future of Copyright in Cyberspace

Copyright law will disintegrate.

–Nicholas Negroponte[39]

New technologies have been disrupting existing equilibria for centuries, yet balanced solutions have been found before.

–Pamela Samuelson[40]

There is currently much discussion among users and observers of the Net about whether copyright can survive the enormously increased ease of copying and the habits and expectations that have developed about access to and distribution of information. Opinions vary widely about what changes are needed in copyright law to address the new issues of intellectual property in cyberspace. Technical and managerial solutions are being developed to provide inexpensive and convenient ways to pay for use of copyrighted material, but will they be ignored? Or will they be enforced in such a way that severely restricts access?

Attorney Lance Rose argues that copyright will survive for several reasons. The "cops," including providers of software and literary and artistic work, are patrolling cyberspace, as we indicated. Large public BBSs and information services will police their own subscribers to avoid suits; they will, as Rose puts it, be "scared straight." Rose points out that illegal activities have extra costs that most people will not want to pay. If trading in unauthorized copies is kept "underground," most people will pay the legal price rather than make the effort to find an illicit BBS that supplies what they want, learn how to access it, make the extra effort to avoid detection, and risk prosecution for copyright infringement. Some copyright infringement will continue in cyberspace, but that does not matter. There are always some lawbreakers. The amount will be small enough to keep publishers in business, Rose argues.[41]

Esther Dyson, editor of *Release 1.0* (a newsletter that covers computer-related issues), takes a different point of view.[42] She says the ease of copying will win out over attempts to protect copyright. Most content, including software, will be free or almost free. Software producers will have to earn their income by providing support services, such as training, custom work, and upgrades—as movie companies earn millions of dollars from toys, tee-shirts, and other paraphernalia based on their movies. Some companies that give away software for free are already doing many of the things Dyson mentions. Writers and other creators of traditionally copyrighted work will have to develop appropriate services to offer for pay in conjunction with their works. It is not clear that this is a good change for all authors and publishers, many of whom may have expertise in authorship, but not in ancillary services. Movie makers still earn the majority of their income from the movie itself.

Problems with the focus on copying in copyright law

Restriction on copying has been the key element of copyright law for literary work and software, but the clause in the Constitution on which copyright is based makes no mention of "copies" or "copyright." The focus on the making of copies has always caused some seemingly odd distinctions, but in the past they have not been significant. Why, for example, is it okay to pass a magazine around among 12 friends so they can read a particular article, but of questionable legality to make 12 copies and mail them to friends who do not live nearby? Cyberspace provides new examples: Why is it okay for a college professor to clip out and post a newspaper or magazine article on the bulletin board outside her office for any member of the campus community to read, but of questionable legality to scan the article and post a copy of it on a computer bulletin board?[43]

A strict focus on copying as the infringing action could fundamentally change the effect of copyright law in cyberspace. For example, activities now permitted include browsing (e.g., reading part of a book in a bookstore) and lending, renting, and reselling a purchased copy of a copyrighted work. If we could not lend, rent, or resell a book to a friend, the friend might buy a copy, providing income to the publisher. But courts have established the principle that the publisher has the right only to the "first sale" of a copy. The buyer of the book may not make additional copies, but may transfer the purchased copy. Publishers, especially of textbooks, which are resold often, have lobbied for legislation requiring that a royalty be paid to the publisher on each resale. They have been unsuccessful. But browsing and transferring a copy on a computer network require the *making of another copy* of the digital work. Thus traditional privileges may be threatened.

If the spirit and purpose of copyright, and the traditional rights and privileges of both publishers and users of copyrighted material, are to be preserved in cyberspace, the rules, or their interpretation, will need changes. A federal government task force developed proposals for new copyright legislation for electronic media. They are very controversial. We will look at them next.

5.4.5 Proposed Legislation

The government's 1995 report, "Intellectual Property and the National Information Infrastructure," proposes a number of changes in copyright law and the precedents established by court decisions.[44] Its recommendations have been introduced as legislation in Congress. Creators and publishers of copyrighted works, including print publishers, Hollywood movie companies, and sound recording companies, support the proposals. On the other side, libraries, education groups, and other Net users who value the easy flow of information that is possible in cyberspace fear that the recommendations would drastically reduce access to information by the public. Information services, BBS operators, and privacy advocates are concerned about issues related to requirements for monitoring online service users (which we mention below). The debate and legislative battle will probably last several years.

The report recommends expansion of copyright protection in ways that explicitly and implicitly remove some rights the public have traditionally held, including virtually all fair use rights. It would extend copyright owners' control to all digital copies, including temporary copies in a computer's memory and copies necessary for transmission of files. Thus, free browsing and the "first sale" doctrine would be eliminated. It would change the law to interpret all digital transmission as transmissions to the public, thus infringing copyright.

The report puts the responsibility for enforcement of copyright law on the online services. It holds them legally liable for copyright infringement by subscribers and would require that the services report infringements to government authorities.

Ban technology?

The government's report recommends making it illegal to produce or provide any device or service to circumvent any copy-protection technique used by publishers to protect copyrighted material. This is an extreme measure. It would ban devices and techniques that have legitimate purposes without requiring proof that they were ever used to infringe a copyright. Publishers of music, movies, software, and so on, have made many attempts in the past to ban, restrict, or tax technology that could be used to infringe copyrights. Courts have held that machines and software that have legitimate, noninfringing uses should not be banned (e.g., the Sony case and the case about software to defeat copyprotection).

At issue is the principle of whether a technology or device should be banned or restricted because it has the potential for illegal use. We saw this issue before in Chapter 3, that is, in the FBI's and NSA's pressure for banning telephone technology that is difficult to tap and encryption schemes that are difficult for them to crack. The same fundamental issue has arisen in numerous issues unrelated to computing. It is behind arguments for banning sales of spray paint to minors (to reduce graffiti), guns, and drug paraphernalia. Those who reject the principle of banning a tool that has some legitimate uses and some illegal ones try to show its absurdity by taking it to its extreme: arguing that matches should be banned because they are used by arsonists. Others argue that each application of the principle should be considered individually, with consideration of the risks of harm. Proponents and lobbyists for bans on tools usually rank the damage they may cause (in general or to the interests of their clients) more highly than the loss of freedom and convenience to those who would use the tool honestly and productively.

5.5 ISSUES FOR SOFTWARE DEVELOPERS

There are several issues about copyright and patent that are of particular interest to software developers. Legal scholars and software industry commentators emphasize that clear rules are needed so that companies can do their work without the threat of changing law and unforeseen suits. Unfortunately, many of the issues are still unresolved.

5.5.1 Reverse Engineering

We saw that in the Sony case, the court ruled that noncommercial copying of an entire movie was fair use. In *Sega Enterprises, Ltd. vs. Accolade, Inc.,* decided by a federal appeals court in 1992, a *commercial* use that involved copying an entire program was ruled fair. Accolade made videogames to run on Sega machines. To make their games run properly, Accolade needed to figure out how part of Sega's game machine software worked. Accolade copied Sega's program and decompiled it (i.e., translated it from machine code to a form in which it could be read and understood). This is called "reverse engineering." Sega sued; Accolade won. Accolade was making new games. The court viewed Accolade's activities as fitting the purpose of fair use, that is, to encourage production of new creative work. The fact that Accolade was a commercial entity was not important. Although Accolade's games might reduce the market for Sega's games, that was fair competition; Accolade was not selling copies of Sega's games.[45]

In another 1992 case, *Atari Games vs. Nintendo,* the court also ruled that making copies of a program for reverse engineering (to learn how it works so that a company can make a compatible product) was not copyright infringement. It is a fair "research" use. Many software products are written to interact with other software (and hardware). These important decisions make it easier for such software to be developed.

In a slightly different case, a software service company copied a software vendor's program as part of its business of providing software maintenance service to customers of the software vendor. In this case, as in the ones above, the company that made the copy was not doing so to resell another company's software; it was providing service. Yet here the court ruled that they infringed the copyright.[46]

5.5.2 Similar Software Products

There are subtle problems of defining and identifying copyright violations when one software company's product resembles another's. If another work is similar, a determination must be made as to whether only ideas and functions were copied or whether the copyrighted expression of the ideas and functions was copied. This determination is difficult for literary works and even more difficult for software. Some principles about software copyright infringement are emerging from court cases filed by software developers against other software developers, but the boundaries of permissible uses are still not certain. The decisions of different federal appeals courts follow different guidelines; uncertainty will remain at least until the Supreme Court decides some key cases.

In a 1986 case, *Whelan Associates vs. Jaslow Dental Laboratory,* the court ruled that a program that was very similar to another in structure and performance, although written in a different programming language for a different computer, infringed the copyright on the first program.[47] The ruling treated programs something like novels and movies, which can infringe copyrights if they are too similar, even if they are not literal copies. That much is reasonable, and in a case where a program is simply translated to a new language for another computer system, it makes sense to treat it like an infringing translation of a book. A serious problem with the Whelan decision, though, is the court's interpretation of what the "idea" in a program is: the purpose of the program. Anything else in the program not essential to the purpose was copyrightable. This meant that a program that used well-known and widely used techniques and routines could be found to be infringing another program's copyright. The Whelan decision went too far.

A 1987 decision took an extreme position in the other direction. A court ruled in *Plains Cotton Co-op Association vs. Goodpasture Computer Service* that only literal copying of code was infringement. This is a far narrower protection than is given literary work. Any programmer knows that there is a lot of creative expression in the organization and structure of a program, as there is in the plot and characters in a novel, but if this ruling were interpreted for novels, it would mean that anyone else could use the plot and characters if they changed the words.

A reasonable interpretation of the boundaries for infringement lies somewhere between these two decisions. Such an in-between position is likely to be complicated, like the 1992 decision in *Computer Associates International vs. Altai.* The court specified a complex process for deciding whether a program infringed a copyright. A brief and simplified summary is: First, identify the purpose of the program, remove from consideration the parts that are in the public domain, are common practice, or are the only efficient way of accomplishing some part; they are not protected by copyright. Then compare the remaining parts of the two programs to see how similar they are. Any particular case would need expert witnesses and a complex analysis of the programs. Several subsequent court decisions have used this approach.

"Look and feel"

The term "look and feel" of a program refers to the user interface: the use of pull-down menus, windows, and icons, as well as the specific commands, menus, icons, and so on, that the user uses to select actions. Two programs that have a similar user interface are sometimes called "workalike" programs. The internal structure and programming may be entirely different. The new program may be faster or have other advantages. A big issue in software copyright is whether the look and feel of a program can be copyrighted; that is, does a workalike program infringe the copyright of the earlier program it resembles? Rulings by different courts have been inconsistent.

In the 1986 Whelan decision mentioned above, the court found that a user interface designed for the dental profession was copyrightable.[48] In the early 1990s, Lotus Development Corp., producer of the Lotus 1–2–3 spreadsheet program, won significant copyright infringement suits against Paperback Software International and Borland International Inc. for using its menus and commands. Borland deleted the infringing features from its Quattro Pro spreadsheet and faced a huge damages penalty, but the *Lotus vs. Borland* decision was reversed on appeal in 1995. In the meantime, Apple sued Microsoft and Hewlett-Packard for user interfaces that Apple claimed were too similar to its Macintosh window and icon interface. Apple lost. The Apple cases were complicated by other factors, so although many in the industry welcomed the decision, its implications for future cases was not entirely clear. In overturning the *Lotus vs. Borland* decision, the federal appeals court ruled that menu commands are "a method of operation," which is explicitly excluded from copyright protection. They are, the court said, like the controls of a car, or the buttons on a VCR.[49] Other analogies that have been offered by opponents of user interface copyright are the arrangement of the keys on a piano—or the keys on a typewriter or computer keyboard. Lotus appealed to the Supreme Court. A clear decision from the Supreme Court could have finally clarified the issue for the many software developers who were watching this case, but the Supreme Court deadlocked and let the appeals court ruling stand without setting any precedent. Software developers are expected to put increasing efforts into getting patents for software. Patents protect methods of operation, but they are more expensive and difficult to get. Many who oppose copyright of user interfaces also oppose patents for them.[50]

There are arguments on both sides of the look-and-feel protection debate. The main argument in favor of protecting a user interface is that it is a major creative effort. Thus, the usual arguments for copyright and patent apply: The programmers who create an interface should be protected so that they profit from their effort. Without protection, companies will be reluctant to make the large investment necessary to develop innovative new systems. On the other side, there are arguments about social benefits. Standard user interfaces increase productivity of users and programmers. We do not have to learn new interfaces for each program. Programmers do not have to "reinvent the wheel," that is, design a new interface just to be different; they can concentrate on developing the truly new aspects of their programs. Development costs for new programs can be reduced, keeping prices down. All these benefits, of course, are not eliminated by copyrighting or patenting a user interface. Companies that want to use a protected interface can sometimes negotiate an agreement and pay a royalty to the patent holders. Some industry observers, however, believe that copyright or patent protection for user interfaces would significantly slow development of new software and hurt small software companies.

EXERCISES

Review exercises

1. What is the main difference between copyright and patent?

2. What is one noncomputer technology that made copyright infringement easier than it had been before?

3. What is the maximum jail term for commercial software copyright infringement (a first offense)?

4. What are the four factors to be used in deciding if a use of copyrighted material is a fair use?

5. Summarize the main reasons why a court ruled that videotaping a movie from television to watch later was not an infringement of copyright.

6. Describe two technical means of protecting software copyrights. Describe two emerging methods for protecting copyright of literary and artistic material on the Net.

7. Describe two changes in copyright recommended by the government's report on "Intellectual Property and the National Information Infrastructure."

General exercises

8. A high school computer class is learning how to use a word processor. A student asks the teacher if he can make a copy of the word processor program to take home. The teacher says no. Write what the teacher could say to the student to explain her refusal. Include at least two reasons.

9. Which of the following activities do you think would be fair use? Give reasons using copyright law and/or court cases.
   (a) Making a copy of a friend's spreadsheet software to try out for two weeks, then either deleting it or buying your own copy.
   (b) Making a copy of a computer game, and playing it for two weeks, then deleting it.
   (c) Your printer is not working. You install your word processor on a friend's computer to use the friend's printer, then delete it when you are done.

10. Consider the legal cases in which the Church of Scientology is suing people for copyright infringement. The defendants posted church documents on the Internet in news groups and discussion groups where the doctrines and practices of the Church are discussed. Some of the documents are considered "secret" by the Church and are shown only to high ranking members, who pay fees to move up the ranks in the Church.
   (a) Give arguments for the defendants' case that the postings are acceptable under the fair use guidelines.
   (b) Give arguments for the Church's case that the postings are not fair use.
   (c) Now you're the judge. Give a decision and reasons for it.

11. Your uncle owns a sandwich shop. He asks you to write an inventory program for him. You are glad to help him and do not charge for the program. The program works pretty well, and you discover later that your uncle has given copies to several friends who also operate small food shops. Do you believe your uncle should have asked your permission to give away your program? Do you believe you should have been paid for the copies?

12. You are a teacher. You would like your students to use a software package, but the school's budget does not include enough money to buy copies for all the students. Your school is in a poor neighborhood, and you know most of the parents cannot afford to buy the software for their children.
   (a) List some ways you could try to obtain the software without making unauthorized copies.
   (b) Suppose none of the methods you try work. Will you copy the software or decide not to use it? Give some arguments for and against your position. Explain why you think the arguments on your side are stronger.[51]

13. Suppose a software publisher files a copyright infringement suit against a company that allowed a dozen employees to make copies of a database program for their home computers. The copies are for personal use; the employees do not work at home. The company's attorneys argue that the copying is fair use.
   (a) Using the fair use guidelines and discussion of cases in the text, present the software publisher's case against fair use.
   (b) Present the defense arguments for the company.

14. Think up and describe a situation, other than those in the exercises above, where there is a question about whether copying a computer program is a fair use.

15. When the Sony case was decided, there was not a big business in rental and sale of movies on videocassettes. Do you think a court would or should rule differently now on whether taping a movie from television is fair use, considering that doing so may diminish the market for movie rentals? Give reasons.

16. Suppose you are a system manager for a university computer. You discover that someone has set up a directory on the system containing copyrighted software and that many people are logging in and downloading copies. List some options for your action. Give pros and cons of each. Which would you do?

17. Suppose you learn of a BBS on which new commercial software is available to be downloaded for free (without authorization from the software publishers). Do you feel tempted to log on to the BBS, see what is available, and possibly download something? Or do you feel tempted to report the BBS to the software publishers? Why?

18. Try to write a law that tells when a BBS operator is guilty of copyright infringement for copyrighted software traded on the system. What are some potential difficulties in interpretation or enforcement of your law?

19. Just as software itself was a new form of intellectual property requiring new thinking about copyright and patent, other new forms of intellectual works are created in electronic media. What copyright or patent protection, if any, do you think the following should have?[52]

   (a) The collection of links for a hypertext application (which is itself a creative work, independent of the perhaps copyrighted documents and images it links).

   (b) Virtual realities?

20. Suppose the "public good" solution to creating software without copyright protection, described in Section 5.3.3 were adopted. How do you think it would affect the quantity and quality of software that would be produced? Give reasons, perhaps including analogies with other federally subsidized goods and services.

21. Which of the actions mentioned in the first paragraph of this chapter are illegal? Why? If there is not enough information given, explain what your answer would depend on.

22. Describe one kind of software or technique used in software that you think is innovative, like an invention, for which patent protection might be appropriate.

Assignments

These exercises require some research or activity that may need to be done during business hours or a few days before the assignment is due.

23. Get a copy of a license agreement for a software package. It could be a spreadsheet, word processor, game, operating system, utility, and so on. Use a package you bought for your own computer at home, or go to any store that sells software and look at one.

   (a) What does the license agreement say about the number of copies that can be made?

   (b) Does it specify penalties for making unauthorized copies?

   (c) Was the agreement on the outside of the package where it is visible to the customer before buying it?

   (d) Do you consider the license agreement to be clearly stated? Reasonable?

24. Read the articles by Esther Dyson and Lance Rose from *Wired* (listed in the references below). Write a short essay telling which author's views about the future of intellectual property in the "digital age" are more convincing to you and why.

Class exercises

1. Hold a debate in class about whether software should be copyrightable or freely available for copying.

2. Assign a group of students to prepare the arguments for the software publisher's case against fair use in Exercise 13 and another group to prepare the defense arguments. Each team presents its arguments in class. Then the remainder of the class acts as a panel of judges, discusses the merits of the arguments, and votes on a ruling.

NOTES

1 The philosophical issue of the nature of the "intangible book" is addressed in Jorge J.E. Garcia, "Textual Identity," *Sorites,* July 1995, pp. 57–75.

2 G. Pascal Zachary, "Patent Commissioner Outlines Steps to Help Avoid Disputes over Software," *Wall Street Journal,* April 11, 1994, p. B6. Diane Wilkins Savage, "Protecting Intellectual Property," *The Red Herring,* March 1995, pp. 125–26.

3 Savage, "Protecting Intellectual Property." Jim Carlton, "Jury Returns $208.2 Million Judgment Against Nintendo in Patent Dispute," *Wall Street Journal,* August 2, 1994, p. B10.

4 Several sources were used for the history in this section. National Research Council, *Intellectual Property Issues in Software,* National Academy Press, 1991. Neil Boorstyn and Martin C. Fliesler, "Copyrights, Computers, and Confusion," *California State Bar Journal,* April 1981, pp. 148–52. Judge Richard Stearns, *United States of America vs. David LaMacchia,* 1994. Robert A. Spanner, "Copyright Infringement Goes Big Time," *Microtimes,* March 8, 1993, p. 36.

5 The piano roll case is *White-Smith Publishing Co. vs. Apollo,* reported in Boorstyn and Fliesler, "Copyrights, Computers, and Confusion."

6 *Data Cash Systems vs. JS & A Group,* reported in Neil Boorstyn and Martin C. Fliesler, "Copyrights, Computers, and Confusion."

7 For a summary of copyright protection in other countries, see Derrick Grover, *The Protection of Computer Software—Its Technology and Applications,* second edition, British Computer Society Monographs in Informatics, Cambridge University Press, 1992, pp. 264–270.

8 Criminal penalties for copyright infringement are in Title 18 of the U.S. Code.

9 U.S. Code Title 17, Section 117.

10 Pamela Samuelson, "Computer Programs and Copyright's Fair Use Doctrine," *Communications of the ACM,* September 1993, 36:9, pp. 19–25.

11 U.S. Code Title 17, Section 107.

12 *Sony Corporation of America vs. Universal City Studios, Inc.,* 1984. Pamela Samuelson, "Computer Programs and Copyright's Fair Use Doctrine," *Communications of the ACM,* September 1993, 36:9, pp. 19–25.

13 "Award Is Weighed in Case Involving Church, Internet," *Wall Street Journal,* January 22, 1996, p. B6. David G. Post, "New World War," *Reason,* April 1996, pp. 28–33. *EFFector Online,* October 7, 1995, 8:16.

14 Software Publishers Association, "PC Software Industry Lost $8.08 Billion To Pirates In 1994" (news release), February 24, 1995. Software Publishers Association, "SPA Report on Global Software Piracy." Jeffrey A. Trachtenberg et al, "Software Companies, Entertainment Firms Welcome Agreement," *Wall Street Journal,* February 27, 1995, p. A3.

15 Software Publishers Association, "SPA Report on Global Software Piracy."

16 "Software-Piracy Case in Los Angeles Leads to Felony Charges," *Wall Street Journal,* November 15, 1995, p. B11. Kathy Chen, "U.S., China Resume Negotiations In Effort to Avert a Trade War," *Wall Street Journal,* February 16, 1995, p. A12. Russell Watson et al, "A Little Fight Music," *Newsweek,* February 13, 1995, pp. 38–39. Estimates of the number of counterfeit CDs produced in China were in the range of 45–75 million per year in the mid-1990s. Kathy Chen, "China Is Faulted By U.S. Group On Piracy Pact," *Wall Street Journal,* October 13, 1995, p. A6. Craig S. Smith, "Microsoft Finds Pirated Software in Raid in China," *Wall Street Journal,* May 1, 1996, p. A13.

17 Russell Watson et al, "A Little Fight Music," *Newsweek,* February 13, 1995, pp. 38–39.

18 Watson et al, "A Little Fight Music." Helene Cooper and Kathy Chen, "China Averts Trade War with the U.S., Promising a Campaign Against Piracy," *Wall Street Journal,* February 27, 1995, p. A3. R. W. Bradford pointed out the unfairness of the tactic used to pressure the Chinese to enforce copyright in "Whose Ox is Xeroxed," *Liberty,* May 1995, 8:5, pp. 8–9. "Asides," *Wall Street Journal,* August 25, 1995, p. A8. (This article reported that an estimated 50,000 pirated copies of Windows 95 were available in the Netherlands and Belgium before the official release date.) Kathy Chen and Helene Cooper, "U.S. and China Reach an Agreement, Averting Trade Sanctions by Both Sides," *Wall Street Journal,* June 18, 1996, pp. A2, A6. William P. Alford, "A Piracy Deal Doesn't Make a China Policy," *Wall Street Journal,* July 17, 1996, p. A14.

19 Helen Nissenbaum, "Should I Copy My Neighbor's Software?" in Deborah G. Johnson and Helen Nissenbaum, *Computers, Ethics & Social Values,* Prentice Hall, 1995, pp. 201–213.

20 Pamela Samuelson, "The Copyright Grab," *Wired,* January 1996, pp. 134–138, 188–191. The companies were Vault and Quaid.

21 Glenn R. Simpson, "A '90s Espionage Tale Stars Software Rivals, E-Mail Spy," *Wall Street Journal,* October 25, 1995, pp. B1, B5.

22 Laura Didio, "Crackdown on Software Bootleggers Hits Home," *LAN Times,* November 1, 1993, 10:22.

23 Robina Gibb, "Bounty to Trap Software Pirates," *The Sunday Telegraph,* October 9, 1994, p. 1. Jared Sandberg, "Pirated Copies of the Latest Software From IBM, Others Posted on the Internet," *Wall Street Journal,* October 31, 1994, p. B6.

24 Software Publishers Association, "Settlement Announced In Copyright Infringement Case," (news release), May 16, 1996. Jonathan Groner, "Swatting Back at Software Pirates," *Legal Times,* May 18, 1992, p. 7.

25 Aaron Goldberg, "Let's Say 'Bye-bye' to the SPA," *PC Week,* January 18, 1993, 10:2, p. 126. Mitzi Waltz, "Making Piracy a Management Issue," *MacWeek,* June 22, 1992, 6:24, p. 10.

26 Karl Peterson of McGraw-Hill, quoted in Didio, "Crackdown on Software Bootleggers Hits Home."

27 Joan E. Rigdon, "A Trusting Oracle to Enter Market Via Internet," *Wall Street Journal,* January 4, 1995, p. B1. The quote is from Bill Larson, president of McAfee Associates, an antivirus software company.

28 Richard Stallman, "Why Software Should Be Free," Free Software Foundation, Inc.

29 Barbara R. Bergmann and Mary W. Gray, "Viewpoint: Software As a Public Good," *Communications of the ACM,* October 1993, 36:10, pp. 13–14.

30 Jared Sandberg, "Pirated Copies of the Latest Software From IBM, Others Posted on the Internet," *Wall Street Journal,* October 31, 1994, p. B6. "Netwatch," *Time,* July 25, 1994, p. 18.

31 "Bulletin-Board Owner Sentenced for Selling Illegal Software Copies," *Wall Street Journal,* March 13, 1995, p. B7. "Software Publishers Association Copyright Protection Fund," SPA, July

1994. Junda Woo, "Copyright Laws Enter the Fight Against Electronic Bulletin Board," *Wall Street Journal,* September 27, 1994, p. B10. Telephone interview with SPA staff.

32 William M. Bulkeley, "Two Face Computer-Fraud Allegations over Software Piracy on the Internet," *Wall Street Journal,* April 11, 1994, p. B6.

33 Judge Richard Stearns, *United States of America vs. David LaMacchia,* Memorandum of Decision and Order on Defendant's Motion to Dismiss, December 28, 1994.

34 Reported in Bulkeley, "Two Face Computer-Fraud Allegations Over Software Piracy on the Internet."

35 Junda Woo and Jared Sandberg, "Copyright Law in Sprawling Cyberspace Is Easy to Break," *Wall Street Journal,* October 10, 1994, p. B6.

36 Jan F. Constantine, quoted in Woo and Sandberg, "Copyright Law in Sprawling Cyberspace Is Easy to Break."

37 Junda Woo, "Case Reveals Flaws in Royalty System," *Wall Street Journal,* January 3, 1995, p. 18. "Publication Rights Clearinghouse," news release from the National Writers Union, December 27, 1995.

38 Edwin Wilson, "Authors' Rights in the Superhighway Era," *Wall Street Journal,* January 25, 1994, p. A16.

39 Nicholas Negroponte, "Being Digital," *Wired,* February 1995, p. 182.

40 Pamela Samuelson, "Copyright and Digital Libraries," *Communications of the ACM,* April 1995, 38:3, pp. 15–21, 110.

41 Lance Rose, "The Emperor's Clothes Still Fit Just Fine," *Wired,* February 1995, pp. 103–6.

42 Esther Dyson, "Intellectual Value," *Wired,* July 1995, pp. 136–41, 182–84. Excerpted from *Release 1.0,* December 1994.

43 These examples were suggested by Carol H. Sanders, who made a number of helpful suggestions for this chapter.

44 The report was drafted by the Intellectual Property Working Group, part of the Clinton administration's NII task force. Pamela Samuelson, "The Copyright Grab," *Wired,* January 1996, pp. 134–38, 188–91. George Leopold, "Copyright Bill Comes Under Fire," *EE Times,* November 27, 1995, pp. 1, 8.

45 "9th Circuit Allows Disassembly in *Sega vs. Accolade,*" *Computer Law Strategist,* November 1992, 9:7, pp. 1, 3–5. "Can You Infringe a Copyright While Analyzing a Competitor's Program?" *Legal Bytes,* George, Donaldson & Ford, L.L.P., publisher, Winter 1992–93, 1:1, p. 3. Pamela Samuelson, "Copyright's Fair Use Doctrine and Digital Data," *Communications of the ACM,* January 1994, 37:1, pp. 21–27.

46 *Southeastern Express Co. vs. Triad Systems Corp.,* reported in "Software Copyrights," *Wall Street Journal,* February 27, 1996, p. A2.

47 The source for information about the cases in this section is "When Is a Computer Program a Copy?" *Legal Bytes,* George, Donaldson & Ford, L.L.P., Winter 1992–93, 1:1, pp. 1,2,4.

48 Anne Wells Branscomb, *Who Owns Information?,* Basic Books, 1994, p. 147.

49 William M. Bulkeley, "Borland Wins Appeal Against Lotus over Bid to Copyright Software Menu," *Wall Street Journal,* March 10, 1995, pp. A3, A16.

50 See, for example, "Against User Interface Copyright" and "Against Software Patents," distributed by the League for Programming Freedom.

51 This exercise was sparked by a brief note in Helen Nissenbaum, "Should I Copy My Neighbor's Software?" in Deborah G. Johnson and Helen Nissenbaum, *Computers, Ethics & Social Values,* Prentice Hall, 1995, p 213.

52 The idea for this exercise comes from Samuelson, "Copyright's Fair Use Doctrine and Digital Data" (re collections of hypertext links) and Jack Russo and Michael Risch, "Copyright Protection For Virtual Realities," *Computer Law Strategist,* October 1992, pp. 1, 3, 4, and November 1992, pp. 2–3.

FOR FURTHER READING

Several articles listed here are from Wired. Wired *articles are available on the World Wire Web at* wired.com.

John Perry Barlow, "The Economy of Ideas: A Framework for Rethinking Patents and Copyrights in the Digital Age," *Wired,* March 1994, pp. 84–90, 126–29.

Anne Wells Branscomb, *Who Owns Information?,* Chapter 8: Who Owns Computer Software?, Basic Books, 1994.

G. Gervaise Davis III, *Software Protection,* Van Nostrand Reinhold, 1985.

Randall Davis, Pamela Samuelson, Mitchell Kapor, and Jerome Reichman, "A New View of Intellectual Property Rights," *Communications of the ACM,* March 1996, 39:3, pp. 21–30.

Peter J. Denning and Bernard Rous, "The ACM Electronic Publishing Plan," "ACM Interim Copyright Policies," and "Author's Guide to ACM Interim Copyright Policies," *Communications of the ACM,* April 1995, 38:4, pp. 97–109. A discussion of problems and issues raised by electronic publishing of research articles and a sample of electronic publishing policies.

Esther Dyson, "Intellectual Value," *Wired,* July 1995, pp. 136–41, 182–85.

Derrick Grover, *The Protection of Computer Software—Its Technology and Applications,* second edition, British Computer Society Monographs in Informatics, Cambridge University Press, 1992.

L. R. Patterson, *Copyright In Historical Perspective,* Vanderbilt University Press, 1968.

David G. Post, "New World War," *Reason,* April 1996, pp. 28–33. Covers the Church of Scientology cases and aspects of the Internet that affect the flow of information and protection of intellectual property.

Lance Rose, "The Emperor's Clothes Still Fit Just Fine," *Wired,* February 1995, pp. 103–6.

Pamela Samuelson, "Computer Programs and Copyright's Fair Use Doctrine," *Communications of the ACM,* September 1993, 36:9, pp. 19–25.

Pamela Samuelson, "Copyright and Digital Libraries," *Communications of the ACM,* April 1995, 38:3, pp. 15–21, 110.

Pamela Samuelson, "The Copyright Grab," *Wired,* January 1996, pp. 134–38, 188–91. Describes the provisions of the NII task force report "Intellectual Property and the National Information Infrastructure."

6

CONSTITUTIONAL (AND RELATED) ISSUES

6.1   CHANGING COMMUNICATIONS PARADIGMS

Congress shall make no law . . . abridging the freedom of speech, or of the press. . . .

–First Amendment, U.S. Constitution

The right of the people to be secure in their persons, houses, papers, and effects, against unreasonable searches and seizures, shall not be violated, and no Warrants shall issue, but upon probable cause, supported by Oath or affirmation, and particularly describing the place to be searched, and the persons or things to be seized.

–Fourth Amendment, U.S. Constitution

In this chapter we consider how the protections of the First and Fourth Amendments to the U.S. Constitution will affect, and will be affected by, computer systems and telecommunications networks. We will describe various incidents and cases (involving pornography and hackers, among others) and discuss issues they raise. We will examine arguments in the debate about censorship of the Internet.

In this section we introduce the traditional three-part framework for regulation and First Amendment protection of communications media. As we will see, this framework does not fit the Net.

Regulatory paradigms

It by now almost a cliché to say that the Internet lets us all be publishers. We do not need expensive printing presses or complex distribution systems. We need only a computer and a modem. Any business, organization, or individual can send comments to newsgroups and bulletin boards or set up a home page on the World Wide Web. We can "publish" whatever we wish; it is available to be read by anyone who chooses. The dramatic change brought about by computer communications is described by Mike Godwin, an attorney with the Electronic Frontier Foundation, as follows:

It is a medium far different from the telephone, which is only a one-to-one medium, ill-suited for reaching large numbers of people. It is a medium far different from the newspaper or TV station, which are one-to-many media, ill-suited for feedback from the audience. For the first time in history, we have a many-to-many medium, in which you don't have to be rich to have access, and in which you don't have to win the approval of an editor or publisher to speak your mind. Usenet and the Internet, as part of this new medium, hold the promise of guaranteeing, for the first time in history, that the First Amendment's protection of freedom of the press means as much to each individual as it does to Time Warner, or to Gannett, or to the *New York Times*.[1]

The new computer communications technologies *may* guarantee freedom of the press for all of us, but the guarantee is far from certain. Telephone, radio, television, cable, satellites, and, of course, computer networks did not exist when the Constitution was written. Freedom of the press applied to publishers who printed newspapers and books and to "the lonely pamphleteer" who printed and distributed pamphlets expressing unconventional ideas. One might think the First Amendment should be interpreted for each new communications technology according to its spirit and intention: to protect our freedom to say what we wish. The government, however, regularly tries to restrict freedom of speech and the press for new technologies that were not explicitly mentioned in the Constitution. Historically, communications technologies have been divided into three categories with respect to the degree of First Amendment protection and government regulation:

- Print media (newspapers, books, magazines, pamphlets)
- Broadcast (television, radio)
- Common carriers (telephone, telegraph, and the postal system)

The first category has the strongest First Amendment protection. Although books have been banned in the U.S. and people were arrested for publishing information on certain topics, such as contraception, the trend has been toward fewer government restraints on the printed word.

Although television and radio are similar to newspapers in their role of providing news and entertainment, both the structure of the broadcasting industry and the content have been highly regulated. Broadcasting licensees are selected by the government and must meet government standards of merit, a requirement that would not be tolerated for publishers because of the obvious threat to freedom of expression. The government has used threats of license revocation to get stations to cancel sexually oriented talk shows or to censor them. Cigarette ads are legal in magazines, but they are banned from radio, television, and all electronic media under the control of the Federal Communications Commission. There are words that may be used in print but may not be said on the radio. There are frequent threats from the federal government of requirements to reduce violence on television or increase programming for children, but the government cannot impose such requirements on publishers. Whether you favor or oppose any of these particular regulations, the point is that the government has more control of TV and radio content than it has over communication methods that existed at the time the Bill of Rights was written. The main argument used to deny full First Amendment treatment to broadcasters was scarcity of broadcast frequencies, that is, that broadcasters had a monopoly. With cable, satellites, and promises of hundreds of channels, the monopoly argument is irrelevant now, but the precedent of government control remains. The argument now used to justify government-imposed restrictions on content is that broadcast material comes into the home and is difficult to keep from children.

Common carriers provide a medium of communication (not content), and must make their service available to everyone. In some cases, as with telephone service, they are required to provide "universal access" (i.e., to subsidize service for people with low incomes). On the argument that they are a monopoly, common carriers have been prohibited from controlling the content of material that passes through their system. Telephone companies have been prohibited from providing content or information services on the grounds that they might discriminate against competing content providers who must also use their telephone lines. Because common carriers have no control over content, they have no responsibility for it.*

The Internet, the Web, computer bulletin board systems, and commercial online information services have become major arenas for distribution of news, information, and opinion. It is not yet clear how constitutional protections will be applied to the Net. One reason is simply that it is new, and various political forces are fighting over the issue of control versus freedom. There are always people who want to restrict or prevent the distribution of certain kinds of information; each new communications technology provides a new battleground for battles that have been fought before. Another reason is the immense flexibility of computer communications systems. They do not fit neatly into the publishing, broadcasting, and common carriage paradigms. Cable television strained these categories previously. In commenting on a law requiring cable stations to carry certain broadcasts, the Supreme Court said cable operators have more free-speech rights than television and radio broadcasters, but less than print publishers.[2] But the Net does not fit between the existing categories any better than it fits within them. It has similarities to all three, and, in addition, to bookstores, libraries, and rented meeting rooms—which are all treated differently in law.

As we proceed with our discussion of First Amendment issues, it is helpful to remember two important points. First, the First Amendment was written precisely for offensive and/or controversial speech and ideas; it would not be needed to protect speech and publication that no one objected to. Second, the First Amendment is a restriction on the power of government, not individuals or private businesses. Although some laws and court decisions take the opposite position, it would seem that for individuals and organizations, freedom of speech inherently includes freedom not to promote ideas they do not agree with.[3] We also have property rights, that is, rights to use our property as we choose. Publishers are not required to publish material they consider offensive, poorly written, or unlikely to appeal to their customers for any reason. Rejection or editing by a publisher is not a violation of a writer's First Amendment rights.

The issues in this chapter have far-reaching implications for freedom. As Ithiel de Sola Pool wrote, in his important book *Technologies of Freedom,*

> Networked computers will be the printing presses of the twenty-first century. If they are not free of public [i.e., government] control, the continued application of constitutional immunities to nonelectronic mechanical presses, lecture halls, and man-carried sheets of paper may become no more than a quaint archaism.

> The onus is on us to determine whether free societies in the twenty-first century will conduct electronic communication under the conditions of freedom established for the domain of print through centuries of struggle, or whether that great achievement will become lost in a confusion about new technologies.[4]

---

*As new technologies blur the technical boundaries between cable, telephone, computer networks, and content providers, the law is adapting. The Telecommunications Act of 1996 changed the regulatory structure. It removes many artificial legal divisions of service areas and restrictions on services that may be provided by telecommunications companies.

6.2   OFFENSIVE SPEECH IN CYBERSPACE

> *I disapprove of what you say, but I will defend to the death your right to say it.*
> –Voltaire's biographer, describing his view of freedom of speech[5]

What is offensive speech? What should be prohibited or restricted by law on the Net? It depends on who you are. It could be political or religious speech, pornography,* sexual or racial slurs, libelous statements, advertising, depictions of violence, or information about how to build bombs. There are vehement advocates for banning each of these—and more. The state of Georgia tried to ban pictures of marijuana from the Internet.[6] A doctor argued for regulating medical discussion on the Net so that people would not get bad advice.

The first reaction of many people to something they do not like is "Ban it!" Many of the targets of new controls for the Net are legal in other media; the proposed new bans would impose stricter censorship on the Net than elsewhere. Other targets, such as child pornography and libel, are already illegal, whether on the Net or not. They may proliferate more easily and anonymously on the Net, so there are new problems and issues of enforcement and liability.

We will discuss a sampling of these topics and controversies, with emphasis on pornography and attempts to censor the Net. Issues and arguments that arise in the pornography/censorship debate are applicable to other areas of offensive information on the Net.

6.2.1   Libel

Under libel law, a person can be sued for damages for saying something in print, or in other media like television, about another person, business, or organization that is false and defamatory, that is, that tends to be damaging to the victim's reputation. Libel is not generally considered a free speech issue.† However, in cyberspace some of the issues about libel (and copyright infringement) are similar to issues about the various other types of offensive speech mentioned at the beginning of Section 6.2. Thus we discuss libel briefly here.

As we observed at the beginning of this chapter, we can all be publishers now. The quotation from Mike Godwin ends by saying that freedom of the press will mean as much to each individual as it does to the *New York Times*. The *New York Times* can be sued for libel—and so can we. Thus the increased power to disseminate our ideas in cyberspace comes with the cost of increased responsibility. If one accepts the validity of libel laws, then applying them to libel on the Net is a natural extension. Under libel law, however, it is not only the person who made the defamatory statement who can be sued. A newspaper or

---

*The distinctions between erotica, pornography, obscenity, and so on, are not clear, and I will not make an attempt here to define them. Some are illegal; some are not. For simplicity, I will often use the word "pornography" to include them all.

†There are some who claim that even libel is protected by the First Amendment, but this view is not widely held, nor is it supported by law or the courts.

television station that prints or broadcasts the statement can be sued also. On the other hand, libraries and bookstores are immune from libel suits, on the theory that they do not (and cannot) read every book they carry to check for defamatory statements.

It is not yet clear whether operators of computer bulletin board systems (BBSs) and online service providers will be treated like publishers or bookstores with respect to libel. Until a 1995 court decision allowing a libel suit against Prodigy for a subscriber's posting, it seemed that in the area of libel, the large online services would be treated like bookstores and libraries. A federal court had used the bookstore/library analogy in dismissing an earlier libel suit against CompuServe.[7] Even if the Prodigy decision is reversed, it is unclear whether small BBSs will receive the same protection as large commercial services. The issue of service provider liability for content posted by subscribers arose in Section 5.4.2 with respect to copyright. We see it here with respect to libel, and we will see it again with respect to pornography. We discuss it in Section 6.2.4.

6.2.2   Pornography and Censorship

There is pornography on the Internet. There are numerous BBSs and Internet sites from which users can download sexually explicit images. A Usenet newsgroup containing erotic pictures is the ninth most widely accessed of the many thousands of groups available.[8] There are discussion groups where people discuss sexual activity, of conventional and unconventional sorts, including pedophilia, in graphic detail.

Is this a problem, and if so, how serious is it? Newspapers and magazines have carried many stories about pornography on the net. *Time* magazine ran a dramatic cover story on "Cyberporn" reporting on what it described as an exhaustive study of online porn. The study found more than 900,000 sexually explicit pictures, short stories, and film clips online. Scholars immediately excoriated the study for methodological and ethical problems. Internet users attacked it and *Time* for grossly exaggerating the problems of porn on the Internet and its accessibility by children. Nine hundred thousand files may sound like a lot to someone unfamiliar with the Internet, but it is a very small fraction (estimated in the article at about one-third of one percent) of the files available. The researchers found no material that is not already available in adult magazines and bookstores. Much of the sexually explicit material is on private adult bulletin board services to which one must pay a subscription fee and provide proof of age. There is, however, a lot available on free newsgroups that many parents would not want their children to see.

Discussion of sexual activity, even unusual or illegal sexual activity, is usually not illegal; it is protected by the First Amendment. Distribution of obscene material is sometimes illegal. (We describe the legal guidelines below.) Some people are shocked that pornography is common in cyberspace, especially on the Internet, which began as a forum for research and scientific discussion. It is not, however, a surprising development. As a writer for *Wired* contends, sexual material quickly invades all new technologies and art forms.[9] He points out that from cave paintings to frescos in Pompeii to stone carvings at Ankor Wat, erotica have flourished. The printing press produced Bibles and porn. Photography produced *Playboy*. Many of the first videocassettes were pornographic. (The legal X-rated video business amounts to a few billion dollars a year.) Whether all this is good or bad, a natural part of human nature or a sign of degeneracy and evil, whether it should be tolerated or stamped out, are moral and political issues beyond the subject of this book.

Pornography is debated endlessly. We will try to focus specifically on issues related to computer systems, on how existing laws, precedents, and the Bill of Rights will be interpreted in this new arena.

Guidelines for illegally obscene material and their application to the net

More than 20 years ago, the Supreme Court, in *Miller vs. California,* established three-part guidelines for determining if material is obscene under the law (and not protected by the First Amendment): (1) It depicts sexual (or excretory) acts whose depiction is specifically prohibited by state law; (2) it depicts these acts in a patently offensive manner, appealing to prurient interest as judged by a reasonable person using community standards; and (3) it has no serious literary, artistic, social, political, or scientific value. The second point—the application of community standards—was a compromise intended to avoid the problem of setting a national standard of obscenity in so large and diverse a country. Thus, small conservative or religious towns could restrict pornography to a greater extent than cosmopolitan urban areas.

Computer networks are changing the meaning of "community." On the Internet, communities have no physical locations. Instead, they are defined by the people who choose to associate by subscribing to a BBS or participating in a newsgroup. The definition of community proved critical in one case. A couple in California operated a computer BBS called Amateur Action that made sexually explicit images available to members. Legal observers generally agree that the Amateur Action BBS operators would not be found guilty of a crime in California. But the federal government apparently wanted to shut it down. The BBS was accessible over the Internet. A postal inspector in Memphis, Tennessee, working with a U.S. attorney there, became a member (the only member in Tennessee[10]) and downloaded sexually oriented images in Memphis. The couple, who lived and worked in California, were prosecuted in Tennessee and found guilty in 1994 of distributing obscenity under the local community standards. Both received jail sentences. A spokesman for the ACLU commented that prosecutions like this one mean that "nothing can be put on the Internet that is more racy than would be tolerated in the most conservative community in the U.S."[11]

The Net is also changing the meaning of "distribution." Did the BBS operators *send* obscene files to Tennessee? A BBS is accessed by the telephone system; anyone, from anywhere, may call in if they choose. The postal inspector in Tennessee initiated the telephone call to the BBS and initiated the transfer of the files. He selected and downloaded them. Critics of the prosecution of the BBS operators argue that it is as if the postal inspector went to California, bought pornographic pictures, and brought them home to Memphis—then had the seller prosecuted under Memphis community standards.[12] Like some other issues in this chapter, whether such prosecutions are constitutional is not likely to be resolved until cases reach the Supreme Court and new precedents and guidelines are developed.

The Amateur Action BBS case illustrates that applying old laws and judicial precedents to activities made possible by new technologies can have results that they were not meant to have. In an Oklahoma case, the operator of a BBS was convicted of offering obscene material on his system. He appealed on the grounds that the state's obscenity laws did not mention binary files and electronic devices such as CD-ROMs. The government argued that obscene material is obscene material whether it is on a videocassette or a CD-ROM.[13] Whatever one thinks of how loose or how restrictive laws about obscenity should be, or whether they should exist at all, the view that the essence of the issue should not depend on the technology is a sensible one. In the Oklahoma case, that view works against the defendant; more often, it extends constitutional protections to the new technologies.

New attempts to censor the net

In the 1990s, as more non-technical people began using the Internet, a variety of religious organizations and anti-pornography groups began to notice that the Net included pornography and other material they found offensive. A movement to pass federal legislation to censor the Net (in particular, a bill introduced by Senator Exon) began. Another variety of people and organizations, including librarians, publishers, Internet companies, and civil liberties groups, opposed such legislation. In 1995 the FBI reported that "utilization of online services or bulletin board systems is rapidly becoming one of the most prevalent techniques for individuals to share pornographic pictures of minors, as well as to identify and recruit children into sexually illicit relationships."[14] After increasing publicity about pornography on the Net and the use of e-mail by pedophiles to contact children, Congress passed a version of the Exon Bill as the Communications Decency Act of 1996 (CDA).*
The law attempts to avoid an obvious conflict with the First Amendment by focusing on material available to children. It provides that anyone who makes available to anyone under 18 any communication that is obscene or indecent would be subject to a fine of $100,000 and two years in prison. The operator of a telecommunication system used for such communication would face the same penalty. That means that information services and BBS operators could be held criminally liable for material posted and transmitted by members and subscribers.

In two suits against the CDA, federal judges ruled that the law is unconstitutional, but the government appealed to the Supreme Court. One of the judges ruling against the CDA said, "as the most participatory form of mass speech yet developed, the Internet deserves the highest protection from government intrusion."[15] The Supreme Court ruling, not yet made when this book was written, will have a critical influence on the future of the Net. If the Court rules against the law, the Net will have a chance of achieving First Amendment protection similar to that enjoyed by print publishers, although there will probably be continuing efforts to censor. If the Supreme Court upholds the law, material that is protected by the First Amendment in print would be subject to criminal penalties if transmitted electronically.

Supporters of the CDA (and other attempts to censor the Net) see it as necessary both to protect children from viewing pornography and indecent e-mail and to protect children from real physical assault and abuse by adults who win a child's confidence via e-mail, then arrange a meeting with him or her. Opponents see the CDA as a profound threat to freedom of expression. The real problems of access to inappropriate material by children and access to children by undesirable people, according to opponents of censorship, can be solved with other less sweeping methods.

----

*Passed as part of the Telecommunications Act of 1996.

Implications for freedom of speech

The Exon Act would be the most sweeping imposition of governmental censorship in American history because it is deliberately and directly aimed at a new technology that goes far beyond any previous ways of communication.

–Nat Hentoff[16]

Although there is disagreement over the standards for what material adults have the right to view, most people agree that a tighter standard is appropriate for children. It is sometimes difficult to design a law that keeps inappropriate material from children while allowing access for adults. The Supreme Court has ruled on this problem. In a significant 1957 case striking down a Michigan law that made it illegal to sell material that might be damaging to children, Justice Frankfurter wrote, "The state may not reduce the adult population of Michigan to reading only what is fit for children."[17] The CDA restricts indecent material accessible by children, but a child can access almost anything on the Net. Thus, its critics say, the CDA would do exactly this, not just in Michigan, but throughout the country.

There is no generally accepted legal definition of "indecent" or "filthy" words used in the law. An enthusiastic love letter or an adult joke sent by e-mail might qualify. Opponents of the CDA gave examples of information that is legal in print but might be cause for prosecution if available online: the Bible, some of Shakespeare's plays, and serious discussions of sexual behavior and health problems like AIDS. The difficulty in determining what to censor is illustrated by America Online's action in response to government pressure to prohibit obscene or vulgar language. AOL included the word "breast" in its list of words banned from subscriber profiles. A week later the ban was reversed after protest, ridicule, and outrage from breast cancer patients.[18]

Supporters of the CDA argued that this was over-reaction; no one would be prosecuted for transmitting Shakespeare or the Bible, or discussing health problems, online. The lack of clear standards, however, can lead to uneven and unfair prosecutions. When a government action or law causes people to avoid legal speech and publication out of fear of prosecution, the action or law is said to have a "chilling effect" on First Amendment rights. As we will see in Section 6.2.4, when service providers are held legally responsible for content posted by their subscribers, the results have even more chilling effects on the exercise of First Amendment rights. Courts generally rule against laws or government actions that have such effects.

Are new restrictions on freedom of speech needed to protect children on the Internet (and to protect adults from material that is offensive to them)? Are there other solutions that do not threaten to diminish free discussion of serious subjects or deny sexually explicit material to adults who want it?

Protecting children

It is illegal to create, possess, or disseminate child pornography. It is also illegal to lure children into sexual acts. In 1995, federal agents conducted numerous raids and made many arrests for these crimes where suspects used e-mail and chat groups on commercial online services. The highly publicized arrests were used by some as an argument in support of stronger laws to control the Net. Others argued that the arrests illustrate that law enforcement has the tools to fight these crimes. Federal agents used surveillance, court orders to read e-mail (as required by the Electronic Communications Privacy Act), search warrants, and undercover investigations to build their cases and make the arrests. The federal judges who decided that the Communications Decency Act was unconstitutional said, "The government can continue to protect children from pornography on the Internet through vigorous enforcement of existing laws criminalizing obscenity and child pornography.[19]

The anonymity of the Net is often cited as a factor in making it easier for people to prey on children. It is. It also makes it easier for an "undercover" officer to pretend to be a 10-year-old online.

CompuServe and other services allow subscribers to lock children out of certain areas. Several of the online services distribute information with tips on how to control what children can view. With funding from several online services, the National Center for Missing and Exploited Children distributes a pamphlet, "Child Safety on the Information Highway," with information on risks to children and guidelines for reducing them.

Commercial services cooperate with investigations of child pornography. America Online, for example, warns that when subscribers notify the company of illegal activity, AOL will report it to the FBI and comply with subpoenas. It expelled subscribers who e-mailed child pornography to others. Its customer agreement gives it the right to remove anything it considers offensive. Prodigy automatically screens out messages posted on discussion groups if they contain forbidden words.*[20]

Software products with names such as CyberSitter, SurfWatch, and Net Nanny block access to sites that contain pornography or check for phrases and files that might be inappropriate for a child. A consortium of Internet companies is working on a voluntary rating system; automated software filters can be developed to screen features according to ratings.[21] In response to market demand, companies like CompuServe are offering new online services targeted to families and children.

> Two-point-five million use America Online. That's like a city. Parents wouldn't let their kids go wandering in a city of 2.5 million people without them, or without knowing what they're going to be doing.
>
> –PAM MCGRAW, *America Online*[22]

Is censorship effective on the net?

The Net is global. The U.S. government cannot control sites outside the country. Many archives of sexual material and BBSs with potentially illegal content exist outside the United States.† One of the side effects of increased government restrictions and censorship in the U.S. is that more services will leave, going perhaps to Europe or the Caribbean. They are still accessible from a computer with a modem. Users of the Net argue that censorship laws can no more eliminate sexually explicit material than antidrug laws

---

*Not everyone applauds automatic filtering. When subscribers first learned that Prodigy was screening messages, some vehemently criticized the action as censorship. Others consider it a reasonable policy decision for a commercial service that has family subscribers.

†The same is true for other banned or restricted activities. Online gambling casinos have already been established offshore to get around U.S. antigambling laws.

can eliminate drugs. Caches, like caches of copyrighted software, will appear on legitimate systems. Underground BBSs will provide what some people want. On the other hand, Lance Rose's arguments about copyright (Section 5.4.4) apply here too. If an activity is illegal, it will be virtually eliminated on the larger commercial services. The threat of prosecution will scare many BBS operators. People who want to obtain the contraband will have to make extra efforts and take extra risks.

6.2.3 Liability of Service Providers

The issue of legal liability of operators of telecommunications and information services (including the Internet; thousands of independent BBSs; commercial online services, like CompuServe, America Online, and Prodigy; and many other companies) for material posted or e-mailed by subscribers is critically important. It remains unresolved, not only for pornography, but for copyright infringement, libel, and harassment as well. Will service providers be treated like common carriers or publishers, or like each in different contexts to match the complexity of the Net? What are the implications of holding service providers responsible for content?

Legal sanctions against service providers are much more effective than trying to catch the people who post prohibited material. Service providers are visible and can be fined or prosecuted by the government. Thus they will be motivated to be effective in restricting prohibited material. They will, in effect, be pressured to police their services. To people for whom suppressing offending material is of greatest importance, and to people who fear children will be hurt by the availability of indecent material on the Net, these concerns outweigh the counterarguments. The side effects of provider responsibility, however, are numerous.

To protect themselves from prosecution, the services might have to monitor and censor every message and file, including personal e-mail. With the volume of transmissions, it is simply impossible for each to be individually screened. To do so would degrade service enormously. It would also be a gross invasion of member privacy. Rather than read and evaluate every transmission, the service providers would use automated software filters to screen out suspect material. They may ban all files in the formats commonly used for sexually oriented images. They may cut off access to long lists of newsgroups or sites that may include proscribed material.* With no clear definition of "indecent" to guide them, and with the need to automate the screening, service providers would err on the side of caution to protect themselves, thus eliminating many communications that are legal. The effect would be to enforce the most restrictive standards on all communications. Some potential users of the Net may give up entirely. For example, a Washington state government official argued that a state law making it illegal to deliver obscene pictures to minors might scare schools into terminating their Internet connections out of fear of liability.[23]

We observed that the global nature of the Net makes it more difficult for one government to control content. In some ways, however, the globalness, combined with laws holding service providers responsible for content, makes it easier for one nation to impose

---

*One side effect of cutting access to sex-oriented sites is that posters may distribute such material in other, unbanned newsgroups, thus making it more available to children and others who prefer to avoid it.

conservative standards on others, threatening not only the notion of community standards, as did the Amateur Action BBS case, but also the notion of different national standards. When German prosecutors told CompuServe to remove access to newsgroups with indecent and offensive material, CompuServe responded by cutting off access to more than 200 newsgroups—not only for its German subscribers, but for everyone.* This action was severely criticized by civil libertarians; it is a precedent that other governments could follow to suppress political or religious discussion they oppose. Indeed, the German government investigated CompuServe for violating German law because it is possible to access a neo-Nazi site in Canada using CompuServe's Internet connection.[24]

The Church of Scientology copyright cases, mentioned in Section 5.2.3, illustrate several of these problems. The church pressured BBS operators and Internet access providers to discontinue carrying newsgroups in which the church and its teachings were discussed. Unlike some of the BBSs described in Chapter 5, where at least a significant part of the material available was copyrighted software, in this case the alleged copyright infringement is clearly incidental to the purpose of the newsgroups and certainly a small part of the activity on the BBSs. The church obtained restraining orders against the operator of a BBS that provided a former minister with Internet access and against Netcom, a major Internet provider. The BBS operator said his system handles 15,000–30,000 messages a day. In responding to the restraining order to prevent the minister from posting messages and to screen postings for church material, the BBS operator said:

> Requiring me to censor all the traffic that crosses my wires . . . is a physically impossible task. . . . Sysops like me will be simply unable to put in the nonremunerative hours, nor will they have either the insurance, or the deep pockets, to stand up to libel, copyright infringement or trade secret litigation. . . . If I am forced to monitor [the former minister's] or any other person's text messages or files for content, I will be forced to turn the power off. . . .[25]

The restraining orders against the BBS and Netcom were lifted, but a court ruled that the church could sue Netcom for not removing the allegedly infringing files.

Under the common carrier model, service providers could be exempt from responsibility for content if they do not exercise any editorial control over content. But this model is not adequate for online information services. It means that companies like Prodigy that try to remove material offensive to their subscribers would have to give up that practice if they wanted protection under the law, thus perhaps making more offensive material available than there is now. Prodigy's policy of screening out offensive language has already been used as justification for suits against the company for ethnic slurs and allegedly libelous material posted by users.

Some proposals make service-provider liability dependent on whether or not the provider knew about the offending files. It seems reasonable to make this an important criterion in determining liability. However, it is not a simple criterion. The provider may know about the disputed files, but, as we have seen, fair use rules for copying and defini-

---

*CompuServe later restored access to most of the newsgroups.

tions of obscene or indecent material are not sharp and clear. Similarly, whether an accusation against a company is true or libelous often cannot be determined without an investigation. To protect themselves, will providers delete any file that anyone complains about? Should a service provider have the responsibility of making such determinations for all questionable postings—and legal liability if a court later comes to a different conclusion than the provider did? Publishers *do* have this responsibility. But publishers publish a much smaller volume of material, and they decide what they publish. To require cyberspace service providers to take as much control and responsibility as print publishers would destroy some of the benefits of the new technology, in particular, its immediacy, its many-to-many character, and the tremendous opening-up of a diverse flow of information to and from millions of people.

6.2.4   Bomb-making Information

Within a few weeks of the bombing of the Oklahoma City federal building in 1995, the Senate's terrorism and technology subcommittee held hearings on "The Availability of Bomb Making Information on the Internet." There are many similarities between the controversy about bomb-making information on the Net and the controversy about pornography. Several senators expressed shock to discover that such information exists. As with pornography, it is a tiny fraction of the broad range of topics one can find on the Net, and it is already widely available in traditional media, protected by the First Amendment. It even has legitimate uses. Also in both cases, there is a real, but often exaggerated, concern about access by children. Information about how to make bombs can be found in the *Encyclopedia Britannica* (which describes how to make an ammonium nitrate and fuel oil bomb, the kind reportedly used in Oklahoma City) and in books in libraries and bookstores. Such information, again including the ammonium nitrate and fuel oil bomb, is available to the public in a booklet called the "Blaster's Handbook"; it is published by the U.S. Department of Agriculture.[26]

Arguing to censor information about bombs on the Internet, Senator Dianne Feinstein said, "there is a difference between free speech and teaching someone to kill."[27] Arguing against censorship, Senator Patrick Leahy emphasized that it is "harmful and dangerous *conduct,* not speech, that justifies adverse legal consequences." This is more or less established legal principle outside of cyberspace. There are, of course, existing laws against the actual acts of using bombs to kill people or destroy property and laws against making them or conspiring to make them for such purposes.

6.2.5   Sexist, Racist, and Harassing Speech Online

In this section we look briefly at two incidents that illustrate problems and issues related to dealing with online speech perceived by some people to be sexist, racist, or harassing.

Discrimination and harassment in college discussion groups

In 1993, Roger Karraker, a journalism instructor, set up a computer system with almost 200 discussion groups for students at Santa Rosa Junior College. At the request of students, he later set up a men-only and a women-only discussion group; students who signed up for these agreed to keep the content confidential. Some male students posted offensive remarks about two female students on the men-only group, and a man told the women about it. Karraker shut down the men-only and women-only groups as soon as he learned of the offensive remarks, but he was put on "administrative leave" by the college while the incident was investigated. The women filed a complaint with the U.S. Department of Education's Office for Civil Rights. The college settled with the women (and the man who informed them of the remarks) by paying them each $15,000. The Office for Civil Rights (OCR) issued a preliminary report stating that it expected to conclude that the college had violated federal law banning sexual discrimination by establishing the men-only and women-only computer discussion groups. It also said it was likely to conclude that the offensive remarks posted in the men-only group, which had only ten members, created a "hostile educational environment" and constituted sexual harassment. The agency proposed as remedial action that the college adopt a speech code for its computer systems.[28]

This is another case where speech on computer systems is being treated differently from other forms of speech and is not being given the same First Amendment protection. If the same comments were made in a men's locker room, they would have been protected by the First Amendment. College speech codes (for ordinary, i.e., nonelectronic, speech) like the one the OCR proposed have been thrown out by courts as violations of the First Amendment. The discrimination issue was also treated differently than it might have been in another context. The college has single-sex counseling sessions, but single-sex computer discussion groups were considered discriminatory. Outside the university, there are many specialized women's discussion groups on the Internet. They exist because women want them, whether to talk about women's health issues, motherhood, how to deal with sexual harassment at work, or just to chat in a comfortable environment. After criticism from First Amendment supporters and negative publicity about the Office of Civil Rights' preliminary findings, the OCR decided not to issue a final report in this case.

Campus speech codes

The extension of speech codes to e-mail and campus computer systems brings the debate over "political correctness" to the Net. There is serious disagreement over whether insulting speech should be banned or whether such a ban on "mean talk," as one critic described it,[29] suppresses free discussion. The difficulty of setting policies on proper speech on campus networks is illustrated by the policy change at the University of California, San Diego. In 1995, the chancellor's office issued the following statement, which is fairly typical of speech codes adopted at colleges for nonelectronic speech and signs.

> The use of University resources such as electronic mail to disparage individuals or groups on the basis of gender, race, sex, sexual orientation, age, disability, or religion, is strictly prohibited and violates University policy.[30]

A few months later, the chancellor issued another statement noting that the policy "has the potential to discourage members of the University from the exercise of their academic freedom and First Amendment rights." The revised statement says:

> I have been informed that the UCSD computer network has been used to distribute messages offensive to individuals to whom they were sent. In order to maintain an

atmosphere conducive to learning and scholarship, the University discourages discourtesy or personal invective in all discussions on the campus, including those conducted through electronic mail. The University is committed to providing a community free of harassment while upholding the principles of academic freedom and free speech.

6.2.6   Different Rules for Cyberspace?

Should cyberspace have full freedom of speech and press? Or are there good arguments for increased restrictions? Information on the Internet is relatively easy to access and distribute, and one can do both with anonymity. Anyone can sit in a library or a bookstore and read about sex or bombs, make photocopies of pages, and send them by mail without a return address. Are would-be terrorists more likely to bomb a building because of the availability of information on the Internet? It does not seem so (and there was no evidence or suspicion that the Oklahoma City bomber used the Internet). Is a child more likely to find a lewd picture or a bomb recipe on the Internet or in a bookstore or library? A librarian might keep a child out of the section where such books are shelved. Software might keep a child out of the area of cyberspace where such material is available. Would a librarian or the software stop a child, perhaps a teenager, old enough to try to build a bomb or actively seek pornography? Is the number of children who might do so significant enough to censor the Internet? How much responsibility should parents take to control what their children read?

These are just a few of the questions to weigh when considering whether the risks of offensive information or pictures on the Net are greater than risks from printed material, and whether they are worth weakening the freedom of speech that is so important to protecting political, religious, and personal freedom. It is essential to consider that, as de Sola Pool said in the quotation at the end of Section 6.1, "networked computers will be the printing presses of the twenty-first century." If censorship of the Net takes hold, First Amendment protection for print media "may become no more than a quaint archaism."

6.3   ANONYMITY AND PSEUDONYMITY

The Colonial press was characterized by irregular appearance, pseudonymous invective, and a boisterous lack of respect for any form of government.
–"Science, Technology, and the First Amendment," U.S. Office of Technology Assessment

6.3.1   From the Federalist Papers to the Internet

From the description in the Office of Technology Assessment's report, quoted above, the Colonial press—the press the authors of the First Amendment to the U.S. Constitution found it so important to protect—had a lot in common with the Internet, including its controversial anonymous e-mail and anonymous postings to newsgroups.

The Federalist Papers, published in newspapers in 1787 and 1788, are a set of 85 letters arguing for adoption of the new U.S. Constitution against critics who thought the Constitution gave far too much power to the federal government. The authors, Alexander

Hamilton, James Madison, and John Jay, had already served the newly free confederation of states in important roles. Jay later became chief justice of the Supreme Court, and Madison later became president. But when they published the Federalist Papers, they used a pseudonym, Publius. Their identities remained secret for several years.

In the nineteenth century, when it was not considered proper for women to write books, women writers such as Mary Ann Evans and Amantine Lucile Aurore Dupin published under male pseudonyms, or pen names, (George Eliot and George Sand). Prominent professional or academic people, including cyberneticist Norbert Wiener, used pseudonyms to publish murder mysteries, science fiction, or other nonscholarly work, and some writers like the iconoclastic H. L. Mencken used pseudonyms for the fun of it.

On the Internet people can send e-mail anonymously and post messages to newsgroups anonymously. The messages are processed by remailing services. The sender sends the message to the remailer, where the return address is stripped off, and the message resent with a coded user ID number. Replies go to the remailer site, where the message is forwarded to the intended recipient, with the replier's return address removed. Thus people can have conversations where neither knows the identity of the other. (Although such services are called anonymous remailers, it is more accurate to call them pseudonymous remailers. The ID assigned by the remailer is a pseudonym for the sender. A record is maintained linking the sender to the pseudonym. A fully anonymous remailer removes and destroys the sender's return address when forwarding the mail. With this kind of system, replies cannot be received.)

There appears to be strong demand for anonymous remailing services. The well-known remailer in Finland, run by Johan Helsingius, was set up originally for users in the Scandinavian countries. Within a week, the service was discovered by others, and soon after, European users were the minority. The service handled 7000 messages a day in the mid-1990s.*

6.3.2   Good Uses and Bad

Political speech is protected under the First Amendment, but there are still many ways in which the government can retaliate against its critics. There are also many personal reasons why someone might not want to be identified as holding certain views. Anonymity provides protection against retaliation and embarrassment.

Victims of rape and other kinds of violence and abuse, and users of illegal drugs who are trying to quit, are among those who can benefit from a forum where they can talk candidly without giving away their identity. (In traditional in-person support groups and group counseling sessions, only first names are used, to protect privacy.) Whistleblowers, reporting on unethical or illegal activities within the government agency or business where they work, may choose to release information via anonymous postings (although, depending on whether the information is verifiable, credibility for such anonymous postings may be low).

Anonymous remailer services can be used for criminal and antisocial purposes too. They can be used for fraud and harassment, and to prey on children. They can be used to li-

---

*Helsingius closed the service in 1996 after the Church of Scientology and the government of Singapore took action to obtain the names of people using it.

bel or threaten others with impunity, or, as we saw in Chapter 5, to infringe copyrights by posting and downloading copyrighted software without authorization. Rumors have ruined business and personal reputations. Online anonymous rumors can do so more quickly and easily. Critics of anonymity argue that it aids in criminal activity and it discourages responsible discourse and accountability.

6.3.3 Issues

Should anonymity be discouraged? Should it be prohibited by policy on commercial online services, BBSs, and so on? Given the potential for misuse, should it be illegal?

Some services may decide to prohibit anonymity (e.g., not accept any mail from known anonymous remailer sites) because of its potential to shield criminal activity or because they consider it incompatible with politeness and netiquette (online etiquette). The WELL,* for example, takes the position that people should take responsibility for their opinions and statements by letting their identities be known. Esther Dyson, editor of *Release 1.0* and a frequent writer on the computing environment, commented that "anonymity is the opposite of community" (while also commenting that there are situations where anonymity is okay).[31] Commercial, family-oriented services may prohibit anonymity to protect their members from harassment and to protect the service from liability. On the other hand, some services and BBSs that emphasize debate on controversial issues or have discussion groups on socially sensitive topics may consider anonymity as reasonable to protect privacy and encourage open, honest discussion. According to Johan Helsingius, the founder of the Finnish remailer, only five Usenet newsgroups voted not to accept anonymous messages.

The fact that there are strong arguments for and against anonymity in different circumstances suggests that it should not be illegal. If policy decisions are made by those responsible for individual services and BBSs, the policies can be flexible, diverse, and adapted to a particular service and clientele. The argument for a legal prohibition is that the potential for harm is great enough to outweigh the inconvenience to honest people who would use anonymity responsibly. Again, we see the issue of whether a technology should be banned or restricted because it has the potential for illegal use. Recall that this issue arose in Chapter 3 with respect to restricting strong encryption (or requiring that the government have all the keys), and in Chapter 5 with respect to banning equipment that can be used to circumvent copyright protection mechanisms.

Most states in the U.S. have laws against anonymous political speech. Some of those laws will be changing. In 1995 the Supreme Court decided a case in which a woman was fined for distributing pamphlets against a proposed school tax without putting her name on them. The Court ruled that distribution of anonymous political leaflets (by an individual) is an exercise of freedom of speech protected by the First Amendment. If the same principle were applied to the Internet, anonymous political postings would probably be protected. However, the Supreme Court ruling did not address anonymous distribution by organizations or businesses, mass mailings, or broadcast advertising. It is not clear how the ruling will apply in cyberspace.[32]

---

*The WELL is the Whole Earth 'Lectronic Link, one of the earliest online communities.

6.4 THE FIRST AMENDMENT AND CRYPTOGRAPHY

In Chapter 3 we described the efforts of the federal government and especially the National Security Agency to restrict the availability of strong cryptography. Some of the government actions are being challenged as violations of the First Amendment.

The book *Applied Cryptography: Protocols, Algorithms, and Source Code in C,* by Bruce Schneier, was published in 1994. It contains more than 100 pages of source code for cryptographic algorithms. As mentioned in Chapter 3, cryptographic algorithms cannot be exported without permission from the government (in practice, the NSA). Schneier and Philip Karn, author of some of the algorithms in the book, requested and received permission to export the book. Later Schneier and Karn made the source code for the algorithms available on disks. The disks contain the same material as the book. Many of the algorithms are in the public domain and have been published in other places; some originated outside the United States. The government ruled that the disks could not be exported. The reason given was that providing the code on disks makes it easier for someone to use it to provide encryption in a product. Critics of the decision point out that it is already quite easy to use optical character scanners to scan printed information such as the book and produce files identical to those on Schneier's and Karn's disks.

The government is using a distinction of technology to determine where the First Amendment applies. The State Department argues that its decision is consistent with the First Amendment. An attorney with the ACLU disagrees, saying "any claim that the First Amendment is inapplicable because of the medium is just not valid." Schneier's and Karn's suit against the government was rejected by the judge because the export law provides that export decisions are not subject to judicial review. They are appealing.[33] In another cryptography/First-Amendment case, a judge issued a strong statement in support of applying freedom-of-speech rights to cryptography algorithms and computer programs in general. We describe that case next.

Although in the past several years, the government has not been as aggressive as before in suppressing printed information on cryptography, it still has the legal power to do so. Cryptography researcher Daniel Bernstein filed suit against the government to challenge its power to restrict publication. He wants to publish his work, including encryption algorithms, on the Internet and discuss it at technical conferences and other public meetings. Currently, he must obtain a license from the State Department and report to the government everyone who receives a copy of his work. Penalties for failure to comply include a large fine and a long jail sentence. The requirement that each recipient of the work be tracked and reported makes distribution or discussion of the work on the Internet impossible. Bernstein's suit argues that the export restrictions (intended for military equipment, airplanes, bombs, etc.) violate the First Amendment when applied to publications. It claims that by denying the right to publish, the government's regulations abridge the constitutional freedom to speak, publish, associate with others, and engage in academic inquiry.[34] The government argues that software is not speech and that control of cryptography is a national-security issue, not a freedom-of-speech issue; the restrictions are necessary to keep strong cryptography from potential foreign enemies and terrorists. At an early stage in the case, the federal judge stated that "This court can find no meaningful difference between computer language . . . and German or French. . . . Like music and mathematical equations, computer language is just that, language, and it communicates information either to a computer or to those who can read it. . . . For the purposes of First Amendment analysis, this court finds that source code is speech."[35]

Other interesting constitutional questions arise if the government tries to require registration of encryption keys or key escrow for Americans. Freedom of speech should certainly include the freedom to have a conversation in a foreign language that American law enforcement officials do not understand. Is the right to send a message in code as much protected by the First Amendment as the right to speak in a foreign language? Should it be? Can the government require that everyone who speaks an unusual language provide the government with a dictionary or a translation of their conversations? Is this an appropriate analogy for requiring people to register or escrow their encryption keys?

6.5   HACKER CASES AND THE FIRST AND FOURTH AMENDMENTS

6.5.1   Freedom of the Press When There Is No "Press"

In 1989, an electronic hacker newsletter called *Phrack* published part of a document about the 911 emergency telephone system. The document had been downloaded by a hacker who accessed a BellSouth telephone company computer without authorization. BellSouth claimed that the document contained sensitive information and its publication threatened the security of the emergency system. After an investigation by the Secret Service,* *Phrack's* editor and publisher, Craig Neidorf, was charged with ten felony counts (wire fraud and interstate transportation of stolen property) with a potential prison sentence of 65 years and a large fine. The Secret Service seized *Phrack's* computer equipment, software, and list of subscribers. The indictment charged that the E911 document was worth $23,900. The document was the focus of the case, but charges were also related to other material published in *Phrack,* including hacker tutorials.[36]

Many who were familiar with this case saw it as a significant threat to electronic publishers. The E911 document published in *Phrack* did not contain sensitive information; it contained a lot of dull bureaucratic language. Fear of hackers may have been the motivating factor in the prosecution. The trial ended in an embarrassment for the government. On the fourth day, the charges were dropped. The defense showed that the information in the E911 document was available in other published sources and in pamphlets sold by another telephone company for under $25.

Issues

Several observers have compared the *Phrack* case to the Pentagon Papers case. In the 1970s the *New York Times* and the *Washington Post* published the Pentagon Papers, documents describing government policies and activities related to the war in Viet Nam. The documents were given to the newspapers without authorization. The government argued that their publication threatened national security, but the newspaper publishers were not charged with criminal offenses.

---

*The Secret Service has responsibility for investigating some kinds of computer crime, in addition to its better-known role of protecting the President.

Why was *Phrack* treated differently from the *Times* and the *Post?* And why did journalists, many civil libertarians, and the public not react with the concern they might normally show for a threat to freedom of the press? One reason is that *Phrack* was not published on paper; it was distributed electronically. There was no printing "press" to be protected by the First Amendment. Electronic newsletters were not seen by tradition-bound people as legitimate news publications. Another reason is the fear, encouraged by news reports about the E911 document, that the case involved dangerous hackers out to sabotage the 911 system.

Thus, one issue raised by this case is whether or not electronic publishers will receive the same protections as print publishers. Another issue is whether the government will treat publication of information about hacking as protected by the First Amendment. The government considered *Phrack's* hacker tutorials to be evidence of criminal activity. However, the information in the tutorials about computer system vulnerabilities and basic hacking methods was widely available from other sources, including professional journals. The same information is used by computer security specialists. Publishing the information may be irresponsible, but should it be a crime? Courts have almost always ruled that publication, even when it promotes illegal activities, is protected by the First Amendment. (Recall the discussion of bomb-making information on the Net in Section 6.2.4.)

A third issue is the chilling effect of prosecutions like Neidorf's on the flow of information. Even though the charges against him were dropped, Neidorf's legal expenses were $100,000. He quit publishing *Phrack*. The threat of prosecution causes some publishers and BBS operators to avoid sensitive issues.

The *Phrack* case involved, mainly, the application of the First Amendment to suspected hackers. Next we will see similar issues in a related case involving application of Fourth Amendment protections against unreasonable search and seizure.

6.5.2   Steve Jackson Games and Operation Sun Devil

Steve Jackson Games is a company that operates a computer bulletin board system and publishes role-playing games. It was raided by the Secret Service in 1990. The agents seized computers, printers, disks, the manuscript for a book about to be published, a BBS, business records, and paper records. The government claimed that an employee of the company had a copy of the E911 document stolen from BellSouth; they thought he had put it on the company's BBS. The document was not on the system, and no charges were ever filed against the company, its owner, or the employee. However, the seizure and long delay in returning the seized material caused disruption of business, financial loss, and the layoff of some employees.[37]

The raid on Steve Jackson Games was just one of a series carried out by the Secret Service and other law enforcement agencies against suspected hackers in 1990 as part of Operation Sun Devil. The operation, involving 150 Secret Service agents, was directed at an informal group of hackers colorfully called the Legion of Doom. With more than two dozen search warrants that allowed searches for stolen files and other evidence of criminal activity, the government seized 40 computer systems, along with diskettes, telephones, telephone-answering machines, audio equipment and tapes, and printers. In most of the cases, charges were never filed against the people whose property was seized, but it was many months or longer until the property was returned.

Although many of the raids may have violated the Fourth Amendment, which requires that the material to be seized be described in particularity, the fact that Steve Jackson Games is a publisher and BBS operator provided an especially strong basis for a court challenge. Steve Jackson Games argued that the government violated two major laws intended to implement First and Fourth Amendment protections.

The Privacy Protection Act of 1980 says that law enforcement agencies may not search for or seize materials from newspapers, broadcasters, and publishers (with a few exceptions). A court may issue an order to provide certain material, but the person or business served with such a order has an opportunity to contest it and can supply copies of the information demanded without losing the ability to function. The act was passed after a government raid on a newspaper office. It applies to anyone who is preparing information for public dissemination. One of the issues in the Steve Jackson Games case was whether this act applied to nontraditional kinds of publications. The government argued that the games and magazines published by the company were not worthy of protection by the Privacy Protection Act. The judge said, to the contrary, the company was a legitimate publisher. The search and seizure were illegal.

Recall that the Electronic Communications Privacy Act of 1986 (ECPA) specifically prohibits the government from reading electronic mail without a court order. The Secret Service seized the Steve Jackson Games BBS, which contained private e-mail of more than 100 people who were not suspects. The government argued that BBS users had no "reasonable expectation of privacy" for their e-mail and that the ECPA did not prohibit the government from seizing and reading e-mail on the BBS because they had a search warrant for Jackson's computers. The judge concluded that e-mail stored on the BBS *was* protected by the ECPA, and government agents read and destroyed some of the messages in violation of the law.

The Steve Jackson Games case is significant for clarifying protection for the fast-growing area of small, nontraditional computerized news, information, and communications businesses and services.

6.6   THE FOURTH AMENDMENT

> *[Constitutional guarantees in the 4th amendment] apply to all invasions on the part of government and its employees of the sanctity of a man's home and the privacies of life. It is not the breaking of his doors, and the rummaging in his drawers, that constitutes the essence of the offense; but it is the invasion of his indefeasible right of personal security, personal liberty and private property.*
>
> –JUSTICE JOSEPH BRADLEY, *Boyd v. United States*[38]

In Chapter 2 we mentioned that Fourth Amendment protections are weakened by the existence of large government and private databases, because the government has access to the kinds of personal information that used to be kept protected in our homes or in the offices of our doctors and bankers. Now government agencies can search masses of personal information and records without a search warrant. In this section we look at other new issues and problems computer technology raises for Fourth Amendment protections.

6.6.1   Search and Seizure of Computers

Operation Sun Devil focused on hackers. In the next few years, raids were conducted against BBS operators who were suspected of distributing obscene material in violation of local laws. In an Oklahoma case, police seized CD-ROMs containing allegedly obscene material, but also seized the computer system that ran the BBS, thus shutting down the entire system. In 1994, law enforcement agents raided homes and businesses of several BBS operators in Florida on the suspicion that they were transmitting obscene material. They seized equipment necessary for the operation of the BBSs and, according to one of the operators who ran a retail computer store, they even seized new, boxed equipment that was part of his retail store stock. Months later, no charges had yet been filed. State and local police officials have conducted similar raids in many cities around the country.[39]

Seizure of a computer presents new problems for both law enforcement and suspects because of the computer's multipurpose use. Investigators may suspect that a hard disk contains files of illegally obscene material, material that infringes copyright, or stolen credit card numbers. With an appropriate warrant, it is reasonable for such material to be seized as evidence and removed from the suspect's premises. But the computer may also contain files belonging to many other people, business records, subscriber lists, and a myriad of other things that are not covered by the warrant. Their seizure by law enforcement can be a serious threat to First Amendment rights. In the 1950s, when the state of Alabama tried to get the membership list of the NAACP, the Supreme Court ruled that it could not. The Court said "Privacy in group association may . . . be indispensable to preservation of freedom of association, particularly where a group espouses dissident beliefs."[40] Now, such membership lists and subscription lists are on the same computer that may be seized and searched for another reason.

It is likely that one reason for seizing everything electronic, even audio equipment, in the Operation Sun Devil raids was that the Secret Service agents did not know enough about computers to know where suspicious data and files might be stored. As law-enforcement officials learn more about computer systems, they are getting better at pinpointing the information they are searching for in a criminal investigation and copying disks rather than carrying off all of a family's or business' electronic equipment. But the limits on what should be seized are not always clear, and, as one journalist commented, "It's not easy to seize part of a computer."[41] In some cases, the seizures appear to be intended to cause as much inconvenience as possible to the people whose property is taken, especially in cases where no charges are filed and equipment is not returned for a long time. The government can shut down a business without a trial. Without income from their business, victims often cannot afford to take legal action for the return of their property.

In 1994 the U.S. Department of Justice produced a long document called "Federal Guidelines for Searching and Seizing Computers." The recommendations are not official and do not have legal status. They are intended to guide federal agencies while "law struggles to catch up to technology." In the meantime, as the report says, "There is often so little law directly on point." The report emphasizes that the basic principles of search and seizure, as specified in the Fourth Amendment, are the same for computer-related crimes as for other crimes: "The cause must be just as probable; the description of items [to be searched or seized], just as particular." The report covers seizure of hardware, searching and seizing information, how to deal with confidential information (e.g., records of doctors, lawyers, and clergy), and return of equipment not relevant to the investigation.[42]

The decision in the Steve Jackson Games case influenced the guidelines. The report warns law enforcement agencies to consider the restrictions on government in the Privacy Protection Act of 1980 before searching a BBS. It also warns them that they must be careful when searching computer systems that may contain private e-mail.

The guidelines consider a few issues relevant to other topics we have covered: encryption and privacy. They suggest that the Fifth Amendment's protection against self-incrimination may prevent the government from compelling a suspect to disclose his or her encryption key; a definite resolution of this question will not be clear until a case is decided by the Supreme Court. Privacy issues are discussed for situations where the computer system being searched is used by more than one person, and one user gives permission for the search. In general, the guidelines suggest that consent of one user is sufficient to search the entire system. If other users have taken steps to protect their privacy (e.g., by using passwords or encryption) a search warrant should be obtained. However, in what sounds more like a weak excuse than a good argument, they say that prosecutors who do not obtain a warrant for the search can argue that users do not have an "expectation of privacy" because they know that system administrators can access all files on the system. Users who know that system operators can read their files still expect privacy with respect to outsiders, including government agents.

The issuance of the federal guidelines, and some of the information and reminders included in them, are a positive step on the part of the government to clarify what is and is not permissible for law enforcement agents. The guidelines do not answer all the questions about searches and seizures of computer equipment, and they are not always followed by local law enforcement organizations. For example, after the report was issued, Ohio authorities seized a hard disk of a BBS with about 7,000 subscribers. The disk contained electronic mail and personal files. The raid was conducted because of suspicion that the disk contained obscene images. Subscribers filed suit arguing that the government should have seized only those images, not the whole disk. Local government officials contend that they need the "original evidence."[43]

6.6.2 The Exclusionary Rule and Computer Errors

The exclusionary rule prohibits the use of evidence in court if it was obtained by law enforcement agents illegally. People are concerned and angry about cases where clearly guilty, violent criminals are set free because of violations of proper procedure. Thus there is pressure to modify or eliminate the exclusionary rule. We have seen that law-enforcement databases have high error rates. The Supreme Court has ruled that evidence can be used in court although it was found in a search done because of an error in a law-enforcement database. Based on a computer check showing an arrest warrant, police conducted a search of a man's car after a routine traffic stop—a search that would normally be illegal. The computer was wrong, but the Supreme Court ruled that evidence of a (nonviolent) crime found in the car could be used against the man.[44] An important issue here is how such a ruling affects the incentive of law-enforcement officials to improve the accuracy of their records. The Arizona Supreme Court argued that

> It is repugnant to the principles of a free society that a person should ever be taken into police custody because of a computer error precipitated by government carelessness. As automation increasingly invades modern life, the potential for Orwellian mischief grows. Under such circumstances, the exclusionary rule is a "cost" we cannot afford to be without.[45]

The Supreme Court reversed the Arizona court ruling, saying that the error was made by a court employee, not a law-enforcement official, and therefore excluding the evidence would not deter future errors by law enforcement. In a dissenting opinion, Justice Ginsburg argued that it was artificial to distinguish between court employees and police employees. In practice, it may be difficult to determine who made the error. "Applying an exclusionary rule as the Arizona court did may well supply a powerful incentive to the State to promote the prompt updating of computer records."

The Electronic Frontier Foundation observes that proposed changes in the exclusionary rule being debated in Congress may permit evidence from illegal wiretaps to be used in court. The requirement for a court order for wiretaps was emphasized by proponents of the Communications Assistance for Law Enforcement Act (Chapter 3), but it may be worthless without the exclusionary rule.

The public is understandably unhappy that clearly guilty criminals sometimes go free. The purpose of the Bill of Rights is to protect innocent people from intrusions and abuse by the government and to provide a set of rules that will protect the guilty from unreasonable treatment. There will always be a tension between aggressive criminal investigation and protection of the rights of both innocent and guilty people. The problem is to balance the need to investigate and punish crime with the need to prevent abuse by law enforcement agents. At issue here is whether and how rules adopted for the use of law enforcement databases will tilt the balance.

EXERCISES

Review exercises

1. Briefly explain the differences between common carriers, broadcasters, and publishers with respect to freedom of speech and control of content.

2. Describe two methods parents can use to restrict access by their children to sexually oriented material on online information services.

3. Mention three cases described in this chapter where electronic communications or publications were treated differently by the government from the way print communications or publications would be treated.

4. List four cases or incidents described in this chapter where a government action could be said to have a "chilling effect" on the exercise of First Amendment rights.

5. Describe briefly how an anonymous remailer works.

6. Why were the charges against *Phrack* dropped?

7. What is the main provision of the Privacy Protection Act of 1980?

General exercises

8. Would you subscribe to a commercial online service that screens messages posted to its discussion groups and eliminates those it considers offensive? Do you think this a violation of freedom of speech or a permissible policy for a private company to adopt?

9. How has the Internet changed the notion of community standards for determining if material is legally obscene? Do you think the community standards criterion can be preserved on the Internet? If so, explain how. If not, explain why?

10. In many cities one can buy both ordinary newspapers and sexually oriented publications from coin-operated machines on sidewalks. College campuses often have newspaper machines, but not the machines for sexually oriented publications.

   List several aspects of coin-operated machines selling sexually oriented newspapers and of sexually oriented online newsgroups that might be relevant to a college's decision whether or not to allow them on campus. Indicate which factors are similar for both kinds of material and which are different.

11. A large cache of pornographic images was stored on a Lawrence Livermore National Laboratory computer system by an employee. Give some arguments consistent with the First Amendment that the lab director could use to remove the cache and discipline the employee.

12. List several similarities and differences among the issues of pornography, bomb-making information, and hacking information on the Net.

13. Suppose that near Christmastime many Web sites and religious discussion groups carry a large amount of material about the religious meaning of Christmas and the religious importance of Jesus Christ. To the majority of Americans, this is not only acceptable, but valuable and positive. To members of non-Christian religions and to atheists, it may be offensive; they may not want their children to view this material. What would be your reaction to a law restricting availability of such material on the Internet? In what ways do the issues about restricting religious material, sexual material, sexist or racist comments, or bomb-making material on the Internet differ? In what ways are these issues similar?

14. One of the arguments used to justify increased government control of television content is that television is "invasive." It comes into the home and is more difficult to keep from children. Do you think this argument is strong enough to outweigh the First Amendment? Give reasons. Is this argument more or less valid for the Internet than for television? Give reasons.

15. It is illegal to make pornographic pictures, videos, and movies using minors (people under the age of 18), but it is not automatically illegal to make such movies where a minor character is played by an adult actor. In other words, current child pornography laws are intended to prevent children from being used (abused and exploited), not from being portrayed. What do you think the law should say about computer-generated pornographic videos or virtual reality programs featuring children as characters, where no real children are used in making them? Give some arguments that would be made by a person who takes a position different from yours.

16. In a highly publicized case, a college student wrote a story of violent rape and murder, using the name of a fellow student as the victim, and posted it to an Usenet newsgroup. Some people saw this case as having important freedom-of-speech implications for the Internet. In what ways are the issues in this case computer-related? How would it have differed if the student wrote the story before the Internet existed?

17. Suppose a group of students creates a World Wide Web home page for their university as a class project. The page includes the university logo, student resumes, an online poker game, and a variety of links. The university administration learns of the home page and decides that it should be controlled by the Public Relations office. What are some of the issues here? Was the students' freedom of speech violated? Are there analogies not involving computer networks where similar issues would arise?

18. Consider the University of California at San Diego's policy statements about online speech (Section 6.2.5). What are the strengths and weaknesses of each version of the statement? Which do you think is better? Why?

19. Suppose you are setting up an online dating service. Members will post a description of themselves and their interests, and other members may respond. Discuss the pros and cons of setting up pseudonyms for your customers. Do traditional dating services or personal advertisements in your area's newspapers use real names or codes to identify people? If you consider use of pseudonyms acceptable for a dating service, but not in certain other circumstances, try to identify the principles or characteristics that could be used to distinguish where they are okay and where they are not.

20. Secret voting is considered an important part of a free and democratic political system. Give arguments on both sides of the following proposition: If we can vote anonymously, we should be free to argue anonymously for or against political candidates on BBSs.

21. What was the significance of the Steve Jackson Games case?

22. Suppose there were a proposal for a law about search of computers that said law enforcement officials could copy files specified in the search warrant, but could not remove computer equipment from the suspect's premises. Give some reasons why this would sometimes not work well.

23. Considering all the services available on the Internet (including the World Wide Web and Usenet), BBSs, and commercial online information services, describe a service or feature that is similar to each of the following.

   (a) A magazine publisher

   (b) A library

   (c) The post office

   (d) A telephone company

   (e) A television station

   (f) A landlord who rents office space to a club

24. Suppose you operate a BBS for backpackers with about 1000 paid subscribers. Members discuss equipment, trip locations, safety, and related subjects. They also use the BBS to plan specific trips and find compatible trip companions. Discuss how serious the risk is of legal problems for you, as the operator, from the following postings. Mention relevant cases or laws from the chapter where appropriate.

   (a) Copyrighted material (e.g., a first aid manual)

   (b) Libelous comments (e.g., about an outdoors equipment manufacturer or store)

   (c) Sexually harassing messages

   (d) Discussions about how to sneak into legally closed natural areas

Assignments

These exercises require some research or activity that may need to be done during business hours or a few days before the assignment is due.

25. Find out if your college restricts access to any Usenet newsgroups. What is its policy for determining which groups to restrict? What do you think of the policy?

26. The government sometimes uses the notion of whether someone has a "reasonable expectation of privacy" to determine if it is legitimate for the government to gain access to various documents. Thus it is interesting to find out how much privacy computer users think they have. Interview five students on your campus (try to choose people who are not computer science majors), and ask whether they think their e-mail can be read by the people listed below. In each case, ask if they think it is actually *possible,* and if so, under what circumstances it would be permitted. Write up a report on the interviews. What is your evaluation of the accuracy of the students' knowledge of the privacy of e-mail?

(a) Another student with an account on the system

(b) The system manager

(c) A law enforcement official

(d) Anyone, after the student deletes it

Class exercises

1. *Background.* A computer system manager at a public university noticed that the number of World Wide Web accesses to the system jumped dramatically. In one day, there were 13,000 WWW accesses to one student's home page. The system manager discovered that the student's home page contained several sexually oriented pictures. The pictures were similar to those published in many magazines; it is not likely that they were legally obscene. The system manager told the student to remove the pictures.

The grievance cases. A female student who accessed the pictures before they were removed filed a grievance against the university for sexual harassment. The student who set up the home page filed a grievance against the university for violation of his First Amendment rights.

The hearings. Divide the class into four groups: representatives for the female student, the male student, and the university (a separate group of representatives for each grievance). Each group meets to plan its arguments. A spokesperson for each presents the arguments in class in, say, five minutes each. After open discussion of the arguments, take a vote of the class on each grievance.

NOTES

1 From a speech by Mike Godwin at Carnegie Mellon University, November 1994, quoted with permission. (The speech is excerpted, including part of the quotation used here, in Mike Godwin, "alt.sex.academic.freedom," *Wired,* February 1995, p. 72.)

2 "High Court Rules Cable Industry Rights Greater Than Broadcast's," *Investors Business Daily,* June 28, 1994.

3 In a 1995 Supreme Court case, Justice David Souter wrote, "One important manifestation of the principle of free speech is that one who chooses to speak may also decide what not to say." (The case concerned the right of organizers of privately sponsored parades to exclude groups from participation. The quote is in *Time,* July 3, 1995, p. 12.) Other court decisions have upheld requirements that owners of property such as shopping centers allow distribution of leaflets on their property whether or not they disagree with the content.

4 Ithiel de Sola Pool, *Technologies of Freedom,* Harvard University Press, 1983, pp. 224–25 and p. 10.

5 The quotation is often incorrectly attributed to Voltaire himself. See Paul F. Boller, Jr. and John George, *They Never Said It: A Book of Fake Quotes, Misquotes, and Misleading Attributions,* Oxford University Press, 1989, for the history.

6 Jared Sandberg, "Regulators Try to Tame the Untamable On-Line World," *Wall Street Journal,* July 5, 1995, pp. B1, B5.

7 *Cubby Inc. vs. CompuServe.* Anne Wells Branscomb, *Who Owns Information?* Basic Books, 1994, pp. 103–4. Mike Godwin, "What's Important About the Medphone Libel Case?" *EFFector Online,* April 2, 1993, v. 5.05.

8 Jared Sandberg, "Electronic Erotica: Too Much Traffic," *Wall Street Journal,* February 8, 1995, p. B1.

9 Gerard van der Leun, "This Is a Naked Lady," *Wired,* Premiere Issue, 1993, pp. 74, 109.

10 Mike Godwin, "Sex, Cyberspace, and the First Amendment," *Cato Policy Report,* January/February 1995, 17:1, p. 10.

11 Robert Peck, quoted in Daniel Pearl, "Government Tackles a Surge of Smut on the Internet," *Wall Street Journal,* February 8, 1995, p. B1.

12 For a commentary on the many issues in this case, see Mike Godwin, "Virtual Community Standards," *Reason,* November 1994, pp. 48–50.

13 Andrea Gerlin, "Electronic Smut's Spread Raises Questions," *Wall Street Journal,* May 27, 1994, p. B3.

14 FBI statement, reported in "On-line Child-porn Probe Yields Searches, Arrests" (Associated Press), *San Diego Union-Tribune,* September 14, 1995, p. A10.

15 Adjudication on Motions for Preliminary Injunction, American Civil Liberties Union et al. v. Janet Reno (No. 96–963) and American Library Association et al v. United States Dept. of Justice (No. 96–1458).

16 Nat Hentoff, "When Privacy Doesn't Compute," *San Diego Union-Tribune,* September 3, 1995, p. G4.

17 *Butler v. Michigan.*

18 Associated Press and New York Times News Service, "Cybercensors Reverse Ban on 'Breast'," December 2, 1995.

19 Adjudication on Motions for Preliminary Injunction, American Civil Liberties Union et al. v. Janet Reno (No. 96–963) and American Library Association et al v. United States Dept. of Justice (No. 96–1458).

20 Pearl, "Government Tackles a Surge of Smut on the Internet." Gerlin, "Electronic Smut's Spread Raises Questions."

21 Joshua Quittner, "How Parents Can Filter Out Naughty Bits," *Time,* July 3, 1995, p. 45.

22 Quoted in David Foster, "Children Lured from Home by Internet Acquaintances," Associated Press, June 13, 1995.

23 Letter from George Lindamood, Department of Information Services Director, to Washington governor Mike Lowry, May 1, 1995 (distributed by CPSR/Seattle).

24 Silvia Ascarelli, "Two On-Line Services Investigated in Racial Hatred Case," *Wall Street Journal,* January 22, 1996, p. B13.

25 Tom Klemesrud, reported in *EFFector Online,* February 23, 1995, 8:2.

26 The sources of bomb-making information and the senate committee hearing are described in two (overlapping) reports by Brock Meeks: "Internet As Terrorist," *Cyberwire Dispatch* (an electronic newsletter), May 11, 1995, and "Target: Internet," *Communications of the ACM,* August 1995, 38:8, pp. 23–25.

27 The quotations in this paragraph are from Meeks, "Internet As Terrorist."

28 Letter from John E. Palomino, Office for Civil Rights, to Santa Rosa Junior College, June 23, 1994. Mike Godwin, "SOLO Contendere: Free Speech versus Sex Discrimination at an Online Forum," *Internet World.* Joanne Jacobs, "The 'Hostile Environment' Runs Amok," *San Diego Union-Tribune,* October 7, 1994, p. B5. Tamar Lewin, "Single Sex Bytes: College Must Pay the Price of Men-only, Women-only Computer Discrimination," *Chicago Tribune,* p. 5. Howard Reingold, "Taking a Byte out of Free Speech Online," *San Francisco Examiner,* October 19, 1994, p. C2.

29 Jacobs, "The 'Hostile Environment' Runs Amok."

30 This and the two following quotations are from a memo on the subject "Replacement Notice on Improper Use of Electronic Mail," issued by the Chancellor's Office, University of California, San Diego, July 19, 1995.

31 In a speech at the Computers, Freedom, and Privacy Conference, San Francisco, March 1995.

32 Brian Doherty, "Outlawing the Federalist Papers," *Reason,* April 1995, p. 14. Paul M. Barrett, "Justices Make It Harder to Collect Awards," *Wall Street Journal,* April 20, 1995, p. B10. The case is *McIntyre vs. Ohio Elections Commission.*

33 "State Dept: 1st Amendment Doesn't Apply to Disks," *EPIC Alert,* October 28, 1994, v. 1.06. Telephone interview with Philip Karn, March 17, 1995. The quote is from Robert Peck and appears in the *EPIC Alert* article.

34 "EFF Sues to Overturn Cryptography Restrictions," *EFFector Online,* February 23, 1995, 8:2. Peter Cassidy, "Reluctant Hero," *Wired,* June 1996, pp. 112–18.

35 Judge Marilyn Patel, quoted in Jared Sandberg, "Judge Rules Encryption Software Is Speech in Case on Export Curbs," *Wall Street Journal,* April 18, 1996, p. B7.

36 Dorothy Denning, "The United States vs. Craig Neidorf," *Communications of the ACM,* March 1991, 34:3, pp. 23–32. Other published accounts of the case, including one in the *New York Times,* state that the government and/or BellSouth gave the document's value as more than $77,000. I am using the lower figure, and other factual material, from Denning's article; she participated in Neidorf's trial. Some additional information is from John Perry Barlow, "Crime & Puzzlement," *Whole Earth Review,* Fall 1990, pp. 44–57.

37 Information on the Steve Jackson Games case and Operation Sun Devil in this section is from Mark Leccese, "Telecomputing and the U.S. Constitution: Steve Jackson Games Goes to Trial," *Connect,* May/June 1993, pp. 38–43; "Electronic Publishing, Bulletin Board E-Mail, and the Steve Jackson Games Case," *Legal Bytes,* published by George, Donaldson & Ford, Winter 1992–93, 1:1, p. 5; Denning, "The United States vs. Craig Neidorf;" Bob Ortega, "Secret Service Held Guilty of Violating Computer Privacy," *Wall Street Journal,* March 16, 1993, p. A10.

38 Quoted in Sheldon Richman, "Dissolving the Inkblot: Privacy as Property Right," *Cato Policy Report,* January/February 1993, 15:1, p. 14.

39 Gerlin, "Electronic Smut's Spread Raises Questions." "Newsbytes," *EFFector Online,* February 10, 1995, 8:1. Charles Platt, "Americans Are Not As Free As We Think We Are," *Wired,* April 1996, pp. 82–91.

40 *NAACP vs. Alabama,* 1958.

41 Gerlin, "Electronic Smut's Spread Raises Questions."

42 "Federal Guidelines for Searching and Seizing Computers," U.S. Dept. of Justice, Criminal Division, Office of Professional Development and Training, July 1994. Published in *the Criminal Law Reporter,* December 21, 1994, 56:12.

43 Constance Johnson, "Seizure of Electronic Messages in Obscenity Case Raises Questions," *Wall Street Journal,* August 18, 1995, p. B2. Platt, "Americans Are Not As Free As We Think We Are."

44 Paul M. Barrett, "Aiding Prosecutions, Justices Allow Use of Some Improperly Obtained Evidence," *Wall Street Journal,* March 2, 1995, p. B4.

45 *Arizona v. Evans,* reported in "Supreme Court Rules on Use of Inaccurate Computer Records," *EPIC Alert,* March 9, 1995, v. 2.04.

FOR FURTHER READING

Alan Dershowitz, "The Right to Transmit Hate Anonymously," United Feature Syndicate, 1995.

Jonathan Emord, *Freedom, Technology, and the First Amendment,* Pacific Research Institute, 1991.

Mike Godwin, "The First Amendment in Cyberspace," available from the Electronic Frontier Foundation.

Thomas W. Hazlett, "The Rationality of U.S. Regulation of the Broadcast Spectrum," *Journal of Law & Economics,* April 1990, pp. 133–75.

Nat Hentoff, *Free Speech for Me—But Not for Thee: How the American Left and Right Relentlessly Censor Each Other,* Harper Collins, 1992.

Mitchell Kapor, "Civil Liberties in Cyberspace," *Scientific American,* September, 1991, pp. 159–64.

"Science, Technology, and the First Amendment, Special Report," Office of Technology Assessment, U.S. Dept. of Commerce, Washington, DC, January 1988 (Report NO. OTA-CIT-369).

Charles Platt, "Americans Are Not As Free As We Think We Are," *Wired,* April 1996, pp. 82–91.

Ithiel de Sola Pool, *Technologies of Freedom,* Harvard University Press, 1983. This book describes the history, rights, restrictions, and responsibilities of the various communications technologies in depth.

7

COMPUTER CRIME

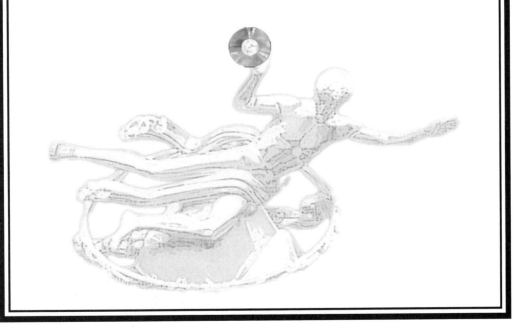

7.1   INTRODUCTION

Computers make many activities easier for us. They also make many illegal activities easier for criminals. They provide new ways to commit old crimes—like copyright infringement and distribution of child pornography, as we saw in Chapter 5 and Chapter 6, and like fraud, embezzlement, theft, forgery, vandalism, and industrial espionage. Computers present new challenges for prevention, detection, and prosecution of crimes.

Computer crimes against businesses and organizations include offenses committed by "insiders" (usually employees) and outsiders (hackers, competitors, criminal gangs). They range in seriousness from harmless trespass to vandalism, theft, and shutdowns of important services. It should not be surprising that computers are used by criminals. Computers are tools, like cars and telephones. Crimes that used to be planned at in-person meetings were later planned on the telephone. In the 20th century, bank robbers fled the scene of their crime in get-away cars instead of on horseback. Employees used to embezzle funds from their employers by "doctoring" the books. Now they can do it by modifying or misusing the software.

The new tool is a powerful one. It makes some crimes not only easier to commit, but also more devastating and harder to detect. Criminals can steal from a bank from miles away or from another country, by modem. Global networks extend the reach of thieves and make arrests and prosecutions more difficult. In one case, a Russian man allegedly stole $400,000 from Citicorp by breaking into its central computer—without entering the United States. While unknowingly under computer surveillance by authorities, he transferred another $11 million to bank accounts in several other countries before his arrest. Alleged accomplices were arrested in several countries.[1]

A robber who enters a bank and uses a gun gets $5000 on average. The average take from a computer fraud is more than $100,000.[2] A thief who steals a credit card gains access to a much larger amount of money than the thief who steals a wallet with some cash. Confidential business information can be stolen from computers and voice mail systems without any signs of "forced entry."

In this chapter we will see how computers are used in a variety of crimes and consider some of the steps being taken to reduce the problem. Although hacking is not as costly as other classes of computer crime (e.g., credit fraud and embezzlement), it is likely to be more intriguing to students. Thus we will discuss many aspects of hacking. As in Chapter 4, where we talked about computer failures, the examples of cases described here are representative of dozens or hundreds more.

7.2   FRAUD AND EMBEZZLEMENT

7.2.1   Swindling the Employer

Although hacking gets more publicity than other computer crimes, the most significant losses to businesses come from crimes committed by employees. Embezzlement is "fraudulent appropriation of property by a person to whom it has been entrusted."[3] With the use of computers, trusted employees have stolen hundreds of thousands, and in some cases millions, of dollars from their employers. In a few spectacular cases, losses were in the hundreds of millions. (Volkswagen is believed to have lost more than $200 million in a foreign exchange fraud perpetrated by high-level employees.) Because of the extremely high security of the Citicorp system, investigators suspected the Russian man who allegedly illegally transferred more than $11 million from the system had insider help. Some frauds require specialized knowledge or programming skills. Others do not; they can be committed by clerks and other employees taking advantage of poor security on the computer systems they use as part of their jobs.[4]

The complexities of modern financial transactions increase the opportunities for embezzlement. The complexity and anonymity of computers add to the problem and help hide scams. The victims of some of the most costly scams are banks, brokerage houses, insurance companies, and other large financial institutions. Employees of insurance companies can set up phony insurance policies and make claims on them. Employees transfer large sums to Swiss bank accounts and then disappear. Employees create fake purchase orders for purchases from phony companies and cash the checks themselves. Employees also steal data from their employer's computer and sell it to competitors. Three employees of the *Encyclopaedia Britannica* sold the customer list (containing two million names and addresses) to a direct mail company, for example.[5]

It is not easy to get reliable data on the amount of computer crime, in part because banks and other victims prefer not to publicize their losses and weaken customer (and stockholder) confidence. Some estimates put the losses from computer fraud, embezzlement, and so on, at billions of dollars a year in the U.S. alone.

Defending against dishonest employees

There are many practices, both technical and managerial, that can be used to reduce the likelihood of large frauds. For example, it is recommended that responsibilities of employees with access to sensitive computer systems be rotated, so suspicious activity may be noticed by someone. Each employee should have his or her own user ID and password, and, where possible, IDs should be coded to allow only access and actions that employee needs to perform. Passwords should be changed immediately after an employee quits or is fired. No one person should have responsibility for enough parts of a system to build and hide elaborate scams. (For example, in an insurance company, establishing an insurance policy and authorizing payments on claims should not be done by the same employee.) We mentioned audit trails as a privacy protection; they also protect against fraud by providing a record of transactions and the employee who authorized them. In one case, a brokerage firm turned off its audit trail software to speed processing of orders; an employee took the opportunity to swindle the company out of an estimated $28 million.[6] In large, impersonal institutions, it is often foolish to trade security for convenience or increased efficiency.

Many people who embezzle from employers have no criminal history. Some have a gripe against the employer; some have financial problems; some just cannot resist the temptation. Careful screening and background checks on prospective employees can be helpful, although recent laws make some kinds of screening more difficult (or completely illegal).

Some businesses have very good security policies; others are quite lax. There are several reasons for the latter. Some managers simply do not take the risks seriously enough. They do not believe that any of their trusted employees would steal from them, or they do not realize how badly they can be hurt, or they do not want to spend the time or the money for good security.

7.2.2   Fraud: Credit Cards, Automated Teller Machines, and Telecommunications

Credit cards, automated teller machines (ATMs), and telephone calling cards illustrate many aspects of the computer crime problem. They give us convenience, but expose us (and the companies that issue them) to risks we did not take before. Most people would not casually carry around many hundreds or thousands of dollars in cash, but a credit card, ATM card, or calling card gives the holder access to such large sums. When we had to go to a bank to withdraw cash, we did so during bank hours—in the daytime—and put the cash away before leaving the building. Now many people use ATM machines at night, outdoors, where they can be observed and robbed.

Credit card fraud and identity theft

Losses from credit card fraud are estimated to be between $1 billion and $4 billion each year. It is probably the most serious form of computer-related crime in terms of dollar losses.[7] Although most credit card fraud is committed by criminals who buy merchandise from legitimate retailers, there are cases where retailers themselves have submitted fraudulent charge slips to the credit card companies; one merchant was convicted of making $95,000 in fraudulent charges.[8]

There are many varieties of credit card fraud. Cards are stolen by large, well-organized theft rings and by individual purse snatchers. Several dozen people were convicted in one case where Northwest Airlines employees stole new cards from the mail transported on Northwest's airplanes. Some of the cards were used by the thieves; some were sold. An estimated $7.5 million was charged on the stolen cards.[9]

Another major technique for credit fraud is the use of counterfeit cards. When cards are stolen from people directly, the card owner usually closes the account quickly. Often the thieves reprogram the magnetic strip with a different account number. They get card numbers in a variety of ways, sometimes by just calling people and asking for them, with some pretext (e.g., telling the person he or she won a prize but the card number is needed). Other relatively easy ways to get numbers are by accessing credit bureau databases and taking charge receipts from garbage cans in and near stores. Credit card numbers are posted and traded on BBSs operated by hackers and thieves.

Another tactic is impersonation, or "identity theft." In our modern world, where most of us live in large communities, cash checks at stores where we are not personally known, and borrow money from strangers, our identity has become a series of numbers (Social Security number, driver's license number, account number) and computer files (credit history, driving record). Identity theft, where a criminal assumes the identity of the victim and runs up large credit card charges or cashes bad checks, is a growing problem. It often costs the victim little in direct monetary losses but much in anguish and disruption of his or her life. The victim may lose a good credit rating, be prevented from borrowing money or cashing checks, lose a job, or be unable to rent an apartment.

In one case a man applied for numerous credit cards in the names of real people who had good credit records; the people whose names were used did not know the accounts existed. The man lived well for two years, took several trips to Europe, and fraudulently charged more than $500,000 before being caught and sent to prison. A part-time English teacher at a California junior college used the Social Security numbers of some of her students, provided on her class lists, to open fraudulent credit-card accounts. Each of the big three credit bureaus handles hundreds of cases a day where victims complain that fraudulent accounts have been opened in their names. Some bold thieves obtain numbers of accounts whose owners rarely used them, then send change-of-address notices to the credit card companies so that the true card owner does not receive bills, thus delaying any question about the charges for several months.[10]

In Chapter 2 we saw that a Social Security number is the key to numerous records containing personal information. It is the key to the information the criminal needs to impersonate the victim. The access it gives to credit records alone is enormously helpful to the criminal for choosing a victim, getting the victim's credit card numbers, and learning enough personal details to successfully impersonate the victim. Many credit card companies issue additional cards and record a change of address without verification that the request comes from the real card holder.

One of the very frustrating aspects of identity theft is that victims get very little help from credit bureaus, police, motor vehicle departments, and the Social Security Administration. The motor vehicle departments and Social Security Administration are reluctant to issue a new driver's license number or SSN to a victim because their record systems are designed for a person to have the same number all his or her life. Their attitude seems to be that the fact that another person is using the number to defraud merchants and credit companies is not their problem.

Reducing the incidence of fraud by identity theft—and its monetary and personal costs—will require a combination of increased security for identification numbers and personal records, better methods for verifying the identity of a person requesting changes in an account, and better methods for distinguishing the victim from the criminal in future transactions.

ATM fraud

Losses from ATM scams have been estimated at $60 million a year.[11] A few cases illustrate how ATM frauds work.

The first is an "insider" case. A man who worked for a company that installed ATM machines had access to the machines using the installer's password. He wrote software to capture the account numbers and PINs (personal identification numbers) used by customers, then made fake cards encoded to mimic the real ones. He and a small group of friends planned to withdraw cash from the accounts on a holiday weekend, when they would have time to raid many accounts and get away. A tip from a friend who had been told of the plan led to a raid where 6000 counterfeit cards were found.[12]

Another group of thieves, lacking insider access to a real ATM system for the capture of account numbers, set up their own machine. They installed an ATM in a shopping mall in Connecticut. Initially, to gain customer confidence, the machine gave out cash. Later, after reading each customer's card and requesting the customer's PIN, it displayed a message saying that the transaction could not be processed. After about two weeks, the machine was removed. It had served its purpose, which was to read the account numbers magnetically recorded on the cards and store the PIN typed by the customer. It was not connected to any banking system. The people who installed the machine created counterfeit cards and used them at real ATMs to steal approximately $107,000 from their victims. (They were caught and convicted.)[13]

There are simpler ways for thieves to get account numbers and PINs. They use binoculars, telescopes, and video cameras to spy on customers typing at the ATMs. Then they collect discarded receipts, which contain the account numbers. The locations of the ATMs, often in public outdoor places, make the spying easy.

Telecommunications fraud

There are several varieties of telecommunications fraud. Industry and government estimates of the value of these activities range from $1 billion to $9 billion. (As with software piracy estimates, the actual loss to the companies is probably somewhat lower; people use more of free or low-priced stolen services than they would if they had to pay full price.)

Just as criminals spy on customers at ATMs to get their PINs, they also spy on people entering calling card numbers and PINs at pay telephones. They sell the calling card codes outright or set up long-distance phone centers in storefronts.

Cellular phones transmit their serial number and billing information at the beginning of each call. A popular criminal technique for avoiding charges is cloning, that is, reprogramming the phone to transmit another customer's number. Cell phone fraud alone is estimated to cost $400 million per year.

Defending against fraud

Solutions for credit card, ATM, and phone fraud illustrate the continual leapfrogging of increased sophistication of security techniques and increased sophistication of the techniques used by criminals. They also illustrate the use of technology itself to solve problems created by technology.

The use of stolen credit cards to make large purchases was fairly safe for thieves. To provide merchants with a way to check if a particular card was stolen, credit card companies printed books of stolen card numbers and delivered updated copies to merchants regularly. The books were thick, with small type. Looking up the card number for each large purchase was a time-consuming inconvenience, and because the books were never quite up-to-date, there was still ample opportunity for thieves to run up large charges. Now the books have disappeared; advances in telecommunications and automation enable the cards to be checked immediately by machines connected to credit card company computers over telephone lines. The thief's window of time to use the card has shrunk to the time it takes the owner to report it stolen.

Procedural changes help protect against theft of new cards from the mail, as in the case involving Northwest Airlines employees. Some credit card issuers now will not activate a card until the customer calls in and provides some identifying information to verify that the card has been received by the legitimate owner. This procedure is only as good as the security of the identifying information. Several Social Security Administration employees provided the social security numbers and mothers' maiden names of thousands of people to a credit-card fraud ring so that they could activate stolen cards, according to federal prosecutors.[14]

Software for credit card systems can detect unusual spending activity. When this happens, a customer may be asked for additional identification in a store, or a card holder may be called to verify purchases. Holograms and customer photos make cards more difficult to counterfeit and stolen cards more difficult to use. Similarly, ATM software can include checks for unusually high activity at a particular machine, indicating possible use of counterfeit cards. (The people who installed the phony ATM in Connecticut were caught because an alert bank employee noticed a large number of transactions at a location where the thieves used their counterfeit cards.)[15]

As counterfeiters improve their skills, new security techniques are needed. One technique being developed to detect counterfeit credit cards uses magnetic noise. Each card has a distinct "magnetic fingerprint" caused by the noise on the magnetic strip. The fingerprint can be read and matched against the stored fingerprint for the card number.[16]

To thwart thieves who spy on customers at ATMs to get their PINs, ATMs are being redesigned so that the keyboards are built into the counter instead of the wall. One simple protection against large losses from stolen or counterfeit cards is the $200 cash withdrawal limit at most ATMs. To get a large amount of money quickly, a thief must raid many accounts.

Various measures are being used to reduce robberies at ATMs: better lighting, surveillance cameras, and emergency buttons connected to the 911 system, for example. ATM industry organizations have developed security policies, standards, and guidelines for member financial institutions.[17] Customer awareness is always an important factor in reducing crime. ATM customers are learning to watch for potential muggers or PIN spies and not to leave receipts at the machines. Although there have been some tragic, violent robberies at ATMs, the overall numbers are not high compared to other crimes. In some large cities, ATM robberies are not counted as a separate category by police; they are included with purse snatchings and other street robberies.

Why the problem is so big

Credit card issuers make trade-offs between security and customer convenience. Most customers do not want to take the time to provide other identification when they use a credit card or to wait while merchants check every ID. Customers may be offended by requests for ID. Credit card companies are willing to absorb a large amount of fraud losses as part of doing business. Such trade-offs are not new. Some retail stores keep small, very expensive items in locked cabinets, but most goods are easily accessible to customers for convenience and efficiency; openness encourages sales. Retail stores have always accepted some amount of losses from shoplifting rather than offend and inconvenience customers by keeping everything locked up or by searching customers when they leave the store. When the company perceives the losses as being too high, they may improve security.

Unfortunately, the bias toward convenience and not giving offense means that simple security measures are often ignored. Most merchants do not check signatures or photos on credit cards. There is a reported case of a restaurant accepting a credit card receipt signed "Daffy Duck." In an experiment, a white man used a credit card with a picture of a black man; no one questioned him. Most of the losses from credit card fraud are absorbed by the credit card issuers, not the retail merchant. Thus the merchant does not have much incentive to check the cards.

Credit bureaus also make trade-offs between security and convenience. Access to credit records of people with good credit histories is one key component in many credit card fraud schemes. Thousands of businesses access credit bureau records frequently for legitimate purposes. For the convenience of these businesses, which are the customers of the credit bureaus, and ultimately, for the convenience of the consumer who is awaiting some decision dependent on his or her credit report, credit records are extremely easy to get. Security (and privacy) suffer. It is possible to provide extremely tight security for credit records. Credit bureaus keep records of certain people, such as law-enforcement agents who investigate hackers and credit fraud, on stand-alone computers, not connected to the standard credit network. Obviously, this security comes at a cost of slower or less convenient service. The desirable level of security is probably somewhere between the current level and the high-security procedures used for special customers.

7.2.3   Swindling the Customer

How do you know that when your groceries are scanned at the supermarket checkout counter the prices charged are the same as the ones posted on the supermarket shelves? How do you know that your computer-generated credit card bill is accurate? How do you know you are not being robbed? In the 17th century, people were suspicious that Pascal's calculating machines could be rigged to give incorrect results. We now know how easy it is to modify a computer program to rig the results. How serious is this problem?

Hertz Corporation allegedly programmed its computers to do two calculations of the cost of repairs to cars damaged by renters: the actual cost to the company and a higher cost charged to the customer.[18] On the other hand, we saw in Chapter 4 that a large grocery chain delayed implementation of a new inventory system because the check-out software sometimes generated the wrong price. Some people trust the computer and assume that the computer-printed statements and bills are correct. Others are more skeptical; they are suspicious of anything that comes out of a machine. Both miss an important point: It is not the computer that one should trust or not trust; it is the company that is using it. Some businesses have high ethical standards and exercise care to avoid mistakes. Some businesses are complete scams, and others are unethical or sloppy. The reputation and character of the business are more important than the computer.

Computer-generated bills may be impressive and daunting to some people, but cheating customers is not a new phenomenon. A rigged program is the computer analogue of rigged gas station pumps and taxi meters. Low-tech cheaters of customers included the old-time butcher who put his thumb on the scale while weighing a customer's meat and grocers who kept a can of coffee on the edge of the check-out counter and added its price to customers' bills.

7.3   SABOTAGE AND INFORMATION THEFT

7.3.1   Sabotage

The most common perpetrators of sabotage of computer systems are employees who were fired or are angry at their employer for some other reason. They may directly destroy files or plant "logic bombs," software that destroys critical files, such as payroll and inventory records, after the employee leaves. An employee fired from an insurance company was convicted for destroying more than 160,000 records with a logic bomb. There have been cases where an employee secretly sabotaged a system in the hopes of earning extra money to fix it. In one odd case, an employee continued to sabotage a printing company's computer system, deleting or garbling files, jamming terminals, crashing the system, blanking screens, and generally creating havoc over a six-month period—while he continued to work at the company unsuspected. The company lost customers, and some employees quit or were fired because of the stress. The owner said he believed the guilty employee (sentenced to five years in prison) just enjoyed making people miserable.[19]

The motivations for sabotage are not new. (Part-time fire fighters have been accused of setting wildfires, knowing they would be hired to fight them.) What is new with computer sabotage is the ease with which a great amount of damage can be done. The lack of violence or physical destruction may make the crime seem less serious both to its perpetrators and to jurors.

The concentration of critical, valuable information at a computer center makes it a target for extortion; some criminals have threatened to blow up computers with real bombs if they were not paid off.

7.3.2 Attacks By Competitors

Businesses keep sensitive and valuable information on computers: plans for new products, product and market research, customer lists, pricing policies, and so on. This information is an appealing target for unethical competitors.

Industrial espionage is not new, but it used to require the physical infiltration of the victim's business, theft of paper documents, physically copying documents by hand or with a camera, or paying off an insider to provide critical information. Paying off an insider is still a useful technique; now the insider might be paid for passwords. Now the spying can be accomplished from a remote location using a computer network. Large quantities of digital information can be copied quickly. There may be no clues to indicate that a theft took place; nothing is missing.

British Airways agreed to pay a competing airline $4 million for hacking the smaller company's computers and stealing passenger lists. American Airlines complained that an ex-employee hired by Northwest copied American's proprietary fare-setting information to a floppy disk and mailed it to Northwest. Voice-mail systems are a frequent target in industrial espionage, as they seem quite vulnerable to break-ins. Customer names, business plans, and details of contract negotiations are among the prizes. Forging e-mail, pretending to be someone in the company and asking for sensitive information, is another tactic.[20]

Defenses against theft of information by competitors are similar to defenses against hackers or other intruders. We will discuss them in Section 7.4.

7.4 INTRUDERS, HACKING, AND CRACKING

7.4.1 What is "Hacking"?

Are hackers bright, inquisitive young people who explore computer systems for fun and intellectual challenge? Or are they irresponsible criminals who invade privacy, steal information and money, destroy files, and crash computer systems?

The answer is: both. The meaning of the word "hacker" has undergone changes as more people began using computers and more people began abusing them. In the early days of computing, a "hacker" was a creative programmer who wrote very elegant or clever programs. A "good hack" was an especially clever piece of code. Hackers have been called "computer virtuosos." They tended to be outside the social mainstream, spending many hours learning as much as they could about computer systems and making them do new things. Many hackers were high school and college students who "hacked" the computers at their school. If they found ways into systems where they were not invited, the early hackers were interested primarily in learning and in intellectual challenges—and the thrill of going where they did not belong. Most had no intention of disrupting services; they frowned on doing damage. As more computers became attached to networks, hacker activities expanded to the networks, and the word "hacking" often suggested breaking into computers on which the hacker did not have legitimate access. Hacking a computer at a big research center, corporation, or government agency was a challenge that brought a sense of accomplishment, a lot of files to explore, and respect from one's peers.

Although the term "break-in" is often used to describe unauthorized access to a computer system, "break-in" suggests more destructive or more surreptitious action than was often necessary, especially in the early days. Many computer users chose simple passwords that were easy to guess, for example, their own names or the name of the project they were working on. They wrote passwords on papers kept on their desks. Hackers looked around or tried easy guesses. The same practices were exploited by Nobel prize winner Richard Feynman when he was a young physicist working on the highly secret atomic bomb project at Los Alamos National Laboratory in the 1940s. Instead of computer passwords, he found or guessed combinations to safes containing classified work on the bomb. Feynman delighted in opening the safes at night and leaving messages for the authorized users informing them that security was not as good as they thought.[21] If Feynman had been born thirty years later, he would probably have been a brilliant and inquisitive hacker in the best sense of the word.

Although many hackers do not intend to do harm, they do not always share the views of the people in charge of the systems they target. Hackers argue that systems should be open, that "information should be free." Protection of proprietary information or privacy are not as important to many hackers as it is to corporate system administrators and to the public.

The activities of many hackers were and are no more destructive than those of other generations of young people who snooped where they did not belong or carried out clever pranks, sometimes breaking a law. Many go on to successful, productive careers in the computer industry, some as computer security experts. Gradually, the term "hacking" stretched to include breaking into computer systems for any unauthorized purpose, malicious as well as nonmalicious. Thus "hacker" is now used to describe people who explore the intricacies of computer and telephone networks and carry out mild pranks—and people who intentionally destroy files; release computer viruses; reroute phone calls; change credit files; interfere with business and personal activities; steal software, passwords, and other information; expose personal information; and steal money. Some people use the term "cracker" for those who break into systems without authorization to steal or cause damage. One writer describes crackers simply as "mean-spirited hackers."[22]

Some crackers fit the common stereotype of social misfits or computer "addicts" lacking the self-discipline to function in a normal job. Some have no ethical concerns and use their skills to take revenge on people they dislike and to commit acts of computer vandalism. Now that unauthorized access to computer systems is against the law in most cases, almost all hackers commit illegal acts. Merely to say that someone is a hacker, or that a hacker broke a law, tells us very little about the person's ethical quality or the degree of seriousness of the crime. For that, we must look at what the person actually does.

Some examples

The targets of hackers include individuals, businesses, universities, and government (including military) agencies. Here is a sampling of hacking activities, illustrating their range.

In 1986, a hacker broke into at least 30–60 computers on the Stanford University campus, several other universities, 15 Silicon Valley companies, three government laboratories, and several other sites. It appeared that his goal was simply to get into as many computers as he could.[23]

Hackers spoofed mail from the premier of Ontario, Canada, sending out unflattering comments about Ontario's parliament. A World Wide Web page set up by a British government department was hacked within minutes after it went online; the hackers redesigned the page. Kevin Poulsen manipulated telephone connections so that he would win thousands of dollars in prizes in a radio station contest. Poulsen also broke into a computer and got a list of undercover businesses operated by the FBI.[24]

Using programs called "sniffers," hackers can read information traveling over computer networks and extract passwords. Some security analysts estimate that one million passwords may have been compromised in 1994. In only one day at the University of California at Berkeley, a hacker program collected more than 3000 passwords.[25]

The Secret Service reported that a 15-year-old hacked a credit reporting service and the telephone system in a scheme to get Western Union to wire money to him from other people's accounts. He is also believed to have hacked a McDonald's payroll computer and given raises to his friends.[26]

Kevin Mitnick, one of the more notorious hackers, was arrested in 1995. He allegedly stole thousands of files from the home computer of Tsutomu Shimomura, a computer security expert at the San Diego Supercomputer Center, and thousands of customer credit card numbers from Netcom, an Internet access company. At that time he was a fugitive who had gone into hiding while on probation for a 1988 hacking conviction. In their book *Cyberpunk,* Katie Hafner and John Markoff describe Mitnick's hacking career until his 1988 arrest. His coups included stealing the new version of Digital Equipment Corporation's VAX/VMS operating system software and other DEC software. Hafner and Markoff describe how Mitnick took revenge on people he disliked, for example, by switching telephone records to send large bills to the victim. Mitnick is reported to have tapped the phones of law-enforcement agents who were investigating him.[27]

Credit bureau databases are a popular hacker target; accessing and disclosing someone's credit record is a revenge tactic. (Changing data in credit files is harder than getting a copy, but it is not beyond the skills, or ethics, of some hackers.) Universities are popular targets because security tends to be looser in an educational environment. In the case made famous by Clifford Stoll in his book *The Cuckoo's Egg,* a German hacker broke into dozens of U.S. computers, including military systems, looking for information to sell to the Soviet Union. Hackers commonly manipulate telephone records and reroute calls to hide their location and avoid payment. Just as some hackers set up secret caches of pornography or stolen software on legitimate systems, others store their stolen files on legitimate systems, in part to make use of the large amount of space available and in part to make it more difficult for investigators to find the hacker or to catch him* with the stolen goods. Kevin Mitnick, for example, allegedly stored 150 megabytes of stolen files on an unused account on the WELL.†

Since the 1970s, when John Draper (who called himself Captain Crunch) discovered that a whistle in a cereal box could be used to fool the telephone system into giving free access to long distance telephone lines, "phone phreaking," or hacking the phone system, has been a popular pastime of young hackers and serious criminals. (We mentioned telecommunications fraud as a major criminal activity in Section 7.2.) Hackers stole an estimated $12 million of telephone service from NASA's Lyndon B. Johnson Space Center and were blamed for stealing millions of dollars worth of phone service from the Drug Enforcement Agency.[28] Private business networks and voice-mail systems with inadequate security are cracked for a variety of services. Once into the system, the hackers can switch to an outside line and make calls that will be billed to the company. They can eavesdrop on voice mail or erase it. A group of hackers can set up their own voice mailboxes in the cracked system to communicate with each other with less chance of being traced. Malicious phone phreaks have done worse. Some have shut down companies by taking control of the company's phone and voice-mail systems and preventing legitimate calls from getting through.

7.4.2   How Serious Is the Problem?

Perhaps before tackling the question of how serious the problem is, we should identify *what* the problem is. One problem to consider is the extent of hacker activities and the amount of damage they do. Another problem is the *potential* damage they could do using their skills. Another way of looking at the problem is the level of security or vulnerability of vital computer and communications systems. Hacking is a problem; so is poor security.

The Computer Emergency Response Team (CERT) was established by the federal government in 1988 to respond to computer security problems on the Internet. CERT helps system administrators investigate and protect against intrusions. In a recent year, it handled reports of more than 2000 computer break-ins. The federal government reports that the rate of hacker attacks on Defense Department computers is doubling each year. A Rand Corporation study reports that hacking incidents in the first six months of 1994 had almost tripled from the year earlier. In a survey of more than 1200 businesses, 20% reported that they had suffered damage from computer break-ins by hackers, competitors, and employees. Many more break-ins are unreported. Businesses, government agencies, and other organizations whose computers are invaded do not want the extent of their vulnerability known because it might encourage other hackers and cause loss of trust and support from customers, stockholders, and the public. (Computer security experts and law enforcement agents cite secrecy on the part of the victims as one of the biggest problems in reducing break-ins.)[29]

---

*Most hackers are male.

†The WELL is the Whole Earth 'Lectronic Link, one of the earliest online communities.

The vulnerability of the Internet as a whole was demonstrated dramatically by the Internet Worm in 1988. Robert T. Morris, a graduate student at Cornell University, wrote a worm program* and released it onto the Internet. The worm did not destroy any files or steal any passwords, and there are some indications that Morris did not intend or expect it to cause the degree of disruption that it did. However, the worm spread quickly to computers running a particular version of UNIX, jamming them up with so many copies that normal processing could not proceed. It was estimated that as many as 2000–3000 computers on the Internet were affected. It took about a full day for systems programmers to discover, decode, and rid their systems of the worm. Some infected sites were not functioning normally until several days later. The worm disrupted research and other activities and inconvenienced a large number of people. The damage done includes the cost of computer time on the infected systems for the time they were not functioning productively, plus the value of the time of the programmers and system managers who fought the worm through the night. The security holes used by the Internet Worm were well-known, and fixes were available. Some system operators had closed the holes on their systems, but many had not. How much responsibility for this incident should be borne by the administrators of the systems crippled by the worm? However one apportions blame, this incident illustrated the vulnerability of the Internet and raised concern about the potential to disrupt critical computer services and cause social disruption. It could happen by accident or be caused by a terrorist or extortionist.

BellSouth, the telephone company whose computers were broken into by members of a hacker group called the Legion Of Doom, described the group as "a severe threat to U.S. financial and telecommunications industries." A U.S. attorney prosecuting a hacker case involving access to telephone company computers stated that "The Legion of Doom had the power to jeopardize the entire phone network." There is, of course, a difference between having the power to do something and having the intent. Anyone with a match has the power to burn a house down. Frank Darden, one of the members of the Legion of Doom, agrees that "If we'd wanted to, we could have knocked out service across the Southeastern U.S." "But," he says, "we were careful not to damage anything." Again, we can look at the problem as being the capabilities and activities of the hackers, or we can look at the problem as being weak security. In fact, Darden seemed as surprised as any other telephone customer might be at the vulnerability of the BellSouth computer: "The fact that I could get into the system amazed me."[30]

When the Defense Department tested security by trying to hack into 12,000 Defense Department computers on the Internet using common hacker techniques, they succeeded 88% of the time. Only 4% of their successful attacks were detected by the target computer.[31]

It is useful to be aware that hacker problems are sometimes exaggerated—by the news media, by security companies, and by law enforcement agencies. The news media emphasize crises and dangers. (On the other hand, sometimes they abandon a story or issue because the public has tired of it, even though the problem has not diminished.)[32] Some journalists remind readers that security companies may exaggerate hacker incidents and

---

*A worm is a program that copies itself repeatedly and clogs a system so that it cannot function efficiently (or at all).

threats to get more business, and government agencies may exaggerate to get higher budgets. On the other hand, we have noted that a large number of hacking and criminal intrusions go unreported by companies desiring to avoid publicity. Both exaggeration and secrecy make it more difficult to determine the precise extent and nature of the problems. It is clear that hacking is costing computer users, and indirectly the general public, a large amount in money and downtime and that there is potential for disruption of critical systems.

7.4.3 Nonmalicious Hacking—Pros and Cons

The hacker arguments

Many hackers who access computer systems without authorization, but without intent to do damage, do not think what they are doing is wrong. Here are some common arguments in defense of this type of hacking.

- No harm is done. The hacker is just curious to see what is there. Hacking is harmless recreation, an intellectual challenge.
- Hackers are performing a service by exposing security weaknesses in the system.
- If the owners of the system want to keep outsiders out, it is their responsibility to provide better security. (This argument is used sometimes when harm is done as well.)
- "Information wants to be free."[33] Copying information does not deprive anyone else of the use of it; hackers who read or copy files are not stealing anything. Hackers are providing a public service by exposing internal documents of corporations and government.
- Phone companies are ripping us off. Getting a few free calls is different from selling access codes. Hackers are not doing it for profit.

We will look at counterarguments to these points.

Is it harmless?

When a system administrator for a computer system at a university, a corporation, or the Pentagon detects an intruder, he or she cannot immediately distinguish a nonmalicious hacker from a thief, terrorist, or spy. The intrusion must be stopped. The administrator's responsibility is to protect the system and its data. Thus, at a minimum, time and effort will be expended to track down the intruder and shut off his or her means of access. In many cases, companies have shut down their Internet connection, at great inconvenience, while investigating and defending against an intruder.

Uncertainty about the intruder's intent and activities has additional costs for systems that contain sensitive data. According to the head of the computer crime unit at the Department of Justice, after a hacker accessed a Boeing computer, apparently just to hop to another system, Boeing spent $75,000 to verify that no files had been changed. Would we be comfortable flying a new Boeing airplane if this were *not* done? A group of young Danes broke into the National Weather Service computers and computers of numerous other government agencies, businesses, and universities in the U.S., Japan, Brazil, Israel, and Denmark. The efforts to track the Danish hackers cost time, energy, and computer resources of the Weather Service, the FBI, MIT, and the Danish police. They were eventually caught, and it appeared they had done little damage to the systems they cracked. But consider the risks of a possible logic bomb or modified files. If the hackers had damaged Weather Service files, for example, they could have halted air traffic that is dependent on weather reports. In fact, their activities did cause the Weather Service computers to slow down. There was the potential that serious weather conditions, such as tornadoes, could have gone undetected and unreported.[34] Similarly, if unauthorized access is detected in a medical records system, a credit database, a computer containing design plans for a new product, payroll data, and others, responsible administrators must stop the intruders and verify that no changes have been made to the records.

These examples illustrate the harm, or expense, caused by uncertainty, even if the hackers have no destructive intent. Another problem, of course, is that a hacker with good intentions may make a mistake; significant damage can be done accidentally, as may have been the case with Morris's worm. Because of the effort and expense of tracking intruders and the potential for huge damage and disruption, and because unauthorized access is a form of trespass, it is now illegal. Hackers with nonmalicious intention must understand that they will often not be viewed kindly.

Security arguments

Are hackers doing us a favor by exposing security weaknesses? The Internet Worm and many hacker break-ins resulted in security improvements. In response to the Internet Worm, some people argued that we should be grateful to Morris for demonstrating the vulnerabilities of the UNIX system. Most computer professionals disagree. UNIX users know the system has security flaws. The commission at Cornell University that investigated the incident commented that "It is no act of genius or heroism to exploit such weaknesses."[35] On the other hand, CERT was formed in response to the worm. There is no doubt that the worm increased awareness of the vulnerability of the Internet and encouraged steps to reduce it. Critics of hackers argue that if a hacker discovers a security weakness in a system, he or she should inform the system manager of the flaw, not exploit it. Unfortunately, many system operators do not close loopholes they are aware of until there is a break-in. Chris Goggins, a well-known hacker and security consultant, reports that he repeatedly warned America Online of a flaw that allowed hackers to create free accounts, disconnect real subscribers, and access private files. The problems were not solved until a group of hackers exploited the flaws and caused significant problems.[36]

We can hope that the publicity about hacking incidents encourage companies to improve protection for sensitive data, but should Netcom or its customers thank a hacker for demonstrating that thousands of customer credit card numbers could be stolen? Did the earthquake in Kobe, Japan, do the people a favor by exposing weaknesses in building construction methods? No hacker activity so far has been anywhere near as destructive as the earthquake. Is this extreme analogy unreasonable, or does it make the point that demonstrating a weakness by exploiting it is often not a favor?

Hackers are correct that system managers are responsible for keeping their systems secure. There are many levels of computer security, just as there are many levels of home security—from leaving the doors unlocked, to using deadbolt locks, to installing a sophisticated alarm system. The appropriate level depends on many factors, including the likelihood of an intrusion, which is increased by the hackers themselves. When the computer system contains valuable or sensitive data, or if many people depend on its smooth operation, the system administrators have a professional and ethical obligation, and in some cases a legal obligation, to take reasonable security precautions to protect the system. But does weak security justify intrusion? Whether or not we choose to put deadbolt locks on our doors, the fact that an intruder is able to enter the house—or a computer system—does not give him or her the right to do so.

How free should information be?

In the early years, hackers primarily sought information about programming and computer systems, and programmers often shared such information. As software became big business, more programmers and software companies began treating technical information as proprietary.

The kind of information available on computer networks now is quite different from 30 years ago. It includes credit reports, consumer profiles, medical records, tax records, confidential business information, personal e-mail, and all the other types of information we described in Chapter 2 when we discussed threats to privacy. Thus, although hackers do offer some good arguments for openness of technical information, the arguments do not address the privacy concerns relevant to so much of the information on the computers they access.

Computer networks also contain intellectual property. As we saw in Chapter 5, although many hackers may be opposed to copyright in principle, that view is not accepted by many producers of intellectual property. The case for hacking to copy software or other intellectual property is, at best, controversial.

Openness of files about government activities is an important principle that the Freedom of Information Act is intended to implement. The FOIA is sometimes ignored by government agencies, and it has exemptions. There are times when unauthorized release of government documents, such as the Pentagon Papers (about the Viet Nam War) or the Justice Department report on the Ruby Ridge incident, may be justified, although the action is controversial. There may be cases where release of documents of private companies exposes threats to health and safety or evidence of criminality, but, in general, the case for accessing and releasing private documents is more questionable. In any case, files whose release serves an important public purpose make up a very small percentage of files accessed by hackers, and such documents are more likely to be made public by someone on the "inside" who leaks them than by hackers.

Ripping off the big corporations

Justifications for stealing small amounts or stealing from corporations are not original with hackers. People who exaggerate their injuries when filling out an insurance claim do the same thing. Here are a few arguments to weigh. The amount stolen does affect the legal penalty and the degree of the ethical offense, but not its essence: Theft is theft. Stealing from a corporation is stealing from the thousands of stockholders who are its owners. (A large fraction of shares on U.S. stock markets is owned by pension funds, so stealing from corporations is stealing from working people and retirees.)

7.4.4 Locking the Doors

It's no use locking the barn door after the horse is gone.

Why is security weak?

We have noted that computer security is often very poor. There are many reasons for this. They come from the history of the development of systems such as the Internet, from human nature, economic factors, government policy, and other sources.

In its early years, the Internet was used primarily as a communications medium for researchers. Open access, ease of use, and ease of sharing information were desirable qualities. It was not designed for security against malicious intruders or teenage explorers. Similarly, the UNIX operating system, in wide use now on thousands of computers connected to the Internet, was designed for use by programmers, with sharing of information a high goal. Security depended primarily on trust. Many systems did not even have passwords. Few early systems were connected to telephone networks. The expansion of the use of computers, access to networks, and decrease in the amount of technical skill needed to use computers have combined to make systems more vulnerable. Now that so much personal and sensitive information is stored on computers and so many critical communications systems depend on computer networks, the potential cost of intrusions (in privacy invasion, risks to health and safety, business loss, social disruption, etc.) is much greater than it was in the early days of computing. Attitudes about security have not caught up with the risk.

Now, as use of the World Wide Web explodes, it is wise to remember that the Web was established as a communications tool for physics researchers. Again, security was not a primary concern. The Web has security holes. Several security flaws were found in Java, the popular programming language used for Web applications.[37] Past experience suggests that some holes will not be discovered or plugged until a few serious and costly breaches occur.

Oddly, the one organization that we would expect to be highly security conscious—the Pentagon—gives a similar excuse for the poor security of Defense Department systems. The Assistant Secretary of Defense for Communications said that many Pentagon systems were built for rapid communication, with little thought given to protection against intruders. He describes the current state of vulnerability as the "result of 20 years of neglect."[38]

A significant change of focus from openness to security is needed among system designers and managers. This change is occurring, but it is slow. Some system managers are reluctant to spend effort and money on improved security. New technical developments are also continually needed to protect new technologies and to protect older technologies against new hacker and criminal techniques.

It seems to be a common human trait not to take sufficient security precautions until after a serious problem has occurred. How many people do not back up their hard disks before they lose files? How many do not lose weight until after a heart attack? The reminder at the beginning of this section, about the futility of locking the barn door after the horse is gone, comes from the days when people used horses for transportation. The security problem predates cars, as well as computers.

Improving security

There are many technical approaches to improving security of computer and telecommunications systems. As with other problems we have discussed, awareness of the extent of the problem, education of users, and acceptance of responsibility are important too.

New systems can be designed with security as a major design goal, unlike UNIX. In Chapter 4 we saw that safety techniques exist and responsible software designers must learn to use them. The same is true for designing systems to be secure from intruders. In both cases, where systems are very complex, it is not an easy task, but the goal will not be achieved if it is not even accepted as a goal.

Recognizing the risk of being open to the world, many network administrators are installing "firewalls"—software or separate computers that monitor incoming communications (e-mail, files, requests for services, etc.) and filter out those that are from untrusted sites or fit a profile of suspicious activity. Likewise, they can monitor information leaving the protected network to check for leaks. There is obviously a trade-off between the openness and accessibility of communication, on one hand, and the security, on the other.

No protection is perfect. Hackers can fake the return address on e-mail and fake their machine's Internet address, pretending to be a trusted machine—a technique called Internet Protocol spoofing. In cases where hackers succeed in breaching the firewalls or other security measures, encryption reduces the value of stolen files to the thieves. Encryption of transmissions provides protection from net sniffers. Digital signatures and other nonforgeable identification techniques are being developed and implemented. The importance of encryption and digital signatures is emphasized in numerous articles on computer security. Several writers criticize government policies that thwart the implementation of strong encryption while the damage done by intruders rises.

To counter cellular phone cloning, a technique has been developed to store each phone's unique electronic "signature" along with its serial number. The system checks that they match when a call is made. Other methods under development use sophisticated mathematical techniques that can identify a phone without having the phone broadcast its serial number. Security in the telephone system itself is improving gradually as older, less secure equipment is replaced.

Computer users and even system administrators vary quite a bit in their knowledge of the systems they use and administer. Education about security risks and countermeasures is one underused tool in reducing security breaches. Users need to understand the importance of keeping their passwords secret; system administrators need to implement standard programs that prevent users from choosing passwords that are easy to guess. A system administrator at a university who tested a simple password-guessing program on 80 workstation accounts found passwords for one quarter of them.[39]

Password security is another area that illustrates the leapfrogging of hacker techniques and defenses. As personal computers got faster and hackers could run programs to try a large number of short letter combinations quickly, security-conscious users chose longer passwords. When dictionaries appeared online and hackers could run a program to test every word in the dictionary, security-conscious users stopped using dictionary words, but foreign words were okay. Now, dictionaries for other languages are available online, so a good password is one that is not a word in any language. The entire computer system can be at risk if a hacker gets into one account. Good system managers do not rely on users to select good passwords; they run programs that make sure that the user's password meets their security specifications.

Several people who work on computer security, including the manager of CERT and security expert Eugene Spafford, see a role for consumer pressure in improving security. As consumers become more aware of the issues, they will consider the quality of security as one of the factors in choosing computing services. Security is not cheap; market demand can justify the costs.[40]

Some attempts to encourage or assist computer system managers in improving security have been quite controversial. The Security Administrator Tool for Analyzing Networks (better known as SATAN) is a program written by two computer security experts to examine computer networks and report on potential security problems. A CERT advisory explains the dilemma: "SATAN was designed as a security tool for system and network administrators. However, given its wide distribution, ease of use, and ability to scan remote networks, SATAN is also likely to be used to locate vulnerable hosts for malicious reasons."[41] The controversy centered on the authors' decision to release SATAN on the Internet. The security holes SATAN searches for are known, so the systems most threatened by the release were those whose administrators have not corrected them. The publicity and controversy about SATAN may have motivated such administrators to do so. However, SATAN can be modified easily to search networks for new loopholes that hackers may discover in the future.

Security through secrecy?

The SATAN controversy illustrates the issue of using secrecy as a security measure. Is it reasonable and practical to try to keep information about system vulnerabilities from hackers? Should computer and network security information be classified, with perhaps the National Security Agency (NSA) prescreening articles to be published in academic journals? How much is this issue similar to or different from the issue of the NSA trying to keep research on cryptography from being published?

AT&T used to rely on secrecy, or obscurity, to prevent people from making long distance calls without paying for them. The exact frequencies of the tones that made the connections were buried in technical manuals and journals. Phone phreaks found them.[42] Experience suggests that secrecy is not a good defense; security must be built into the system. But is there a value to discretion? Is it responsible to widely circulate information or tools that will assist crackers as well as systems managers?

7.4.5   Law Enforcement

In Section 6.5 we described some hacker cases—Steve Jackson Games, the 911 document, the Operation Sun Devil raids—where many civil libertarians and computer professionals believe law-enforcement agencies overreacted. The Steve Jackson Games case included a sealed search warrant (Jackson was told nothing about the purpose of the raid or who or what was suspected), a raid on a publisher, seizure of equipment and records unrelated to the suspected offense but necessary to the operation of the business, and seizure and reading of customer e-mail protected by the Electronic Communications Privacy Act—all in a case where an employee, not Jackson or his company, was suspected of a hacking offense. In the *Phrack* case, the charges were drastically exaggerated. In some Operation Sun Devil raids, Secret Service agents reportedly held families of hackers at gunpoint.[43]

The paranoia, or hysteria, about hackers came in part from ignorance and in part in reaction to the Internet Worm. John Perry Barlow colorfully describes how he spent two hours explaining the basics of computing and computer networks to an FBI agent who came to question him.[44] The cases mentioned above, and Barlow's interview with the FBI, occurred in 1990. Understanding of technical aspects of hacking and the hacker culture have improved somewhat. Law-enforcement agencies, including the FBI, have established special units to deal with computer crime. More police detectives are being trained in this area. Police are beginning to use old-fashioned techniques to track potential hacker crime. A police detective who specializes in financial crime and hacking told me that 30% of hackers are government informers, and the majority of subscribers to *2600*, a hacker magazine, are law-enforcement personnel. He may have exaggerated, but he makes the point that the sheriff has come to the frontier, and the sheriff now speaks the language. We can hope that improved understanding on the part of law enforcement will help stop malicious, destructive hacking activities without the ill-informed, heavy-handed tactics and civil liberties violations of 1990.

7.4.6 Penalties Appropriate to the Crime

Clearly, offenses related to unauthorized access vary in degree, and penalties should vary as well, as they do for trespass, vandalism, invasion of privacy, fraud, and theft. There are still difficult questions in deciding on appropriate penalties.

How should ethical and legal distinctions be made between hackers who use their knowledge to make long-distance calls without paying for them and criminals who sell calling card codes and cloned cellular phones? How can we distinguish between the young Steve Wozniak and a criminal who should be sent to jail for many years? Wozniak is the creator of the Apple computer, co-founder of Apple Computer Corporation, and now a wealthy donor to medical research and other valuable efforts. But before he was building Apples, Wozniak was building blue boxes, the devices that enabled people to make long-distance phone calls without paying for them.[45]

What is an appropriate penalty for a person who damages files or disrupts a system? Should it depend on whether the disruption was intentional or accidental? Should the punishment be designed primarily to compensate for damage done, or to punish the person, or to "send a signal" to others who might be thinking of trying something similar? Because of the uncertainty about an intruder's intentions and the cost of tracking and catching him or her, should penalties be harsh even for minor offenses? These are basic questions about the purpose of a penalty for any crime or accidental damage. They are debated by philosophers, criminologists, and economists.

Although compensating the victims may seem most important to many people, the criminal justice system does not provide for it. Fines imposed in criminal trials go to the government. Victims must sue in civil court to recover for damages. Unfortunately, with or without computers, it is possible for someone to cause far more damage than he or she can pay for. Robert Morris, for example, was sentenced to three years of probation, fined $10,000, and required to perform 400 hours of community service. There was a lot of disagreement about whether the punishment was reasonable or too lenient. In any case, he did not pay the costs of the disruption caused by his worm program. It is partly because the potential costs can be too high to be repaid that actions such as unauthorized access may have penalties more severe than the access alone seems to merit.

7.5   COMPUTER CRIME LAWS

7.5.1   Old Laws and New Offenses

We saw in Chapter 5 how new technology required changes in copyright law, interpretation of the law, and penalties. As traditional crimes began to be committed using computers, the old laws—against theft and fraud, for example—were sometimes sufficient to obtain prosecutions; courts interpreted the law to include the new activity. In other cases, as in the LaMacchia copyright case (Section 5.4.2), the courts decided that the current law did not apply to the new circumstances and it was up to the legislature, not the court, to extend the law. For some new activities made possible by computers, such as using an employer's computer for personal work or hacking without doing harm, there was real disagreement not only about whether the activity was a crime under existing law, but also whether it should be a crime at all. I will describe cases where the old laws led to convictions and cases where they did not, then describe the new computer crime laws. The information in this section on cases and state laws is from a study done for the U.S. Department of Justice.[46]

Several cases where courts rendered different rulings involved use of a company's computer by an employee for the employee's own commercial business. Although this is not one of the more significant categories of computer crime, it illustrates how computer technology challenged existing laws and led to new ones. Also, some of the basic arguments in these cases apply to intrusions and use of computer time by outsiders (e.g., hackers) as well.

The employees were charged with theft or larceny. Larceny is a legal term that means taking away a person's property (a "thing of value") with the intent to steal it. One defense argument was that the employees did not deprive the employers of any tangible property; they did not steal a "thing of value." They did not "carry away" anything, as the law, written for physical property, stated. In some cases the courts agreed with the defendants, ruling that computer time and services were not tangible and could not be "carried away." In other cases the courts rejected this argument, ruling that the computer itself is clearly tangible property and use of computer time is a thing of value.

Particularly where some detail supported the employee's claim, the courts sided with the employee. For example, in a case where an employee was charged with theft for using the employer's computer for his own business, the employer leased computer time at a fixed rate, independent of usage. The employee convinced the court that he did not deprive his employer of anything because there was no additional charge to the employer for the computer services he used. Also, he did not use any of the employer's data. He argued that his use of the computer was analogous to using a tool, such as a hammer or typewriter, belonging to the employer for personal business and storing personal items on an empty shelf. An employer might object and possibly fire someone for such actions, but, the employee claimed, it was not a criminal offense. The Indiana Supreme Court agreed and reversed the defendant's conviction. A dissenting judge, however, found the arguments unconvincing and stated that "Time and use are at the very core of the value of a computer system. . . . The fact is that the [employer] owned the computer system. . . . The time and use of that equipment . . . belonged to the [employer]."[47]

In some cases where the objectionable action was clearly, from a nonlegal viewpoint, fraud or theft, prosecutors feared they would not get a conviction under the existing fraud and theft laws. They sometimes used federal wire fraud or mail fraud laws, although the use of telephone or mail was a minor and unimportant part of the activity. For example, two TWA employees were convicted of federal wire fraud for a scheme where they pocketed cash paid by customers for tickets and voided those tickets so the books would balance. The airline's computer was in a different state, so federal wire fraud law could be used. Such use of the wire fraud law is questionable. Because so many computer networks now cross state lines (the factor that allows federal laws to be applied), the government can try to use wire fraud laws when an action is not clearly criminal under another law. We might applaud the cleverness of prosecutors in doing so in cases like this, where the employees were clearly stealing from the airline. But recall that the judge in the LaMacchia case pointed out that stretching a law can threaten many ordinary people doing things the legislature did not intend to criminalize.

In an ATM fraud case, a defendant argued that he did not use deception because he did not make any false claims; he just put someone else's card in the ATM and typed the person's PIN. The court found existing laws good enough here. It ruled that deception does not have to be verbal; the defendant's conduct sufficed.

7.5.2 Now It's a Crime

Because of the problems that arose in some prosecutions, state governments began passing laws that specifically addressed computer crimes. Access to and use of a computer without authorization have been made criminal offenses by state and federal laws. This means that hacker activity that includes access to computers where the hacker is not an authorized user is illegal in most cases. Some laws were written clearly and explicitly for the cases where defendants had previously been freed. For example, to counter the argument that computer time was intangible and could not be stolen, the new crime of "theft of computer services" was defined. The Virginia law is simple and clear on this point: "Any person who willfully uses a computer or computer network, with intent to obtain computer services without authority, shall be guilty of the crime of theft of computer services. . . ."

Some of the actions that are distinguished (and made illegal) in the laws are listed below. (The first six are all legitimate and routine activities when performed with authorization; they are illegal when done without authorization or by exceeding one's authorization. The seventh item in the list can occur accidentally; it too is illegal when done while accessing a computer without authorization or by exceeding one's authorization.)

1. Access of a computer system
2. Use of computer services
3. Accessing (reading) files

4. Copying data, programs, or other information

5. Modifying data or other files

6. Destroying data or other files

7. Interrupting the operation of a computer or causing a computer to malfunction (e.g., by viruses or worms)

8. Access to commit fraud

9. Disclosing passwords or other access codes to unauthorized people

10. Interrupting or impairing government operation, public communication, transportation or other public utilities

There are more than a dozen federal laws that can be used to prosecute people for crimes related to computer and telecommunications systems. They cover electronic funds transfer and bank fraud, interference with satellite operations, damage to government property, unlicensed export of certain technical data, and a variety of other actions. Congress passed the Computer Fraud and Abuse Act, the main federal computer crime law, in 1986.

The Computer Fraud and Abuse Act is poorly organized and not particularly easy to read. It groups offenses in several slightly different categories and is therefore difficult to summarize. As a federal law, it covers areas over which the federal government has jurisdiction: government computers (or those used by government agencies), financial systems, medical systems, and activities that involve computers in more than one state (because the federal government has the power to regulate interstate commerce). There are three groups of offenses, with prison sentences of up to one, five, or ten years for a first offense. The first group is accessing and obtaining information without authorization (or by exceeding one's authorization) from computer systems of financial institutions, credit reporting businesses, and government agencies. The next group involves altering, damaging, or destroying information, or preventing authorized use of a computer or information. The heaviest penalty is for obtaining information that the federal government considers important to national defense or foreign relations.

7.5.3 The Issue of Venue

Normally, criminal charges are filed and a trial takes place in the place (county or state) where the crime was committed. State laws differ. If someone in Boise logs on to a computer in San Francisco, hops over the Internet, using unauthorized access to other computers, to steal files from someone in Chicago and stores them on a computer in Florida, where is the crime committed? Where should the trial be held? Where the defendant is physically located? Or where the computer whose files were stolen is located? We saw that for First Amendment cases involving distribution of obscene material, the jurisdiction was a critical issue because community standards are an essential factor in determining guilt. In cases that do not explicitly involve community standards, venue (the place where the charges are brought) can still be very important. The government may choose a location where prosecutors have more expertise in computer crime, but that choice may adversely affect a defendant who must hire distant lawyers and travel a long distance to a trial. This is one more issue raised by our increasing interconnectivity, by the access computer networks provide to sites all over the world. The problem is getting worse as more computer crimes are committed internationally.

7.6 DIGITAL FORGERY

> *Seeing is believing may soon become an anachronism of the precomputer era.*
>
> —Sanford Sherizen[48]

7.6.1 The Problem

A photograph shows Marilyn Monroe arm in arm with Abraham Lincoln. Forrest Gump chats with John F. Kennedy in a movie. These impossible images were produced by digital manipulation of photographs and video. We know that Marilyn Monroe and Abraham Lincoln lived a hundred years apart, that the movie *Forrest Gump* used sophisticated computerized special effects. Where is the crime? The same technology that is used for entertainment is also used for fraud.[49]

Desktop publishing systems, color laser and ink-jet printers, color copiers, and image scanners enable crooks to make fakes with relative ease—fake checks, currency, passports, visas, stock and bond certificates, purchase orders, birth certificates, identification cards, corporate stationery—to name a few examples. A group of counterfeiters made off with $750,000 from one counterfeit check. They produced it by scanning a real check from a corporation, changing the amount and payee, then printing it on a laser printer. Forgers and counterfeiters used to need specialized skills; computer software and hardware have dramatically reduced the requirements. The equipment has improved in quality while prices have tumbled from many thousands of dollars to hundreds. Only about 10% of counterfeit U.S. currency is produced by desktop forgery (rather than the old method of printing using engraved plates), but it is hard to detect and the amount is increasing rapidly. As protection against copying, U.S. currency contains microprinting that is seven-thousandths of an inch high, but some new copiers have resolution good enough to reproduce it.[50]

The increased ease of forgery and counterfeiting threatens the security of financial institutions and U.S. currency, and ultimately, the stability of the economy. Cybercitizens might argue that currency and checks will become unimportant as they are replaced with digital cash and other electronic transactions, but presently, large-scale counterfeiting would have significant economic impact.

7.6.2 Defenses

The defenses against forgery and counterfeiting include the usual array of approaches: technical tricks that make copying more difficult, education (increased training of clerks who process documents that are likely targets), business practices to reduce risk, and changes in laws.

Antifraud techniques, such as microprinting and using paper with watermarks, have been used in the past. New techniques are being developed to fight new threats. Microprinting techniques are being updated. Currency contains a "security thread" that is not reproduced by a copier or scanner, but can be seen when a bright light shines through the bill. The paper used for checks, money orders, and identification documents can have embedded fibers or use special inks that glow under ultraviolet light. The new U.S. $100 bill incorporates some of these security features. Some copiers contain a chip that recognizes currency and prevents the copier from making a copy.

Copiers can print the machine's serial number on each copy, so that counterfeits can be tracked. There had been discussion of imposing a legal requirement that copies made by copying machines not be the same size as the original. Like many of the attempts we have seen to ban or restrict machines or technology that could be used in criminal ways, this would have been a problem for many of the millions of legitimate users who want same-size copies.

An example of a procedural change to reduce check fraud is for a business to send its bank a list of the number and amount of all checks issued; the bank can then quickly verify incoming checks.

In the past banks that accepted forged checks usually absorbed the loss. Changes in state laws now place some of the responsibility on the businesses whose checks are copied, thus providing more incentive for them to improve security of their checks.

7.6.3 Faking Photos

The ease with which digital images can be modified raises other issues, some related to crime and some that are intriguing ethical and social issues. Many cameras now record digital images; they do not use film. (The ID photos taken by motor vehicle bureaus, for example, are digital photos stored on computers.) Photos taken on film are scanned for storage and use in computerized publishing systems. How can we be sure the images we see have not been modified or faked?

Photographs (e.g., crime scene photos) are used as evidence in legal proceedings. A trusted and reliable means of authentication of digital photos will be essential for the justice system. A technical solution is available: encryption. The public key encryption schemes for signing or authenticating a message can be used to authenticate a digital image file.

Should news organizations (newspapers, TV news programs, magazines, and online news services) modify photographs? Is it acceptable if the purpose is artistic, or to enhance or improve the image without changing the content? Was darkening O.J. Simpson's skin on the cover of *Time* an artistic measure or a racist one?

News organizations and individual publishers are working out their policies. The National Press Photographers Association has a policy that considers any alteration of a photo's editorial content to be a breach of ethical standards. But where is the line between editorial content and aesthetics? Some magazines treat their cover photos as advertisements for the magazine and are more likely to manipulate them than the photos inside. (*National Geographic* generated one of the first computer-era controversies about faked photos when it moved two pyramids closer together to fit them both on the cover.)[51]

Some magazine editors are realizing that a reputation for manipulating photos, like any form of deception, makes all of one's work suspect. The art director of *Texas Monthly* commented that "The altered photographs we had done were really hurting the integrity of the magazine's cover to the point that when we had a great photograph, nobody believed it." The editor of *Audubon,* also citing the credibility problem, announced in an editorial that *Audubon* would not print any manipulated photos.[52]

There are numerous examples in history of photographs that were faked before digital technology. The ethical issues are not new, but they now are faced by many more people because image manipulation has become so easy; it is no longer reserved to the specialist with a darkroom. The general public must become more aware of the possibility of fakery and learn to have a reasonable skepticism.

EXERCISES

Review exercises

1. What is one significant kind of computer crime committed by "insiders" in a company? What is one significant kind of computer crime committed by "outsiders"?

2. What are two ways computer technology is used to reduce the problem of credit card fraud?

3. What did the word "hacker" mean in the early days of computing?

4. What is a historic reason for weak security on the Internet?

5. Give two arguments hackers use to justify their activities. Give counterarguments to each one.

6. What kinds of computer systems are protected by the Computer Fraud and Abuse Act?

General exercises

7. At many gas stations customers can pay with a credit card using an automated machine without signing a receipt. Compare the risk of use of stolen or counterfeit cards with the convenience of using the machines. Do you think gas stations should require a signature? Why or why not?

8. Cable decoder boxes are used to unscramble cable TV signals and watch cable programs without paying for them. Should it be illegal to sell such devices (without authorization of the cable company)? Why or why not? Should it be illegal to use such devices (without authorization of the cable company)? Why or why not?

9. Chris logs on to your computer at night while you sleep and uses some of your software. Robin takes your car at night while you sleep and drives it around for a while. (Neither has your permission; they do not damage the computer or the car.) List several characteristics of the two events that are similar (characteristics related to the effects of the events, ethics, legality, risks, etc.). List several characteristics of the two events that are different.

10. Choose one of the arguments in support of nonmalicious hacking (in Section 7.4.3) and write a short essay elaborating on and defending the argument.

11. Do you agree or disagree with the following statement by Ken Thompson, one of the inventors of UNIX? Give your reasons.

    The act of breaking into a computer system has to have the same social stigma as breaking into a neighbor's house. It should not matter that the neighbor's door is unlocked.[53]

12. How many words are in a typical English dictionary? Tell what dictionary you used and how you determined (or estimated) the number of words. Roughly how many random six-letter combinations are there that may contain uppercase and lowercase letters? (Show your calculation.) What is the implication of these numbers for password selection?

13. Suppose a hacker is convicted of copying files related to computer security after accessing the computer of a security specialist without authorization, and of copying thousands of customer credit card numbers from an online business (but not of using any of them). What penalty do you think is appropriate? Why? What factors do you consider relevant? What are reasonable analogies with noncomputer crimes?

14. Do you think the release of SATAN on the Internet was a responsible or irresponsible act? Give your reasons.

15. Suppose two employees of a state lottery access the lottery computer and rig the lottery so that they win.* They are caught. You are the prosecutor; the state does not have a computer crime law. What charges will you bring? What arguments will you make in court to convince the jury that the defendants committed a crime?

16. "Spamming" means sending e-mail, both "junk mail" advertisements and comments or discussion, to many people or newsgroups who do not want to receive it. Do you think it should be illegal? Why, or why not? How would you specify the offense in a law so that it does not criminalize reasonable activities or infringe on freedom of speech?

17. Should it be illegal to fake the return address on e-mail posted to a newsgroup, to make it appear to be from another person? Give reasons; include analogies with similar activities that do not involve computers.

18. Consider the discussion in Section 7.5.1 about use of computer time, services, and storage on an employer's computer for an employee's business. Write an essay in which you present arguments for considering such activity a matter of employer/employee relations (analogous to using a tool belonging to the employer for personal business), present arguments for treating such action as a theft, and then take a position on one side and defend it.

19. Suppose a person finds (not steals) an ATM card on which the owner has (foolishly) written his PIN. What case or principle mentioned in this chapter suggests that the person would be committing a crime if he used the card to withdraw cash from the account?

20. To track potential counterfeit currency, checks, and so on, some copying machines automatically print their serial number on all copies they make. What are some privacy implications, or possible dangers to privacy, of this technique?

Assignments
These exercises require some research or activity that may need to be done during business hours or a few days before the assignment is due.

21. Contact your city's police department and find out how many of each of the following crimes were reported in your city last year: robberies at ATMs, car thefts, house burglaries, muggings or purse snatchings (not at ATMs).

22. If you have a credit card, over the next few weeks count the times each of the following occurs: You use the card without providing a signature to be verified (e.g., at an automated gas station or for a telephone order). You sign a receipt, but the merchant does not compare your signature to the signature on the card. You sign a receipt, and the merchant does compare your signature to the signature on the card.

23. Find a dozen newspaper and/or magazine articles about hackers from the past few years. How are hackers described, as criminals or heroes? Give examples.

---

*The Pennsylvania lottery was rigged in the early 1980s.

24. (a) Find out the rules for choosing a password on the computer system at your school. Are students permitted to choose their own passwords? Can you use a dictionary word? What is the minimum password length?

(b) Log on to your computer account on your campus (or work) computer system, but make a mistake typing your password. Is there a noticeable pause before you get an error message and a new login prompt (longer than the pause that occurs for a successful login)? On many systems there is such a pause. Can you figure out why?

25. Read the Computer Fraud and Abuse Act of 1986, and answer the following questions.

(a) What is the definition of a "federal interest computer"?

(b) What is the maximum penalty for unauthorized changes in medical records?

(c) What is the maximum penalty for "trafficking" in passwords?

(d) Is the act's legal writing style easier to read than it would be if it were encrypted? :-)

Class exercises

1. The families of two hospital patients who died as the result of a virus in a hospital computer are suing each of the people listed below and urging the district attorney to bring criminal charges for negligence against each of them.[54]

- A student in a course on computer security at a small college who posted a copy of the virus program on a campus BBS with a discussion of how it works.
- The student who activated the virus program and released it onto the Internet.
- The president of the college.
- The president of the company that provides Internet access for the college.
- The director of the hospital whose computer system was infected by the virus, causing patient medical records to be unavailable for a full day, which led to the deaths of the two patients.

  Divide the class into ten teams, five (one for each person listed above) to present arguments for civil and/or criminal penalties, and five (one for each person) to present defense arguments. After the presentations, use a class vote or discussion to decide which, if any, of the characters should not be considered guilty at all, which, if any, should bear a high degree of responsibility, and which are "fuzzy" cases, hard to decide.

2. Divide students into a prosecution team and a defense team for the two state employees who rigged the lottery, as described in Exercise 15. The prosecution team should inform the defense team, well before the class meeting, of what charges they will bring. In class, each team presents its arguments.

NOTES

1   William M. Carley and Timothy L. O'Brien, "How Citicorp System Was Raided and Funds Moved Around the World," *Wall Street Journal,* September 12, 1995, pp. A1, A6. Timothy L. O'Brien, "Russian Hacker, in Hitting Citicorp, Shows Global Vulnerability of Banks," *Wall Street Journal,* August 21, 1995, p. A4.

2   I have seen estimates ranging up to $250,000 for the average, some from computer security firms, which have an incentive to exaggerate. It is difficult to get precise figures, in part because victims are reluctant to report losses.

3   *Webster's Third New International Dictionary.*

4   Tom Forester and Perry Morrison, *Computer Ethics: Cautionary Tales and Ethical Dilemmas in Computing,* 2nd ed., MIT Press, 1994, p. 34. Carley and O'Brien, "How Citicorp System Was Raided."

5   Hugh Cornwall, *Datatheft: Computer Fraud, Industrial Espionage and Information Crime,* Heinemann, 1987, p. 102.

6   Forester and Morrison, *Computer Ethics,* p. 37.

7   The loss estimate appears in Jeffrey Rothfeder, *Privacy For Sale,* Simon & Schuster, 1992, p. 52. A detective who works in this area told me that he believes that only one-tenth of the losses are actually reported and that total credit card fraud amounts to $40–$50 billion a year.

8   Hugh Nugent, "State Computer Crime Statutes," National Institute of Justice, U.S. Dept. of Justice, November 1991, contract no. OJP-85-C-006, p. 3.

9   Barbara Carton, "An Unsolved Slaying of an Airline Worker Stirs Family to Action," *Wall Street Journal,* June 20, 1995, pp. A1, A8.

10 Interview with Detective Dennis Sadler, San Diego Police Department, June 2, 1995. "'Theft of Identity' Rises to Thousands a Day," *Privacy Journal,* February 1996, 22:4, pp. 1, 4. "Credit, SSN Fraud Victims," *Privacy Journal,* April 1996, p. 6.

11 This estimate is attributed to a Bank of America vice president by Jeffrey Rothfeder, *Privacy For Sale,* Simon & Schuster, 1992, p. 116.

12 Jeffrey Rothfeder, *Privacy For Sale,* Simon & Schuster, 1992, pp. 113–16.

13 Elizabeth Attebery, "2 Suspects Held in Phony ATM Scam," San Diego Union-Tribune, June 30, 1993, p. C2. F. Barry Schreiber, "The Future of ATM Security," *Security Management,* March 1994, 38:3, p. 18A.

14 Saul Hansell, "U.S. Workers Stole Data on 11,000, Agency Says," *New York Times,* April 6, 1996, p. 6.

15 Matt Barthel, "Bank Worker Gets Kudos for Cracking ATM Scam," *The American Banker,* October 25, 1993, p. 24.

16 Jerry E. Bishop, "Lab Notes: Foiling Card Forgers With Magnetic 'Noise'," *Wall Street Journal,* February 8, 1994, p. B1.

17 Schreiber, "The Future of ATM Security."

18 Peter G. Neumann et al, "Risks to the Public in Computers and Related Systems," *Software Engineering Notes,* April 1988, 13:2, pp. 7–8.

19 William M. Carley, "As Computers Flip, People Lose Grip In Saga of Sabotage at Printing Firm," *Wall Street Journal,* August 27, 1992, p. A7.

20 "Like a Virgin," *Security Insider Report,* February 1993, p. 5. William M. Carley, "Did Northwest Steal American's Systems? The Court Will Decide," *Wall Street Journal,* July 7, 1994, p. A1.

21 Richard P. Feynman, *Surely You're Joking, Mr. Feynman: Adventures of a Curious Character,* W. W. Norton, 1984, pp. 137–55.

22 David L. Wilson, "'Crackers': a Serious Threat," *The Chronicle of Higher Education,* August 17, 1994, pp. A23–A24.

23 Brian Reid, "Reflection on Some Recent Widespread Computer Break-Ins," *Communications of the ACM,* February 1987, 30:2, pp. 103–05; reprinted in Peter J. Denning, ed., *Computers Under Attack: Intruders, Worms, and Viruses,* Addison Wesley, 1990, pp. 145–49.

24 "Politicians and the Net," *Wired,* February 1995, p. 46. Laura Evenson and Michelle Quinn, "Outlaws on the Cyberprairie," *San Francisco Chronicle,* April 2, 1995, pp. 1, 4.

25 Wilson, "'Crackers': a Serious Threat." Jared Sandberg, "Security Breach at the Internet Raises Worries," *Wall Street Journal,* February 7, 1994, p. B5.

258   CHAPTER 7   COMPUTER CRIME

26 John R. Wilke, "In the Arcane Culture of Computer Hackers, Few Doors Stay Closed," *Wall Street Journal,* August 22, 1990, pp. A1, A4.

27 Katie Hafner and John Markoff, *Cyberpunk: Outlaws and Hackers on the Computer Frontier,* Simon & Schuster, 1991.

28 "Newstrack," *Communications of the ACM,* February 1991, 34:2, pp. 13–14.

29 Wade Roush, "Hackers," *Technology Review,* April 1995, pp. 32–40. Jared Sandberg, "Losses Linked to Lax Security of Computers," *Wall Street Journal,* November 18, 1994, p. B2. Wilson, "'Crackers': a Serious Threat." John J. Fialka, "Pentagon Hacker Attacks Increase and Some Pose Threat, GAO Says," *Wall Street Journal,* May 23, 1996, p. B7.

30 All the quotes are from Wilke, "In the Arcane Culture of Computer Hackers, Few Doors Stay Closed."

31 John J. Fialka, "Pentagon Studies Art of 'Information Warfare' To Reduce Its Systems' Vulnerability to Hackers," *Wall Street Journal,* July 3, 1995, p. A10.

32 Donn B. Parker makes this point in his article, "The Trojan Horse Virus and Other Crimoids," in Peter J. Denning, ed., *Computers Under Attack: Intruders, Worms, and Viruses,* Addison Wesley, 1990, pp. 544–54.

33 I am not certain of the origin of this statement; it has been attributed to Stewart Brand.

34 John J. Fialka, "The Latest Flurries at Weather Bureau: Scattered Hacking," *Wall Street Journal,* October 10, 1994, pp. A1, A6.

35 Ted Eisenberg, David Gries, Juris Hartmanis, Don Holcomb, M. Stuart Lynn, Thomas Santoro, "The Cornell Commission: On Morris and the Worm," *Communications of the ACM,* June 1989, 32:6, pp. 706–9.

36 Larry Lange, "Corporate America: Beware Inside Job," *Electronic Engineering Times,* January 15, 1996, pp. 20, 22. Jared Sandberg, "AOL Tightens Security after Hackers Foil the Service with Fake Accounts," *Wall Street Journal,* September 8, 1995, p. B3.

37 Paul Wallich, "Wire Pirates," *Scientific American,* March 1994, pp. 90–101. Don Clark, "Researchers Find Big Security Flaw in Java Language," *Wall Street Journal,* March 26, 1996, p. B7.

38 Emmett Paige, Jr., quoted in Fialka, "Pentagon Studies Art of 'Information Warfare'."

39 Wallich, "Wire Pirates."

40 David L. Wilson, "Internet Security Arm Decides to Focus on Emergencies," *The Chronicle of Higher Education,* August 17, 1994, p. A24. Jared Sandberg, "Newest Security Glitch on the Internet Could Affect Many 'Host' Computers," *Wall Street Journal,* February 23, 1995, p. B6.

41 CERT Advisory CA-95:06, "Security Administrator Tool for Analyzing Networks (SATAN)," April 3, 1995.

42 Wallich, "Wire Pirates."

43 John Perry Barlow, "Crime and Puzzlement," *The Whole Earth Review,* Fall, 1990, pp. 44–57. (This article describes and comments on several hacker cases we have mentioned.) Wilke, "In the Arcane Culture of Computer Hackers, Few Doors Stay Closed."

44 Barlow, "Crime and Puzzlement."

45 Craig Bromberg, "In Defense of Hackers," *The New York Times Magazine,* April 21, 1991, pp. 45–49.

46 Hugh Nugent, "State Computer Crime Statutes," National Institute of Justice, U.S. Dept. of Justice, November 1991, contract no. OJP-85-C-006.

47 *State v. McGraw,* 1985.

48 "Beware of a Blizzard of Fake Documents" (letter to the editor), *New York Times,* August 16, 1991, pg. 12.

49 The photo of Marilyn Monroe and Abraham Lincoln and an explanation of how such fakes are produced is in William J. Mitchell, "When Is Seeing Believing?" *Scientific American,* February 1994, pp. 68–73.

50 Doug McClellan, "Desktop Counterfeiting," *Technology Review,* February/March 1995, pp. 32–40.

51 Jacques Leslie, "Digital Photopros and Photo(shop) Realism," *Wired,* May 1995, pp. 108–13.

52 D. J. Stout, quoted in Leslie, "Digital Photopros and Photo(shop) Realism." Michael W. Robbins, "The Apple of Visual Technology," *Audubon,* July/August 1994, p. 4.

53 In Donn Seeley, "Password Cracking: A Game of Wits," *Communications of the ACM,* June 1989, 32:6, pp. 700–703, reprinted in Peter J. Denning, ed., *Computers Under Attack: Intruders, Worms, and Viruses,* Addison-Wesley, 1990, pp. 244–252.

54 This exercise is a simplified version of a scenario used in a mock hearing presentation at the Computers, Freedom, and Privacy conference, San Francisco, 1993, in a session chaired by Don Ingraham.

FOR FURTHER READING

"Is Computer Hacking a Crime?" *Harper's Magazine,* March 1990, pp. 45–57. An online discussion among several well-known hackers and others.

William R. Cheswick and Steven M. Bellovin, *Firewalls and Internet Security: Repelling the Wily Hacker,* Addison-Wesley, 1994. A technical book with a few chapters on a hacker tracking case.

Hugh Cornwall, *Datatheft: Computer Fraud, Industrial Espionage and Information Crime,* Heinemann, 1987.

Peter J. Denning, ed., *Computers Under Attack: Intruders, Worms, and Viruses,* Addison-Wesley, 1990. An excellent collection of articles and reports on hacker activities and issues.

Katie Hafner and John Markoff, *Cyberpunk: Outlaws and Hackers on the Computer Frontier,* Simon & Schuster, 1991.

Lance J. Hoffman, ed., *Rogue Programs: Viruses, Worms, and Trojan Horses,* Van Nostrand Reinhold, 1990.

Richard C. Hollinger and Lonn Lanza-Kaduce, "The Process of Criminalization: The Case of Computer Crime Laws," *Criminology,* 1988, 26:101. A history of the making of state computer crime laws.

Steven Levy, *Hackers: Heroes of the Computer Revolution,* Doubleday, 1984.

Jonathan Littman, *The Fugitive Game: Online with Kevin Mitnick,* Little, Brown, 1996.

Doug McClellan, "Desktop Counterfeiting," *Technology Review,* February/March 1995, pp. 32–40.

Tsutomu Shimomura and John Markoff, *Take-down: The Pursuit and Capture of America's Most Wanted Computer Outlaw—By the Man Who Did It,* Hyperion, 1996.

Bruce Sterling, *The Hacker Crackdown: Law and Disorder on the Electronic Frontier,* Bantam Books, 1992.

Clifford Stoll, *The Cuckoo's Egg: Tracking a Spy Through the Maze of Computer Espionage,* Doubleday, 1989.

Paul Wallich, "Wire Pirates," *Scientific American,* March 1994, pp. 90–101.

Martin Wasik, *Crime & the Computer,* Oxford University Press, 1991.

8

COMPUTERS AND WORK

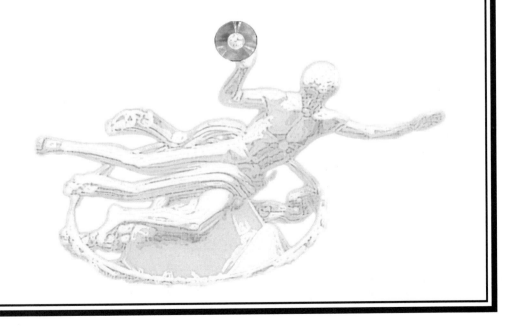

8.1   THE CHANGING NATURE OF WORK

Computers and computerized information and communications networks are having a profound impact on work. Computers are eliminating many jobs and creating others. Will increased productivity from computerization lead to reduced working hours and more leisure, or fewer jobs and more unemployment, or little change in working hours, but more wealth, or less wealth? In the short term, how will we deal with the dislocations caused by the loss of jobs and the need to retrain? In the long term, will we have masses of people out of work? Will the need for increased training and skills create wider divisions between those who can obtain the new skills and those who cannot?

"Telework" and "telecommuting" have become part of our vocabulary, describing the growing phenomenon of working at a distance from the traditional company office, connected by computer. Computers and communications networks are expected to cause changes in the size of businesses and the number of people who are self-employed. The physical distribution of population is likely to change: Communications networks make it possible for companies to locate in small towns and work with dispersed consultants instead of having hundreds or thousands of employees in larger population centers. As more people work at home, they can live farther from business centers.

At the same time that information technology is giving some workers more autonomy, computers are giving employers increased power to monitor the work, communications, and movements of employees. These changes affect the productivity, privacy, and morale of employees.

Several health issues have been raised concerning the use and manufacture of computers. How significant are they?

We explore these issues in this chapter. Although there is much we can say about what is happening now and what may happen in the future, the long-term impact and resolution of many of these issues is uncertain—more so, I think, than for many of the topics we discussed in other chapters. The effects of computerization on work are also heavily interconnected with a more diverse collection of political and economic factors, from local zoning to national tax policy. It is difficult to isolate effects that result solely from computers. We can make guesses about the future from the impact of earlier technologies, but making projections is difficult.

8.2   THE IMPACT ON EMPLOYMENT

But nowhere is there any mention of the truth about the information highway, which is mass unemployment.

—DAVID NOBLE, *"The Truth About the Information Highway"*[1]

8.2.1   Job Destruction and Creation

Computers and employment

One of the first issues many people think of when considering the impact of computers on work is unemployment. Does computerization destroy jobs? Does it cause mass unemployment? The quotation above is about the information highway, but many social scientists believe it applies to computers and technology in general.

As we saw in Chapter 1, the number of bank tellers dropped by about 37% between 1983 and 1993. A study by Deloitte and Touche predicted that another 450,000 bank jobs would be lost by the year 2000 because of automation and electronic banking services. Electronic calculators made slide rules, used by engineers since the 17th century, obsolete; the jobs involved in making and selling them are gone. The number of telephone operators dropped from 250,000 in 1956 to 60,000 in 1995 and is expected to drop further. The jobs of 35,000 electric meter readers will soon disappear as utility companies continue to install electronic devices that broadcast meter readings to company computers. Similar technology will be used to monitor vending machines and oil wells, reducing the number of people needed to check on them in person. As more shopping is done online, there may be fewer jobs for sales clerks. A bank holding company receives 1.5 million customer inquiries by telephone each month; 80% are handled by computer. The company reduced the number of customer service employees by 40%. Railroads have computerized dispatch operations and eliminated hundreds of employees. The New York Stock Exchange is eliminating the jobs of 140 runners who carry paper messages between brokers; they are being replaced by cellular phones. Travel agencies are closing as consumers make airplane reservations via online services. As more cameras record images in digital form, film processors will go out of business.[2] In fact, we can go through the discussion of benefits of computers in Chapter 1 and see that many of them, by making tasks more efficient, reduce the number of people required to carry out the tasks.

On the other hand, there are now people who build automated teller machines and write software for them, and people who design, build, and program the electronic calculators and computers that replaced slide rules and telephone operators. Besides computers themselves, there are countless new products that use computer technology: VCRs, computer games, fax machines, cellular phones, medical devices, and so on. New products create new jobs in design, marketing, manufacture, sales, customer service, repair, and maintenance. Industries that benefit from improved information management are hiring thousands of people in job categories that barely existed a decade ago. United Parcel Service of America, for example, now has 3000 information technology workers; it had only 90 in 1983.[3]

What is the overall effect? Do computers destroy more jobs than they create? These are extremely complicated questions. We will look at some aspects of possible answers in the rest of this section.

There is no question that technology in general and computers in particular eliminate some jobs. One of the goals of technology is to reduce the resources needed to accomplish a result, to increase productivity and our standard of living. If we look back at the examples of lost jobs described at the beginning of this section, we see that many of them accompanied increased productivity. The bank handles 1.5 million customer inquiries with fewer service representatives. The railroad ships more tons per worker with its new computer system. Stock brokerages and insurance companies process more orders with fewer people. Human labor is a resource. If a technology is successful, it should eliminate some jobs, but it should also create others. What jobs have been created by computers? The number of new Internet-related jobs created in 1995 was estimated at 36,000, and 100,000 more were expected to be created in 1996.[4] According to the Bureau of Labor Statistics, in

1992 there were 211,000 computer engineers and 455,000 computer systems analysts. By 2005, the Bureau expects these figures to grow to 447,000 and 956,000, respectively. These figures do not include support staff—receptionists, janitors, and stock clerks—who work in computer companies nor all the people who work in the myriad of computer hardware and software retail stores and mail-order houses that did not exist before the 1970s and 80s.

Even after examining publications of the Bureau of Labor Statistics telling how many people work in various job categories and industries, it is difficult to precisely count jobs gained and lost from computers. Job categories are not clearly defined. Industry totals and job categories overlap. More importantly, figures on computer-related jobs do not tell us the impact of computers on jobs in other areas. How many more people buy a microwave oven (generating more jobs in the microwave oven industry) because microprocessors have made them more convenient to use? How many more watches or clocks are sold because they are now so cheap? How many more compact disk players and music CDs are sold because the sound quality is better than on records and tapes? When a package delivery service installs computer systems to make its operations more efficient, fewer counter clerks, drivers, and managers can process the same number of packages. Does this eliminate jobs, or do the lower rates resulting from increased efficiency encourage more people to send packages, ultimately increasing business and jobs? A few hundred years ago, listening to professional quality music was a rare luxury for most people. The wealthy could hire professional musicians to perform for them. Technology, including electricity, radio, and now CDs, brought the cost of an individual "performance" in a private home down so low that music is available to almost anyone. The effect on employment? There are now thousands of musicians making a living, and many making a fortune, in jazz, country, classical, new age, rock, and rap music. In the long term, if technology brings the cost of a product or service down enough to expand the market, more people will work in that field. Other new jobs created by technology are often ones not imagined or possible before.

We are still in the transition to a computerized society. Incredible innovations in communications are likely to burst onto the market in the next decade. Cyberspace is still a frontier, just on the verge of being developed. The world of online and interactive entertainment, commercial, and information services is likely to expand enormously. It is too soon to try to total up the number of jobs created and eliminated by computers, but the examples and possibilities we cited above, and some of the discussion of other factors below, suggest that the net effect of computers on employment will be a gain.

Will computers be the most important factor in determining future employment levels? We can gain some insight into this question by considering other factors that affect employment and the historic impact of technology in general.

Technology, economic factors, and employment

Since the beginning of the Industrial Revolution, technology has been blamed for massive unemployment. In the early 1800s, the Luddites (of whom we will say more in Chapter 9) burned weaving looms because they feared the looms would eliminate their jobs. A few decades later, a mob of seamstresses and tailors destroyed sewing machines because of the same fears. But with a sewing machine, a seamstress could make more than two shirts a day. Rather than loss of jobs, the sewing machine meant a reduction in the price of clothes, more demand, and ultimately hundreds of thousands of new jobs.[5]*

As we have noted, technology is a significant factor in unemployment in specific areas and in the short term. Is it the most significant factor? Consider the times of significant unemployment in the U.S. in this century. The Great Depression in the 1930s was not caused by technology (and certainly not by computers). Economists and historians attribute the depression to a variety of factors including "business cycles," the then-new Federal Reserve Bank's inept manipulation of interest rates, and that old standby, "greed." There was a recession in the early 1980s and another in the early 1990s. In the interim, during most of the 1980s, when the Baby Boomers were in their 20s and 30s, the economy grew and unemployment was very low. But the growth in use of computers has been dramatic and continuous, especially since the mid-1970s when personal computers began to appear. While most of the country recovered from the recession of the early 1990s, the California economy remained depressed. Was it because California was "computerizing" faster than the rest of the country? No; California suffered from loss of jobs in the defense and aerospace industries, as federal funding in these areas declined, and from the large number of businesses fleeing the state because California's tax and regulatory policies were more costly than those of other states. A variety of anticompetitive laws in the U.S. make the formation of new businesses difficult. Demographics also have an impact on growth and decline of various job sectors. The Bureau of Labor Statistics predicts increases in a whole range of medical jobs because of the aging Baby Boomers and the increase in the elderly population. For the past ten years, unemployment rates have averaged around 10% in Europe and about 6% in the U.S., but Europe is not more technologically advanced or computerized than the United States. The Organisation for Economic Co-operation and Development (OECD), an international organization whose members include most of Western Europe, North America, Japan, Australia, and New Zealand, studied employment trends in 25 countries from 1950 to 1995. OECD concluded that unemployment stems from "policies . . . [that] have made economies rigid, and stalled the ability . . . to adapt." The study suggested that "unemployment should be addressed not by seeking to slow the pace of change, but rather by restoring economies' and societies' capacity to adapt to it."[6] These few examples indicate that economic and political policy and other nontechnological factors have a strong impact on employment rates, perhaps stronger than computers.

Although it is difficult to separate the effects of technology from other factors, we will try to get some idea of the impact of technology on jobs in the U.S. over the past century. We cannot quantify the increase in technology, but we can observe that airplanes, automobiles, radio, television, computers, much medical technology, and so on, did not exist at the beginning of the century. The use of telephones and electricity was minimal. Agricultural technology drastically reduced the percentage of the population that works in agriculture. Clearly, there has been an enormous increase in technology in this century and a decrease in jobs in areas like agriculture and saddle making. What has happened to

---

*Sewing machines were first marketed to factory owners, just as computers were first used by large companies. Isaac Singer had the insight to sell them directly to women, in a parallel to the eventual shift from corporation-owned mainframes to personal computers for consumers.

employment overall? The population of the U.S. is now approximately four times as high as it was near the beginning of the 20th century. If technology destroyed jobs, there should be fewer people working now than there were in 1900. I tried to compare unemployment figures for the early part of the century and now. The U.S. government changed the ways the data are reported, making exact comparisons difficult, but the changes themselves are interesting. In 1870, the average age for starting work was 13; in 1990 it was 19.1. The 1947 edition of *Statistical Abstracts of the United States* includes in the labor force people 14 years old and above; approximately 9.5% was described as seeking work (i.e., unemployed). In 1995 the national unemployment rate was under 6%. Now, labor force calculations do not include anyone under 16. In part because of the benefits of technology, we no longer routinely include children as young as 13 or 14 as part of the labor force.

8.2.2   Income and Productivity

Are we making more now or less?

In the past several years, newspapers have reported huge layoffs almost weekly as many large companies "downsized." There is a trend toward more part-time and temporary jobs, as firms are reluctant to commit to hiring regular, permanent employees. Negative attitudes about the future of the economy and quality of life are gaining popularity. For example, it is common to read (and polls show that many people believe) that we do not live as well as people did 25 years ago; both parents in a typical family must work to maintain a middle-class lifestyle; and today's children are likely to become the first generation that will not live as well as their parents. Many factors affect standard of living, but critics of computers put much of the blame on computerization. In deciding whether computers are guilty, it is worth first examining whether the evidence is valid.

Many economists agree that average hourly wages have declined, perhaps as much as 10% since 1970. This is sometimes cited as an indication that the value of human work is declining as computers take over tasks people used to do. However, while hourly wages declined, fringe benefits increased from 29.3% of payroll in 1970 to 40.2% of payroll in 1992. Total compensation, some economists report, is up about 15%.[7] There are different ways to count income and correct for inflation, and advocates of different points of view can often find data that seem to support their position. Two researchers decided that using such data was a poor substitute for looking at direct measures of consumption and leisure. Figure 8.1 includes a sampling of the data they collected from a variety of government and industry sources. They indicate that while computerization has been increasing, so have many measures of real income and quality of life.

Working hours and productivity

While some social scientists argue that computerization is reducing salaries for people because computers do their jobs more cheaply, others argue that computers are a huge waste of resources, that they are not increasing productivity. In the 1980s, U.S. firms spent more than $750 billion on computer and communications hardware and software, but studies showed only a very small increase in productivity in the industries that

	1970	1990
Average new home size (sq. ft.)	1500	2080
New homes with central air conditioning	34%	76%
Households with 2 or more vehicles	29.3%	54%
Work time to buy gas for 100-mile trip	49 min.	31 min.
Households with color TV	39.9%	96.1%
Televisions per household	1.4	2.1
Households with VCRs	0	67 million
Households with microwave oven	less than 1%	78.8%
Households with dishwashers	26%	45%
Housing units lacking complete plumbing	6.9%	1.1%
Homes lacking telephone	13%	5.2%
Median household net worth (real)	$24,217	$48,887
Annual paid vacation and holidays	15.5 days	22.5 days
Recreational boats owned	8.8 mill.	16 mill.
Shipments of RVs	30,300	226,500
Adult softball teams	29,000	188,000
Attendance at symphonies	12.7 mill.	43.6 mill.
Americans taking cruises	0.5 mill.	3.6 mill.

FIGURE 8.1: Data on Living Standards and Leisure (Adapted from
W. Michael Cox and Richard Alm, "The Good Old Days Are Now,"
Reason, December 1995, pp. 20–27. Used with permission
of the Reason Foundation.)

computerized heavily. The National Research Council argues that traditional methods of measuring productivity do not accurately measure some of the improvements brought about by computers, particularly in service.[8] Some studies show productivity increases beginning to appear; it may have taken several years for the impact of the new systems to show up.

If productivity increases, what would be the impact on working hours? Since the beginning of the Industrial Revolution, working hours have declined. Most of us no longer work 10–12 hour days, six days a week. Figures on working hours, like income data, can be counted in various ways to help support different conclusions. Some economists report a decline in average annual working hours from 1903 in 1950 to 1743 in 1973, and 1562 in 1990. Another report says that although output per hour of work has roughly doubled since the end of World War II, working hours have not declined significantly since then. One reason why working hours may not drop with increased productivity is that people have higher expectations. Many people consider the lifestyle represented by the 1990 data in Figure 8.1 to be essential. Another reason, according to labor economist Ronald Ehrenberg, is that quirks in the tax and compensation structure encourage employers to have regular workers work overtime (even with a premium on overtime pay) rather than hire additional employees.[9] A third reason is that taxes take a much larger percentage of income than they did in the past; thus people have to work more hours for the same take-home pay.* As we have said before, social, political, and economic factors can dwarf the possible impact of computers. The changes brought by computers are too new, and there is too little information to draw firm conclusions yet about the long-term impact of computers on working hours.

8.2.3   Is the Impact of Computers Different from Other Technologies?

Some who are concerned about the impact of computers on employment accept the fact that, in the past, technology has led to new jobs and products, but argue that the impact of computers is different—that computers will have a more negative impact on jobs. Computers differ from earlier technologies in several key ways.

Computers eliminate a much wider variety of jobs than any single new technological advance in the past. The impact of new machines or technologies tended to be concentrated in one industry or activity. Earlier automation eliminated primarily manufacturing jobs, but computers can automate services, such as those of telephone operators and receptionists, as well. The transition to new jobs will be more difficult because of the broad impact of computers.

Computers eliminate more high-skilled jobs than older technologies. Computers make decisions that used to require skilled or trained human workers. For example, computer programs analyze loan applications and decide which to approve. (Some programs are better than people at predicting which applicants are likely to default on their loans.)

The pace of improvement in speed, capability, and cost for computers is much faster than for any previous technology. The pace itself will cause more job disruption as people continually find their jobs being eliminated and need to be retrained.

How significant are these differences between computers and earlier technological changes? Although it often seems that our times and problems are new and different from what came before, similar concerns could have been raised for other technologies. The steam engine and electricity brought enormous change in jobs, making many obsolete. The printing press put scribes out of work when writing was a skill had by only a small, "highly trained" elite. Machines to do arithmetic were seen by some as taking over tasks that required uniquely human intelligence. When economist Claudia Goldin researched earlier periods of rapid technological development, she found that the education system quickly adapted to train children in the necessary skills.

The pace of change brought by computers is new, and their broad flexibility and applications may exacerbate the stresses of change by affecting so many areas at once, but it is difficult to tell at this time whether the negative impact of computers on jobs will be different in quality or only in degree from earlier technological changes.

---

*Estimates vary. The Tax Foundation reports that we now work, on average, two hours and 47 minutes out of each 8-hour workday to pay taxes, compared to only 57 minutes 50 years ago.

8.2.4   Changing Jobs

Jobs of the future

Almost all jobs will require the ability to use a computer in the near future. This in itself may not be a serious problem. People always must learn the tools of their trades or professions, and the tools have changed in the past. With good software and user interfaces, it may be easier for a waiter or waitress to enter customer orders on a computer than on paper.

The new jobs created by computers are different in important ways from the jobs eliminated. For example, the hundreds of thousands of new computer engineering and systems analyst jobs require a college degree. The jobs of telephone operator, bank teller, and customer service representative did not. Thus, one fear is that, while there may be jobs for the intellectual elite, there will be fewer jobs for people with lower skills and education. It may be that comparing the bank teller job with the computer engineer is the mistake; perhaps the people who would have been bank tellers in the past will now be sales clerks in computer stores.

There are some concerns that many white collar, professional jobs may be taken over by computers and that human intelligence in employment will be "devalued." Design jobs are being automated. For example, software to design the electrical layout for new housing developments can do in a half hour a job that would take a high-paid employee 100 hours.[10] Some computer programs write computer programs, reducing the need for trained programmers. Thus, some worry, computers may increase divisions in our society. Jobs may diverge into two distinct groups: those with high pay that require very highly skilled and highly trained people and those that have very low-skill requirements and very low pay. Others see computers freeing us from the repetitive, boring aspects of jobs so that we can spend more time being creative and doing the tasks for which human intelligence and problem solving are necessary. Architects learned to use computer-aided design; they still design buildings. Accountants learned to use spreadsheets and have more time for thinking, planning, and analysis as a result. The skill level and variety of tasks and responsibilities in some jobs are increasing. For example, women who used to be stenographers and typists learned how to use word processors and information systems. Secretaries do more interesting work now.

Difficult transitions

When new technologies eliminate jobs slowly, attrition (not hiring a new person when one retires, quits, or is reassigned) can reduce the number of workers without disruption. When the changes come faster and are more pervasive, as with computers, people are fired. Labor-saving technologies eliminate old jobs before generating the gains from new jobs and new (and/or cheaper) products and industries. Long-term net social gains from new jobs are not of much interest to a person who is fired. The loss of a job is immediate and personal, and can be devastating. When large numbers of people lose their jobs in one small community or within a short time, difficult social problems occur. There is clearly a need for retraining. In societies that change very slowly, a person may hold the same job for all of his or her working years. This will not happen in a dynamic society where technology is developing at a fast pace. Thus, there is also a need for people to be more flexible and plan for change.

Should Thomas Edison have hidden his light bulbs so that candle makers would not lose their jobs? If someone discovers a cure for the common cold, should he or she hide it to protect the jobs of all the people who work in the huge cold-medicine industry? Most people (though not all) would say no.

> *I pity the poor, and should hardly think myself innocent if any man felt more for them than I do; but the remedy for their grievances, lies not in the destruction of Machinery. They are oppressed exceedingly, but not by Machinery. Those who accuse Machinery of causing any part of the distresses of the poor, have very contracted views and narrow minds, and see but a little way. They do not seem to consider that almost every thing was new Machinery once. There was a time when corn was ground by the hand; and when Corn Mills and Wind Mills were first invented they were New Machinery; and therefore why not break and burn these as soon as any other kind of Machinery; for if they were all stopped, and corn again ground by the hand, there would be plenty of employment for many hands! Much the same observations might be made respecting every other kind of Machinery, and I have asked this question in order to shew the silliness of the practice.*
>
> —GEORGE BEAUMONT *(from "Reflections on Luddism," 1812)*[11]

8.3   THE WORK ENVIRONMENT

Computers are changing the work environment, in some ways for the better, in some for the worse. We will look at a few of these changes: telecommuting, "empowerment" of workers via access to information technology and flatter organizational hierarchies, and the emerging issues related to monitoring of employees.

8.3.1   Teleworking

Home computers, modems, fax machines, and wireless communications have made it possible for millions of people to work without "going to work," that is, without going to their employer's (or their own) business offices. I will use the term "telecommuting" for several variations of new work paradigms. The most common meaning is working for an employer at a computer-equipped office in the employee's home. Some large businesses have set up satellite "telecommuting centers" with computer and communications equipment located closer to where their employees live than to the main business office. In some jobs, such as sales, the office is mobile: The employee travels with a laptop computer and wireless communications equipment. Telecommuting also includes running a business from one's home that relies heavily on computers and communications.

The rapidly dropping costs of communications and information transfer have encouraged these practices. The figures I cite here are from a variety of sources and count in different ways, but they give a general idea of the size and growth of the phenomenon. Twenty-one million Americans work at home at least one day a week, using computers and telecommunications technology. The number of home offices approximately doubled between 1988 and 1995. The number of full-time telecommuters has increased from approximately 3–4 million in 1990 to 8–10 million in 1995. Nearly four million people run home-based businesses.[12]

Telecommuting has a large number of benefits for teleworkers, their employers, and for society in general. There are a number of problems as well.

Benefits

The main advantages for employers are reduced overhead and, in some cases, increased productivity. For companies that set up scattered telework centers in suburbs to replace large downtown offices where real estate and office rental prices are high, the savings can be significant. For those that have moved employees all the way to their homes or cars (e.g., sales people), savings include closure of dozens of branch offices. Studies in areas where work is easy to measure (e.g., data entry) show productivity gains of 15%. (Measuring productivity in professional and management work is more difficult.)[13]

Telecommuting reduces rush-hour traffic congestion and the associated pollution and energy use. A one-percent decrease in urban commuting could reduce gasoline usage by a few million barrels per year.[14] Telework reduces expenses for commuting and for work clothes. It saves time. It provides previously unavailable work options for some disabled people for whom commuting is physically difficult and expensive. It allows work to continue after blizzards close roads. Roughly 55% of woman-owned businesses are home-based businesses. Telecommuting, and the flexible hours it permits, can help reduce child-care expenses and give parents more time with their children. Telecommuting gives people increased flexibility of work location. They can live in rural areas instead of big cities and suburbs if they prefer (in "electronic cottages," to use futurist Alvin Toffler's words). Two-career couples can work for companies hundreds or thousands of miles apart.[15] Joel Kotkin observes that telecommuting can help bring back a sense of community as people who work at home (or nearby) develop stronger roots in their communities than many commuters now have.[16]

Telework, and telecommunications generally, make it easier to work with clients, customers, and employees in other countries. At home, it may be more convenient to work a few hours that are compatible with foreign time zones. (One of the concerns about improved communications and the ease of working with people in other countries is that the U.S. may lose jobs to countries where pay rates are lower.)

Problems

Many early telecommuters were volunteers, people who wanted to work at home. They were more likely to be independent workers. (Many were computer programmers.) As more businesses began to require employees to move their offices to their homes, isolation became more of a problem.

Lacking immediate supervision, some people are less productive, while others work too hard and too long. Employees need better direction about what work and how much work they are expected to do at home. Kathleen Christensen, in her book on home-based work, says that telecommuting will not work well for all people; it takes a particular personality to work without supervision.[17] Being at home with children may be an advantage for some telecommuters, but a distraction for others.

For many people, the social interactions at work are a significant part of pleasant working conditions, so social isolation and low morale are problems. Some workers fear that when only some employees in a division or business work at home, lack of "visibility" in the office may be a disadvantage when promotions and bonuses are awarded. A study for the Small Business Administration of telecommuters in the late 1980s showed that they were promoted faster than their in-office colleagues, but these early telecommuters may have been more independent and highly motivated workers. Although ideally promotions should depend on productivity, personal relationships can be important, especially in less competitive industries. E-mail and telephone calls can be used to maintain visibility. Employers can address the social isolation problem by holding regular meetings or other events where employees interact in person. Telecommuters may reduce isolation by participating in activities of professional associations and other social networks.

Some employees complain that the costs of office space and overhead that have been reduced for the employer have simply been shifted to the employee who must give up space at home for the office, learn how to maintain equipment that the company used to maintain, and so on.

Like many of the options provided by new technologies (or social trends), telework may be very desirable for some people and of no use to others.

Side effects

Aside from the direct advantages and disadvantages, teleworking has several side effects that may change various business and social aspects of how we live and work.

How will telecommuting affect our sense of community? The Industrial Revolution led to a major shift in work patterns; jobs moved to offices and factories. Working at home now seems like something new and unusual, but before the Industrial Revolution, most people worked at, or close to, home. Even in the past few centuries, working at home has not been uncommon. Writers traditionally work at home. Farmers worked in the fields, but the farm office was in the house. Doctors, especially in small towns, had their medical offices in their homes. Shopkeepers often had an apartment behind or above the store. Perhaps writers are closest to modern information workers who telecommute in that they tend to work in isolation. Is that why we have an image of writers spending the evenings at coffee houses or at intellectual "salons" talking with other intellectuals? Will such activities spring up in suburbs and small towns to fill the social needs of teleworkers? In the past, social isolation was not considered a problem for people who worked in or near their homes; they lived, worked, and socialized in communities. They had the grange, the church, and the community center. Is Kotkin correct that telecommuting may encourage a return to involvement in one's local community? Will being there all day, doing errands locally, eating in local restaurants, and so on, generate an interest in the safety, beauty, and vitality of the community that is less likely to develop when one returns home after dark, tired from a day at the office? On the other hand, now that we can communicate with people all over the world on the Internet, will home workers stay inside, communicating with unseen business and social acquaintances, and be just as unlikely to know their neighbors as many commuters are now?

Telecommuting might not seem new and unusual if more people had been working at home in recent decades. And they might have been—except that unions and government policy discouraged it. For a while in the 1980s, some unions talked of trying to make telecommuting illegal. Because telecommuters tend to be independent, middle-class workers, and because their numbers have grown so fast, these efforts quickly seemed futile, and I have not heard them discussed recently. But why would working at home be banned or discouraged?

Two kinds of laws are involved: local zoning laws and labor laws, the first directed mostly at middle-class neighborhoods, and the second directed mostly at low-income women. Many communities argue that home businesses bring noise and traffic problems to residential neighborhoods. Thus, for example, local zoning laws often prohibit a home business from receiving deliveries or customers at the home. In many cities, a person with a full-time job who starts a small side-business at home is breaking the law when a customer comes to the home to make a purchase. An accountant who works in an office all day but has a tax-preparation business at home is breaking the law when clients come to the house in the evening.* These laws predate telecommuting, but they apply to telecommuters as well. Some kinds of home work are outright illegal. For example, labor laws prohibit most home sewing work, where women sew garments for clothing manufacturers and are paid by the piece. Tens of thousands of women do this work in spite of the laws. The arguments in support of the laws are that the women often get less than minimum wage, and it is difficult for the government to make sure that children are not working in violation of child-labor laws, and that working conditions are safe. Critics of such laws argue that they deny the women a choice, and that unions, the main supporters of the laws, are primarily concerned with the difficulty of organizing workers who are dispersed. There are other factors that may contribute to legal restrictions on home work. In some cases, local politicians do not like the fact that home businesses are less visible and therefore harder to regulate and tax. Large, established businesses sometimes support restrictive laws to reduce competition from low-overhead home-based work.

The increase in telework may reduce the restrictions on other forms of home work— to the benefit or detriment of residential neighborhoods and those who work at home, depending on how you weigh the arguments. Here we have an example where a change in work patterns enabled by computer technology might cause a reexamination and change of long-standing regulations unrelated to computers.

8.3.2   Management and Hierarchies

Computers are affecting many aspects of business organization, management, and employment trends. I will briefly mention a few of the possible trends.

Changing business structures

Currently there is much speculation about the impact of computer and telecommunications networks on the size and structure of business. Different observers see trends going in opposite directions.

Some see trends toward smaller businesses and more independent consultants and contractors—"information entrepreneurs," as they are sometimes called. Working at home or at telework centers not operated by one's own company loosens the tie between

---

*Zoning laws vary in different communities; these activities are not illegal everywhere.

employer and employee. Company loyalty and identification may decrease. It may be easier for workers to find other work opportunities or to work part-time for different employers or clients, thus encouraging more information workers to become self-employed. The communications revolution has made it so much easier to do business with people in other parts of the country and the world. This had led some observers to project an increase in "Mom and Pop multinationals," small businesses that operate globally.

The Economist reports that the average number of employees per firm has been declining since the late 1960s. A study of a large sample of U.S. businesses found that between 1975 and 1985, the average number of employees per firm declined by 20%. It also found a correlation between more computer use and small firm size. The reason was not that computers were putting people out of work, but rather that firms narrowed the focus of their activities, purchasing more components and services from other firms. The study argues that computers and information networks reduce the cost and uncertainties of finding and relying on suppliers and consultants; hence, businesses are doing more of it.[18]

The legal, tax, and regulatory framework in which businesses operate has an enormous impact, sometimes quite indirect and unidentified, on business size, structure, and employment patterns. These effects may prevent or slow changes that computers might otherwise cause. Complex regulatory laws, for example, tend to encourage large firms because they can spread the cost of a large legal department over a large sales volume.

Some observers foresee computers contributing to the growth of large, multinational corporations, with mergers between giant companies—for example, communications and entertainment companies. There have been many big mergers and buy-outs in the past decade, and more are being negotiated regularly. At the same time, some large companies, like AT&T, are splitting up into smaller units. It is unclear how much of this business concentration or downsizing comes from the power of centralized computer systems and how much from economic and political factors.

Hierarchies within companies

Two related trends getting some notice are "flattening hierarchies" and "empowerment of workers." The availability of information technology is leading many businesses to give workers more information and more decision-making authority. Manufacturing plant workers have access to online inventory and purchasing information and make decisions about production schedules. Credit card company service representatives, with immediate access to account information, can make decisions to cancel a late charge or finance charge, for example. The need for middle managers is decreasing, and their jobs are changing. Some say they now think of themselves as "facilitators" rather than managers; they find the information technology tools to help their workers manage their own work.[19]

The ease of communicating by e-mail has been noted as a factor in reducing stratification in businesses. Any employee (in a business where employees have e-mail) can send a note to the president of the company, keeping him or her more in touch with the ideas and attitudes of employees. E-mail has proved a mixed blessing for many executives and professionals. Being flooded with dozens or hundreds of messages a day is a serious time waster. As a result, many executives no longer use e-mail.

8.4   EMPLOYEE MONITORING

*Technology now allows employers to cross the line from monitoring the work
to monitoring the worker.*

—CINDIA CAMERON, *National Association of Working Women*

8.4.1   Background

One of the big issues of computers in the workplace is employee monitoring. Supervisors
and managers have, of course, always monitored their employees. The degree of detail and
frequency of the monitoring has varied depending on the kind of work, economic factors,
and available technology. Computers have made new kinds of monitoring possible and
old methods more efficient. Before we look at the new issues raised by computers, we
will briefly recall some of the past and present monitoring that does not depend on
computers.

Total hours worked are monitored by logs or time clocks. In many jobs, total output
for a day can be counted (widgets produced, forms typed, sales concluded). In some jobs,
such as factory assembly lines, the pace of work is implicitly monitored by the speed of the
line; if a worker is not keeping up, the failure will be obvious farther down the line. Supervisors record or listen in on the work of telephone operators and customer service representatives. Surveillance cameras are used in factories and offices for security. In some of
the accounts of the worst conditions in factories and clerical offices of the past two centuries, bosses patrolled the aisles watching workers, prodding them to work faster, and dis-
couraging conversation and breaks.

Electronic monitoring capabilities are the modern time clock, telephone extension,
and camera. Most precomputer monitoring, however, was not constant because the supervisor had many workers to oversee and other work to do; workers usually knew when the
supervisor was present to observe them. With computers, monitoring can be constant,
more detailed, and unseen by the worker. Although some monitoring techniques, like video
surveillance and listening in on phone calls, do not need computers, we include them in the
discussion in this chapter for several reasons. Telephone systems are now so essentially
combined with computer systems that telephone monitoring has become a de facto computer issue. Customer service representatives now use computer terminals while talking
with a customer to review and update account information; supervisors can set their terminals to show exactly what the monitored worker sees and is doing on his or her screen. The
vast growth of computer storage capabilities means that telephone conversations (and
voice mail and physical surveillance information) can be stored longer. Such information
can also be searched more easily, with the potential of making the monitored details part of
the employee's permanent record.

The subjects of most precomputer monitoring were so-called "blue collar" (factory)
and "pink collar" (telephone and clerical) workers. Some of the new monitoring capabilities, such as reading an employee's e-mail, affect professional workers too. Some editors
remotely monitor the computer screens of journalists, and some senior lawyers monitor
other attorneys in their firm.[20]

We will discuss four kinds of monitoring:

- Electronic monitoring of details of performance, such as keystrokes or time spent on customer service calls.
- Physical surveillance of the movements and activities of employees.
- Monitoring of customer service telephone work.
- Access to e-mail, voice mail, and computer files of employees.

We will devote most of the discussion to the last two, as they have generated the most controversy. Federal legislation has been proposed to severely control and limit monitoring of employees. So far, it has not passed. We will discuss current law and proposals for policies and regulations on monitoring.

8.4.2 Monitoring Keystrokes

Every keystroke of data entry and data processing clerks can be counted automatically. Some employers set keystroke quotas. Some make the records of employees' performance public in the workplace to encourage competition among workers. Terminals beep if the employee pauses in his or her work. The purposes are to evaluate individual employees and to measure and increase productivity. When the quotas are unreasonable and the pace relentless, the pressure can be intense. The management style of intense surveillance— constant watching, very demanding work quotas, threats of being fired—is older than computers, and the workplaces where it dominates earned the term "sweatshops." The modern, computerized version is described as "electronic sweatshops." The results include increased stress, wrist injuries (discussed in more detail in Section 8.5.1), and low morale.

Similarly, workers who answer telephone calls all day can be monitored in detail. Now the exact number and duration of each call, and the idle time between calls, can be automatically logged, analyzed, and made part of the employee's record. (The separate issue of listening in on calls is discussed below.)

Workers complain that such constant, detailed surveillance causes a loss of a sense of dignity and independence and destroys confidence. They are treated like machines, not people. The surveillance causes stress and boredom. Critics point out that the pressure increases health costs for the employer. Critics also raise questions about the effectiveness of such monitoring, arguing that it puts too much emphasis on quantity instead of quality. It reduces workers' commitment to do a good job. Pressure on telephone information operators to reduce the amount of time spent on each call, according to one critic, caused operators to cut customers off by claiming the computer was down.[21]

There are different views on the reasons for detailed monitoring and on how likely it is to continue or increase. The views seem to depend somewhat on the observer's theories of industrial organization and management. Paul Attewell summarizes several of the theories and their application to this issue.[22] Marxist theory, for example, views surveillance as part of management's attempt to control the workers and to squeeze out as much value as possible from them. It sees monitoring increasing unless stopped through negotiation by organized labor or through legislation by government. The corporate culture theory is the

view that different companies have distinct personalities. Those that have paid little attention to the humanity of workers in the past will be quick to adopt electronic surveillance
techniques; those that have a history of good employee relations are not likely to do so. Industrial sociologists study worker reaction and the kinds of workplaces where "sweatshop"
management tends to occur. They find it generates resistance from workers and is not productive in most modern jobs.

Whether it be for practical or humane reasons (or both), several large banking and insurance businesses have redesigned "assembly-line" clerical jobs to include a variety of
tasks and skills—and have increased productivity as a result.

8.4.3   Physical Surveillance

Electronic identification badges that serve as door keys provide increased security for a
business, but they allow monitoring of the movements of employees. Some badges broadcast the employee's location, so that his or her exact location is always known. Some businesses equip company cars with locating devices for security. If the company supplies a car
to a manager for both business and personal use, his or her personal travel can be tracked.
Automatic monitoring of the speed of company vehicles may be done to enforce safety
rules, but it may be seen as intrusive by drivers.

8.4.4   Monitoring Customer Service Calls

Telephone customer service workers include airline and car-rental reservation clerks, catalog mail-order operators, telemarketers, credit bureau service representatives and collections agents, long distance telephone service representatives—to list just a few examples.
MCI, for example, gets about three million phone calls per month from customers and
prospective customers.[23] The employer has a strong interest in ensuring that customer calls
are handled accurately, efficiently, and courteously. Many companies with large customer
service operations have a regular program in which supervisors listen in on calls periodically to train and evaluate new workers and to check on the performance of more experienced workers. Some advocacy groups argue that listening in on customer service calls is
a privacy issue: It infringes the privacy of the employees and customers. Employers argue
that there is no privacy issue: The calls are not personal; they are the job the worker was
hired to do, and the customer is talking to a complete stranger. (Information about an account or purchase discussed in the call would be available to the supervisor independent of
the monitoring.)

Complaints about monitoring have led many large firms and industries (e.g., financial services) to establish clear and detailed monitoring policies. It has also led to proposed
regulation of monitoring. Figure 8.2 lists a variety of guidelines for monitoring that are advocated by worker organizations. Some are included in proposed federal legislation, and
some have been adopted as policy by businesses. The first six guidelines were included in
a Harris survey about monitoring of customer service workers.[24] They were considered
necessary by at least roughly three-quarters (and in some cases, more than 90%) of respondents. The last two are more controversial and are opposed by many employers.

1. Monitoring and evaluation procedures should be explained fully to employees.

2. Employees should be told when they are hired that business calls may be monitored.

3. Only business calls can be monitored, not personal ones. Employers should provide unmonitored telephones for personal calls.

4. Employees whose performance is criticized should have access to monitoring data and an opportunity to challenge the evaluation.

5. Problems uncovered by monitoring should lead to more training. There should be no disciplinary action unless the employee fails to improve.

6. Employees should be involved in setting up procedures for monitoring.

7. Monitoring should not be continuous; it can be periodic.

8. Statistics on productivity should not be maintained for individual workers, but only for groups.

9. Employees with more than five years' experience should not be monitored at all.

10. Workers should be informed each time they are to be monitored, not just in general.

FIGURE 8.2: Guidelines for monitoring.

8.4.5 Employee E-mail, Voice Mail, and Files

[E-mail] combines the casualness of speech with the permanence of writing. It's got a lot of potential for embarrassing the other side.

—ALLAN B. TAYLOR, *attorney*[25]

A legal newsletter estimated that more than 10 billion e-mail messages per year would be transmitted within businesses in the mid-1990s. Many people think that, because they use a password to access their e-mail or voice mail, their messages are not accessible to anyone else. This in not true. In virtually all systems, the system manager can access anything on the system. Employers can read the e-mail of employees, they can listen to voice-mail messages, and they can read computer files. How many of them do? In a widely cited 1993 survey of 301 businesses conducted by *Macworld,* 22% of the businesses said they sometimes monitor or search the e-mail, voice mail, or computer files of their employees. 30% of the larger companies in the survey do so. (The average number of employees in the companies surveyed was 3240.) However, most of the companies that do such monitoring do so infrequently; 71% did five or fewer searches in the two years preceding the survey.[26]

There are legitimate reasons for employers to sometimes listen to voice-mail messages or read e-mail or files on an employee's computer. Some are listed in Figure 8.3.

- Find needed business information in an employee's messages or files when the employee is not available.
- Protect security of proprietary information and data.
- Investigate possible criminal activities by employees.
- Prevent personal use of employer facilities.
- Investigate complaints of harassment.
- Check for illegal software.

FIGURE 8.3: Reasons for monitoring e-mail, voice mail, and computer files.

A spokesman for Eastman Kodak says that the company reserves the right to inspect company resources at any time, but does not monitor contents of e-mail on a regular basis. It intervenes when someone reports an abuse. Very few abuses are found. The most common e-mail problem is harassment (including sexual harassment, cases with pending divorces, and love triangles). Other abuses found include mailing jokes to thousands of people, running a business using Kodak's address, personal communications, and running betting pools on football and basketball games.[27]

The computers, mail, and phone systems used at work are the property of the employer and are provided for business purposes. Employees who have e-mail, voice mail, and their own computer files tend to be workers with more varied job functions and responsibilities than customer service or data entry workers. They include, for example, computer programmers, managers, sales people, secretaries, lawyers, researchers, and college professors. It is common for such workers to use e-mail and the telephone for communications with family and friends, especially where there is no clear policy against it. The content of their files and messages is more likely to include personal things. Thus privacy is often an issue. Employers claim they have a right and a need to monitor the use of their facilities. Opponents point out that employees do not give up all privacy when they enter an employer's premises. The bathrooms belong to the employer too, but camera surveillance in bathrooms is not acceptable.[28] The controversies stem from disagreements about the appropriate boundary between the employers' rights and the employees' privacy.

Some supervisors snoop to find out what employees are saying about them or the company; some snoop into personal messages. These activities are far more questionable than those in Figure 8.3, but can also be defended as having a business purpose. For example, businesses have faced increased liability for sexual harassment by employees, so employers could claim a right to monitor messages involving romantic relationships between two employees. There have been some cases where an employer routinely intercepted all e-mail entering and leaving the company site.[29] Is this an inappropriate intrusion on privacy, a justifiable security measure to protect trade secrets, or an acceptable method to check for prohibited personal use of company facilities? The problem here consists of defining a reasonable boundary between, on the one hand, the employer's property rights, protection of company assets, the need for access to business information, and the need to monitor for possible legal and liability problems, and, on the other hand, actions that invade personal privacy.

There is little law now controlling workplace monitoring. Monitoring for purposes listed in Figure 8.3 are generally legal. Specific policies are set by management or by negotiations between management and employees. Employers are permitted by law to monitor telephone calls for business purposes. Courts have interpreted the ban on eavesdropping on nonbusiness calls to mean that an employer must cease monitoring a call as soon as it is apparent that the call is personal. Courts have sometimes ruled against employers if there was a convincing case that monitoring was done to snoop on personal and union activities or to track down whistleblowers. The Electronic Communications Privacy Act prohibits interception of e-mail on commercial e-mail services, but it does not prohibit employers from reading internal employee e-mail on company systems. In a case where two employees were fired after a supervisor read their e-mail messages that criticized him, a judge ruled that the company could read the e-mail because it owned and operated the system. In another case, monitoring discussion about a boss was accepted because the discussion could affect the business environment. Courts have handed down similar decisions in other cases.[30]

Court decisions sometimes depend on a determination of whether an employee had a reasonable "expectation of privacy," but different levels of technical knowledge and different social views can lead people to have very different ideas of when an expectation of privacy is reasonable. At a minimum, an employer should inform employees whether or not personal use of employer-provided communications and computer systems is permitted, and whether or not, and under what circumstances, the employer will access employee messages and files. Some large companies have explicit policies that employee e-mail is private and will not be read by the employer.[31] Others provide a notice to employees every time they log on to the e-mail system, reminding them that the system is for business, not personal, use, and that the company reserves the right to monitor messages.[32] A clear statement of policy by the employer removes the guesswork about expectation of privacy.

Two cases illustrate some legal issues concerning the scope of an employer's right to access e-mail and voice mail. Eugene Wang, a vice president of Borland International, quit to take a job at Symantec Corporation, a direct competitor of Borland. Borland officials suspected that Wang was giving Symantec highly sensitive Borland documents. They read some of Wang's e-mail and found evidence they felt confirmed their suspicions. The police, using a search warrant, then seized documents from Wang and Symantec. At issue is whether Borland violated the law in reading Wang's e-mail. If they did, the evidence seized in the search could be ruled inadmissible in court. A reason for the ambiguity about the right of Borland to read the mail is that Wang was using MCI Mail, a commercial e-mail provider, but the e-mail account was provided and paid for by Borland.[33]

An employee at a McDonald's restaurant was fired after a manager listened to voice-mail messages between the employee and his mistress, also a McDonald's employee. The messages were played for the man's wife. He objected that his privacy had been invaded, and he sued. Possible issues in this case included whether or not the rule about personal telephone calls (once a supervisor realizes it is personal, he or she should cease listening) applies to voice-mail messages, and whether or not listening to the messages served a business purpose. The issues were not resolved because the case was settled out of court; the settlement was not disclosed.[34]

8.4.6 Regulation

The main piece of legislation proposed to regulate monitoring is the Privacy for Consumers and Workers Act (PCWA), introduced in Congress in 1993, but not passed. It is strongly supported by various worker advocacy organizations. The bill covers both monitoring of customer service workers and monitoring of voice mail and computer files of other employees. It generated strong opposition from employers because it would have banned many kinds of monitoring and access to employee messages and files and severely restricted what it permitted. Most of the guidelines in Figure 8.2 were incorporated into the bill as legal requirements. For example, it banned periodic monitoring of employees with five years' experience. It required detailed written notice to employees, including the hours they will be monitored. It restricted the use of monitoring data for evaluating and disciplining employees. The provisions about access to the computer files of professional workers were so restrictive, according to critics of the bill, that they would interfere with ordinary business functioning and prevent disciplinary action against employees found to be doing improper or illegal things. Supporters argue that most prohibited or restricted monitoring is counterproductive and the bill is needed to protect employee privacy.[35]

The controversy over the PCWA is a good case for thinking about the distinction between policies and laws. Advocates argue that the bill will actually benefit employers ("a blessing in disguise" for employers, according to Lewis Maltby of the ACLU[36]). Written procedures for monitoring and for use of the collected data will make monitoring more useful to the employer. Giving more freedom and respect to long-time employees will maintain their loyalty and make them more productive. Counting keystrokes is counterproductive because it causes increased stress, reduces worker productivity, and causes health problems and costs. All of these are good arguments in many cases. If employers are convinced that any of the specific proposals in the bills are beneficial to their company, they can adopt them. (This is, in fact, already happening in many large companies.) What if some employers are not convinced? If the issue is whether or not specific practices are "good business," rather than a question of rights or safety, who should make the decisions: legislators or the people responsible for a particular business? Which of the guidelines and provisions of the PCWA involve issues of rights that should have legal protection, and which should be matters of policy to be determined by the employer?

8.5 HEALTH ISSUES

Several health problems are associated with manufacture and use of computers. Two problems that have received a lot of attention are radiation from computer terminals and wrist problems (repetitive strain injury) from frequent use of computer keyboards. There is controversy about these problems because the scientific evidence is inconclusive. We will discuss repetitive strain injury (which includes the perhaps better known carpal tunnel syndrome) in detail because it illustrates the variety of possible causes for a new problem and the management and legal issues that result.

8.5.1 Repetitive Strain Injury

What is RSI?

You may have seen computer programmers, secretaries, or supermarket checkers wearing wrist braces, called splints—a common sign of the increase in repetitive strain injury (RSI) and carpal tunnel syndrome. By 1990 more than half of workplace injuries in the U.S. were related to RSI, up from 21% in 1982.[37] In 1992, more than 280,000 RSI cases were reported to the Bureau of Labor Statistics. Carpal tunnel syndrome and RSI have received a lot of attention in the news media—more than 1200 articles in one year— much of it focusing on computer keyboard operators as the victims. RSI has also been getting increased attention in the courts. More than 3000 lawsuits have been filed against employers and equipment manufacturers because of these conditions.

RSI causes pain in the wrist, hand, and arm (and sometimes the neck and shoulders too). It is associated with frequent, repetitive, forceful and/or awkward motion. Carpal tunnel syndrome involves damage to a nerve in the hand and can result in numbness in the fingers and eventually in permanent disability. Other types of strain injuries involve damage to muscles, tendons, joints, and nerves. These injuries can cause extreme pain. If not treated properly and before extensive damage is done, they can make ordinary activities such as opening a door or shaking hands painful or impossible, and they can prevent people from working. We will use "RSI" to refer to all the various hand and wrist problems that are being attributed to computers and automation.*

Some reasons for the controversy and confusion surrounding RSI are (1) RSI includes more than a dozen different conditions, each with different symptoms and treatment, (2) RSI involves soft tissue damage for which, in many cases, there are no clear, objective physiological diagnostic tests,† and (3) symptoms may take weeks, months, or years to show up. There are uncertainties about the nature, causes, diagnosis, treatment, and prevention of RSI. We will review some of what is known and some ways to deal with the problem.

Who gets RSI, and why is it increasing?

RSI is not a new disease. There are references to similar problems in the 18th and 19th centuries afflicting clerks and scribes (we used to call this "writer's cramp"), women who milked cows, and others whose work required repetitive hand motions. Computer-related RSI has received attention recently, and there is a common perception that the use of computers and computerized automation systems are responsible for most current RSI problems. This is not true. Most RSI cases occur among meat processors. RSI can be a problem in any activity that requires frequent repeated motions, unusual hand positions, or stress on the hands and wrists. There are medical articles on RSI problems among weight lifters, gymnasts, and "pushup enthusiasts." Auto workers, seamstresses, musicians, carpenters, and workers in bakery factories suffer. A study of sign language interpreters for the deaf found that 35 of the 40 people studied had more than one symptom of RSI. An

---

*A variety of other terminology is used. One may see "repetitive stress injury," "overuse syndrome," "repetitive motion injury," and "cumulative trauma disorder."

†There are tests for carpal tunnel syndrome.

illustrated RSI patient information pamphlet given me by a doctor shows as typical victims an auto mechanic, a house painter, and a woman reading a heavy book. There is no mention or picture of a computer keyboard in the pamphlet, which was printed in 1986. An article in the *Journal of the American Medical Association* lists 29 occupations with common RSI problems.[38]

Computer users are the newest significant group of RSI sufferers. Office work accounts for about 12% of current cases. There are many professions now where people use a computer all day or for many hours each day. RSI afflicts data entry personnel (some of whom type 10,000–15,000 keystrokes per hour), airline reservations clerks, stock brokers, emergency dispatchers, journalists, computer programmers, and many others. It is also a problem for supermarket checkers. Computerized checkout systems have reduced the variety of motions checkers used to perform; now they primarily move products quickly past a bar-code scanner.

Although RSI is not a new problem, in the past decade the number of reported cases has increased tenfold. What has caused the dramatic increase? Two obvious factors are the increased use of computers and increased automation leading to a faster pace of work. Other factors are improved accuracy in reporting, coverage by the news media, and increased awareness of the problem by employees and employers. Some writers suggest that RSI is receiving more attention now because the newer sufferers are white collar workers (including journalists!) whose complaints are taken more seriously than those of factory workers and women. Unfortunately, measuring the extent and growth of RSI problems is complicated by social, psychological, and legal issues. Some medical writers warn other doctors that for some people RSI is an excuse to get out of boring or stressful work; for some, it is a route to monetary compensation. (Medical expenses and lost salary may be covered by Workers Compensation, and there is the prospect of winning large awards in lawsuits against keyboard makers and/or employers.) On the other hand, before RSI received a lot of attention, company doctors may have been reluctant to diagnose such a vaguely defined injury because of the costs to the employer. Some social factors are likely to cause improved reporting of a real problem, whereas others may cause reports to be exaggerated. It is difficult to separate the factors and sometimes difficult to distinguish the real and serious injuries from the imagined or exaggerated ones. The uncertainties lead to articles like one that asks in its headline whether RSI is "An Epidemic or a Fad?"[39] In spite of the unknowns and the incentive to exaggerate, it is unquestionable that a lot of people who work at a keyboard are suffering from hand, arm, and wrist injuries causing pain. Many people who work on computer keyboards, or employ those who do, think that sitting at a desk all day and typing is physically easy. They do not realize that typing millions of keystrokes per year is strenuous activity and that some attention must be paid to proper technique and safety concerns.

Working at a computer keyboard is considered a source of RSI, but it is not clear whether the real culprit is the design of the keyboard itself, improper user technique, bad posture, bad work habits, or poor ergonomic design of chairs and work tables. All these factors seem to contribute to the problem. No one is certain why one employee performing a specific job suffers from RSI, while another person doing the same job on the same equipment does not. Scientists are still studying a long list of possible causes or related factors including a person's weight, stress, congenital defects, wrist size, varicose veins, vitamin deficiency, and whether or not a person is double-jointed.[40]

As with many problems we consider in this book, there are several categories of potential solutions: technical, managerial, legal, and educational.

Ergonomic solutions

Some people emphasize physical design of keyboards, furniture, and so on, as the cure-all for RSI. There has been a lot of attention on proper ergonomic design of keyboards and workstations lately. Responding to concerns about RSI, some laptop computer makers redesigned the machines to include a wrist rest. We can now buy split, twisted, and otherwise nontraditionally shaped keyboards—each one implementing some manufacturer's idea of what will be more comfortable and less likely to cause RSI. The variety of keyboards suggests uncertainty about what is best. Or, perhaps, what is best depends on the user, and a variety of options is desirable. Modifying equipment alone will not solve the problem. Human factors such as health, posture, and harmful keyboard usage styles must be considered. One RSI expert, Dr. Emil Pascarelli, reports that virtually all the RSI patients he sees unintentionally contribute to their injuries by using poor keyboard technique. He says that RSI is almost totally preventable by both improving the physical arrangement of the work area and training the user in proper technique (including the importance of rest breaks, posture, and exercises). The National Safety Council reported that 90% of companies surveyed said that redesigning workstations and jobs was successful in reducing severe RSI problems.[41]

In the future, we may have an excellent technological solution for preventing RSI from keyboard use: replacement of keyboards by speech input. (But we may discover an increase in strain of the vocal cords.)

The role of management

Many employers resisted making changes to tackle the RSI problem. They may have been skeptical about the reality of the problem, and they were reluctant to spend money or modify work procedures in ways they thought would reduce productivity. Gradually more employers are recognizing that the problem is real and that preventive measures cost less than medical expenses and lost work time for affected employees. The Sara Lee Corporation is a good illustration of this change. The employees who suffered from RSI were bakery assembly line workers, including those who repeatedly, quickly twisted their wrists to bend croissants into their curved shape. Although they were not keyboard operators, the solutions have general applicability. At first Sara Lee's management did not take the problem seriously and refused to slow down the bakery production line. Injuries, lost work time, and surgeries increased. Eventually the company made a major effort to solve the problem. Employees and outside experts evaluated and modified work tools and procedures. The result was that the number of work days lost to RSI dropped to a small fraction of the number for the previous year.* The company estimates that its measures to prevent RSI problems save $750,000 per year at one bakery employing about 600 people.[42] This

---

*Eight days in the first seven months of 1992, down from 181 days in all of 1991. At the peak, in 1987, 731 work days were lost to RSI.

example illustrates that once the problem is recognized, it may not be difficult or expensive to solve.

The success at Sara Lee and the data from the National Safety Council may suggest that appropriate modifications to reduce or eliminate RSI are so clear and well known that there is no excuse for not having implemented them sooner. Not quite. Some studies show job stress is related to RSI (but not that it is a cause). Could it be that higher morale and reduced stress at the Sara Lee bakery, resulting from management's show of concern about the problem, contributed to the improvement? Also, before problems occur, it may not be at all obvious what tools need to be changed. For example, one of the modifications made at the bakery was a redesign of an icing gun to reduce its weight and the strength needed to squeeze out the icing. Equipment manufacturers have an incentive to design their products for comfortable use and reduced injury: It makes their products better. But would anyone have thought to redesign the icing gun before a significant number of icers began to have RSI problems? It may be easier to solve RSI problems than to predict where they will occur.

Legal issues

Thousands of workers suffering from RSI are suing keyboard makers and employers, charging that they are at fault and should pay medical costs and damages to the victims. The suits argue that the manufacturers should have warned the users about the potential for injury. In the first such case to reach a jury verdict, the jury took less than an hour to decide in favor of the computer maker. The uncertainty of causation makes winning such suits difficult. Defense attorneys and some judges say that RSI is too vaguely defined, and causation has not been proved. Plaintiffs, on the other hand, argue that the connection between keyboard operation and RSI is clear, and they should not have to wait the years it will take until conclusive scientific studies can be done.[43]

Some judges and others compare the complaints to ordinary aches and pains from over-exercising or overusing a normally safe tool or device. What would we think of an RSI lawsuit against the maker of a tennis racket or a violin? It is not clear whether keyboard makers should be held legally liable for RSI injuries, or for not including warnings. However, partly because of growing recognition that there is a problem, even if its exact source is not known, and partly as protection against suits, several major computer companies have been providing information about proper use and arrangement of keyboards. Compaq has begun to put "warning labels" on keyboards, telling users to read the safety information.

The federal government's Occupational Safety and Health Administration (OSHA) has imposed stiff fines on some companies where a large number of employees suffer from RSI. In one case where the fine was $1.4 million, the company (Pepperidge Farms, another bakery) argued that they should not be fined when OSHA itself did not know how to prevent the injuries. A judge partly agreed and slashed the fine. OSHA has spent several years working on federal workplace rules for RSI. In 1994, it conceded that specific rules could not be developed because scientists still do not understand the causes of the injuries or how to prevent them. Commenting on the risks of writing detailed regulations, the head of OSHA said, "Specification standards can lock you into time and technology and inhibit innovation."[44]

The Australian epidemic

In the early 1980s Australia experienced a sudden sharp epidemic of RSI. The number of cases reported in one state of Australia more than quadrupled in a five-year period (1979–1984). Most of the people reporting problems were women in government office jobs.[45] At the peak in 1985, more than 50% of workers in some areas reported RSI problems. In the next few years, the number of cases declined. The Australian RSI epidemic seemed unique at the time; cases in the U.S. were comparatively rare. Several researchers, including Kiesler and Finholt of Carnegie Mellon University,[46] studied the Australian situation. Kiesler and Finholt found that poor equipment design alone did not explain the startlingly high rate of reported RSI cases in Australia. Australia imported most of its computer equipment from other countries, which were not experiencing similar RSI increases. In fact, Australia was making ergonomic improvements at the time the epidemic occurred. The rates of injury varied in different parts of the country, even though there did not appear to be any important differences in the work or workplaces. Because of the odd characteristics of the epidemic, this study and others considered hysteria, a phenomenon where the physical symptoms are real, but the causes are psychological—what we informally call the power of suggestion. Dr. Pascarelli offers another explanation for RSI "epidemics"; it may have been a factor in Australia. When some workers in large offices begin to suffer serious pain and disability, coworkers who are having milder problems begin to worry and seek treatment sooner than they might otherwise. As the problem gets more publicity, people with very early symptoms, who might have ignored them, will seek treatment immediately. Thus the number of new cases may spike, then level off.[47]

Kiesler and Finholt found a number of factors to be relevant in the Australian epidemic. RSI became a focus for union and feminist activity in the early 80s. The medical establishment gave RSI official validation and were willing to diagnose it early. The news media covered the problem in detail. RSI was recognized as a legitimate injury by the workers' compensation system in Australia. Workers could be compensated even if they had no physical symptoms. For a six-month period in Australia, no federal worker who applied for compensation for RSI was refused. Although all these factors were relevant, a main conclusion of this study and others was that many RSI complaints resulted from generally poor job conditions and low job satisfaction. Rapid conversion to computer technology and insufficient training increased stress. One government office increased required data entry rates to 14,000 keystrokes per hour. Keyboard operators had low status, little autonomy, and a poor physical environment. While not denying the reality of the pain suffered by many workers, nor claiming that workers intentionally defrauded employers, the study points out that "the ambiguous nature of RSI makes it the perfect candidate for many workers as they seek an approved exit from the computing pool while preserving benefits and some salary."[48] The study suggests that ergonomic changes, while important, will probably not solve RSI problems as long as the jobs themselves are poorly designed.

Education and choices

Both employers and computer users need to be aware of the potential problems from improper or intensive keyboard work. They need to learn what is known about prevention and treatment of RSI. Employers are learning the costs of poor equipment and work practices.

Users of any tool should learn the proper techniques for its use. We, as computer users, have some responsibility for learning good keyboard work habits. Realistic observation of human behavior suggests that even after users are educated about proper keyboard techniques and the need for rest breaks, they may ignore what they learn. We are told repeatedly by mothers and doctors that we should sit up straight, exercise often, and eat our vegetables. Many people do not follow this advice. But once we have the information, we can choose what to do with it.

> *Balance is very important for hand comfort. You'll be surprised at how quick your wrist will ache if the knife is not balanced properly.*
> —GEORGE McNEILL, *Executive Chef, Royal York Hotel, Toronto*
> (on an advertisement for fine cutlery)

EXERCISES

Review exercises

1. List two job categories where the number of jobs has declined drastically due to computers.

2. List two job categories where the number of jobs has increased drastically due to computers.

3. What are some advantages and some disadvantages of telecommuting?

4. What are two advantages or purposes of electronic monitoring of keystrokes, the number of items scanned by supermarket checkout workers, and so on? What are two of the main problems caused by such monitoring of employees?

5. What types of employee monitoring most affect professional ("white collar") employees?

6. What are two occupations where repetitive strain injury is common, but workers are not using computers?

General exercises

7. List four examples from Section 1.3 where the benefit described reduces the number of jobs needed to accomplish the task. Tell specifically what jobs are reduced or eliminated.

8. Why is it difficult to determine the number of jobs eliminated and created by computers?

9. Should there be legal bans on some kinds of home-based work and not others (e.g. sewing vs. office work)? Why, or why not? If you think there should be some restrictions on home work, what principles should be used in deciding what to ban or regulate?

10. Some businesses complain that when they give their employees Internet connections, some employees waste a large amount of time "surfing the Net," instead of working. Suggest ways a business might reduce this problem. Is reviewing logs of employees' online activities an acceptable method?

11. Proposed federal legislation to control employee monitoring includes a provision that employees with more than five years of experience may not be monitored. Give reasons for not monitoring experienced employees. Give reasons in favor of monitoring them.

12. Which of the telephone monitoring guidelines listed in Figure 8.2 do you think should be enforced by law, and which should be left to company policy? If you make your decisions on a

case-by-case basis, give your reason for each. If you can identify a general principle to make the distinction, explain the principle.

13. Using the Freedom of Information Act and similar state laws, some people have requested the e-mail of governors, legislators, and past and current presidents. These requests raise the issue of whether the e-mail of government employees and elected officials should be treated as personal conversation or official government documents. What do you think? Why?

14. Consider the following scenario. An employee at an investment firm reported to a supervisor that some employees have unlicensed software on their office computers. Over a weekend, without informing the employees in advance, the company searches all computers (via its network) looking for unlicensed software.

    Discuss arguments for and against the company's action. What are the issues involved? Do you think the search was reasonable? What alternative actions could the company have taken? Give reasons why they would have been better, or not as good, as doing the search.

15. In response to the lack of scientific knowledge about whether or how keyboards cause RSI, a plaintiff's lawyer who is handling more than 1000 RSI lawsuits commented that "The law can't wait on science."[49] Give some arguments to support this statement (as it applies to RSI lawsuits). Give some arguments against it. Do you agree with the statement? Why?

Assignments

These exercises require some research or activity that may need to be done during business hours or a few days before the assignment is due.

16. Get a current copy of your local newspaper and review the employment ads. What kinds of jobs are most common in the ads? What percent of the ads are for jobs that require computer skills? What percent are for computer professionals (programmers, computer engineers, etc.)?

17. Collect newspaper articles or news stories from the next few weeks* about businesses laying off workers. Write a summary including the company, the industry it is in, the number of employees laid off, the reasons given, and whether or not the layoffs were the result of computers. (Explain how, in cases where it is not obvious.)

18. (a) Interview someone who uses a computer at work, but worked at the job (or a similar job) before computers were used for it. Write up their answers to the questions below. Include the person's name, employer, and job title. (Some possible choices for an interview subject are a waiter or waitress in a restaurant where orders are entered on a computer, a supermarket checkout clerk who worked before and after checkout scanners were introduced, a secretary or clerical worker who has worked with and without computers, a librarian, a police officer, a customer service person. Consider family members, friends, etc.)

    1. Have computers made the work easier or more enjoyable, or more stressful and unpleasant? In what ways?

    2. Were you (and others who work with you) given adequate training in the use of the computer?

    3. What seems to be the general attitude toward computers among the people you work with?

    4. Did computerizing at the job cause some people to be fired?

    (b) If possible, talk to a manager or supervisor at the same place and ask what the manager thinks the employees' answers would be to the questions above. Summarize the manager's answers. Are the manager's perceptions of the employee's opinions accurate?

*Or the past few weeks, if that is more convenient.

19. The purpose of this exercise is to determine if the *Borland vs. Symantec* case (Section 8.4) has been resolved. Do a search of newspapers or legal records (using a service like Nexis/Lexis if one is available to you), and try to find articles about the case. If it has been resolved, write a summary of the result and the arguments it was based on.

20. Was RSI "a fad or an epidemic"? Find data from the past ten years on the number of RSI cases in the United States, or look for newspaper and magazine articles on RSI. What trends do you see?

Class exercises

1. Have a mock trial in class for an RSI lawsuit against a computer keyboard manufacturer. Assign teams of students to be lawyers for the plaintiff and the defense. Assign some to be medical expert witnesses and ergonomics specialists for each side. Assign the rest of the class to be the jury.

NOTES

1 *CPU: Working in the Computer Industry* (an electronic publication for workers in the computer industry), February 15, 1995.

2 Associated Press, "Electronic Dealings Will Slash Bank Jobs, Study Finds," *Wall Street Journal,* August 14, 1995, p. A5D. G. Pascal Zachary, "Service Productivity Is Rising Fast—and So Is the Fear of Lost Jobs," *Wall Street Journal,* June 8, 1995, p. A1.

3 Joan E. Rigdon, "Technological Gains Are Cutting Costs, And Jobs, in Services," *Wall Street Journal,* February 2, 1994, p. A1.

4 Robert Fox, "Newstrack," *Communications of the ACM,* April 1996, p. 9.

5 J. M. Fenster, "Seam Stresses," *Great Inventions That Changed the World,* American Heritage, 1994.

6 Unemployment data from Eurostat, the Organisation for Economic Co-operation and Development (OECD), and EU member nations, reported in *Wall Street Journal,* November 30, 1995, p. A10. Nick Gillespie, "Change Is Good," *Reason,* April 1995, p. 15.

7 W. Michael Cox and Richard Alm, "The Good Old Days Are Now," *Reason,* December 1995, pp. 20–27.

8 "Probing a Computer Productivity Paradox," *Science News,* January 1, 1994, 145:1, p. 7.

9 Paul Wallich, "The Analytical Economist," *Scientific American,* August 1994, p. 89.

10 Zachary, "Service Productivity Is Rising Fast—and So Is the Fear of Lost Jobs."

11 Reprinted in *British Labour Struggles: Contemporary Pamphlets 1727–1850,* Arno Press, 1972

12 Stephanie N. Mehta, "Chicago Targets Home Offices," *Wall Street Journal,* April 3, 1995, p. B2. Joel Kotkin, "Commuting Via Information Superhighway," *Wall Street Journal,* January 27, 1994, p. A14. *Technology in the American Household,* Times Mirror Center for the People and the Press, May 1994, p. 4.

13 Jack Nilles, "Teleworking: Working Closer to Home," *Technology Review,* April 1982, pp. 56–62.

14 Nilles, "Teleworking: Working Closer to Home."

15 Some friends of mine moved to Florida where the wife is a college professor, while her husband continues to work for his long-time employer, a software company in California.

16 Kotkin, "Commuting Via Information Superhighway."

17 Kathleen E. Christensen, *The New Era of Home-Based Work: Directions and Policies,* Westview Press, 1988.

18 "The Incredible Shrinking Company," *The Economist,* December 15, 1990, pp. 65–66.

19 These trends, with several examples, are described in James B. Treece, "Breaking the Chains of Command," *Business Week,* special issue on the Information Revolution, 1994, pp. 112–14.

20 "A Conversation With Lewis Maltby" (director of the ACLU's Task Force on Civil Liberties in the Workplace), *Privacy and American Business,* September 1994, pp. 9, 12.

21 David D. Redell, "Safeguard Employees' Privacy," *San Diego Union-Tribune,* October 13, 1993, p. B5.

22 Paul Attewell, "Big Brother and the Sweatshop: Computer Surveillance in the Automated Office," *Sociological Theory,* 1987, v. 5, pp. 87–89.

23 John Gerdelman, "MCI's Monitoring Program," *Privacy and American Business,* September 1994, p. 17.

24 Louis Harris and Associates, "Privacy and Fair Employer Monitoring Practices," April, 1994.

25 Quoted in *Connecticut Law Tribune,* December 18, 1995.

26 "Employers' Access to Employee E-Mail," *The DataLaw Report,* July 1993, 1:1, p. 1. Charles Pillar, "Bosses With X-ray Eyes," *Macworld,* July 1993, pp. 118–123.

27 Robert Mirguet, Eastman Kodak, *Privacy and American Business,* October 1994.

28 Except in limited cases where possible criminal activity is being investigated.

29 Anne Wells Branscomb, *Who Owns Information?,* Basic Books, 1994, reports that Epson America, Inc. did this, p. 93.

30 "The Legal Status of Work Monitoring," *Privacy and American Business,* September 1994, p. 6. "Work Monitoring, Privacy, and Fairness," *Privacy and American Business,* September 1994, pp. 1–3. Frances A. McMorris, "Is Office Voice Mail Private? Don't Bet On It," *Wall Street Journal,* February 28, 1995, p. B1. Rick Raber, "When Does Surveillance Turn to Intrusion?" *Chicago Tribune,* May 2, 1995, p. 3.

31 General Motors has such a policy, according to Raber, "When Does Surveillance Turn To Intrusion?"

32 Branscomb, *Who Owns Information?,* reports that Federal Express, American Airlines, Pacific Bell, and United Parcel Service do this, p. 94. IBM and Citicorp provide similar reminders.

33 Mitchell Kapor, "Computer Spies," *Forbes,* November 9, 1992, p. 288. "To Catch a Spy: Is Workplace E-Mail Private?" *Macworld,* July 1993, p. 122.

34 Raber, "When Does Surveillance Turn to Intrusion?" "Voice-Mail Case Settled," *Privacy Journal,* March 1996, 22:5, p. 1.

35 For a "pro and con" debate on the bill between David D. Redell, from Computer Professionals for Social Responsibility, and Jerry Jasinowski, president of the National Association of Manufacturers, see "Pro/Con: Electronic Monitoring of Workers," *San Diego Union-Tribune,* October 13, 1993, p. B5.

36 "A Conversation With Lewis Maltby."

37 Data from Bureau of Labor Statistics reported in Joan E. Rigdon, "How a Plant Handles Occupational Hazard With Common Sense," *Wall Street Journal,* September 28, 1992, p. A1.

38 Edward Felsenthal, "An Epidemic or a Fad? The Debate Heats Up Over Repetitive Stress," *Wall Street Journal,* July 14, 1994, p. A1. R. L. Linscheid and J. H. Dobyns, "Athletic Injuries of the Wrist," *Clinical Orthopedics,* September 1985, pp. 141–151. *American Annals of the Deaf.* David M. Rempel, Robert J. Harrison, Scott Barnhart, "Work-Related Cumulative Trauma Disorders of the Upper Extremity," *Journal of the American Medical Association,* 267:6, February 12, 1992, pp. 838–42.

39 Felsenthal, "An Epidemic or a Fad?"

40 Sara Kiesler and Tom Finholt, "The Mystery of RSI," *American Psychologist,* December 1988, 43:12, pp. 1004–15. Felsenthal, "An Epidemic or a Fad?"

41 *Inc.,* June, 1994, reported in *Investors Business Daily,* June 28, 1994.

42 Joan E. Rigdon, "How a Plant Handles Occupational Hazard With Common Sense," *Wall Street Journal,* September 28, 1992, p. A1.

43 Kyle Pope, "Compaq Wins Verdict in Wrist Injury Case," *Wall Street Journal,* February 22, 1994, p. B5.

44 Edward Felsenthal, "Ergonomics Guidelines Lack Solutions," *Wall Street Journal,* July 19, 1994, p. B7.

45 Mark Ragg, "Plague of RSI Suddenly 'Disappears'," *The Australian,* September 7, 1987.

46 Sara Kiesler and Tom Finholt, "The Mystery of RSI," *American Psychologist,* December 1988, 43:12, pp. 1004–15.

47 Emil Pascarelli and Deborah Quilter, *Repetitive Strain Injury: A Computer User's Guide,* John Wiley & Sons, Inc., 1994, p. 11.

48 Kiesler and Finholt, "The Mystery of RSI," p. 1012.

49 Steven Philips, quoted in Felsenthal, "An Epidemic or a Fad?"

FOR FURTHER READING

Michael L. Dertouzos, *Computers and Productivity,* MIT Laboratory for Computer Science, 1990.

Ronald Kutscher, *The Impact of Technology on Employment in the United States: Past and Future,* Farmer Press, 1987.

Thomas K. Landauer, *The Trouble With Computers: Usefulness, Usability, and Productivity,* MIT Press, 1995.

Jack Nilles, "Teleworking: Working Closer to Home," *Technology Review,* April 1982, pp. 56–62. An early article that already saw many of the advantages and disadvantages of telework.

Emil Pascarelli and Deborah Quilter, *Repetitive Strain Injury: A Computer User's Guide,* John Wiley & Sons, Inc., 1994.

Don Sellers, *Zap! How Your Computer Can Hurt You and What You Can Do About It,* (ed. Stephen F. Roth), Peachtree Press, 1994.

Suzanne P. Weisband and Bruce A. Reinig, "Managing User Perceptions of Email Privacy," *Communications of the ACM,* December 1995, 38:12, pp. 40–47.

9 BROADER ISSUES ON THE IMPACT AND CONTROL OF COMPUTERS

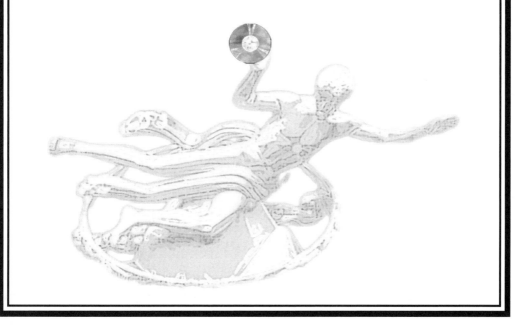

In a way not seen since Gutenberg's printing press that ended the Dark Ages and ignited the Renaissance, the microchip is an epochal technology with unimaginably far-reaching economic, social, and political consequences.

—MICHAEL ROTHSCHILD[1]

Most of the topics we considered in previous chapters focus on one subject, such as crime, copyright, or censorship of the Internet. This chapter introduces broader, perhaps fuzzier, issues, more akin to some we considered in Chapter 4 on reliability of computer systems (e.g, How much risk is too much? Are we too dependent on computers?). Here we will consider such questions as: How do computers and telecommunications affect human interaction and community? Will they increase the distance between rich and poor people? Are guarantees of universal access needed and desirable? What is the impact of computing on the quality of life? Is computer technology, overall, a benefit to us or a harm? How should computing technology be controlled to ensure positive uses and consequences?

9.1   A VARIETY OF SOCIAL ISSUES

9.1.1   Community or Isolation

While all this razzle-dazzle connects us electronically, it disconnects us from each other, having us "interfacing" more with computers and TV screens than looking in the face of our fellow human beings. Is this progress?

—JIM HIGHTOWER[2]

If children are separated from their parents by hours of TV, from their playmates by video games, and from their teachers by teaching machines, when are they supposed to learn to be human?

—MARIAN KESTER[3]

Something goes on among humans that is definitely not present in human-machine relationships.

—JERRY MANDER[4]

Community and personal relationships

    As the quotations above indicate, many observers worry that the impact of computers on community, social, and interpersonal interaction is negative and will get worse. Some fear that use of computers in schools will have negative effects on children, and ultimately on society. We will briefly describe these concerns, then present other perspectives on them.

Richard Sclove, executive director of the Loka Institute, an advocacy organization concerned with the social impact of science and technology, criticizes the "Wal-Mart effect" of computers (and other technologies). They hurt local community vibrancy. He fears that online shopping will kill real stores and community-based professionals, that the affluent will withdraw support for public schools and other local public services. Sclove and other critics of the Internet worry that computers reduce face-to-face gathering. Neil Postman says that voting, shopping, banking, and getting information at home is a "catastrophe"; there are fewer opportunities for people to be "co-present," resulting in isolation from neighbors. Technology, he worries, puts a much greater stress on the individual and downplays the importance of community.[5]

Increased computer use in schools may lead to children spending more time working alone with the machine instead of interacting with their teachers and fellow students. As a result, some observers worry, their social skills may not develop as well as they would without computers. They may not learn to value other people.

We are all familiar with the image of teenagers and young men (and some women) spending hours into the night in front of their computer screens, playing games, exploring systems, hacking, or surfing the net. Some of them virtually eliminate direct contact with their families and other people. Some who are already socially awkward find the computer easier to deal with than people; the computer provides an excuse not to overcome the social awkwardness. There are people who fit this extreme image. In addition, there are many more, ordinary teens and adults, who spend hours online instead of with their families and in-person friends.

How serious are these problems? Is the Internet creating a subpopulation of people who are narrow and unsocial? Is working on a computer more isolating than reading a book, an activity that is usually applauded? Is the Internet destroying communities?

"Addiction" to cyberspace is a problem for some people. On the other hand, online communities can benefit their participants, especially communities focused on special interests or problems for which a person might not find many contacts in his or her local community. According to the CEO of America Online, more people use the service for "community" than for information retrieval. Online relationships tend to be based on similar interests rather than merely proximity in a neighborhood. A Times Mirror survey found that users of computers and modems are "voracious consumers of information," but not just from online sources. They read newspapers, magazines, and books and watch serious news programs on TV as much or more than people with similar demographic characteristics who do not use computers.[6]

Serious research is being done on what makes a strong community. Given the complexity of human society, answers are theories, not proven facts. Social scientist Robert Putnam argues that one important factor is the number of clubs and other organizations people join and are active in.[7] As Alexis de Tocqueville observed more than 150 years ago, "Americans of all ages, all stations in life, and all types of disposition are forever forming associations."[8] We join hobby clubs, churches, Boy Scouts and Girl Scouts, unions, professional organizations, service clubs, hiking and running clubs, and a myriad of others. Such memberships create informal personal and information networks that are helpful for both economic growth and solving social problems in a community. But participation in clubs has been declining. Critics of computers and the Internet blame them for this decline, but social scientists point to a number of other factors: modern transportation and communications (encouraging increased mobility), changes in family patterns (later marriage, more divorce, working mothers), and television. The loss of close, local community ties began before widespread use of personal computers and the Internet. The Times Mirror survey found that Net users were at least as likely as demographically similar nonusers to visit with family and friends and be members of a club or organization. Overall, it does not appear that adults who spend a lot of time in cyberspace are less social than those who do not.

To the extent that computers contribute to formation of electronic relationships with people scattered around the country and the world, they may further weaken local community bonds, but the degree of change seems small compared to the effects on communities of other technological and social changes. Automated and online services reduce the opportunities for personal interaction with neighbors and local merchants in the course of ordinary daily activities, but they free up time that we can fill with activities shared with people we know well and associate with by choice.

The desire for the advantages of small community life—a slower pace, less commuting, being closer to nature, involvement with neighbors, and so on—is prompting many professionals and knowledge workers to move to small towns.

Some businesses are relocating to small towns, because telecommunications and transportation reduce the need to be in a larger city. In the 1980s, population in 20 of the 40 largest metropolitan areas declined; a study by the Office of Technology Assessment attributed the decline to advances in information technology.[9] Computer technology is beginning to make a return to small community life easier. The Internet and satellite communications, and so on, bring education, information, and entertainment options that were not available before. Computer enthusiasts see the ability of the Net to "conquer distance" as one of its advantages, potentially allowing a reversal of the population concentration in cities. On the other hand, some people, especially young adults, prefer city life for its vibrancy and career and social opportunities. It is not likely that cities will disappear as long as they have advantages for many people.

Some extreme critics of the impact of the Internet on community propose laws and regulations to strengthen the elements they consider important to community. For example, in order to "conserve cultural space for face-to-face social engagement, traditional forms of community life, off-screen leisure activities, and time spent in nature," Sclove and Scheuer suggest regulations to manipulate rates to discourage use of the Net one evening a week. They suggest taxing online shopping and consumer services to subsidize local community activities.[10] These proposals, of course, are controversial. Economists point out that tax subsidies and artificial manipulation of prices waste resources by shifting production from services consumers value more highly to those they value less. Supporters of such schemes view the individual choices as less important than the strength of the community. Others object to the view that individualism and strength of community are in opposition. Community is important to people. Thoughtful criticism of the impact of the Net on community can make us think about our own activities, choices, and trade-offs. Those who value freedom to make individual choices argue that coercive manipulation of people's choices and activities breeds resentment rather than community.

9.1.2   Information Haves and Have-Nots: The Access Issue

Under the universal service guarantee in the Communications Act of 1934, telephone companies are required to provide telephone service to poor people at low rates, subsidized by other customers. At issue now is whether and how to extend this principle to the Net. Will there be "universal access"? What should it include? How should it be achieved? What should the government's role be?

The focus on this issue stems from the concern that access to information may give some people such a large advantage over those without access that our society will divide sharply into the "information haves" and "information have-nots," leaving the have-nots to a lowly and unsatisfying existence. Some see this social and economic division leading to violence and political disruption.[11] Whether or not such disruption occurs, the human cost in joblessness, wasted potential, and poverty could be high.

In 1994, according to the Times Mirror survey, a family with a college graduate parent and family income over $50,000 was five times more likely to have a home computer and ten times more likely to have a modem than the family of a nongraduate earning less than $30,000. Computer skills will be needed for many jobs. Children who do not acquire basic skills will be at a disadvantage. Almost half the children of college graduates use a computer at home; only 17% of children of parents with high school education or less do.[12] Poor and minority children have less access to computers both in schools and at home.

Computer Professionals for Social Responsibility (CPSR) explains the principle of universal access this way:[13]

> Universal access to the NII* is a necessary and basic condition of citizenship in our information-driven society. Guaranteeing such access is therefore an absolute requirement for any degree of equity. At a minimum, universal access requires the following conditions:
>
> - Everyone in the country must have a place they can go to gain access to the NII.
> - Hardware and software for the NII must be easy to use and fit the needs of all users, including the disabled.
> - Simple training in the effective use of these tools must be available.
> - Pricing for the NII must be structured so that service is affordable by everyone.
> - Access to the full range of features supported by the NII must be available to all.

CPSR notes that "access will require not merely a connection to the NII but the hardware to use that connection."[14] Various other organizations have made similar arguments and proposals for universal access. The government's National Information Infrastructure

---

*"National Information Infrastructure," or NII, is the political term for the Net in the U.S.

Advisory Committee defines universal access to include interactive, multimedia equipment and software. A study by the RAND research organization concluded that universal e-mail access is essential; it recommended that Web browsers be considered as a minimum requirement.[15]

The market and voluntary community activities

Some of the goals of universal access are partially met by technical developments, the market, and other voluntary activities.

The main accomplishment of the market is provision of an enormous variety of new products and services at steadily dropping prices. A typical home computer available now is thousands of times better than the Apple I, measured by the amount of memory, the speed, and the amount of software available. Yet the basic computer now costs about the same, if not less than the Apple I. The vast resources of online information services are available for less than the cost of monthly telephone service. The introduction of Microsoft Network in 1995 sparked a price war among online services, with prices for basic e-mail and World Wide Web access dropping to only $4.95 a month. The price of modems has tumbled while the speed has gone from 300 baud to 28,800. A poor family that can afford a used car and a television can afford more computing power and network access than all but big companies, universities, and government agencies had a generation ago. Several companies are now planning to produce network access computers for only a few hundred dollars.

Virtually all technological innovation is first available to the rich (or others willing to pay the initially high price). When first introduced little more than a decade ago, compact disk music players cost $1000; now they are close to $100. A good watch used to be an expensive luxury; now digital watches cost a few dollars. Prices of many consumer products follow this pattern. The early purchases finance improvements in design and production techniques that bring the price down. Computer prices have plunged more dramatically than prices of most other products. Telephones and televisions were originally luxuries of the rich; now almost every household has them. The unexpectedly large increase in the number of homes with PCs in 1995 was attributed in part to increased purchases by less-affluent people. This phenomenon has led some observers to conclude that it is more accurate to think of people as "haves" and "have-laters" rather than "haves" and "have-nots."[16]

The market provides options for people who want to use a product or service but cannot afford to buy one. For example, people who do not own a washing machine use coin-operated laundries. Few of us own a copying machine; we pay per page at a copy store. "Computer bars" and "cyber cafes" are opening all over the country and in several other countries. They provide Internet access for an hourly fee, or free with purchases of food or coffee. The cafes provide a friendly, informal setting for novices to learn about the Internet, and their initial popularity suggests that many people enjoy "co-present" social interaction even while they are exploring the Net. Copy stores are beginning to provide pay-per-use terminals. Stores like Mailboxes, Etc. and Pak-Mail might add e-mail and other services. A few years ago, we would not have predicted the appearance of bank machines in supermarkets. Some companies are experimenting with providing free equipment, software, and/or e-mail service that include online advertising. It is hard to predict exactly where and how access will be provided by innovative businesspeople who see a demand for services.

The development of easy-to-use point-and-click graphical interfaces for commercial online services and the World Wide Web may reduce the problem of training. Although poor user interfaces are frustratingly common now, it will probably eventually become easier to use the Net than it is to drive a car, a skill most people acquire. Software of all sorts, including Web browsers, is available for free. Some is provided by programmers who donate it; some is provided by companies who see it as advertising for other products.

Individuals and businesses contribute equipment and services to schools and community organizations that cannot afford them. The donations range from small to huge. A high-tech company buys new computers and donates the old ones, which were state-of-the art only a few years earlier, to local schools. A local computer society takes on the project of wiring local schools for Internet access. AT&T is making a $150-million donation of Internet services for almost all public and private elementary and secondary schools in the country. In California several high-tech companies sponsored NetDay96, a modern "barn-raising," a day on which thousands of volunteers went to schools around the state to install wire for Internet access. Similar projects are planned in other states.

There are millions of old, used computers in the United States. Some cities have computer swap meets where one can buy equipment at very low prices. Used equipment does not have the speed and features of the latest models, but it can be used to access the Net.[17] With second-hand users in mind, some people are writing text-based software for the Web. If demand develops, perhaps stores in low-income neighborhoods that sell used refrigerators will add used computers to their stock.

The gap between the market and universal access

The market and other voluntary efforts will not provide the universality and quality of access that some consider essential. Supporters of universal access, in the sense of modern multimedia equipment for everyone, find the examples above unsatisfying. There probably are no cafes with Internet access in poor neighborhoods. Second-hand computers do not meet the requirement of access to the full range and quality of features and services that are available. CPSR and others emphasize the need to provide access in all homes; it is not enough that going to a library or store allows access. Many school districts cannot afford computers and training. Universal access proponents argue that what is not provided by the market and community efforts must be provided by government. Some proposals from RAND, CPSR, and the government's NII advisory committee, for example, include the following:

- Requiring companies to provide discounted rates to poor people
- Government subsidies for the poor, paid for by taxpayers in general
- Taxes on information providers
- Taxes on e-mail and communications providers
- Government programs to pay for computers in libraries, public schools, and community centers

The RAND study anticipates that the cost of the subsidy for universal e-mail access (network access and equipment) could be about $1 billion a year.[18]

Criticisms of universal access proposals

Proposals for government involvement through compulsory access requirements or subsidies provided by taxes are not universally supported. The objections include disagreements about the seriousness of the problem of access for the poor and ethical objections to compulsory solutions. Some critics reject the idea that access to computers and the Net are either the cause of or the cure for divisions in our society. They reject the premise that computers will cause a sharp division between information haves and have-nots. We have always had rich and poor and a large middle class, and previous predictions of sharp divisions caused by new technologies have not occurred. Knowledge and education are important: High school dropouts are five times as likely to face long-term unemployment as college graduates.[19] But complex social, political, and economic factors, not lack of computers, cause high dropout rates, crime, and the generally poor quality of public schools in inner-city neighborhoods. Steve Jobs, cofounder of Apple Corp., who, in his words, "probably spearheaded giving away more computer equipment to schools than anybody else on the planet," commented that "What's wrong with education cannot be fixed with technology. . . . It's a political problem."[20]

Critics of mandatory subsidies and taxes argue that they are inequitable, inefficient, and unnecessary. These views are usually associated with more general views about the role of government and egalitarianism. Some believe that all tax subsidies are unjust to the taxpayers who must pay for them. Some believe that subsidies should be restricted to the basic necessities of life, such as food.

Critics of subsidies argue that not everyone needs or wants access to the Net. If they did, the low prices would not be a barrier. Poor people set spending priorities and buy what they value most. More than 98% of American households have televisions, which are not subsidized. The Times Mirror survey found that while the number of children who have access to computers at home differed significantly depending on socio-economic status, there was little difference in the number of homes that have video games. Teenagers, including poor teenagers, are eager to learn to drive. Perhaps a significant factor in development of their computer skills is whether they will decide that computers are as useful as driving.

Both critics and advocates of subsidized universal access see two important tasks: (1) convincing parents and children that computers are a valuable tool for bettering one's chances at a productive future, and (2) establishing the social support environment needed to encourage their use.

9.1.3 Loss of Skills and Judgment

Computers, like other tools and technologies, encourage certain uses and consequences by making them easier. Some skills that were important before are displaced by the new tools. We will look at some examples of the ways computers and other technologies may affect the way we do things.

Writing, thinking, and memory

I have a spelling checker.
It came with my PC.
It plainly marks four my revue,
Miss steaks aye can knot sea.
Eye ran this poem threw it,
I'm sure your pleased too no.
It's letter perfect in it's weigh,
My checker tolled me sew.

–JERROLD H. ZAR, *"Candidate for a Pullet Surprise"*[21]

The spelling checker poem humorously illustrates the problem of doing what the tool makes easy and ignoring other important tasks. A computer can check the spelling of all the words in a document in less time than it takes a person to flip through the pages of a printed dictionary to find the first one. But it looks up each word only to determine if it is in its dictionary; it does not check whether the word is properly used. Many of the steps in publishing have been made easier by computers. The ease and fun of playing with layout, fonts, and graphics have led many people to concentrate on those aspects of the document at the expense of thoughtful writing, correct grammar, word usage, correct information, and editing—the parts that still require hard mental effort. The convenience of using a computer can encourage mental laziness.

Critics of computers see the loss of skills as part of a long trend of skill losses due to technology. For example, Chet Bowers argues that the telephone increases communication, but reduces use of visual signals. The use of a stick to increase our reach reduces our ability to use our sense of touch and smell. Modern critics, taking their cue from Socrates (through Plato's *Phaedrus*), find fault with the invention of writing. It destroyed memory and oral skill and obscured the distinction between wisdom and knowledge, according to critics. With reading and writing, the complaint argues, a presentation tends to be more one-sided, more dogmatic, because there is no dialogue, no one to question arguments and conclusions.[22] Numerous critics of the Internet make similar charges against it: A vast amount of information is available, but it comes without wisdom. Computers emphasize thinking based on data, numbers, quantifiable entities. They discourage focus on judgment and values. They encourage the making of fancy charts based on complex computations, but they discourage deep thought about the purpose to which the charts will be put or the validity and meaning of the data. They encourage surfing the Net, looking for facts; they discourage discussion with others of what we found and the ability to defend a point of view in conversation.

It is interesting and valuable to observe the variety of changes in social patterns that occur because of the invention of a new tool or technology. It helps us understand how human beings behave and how society evolves. Although it is valuable to be aware of changes in the relative importance of various skills, it is not obvious, as some critics suggest, that all the changes are bad. Some old skills are replaced by better ones. How much more poetry is available to us now in books than we could have memorized? While most of us no longer develop strong memorization skills, these skills have not been lost to those who need them: A few days ago, I attended a one-man play that lasted two hours. Language scholar Walter Ong pointed out that the old skills are not lost; they are enhanced, but not used where the new ones function better. He argues that writing made oral communication much more effective.[23] Certainly the Internet can be used to enhance communication. Anyone who participates in online newsgroups and discussion groups knows that dialogue and argument survive. The quality, not surprisingly, includes both thoughtful, deep analysis and insulting "flame wars." Perhaps surprisingly, as more people are signing up for online services and buying multimedia CD-ROMs, sales of books have been steadily rising as well.[24]

This is not to say that all the criticisms are unfounded. We need to evaluate carefully the changes and identify those that are truly problems. For example, we should be alert to the tendency to overemphasize tasks that computers can do well, while ignoring other important tasks, that is, the tendency to mental laziness. We need to resist the temptation to emphasize data rather than analysis, facts rather than understanding and evaluation.

Abdicating responsibility

People are often willing to let computers do their thinking for them. They place too much reliance on output from computers, which were called "giant brains" in the 1950s. Neil Postman compares the claim, "The computer has determined . . ." to the claim, "It is God's will," in its effectiveness in eliciting acceptance.[25]

Abdication of responsibility to exercise judgment, and sometimes, a reasonable amount of skepticism, has serious consequences. Loan approvals, insurance approvals, and similar decisions are made with the help of computerized credit and health reports. Police officers make arrest decisions using information in the FBI's NCIC computer system. Bad decisions are sometimes made because of ignorance of the kinds of errors that can occur in the computer system, ignorance of the purpose of the system, and the mystique that anything coming from a computer must be correct. For example, people have been arrested when a check of NCIC showed an arrest warrant for someone with a similar name. Does the officer think that because the warrant was displayed, the computer has decided that the person being checked is the wanted person? Or does the officer know that the system simply displays any close matches and that the responsibility for the arrest decision lies with the officer?

In bureaucracies, a decision-maker may feel that there is less personal risk (and less bother) in just accepting a computer report rather than doing additional checking or making a decision not supported by the computer.

To produce good work and make wise decisions, both computer professionals and ordinary nontechnical users must consider what computers can do well and reliably and where humans must exercise good judgment and take responsibility.

9.2   POLITICAL FREEDOM

Will computers and the Internet reduce the power of governments, especially oppressive governments? Or will they help governments consolidate power over their citizens? The "conventional wisdom" among most users and observers of the Net (if anything about the Net can be called conventional) is that computers are a force for greatly increased freedom.

There are good reasons for this optimistic view. There are also, however, events and trends that suggest the potential for increased control of people's activities and suppression of free information flow. We will look at support for both points of view, first examining some of the ways the Net contributes to political freedom and reduces misbehavior by governments.

A force for freedom

Electronic mail and fax machines played a significant role during the collapse of the Soviet Union and the democracy demonstrations in China's Tiananmen Square. Information about what was happening was sent to western countries without being censored. Articles and whole newsletters were faxed to China and distributed there. Both countries have far fewer computers and fax machines than the U.S., and totalitarian governments restrict ownership of publishing and communication equipment, but there were enough such machines available to provide a steady flow of information.

In some Asian countries, governments control and frequently censor the news media. Newsgroups on the Internet have become a vibrant forum for political discussion and criticism of governments. Although, as we shall describe below, many governments are taking steps to cut off such discussion, people who have experienced open communication may not give it up easily. Commenting on the Chinese government, a Hong Kong publisher said that even if they control 90% of the media in the future, when it is virtually all computerized, "the 10% surviving will be enough to inform everyone."[26] In the tradition of Samizdat, the underground publishing network in the former Soviet Union, underground electronic communication will spread information in countries with oppressive governments, probably more effectively than was possible with older technologies.

As we saw in Chapter 3, encryption is a valuable tool for protecting communications and files of opposition movements in countries with oppressive governments. Anonymous remailers protect dissidents from punishment for expressing their views.

In general, access to information and communications decrease a government's ability to abuse its people. Arthur C. Clarke comments, "No government will be able to conceal, at least for very long, evidence of crimes or atrocities—even from its own people. The very existence of the myriads of new information channels, operating in real time and across all frontiers, will be a powerful influence for civilized behavior."[27]

In the U.S., if a questionable bill is introduced in Congress, reports and analysis of it quickly appear on relevant newsgroups. Opposition is organized and public response, sometimes via e-mail to members of Congress, is swift. If a government tries to cover up a mistake or abuse, critical information will be more widely disseminated than when we depended on radio or TV networks, licensed by the government. We can read the full text of bills, budgets, investigative reports, congressional testimony and debate, instead of relying on a few sentences quoted from an official news release or a sound bite from a biased spokesperson.

The Internet was designed for military researchers. A critical requirement was that messages should get to their destination even if some computers or communication lines fail or are destroyed. Thus, messages are broken into small pieces, called packets, and sent individually through the Net following any available path that eventually leads to the destination, where the packets are reassembled. Ironically, this decentralized, distributed protocol, designed for government purposes, makes it difficult for a government to block communication. In the often quoted comment of John Gilmore, the Net treats censorship as an error and routes around it.

We look next at some of the reasons for concern about the potential for governments to become more intrusive and controlling, or at least to slow down the growth of political and economic freedom that computers and the global communications revolution seem capable of bringing.

A force for control

Computers dramatically increase a government's ability to amass information on its citizens and to monitor their movements and activities. In Chapter 2 we discussed the potential abuses of computer matching and profiling by government agencies using both private and government databases and the risks of surveillance and loss of freedom from national ID cards. All the computerized tools that aid desirable law enforcement can be used as well by governments to enforce oppressive laws and carry out illegal activities against the population.

The convenience of text searching by computer makes it easier for a government to scan electronic newsletters and messages posted to newsgroups to identify people critical of the government. The administrators of Singapore's Technet, a government-funded service, examined 80,000 files belonging to users in a search for "countersocial activity." In this case they were looking for pornography, but clearly, in countries where criticism of the government is illegal or not tolerated, searches for "countersocial activity" have ominous implications.[28]

While governments use computer technology to protect and increase their own power, they can restrict uses that contribute to freedom. As we saw in Chapter 3, the U.S. government may simply ban the use or distribution of encryption software unless it has access to all the keys. The vibrant communication made possible by the Internet threatens governments in countries that lack political and cultural freedom. Many governments are taking steps to cut, or seriously reduce, the flow of information and opinion on the Net. China is developing what it calls its "intranet," while channeling all foreign Internet traffic through a small number of gateways under its control. The Chinese government filters all online international economic news through its news agency. All users of the Internet and other international computer networks are required to register with the police. Sale of satellite dishes was banned (just as residential telephones were banned in China in the past). New regulations prohibit "producing, retrieving, duplicating and spreading information that may hinder public order." China uses firewalls to block access to Internet sites it disapproves. Viet Nam uses filtering software to find and block anticommunist messages coming from other countries. The government of Iran made people dismantle satellite dishes to avoid "cultural contamination" from U.S. television. Singapore requires that online political and religious groups register with the government. Content providers are prohibited from distributing material that could "undermine public morals, political stability or religious harmony." The government of Singapore justified its censorship attempts in part by citing the censorship efforts in the United States, in particular, the passage of the Communications Decency Act.[29]

Stewart Baker, formerly General Counsel of the National Security Agency, points out that when an oppressive government bans some communication or information, its actions can stop the flow of information to other countries as well.[30] For example, when the government of China objected to a particular program on the British Broadcasting Corporation (BBC) that was critical of Mao Tse-tung, the satellite provider cut the BBC completely out of its transmission to China. The area affected by the cut also included Taiwan and Hong Kong. We saw in Chapter 6 that CompuServe cut access to hundreds of newsgroups for all its subscribers worldwide when the German government ordered them cut for German subscribers. When businesses want to provide communications and information services in countries where the government owns or controls the communications systems, the businesses will censor what those governments want censored. We saw in Chapter 6 that application of the "community standards" criterion for obscenity may impose the most restrictive standard on the Internet for all of the United States. Similarly, the demands of governments in unfree countries may impose restrictive standards on political information throughout their part of the world.

The risk of abuse by governments of computer technology is enormous. Protection from such abuses depends in part on strong support for individual freedom and freedom of speech, the recognition of the importance of strictly controlling government power, and the appropriate laws and enforcement mechanisms to do so.

9.3   EVALUATIONS OF THE IMPACT OF COMPUTER TECHNOLOGY

The microchip is . . . made of silicon, or sand—a natural resource that is in great abundance and has virtually no monetary value. Yet the combination of a few grains of this sand and the infinite inventiveness of the human mind has led to the creation of a machine that will both create trillions of dollars of added wealth for the inhabitants of the earth in the next century and will do so with incomprehensibly vast savings in physical labor and natural resources.

—STEPHEN MOORE[31]

Quite apart from the environmental and medical evils associated with them being produced and used, there are two moral judgments against computers. One is that computerization enables the large forces of our civilization to operate more swiftly and efficiently in their pernicious goals of making money and producing things. . . . And Secondly, in the course of using these, these forces are destroying nature with more speed and efficiency than ever before.

—KIRKPATRICK SALE[32]

9.3.1   The Neo-Luddite View of Computers and Technology

The quotations above illustrate the disparity of views about the value of computer technology. Evaluations of computers cover the spectrum from "miracle" to "catastrophe." Although most of this book has been devoted to discussing problems that arise with the use of computers, the implicit (and sometimes explicit) view has been that computers are a positive development bringing us many benefits. What we saw of failures of computer systems in Chapter 4 warns us that some potential applications can have horrifying risks. The potential for loss of freedom and privacy via government surveillance, computer matching and profiling, consumer dossier building, and national ID systems are serious dangers. We saw disruptive changes in employment, computer crime, and social and economic risks from computer failures. We may urgently try to prevent some applications of computers from being implemented and urgently advocate increased protection from risks and better solutions for problems, but we did not consider the threats and risks as reasons for condemning the technology as a whole. For the most part, we have looked at new risks and negative side effects of computers as problems that occur in the natural process of change, either problems to be solved (with some combination of technology, law, education, management, and public pressure) or the price we pay for the benefits, part of a trade-off. This attitude is shared by many people with quite different political views, people who disagree about the significance of specific computer-related problems and about exactly how they should be solved.

On the other hand, there are people who utterly reject the view that computers are a positive development with many important benefits. They see the benefits as few and overwhelmingly outweighed by the damage done by computers. The difference in perspective is illustrated by a comment made by one reviewer of this book. He objected to the "gift of fire" analogy I use to suggest that computers can be very useful and also very dangerous. The reviewer thought "Pandora's box" was more appropriate. Pandora's box held "all the ills of mankind." Kirkpatrick Sale, author of *Rebels Against the Future,* demonstrates his opinion of computers by smashing one with a sledgehammer at public appearances.

In England in 1811–1812, people burned factories and mills in efforts to stop the technologies and social changes that were eliminating their jobs. Many were weavers who had worked at home on small machines. They were called Luddites.* For almost 200 years, the violent Luddite uprising has endured as the most dramatic symbol of opposition to the Industrial Revolution. The term "Luddite" has long been used derisively to describe people who oppose technological progress. More recently, it has been adopted as an honorable term by critics of technology. Kirkpatrick Sale, and many others who share his viewpoint, call themselves neo-Luddites, or simply Luddites. They have published several books in the past few years criticizing computers and the Internet.

What do the neo-Luddites find so reprehensible about computers? Some of their criticisms are problems that also trouble people whose view of computers is generally positive; we discussed them in earlier chapters (especially Chapter 8) and in Section 9.1. One of the differentiating characteristics of the neo-Luddites is the depth of their criticism—their overall evaluation of computers as a terribly bad development for humankind. Some of the specific criticisms include the following:

- Computers cause massive unemployment and deskilling of jobs. "Sweatshop labor is involved in their manufacture."[33]
- Computers "manufacture needs," that is, we use them just because they are there, not because they satisfy real needs.
- Computers cause social inequity and social disintegration.
- Computers separate humans from nature and destroy the environment.
- Computers are dehumanizing. They weaken communities and lead to isolation of people from each other.

---

*The name Luddite comes from General Ned Ludd, the fictitious, symbolic leader of the movement.

- Computers benefit big business and big government most.

- Use of computers in schools will thwart development of social skills, human values, and intellectual skills in children. They will create an "ominous uniformity of knowledge" consistent with corporate values.[34]

- Computers do little or nothing to solve real human problems. For example, Neil Postman, in response to claims of the benefits of access to information, argues that "If families break up, children are mistreated, crime terrorizes a city, education is impotent, it does not happen because of inadequate information."[35]

Some of these criticisms may seem unfair. The conditions in computer factories hardly compare to conditions in the sweatshop factories of the early Industrial Revolution. In Chapter 8 we saw that computers eliminate jobs, and the pace of computerization causes disruptions, but the case that computers, and technology in general, cause massive unemployment is not convincing, or is at least controversial. Blaming computers for social inequity in the world seems to ignore thousands of years of history. Postman is right that inadequate information is not the source of most social problems. A computer in the classroom does not replace good parents in the home. But should this be a criticism of computers and information systems? Access to information and communication can assist in solving problems, and is not likely to hurt. The main problem for ordinary people, Postman says, is how to find meaning in life. We need answers to questions like "Why are we here?" "How are we supposed to behave?"[36] Is it a valid criticism of computers that they do not solve fundamental social and philosophical problems that have engaged us for centuries?

To the neo-Luddites, the brief counterarguments we just mentioned miss the point. The view that computers are fundamentally malevolent is part of a wider view that almost all of technology is malevolent. To the modern-day Luddites, the computer is just the latest, but in many ways the worst, stage in the decline of what was good in human society. Computers are worse than earlier technologies because of their enormous speed and flexibility. The negative trends caused by technology are increased by computers. Thus, if one points out that a particular problem blamed on computers already existed because of an earlier technology, Luddites consider the distinction to be a minor one.

The depth of the antipathy to technology in the Luddite view is perhaps made clearer by attitudes toward common devices most of us use daily. For example, Sale has said, "I find talking on the phone a physical pain, as well as a mental anguish." Sven Birkerts, another critic of computers, says that if he lived in 1900, he probably would have opposed the telephone. Speaking of the invention of the printing press, Sale laments that "literacy . . . destroys orality." He regards not only computers, but civilization as a catastrophe. The invention of the clock has come under criticism from Luddites. Some of us see modern medicine as a life-saving and life-enhancing boon to humanity; some Luddites point out that it gave us the population explosion and extended senility.[37]

Having read and listened to the arguments of technology enthusiasts and technology critics, I find it striking that different people look at the same history, the same society, the same products and services, the same jobs—and come to diametrically opposed conclusions about what they see. There is a fundamental difference in the world view of supporters and opponents of technology. It is more than the difference in seeing a glass as half full or half empty. The difference seems to be one of contrasting views of what should be in the glass. Supporters of technology see an upward trend in quality of life beginning with people living at the mercy of nature with an empty glass that technology has been gradually filling. Neo-Luddites view the glass as originally full when people lived in small communities with little impact on nature; they see technology as draining it.

The neo-Luddite view is tied to a particular view of the appropriate way of life for human beings. For example, Sale's first point, in the quotation at the beginning of the chapter, makes the moral judgment that making money and producing things is pernicious. His introductory remark and his second point only hint at the unusually high valuation he places on not disturbing nature (unusually high even in the current context where there is much awareness of the importance of protecting the environment). We explore these views further.

9.3.2 Luddite Views of Economics, Nature, and Human Needs

Business, consumers, and work

Luddites generally have a negative view of capitalism, business, markets, consumer products, and factories and other modern forms of work. They see the profit-seeking goals of corporations as in fundamental conflict with the well-being of workers and the natural environment. They see work in factories, large offices, and corporations in general as dehumanizing, dreary, and bad for the health of the workers. Hence, for example, the criticisms of the clock. Neil Postman describes the invention of the clock as "the technology of greatest use to men who wished to devote themselves to the accumulation of money."[38]

The difference in perspective of Luddites and non-Luddites is sometimes illustrated by choice of words, making subtle differences in a statement. What is the purpose of technology? To the Luddites, it is to eliminate jobs to reduce the costs of production. To proponents of technology, it is to reduce the effort needed to produce goods and services. The two statements say nearly the same thing, but the first suggests massive unemployment, profits for capitalists, and a poorer life for most workers. The second suggests improvements in wealth and the standard of living.

The Luddite view combines a negative attitude toward business with a high estimation of the power of corporations to manipulate and control workers and consumers. For example, Richard Sclove describes telecommuting as being "imposed by business." (Interestingly, one of the common criticisms of the Industrial Revolution was that working in factories instead of at home weakened local community bonds.)

Luddites have particularly strong criticism for automobiles, cities, and most of the technologies involved in communications and transportation. Thus it is worth noting that most of us get both personal and social benefits from them. Cities are centers of culture, wealth production, education, and job opportunities.[39] Modern transportation and communication reduce the price of products and increase their variety and availability. For example, we can eat fresh fruits and vegetables all year. We can drive to a large discount store instead of buying from a more expensive local shop. We can phone around town to find a store, movie theater, or restaurant that has exactly what we want. Now we can use the Internet to shop more widely. We can drive long distances to take a better job. We can move to a new city, away from our family and friends, for college or a job. Airplanes, the telephone, and now the Internet, make the separations less unpleasant because we can visit or hear the voices of friends and family members, or send long e-mail messages for less than the price of a long-distance call.

These advantages are not highly valued by Luddites and other critics of technology. In some cases, in their point of view, the advantages are merely ameliorating other problems caused by technology. For example, Postman quotes Sigmund Freud's comment, "If there had been no railway to conquer distances, my child would never have left his native town and I should need no telephone to hear his voice."[40]

A common criticism of capitalism is that it survives by convincing us to buy products we do not need. Sale and other Luddites argue, similarly, that technology causes products to be produced that we do not need. This contrasts with the market-oriented view that sees the choices made by consumers as determining which products, services, and businesses succeed or fail (in the absence of government favoritism, subsidies, and restrictions). We will examine the issue of created needs next.

Does the technology create the need for itself?

Sale argues that notebook computers do not "meet any known or expressed need," but were made simply because miniaturization of computing components made them possible. I own a notebook computer. I use it when I travel, for example, to take notes at a conference (so I do not have to recopy notes from paper, and I do not lose the notes) and to work while I am away from my home or office (without having to haul along several books, files, and pads of paper). I recently took my computer to class and wrote a report while my students were taking an exam. A typewriter would have been noisy; paper would have been wasted on notes and rough drafts, to be copied later. So, does a notebook computer meet a need? It depends on what we mean by "need."

Those who emphasize the value of individual action and choices argue that needs are relative to goals, and goals are held by individuals. Thus, should we ask whether "we," as a society, need notebook computers? Or should this be an individual decision with different responses? Many people demonstrate, by their purchases, that they want one. Anyone who does not feel a desire or need for a computer does not have to buy one. This individual-oriented approach is rejected by the Luddites, who believe buyers are manipulated by advertising, work pressure, or other forces beyond their control.

Many environmental and antitechnology groups use computers. The editor of *Wild Earth,* for example, who considers himself a neo-Luddite, says he "inclines toward the view that technology is inherently evil," but he "disseminates this view via E-mail, computer, and laser printer."[41] The question is: Is he using computer equipment because of an artificial need or because it is useful and helpful to him? Sale sees the use of computers by such groups as an uncomfortable compromise; the use of computers, he says, insidiously embeds into the user the values and thought processes of the society that makes the technology.[42]

The argument that people are manipulated by capitalists or technologies to buy things they do not really want, like the argument that use of computers has an insidiously corrupting effect on computer users, is based on a low view of the judgment and autonomy of ordinary people. It is one thing to differ with another person's values and choices. It is another to conclude that because of the difference, the other person is weak and incapable of making his or her own decisions. The Luddite view of the appropriate way of life puts little value on modern comforts and conveniences or on the availability of a large variety of goods and services. Perhaps consumers value these things more highly than the Luddites do. To get a clearer understanding of the Luddite view of a proper lifestyle, we will consider some of their comments on the relationship of humans and nature.

Nature and human lifestyles

Luddites argue that technology has made no improvement in life, or at best improvements of little importance. Sale's list of benefits includes speed, ease, and mass access—all of which he disdains. Sale says that while individuals may feel their lives are better because of computers, the perceived benefits are "industrial virtues that may not be virtues in another morality." He defines moral judgment as "the capacity to decide that a thing is right when it enhances the integrity, stability, and beauty of nature and is wrong when it does otherwise."[43]

Jerry Mander, founder of the Center for Deep Ecology, points out that thousands of generations of humans got along without computers, suggesting that we could do just fine without them too. Mander's objections to technology lead him to the conclusion that there can be no "good" pesticide. While many people work on technological, legal, and educational approaches to reducing pollution from automobiles, Mander says there can be no "good" automobile.[44]

What are the underlying premises behind these comments of Sale's and Mander's? Why do Luddites reject what most people see as benefits? We will consider Sale's comment on moral judgment first. Many debates about the environment set up a humans-versus-nature dichotomy.[45] This is not the true conflict. Nature, biodiversity, forests, a hospitable climate, clean air and water, open space away from cities—these are all important and valuable to humanity. So are shelter from the rain, cold, and heat. So are life-saving medicines and medical techniques. Conflicts about the environment are not conflicts between humans and nature; they are conflicts between people with different views about how to meet human needs. In contrast to Sale's statement, moral judgment, to many people, and for many centuries, has meant the capacity to choose that which enhances human life, reduces misery, and increases happiness. Sale's comment chooses nature, not humanity, as the primary standard of moral value.

Whether an automobile is "good," by a human-centered standard, depends on whether it meets our needs, how well it does so, and at what cost (to the environment and society, as well as to our bank account). Thus, Mander's comment about automobiles again raises the issues of our standard of value and our need for a product or service. Do we need electricity and hot water on tap? Do we need movies and symphony orchestras? Or do we need nothing more than food and shelter? Do we need an average life expectancy of more than 25 years? Do we want to merely exist—do we *need* even that?—or do we want long, happy, comfortable lives filled with time for love, interesting activities, and an opportunity to use our marvelously inventive brains?

The Luddites champion a pretechnological society. Sale, for example, speaks of the sense of comradeship, the harmony, and stability of tribal societies. Half of Jerry Mander's book on the failure of technology is about the alternative lifestyle of the Indian Nations. Living in small communities, close to nature, has enormous appeal to many people, but their image of such a life includes many aspects of our modern, high standard of living, not the lifestyle of thousands of generations ago. When evaluating the neo-Luddite arguments it is useful to consider whether the underlying Luddite views of an appropriate lifestyle are close to one's own.

> *The Web is alive, and filled with life, nearly as complex and, well, natural as a primordial swamp.*
>
> —JOHN PERRY BARLOW[46]

9.3.3 Who Benefits Most?

Technology critics recognize that many people consider computers to be useful. Mander explains one of the reasons why, in spite of this, he still considers computers to be, overall, negative.

> People have them at home and find them empowering for themselves and their organizations. They are helpful in many ways and offer considerable personal control, unlike nonyielding technologies like television. Small social and political groups find computers valuable for information storage, networking, processing mailing lists, . . . , and so on. Yet all this begs the question. The real issue is not whether computers can benefit you or your group; the question is who benefits most from computers in society?[47]

Mander believes the answer to his question is transnational corporations and centralized corporate power. "In capitalist society, the benefits are disproportionately allotted to the people who own the machines." Our level of empowerment, he says, is pathetic by comparison. Mander says that "small businesses would actually be better off if computers had not been invented, since they are essentially one more tool that large businesses can use better."[48]

The subtitle of John Naisbitt's book *Global Paradox: The Bigger the World Economy, the More Powerful Its Smallest Players* contrasts with Mander's view that computers are bad for small businesses. Naisbitt sees telecommunications as the driving force in creating a huge global economy and reducing the size of both political and business units.

Postman acknowledges that computers are very beneficial to disabled people. He sees convenient access to online information as a tremendous advantage for scholars and scientists. But he sees the main beneficiaries of computers as government and big business. In his view they have little value to ordinary workers.[49] This is consistent with the Luddite view that technology in general is bad for most ordinary people, but it is in stark contrast with the views of others who see technology benefiting the poorest and weakest people in society the most. Economist Julian Simon says, "The standard of living of commoners is higher today than that of royalty only two centuries ago—especially their health and life expectancy."[50] C. P. Snow wrote, "Health, food, education; nothing but the industrial revolution could have spread them right down to the very poor."[51] Who benefits more from a speech-activated home-environment control system: a quadriplegic or a rich person for whom it is a toy or convenience? Wireless communications technology will make millions or billions of dollars for corporations, and a car phone is a convenience for a middle-class professional. How does that compare to the impact of wireless communications on the quality of life of an American Indian family living on a rural reservation that is not wired for telephone and electricity?

In the exhibit "Workers" by Brazilian photographer Sebastião Salgado, there is a photograph of dozens of laborers climbing out of a huge pit, a gold mine in Brazil. The men, packed tightly, one above another, climb 60-foot stick ladders, carrying bags of dirt on their backs. In the pit, hundreds more workers dig and fill their sacks. Another photograph shows a worker at a sulfur mine in Indonesia holding a scarf over his mouth for protection from the thick dust. A third shows the huge earth-cutting drill, perhaps 35 feet in diameter, that bored the tunnel in the English Channel. Two skilled men are working on the drill.[52] One of the most striking things about the photographs is how differently a neo-Luddite and someone with a positive view of technology would interpret them. To the latter, the photos show dramatically how technology eliminates back-breaking, unhealthy physical labor and raises the standard of living of workers. To the neo-Luddite, all three photos show the evils of technology: The mining would not be done in a nature-oriented society. The reduction of workers from a few hundred in the mine to two on the drill would be evidence of the unemployment caused by technology. The drill itself would perhaps be seen as raping the earth.

9.3.4 Accomplishments of Technology

Some aspects of the neo-Luddite antitechnology view have become part of the general public outlook: that living and working conditions are getting worse, that we are running out of natural resources, that the environment is deteriorating, for example. A variety of scholars claim that this point of view is simply false. Economist Julian Simon argues that hard data, accepted by most economists, show that the prices of food are sharply down around most of the world, raw materials are more abundant (as measured by their price), and wages and salaries have been going up in rich and poor countries alike. Prices of natural resources (metals, raw materials, energy) have declined over the past 100 years and especially in the 1980s, due to improvements in mining technologies and introduction of new substitutes for some minerals, for example, optical fiber for copper. Technology has increased crop yields per acre and milk per cow. Nicholas Eberstadt, an expert on population, reports that food supplies and gross domestic product have been growing faster than population for decades in most areas of the world, in developing and developed countries.[53]

Air and water quality have improved in the past few decades. Technology has reduced or almost eliminated typhoid, smallpox, dysentery, plagues, and malaria in most of the world. Crowding (not population) has declined worldwide; crowding is measured by the amount of living space per person in homes. Simon summarizes by saying, "Just about every single measure of the quality of life shows improvement rather than the deterioration that the doomsayers claim has occurred."[54] While Kirkpatrick Sale sees the reduction in family farm population in the U.S. (from 23 million to 5 million between 1950 and 1990) as a problem,[55] Simon says a low proportion of a country's labor force working in agriculture is the single best indicator of a higher standard of living. If most of the population works in agriculture, few other goods or services can be produced.

Various studies show increased economic growth is due only in small part to quantitative improvements (e.g., more work hours, more capital) and in larger part to what is called "total factor productivity," that is, workforce skill, quality of capital, better organization, innovation, and technology (communications, refrigeration, manufacturing techniques, computers).[56]

Technology and the Industrial Revolution have had a dramatic impact on life expectancy. Records from 18th century French villages showed that the median age of death was lower than the median age of marriage. Until recent generations, parents had to endure the deaths of most of their children. Starvation was common. Life expectancy for women was lower than for men because many women died in childbirth. (It is now several years higher for women than men in the U.S.) Worldwide average life expectancy at birth increased from approximately 30 in 1900 to 64 in 1990. The increase has been steeper in developing countries.[57]

These data say nothing specific about computers. Measuring quality of life is subjective, and some find other measures more important than those cited above. But for many people, these data suggest that technology has much to contribute to human well-being.

9.4   CONTROLLING TECHNOLOGY

No one voted for this technology or any of the various machines and processes that make it up.

–KIRKPATRICK SALE[58]

9.4.1   Some Proposals and Many Questions

In various sections of this book we have discussed issues of control, for example control of personal information (Chapter 2) and censorship of indecent material (Chapter 6). Here we discuss two more control issues.

The first is a content issue, but not the one discussed in Chapter 6. While the political right tends to favor control in the sense of censoring sexual and other material on the Net, control in the sense we discuss here tends to be a left, or liberal, issue. Many groups advocate legal regulations, taxes, and other mechanisms to ensure that content they consider desirable is available on the Net. They want to ensure that there will be socially useful and valuable information, to set a balance between commercial and educational information, and to ensure that there will be material to benefit children.

The second issue concerns control at a broader level. Some people argue that new technology should not be used at all until it has been studied, its consequences figured out, and a determination made that the consequences are acceptable. (Neo-Luddites, in particular, hold this view.) Some, for example Sclove and Scheuer, suggest that the government require analysis of the potential social effects of electronic services before any major components of new information infrastructures are implemented. The required study would be similar to the environmental impact studies required for projects that affect the land.[59] Some privacy advocates suggest requiring "privacy impact studies" for new uses of databases or new information technologies in general. The idea is that if the report does not meet criteria set by the government, the product or technology would not be permitted.

Are these good ideas? We saw in Section 9.3.2 that the determination of what are true needs is dependent on our choice of values. Chapter 6 indicates that there are profound disagreements about desirable content on the Net. When we consider controlling content and controls on the development of the technology itself, we must make choices between very different paradigms of control, choices that depend in part on our political philosophy and the results we expect from the alternatives. Which decisions about computers and the Internet should be centralized and coercive, made by government or votes, and enforced by law? Which decisions should evolve from the decentralized, voluntary choices made by thousands of businesses and millions of consumers? These are fundamental questions to keep in mind as we look at arguments relevant to these control issues in the next few sections.

9.4.2 Ensuring Valuable and Diverse Content

How should cyberspace be controlled to ensure that there will be socially valuable content and a diversity of views represented? Given the enormous quantity and diversity of material already on the Net, this concern may seem surprising, but advocates of efforts to ensure socially valuable content worry that if left to the decisions of profit-seeking businesses, cyberspace will be all shopping malls, advertisements, and movies, and that a few large companies will dominate the market for information on the Net, reducing diversity of opinion. Lawrence Grossman, former president of the Public Broadcasting System (PBS) and NBC News, argues that large media corporations will not provide the civic, educational, and cultural programming the public needs.[60]

Content in an information technology depends in part on how it is funded (e.g., via government subsidies, advertising, donations, or payment by consumers) and in part on whether there are explicit legal licensing and content requirements (e.g., the Fairness Doctrine, requirements for a certain percentage of news coverage or public service announcements). Currently, government funding for television and radio via the Public Broadcasting System (PBS) is seen by many as a model for providing socially useful programming within a mostly privately funded communications industry.* Computer Professionals for Social Responsibility suggests the establishment of "public spaces" on the Net. Public areas might be set up by the government or established by online service providers in exchange for tax deductions. The idea is somewhat similar to public-access cable TV channels, or to PBS. The purpose is to provide both access to information and a place for anyone to post messages with a guarantee of freedom of speech.[61] Grossman advocates the establishment of a public telecommunications trust fund to provide free online forums for labor unions, civic organizations, community-action groups, public-interest groups, citizen's organizations, political candidates, and political parties.[62]

Opponents argue that government funds for such programs are used to promote particular political and social points of view, that public access requirements are an unfair intrusion on the property rights of the service provider, and that these subsidies and regulations are not needed to meet consumer demands. Labor unions and community organizations, they would argue, pay for goods and services (e.g., stamps, stationery, and telephone

---

*PBS stations are partly supported by members and donors. Here we are considering only aspects related to the part that is government funded.

service) like any other organizations and businesses; they should expect to pay for publicity and computer forums.

There is a censorship issue when the government owns or substantially subsidizes communications systems or networks. When the government pays for something, it sets policy. For example, in the 1980s federally subsidized family planning clinics were not permitted to discuss abortion. No matter what side of that issue you are on, no matter how the policy changes with different presidents, the point is that when the government pays, it can restrict constitutionally protected speech if it chooses. In the past, the government has made it illegal to send information through the mail that was otherwise protected by the First Amendment. In light of controversies over government funding for PBS, art shows sponsored by the National Endowment for the Humanities, and exhibits at the Smithsonian Institution and the Library of Congress, there does not seem to be strong agreement among the public about what constitutes socially valuable content. There is currently debate about whether restricting some forms of speech, such as racist or sexist jokes and comments, is compatible with freedom of speech. A federal agency that provides funds for public radio stations rejected the application of a university because it broadcasts one hour a week of religious programming.[63] Such difficult content and freedom-of-speech issues are not eliminated, but in fact are made more problematic, in the context of "public areas" because taxpayers or service providers who disagree with the adopted policy—whatever it is—are still forced to pay for it.

Lessons from other information media

How important is it to establish a governmental mechanism to ensure valuable content on the Net? We can approach this question by observing some analogies with other information and entertainment media.

There are many parallels between the Internet and publishing. In the first few decades after the invention of the printing press, one could have worried that it would be used almost exclusively for printing junk fiction and government propaganda, that magazines and newspapers would be full of advertising, and that there would be no good books for children. In fact, we did get a junk fiction and magazines and newspapers full of advertising. We also got books, magazines, and newsletters on science, philosophy, astrology, communism, capitalism, Christian thought, gay rights, cooking (from beef to vegetarian), and an enormous number of other subjects and points of view. Excellent children's books are plentiful. We have expensive, beautifully bound books and cheap paperbacks. There are numerous content providers: large and small publishers who hope to make profits and writers or foundations who publish without regard to commercial success. The printing press provides tremendous diversity.

Who controls the printing press to ensure diversity and socially valuable content? Publishers? Consumers? Publishers decide what books their company will publish, but they choose those they think the public will buy. No one publisher or one consumer decides what will or will not be published. We do not have majority votes about what should be published. (What implications would *that* have for publication of material on minority viewpoints and lifestyles?) Who is in control? Nobody and everybody.

Television and radio have been more regulated and less diverse than print media. When radio was new, there was much discussion about how to fund high-quality programming—similar to current discussion about the Internet. Many people strongly opposed advertising on the radio. An alternative suggestion was for the government to subsidize programming. The negative implications for freedom of speech were widely recognized, and this idea was dropped. Soon after the Federal Communications Commission (FCC) was formed, the number of TV networks dropped from four to three and remained there for decades, although spectrum was available for a much larger number of stations.[64]

Today, there is reason for optimism that the goals of public spaces—diversity and freedom of speech—are being met and will continue to be met without any government mandates, subsidies, or regulations. The newsgroups on Usenet are open to everyone for both reading and posting comments. Members of ethnic and political minority groups have established hundreds of discussion groups, bulletin boards, and Web sites. As with publishing, there is enormous diversity of information and opinion on the Net. Advocates of public spaces are less optimistic; they see the experience of television rather than publishing as the more likely model for cyberspace. They fear that as large news and entertainment conglomerates move into cyberspace, only a few points of view will be presented, as is the case with the small number of television news organizations. They fear that commercial interests will dominate over honest and fair reporting and debate.

Although there are some very large publishing companies, they do not dominate publishing as much as the television networks dominate television. There are numerous small publishers filling special niches, as there are many small BBSs and discussion forums online. What may prevent that from continuing? One potential threat is that large companies will use laws and regulations to restrict their competition, as established businesses have often done. The television networks used laws to delay cable for more than a decade. In Argentina there are more than 2000 low-power radio stations in rural areas and poor shantytowns; they provide community-oriented programming and a wide range of political views. Low-power radio stations are illegal in the United States; in the early years of radio, the larger, established broadcasting companies encouraged the federal government to ban them. A jazz radio station in Missouri was staffed by volunteer music lovers who had other paying jobs. The government fined the station and ordered it to pay the volunteers minimum wage, which will probably put the station out of business.[65] It will be important, when considering any proposed regulation or licensing of the Internet and BBSs to look carefully at direct and indirect effects that threaten the survival of small operators who fill specialized niches and provide a diversity of topics and opinions.

Advertising

It is likely, as some people worry, that the Internet will continue to become more commercial. We probably will see more advertisements when we log on to information services. Shopping and banking on the Internet may not be the activities envisioned by the pioneers of cyberspace, but they may come to occupy a large portion of it. Advertising can be a source of useful information or an obnoxious intrusion. Almost no one complains about specialized ads in magazines (say in *Car & Driver* or *Byte*). Consumers find them a valued information source and know that the price of the magazines would be higher without the ads. Advertising is one of several ways of funding entertainment and information content; consumer response and pressure can influence its amount and quality.

Online services paid for by donations and memberships may restrict advertising, as PBS currently does. Services that charge special fees, like cable television movie channels, may remain free of advertising.

9.4.3 Prohibiting Bad Technologies

How should decisions be made about the basic question of whether a whole technology, or major segments of it, will be used at all? Who would make such decisions?

Most people in science, engineering, and business accept, almost without question the view that people can choose to use a technology for good or ill. Critics of technology disagree; they argue that computers, and technology in general, are not "neutral," not simply tools that we can choose to use for good or bad purposes. To these critics, it is important that the decision to allow a technology be made at the beginning, on the technology as a whole, because, as Neil Postman puts it, "Once a technology is admitted [to our culture], it plays out its hand; it does what it is designed to do."[66] In a sense, this view sees the technologies themselves as being in control.

In the view of the neo-Luddites and other strong critics of computers, decisions about technology are made by big corporations and governments without sufficient input or control by workers and other ordinary people. They want some sort of social input in deciding what technologies to develop. This view is expressed by Sale's lament at the beginning of Section 9.4: There was never a vote on whether we should have computers.

Is it possible for a society to choose to have certain specific desirable modern inventions while prohibiting others or prohibiting whole technologies? How finely can decisions about acceptable and unacceptable technologies be made? In response to a criticism that the tribal life he extolled would have no pianos, no violins, no telescope, no Mozart, Sale replied, "If your clan thought that the violin was a useful and nonharmful tool, you could choose to invent that."[67] Many critics of computers recognize the value of computing technology to disabled people. Perhaps they would permit development of such applications. The question is whether it is possible for a clan or society to choose to invent a violin or a book-reader for blind people without the technological base on which these are built, the freedom to innovate, a large enough economy to get materials from distant sources, and the large number of potential applications that make the research, development, and production of the basic ingredients of these products economically feasible.[68]

An example of restricting a technology

Here we look at an example where legislation limits the use of a particular medical technology. Public spirited arguments are given for these laws, but the laws can also be seen as a means to restrict competition and protect special interests—a risk of any mechanism to prohibit a technology or product.

In Chapter 1 we described long-distance medicine, also called telemedicine, as a benefit of computer technology. Computer and communications networks make possible remote examinations of patients and medical test results, such as X-rays and CT scans. After reading Chapter 2 and Chapter 4, you should be able to think of potential privacy and safety problems with such systems. After reading Section 9.1.1, you may think of other objections. Four states have already passed laws prohibiting the practice of telemedicine by doctors who are not licensed in that state. Are these laws reasonable?

The main argument given for the laws is safety, or concern about out-of-state "quacks." The laws are designed "to keep out the charlatans and snake-oil salesmen," according to one supporter.[69] The argument seems weak, considering that the laws are targeted at doctors who are licensed, but in another state.

Telemedicine may increase the influence of large, well-financed medical centers—to the detriment of local physicians in private practice. Large hospitals may become the "Wal-Marts of medicine," says one writer.* Telemedicine may make medical care even more impersonal than it is already becoming. To people who dislike large, impersonal institutions, these may be serious worries, whereas, on the other hand, many people like to shop at Wal-Mart. Was concern for patients the real reason for the laws? Many doctors who support the bans see telemedicine as a significant competitive threat. As the director of one state medical board put it, "They're worried about protecting their turf."[70]

Recall our questions about how decisions about new technologies or applications should be made. Should one uniform decision about whether or not telemedicine can be used be made by legislators, or should individual decisions be made by doctors and patients?

Is technology in control?

Arguments for bans on technology are often based on deterministic views like that of Neil Postman, quoted above ("Once a technology is admitted, it plays out its hand; it does what it is designed to do.") A brief look at the development of communications and computer technology suggests that they do much more than they were "designed to do." The computer was designed to calculate ballistics trajectories for the military. They are still used by the military, but their business and consumer uses dominate. Optical scanners, speech recognition systems, touch screens, and e-mail were developed for a variety of research, business, and consumer uses, but they are the main ingredients in tools for disabled people. Postman's statement leaves little room for human responsibility and choice, innovative applications, discoveries of new uses, unexpected consequences, or social action to encourage or discourage specific applications. Don Norman suggests that society influences the role of a technology when he says, "The failure to predict the computer revolution was the failure to understand how society would modify the original notion of a computational device into a useful tool for everyday activities."[71] We will look next at the problem of predicting the uses of a technology.

9.4.4 The Difficulty of Prediction

How well can a government committee, a think tank, or a computer industry executive predict the consequences of a new technology? Consider the quotations in Figure 9.1. Difficulty of prediction is not limited to computers and communications, of course. Some scientists were skeptical of air travel, space travel, and even railroads. (They believed that

---

*This is the second time in this chapter where I have quoted someone using Wal-Mart as a negative analogy. Many ordinary people see this as an elitist attitude on the part of intelectuals who disdain their preferences.

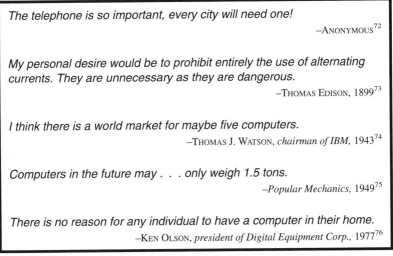

The telephone is so important, every city will need one!

                                        –ANONYMOUS[72]

My personal desire would be to prohibit entirely the use of alternating currents. They are unnecessary as they are dangerous.

                                    –THOMAS EDISON, 1899[73]

I think there is a world market for maybe five computers.

                          –THOMAS J. WATSON, *chairman of IBM*, 1943[74]

Computers in the future may . . . only weigh 1.5 tons.

                                –*Popular Mechanics*, 1949[75]

There is no reason for any individual to have a computer in their home.

            –KEN OLSON, *president of Digital Equipment Corp.*, 1977[76]

FIGURE 9.1 Predictions.*

passengers would not be able to breathe on high-speed trains.) The quotations in Figure 9.1 reflect a lack of imagination about the myriad of uses people would find for each new technology, about what the public would like, and what they would pay for. They demonstrate humorously that many experts can be utterly wrong. We will look at the prediction problem more seriously and in more depth by considering arguments made by computer scientist Joseph Weizenbaum in 1975 against development of a particular computer technology: speech recognition systems.[77] Here are Weizenbaum's objections, accompanied by comments from our perspective today.

- *"The problem is so enormous that only the largest possible computers will ever be able to manage it."* Speech-recognition software runs on personal computers. We can buy pocket-sized personal organizers that take spoken commands.

- *". . . a speech-recognition machine is bound to be enormously expensive, . . . only governments and possibly a very few very large corporations will therefore be able to afford it. . . ."* Some computers come with simple speech-recognition software as a free bonus. The pocket organizers cost a few hundred dollars.

- *"What can it possibly be used for?"* Recall some of the applications described in Section 1.3: training systems (e.g., for air traffic controllers and foreign languages) and tools that help disabled people use computers and control appliances in their homes. People who suffer from repetitive strain injury can use speech-recognition input instead of a keyboard. IBM advertises speech input

---

*Bill Gates, chairman of Microsoft, is widely reported to have said, "640K ought to be enough for anybody" back in 1981 when PCs typically had 640K bytes of memory or less, but I have not found a reliable source for this remark.

software for poets, so they can concentrate on poetry instead of typing. With some business telephone systems, we can speak the name of the person we want to reach and automatically be connected to that person's extension. In countries like China, where the language has thousands of characters, speech recognition may be a useful alternative to a keyboard.

- *The military planned to control weapons by voice command, "a long step toward a fully automated battlefield."* Some argue that we should have the best possible weapons to defend ourselves. Others argue that if wars are easier to fight, governments fight more of them. If wars are fought by remotely controlled automated weapons with no humans on the battlefield, is that an improvement over wars in which people are slaughtered? What if only one side has the high-tech weapons? Would that cause more wars of aggression? Is there any technology that the military cannot or does not use? Should we decline to develop strong fabrics because they may be used for military uniforms?

  Clearly, the use of high-tech tools by the military raises serious questions. The passage of two decades since Weizenbaum expressed his objections has not produced definitive answers.

- *Governments can use speech recognition to increase the efficiency and effectiveness of wiretapping.* (Weizenbaum is concerned with abuses of wiretapping, e.g., tapping done by oppressive governments. He does not explicitly mention wiretapping of criminal suspects.) One can argue that the same tools can be used beneficially in legal wiretapping of suspected terrorists, but there is no question that they are a danger in the hands of abusive governments. As with military applications, we must consider the potential for powerful technologies to be used destructively or oppressively by governments.

Discussion of Weizenbaum's objections is important for several reasons. (1) Although Weizenbaum is an expert in artificial intelligence, of which speech recognition is a subfield, he was mistaken in his expectations about the costs and benefits. (2) His objections about military and government use highlight the dilemma: Should we decline to develop technologies that can be misused, or should we develop the tools because of their beneficial uses, and use other means, including our votes and our voices, to influence government and military policy? (3) Weizenbaum's argument against development of a technology because of its expected cost is similar to arguments expressed by others about current and future computer applications and other technologies. For example, a common objection to some new medical technologies is that they are so expensive that only the rich will be able to afford them. This shortsighted view can result in the denial of benefits to the whole population. Recall that in Section 1.3.3 we mentioned development of a computer chip to float on the retina of the eye and send visual signals to the brain. It has the potential to restore sight to some blind people. The current cost is $500,000. Should it be banned because it would be available only to the very rich? The developer of the chip expects the cost to come down to $50 with mass production.

Weizenbaum was not trying to evaluate computer technology as a whole, but was focusing on one specific application area. If we are to permit the government, or experts, or the people via a majority vote, to prohibit development of certain technologies, it is essential at least that we be able to estimate the consequences—risks and benefits—of the technology fairly accurately. We cannot do this. The experts cannot do it.

One can go back to the 1960s and 70s and find quotations predicting marvelous benefits from computers that have not occurred. Indeed, one can pick up a variety of magazines now full of enthusiastic, optimistic predictions of wonders soon to be available from new developments in computer and communications technology. There has been, and will continue to be, much hype about computers. Corporations (and others) who use the hype to argue for subsidies or huge government-funded development programs are in as weak a position as those who argue for prohibitions.

We have focused on practical consequences—what might be lost by prohibiting a new technology. There is also an issue of basic liberty, the liberty to work at what one chooses, to use one's resources to invent and create, to invest in one's own ideas. Is it socially or morally justifiable to prohibit people from pursuing the development of a new technology with their own efforts and investment? What level of certainty of dire consequences should we require before restricting the freedom of others to develop technology they believe will be beneficial?

We have presented various arguments against the view that new technologies should be evaluated and perhaps banned at the start. Does this mean that no one should make decisions about whether it is good to develop a particular application of a new technology? No. The arguments and examples in this section suggest two things: (1) that decisions about development of new technology be limited in scope, perhaps limited to particular products, and (2) that the decision-making process be decentralized and noncoercive to reduce the impact of mistakes and the violations of liberty. The fundamental problem is not what decision to make about a particular technology, but rather it is to select a decision-making process that is most likely to produce what people want, to work well given the difficulty of predicting consequences, to respect the diversity of personal opinions about what constitutes a desirable life style, and to be relatively free of political manipulation. Given the errors made by so many experts, perhaps it is fortunate for us that there was no central decision maker who could decide whether or not the technology of computing should be developed. The decisions were made by individual engineers, researchers, entrepreneurs, venture capitalists, customers, and teenagers who tinkered in their garages.

EXERCISES

Review exercises

1. What are some of the proposals for ensuring universal access to computing and information services?

2. Give some examples of access to information systems for people who do not own a computer.

3. What are some methods governments are using to slow the flow of information made possible by the Internet and other modern communications technologies?

4. What are some of the Luddite criticisms of computers?

5. Give an example of a mistaken prediction made about computers.

General exercises

6. How does computer technology affect the strength of local communities?

7. One of the points in the CPSR list of requirements for universal access is that hardware and software fit the needs of disabled people. With the discussion of computer use by the disabled in Chapter 1 as background, discuss the roles of the market, community activities, and the government in meeting this goal.

8. A college English teacher has a policy that students may not turn in papers prepared on a word processor. Some students do not have computers, and the teacher considers it unfair if some can use a spelling checker and produce nice looking papers while others cannot. What do you think of this policy? Give reasons.

9. What are some attributes of movie theaters that are lacking when watching a movie at home? Do you think availability of hundreds of movies at home via cable or computer networks will destroy the movie theater business? Give your reasons.

10. Rewrite the spelling checker poem (in Section 9.1.3), correcting all the mistakes. (There are more than a dozen mistakes.)

11. To what extent has the electronic calculator destroyed our ability to do arithmetic in our heads? What are the advantages of using a calculator? What are the disadvantages of reduced arithmetic skills? Do you think children should be taught to use calculators in school? Why?

12. What are some skills, traditions, and/or social conventions that have been, or may soon be, lost because of computers? Include at least one that you think will be a real loss (i.e., a negative result of computers) and include at least one where you think the loss is not a problem. Give reasons.

13. When it became possible for people to make airline reservations themselves using online services, rather than calling a travel agent or the airline, there was a significant increase in "no-shows" (people who made a reservation but did not show up for the flight).

    (a) Why do you think this happened?

    (b) What problems does the increase in no-shows cause?

    (c) Some people are promoting the idea that we could soon use the Internet to hold frequent national votes on social and political issues. What concern does the increase in no-shows for airline reservations suggest about electronic voting?

14. When this book was written, approximately 70% of the computers on the Internet were in the United States. Does this suggest that there will be a growing gap between "have" and "have-not" nations? Give your reasons. (Try to find out what percentage of computers on the Net are in the U.S. now.)

15. What is the likely impact of the efforts of various governments to control access to information on the Internet?

16. In Section 1.3 we gave a few examples of how computer systems have reduced the use of paper. Overall, however, office paper use increased from roughly 2.9 million tons per year in 1989 to more than 4 million tons in 1995. Consider the claim that laser printers and fax machines encourage use and waste of paper. Give arguments for and against this claim. Do you think the increase in paper use is a serious problem caused by computers? Give your reasons.

17. (a) Which of the Luddite criticisms of computers listed in Section 9.3.1 do you consider the most valid and significant? Why?

    (b) Overall, what do you think of the Luddite view of computer technology? Giver reasons.

18. Imagine a society in which the wheel has not been invented or introduced. Describe what you think the society would be like. Include both positive and negative aspects. What are the best

things about the society? What are the worst? Would you prefer to live in that society or in the one you live in now? Why?

19. Reread the discussion of telemedicine in Sections 1.3.2 and 9.4.3. Describe some potential problems with telemedicine (besides those given in Section 9.4.3). Do you think there should be state laws prohibiting the practice of telemedicine within the state by doctors who are licensed but not licensed in that state. Why? If not, what other methods, if any, should be used to control the practice of telemedicine?

Assignments

These exercises require some research or activity that may need to be done during business hours or a few days before the assignment is due.

20. Find out if there is a public access cable TV station in your area. If there is, tell what kinds of programs it carries, and how many viewers it has. Do you think the use of government-provided public spaces on the NII would be similar? Why?

21. Arrange to visit an elementary school where the children use computers. Report on the types of activities and exercises for which the computers were used. Evaluate them. What are the advantages and disadvantages of using a computer for each activity you observed. Were computers necessary for the activity? Do you think the computers were being used well?

22. Contact the Registrar of Voters for your county; find out and describe how computers are used in elections. In addition to what is done in your county, list a variety of ways computers could be used for voting. (You may get some ideas from radio station polls and other kinds of voting.) What are some of the risks of using computers in elections?

23. We sometimes see technology described as our "national religion." On the other hand, the environmentalist viewpoint, often critical of technology, is quite strong in our society. Find one recent news or magazine article that illustrates each of these points of view. Give a brief summary of each; tell how it exemplifies a view of technology. In general, which view do you think is stronger in our society? Give reasons.

24. UNIX is a widely used computer operating system. Find out who wrote the first UNIX system and what it was written for. Was it intended to be a commercial product?

25. Software developed to help Internet service providers and parents block access to material inappropriate for children is now being used by some governments to block access to political and religious discussions. In what way does this example illustrate the views that technology will inevitably be used for negative purposes and that, as Neil Postman said, "Once a technology is admitted, . . . it does what it is designed to do"?

Class exercises

1. Hold a debate in class on one variant of the following question: Does computer technology, overall, have a negative impact on

   (a) most people in the world?

   (b) poor people in the U.S.?

   (c) the middle class in the U.S.?

2. Assign half the class to read a chapter from a book critical of computers or technology in general and half the class to read a chapter from a book that is favorable to technology. (There are several choices in the references below.) Have several students present a short summary of the arguments in the book they read, and hold a class discussion on the arguments.

NOTES

1   Michael Rothschild, "Beyond Repair: The Politics of the Machine Age Are Hopelessly Obsolete," *The New Democrat,* July/August 1995, pp. 8–11.

2   Hightower is a radio commentator, quoted in Robert Fox, "Newstrack," *Communications of the ACM,* August 1995, 38:8, pp. 11–12.

3   Quoted in Jerry Mander, *In the Absence of the Sacred: The Failure of Technology and the Survival of the Indian Nations,* Sierra Club Books, 1991, p. 62.

4   Mander, *In the Absence of the Sacred,* p. 62.

5   Richard Sclove and Jeffrey Scheuer, "On the Road Again: If Information Highways Are Anything Like Interstate Highways—Watch Out!" in Rob Kling, ed., *Computerization and Controversy: Value Conflict and Social Choices,* 2nd ed., Academic Press, 1996. Comments by Sclove in the panel, "The Case Against Computers: A Systemic Critique," at the Computers, Freedom, and Privacy conference, San Francisco, 1995. Alexandra Eyle, "No Time Like the Co-Present" (interview with Neil Postman), *NetGuide,* July 1995, pp. 121–22. Chet Bowers, another critic, also complains that computers contribute to the view of the individual as the basic social unit.

6   "Technology in the American Household," Times Mirror Center for the People and the Press, May 1994, pp. 5–7.

7   Robert D. Putnam, *Making Democracy Work,* Princeton University Press, 1993. I thank Phil Agre for bringing Putnam's work and some of the ideas in this paragraph to my attention in his talk, "Networking in the Community," at the San Diego ACM chapter meeting, January 24, 1996.

8   Alexis de Tocqueville, *Democracy in America,* Volume 2, Chapter 2.

9   Office of Technology Assessment, "The Technological Reshaping of Metropolitan America," 1995.

10 Sclove and Scheuer, "On the Road Again," p. 612.

11 For example, Kirkpatrick Sale, in "Interview with the Luddite" (Kevin Kelly, interviewer), *Wired,* June 1995, pp. 166–68, 211–16.

12 Times Mirror, "Technology in the American Household," p. 8.

13 CPSR, "Serving the Community: A Public Interest Vision of the National Information Infrastructure," pp. 15–16.

14 CPSR, "Serving the Community," p. 21.

15 National Information Infrastructure Advisory Committee, "A Nation of Opportunity: Realizing the Promise of the Information Superhighway," reported in *TelecomPost,* October 26, 1995. Robert H. Anderson, Tora K. Bikson, Sally Ann Law, Bridger M. Mitchell, *Universal Access to E-mail; Feasibility and Societal Implications,* Center for Information Revolution Analysis, RAND, 1995.

16 G. Christian Hill, "Tally of Homes With PCs Increased 16% Last Year," *Wall Street Journal,* May 21, 1996, p. B7. The term "have-lates," as a substitute for "have-nots," was first used by Marvin Minsky, to the best of my knowledge; I prefer to use "have-laters" rather than "have-lates."

17 Sandy Sandfort and Duncan Frissell, "Net Access for Next to Nothing," *Wired,* May 1995, p. 141, estimates that one could put together a used, no-frills system with a few hundred dollars.

18 Anderson et al, *Universal Access to E-mail,* p. 176.

19 Rothschild, "Beyond Repair: The Politics of the Machine Age Are Hopelessly Obsolete."

20 "Steve Jobs: The Next Insanely Great Thing," interview by Gary Wolf, *Wired,* February 1996, 4:2, pp. 102–7, 158–63.

21 Parts of this poem have circulated on computer networks and appeared in newspapers. The full version (36 lines), slightly different from the one I used, appeared in the *Journal of Irreproducible Results,* January/February 1994, 39:1, p. 13. Zar attributes the title to Pamela Brown and the opening lines to Mark Eckman. This excerpt is reprinted with permission of George H. Scherr.

22 See, for example, Neil Postman, *Technopoly: The Surrender of Culture to Technology,* Alfred A. Knopf, 1992, pp. 3–8.

23 Walter J. Ong, *Interfaces of the Word: Studies in the Evolution of Consciousness and Culture,* Cornell University Press, 1977.

24 Americans bought more than a billion books in 1994, up 31% from 1991, according to an annual survey reported in Patrick M. Reilly, "Book-Buying Is at New Highs, Survey Finds," *Wall Street Journal,* June 2, 1995, p. B1..

25 Postman, *Technopoly,* p. 115.

26 Jimmy Lai, publisher of *Next Magazine Ltd.,* quoted in Tim W. Ferguson, "From Street Hawking to Karl Popper," *Wall Street Journal,* July 19, 1994, p. A15.

27 Arthur C. Clarke, "Beyond the Global Village," *1984 Spring: A Choice of Futures,* Ballantine/ Dell, 1984, p. 7.

28 David P. Hamilton, "Asians Taste Free Speech on Internet," *Wall Street Journal,* December 8, 1994, pp. B1, B10.

29 These measures were widely reported in early 1996. The quote about the Chinese regulations is from Marcus W. Brauchli, "China Requires Computer Networks to Get Registered," *Wall Street Journal,* February 5, 1996, p. C15. The quote about the Singapore regulations is from Darren Mc-Dermott, "Singapore Unveils Sweeping Measures to Control Words, Images on Internet," *Wall Street Journal,* March 6, 1996, p. B6.

30 Stewart Baker, "The Net Escape Censorship? Ha!" *Wired,* September 1995, pp. 125–126.

31 Stephen Moore, "The Coming Age of Abundance," in Ronald Bailey, ed., *The True State of the Planet,* Free Press, 1995, p. 113.

32 "Interview With the Luddite," *Wired,* June 1995, pp. 166–68, 211–16 (see pp. 213–14).

33 Kirkpatrick Sale, *Rebels Against the Future: The Luddites and Their War Against the Industrial Revolution: Lessons for the Computer Age,* Addison-Wesley, 1995, p. 257.

34 Mander, *In the Absence of the Sacred,* p. 61.

35 Postman, *Technopoly,* p. 119.

36 Eyle, "No Time Like the Co-Present."

37 Harvey Blume, "Digital Refusnik" (interview with Sven Birkerts), *Wired,* May 1995, pp. 178-179. "Interview With the Luddite."

38 Postman, *Technopoly,* p. 15.

39 See Jane Jacob's classic *The Economy of Cities,* Random House, 1969.

40 Postman, *Technopoly,* p. 6. The Freud quote is from *Civilization and Its Discontent* (e.g., the edition edited and translated by James Strachey, W. W. Norton, 1961, p. 35).

41 John Davis, quoted in Sale, *Rebels Against the Future,* p. 256.

42 Sale, *Rebels Against the Future,* p. 257.

43 The quotes are from "Interview With the Luddite," p. 214 and p. 213. Sale expresses this point of view also in *Rebels Against the Future,* p. 213.

44 Sale, *Rebels Against the Future,* p. 256.

45 This dichotomy has always struck me as strange because it almost suggests that humans are alien creatures who arrived on earth from somewhere else. We evolved here. We are part of nature. A human house is as natural as a bird's nest, though, unlike birds, we have the capacity to build both ugly and beautiful things.

46 In "George Gilder and His Critics," *Forbes ASAP,* October 9, 1995, pp. 165–81.

47 Mander, *In the Absence of the Sacred,* pp. 67–68.

48 Mander, *In the Absence of the Sacred,* p. 57. Comments at the Computers, Freedom, and Privacy conference, San Francisco, 1995; Panel: "Against Computers: A Systemic Critique."

49 Eyle, "No Time Like the Co-Present." Postman, *Technopoly,* p. 10.

50 Julian L. Simon, "The State of Humanity: Steadily Improving," Cato Policy Report, September/October 1995, 17:5, pp. 1, 10–11, 14–15. See Simon's book *The State of Humanity* listed in the references.

51 C. P. Snow, "The Two Cultures and the Scientific Revolution," in *The Two Cultures: And a Second Look,* Cambridge University Press, 1964, p. 27.

52 The exhibit is traveling to several countries. The photos described here, and several others, appear in Miles Orvell, "A Tribute to the World's Workers," *Technology Review,* October 1995, pp. 62–69.

53 Moore, "The Coming Age of Abundance," p. 119. Nicholas Eberstadt, "Population, Food, and Income: Global Trends in the Twentieth Century," p. 34, in Bailey, *The True State of the Planet.*

54 Julian L. Simon, "The State of Humanity: Steadily Improving," *Cato Policy Report,* September/October 1995, 17:5, pp. 1, 10–11, 14–15.

55 Sale, *Rebels Against the Future,* p. 215. Sale describes several government programs that have added to the transition from family farms to large corporate farms. I share his objection to such artificial, coercive methods.

56 Eberstadt, "Population, Food, and Income," pp. 7–47.

57 Snow, *The Two Cultures,* pp. 82–83. The population data, some from the United Nations, are reported in Eberstadt, "Population, Food, and Income," p. 21, p. 23.

58 Sale, *Rebels Against the Future,* p. 210.

59 Sclove and Scheuer, "On the Road Again?" p. 612.

60 Lawrence K. Grossman, "Maintaining Diversity in the Electronic Republic," *Technology Review,* November/December 1995, pp. 23–26.

61 CPSR, "Serving the Community: A Public Interest Vision of the National Information Infrastructure," p. 23.

62 Grossman, "Maintaining Diversity in the Electronic Republic."

63 "One by One," *Wall Street Journal,* January 29, 1996, p. 16.

64 Todd Lappin, "Déjà Vu All Over Again," *Wired,* May 1995, pp. 175–77, 218–22. Thomas W. Hazlett, "The Rationality of U.S. Regulation of the Broadcast Spectrum," *Journal of Law & Economics,* April 1990, pp. 133-175.

65 Jesse Walker, "Don't Touch That Dial," *Reason,* October 1995, pp. 30–35. Charles Oliver, "Brickbats," Reason, November 1995, p. 17.

66 Postman, *Technopoly,* p. 7.

67 "Interview with the Luddite."

68 See Jacobs, *The Economy of Cities* for a discussion of how wealth develops.

69 Bill Richards, "Doctors Can Diagnose Illnesses Long Distance, To the Dismay of Some," *Wall Street Journal,* January 17, 1996, pp. A1, A10.

70 Richards, "Doctors Can Diagnose Illnesses Long Distance."

71 Donald A. Norman, *Things That Make Us Smart: Defending Human Attributes In the Age of the Machine,* Addison-Wesley, 1993, p. 190.

72 Quoted in Don Norman, *Things That Make Us Smart: Defending Human Attributes In the Age of the Machine,* Addison-Wesley, 1993, p. 191.

73 Quoted in Chris Morgan and David Langford, *Facts and Fallacies: A Book of Definitive Mistakes and Misguided Predictions,* St. Martin's Press, 1981.

74 Chris Morgan and David Langford, *Facts and Fallacies: A Book of Definitive Mistakes and Misguided Predictions,* St. Martin's Press, 1981, p. 44.

75 From the March 1949 issue, p. 258, as quoted in Christopher Cerf and Victor Navasky, *The Definitive Compendium of Authoritative Misinformation,* Pantheon Books, 1984, p. 208.

76 Comment made at a convention of the World Future Society, as quoted in Christopher Cerf and Victor Navasky, *The Definitive Compendium of Authoritative Misinformation,* Pantheon Books, 1984, p. 209.

77 Joseph Weizenbaum, *Computer Power and Human Reason: From Judgment To Calculation,* W. H. Freeman and Company, 1976, pp. 270–72.

FOR FURTHER READING

Ronald Bailey, ed., *The True State of the Planet,* Free Press, 1995. A collection of articles by experts in various areas arguing that a variety of social and environmental problems are not as serious as many people think.

Sven Birkerts, *The Gutenberg Elegies: The Fate of Reading in An Electronic Age,* Faber and Faber, 1994. Birkerts is a critic of computers; he writes on a typewriter.

Communications of the ACM, January 1995, 38:1. Contains more than a dozen articles about women in the computing professions.

Computer Professionals for Social Responsibility, "Serving the Community: A Public Interest Vision of the National Information Infrastructure."

Samuel C. Florman, *Blaming Technology: The Irrational Search for Scapegoats,* St. Martin's Press, 1981.

Lawrence Gasman, *Telecompetition: The Free Market Road to the Information Highway,* Cato Institute, 1994.

Steve Gibson, "Universal Disservice: The Hazards of Fretting About Info Haves and Have-Nots," *Reason,* April 1995, pp. 47–49.

Lawrence K. Grossman, "Maintaining Diversity in the Electronic Republic," *Technology Review,* November/December 1995, pp. 23–26.

Peter Huber, *Orwell's Revenge: A 1984 Palimpsest,* Free Press, 1994. Huber argues that Orwell was wrong about technology's role in aiding totalitarian governments. Instead, he argues it is a force for increased freedom. This book includes a "sequel" to Orwell's *1984.*

Kevin Kelly, *Out of Control: The Rise of Neo-Biological Civilization,* Addison-Wesley, 1994.

Todd Lappin, "Déjà Vu All Over Again," *Wired,* May 1995, pp. 175–77, 218–22. A comparison of predictions of the social impact of radio 75 years ago and the predictions for the Internet today.

Jerry Mander, *In the Absence of the Sacred: The Failure of Technology and the Survival of the Indian Nations,* Sierra Club Books, 1991.

Joel Mokyr, *The Lever of Riches: Technological Creativity and Economic Progress,* Oxford University Press, 1990.

John Naisbitt, *Global Paradox: The Bigger the World Economy, the More Powerful Its Smallest Players,* William Morrow and Company, 1994.

A. Lin Neumann, "The Resistance Network," *Wired,* January 1996, 4:1, pp. 108–14. An article on the use of computer networks by human rights organizations, many in countries with oppressive governments.

Donald Norman, *Things That Make Us Smart: Defending Human Attributes in the Age of the Machine,* Addison-Wesley, 1993.

George Orwell, *1984,* 1948. Orwell's distopian novel in which the totalitarian government controlled the people via ubiquitous telescreens. (Orwell introduced the term "Big Brother" for the government.)

Neil Postman, *Technopoly: The Surrender of Culture to Technology,* Alfred A. Knopf, 1992.

Robert D. Putnam, *Making Democracy Work: Civic Traditions in Modern Italy,* Princeton University Press, 1993. Although this book is about Italy, its ideas and observations about what makes communities work well are useful for discussions of the impact of computers on community.

Saul Rockman, "In School or Out: Technology, Equity, and the Future of Our Kids," *Communications of the ACM,* June 1995, 38:6, pp. 25–29.

Nathan Rosenberg and L. E. Birdzell Jr., *How the West Grew Rich,* Basic Books, 1987.

Michael Rothschild, *Bionomics: Economy As Ecosystem,* Henry Holt, 1992.

Kirkpatrick Sale, *Rebels Against the Future: The Luddites and Their War Against the Industrial Revolution: Lessons for the Computer Age,* Addison-Wesley, 1995.

Douglas Schuler, *New Community Networks: Wired for Change,* Addison-Wesley, 1996.

Scott Shane, *Dismantling Utopia: How Information Ended the Soviet Union,* I. R. Dee, 1994.

Julian L. Simon, ed., *The State of Humanity,* Blackwell Publishers, 1995.

C. P. Snow, "The Two Cultures and the Scientific Revolution." In this speech, Snow argues that people in the humanities and people in the sciences have fundamentally different views of science and technology. The speech appears, with an update, in C. P. Snow, *The Two Cultures: And a Second Look,* Cambridge University Press, 1964.

Clifford Stoll, *Silicon Snake Oil: Second Thoughts on the Information Highway,* Doubleday, 1995.

10 ISSUES OF PROFESSIONAL ETHICS AND RESPONSIBILITIES

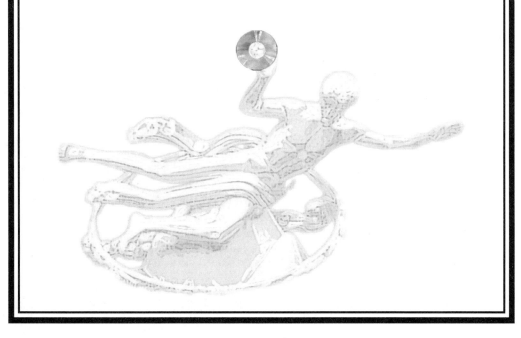

Honesty is the best policy.

–English proverb, pre-1600

10.1   WHAT IS "COMPUTER ETHICS"?

In the previous chapters we discussed issues and problems related to computers from a somewhat detached perspective. We saw how a new technology can create new risks and problems and how social and legal institutions must continually adapt. But technology is not an immutable force outside of human control. People make decisions about what technologies and products to develop and how to use them. People make decisions about when a product is safe to release. People make decisions about access to and use of personal information. People make laws and set rules and standards. In this chapter we look at those decisions and activities from an ethical perspective. We examine ethical dilemmas and guidelines related to actions and decisions of individuals and organizations who create and use computer systems.

The scope of the term "computer ethics" varies considerably. Some people include issues such as the universal access issue discussed in Section 9.1.2, the environmental impact of computers, the impact of computers on employment, whether or not to sell computers to communist or right-wing governments, and use of computers by the military. These are all important issues that involve computers, but one's opinions about them usually have more to do with one's political and social views than with one's knowledge or experience as a computer professional. I believe that "computer ethics" is most usefully defined more narrowly as a category of professional ethics, similar to medical, legal, and accounting ethics, for example.* Professionals have special expertise that the general public and clients or customers of the professionals do not have. Most of the people affected by the devices, systems, and services of professionals do not understand how they work and cannot easily judge their quality and safety. This creates special responsibilities for the professional.

Thus, for our discussion, computer ethics includes ethical issues faced by a computer professional as part of the job. It includes relationships with and responsibilities toward customers and clients, coworkers, employees, employers, others who will use one's products, and others who will be affected by them. We also include issues for professionals in other areas where computers are used.

We look at situations where critical decisions must be made, situations where significant consequences for you and others may result from your decision. For example, what if your company is about to deliver a computer system to a customer and you believe it still has serious bugs that could cause harm to the users? Who is responsible when an unknown bug in a program costs lives or millions of dollars? What if your supervisor asks you to make unauthorized copies of copyrighted software? Is it right to hire foreign programmers who work at lower salaries than American programmers? What if you are assigned to a job for a client whose business you find objectionable? These are a few of the questions we will consider later in this chapter.

---

*This more focused view of computer ethics was well presented and well argued by Donald Gotterbarn and seems to be gaining acceptance among scholars in this field.[1]

There are special aspects to making ethical decisions in a professional context, but the decisions are fundamentally based on general ethical principles and theories. In the next section we introduce several ethical theories. We discuss some distinctions (e.g., between ethics and law) that are important to understand when tackling ethical issues. In Section 10.3 we return to the more specific area of computer ethics. We look at guidelines for computer professionals and new ethical dilemmas raised by computer technology. In Section 10.4 we illustrate the application of the theories and guidelines with discussion of sample cases.

10.2 ETHICAL THEORIES

10.2.1 What Is Ethics, Anyway?

Ethics is the study of what it means to "do the right thing." It is a complex subject that has occupied philosophers for thousands of years. This presentation is necessarily simplified.

Ethical theory is based on the assumption that people are rational and make free choices. Neither of these conditions is always and absolutely true. People act emotionally, and they make mistakes. A person is not making a free choice when someone else is pointing a gun at him. Some argue that a person is not making a free choice in a situation where she might lose a job. However, free choice and use of rational judgment are capacities and characteristics of human beings, and they are reasonably assumed at the basis of ethical theory. We take the view that the individual is, in most circumstances, responsible, or accountable, for his or her actions.

Ethical rules are rules to follow in our interactions with other people. Most ethical theories attempt to achieve the same goal: to enhance human dignity, peace, happiness, and well-being. Ethical rules apply to all of us and are intended to achieve good results for people in general, and for situations in general—not just for ourselves, not just for one situation. A set of rules that does this well respects the fact that we are each unique and have our own values and goals, that we have judgment and will, and that we act according to our judgment to achieve our goals. The rules should clarify our obligations and responsibilities— and our areas of choice and personal preference. (Not all ethical theories fit this description. Ethical relativism and some types of ethical egoism do not. In this chapter, however, we accept these goals and requirements for ethical theories.)

There is a distinction in ethical theory between normative and descriptive ethics. Normative statements are those that tell us what we *should* do, what is right in some essential way. Descriptive statements tell us about *how* people behave, what ethical rules a particular society (or profession or person) has adopted. Most of the discussion of ethics in this chapter is of the normative kind—not that I will tell you what you should do in every case; rather we discuss approaches that can guide you in making decisions.

Doing the right thing is often easy. Most of the time we are honest, we keep our promises, we do not steal, we do our work. This should not be surprising. If ethical rules are good ones, they work for people; that is, they make our lives better. Honesty makes interactions among people work more smoothly and reliably, for example. Behaving ethically is often practical. Also, there are external factors that encourage us to do right: We might be arrested if caught stealing. We might lose friends if we often lie or break promises. We might lose our jobs if we do not do our work. Sometimes, however, it is difficult to do the right thing. It takes courage in situations where we may suffer negative consequences. Courage is often associated with heroic acts where one risks one's life to save someone in a dangerous situation—the kind of act that makes front-page news. Most of us do not have those opportunities to display courage, but we do have many opportunities in day-to-day life. Courage in a professional setting may mean admitting to a customer that your program is at fault after it has caused a serious problem for the customer, declining a job for which you are not qualified, or speaking out when you see someone else doing something wrong.

We cannot solve ethical problems by applying a formula or an algorithm. Human behavior is more complex and less well understood than physics and mathematics. We do know a lot about human behavior; we have developed laws of economics and understand many aspects of human psychology. However, the variability of self-willed humans with their diverse tastes and values, and the complexity of their interactions, sometimes make ethical judgments difficult.

10.2.2 A Variety of Ethical Views

Although there is much agreement about general ethical rules, there are many different theories about how to establish a firm justification for the rules and how to determine what is ethical in specific cases. In this section we give very brief descriptions of a few approaches to ethics.[2] Some ethicists* make a distinction between ethical theories that view certain acts as good because of some intrinsic aspect of the action and ethical theories that view acts as good or bad depending on their consequences. These are called deontological (or nonconsequentialist) and consequentialist theories, respectively. The distinction is perhaps emphasized more than necessary. If the criteria used by deontologists to determine the intrinsic goodness or badness of an act did not consider its consequences for people—at least for most people, most of the time—their criteria would seem to have little ethical merit.

Deontological theories

Deontologists tend to emphasize duty and absolute rules, to be followed whether they lead to good or ill consequences in particular cases. One example is: Do not lie. An act is ethical if it complies with ethical rules and is chosen for that reason.

Immanuel Kant, the philosopher most often presented as the prime example of a deontologist, contributed many important ideas to ethical theory. We mention three of them here. One is the principle of universality: We should follow rules of behavior that could be universally applied to everyone. This principle is so fundamental to ethical theory that we already accepted it in our explanation of ethics in Section 10.2.1. The Biblical instruction, "Do unto others as you would have them do unto you," is another statement of the same general idea.

Deontologists argue that logic or reason determine rules of ethical behavior, that actions are intrinsically good because they follow from logic. Kant believed that rationality is the standard of what is good. We can reason about what makes sense and act accord-

---

*Ethicists are philosophers (and others) who study ethics.

ingly, or we can act irrationally, which is evil. The view that something is evil *because* it is illogical may not be convincing, but Kant's instruction to "Respect the reason in you," that is, to use your reason, rationality, and judgment, rather than emotions, when making a decision in an ethical context, is a wise one.

Third, Kant stated a principle about interacting with other people: One must never treat people as merely means to ends, but rather as ends in themselves.

Kant took an extreme position on the absolutism of ethical rules. He argued, for example, that it is always wrong to lie, that, for example, if a person is looking for someone he intends to murder and he asks you where the intended victim is, it is wrong for you to lie to protect the victim. Most people would agree that there are cases where even very good, universal rules should be broken—because of the consequences. We will now consider the most well-known consequentialist ethical theory: utilitarianism.

Utilitarianism

The guiding principle of utilitarianism, as expressed by John Stuart Mill,[3] is to increase happiness, or "utility." A person's utility is what satisfies the person's needs and values. An action may decrease utility for some people and increase it for others; thus, we should consider the benefits and damages to all affected people, that is, the change in aggregate utility. An act is right if it tends to increase aggregate utility and wrong if it tends to decrease it.

Utilitarianism is a very influential theory, and it has many variations. As stated above, the utilitarian principle applies to individual actions. For each action, we consider the impact on utility and judge the action by its net impact. This is sometimes called "act utilitarianism." One variant of utilitarianism, called "rule utilitarianism," applies the utility principle not to individual actions but to general ethical rules. Thus, a rule utilitarian may argue that the rule "Do not lie" will increase total utility, and for that reason is a good rule. Rule-utilitarians do not do a utility calculation for each instance where lying is considered. Generally, a utilitarian would be more comfortable than a deontologist breaking a rule in circumstances where doing so would have good consequences.

There are numerous problems with act-utilitarianism. It may be difficult or impossible to determine all the consequences of an act. If we can do so, do we increase what we believe will or should contribute to the happiness of the people affected, or what they choose themselves? How do we know what they would choose? How do we quantify happiness in order to make comparisons among many people? Should some people's utility be given more weight than others'? Should we weigh a thief's gain of utility equal to the victim's loss? Is a dollar worth the same to a person who worked for it and a person who received it as a gift? Or to a rich person and a poor person? How can we measure the utility of freedom?

A more fundamental (and ethical) objection to act-utilitarianism is that it does not recognize or respect individual rights. It has no absolute prohibitions and may allow actions that many people consider always wrong. For example, if there is a convincing case that killing an innocent person, or taking all of a person's property and redistributing it to other community members, would maximize utility in a community, these acts could be justified under utilitarianism. A person has no protected domain of freedom.

Rule-utilitarianism suffers far less than does act-utilitarianism from these problems. Recognizing that widespread killing and stealing decrease the security and happiness of all, a rule utilitarian can derive rules against these acts. These particular rules can be stated in terms of rights to life and property. We will now look at natural rights as a basis for ethical decisions.

Natural rights

Suppose we wish to treat people as ends rather than merely means and we wish to increase people's happiness. These goals are somewhat vague and open to many interpretations in specific circumstances. One approach we might follow is to let people make their own decisions, to define a sphere of freedom in which people can act freely according to their own judgment, without coercive interference by others, even others (including us) who think they are doing what is best for the people involved, or for humanity in general. This approach views ethical behavior as acting in such a way that respects a set of fundamental rights of others, including the rights to life, liberty, and property.

These rights are sometimes called natural rights because, in the opinion of some philosophers, they come from nature, or can be derived from the nature of humanity. We each have an exclusive right to ourselves and our labor, and to what we produce with our labor. John Locke argued for a natural right to property that we create or obtain by mixing our labor with it. Respect for these rights implies ethical rules against killing, stealing, and deception.

Those who emphasize natural rights tend to emphasize the ethical character of the *process* by which people interact, seeing acts generally as likely to be ethical if they involve voluntary interactions and freely made exchanges of property, where the parties are not deceived or coerced. This contrasts with other approaches that tend to focus on the *result* or *state* achieved by the interaction, for example, seeing an action as likely to be unethical if it leaves some people poor.

No simple answers

Ethical theories do not provide clear, incontrovertibly correct positions on most issues. The approaches we described can be used to support opposite sides of many an issue. For example, consider Kant's imperative that one must never treat people as merely means to ends, but rather as ends in themselves. It can be used to argue that an employee who is being paid a very low wage, say, a wage too low to support a family, is wrongly being treated as merely a means for the employer to make money. But it can also be used to argue that expecting the employer to pay more than he or she considers reasonable is treating the employer merely as a means to providing a job or income for the employee. Similarly, it is easy for two utilitarians to come to different conclusions on a particular issue by measuring happiness or utility differently. If a very small set of basic natural rights is selected, they provide no guidance for many situations where ethical decisions are needed. But if we try to define rights to cover more situations, there will be fierce disagreement about just what those rights should be. (Recall the question in Chapter 2 about whether there is a right to privacy, and if so, how far it goes.)

Although ethical theories do not completely settle difficult, controversial issues, they help to identify important principles or guidelines. They remind us of things to consider, and they can help clarify reasoning and values. There is much merit in Kant's principle of universalism and his emphasis on treating humanity as an intrinsically valuable end, in utilitarianism's standard of increasing achievement of people values and happiness and in the natural rights approach of setting minimal rules in a rights framework to guarantee people a sphere in which they can act according to their own values and judgment.

10.2.3 Some Important Distinctions

There are a number of important distinctions that affect our ethical judgments, but which are often not clearly expressed or understood. In this section, we identify a few of these. Just being aware of them can help clarify issues in some ethical debates.

Right, wrong, and okay

It is misleading to divide all acts into two categories—ethically right and ethically wrong. Rather, it is better to think of acts as either ethically obligatory, ethically prohibited, or neither. Most of our options and actions are ethically acceptable, but not obligatory.

Negative and positive rights, or liberties and claim-rights

When people speak of rights, they are often speaking about two quite different kinds of rights. These are usually called negative and positive rights, but the terms *liberties* and *claim-rights* are more descriptive of the distinction.[4]

Negative rights, or liberties, are rights to act without interference. The only obligation they impose on others is not to prevent you from acting. They include the right to life in the sense that no one has the right to kill you, the right to be free from assault, the right to use your property, the right to use your labor, skills, and mind to create goods and services and to trade with other people in voluntary exchanges. The natural rights described in Section 10.2.2 are liberties, or negative rights, as are the rights to "life, liberty, and the pursuit of happiness" described in the Declaration of Independence. Freedom of speech and religion, as guaranteed in the First Amendment of the U.S. Constitution, are negative rights: The government may not interfere with you, jail you, or kill you because of what you say or what your religious beliefs are. The right to work, as a liberty, or negative right, means that no one has the right to prohibit you from working, or, for example, to punish you for working without getting a government permit.

Claim-rights, or positive rights, are rights that impose an obligation on some people to provide certain things for others. A positive right to a job means that someone must hire you whether or not they voluntarily choose to or that it is right, or obligatory, for the government to set up job programs for people who are out of work. A positive right to life means that some people are obligated to pay for food or medical care for others who cannot pay for them. When freedom of speech is interpreted as a claim-right, or positive right, it means that owners of shopping malls, radio stations, and online services may be required to provide space or time for content they do not wish to include or that tax subsidies be given to people or organizations who cannot afford to publish what they wish.

Now here is the problem: Some people think that we have both negative and positive rights, that liberties are almost worthless by themselves, and that society must devise social and legal mechanisms to ensure that everyone has their claim-rights, or positive rights, satisfied, even if that means diminishing the liberties of some. Other people think that there can be no (or very few) positive rights because negative and positive rights are fundamentally incompatible; it is impossible to enforce claim-rights for some people without violating the liberties of others, and protection of liberties, or negative rights, is essential to human freedom and dignity.

This is one of the reasons for disagreement on issues like universal access to computing and information services (where "universal access" is to be achieved by taxes or regulations on businesses). More generally, this distinction affects one's view of whether giving money or time to charity is an ethical obligation or simply an ethically admirable act.

Distinguishing wrong and harm

One criterion often used in deciding that an act is wrong is that it harms someone. However, it is important to remember that harm is not a sufficient criterion to determine that an act is unethical. Many ethical, even admirable, acts can make other people worse off. For example, you may accept a job offer knowing someone else wanted the job and needed it more than you do. You may reduce the income of other programmers by writing a better program that consumers prefer. If your program is really good, you may put a competitor out of business completely and cause many people to lose their jobs. Yet there is nothing wrong with doing honest, productive work.

On the other hand, hackers argue that breaking into computer systems without authorization is not wrong because they do no harm. Lack of harm is not sufficient to conclude that an act is ethically acceptable. Aside from the fact that the hacker may do unintended harm, one can argue that hacking is a violation of property rights: A person has no right to enter your property without your permission, independent of harm done.

Separating goals from constraints

Economist Milton Friedman has written that the goal or responsibility of a business is to make a profit for its shareholders. Some ethicists are appalled by this statement, as they believe it justifies, or is used to justify, irresponsible and unethical actions. It seems to me that arguments on this point miss the distinction between goals, on the one hand, and constraints on actions that may be taken to achieve the goals, on the other—or the distinction between ends and means. Our personal goals may include financial success and finding an attractive mate. These goals can be achieved by working hard, investing wisely, and being an interesting and decent person. They may be achievable as well by stealing and lying. By most ethical theories, the latter methods are unacceptable. Ethics tell us what actions are acceptable or unacceptable in our attempts to achieve the goals. There is nothing unethical about a business having the goal of maximizing profits. The ethical character of the company depends on whether the actions taken to achieve the goal are consistent with ethical constraints.

Personal preference and ethics

There are many issues where we have strong feelings, some related to our ethical views. It may be difficult to draw a line between what we consider ethically wrong and what we personally disapprove of. Pick an organization that advocates some policy you consider deeply ethically wrong, perhaps an abortion rights group or an antiabortion group, or a group that advocates legalizing marriages between same-sex couples, or a group that advocates banning homosexuals from teaching in public schools. Suppose the group is solely an advocacy or educational group; it does not perform abortions or block abortion clinics, for example. Now, the organization asks you, a programmer, to write a software package, perhaps a mailing list program. You believe in freedom of speech, but you find the job distasteful; you do not want to do anything to assist the organization.

If you decide to decline the job, are you acting on ethical grounds? In other words, can you claim that performing the job is unethical? Probably not. The organization is exercising freedom of speech. Although its position is controversial and ethical issues are relevant to the social issue the organization supports, the organization is not engaged in unethical activity. Your assistance would help to further a goal you do not support. This is a matter of personal preference. On the other hand, there is nothing ethically *wrong* with declining the assignment; the customer's freedom of speech does not impose an ethical obligation on you for assistance (unless you take an extremely broad view of claim-rights).

When discussing political or social issues, people frequently argue that their position is right in a moral or ethical sense or that an opponent's position is morally wrong or unethical. People tend to want to be on the "moral high ground" and feel the stigma of an accusation that their view is ethically wrong. Thus, arguments based on ethics can be used to intimidate. It is often a good idea to try to distinguish between actions we find distasteful, rude, or ill-advised and actions that we can argue convincingly are ethically wrong.

Law and ethics

What is the connection between law and ethics? Very little. Is it ethical to prohibit marijuana use by terminally ill people who would benefit from it? Is it ethical for the government or a state university to give preference in contracts, hiring, or admissions to people in specific ethnic groups? Is it ethical to sell mailing lists based on a customer's purchasing history? These controversies are not settled by whatever the current law happens to be. In addition, history provides numerous examples of laws most of us consider profoundly wrong by ethical standards; slavery is perhaps the most obvious example in American history. Ethics precedes law in the sense that ethical principles help determine whether or not specific laws should be passed.

Some laws enforce ethical rules (e.g., against murder and theft). There is disagreement about the exact boundary of this category of laws (e.g., whether or not it includes laws that enforce claim-rights). But, by definition, we are ethically obligated to obey laws in this category—not because they are laws, but because the laws implement the obligations and prohibitions of ethical rules.

Other laws fall into several categories; we look at the ethical character of a few of them. One category of laws establishes conventions that are followed in business or other activities. Commercial law, such as the Uniform Commercial Code, defines rules for economic transactions and contracts. Such rules provide a framework in which transactions can be accomplished smoothly and with confidence among strangers. They include provisions for how a contract will be interpreted if a dispute must be resolved by a court. These laws are extremely important to any society. They should be consistent with ethics; but beyond basic ethical considerations, details may depend on historic conventions, practicality, and other nonethical criteria. Another convention enforced by law is that, in the U.S., we are required to drive on the right side of the road. In England drivers are required to drive on the left side. There is obviously nothing intrinsically right or wrong about either choice. But once the convention is established, it is ethically wrong to drive on the wrong side of the road because it endangers other people.

Unfortunately, many laws fall into a category that is not intended to implement ethical rules—or even be consistent with them. The political process is subject to pressure from special interest groups of all sorts who seek to pass laws that favor their groups or businesses. Examples include the laws that delayed the introduction of cable television (promoted by the TV networks) and the prohibition on coloring margarine yellow (sponsored by the dairy industry). Many political, religious, or ideological organizations promote laws to require (or prohibit) certain kinds of behavior that the group considers desirable (or objectionable). Examples include prohibitions on gambling or alcohol, requirements for recycling, and requirements that stores close on Sundays. At an extreme, in some countries, this category includes restrictions on the practice of certain religions.

Copyright law has elements of all three categories we described. It defines a property right, violation of which is a form of theft. Because of the intangible nature of intellectual property, some of the rules about what constitutes infringement are more like the second category: pragmatic rules that are devised to be workable. Powerful groups (e.g., the publishing or music industry) lobby for specific rules to benefit themselves. This is why some violations of copyright law are clearly unethical (if one accepts the concept of intellectual property at all), while others may seem to be entirely acceptable.

Are we ethically obligated to obey a law just because it is a law? Some argue that we are: As members of society, we are obliged to accept the rules that are made by the legislative process so long as they are not clearly and utterly ethically wrong (e.g., slavery). Others argue that whereas this might often be a good policy, it is not an ethical obligation. Legislators are just a group of people, subject to errors and political influences; there is no reason to feel an ethical obligation to do something just because they say so. Indeed, some consider all laws that regulate personal behavior or voluntary economic transactions to be violations of the liberty and autonomy of the people forced to obey, hence, ethically wrong.

Is it always ethically right to do something that is legal? Laws must be uniform and stated in a way that clearly indicates what actions are punishable. Ethical situations are complex and variable; relevant factors may be known to the people involved but not provable in court. There are widely accepted ethical rules that would be difficult and probably unwise to enforce absolutely with laws; for example: Do not lie. We have seen that new law lags behind new technology. This makes sense. It takes time to recognize the new problems, consider possible solutions, think and debate about the consequences and fairness of various proposals, and so on. Once a law is passed, it virtually halts experimentation with alternative solutions and reduces competition and diversity of options. A good law will set minimal standards that can apply to all situations, leaving a large range of voluntary choices. Ethics fills the gap between the time when technology creates new problems and the time when reasonable laws are passed, and ethics fills the gap between general legal standards that apply to all cases and the particular choices that must be made in a specific case.

We conclude that while it is not ethically obligatory to obey all laws, that is not an excuse to ignore laws, nor is a law (or lack of a law) an excuse to ignore ethics.

10.3 ETHICAL GUIDELINES FOR COMPUTER PROFESSIONALS

In this section we look at ethical guidelines from several perspectives. We consider special characteristics of professional ethics, as distinct from general ethics. We look at new areas of activity made possible by computers where new guidelines, or application of basic ethical theories, must be developed by scholars and professionals. Finally, we consider formal codes of professional ethics and, in particular, the ACM Code of Ethics and Professional Conduct.

10.3.1 Some Special Aspects of Professional Ethics

Professional ethics have several characteristics different from general ethics. The role of the professional is special in several ways. First, the professional is an expert in a field, be it computer science or medicine, that most customers know little about. Customers rely on the knowledge, expertise, and honesty of the professional. Second, the products of many professionals (e.g., bridges, cars, and buildings built by engineers and computer systems designed by software engineers) profoundly affect large numbers of people. A professional can cause great harm to the client, or other members of the public, through dishonesty, carelessness, or incompetence. Often the victims have little ability to protect themselves; many are not the direct customers of the professional and have no direct control or decision-making role in choosing the product or making decisions about its quality and safety. Thus, computer professionals have special responsibilities to their customers and to the general public, to the users of their products, whether or not they have a direct relationship with the users. These responsibilities includes doing a careful job on software projects where errors and failures will cause monetary losses, disruption, or physical harm to the customer and/or the public. They include thinking about the potential risks to privacy or security of data and taking action to diminish risks that are too high.

In general, ethical rules may be viewed as fundamental and universal, like laws of science, or they may be viewed as rules we make up, like the rules of baseball, to provide a framework in which to interact with other people in a peaceful, productive way. The different viewpoints are illustrated by the titles of two books. One is *Ethics:* Discovering *Right and Wrong;* the other is *Ethics:* Inventing *Right and Wrong.*[5] We do not have to decide which view is correct to find good ethical rules. In either case, our tools include reason, introspection, and observation of human nature, values, and behavior. Some aspects of professional ethics, however, are definitely in the second category. Specific standards for ethical behavior within a profession are developed gradually and are based not only on ethical theory, but also on what is possible using current technology and what is generally accepted practice.

The professional has a responsibility to maintain an expected level of competence and be up-to-date on professional standards and techniques. The claim to be a professional in a particular area implies that the customer can expect a certain minimum level of expertise, based on current knowledge, technology, and the standards of the profession. Professional responsibility includes knowing or learning enough about the application field to do a good job. Responsibility for a noncomputer professional using a sophisticated computer system includes knowing or learning enough about the software or system being used to understand potential problems.

When acting in a professional capacity as an employee, a professional has responsibilities to the employer. Some may be listed explicitly in a contract, but many are implicit. In general, we have an ethical obligation not to break agreements and contracts we have made. Violating an agreement can be a form of lying or theft. We gain something of value from the agreement, perhaps a paycheck or a payment from a customer. In return we have made certain promises. If we do not keep our part of the bargain, we have obtained something dishonestly, or without paying for it. Examples of employment agreements include promising not to discuss details of your work with people outside the company or not to use the company system for personal uses. Sometimes we might think a company policy is unreasonable, but if we agreed to follow it as part of accepting the job, we have an ethical obligation to honor the agreement.

Do organizations have moral status?

Can a business have ethics? This is a relevant question here because we will be discussing decisions made in a professional context. Computer programs and computer-controlled devices like the Therac-25 (described in Section 4.2) are not produced by one individual alone. They are produced by a company or organization, and the decisions about design, testing, and so on, are made within an organizational structure.

Some philosophers argue that it is meaningless to speak of an organization having ethics. All decisions and actions are made and taken by individual people; those people must have ethical responsibility for everything they do. Others argue that an organization that acts with intention and a formal decision structure, such as a business, is a moral entity.[6] Accepting a business as a moral entity does not necessarily diminish the responsibility of the individual people. Ultimately, it is individuals who are making decisions and taking actions. We can hold both the individuals and the company or organization responsible for their acts.* Whether or not one accepts the idea that a business can have moral rights and responsibilities, it is clear that organizational structure and policies lead to a pattern of actions and decisions that have ethical content. Businesses do have a "corporate culture," or a "personality," or simply a reputation for treating employees and customers in respectful and honest—or careless and deceptive—ways.

In Chapter 4 we saw examples of ethically varied business behavior. Recall the decision by a supermarket company to delay implementation of a new checkout scanner and inventory system because the scanner occasionally charged the wrong price for a product. The opposite decision might have been made by the same person working at a different company. Such decisions are influenced by the policies and principles of the company. People in managerial positions shape the corporate culture or ethics of the business. Thus, decisions by managers have an impact beyond the particular product or contract the decision involves. A manager who is dishonest with customers, for example, in a situation where serious harm is not likely, may be setting an example that encourages other employ-

---

*Regardless of whether businesses and organizations are viewed as moral agents, they are treated as legal entities and can be sued and fined.

ees to be dishonest in general, with more serious harm in other cases. A manager's ethical responsibility includes his or her contribution to the company's ethical personality.

10.3.2   New Ethical Problems and Standards for Computer Technology

New technology creates new ethical issues. Many things were not possible in the past, so we did not have to confront the issue of whether or how to do them. Medical technology, like computer technology, has grown enormously in the past few decades. Medical professionals have to address new questions, such as: Now that we can do heart transplants, who should decide which dying patient gets an available heart? What criteria should be used? Suppose a new medical technique has potentially great benefits for patients, but also has high risks? How should a doctor or hospital decide whether to use it?

Similarly, new ethical questions arise in applications of computer technology. Simple ethical rules are often not sufficient to tell us what to do in new, sometimes difficult situations. We need to try to apply the theories and guidelines of ethics to the new situations and develop new conventions about how to deal with them. This can be quite difficult because the situations are complex. Scholars and professionals in the field are currently involved in discussion and debate about many of the new ethical dilemmas raised by computing technology. In the rest of this section we mention a few areas where ethical guidelines need to be developed to guide the behavior of individuals and organizations.

Privacy

Many of the issues discussed in Chapter 2, related to databases used for marketing and decision making, involve ethical issues. We will mention a few examples.

Suppose you set policy for a company that maintains a large database containing personal information, perhaps a credit bureau. The law permits you to provide credit reports to businesses with a legitimate business interest. How will you define "legitimate business interest"? How will you verify that the person requesting the report has a legitimate purpose? The consumers about whom you collect data are not your customers; you have no contract with them. Your policy decisions depend in part on ethical considerations about how you should treat people who may be seriously affected by your actions.

Suppose your software company is asked, by a private company, to develop a database of information obtained from government records, perhaps to generate lists of convicted shoplifters or child molesters, perhaps marketing lists of new home buyers, affluent boat owners, or divorced parents with young children. The people who will be on the lists did not have a choice about whether the information would be open to the public; they did not give permission for its use in the lists. How will you decide whether or not to accept the job? You may cite the law to avoid an ethical decision: The records are public and available to anyone. You may decide against secondary uses of information that was not provided voluntarily by the people it concerns. Some people might not object to being on the marketing lists, but it is impossible to ask each one; you may make your own utilitarian calculation about whether or not the benefits of the lists outweigh the privacy invasions or inconveniences they may cause for some people. You may refuse to make marketing lists, but agree to making lists of people convicted of certain crimes, using Posner's principle (see Section 2.7) that negative information, such as convictions, should be in the public domain.

In Chapter 2 we discussed some of the social and political issues raised by the ability to search, extremely quickly, the vast amount of information stored electronically and to do computer matching and profiling. The technology available now makes it possible to use information in ways utterly unanticipated at the time the information was provided, sometimes with unexpected and unintended consequences. These new capabilities raise ethical issues, as well as political and social ones. Several companies have developed powerful programs, such as AltaVista by Digital Equipment Corporation (DEC), to search the World Wide Web and archives of Usenet newsgroups. The programs are very useful Web search tools. Web pages are intended to be public and fairly permanent (although the content changes). The situation for the newsgroups, however, is (or was) somewhat different. When the extremely fast search tools and huge Usenet archives were made freely available, it quickly became popular for people to search for the names of their acquaintances and find all the messages they posted. Ethical problems arise because of the sensitivity of some of the newsgroup topics and the privacy expectations of the people who participated in them. Some newsgroups include discussions by or about gay teenagers, victims of physical abuse, unusual sexual practices, or unusual religions and political views. Although participants may have known that anyone can log on and read any newsgroup, the likelihood was small; the presumption was that the postings were read by a relatively small group of people who shared common problems or interests. Also, many participants thought their postings were as ephemeral as a conversation; they would not have thought that postings from years ago still exist. Most systems delete messages after a few days or weeks. (The volume of postings, roughly a gigabyte a day in the mid-1990s, made it impossible for most sites to store them longer.) But companies that provide the search programs collected huge archives, some going back many years. Now they continuously update the archives by storing all new newsgroup postings. One company's software allows creation of user profiles describing the subjects a person frequently writes about.

Given this background, and an understanding of the technology and expectations of several years ago, is it right to make all messages posted to newsgroups in the past easily available to everyone now? Whatever one's answer to this question (and many would argue that the loss of privacy was a small price to pay for the usefulness of the search programs as research tools), this is an ethical issue the companies should have considered when setting up and promoting their search programs and Usenet archives. Anyone contemplating such a project should give consideration to the consequences and privacy expectations involved. An issue for users is: Now that the archives and search capability are available, is it ethical to search for a particular person's name, say a prospective employee, to see what newsgroups the person participated in and what opinions he or she expressed?

In Sections 2.8.1 and 2.8.3 we presented the Code of Fair Information Practices and the Freedom of Information Use Guidelines. Many of their provisions are useful ethical guidelines for dealing with personal information.

How good is good enough?

In Chapter 4 we saw some of the minor and major consequences of flaws in computer systems. In some of those cases, people acted in clearly unethical or irresponsible ways. In many cases, however, there was no ill intent. As we pointed out in Chapter 4, because of its inherent complexity, software—even well-designed, well-implemented, well-tested software that has been in use for a long time—will have bugs. In addition, unexpected circumstances arise when it is operating, and users do not always understand how to use the software correctly. The difficulty, or impossibility, of assuring correctness is combined with increased impact, increased danger and harm, when things go wrong. There are some legal principles that can be used to sue when damage occurs (standards of liability, negligence, misrepresentation, etc.), but the legal standards are not clear or uniform, in part because standards for the profession have not been fully developed.

As an example of the work being done by computer professionals and ethicists from other fields to devise ethical guidelines for safety-critical applications, we describe some guidelines developed by Collins *et al* in the article "How Good Is Good Enough?"[7] Collins *et al* present a lengthy analysis of one hypothetical scenario, a computerized system for filling prescriptions in a hospital pharmacy. I have culled from their discussion what I think are some of their most important guidelines; they follow, with comments.

- **Providers have an ethical responsibility to do a thorough, careful job when writing their bids or contracts.** Inadequate planning of time or budget for testing and other important steps in the development process is likely to lead to pressure to cut corners later.

- **Do not increase harm to the people most vulnerable.** This means accepting as a major concern the safety of patients, passengers, drivers, and so on—the people who would be hurt most seriously if a computerized system does not work properly.

- **Do not increase the risk in an already risky situation.**

  One implication of this is the inclusion of backup systems, such as hardware safety devices to protect against software errors, and manual systems to use when an automated system fails. In the Therac-25 case (Section 4.2), this would have meant that the hardware safety interlock in earlier versions of the machine not be eliminated.

  Another implication, given in Collins *et al,* is that software designed for an application where the danger of harm from a failure is small should not be used in an application where the harm from a failure would be serious. The quality and testing standards for the software might not have been as high as would be necessary in the new application. Again we can use an illustration from the Therac-25: The software used for the Therac-20, which had a hardware safety interlock, should not have been used in the Therac-25, where safety depended entirely on the software. Also, software for non-safety-critical applications may have confusing user interfaces, which may be tolerable in the original application but could have fatal consequences in safety-critical applications.

- **Software developers and buyers* have a responsibility to be open and honest about capabilities, safety, and limitations of the software in communication with customers, employees, others who are affected by it, and the public, where appropriate.**

---

*Think of buyers as hospital or airline company officials, for example, and users as the staff members, pilots, and so on, who will operate the software.

In at least four of the cases described in Chapter 4, there is a strong argument that the treatment of customers was dishonest. (In several cases, poor treatment of customers was bad business.) Honesty of salespeople is hardly a new issue. The line between emphasizing your best side and being dishonest is not always clear, but it should be clear that hiding known, serious flaws and lying to customers are on the wrong side of the line.

Honesty includes taking responsibility for damaging or injuring others. If you break a neighbor's window playing ball or smash into someone's car, you have an obligation to pay for the damage. If a business finds that its product caused injury, it should not hide that fact or attempt to put the blame on others.

- **Developers and buyers have an obligation to properly train users. Buyers and users have a responsibility to understand the limitations of the software and its proper operation.**
- **Developers and buyers should include users** (such as medical staff, technicians, pilots, office workers) **in the planning and testing stages to improve safe functioning of the system.** Recall the discussion of computer controls for airplanes (Sections 4.1.4 and 4.3.2) where confusing user interfaces and system behavior increased the risk of accidents.

One of the most difficult ethical problems that arises in safety-critical applications is deciding how much risk is acceptable. In 1986 the space shuttle Challenger was destroyed by burning gases that leaked from the rocket shortly after launch; the seven people aboard were killed.* A comment from one of the engineers who opposed the launch sheds some light on how subtle shifts in attitude can affect the result of a decision. The night before the scheduled launch, the engineers argued for a delay; they knew the cold weather posed a severe threat to the shuttle. We cannot prove absolutely that a system is safe, nor can we usually prove absolutely that it will fail and kill someone. The engineer reported that, in the case of the Challenger, "It was up to us to prove beyond a shadow of a doubt that it was not safe to [launch]." This, he said, was the total reverse of a usual Flight Readiness Review.[8] For the ethical decision maker, the policy should be not to proceed without a convincing case for safety, rather than not to delay without a convincing case for disaster.

Accountability: Who is responsible?

The discussion in the previous section shows that software developers, buyers, and users all have ethical responsibility for safe and proper functioning of software. Here we look at a few more issues involved in determining who is ethically responsible when a program fails and causes large monetary damages or injuries to people.

If the software itself is faulty, there is the issue of deciding who within the software development company is responsible. Each person has the responsibility to do his or her own job ethically. A programmer is responsible for doing a competent job, for being honest about weaknesses and potential bugs in the results, for example, but not for the test plan

---

*The computer system was not at fault.

developed by others or for management decisions. Managers at various levels are responsible for seeing that reasonable planning, design, and testing are done. At any point in the process, anyone who knows that something is being overlooked, done wrong, or done carelessly has an obligation to speak out; each person is in part responsible for the result. This division and sharing of responsibility within a company is similar for engineering, manufacturing, a hospital, and so on.

Some aspects of software generate new problems in assigning responsibility. It is common to see disclaimers on consumer appliances stating that warranties are not valid if the buyer makes any modifications to the product. It is reasonable that the manufacturer of a microwave oven or stereo not be held responsible (financially or morally) if a failure or injury is probably the result of changes made by the customer. But it is common for custom software to be modified, expanded, and enhanced over time, often by people other than those who did the original design and implementation. Unfortunately, the long life and evolution of software encourages all participants to disclaim responsibility.

Questions about responsibility are particularly complicated for decisions systems, for example, systems that use models and heuristics to guide business and financial decision making, where a wrong decision can have serious results. Is the developer of the system responsible for occasional poor predictions, or is the user responsible for understanding the risks and limitations of the system? Many of the guidelines from Collins *et al* can be applied here. It is especially important that developers explain the limitations and uncertainties to clients and that clients do not shirk responsibility for understanding them and taking appropriate precautions.

To illustrate the difficulties of cases where a decision system is modified over time, Johnson and Mulvey[9] use a scenario where a software developer has written a program to make investment decisions. The client is a company that manages pension funds. The program has functioned well for several years. An investment manager at the client firm instructs his in-house programmers to make some modifications. Shortly afterward, the manager, following the program's recommendation, makes a large investment that turns out to be a disaster, losing a significant portion of the pension funds. Who, if anyone, is ethically responsible for the loss? The answer depends on several factors.

The first factor is the quality of the program. Was it written according to accepted and expected professional standards? Both software standards and investing standards are relevant. One problem here is that quality standards for software have not yet been established as clearly and uniformly as standards in other fields. Is a programmer ethically responsible for an error in the program? We observed repeatedly that some bugs are inevitable. Others are the result of carelessness and incompetence. A determination of ethical responsibility for a program bug includes a decision about whether the programmer should have reasonably been expected to avoid that particular bug and whether a reasonable test plan should have detected it. Again here, while some cases are clear, many are not.

When changes in complex programs are made by a client's staff, the risk of problems may significantly increase. The client's specifications or instructions may not be clear. The staff may be less likely than the software developer to be familiar with the structure of the program and its safety features. If the staff is small and/or does not contain people sensitive to the fact that errors can be introduced by small changes, testing may be insufficient. The client has the responsibility to ensure that changes are made consistent with good professional standards, and to allow what might seem like a large amount of time to make—and test—a small change.

10.3.3 Professional Codes of Ethics

Many professional organizations have written codes of professional conduct. There are many good reasons to have such codes. They can provide a general statement of ethical values reminding people in the profession that ethical behavior is expected of them. They can describe to the profession and the public the standards of behavior developed by the profession over time, such as the kinds of standards for privacy and safety gradually being developed for computer technology. Professional codes can provide valuable guidance for new young members of the profession who want to behave ethically but do not know what is expected of them, whose limited experience has not prepared them to be alert to difficult ethical situations and handle them appropriately. Professional codes of ethics can be written by dedicated people who are honestly trying to devise a good code to guide practitioners in the field and protect the public who rely on the special expertise of the people in the profession.

It is worth noting that professional codes of ethics can be written for less worthy goals, or that some particular provisions may serve the interests of particular members of the profession rather than all practitioners and the public. For example, recall the discussion of bans on telemedicine practice by out-of-state doctors (Section 9.4). Would opposition to competition affect a decision about how telemedicine is treated in a professional code? One medical organization used a telemedicine ban as a bargaining chip in negotiating with a state legislature about legislation affecting doctors. Professional organizations often lobby government representatives and participate in writing laws. Deals may be made that include provisions chosen for political rather than ethical or professional reasons.

Mandatory professional licensing is an issue where economic interests can influence the position taken in a code of ethics. Mandatory licensing for various trades and professions has the effect of reducing the number of people in the profession (particularly of those who are self-taught), raising the fees of those who are licensed, and raising the cost of services. Of course, many in the computing profession who advocate licensing are motivated by a genuine desire to improve the quality of the profession and protect the public from dangerously incompetent practitioners.

There are several organizations for the range of professions included in the general term "computer professional." The professional organization for computer scientists is the Association for Computing Machinery (ACM), founded at the birth of the computer age in 1946. Professional organizations tend to be large; the ACM has approximately 80,000 members. In any profession, members have widely differing views on many ethical, social, and political issues. Sometimes a professional organization's code of ethics includes positions on issues where the members differ strongly; a majority of members (or a majority of members of the governing body within the organization) may use its power to endorse its favored position. For a majority to adopt its position as an ethical tenet of the profession would be dishonest. For example, it would seem inappropriate (even unethical) for the ethics code of a general professional organization of doctors to take a position on, say, gun control. It would not, on the other hand, be inappropriate for a subgroup of the profession organized around a shared viewpoint to include a position in its code of ethics. Similarly, we should consider whether it is appropriate to include ethical positions on issues like working on computer systems for nuclear weapons, or environmental issues, in a general ethical code for computer professionals. It is reasonable that an organization such as Computer Professionals for Social Responsibility would adopt positions or ethical statements that might be inappropriate for the ACM as a whole.

The ACM Code of Ethics and Professional Conduct is included as an appendix at the end of this chapter. It has a section on the basic ethical values of honesty and trustworthiness (Section 1.3) and several sections that emphasize treating others with dignity. These basic values can be derived from the ethical theories we looked at in Section 10.2.2. The code covers many aspects of professional behavior, including the responsibility to respect confidentiality (1.8), maintain professional competence (2.2), be aware of relevant laws (2.3), and honor contracts and agreements (2.6). In addition, the code puts special emphasis on areas that are particularly (but not uniquely) vulnerable from computer systems: privacy, safety, and property. It stresses the responsibility to respect and protect privacy (1.7), avoid harm to others (1.2), and respect property rights (with intellectual property and computer systems themselves as most relevant examples) (1.5, 1.6, 2.8). Although the code and the guidelines that accompany the code have some weaknesses (some of which are explored in the exercises), many of its sections provide excellent guidance for computer professionals.

10.4   CASES

10.4.1   Introduction and Methodology

In this section we analyze situations that a computer professional may confront in his or her work. A few of them are real cases that were encountered by a student in my course on social, legal, and ethical issues in computing.*

The cases presented here are just a few samples of the kinds that can occur. They vary in seriousness and difficulty, and they include situations that illustrate professional responsibilities to potential users of computer systems in the general public, customers or clients, the employer, coworkers, and others. More cases are given in the exercises at the end of the chapter. In the last case, on hiring low-wage foreign programmers, a controversy that overlaps social and ethical issues, we will give a lengthy discussion that attempts to tackle the problem with the formal ethical theories as well as informal methods.

In most of this book, I have tried to give arguments on both sides of controversial issues without taking a position. Ethical issues may be even more difficult than some of the others we have covered, and there may well be disagreement among computer ethics specialists on some points in the cases considered here. In any real case, there are many other relevant facts and details that affect the conclusion. In spite of the difficulty of drawing ethical conclusions, especially for brief fictional scenarios, for some of these cases I will give conclusions. You may face cases like these where you have to make a decision. I do not want to leave the impression that because a decision is difficult or because some

---

*I have mingled them with other cases and changed some details because he requested anonymity.

people benefit or lose either way, there is no ethical basis for making the decision. (It seems ethically irresponsible to do so.)

How shall we analyze specific scenarios to determine what actions are ethical? We now have a number of tools. We can try to apply our favorite ethical theory, or some combination of the theories. We can ask questions that reflect basic ethical values: Is it honest? Is it responsible? Does it violate someone's rights? Does it violate an agreement we made? We can consult the ACM Code of Ethics and Professional Conduct. Some ethicists have developed elaborate methodologies for analyzing cases; they make charts to record responsibilities, benefits, and damages to the various people involved in the scenario. We will use less formal methods here. Although we will not follow the outline below step-by-step, our discussions of the cases will usually include most of these elements:

- Identify all the people and organizations affected. (They are generally referred to as the stakeholders.)
- In cases where there is not a simple yes or no decision, but rather one has to choose some action, list as many possible actions as we can.
- Consider the impact of the options on the stakeholders. List consequences, risks, benefits, harms, costs for each action considered.
- Identify responsibilities of the decision makers and rights of stakeholders. Determine if any of the actions would violate general ethical guidelines or someone's rights.
- Decide which actions are ethically wrong, which are ethically obligatory, and which are acceptable choices, but not required.
- If there are several ethically acceptable options, select an option, considering the ethical merits of each, courtesy to others, practicality, self-interest, personal preferences, and so on.

"Brainstorming" about all the affected people and possible consequences can generate a long discussion. After the discussion, we may then bring in an ethical principle that says that the benefits or costs we just listed are irrelevant or minor. The effort was not wasted. It may bring out ethical and practical considerations we would not have thought of otherwise. And it is as helpful to know why some factors do not carry heavy ethical weight as it is to know which ones do.

10.4.2   Copying an Employee's Files

You are a computer system manager. An employee is out sick and another employee requests that you copy all files from the sick person's computer to hers so she can do some work.

The obvious risk here is privacy. The sick employee may have personal files stored on the computer. It is also possible that the sick employee has files related to secret or proprietary company information to which other employees are not supposed to have access. There is a small risk to you and the company from a complaint or suit for invasion of privacy if personal files are copied. On the other hand, the company and the employee making the request may suffer if important work is not completed on time.

The right thing to do in this case depends in large part on the policies, practices, and expectations at the particular company. If there is a strong policy against personal use of the computer system, if it is routine practice for employees to share files while working on a project, and if it is reasonable to believe that all the files to be copied are related to the project the employees are working on, there may be no ethical problem with copying the files. However, if there is some doubt, you must decide what to do.

There may be a very simple solution to this problem: Call the sick employee and ask permission to copy the files. But he or she may not be reachable. Another option would be to request authorization from the manager of the project on which the employees were working. In the actual case, the system manager refused to transfer all the files, but agreed to transfer specific files if given the filenames.

10.4.3 Insufficient Privacy Protection

Your customer is a community clinic that works with families that have problems of family violence. The clinic has three sites in the same city, including a shelter for battered women and children. The director wants a computerized record system with the ability to transfer files among sites and make appointments at any site for any other. She wants to have an Internet connection for e-mail communication with other social service agencies about client needs. She wants a notebook computer capable of storing copies of records, to be carried by staffers when they visit clients at home. At the shelter, only first names are used by staffers, but the records contain last names and forwarding addresses of women who have recently left. The director's description of the system makes no mention of passwords or encryption. The clinic's budget is small, and she wants to keep the cost as low as possible.*

You, as the computer professional, have specialized knowledge of risks related to computer systems, in this case, privacy risks that can result in embarrassment for families using the clinic and physical harm to women who use the shelter. The clinic director is likely be aware of the sensitivity of the information in the records, but she may not be aware of the vulnerabilities of a computer system. It is as much your obligation to warn the director of the risks as it is for a physician to warn a patient of side effects of a drug he or she prescribes.

Suppose you warn the director about unauthorized access to sensitive information by staff members and hackers and interception of records and e-mail transmitted without encryption. You suggest a list of measures to protect client privacy, including, for example, unique user IDs and passwords for each staff member coded to allow access only to information they need, an audit trail function that keeps track of who accessed and modified the records, an ID code system (not social security number) that can be used when discussing clients with other agencies that do not need their names, and encryption for transmission of

*After writing this scenario, I read of an incident in which someone mailed a list of 4000 AIDS patients to a newspaper. The county health department stored the list on portable computers and did not encode the names.

records. (Note that your ability to provide such suggestions is dependent on your professional competence and currency in the field.) You tell the director that carrying records on the notebook computer has risks of unauthorized leakage, both accidental and via a bribe to a staffer. (Suppose a client is a candidate for the city council or a party in a child custody case.) You suggest procedures to reduce such leaks. The features you recommend will make the system more expensive.

If you convince the director of the importance of your recommendations, and she agrees to pay the extra cost, your professional/ethical behavior has helped improve the security of the system and protect client privacy.

What if the director says she cannot afford the additional features and is willing to have the system developed without them? You have several options. You can develop the cheaper, but more vulnerable, system, or refuse and lose the job, or work out a compromise that includes the protections you consider most important. What should you do? The answer here is less clear than your obligation to inform the director of the risks. Is it now up to the director alone to make an informed choice, weighing the risks and costs? In a case where the risk would be taken only by the customer, some would say yes, it is your job to inform, no more. Others would say that the customer lacks the professional expertise to evaluate the risks. In this scenario, however, the director is not the only person at risk, nor is the risk to her the most significant risk of an insecure system. You have an ethical responsibility to consider the potential harm to clients from exposure of sensitive information if you build a system without adequate privacy protection.

The most difficult decision may be deciding what is adequate. There is not always a sharp, clear line between sufficient and insufficient protection, so the decision in a specific case may be difficult.*

10.4.4   Risky Systems

You are part of a team working on a computer controlled laser device for treating cancerous tumors. The computer controls direction, intensity, and timing of the beam that destroys the tumor. Various delays have put the project behind schedule, and the deadline is approaching. There will not be time to complete all the planned testing. The system has been functioning properly in the routine treatment scenarios that have been tested so far. The project manager is considering whether to deliver the system on time, while continuing testing, and to make patches if bugs are found.

The central issue here is safety. Your company is building a machine that is designed to save lives, but if it malfunctions, it can kill or injure patients. Suppose you are the manager responsible for making the decision about delivering the system. What should you do?

Perhaps the situation seems obvious: Delivering the system on time benefits the company but may endanger the patients—a case of profits versus safety. But we will defer a conclusion until after we analyze the case further.

---

*Note, by the way, that although we have focused on the need for privacy protection here, such protection can be overdone. You also have a professional ethical responsibility not to scare a customer into paying for security measures that are expensive but protect against very unlikely risks.

Who are the people affected (the stakeholders)? First, the patients to be treated with the machine. A malfunction could cause injury or death. On the other hand, if release of the machine is delayed, some patients it might have cured may undergo surgery instead. We will assume treatment with the laser machine is preferable because it is less invasive, requires less hospitalization and recovery time, and overall is less expensive. For some patients, surgery may be impossible, and they may die from their cancer if the laser is not used. Second, the hospitals and clinics who will purchase the machine are affected. Delay could cause financial losses if they have planned on having the machine at a particular time. However, it is reasonable for them to expect that the machine has been professionally designed and fully tested. The customers are being deceived if they are not told that the testing was not completed. Third, your decision affects you and your company (including its stockholders and employees). Negative consequences of delaying delivery may include damage to your reputation for managing a project (with possible impact on salary and advancement), loss of reputation and a possible fall in stock price for the company, loss of other contracts resulting in reduction of jobs for its programmers and other employees. As a project manager, you have an obligation to help the company do well. On the other hand, if the system is delivered without complete testing and an injury to a patient results, the same negative consequences are likely to occur (in addition to the human feelings of guilt and remorse and significant monetary losses from lawsuits).

This brief examination shows that delivering the system without complete testing may have both negative and positive impacts on patients, and it can have both negative and positive impacts on the manager and the company. The issue is not simply profits versus safety. You may be honestly trying to weigh the risks of delivering the system against the costs of delay. However, we should be aware of a few aspects of human nature that can influence the decision. One is to put more weight on short term and/or highly likely effects. Many of the costs of delay are fairly certain and immediate, and the risk of malfunction is uncertain and in the future. Also, people tend to use the inherent uncertainties of a situation and the genuine arguments for one side to rationalize making the wrong decision, that is, for taking the easy way out. It may take experience (with both professional and ethical issues), knowledge of cases like the Therac-25, and courage to resist the temptation to put short term effects ahead of longer term risks.

Now that we have seen that arguments can be made on both sides, we must decide how to weigh them and how to avoid rationalization. First, the machine works well in the routine tests performed so far. The Therac-25 case illustrates that a complex system can function correctly hundreds of times, but fail with fatal consequences in unusual circumstances. Your customer may not know this. You, as a computer professional, have more understanding about the complexity of computer programs and the potential for errors, especially in programs that interact with real-world events, like operator input and control of machinery. We assume the original test plan for the laser machine was devised for good reasons. The tests should be completed before delivery.

Some patients will benefit from on-time delivery. Should they be weighted equally against the patients who may be harmed by a malfunction? Not necessarily. The machine represents an improvement in medical treatment, but there is no ethical obligation that it be available to the public on a certain date. You are not responsible for the disease of people who rely on existing treatments. Your machine is being offered as an improvement. Your obligation to the people who will use the machine is to be sure that it is as safe as good professional practice can make it, and that includes proper testing. You do not have an ethical obligation to cure people of cancer; you do have an ethical obligation to use your professional judgment in a way that does not expose people, without their knowledge, to additional harm.*

What about your responsibility to your company? Even if we weigh the short-term effects of the delay more highly than the risks of losses that would result from a malfunction, the ethical arguments are on the side of fully testing the machine. Yes, you have a responsibility to help your company be successful, but that is not an absolute obligation. (Recall the discussion of goals and constraints in Section 10.2.3.) Perhaps the distinction would be more obvious if the issue were stealing (from a competitor or a customer perhaps). Your responsibility to the company is secondary to ethical constraints. In the present case, avoiding unreasonable risk of harm to patients is the ethical constraint.

10.4.5 Going Public

Suppose you are a member of a team working on a computer-controlled crash-avoidance system for automobiles. You think the system has a flaw that could endanger people. The project manager does not seem concerned and expects to announce completion of the project soon. Are you ethically obligated to do something?

Given the potential consequences, it is a reasonable conclusion that you have an ethical obligation to do something. As is often the case with obligations, it is not clear how much you are obligated to do. We will list a variety of options. First, at a minimum, discuss your concerns with the project manager. If the manager decides to proceed as planned with no examination of the problem, your next option is to go to someone higher up in the company.

If no one with authority in the company is willing to investigate your concerns, you have a more difficult dilemma. Up to this point, there is no question about your activities being ethically wrong. There is nothing wrong with voicing your concerns; it is admirable and probably obligatory. Now you have the option of going outside the company (to the customer, to the news media, or to a government agency). There is personal risk of course: You might lose your job. There is also the ethical issue of the damage you might do to your company, and ultimately to the people who would benefit from the system if negative publicity kills the project altogether.

At this point it is a good idea to consider whether you are confident that you have the expertise to assess the risk. If you conclude that the management decision was an acceptable one (and that you are not letting your concern for keeping your job sway your conclusion), this may be the point at which to drop the issue. If you are convinced that the risk is real, or if you are aware of a careless, irresponsible attitude among the company management, then you are obligated to go further. You are not an uninvolved bystander, for whom the question of ethical obligation may be more fuzzy. Your salary is being paid by the project; you are part of the team; you are a participant.

---

*There are many situations where patients knowingly try risky drugs or treatments. Here we are assuming that the laser device is not being described as risky or experimental, but as a new, presumably safe, treatment device.

There have been several dramatic cases where professionals faced this difficult situation. The engineers who worked on the rockets for the space shuttle Challenger knew that it was not safe to launch the shuttle in cold weather. They argued for a delay and tried to convince their managers and NASA officials of the danger. When the decision was made to approve the launch, the engineers faced the issue we are confronting here. Should they have done more, perhaps gone to others in their company or NASA, or to the news media, to stop the launch?* In another example, computer engineers who worked on the San Francisco Bay Area Rapid Transit system (BART) were concerned about the safety of the software designed to control the trains. Although they tried for many months, they were not successful in their attempts to convince their managers that changes were needed. Eventually, some of their critical memos and reports were published in a newspaper. The engineers were fired. During the next few years, while several crashes occurred, there were public investigations and numerous recommendations made for improving safety of the system.[10]

In these cases we have the benefit of hindsight. We know that BART had serious management and technical problems that resulted in injuries and at least one death. We know that the Challenger should not have been launched in the cold. The difficulty, of course, is deciding how far to go with one's objections when there is a risk, but not a certainty, of a disaster. One of the BART engineers made these comments about the process:

> If there is something that ought to be corrected inside an organization, the most effective way to do it is to do it within the organization and exhaust all possibilities there . . . you might have to go to the extreme of publishing these things, but you should never start that way.[11]

The difficult question the professional in such a case must answer is: How serious must the risk be, and how imminent the danger, before you "go public"?

10.4.6 Release of Personal Information

We will look at two related scenarios here. First,

> You work for the IRS, the Social Security Administration, a medical clinic, or one of the large credit bureaus. Someone asks you to get a copy of a person's file. He will pay you $100.

Who are the stakeholders? Who is affected by your response? You: You have an opportunity to make some extra money. The person seeking the file: Presumably he has something to gain from it. The person whose file is requested: His or her privacy will be invaded. Your employer: If the sale becomes known, the employer may be sued by the victim; if such sales of files become common, the employer will gain a reputation for carelessness

---

*I, by no means, intend to suggest that the engineers bear the responsibility for the loss of the Challenger. They may, however, have been able to prevent it.

and potentially lose business and lawsuits. All people about whom the company has personal files: If you sell one file, chances are you will sell others if asked in the future.

There are many alternative actions open to you: Sell the file. Refuse and say nothing about the incident. Refuse and report the incident to your supervisor. Refuse and report to the police. Contact the person whose file was requested and tell him or her of the incident. Agree to sell the file, but actually work with the police to collect evidence to convict the person trying to buy it.

Are any of these alternatives ethically prohibited or obligatory? The first option, selling the file, is wrong. It almost certainly violates rules and policies you have agreed to abide by in accepting your job. As an employee, you are bound by the guarantees of confidentiality the company or agency has promised its customers or the public. Depending on how the information in the file is to be used, you may be helping to cause serious harm to the victim.

Some would argue that selling the file is wrong because it violates the privacy of the victim, but recall that the boundaries of privacy are unclear because they can conflict with freedom of speech and reasonable flow of information. If you happened to know the victim and knew the same information in the file, you might not be under an ethical obligation to keep it secret. The essential element that makes selling the file wrong in this scenario is your position of trust as an employee in a company that maintains sensitive files.

None of the other actions we listed are ethically wrong. Are any ethically required? Depending on policies in the company, you may be obligated to report any attempt to gain access to the records. There are other good reasons for reporting the incident. Reporting could lead to the capture of someone making a business of buying sensitive information without the knowledge or consent of the person the information concerns and without the knowledge and consent of the companies responsible for the information. It could protect you if it is discovered later that files were sold and the guilty person is not known. (Some ethicists, e.g., deontologists, argue that taking an action because it benefits you is not ethically meritorious. However, one can argue that taking an action that protects an innocent person is meritorious, even if the person is yourself.)

In general, if there is no explicit reporting requirement at your company, there would be disagreement about whether you are ethically required to do more than refuse to sell the file. It is difficult to decide how much you are obligated to do to prevent a wrong thing from happening if you are not participating in the wrong act. A recluse who ignores evils and pains around him may not be doing anything unethical, but he is not what we would consider a good neighbor. One might think of acting to prevent a wrong as (loosely speaking) a social obligation, part of being a good neighbor, good employee, or good citizen, even if it is not an ethical requirement.

Now we consider a variation of this scenario.

You know another employee sells files with people's personal information.

Your options include doing nothing, talking to the other employee and trying to get him or her to stop selling files (by threats of exposure or ethical arguments), reporting to your supervisor (perhaps anonymously), or reporting to an appropriate law enforcement agency. The question here is whether you have an obligation to do anything. This scenario differs from the previous one in two ways. First, you are not directly involved; no one has approached you. This difference might seem to argue for no obligation. On the other hand, in the first scenario, if you refused to sell the file, the buyer might give up, and the victim's information would not be disclosed. In this case, you know that sensitive information is being sold. In this case, the argument in favor of an obligation to take action seems stronger. One reason is that as an employee of the company you have a responsibility to protect the company and its clients.

10.4.7 Conflict of Interest

You have a small consulting business. The CyberStuff company plans to acquire a new computer/network system and it wants to hire you to evaluate bids from vendors. Your spouse works for NetWorkx and did most of the work in writing the bid that NetWorkx plans to submit. You read the bid while your spouse was working on it, and you think it is excellent. Do you tell CyberStuff about your spouse's connection with NetWorkx?

Conflict-of-interest situations can occur in many professions. Sometimes the ethical course of action is clear; sometimes, depending on how small your connection is with the people or organizations who may benefit or lose because of your action, it may be more difficult to determine.

I have seen two immediate reactions to scenarios similar to this one (in discussions among professionals and among students). One is that it is a simple case of profits versus honesty, and ethics requires that you inform the company about your connection to the software vendor. The other is that if you honestly believe you can be objective and fairly consider all bids, you have no ethical obligation to say anything. Which is right? Is this a simple choice between saying nothing and benefiting from the contract or disclosing your connection and losing the contract? Before answering these questions, we will consider the affected parties, possible consequences, and professional ethics.

The affected parties are the CyberStuff company, yourself, your spouse, your spouse's company, and the other companies whose bids you will be reviewing. A key unknown factor in considering consequences is that we do not know whether or not CyberStuff will later discover your connection to one of the bidders. If you say nothing about the conflict of interest, you benefit because you get the consulting job. If you recommend NetWorkx, it benefits from a sale. However, if the conflict of interest is discovered later, your reputation for honesty—important to a consultant—will be damaged. The reputation of your spouse's company may also suffer. Note that even if you conclude that you are truly unbiased and do not have an ethical obligation to tell CyberStuff about your connection to your spouse's company, you should consider whether you have an ethical obligation to NetWorkx, because you may put its reputation for honesty at risk.

What are the consequences of disclosing the conflict of interest to the client now? You will probably lose this particular job, but your honesty may be valued and get you more business in the future. Thus there may be benefits, even to you, from disclosing the conflict of interest.

Suppose your connection to NetWorkx is unlikely to be discovered. What are your responsibilities to your potential client as a professional consultant? When you are hired as a consultant, you are being hired to offer unbiased, honest, impartial professional advice.

There is an implicit assumption that you do not have a personal interest in the outcome or a personal reason to favor one of bids you will review. The conclusion in this case hangs on this point. In spite of your belief in your impartiality, you may be unintentionally biased. It is not up to you to make the decision about whether you can be fair. That decision should be made by the client. Your ethical obligation in this case is to inform CyberStuff of the conflict of interest.

(See Exercise 21 for a slightly different scenario.)

10.4.8 Copyright Violation

Your company has about 25 licenses for a computer program, but you discover that it has been copied onto 80 computers.

The first step here is to inform your supervisor that the copies violate the license agreement. You could offer helpful information, for example, that there is a software package available that could monitor use of the program to ensure that no more than 25 copies were active at any time. Suppose the supervisor is not willing to take any action and does not want to install the monitoring software? What next? What if you bring the problem to the attention of higher level people in the company and no one cares? There are several possible actions: Give up; you did your best to correct the problem. Call the software vendor or the Software Publishers Association and report the offense. Quit your job.

Is giving up at this point ethically acceptable? My students thought it depended in part on whether you are the person who signed the license agreements. If so, you have made an agreement about the use of the software, and you are obligated to honor it. Because you did not make the copies, you have not broken the agreement directly, but you have responsibility for the software. As a practical matter, your name on the license may expose you to legal risk or to being made a scapegoat by unethical managers in your company. Thus you may prefer to report the violation or quit your job and have your name removed from the licenses to protect yourself. If you are not the person who signed the licenses, then you observed a wrong being done, brought it to the attention of appropriate people in the company, and even offered a solution. Is that enough? Once again, we have reached the question of how far you must go to stop an unethical act or a crime committed by others, a question that is often difficult to answer.

10.4.9 Hiring Foreign Programmers

You are a manager at a software company about to begin a large software project. You will need to hire dozens of new programmers. Using the Internet for communication and software delivery, you can hire programmers in India at lower salary than U.S. programmers. Should you do this?[12]

This case differs from the others we considered in that it includes wider social and economic issues. I include it for several reasons. It is a real, current controversy. Hiring of foreign programmers who work in their home country has been increasing, with potentially significant implications for the economies of other countries and the U.S., and for programmers in all countries. This is a good example for trying to distinguish economic advantage from ethical arguments. Also, in other industries, in several countries, legislation has been used to restrict the hiring of foreign workers. The discussion here may provide insight into the ethics of such legislation.

The most obvious people affected by the decision in this case are the Indian programmers and the U.S. programmers you might hire. Before we consider other stakeholders, we will use utilitarianism and Kant's principle about treating people as ends in themselves to generate some ideas, questions, and observations about these two groups. How can we compare the impact on utility from the two choices? The number of people hired will be the same in either case. There does not appear to be any reason, from an ethical point of view, for placing a higher weight on the utility of one group of programmers merely because of their nationality. Shall we weigh the utilities of the programmers according to the number of dollars they will receive? That favors hiring the U.S. programmers. Or should we weigh the utility of the pay by comparing it to the average salary in each country? That favors hiring the Indians. The utility obtained from a job for an individual programmer depends on the availability of other jobs. Are there more opportunities to earn a comparable income in the U.S. or in India? Depending on how one evaluates the utility of the pay, one can argue that either decision increases net utility of the programmers. There does not appear to be a strong ethical argument using utilitarianism for one choice over the other.

What happens when we apply Kant's principle? When we hire people for a job, we are interacting with them in a limited role. We are making a trade, money for work. The programmers are a means to an end: producing a marketable product at a reasonable price. Kant does not say that people must not be treated as a means to an end, but rather that they should not be treated *merely* as such; people are an end in themselves. Kant does not seem helpful here, especially if we observe that the hiring decision does not treat the potential programmers differently in a way that has to do with ends and means.

Some would argue that you are taking advantage of the Indian programmers, perhaps "exploiting" them by paying them less than you would have to pay the U.S. programmers. They believe it is unfair to both the U.S. and Indian programmers that the Indians get the jobs by charging less money. It is equally logical, however, to argue that paying the higher rate for U.S. programmers is wasteful, or charity, or simply overpayment. What makes either pay level more "right" than the other? All buyers would like to pay less for what they buy, and all sellers would like to get a higher price for their goods and services. There is nothing automatically unethical about choosing the cheaper of two products, services, or employees.

We can argue that treating the Indian programmers as ends in themselves includes respecting the choices and trade-offs they make to better their lives according to their own judgment, in particular in offering to work for lower wages. But there are special cases in which we might decide otherwise. First, suppose your company is doing something to limit the other options of the Indian programmers. If your company is lobbying for import restrictions on software produced by Indian firms, for example, thus decreasing the availability of other programming jobs in India, then you are manipulating the programmers into a situation where they have few or no other choices. In that case you are not respecting their freedom and allowing them to compete fairly; you are not treating them as ends in themselves. We will assume for the rest of the discussion that your company is not doing anything like this.

Another reason we might decide that the Indian programmers are not being treated as ends in themselves, or with respect for their human dignity, is that their working conditions would be worse than the working conditions expected by U.S. workers (or required by law in the U.S.). There might be no medical insurance for the programmers. The offices in which they work may be rundown, crowded, and lacking air-conditioning. Is hiring them to work in such conditions unethical, or does it give them an opportunity to improve conditions in their country? Whether or not it is ethically required, there are several reasons why you might pay more (or provide better working conditions) than market conditions in India require: a sense of shared humanity that motivates you to want to provide conditions you consider desirable, a sense of generosity (i.e., willingness to contribute to the improvement of the standard of living of people in a country less rich than ours) and economic benefit: paying more than expected may get you high morale, productivity, and company loyalty.

Many laws have been passed to require that the same salary be paid to all workers when a large group of potential workers (foreigners, ethnic minorities, low-skilled workers, teenagers) is willing to work for lower pay. The main argument is that such laws will prevent the less-advantaged workers from being exploited. Historically, one of the effects of these laws is that the traditionally higher paid group gets most of the jobs. (Often that has been the intent of the law.) In this case, the almost certain result would be that the U.S. programmers are hired. The law, or an ethical requirement that the Indian programmers be paid the same as the U.S. programmers, would protect the high incomes of programmers in the U.S. and the profits of companies that pay higher salaries. Such requirements are generally opposed by new workers or businesses that are trying to compete by lowering prices.

So far, we have been discussing only the impact of your decision on the programmers. Other people are affected too: your customers, the owners or stockholders of your company, and, indirectly and to a smaller degree, many people in other businesses. If you hire the Indian programmers, your customers benefit from the lower price of the product, and the owners of your company benefit from the profits. If the product is successful, the company may pay for advertising, distribution, and so on, providing jobs for others in the United States. On the other hand, if you hire U.S. programmers, they will spend more of their earnings in the U.S. than the Indian programmers, generating jobs and income for others. If the product is not profitable because of higher programming costs, the company may go out of business, with a negative impact on all its employees and suppliers. To which of all these people do you have responsibilities or obligations? As a manager of the company, you have an obligation to help make the product and the company successful, to manage the project to maximize profit (not independent of ethical considerations, as we have noted, but consistent with them). Unless the owners of the company have a policy to improve the standard of living of people in other countries or to "Buy American," your obligation to them includes hiring competent workers at the best price. You have some responsibility for the fate of other company employees who might lose their jobs if you do a poor job of managing your product. You do not have any special obligation to other service providers you may hire, nor to people seeking jobs as programmers in either country.

This discussion suggests that there is no strong ethical argument for an obligation to hire one group of programmers rather than the other.

10.5 APPENDIX: THE ACM CODE OF ETHICS AND PROFESSIONAL CONDUCT*

Preamble

Commitment to ethical professional conduct is expected of every voting, associate, and student member of ACM. This Code, consisting of 24 imperatives formulated as statements of personal responsibility, identifies the elements of such a commitment.

It contains many, but not all, issues professionals are likely to face. Section 1 outlines fundamental ethical considerations, while Section 2 addresses additional, more specific considerations of professional conduct. Statements in Section 3 pertain more specifically to individuals who have a leadership role, whether in the workplace or in a volunteer capacity, for example with organizations such as ACM. Principles involving compliance with this Code are given in Section 4.

The Code shall be supplemented by a set of Guidelines, which provide explanation to assist members in dealing with the various issues contained in the Code. It is expected that the Guidelines will be changed more frequently than the Code.

The Code and its supplemented Guidelines are intended to serve as a basis for ethical decision making in the conduct of professional work. Secondarily, they may serve as a basis for judging the merit of a formal complaint pertaining to violation of professional ethical standards.

It should be noted that although computing is not mentioned in the moral imperatives section, the Code is concerned with how these fundamental imperatives apply to one's conduct as a computing professional. These imperatives are expressed in a general form to emphasize that ethical principles which apply to computer ethics are derived from more general ethical principles.

It is understood that some words and phrases in a code of ethics are subject to varying interpretations, and that any ethical principle may conflict with other ethical principles in specific situations. Questions related to ethical conflicts can best be answered by thoughtful consideration of fundamental principles, rather than reliance on detailed regulations.

1. GENERAL MORAL IMPERATIVES. As an ACM member I will . . .

  1.1 Contribute to society and human well-being

  1.2 Avoid harm to others

  1.3 Be honest and trustworthy

  1.4 Be fair and take action not to discriminate

  1.5 Honor property rights including copyrights and patents

  1.6 Give proper credit for intellectual property

---

*This Code and the supplemental Guidelines were developed by the Task Force for the Revision of the ACM Code of Ethics and Professional Conduct: Ronald E. Anderson, Chair, Gerald Engel, Donald Gotterbarn, Grace C. Hertlein, Alex Hoffman, Bruce Jawer, Deborah G. Johnson, Doris K. Lidtke, Joyce Currie Little, Dianne Martin, Donn B. Parker, Judith A. Perrolle, and Richard S. Rosenberg. The Task Force was organized by ACM/SIG-CAS and funding was provided by the ACM SIG Discretionary Fund. This Code and the supplemental guidelines were adopted by the ACM Council on October 16, 1992. Reprinted with the permission of the Association for Computing Machinery.

1.7 Respect the privacy of others

1.8 Honor confidentiality.

2. MORE SPECIFIC PROFESSIONAL RESPONSIBILITIES. As an ACM computing professional I will . . .

2.1 Strive to achieve the highest quality, effectiveness and dignity in both the process and products of professional work

2.2 Acquire and maintain professional competence

2.3 Know and respect existing laws pertaining to professional work

2.4 Accept and provide appropriate professional review

2.5 Give comprehensive and thorough evaluations of computer systems and their impacts, including analysis of possible risks

2.6 Honor contracts, agreements, and assigned responsibilities

2.7 Improve public understanding of computing and its consequences

2.8 Access computing and communication resources only when authorized to do so.

3. ORGANIZATIONAL LEADERSHIP IMPERATIVES. As an ACM member and an organizational leader, I will . . .

3.1 Articulate social responsibilities of members of an organizational unit and encourage full acceptance of those responsibilities

3.2 Manage personnel and resources to design and build information systems that enhance the quality of working life

3.3 Acknowledge and support proper and authorized uses of an organization's computing and communication resources

3.4 Ensure that users and those who will be affected by a system have their needs clearly articulated during the assessment and design of requirements. Later the system must be validated to meet requirements.

3.5 Articulate and support policies that protect the dignity of users and others affected by a computing system

3.6 Create opportunities for members of the organization to learn the principles and limitations of computer systems.

4. COMPLIANCE WITH THE CODE. As an ACM member I will . . .

4.1 Uphold and promote the principles of this Code.

4.2 Treat violations of this code as inconsistent with membership in the ACM.

Guidelines

1. GENERAL MORAL IMPERATIVES. As an ACM member I will . . .

1.1 Contribute to society and human well-being. This principle concerning the quality of life of all people affirms an obligation to protect fundamental human rights and to respect the diversity of all cultures. An essential aim of computing professionals is to minimize negative consequences of computing systems, including threats to health and safety. When designing or implementing systems, computing professionals must attempt to ensure that the products of their efforts will be used in socially responsible ways, will meet social needs, and will avoid harmful effects to health and welfare.

In addition to a safe social environment, human well-being includes a safe natural environment. Therefore, computing professionals who design and develop systems must be alert to, and make others aware of, any potential damage to the local or global environment.

1.2 Avoid harm to others. "Harm" means injury or negative consequences, such as undesirable loss of information, loss of property, property damage, or unwanted environmental impacts. This principle prohibits use of computing technology in ways that result in harm to any of the following: users, the general public, employees, employers. Harmful actions include intentional destruction or modification of files and programs leading to serious loss of resources or unnecessary expenditure of human resources such as the time and effort required to purge systems of "computer viruses."

Well-intended actions, including those that accomplish assigned duties, may lead to harm unexpectedly. In such an event the responsible person or persons are obligated to undo or mitigate the negative consequences as much as possible. One way to avoid unintentional harm is to carefully consider potential impacts on all those affected by decisions made during design and implementation.

To minimize the possibility of indirectly harming others, computing professionals must minimize malfunctions by following generally accepted standards for system design and testing. Furthermore, it is often necessary to assess the social consequences of systems to project the likelihood of any serious harm to others. If system features are misrepresented to users, coworkers, or supervisors, the individual computing professional is responsible for any resulting injury.

In the work environment the computing professional has the additional obligation to report any signs of system dangers that might result in serious personal or social damage. If one's superiors do not act to curtail or mitigate such dangers, it may be necessary to "blow the whistle" to help correct the problem or reduce the risk. However, capricious or misguided reporting of violations can, itself, be harmful. Before reporting violations, all relevant aspects of the incident must be thoroughly assessed. In particular, the assessment of risk and responsibility must be credible. It is suggested that advice be sought from other computing professionals. See principle 2.5 regarding thorough evaluations.

1.3 Be honest and trustworthy. Honesty is an essential component of trust. Without trust an organization cannot function effectively. The honest computing professional will not make deliberately false or deceptive claims about a system or system design, but will instead provide full disclosure of all pertinent system limitations and problems.

A computer professional has a duty to be honest about his or her own qualifications, and about any circumstances that might lead to conflicts of interest.

Membership in volunteer organizations such as ACM may at times place individuals in situations where their statements or actions could be interpreted as carrying the "weight" of a larger group of professionals. An ACM member will exercise care to not misrepresent ACM or positions and policies of ACM or any ACM units.

1.4 Be fair and take action not to discriminate. The values of equality, tolerance, respect for others, and the principles of equal justice govern this imperative. Discrimination on the basis of race, sex, religion, age, disability, national origin, or other such factors is an explicit violation of ACM policy and will not be tolerated.

Inequities between different groups of people may result from the use or misuse of information and technology. In a fair society, all individuals would have equal opportunity to participate in, or benefit from, the use of computer resources regardless of race, sex, religion, age, disability, national origin or other such similar factors. However, these ideals do not justify unauthorized use of computer resources nor do they provide an adequate basis for violation of any other ethical imperatives of this code.

1.5 Honor property rights including copyrights and patents. Violation of copyrights, patents, trade secrets and the terms of license agreements is prohibited by law in most circumstances. Even when software is not so protected, such violations are contrary to professional behavior. Copies of software should be made only with proper authorization. Unauthorized duplication of materials must not be condoned.

1.6 Give proper credit for intellectual property. Computing professionals are obligated to protect the integrity of intellectual property. Specifically, one must not take credit for other's ideas or work, even in cases where the work has not been explicitly protected by copyright, patent, etc.

1.7 Respect the privacy of others. Computing and communication technology enables the collection and exchange of personal information on a scale unprecedented in the history of civilization. Thus there is increased potential for violating the privacy of individuals and groups. It is the responsibility of professionals to maintain the privacy and integrity of data describing individuals. This includes taking precautions to ensure the accuracy of data, as well as protecting it from unauthorized access or accidental disclosure to inappropriate individuals. Furthermore, procedures must be established to allow individuals to review their records and correct inaccuracies.

This imperative implies that only the necessary amount of personal information be collected in a system, that retention and disposal periods for that information be clearly defined and enforced, and that personal information gathered for a specific purpose not be used for other purposes without consent of the individual(s). These principles apply to electronic communications, including electronic mail, and prohibit procedures that capture or monitor electronic user data, including messages, without the permission of users or bona fide authorization related to system operation and maintenance. User data observed during the normal duties of system operation and maintenance must be treated with strictest confidentiality, except in cases where it is evidence for the violation of law, organizational regulations, or this Code. In these cases, the nature or contents of that information must be disclosed only to proper authorities.

1.8 Honor confidentiality. The principle of honesty extends to issues of confidentiality of information whenever one has made an explicit promise to honor confidentiality or, implicitly, when private information not directly related to the performance of one's duties becomes available. The ethical concern is to respect all obligations of confidentiality to employers, clients, and users unless discharged from such obligations by requirements of the law or other principles of this Code.

2. MORE SPECIFIC PROFESSIONAL RESPONSIBILITIES. As an ACM computing professional I will . . .

2.1 Strive to achieve the highest quality, effectiveness and dignity in both the process and products of professional work. Excellence is perhaps the most important obligation of a professional. The computing professional must strive to achieve quality and to be cognizant of the serious negative consequences that may result from poor quality in a system.

2.2 Acquire and maintain professional competence. Excellence depends on individuals who take responsibility for acquiring and maintaining professional competence. A professional must participate in setting standards for appropriate levels of competence, and strive to achieve those standards. Upgrading technical knowledge and competence can be achieved in several ways: doing independent study; attending seminars, conferences, or courses; and being involved in professional organizations.

2.3 Know and respect existing laws pertaining to professional work. ACM members must obey existing local, state, province, national, and international laws unless there is a compelling ethical basis not to do so. Policies and procedures of the organizations in which one participates must also be obeyed. But compliance must be balanced with the recognition that sometimes existing laws and rules may be immoral or inappropriate and, therefore, must be challenged. Violation of a law or regulation may be ethical when that law or rule has inadequate moral basis or when it conflicts with another law judged to be more important. If one decides to violate a law or rule because it is viewed as unethical, or for any other reason, one must fully accept responsibility for one's actions and for the consequences.

2.4 Accept and provide appropriate professional review. Quality professional work, especially in the computing profession, depends on professional reviewing and critiquing. Whenever appropriate, individual members should seek and utilize peer review as well as provide critical review of the work of others.

2.5 Give comprehensive and thorough evaluations of computer systems and their impacts, including analysis of possible risks. Computer professionals must strive to be perceptive, thorough, and objective when evaluating, recommending, and presenting system descriptions and alternatives. Computer professionals are in a position of special trust, and therefore have a special responsibility to provide objective, credible evaluations to employers, clients, users, and the public. When providing evaluations the professional must also identify any relevant conflicts of interest, as stated in imperative 1.3.

As noted in the discussion of principle 1.2 on avoiding harm, any signs of danger from systems must be reported to those who have opportunity and/or responsibility to resolve them. See the guidelines for imperative 1.2 for more details concerning harm, including the reporting of professional violations.

2.6 Honor contracts, agreements, and assigned responsibilities. Honoring one's commitments is a matter of integrity and honesty. For the computer professional this includes ensuring that system elements perform as intended. Also, when one contracts for work with another party, one has an obligation to keep that party properly informed about progress toward completing that work.

A computing professional has a responsibility to request a change in any assignment that he or she feels cannot be completed as defined. Only after serious consideration and with full disclosure of risks and concerns to the employer or client, should one accept the assignment. The major underlying principle here is the obligation to accept personal accountability for professional work. On some occasions other ethical principles may take greater priority.

A judgment that a specific assignment should not be performed may not be accepted. Having clearly identified one's concerns and reasons for that judgment, but failing to procure a change in that assignment, one may yet be obligated, by contract or by law, to proceed as directed. The computing professional's ethical judgment should be the final guide in deciding whether or not to proceed. Regardless of the decision, one must accept the responsibility for the consequences.

However, performing assignments "against one's own judgment" does not relieve the professional of responsibility for any negative consequences.

2.7 Improve public understanding of computing and its consequences. Computing professionals have a responsibility to share technical knowledge with the public by encouraging understanding of computing, including the impacts of computer systems and their limitations. This imperative implies an obligation to counter any false views related to computing.

2.8 Access computing and communication resources only when authorized to do so. Theft or destruction of tangible and electronic property is prohibited by imperative 1.2—"Avoid harm to others." Trespassing and unauthorized use of a computer or communication system is addressed by this imperative. Trespassing includes accessing communication networks and computer systems, or accounts and/or files associated with those systems, without explicit authorization to do so. Individuals and organizations have the right to restrict access to their systems so long as they do not violate the discrimination principle (see 1.4).

No one should enter or use another's computer system, software, or data files without permission. One must always have appropriate approval before using system resources, including communication ports, file space, other system peripherals, and computer time.

3. ORGANIZATIONAL LEADERSHIP IMPERATIVES. As an ACM member and an organizational leader, I will . . .

Background note: This section draws extensively from the draft IFIP Code of Ethics, especially its sections on organizational ethics and international concerns. The ethical obligations of organizations tend to be neglected in most codes of professional conduct, perhaps because these codes are written from the perspective of the individual member. This dilemma is addressed by stating these imperatives from the perspective of the organizational leader. In this context "leader" is viewed as any organizational member who has leadership or educational responsibilities. These imperatives generally may apply to organizations as well as their leaders. In this context "organizations" are corporations, government agencies, and other "employers," as well as volunteer professional organizations.

3.1 Articulate social responsibilities of members of an organizational unit and encourage full acceptance of those responsibilities. Because organizations of all kinds have impacts on the public, they must accept responsibilities to society. Organizational procedures and attitudes oriented toward quality and the welfare of society will reduce harm to members of the public, thereby serving public interest and fulfilling social responsibility. Therefore, organizational leaders must encourage full participation in meeting social responsibilities as well as quality performance.

3.2 Manage personnel and resources to design and build information systems that enhance the quality of working life. Organizational leaders are responsible for ensuring that computer systems enhance, not degrade, the quality of working life. When implementing a computer system, organizations must consider the personal and professional development, physical safety, and human dignity of all workers. Appropriate human-computer ergonomic standards should be considered in system design and in the workplace.

3.3 Acknowledge and support proper and authorized uses of an organization's computing and communication resources. Because computer systems can become tools to harm as well as to benefit an organization, the leadership has the responsibility to clearly define appropriate and inappropriate uses of organizational computing resources. While the number and scope of such rules should be minimal, they should be fully enforced when established.

3.4 Ensure that users and those who will be affected by a system have their needs clearly articulated during the assessment and design of requirements; later the system must be validated to meet requirements. Current system users, potential users and other persons whose lives may be affected by a system must have their needs assessed and incorporated in the statement of requirements. System validation should ensure compliance with those requirements.

3.5 Articulate and support policies that protect the dignity of users and others affected by a computing system. Designing or implementing systems that deliberately or inadvertently demean individuals or groups is ethically unacceptable. Computer professionals who are in decision making positions should verify that systems are designed and implemented to protect personal privacy and enhance personal dignity.

3.6 Create opportunities for members of the organization to learn the principles and limitations of computer systems. This complements the imperative on public understanding (2.7). Educational opportunities are essential to facilitate optimal participation of all organizational members. Opportunities must be available to all members to help them improve their knowledge and skills in computing, including courses that familiarize them with the consequences and limitations of particular types of systems. In particular, professionals must be made aware of the dangers of building systems around oversimplified models, the improbability of anticipating and designing for every possible operating condition, and other issues related to the complexity of this profession.

4. COMPLIANCE WITH THE CODE. As an ACM member I will . . .

4.1 Uphold and promote the principles of this Code. The future of the computing profession depends on both technical and ethical excellence. Not only is it important for ACM computing professionals to adhere to the principles expressed in this Code, each member should encourage and support adherence by other members.

4.2 Treat violations of this code as inconsistent with membership in the ACM. Adherence of professionals to a code of ethics is largely a voluntary matter. However, if a member does not follow this code by engaging in gross misconduct, membership in ACM may be terminated.

EXERCISES

Review exercises

1. What are two of Kant's important ideas about ethics?

2. What is the difference between act-utilitarianism and rule-utilitarianism?

3. In what sense, if any, is the right of access to computer information networks a negative right (a liberty), and in what sense, if any, is it a positive right (a claim-right)?

4. What are two ways professional ethics differ from ethics in general?

General exercises

5. Give arguments in support of "Do not lie" as a good general ethical rule. Identify which of your arguments are utilitarian and which are deontological.

6. Which kind of ethical theory, deontologist or consequentialist, works better for arguing that it is wrong to drive one's car on the left side of a road in a country where people normally drive on the right? Explain.

7. Describe a case at work or in school where you were asked or pressured to do something you thought unethical.

8. There have been proposals for a compulsory National Service system, where young people would be required to do community service jobs for a year or two. One person opposes both the military draft and the draft for National Service. Another person opposes the military draft, but supports the National Service draft. What ethical arguments and/or ethical theories do you think are the basis for each person's position?

9. A computer science professor in a computer security class assigns students to break into a computer system and bring back specific files to prove they did. (The owner of the system is unaware of the assignment.) Analyze this case from an ethical perspective. Tell what people are affected and how, and what the ethical issues are. Tell what actions a student in the class could take, and which, if any, are ethically wrong, which are acceptable, and what, if any, ethical obligations a student has.

10. In Section 2.3.4, we mentioned an incident in which a woman who filled out a detailed consumer profile questionnaire received an offensive and threatening letter from a convicted rapist. Prison inmates had been hired to enter the questionnaire data into a computer database. What are the ethical issues involved in a direct marketing company's decision about whether to contract with a prison system or use a more expensive commercial data-entry service? What guidelines from Section 10.3.2 are relevant? What provisions of the ACM Code are relevant? In hindsight, we know that the decision in this case had serious negative consequences. Do you think the company should have anticipated such a problem, or was the decision to use prisoners for the data entry task a reasonable one?

11. Analyze the following scenario. List the people affected. What responsibilities and obligations do you have? Is the action ethical?

> You work for a software company designing an appointment system for a large chain of health clinics. You are considering building in a back door so that you can log in to the system after it is installed. (This is not in the specifications for maintenance; it is your secret.)

12. You are offered a job with a company that is developing software for a new generation of space shuttles. You do not have any training in the specific techniques that will be used in the programs you will be working on. You can tell from the job interview that the interviewer thinks your college program included this material. Should you take the job? Should you tell the interviewer that you have no training or experience in this area? Analyze this case using the methods in Section 10.4.1.

13. You are the traffic manager for a small city. The City Council has directed you to buy and install a computer system to control the traffic lights so that the timing of the lights can be adjusted to improve traffic flow at rush hours and for special events.

    (a) List some potential risks of the system.

    (b) Indicate how each of the guidelines from Collins *et al* in Section 10.3.2 applies to this project.

14. You are the head of the psychiatric division of a large hospital. A researcher wants to do statistical research using the records of the patients treated in your division over the past 25 years. The researcher does not need to know the names of the patients. The records of the past 10 years are on electronic media; a program can be written to copy the information the researcher needs from each file to a new file without the patient name. The older records are on paper; it would take a very large amount of effort to make copies and remove names. The research is important; it is part of a continuing study begun 20 years ago. In the past, when all records were on paper, names were not removed. The researchers were expected to treat the records as confidential.

    What are your options? Give ethical arguments for (or against) several. Which options do you think are acceptable? Which unacceptable? How does the change in technology affect the risks and obligations to the patients?

15. Consider the scenario in Exercise 9. Find two provisions in the ACM Code of Ethics and Professional Conduct for which there is a strong argument that the professor's assignment is in violation. Give reasons.

16. Consider the scenario in Exercise 11. Find two provisions in the ACM Code of Ethics and Professional Conduct for which there is a strong argument that the action contemplated by the programmer is in violation. Give reasons.

17. Give arguments for and against including a guideline on censorship of electronic information media in the ACM Code of Ethics and Professional Conduct. Then give your opinion as to which side is stronger. If you think there should be a section, what should it say?

18. Are there any sections of the Guidelines for the ACM Code of Ethics and Professional Conduct that you think should be removed? If so, which and why?

19. Suppose you came to the U.S. from Bosnia 15 years ago. You now have a small software company and are a member of the ACM. You will need to hire a dozen programmers this year. Because of the devastation by the war in your homeland, you have decided to seek out and hire only refugees from Bosnia. The guidelines for Section 1.4 of the ACM Code of Ethics and Professional Conduct says "Discrimination on the basis of . . . national origin . . . is an explicit violation of ACM policy and will not be tolerated." Analyze the ethical issues in this situation. Do you think your action is ethically acceptable? Would you modify this part of the ACM Code? If so, how?

20. Consider the following statements.

    (i) In addition to a safe social environment, human well-being includes a safe natural environment. Therefore, computing professionals who design and develop systems must be alert to, and make others aware of, any potential damage to the local or global environment.

    (ii) We cannot assume that a computer-based economy automatically will provide enough jobs for everyone in the future. Computer professionals should be aware of this pressure on employment when designing and implementing systems that will reduce job opportunities for those most in need of them.

The first is in the Guidelines of the ACM Code of Ethics and Professional Conduct (Section 1.1).[13] The second is from a book on computer ethics.[13] Compare the two statements from the perspective of how relevant and appropriate they are for an ethical code for computer professionals. Do you think both should be in the Guidelines? Neither? Just one? (Which one?) Give your reasons.

21. Suppose there are two large competing network communications firms in your city. The companies are hostile to each other; there have been unproved claims of industrial espionage by each company. Your spouse works for one of the companies. You are now interviewing for a job with the other. Do you have an ethical obligation to tell the interviewer about your spouse's job? How is this case similar to and different from the conflict of interest case in Section 10.4.7?

22. In 1990, the campaign of a gubernatorial candidate in Massachusetts distorted an image of his opponent in a television interview to make the opponent appear more menacing.[14] Such modification is easy with digital images and graphics programs. Explain whether you think this was an ethical action. How does it differ from using a caricature (as is often done in cartoons and is protected by the First Amendment)?

23. Consider the case in Section 10.4.4. Suppose the company has decided to deliver the laser device before completing testing and you have decided you must inform the hospitals who are purchasing it. Discuss ethical and practical factors relevant to deciding whether to send information to the hospitals openly or anonymously.

24. The cases in Sections 10.4.4 and 10.4.5 concern safety-critical systems. Suppose the system is an accounting system, or a consumer tax preparation system, or a game. How would the analysis of the scenarios in Sections 10.4.4 and 10.4.5 differ?

25. In the scenario in Section 10.4.6, someone offers to pay you for a copy of a person's confidential file. One of the actions mentioned was that you could contact the person whose file was requested and tell him or her of the incident. Is this action ethically prohibited, ethically obligatory, or neither? Give reasons.

26. You run a small company that developed and markets a filter program to help parents filter out material they do not wish their children to access on the Internet. A foreign government wants your company to develop a custom version of your program to be used on the country's Internet connection to filter out material the government does not wish its citizens to access.* Give arguments in favor of accepting the contract and arguments against it. Is it ethically wrong to accept the contract? Would you accept it? Why or why not?

Class exercises

1. Almost all the exercises in this chapter are suitable for a class debate or for assignment for small groups of students to prepare and present an analysis in class.

NOTES

1   Donald Gotterbarn, "Computer Ethics: Responsibility Regained," *National Forum: The Phi Kappa Phi Forum,* Summer 1991, 71:3; reprinted in Deborah G. Johnson and Helen Nissenbaum, eds., *Computers, Ethics & Social Values,* Prentice Hall, 1995, pp. 18–24.)

*Such a request was made to a company that produces filtering software.

2 Sources used in preparation of this section include Joseph Ellin, *Morality and the Meaning of Life: An Introduction to Ethical Theory,* Harcourt Brace Jovanovich, 1995; Deborah G. Johnson, *Computer Ethics,* Prentice Hall, 2nd ed., 1994; Louis Pojman, *Ethical Theory: Classical and Contemporary Readings,* 2nd ed., Wadsworth, 1995 (which includes John Stuart Mill's "Utilitarianism," Kant's "The Foundations of the Metaphysic of Morals," John Locke's "Natural Rights"); and James Rachels, *The Elements of Moral Philosophy,* McGraw Hill, 1993.

3 John Stuart Mill, *Utilitarianism,* 1863.

4 The term "claim-rights" is used by J. L. Mackie in *Ethics: Inventing Right and Wrong.* Another term that could be used for positive rights is entitlements.

5 By Louis P. Pojman (Wadsworth, 1990) and J. L. Mackie (Penguin Books, 1977), respectively.

6 Kenneth C. Laudon, "Ethical Concepts and Information Technology," *Communications of the ACM,* December 1995, 38:12, p. 38.

7 W. Robert Collins, Keith W. Miller, Bethany J. Spielman, and Phillip Wherry, "How Good Is Good Enough?" *Communications of the ACM,* January 1994, pp. 81–91.

8 Roger Boisjoly, quoted in Diane Vaughan, *The Challenger Launch Decision: Risky Technology, Culture, and Deviance at NASA,* University of Chicago Press, 1996, p. 41.

9 Deborah G. Johnson and John M. Mulvey, "Accountability and Computer Decision Systems," *Communications of the ACM,* December 1995, pp. 58–64.

10 See Diane Vaughan, *The Challenger Launch Decision: Risky Technology, Culture, and Deviance at NASA,* University of Chicago Press, 1996, for an analysis of the institutional practices that contributed to the Challenger tragedy. See Robert M. Anderson et al, *Divided Loyalties: Whistle-Blowing at BART,* Purdue University, 1980, for the BART case.

11 Holger Hjorstvang, quoted in Anderson et al, *Divided Loyalties,* p. 140.

12 My thanks to my student Anthony Biag whose questions in class on this issue prompted me to include it in this book.

13 Tom Forester and Perry Morrison, *Computer Ethics: Cautionary Tales and Ethical Dilemmas in Computing,* 2nd ed., MIT Press, 1994, p. 202.

14 Anne Branscomb, *Who Owns Information?,* Basic Books, 1994, pp. 73–75.

FOR FURTHER READING

Robert M. Anderson, Robert Perrucci, Dan E. Schendel, and Leon E. Trachtman, *Divided Loyalties: Whistle-Blowing at BART,* Purdue University, 1980.

Ronald E. Anderson, Deborah G. Johnson, Donald Gotterbarn, Judith Perrolle, "Using the New ACM Code of Ethics in Decision Making," *Communications of the ACM,* February 1993, 36:2, pp. 98–107.

Michael D. Bayles, *Professional Ethics,* Wadsworth, 1981.

Vint Cerf, "Ethics and the Internet," *Communications of the ACM,* June 1989, 32:6, p. 710. Although written when the Internet was still primarily used by researchers, and thus a little out-of-date, this is an example of an attempt to establish a standard of ethics for the Internet.

W. Robert Collins, Keith W. Miller, Bethany J. Spielman, and Phillip Wherry, "How Good Is Good Enough?" *Communications of the ACM,* January 1994, pp. 81–91.

Joseph Ellin, *Morality and the Meaning of Life: An Introduction to Ethical Theory,* Harcourt Brace Jovanovich, 1995.

Deborah G. Johnson, *Computer Ethics,* Prentice Hall, 2nd ed., 1994.

Deborah G. Johnson and John M. Mulvey, "Accountability and Computer Decision Systems," *Communications of the ACM,* December 1995, 38:12, pp. 58–64.

Kenneth C. Laudon, "Ethical Concepts and Information Technology," *Communications of the ACM,* December 1995, 38:12, pp. 33–39.

Jan Narveson, *Moral Matters,* Broadview Press, 1993. The first chapter gives a good, very readable introduction to moral issues.

Helen Nissenbaum, "Computing and Accountability," *Communications of the ACM,* January 1994, 36:1, pp. 73–80.

Effy Oz, *Ethics for the Information Age,* William C. Brown, 1994.

David Lorge Parnas, "Computing and the Citizen: SDI: A Violation of Professional Responsibility," *Abacus,* Winter 1987, 4:2, pp. 46–52.

Louis Pojman, *Ethical Theory: Classical and Contemporary Readings,* 2nd ed., Wadsworth, 1995. Includes John Stuart Mill's "Utilitarianism," Kant's "The Foundations of the Metaphysic of Morals," John Locke's "Natural Rights," and other classical essays on various ethical theories.

James Rachels, *The Elements of Moral Philosophy,* McGraw Hill, 1993.

Diane Vaughan, *The Challenger Launch Decision: Risky Technology, Culture, and Deviance at NASA,* University of Chicago Press, 1996.

INDEX